PROFESSIONAL SELLING

An Interpersonal Perspective

K. Douglas Smith

PROFESSIONAL SELLING

An Interpersonal Perspective

Gary F. Soldow
Gloria P. Thomas
Baruch College
The City University of New York

Macmillan Publishing Company
New York
Collier Macmillan Canada
Toronto
Maxwell Macmillan International
New York Oxford Singapore Sydney

Editor: Michele Rhoades
Production Supervisor: John Travis
Production Manager: Valerie Sawyer
Designer: Jane Edelstein
Photo Researcher: Cheryl Mannes
This book was set in 10/12 ITC Century Book by Ruttle, Shaw & Wetherill, Inc., printed and bound by R. R. Donnelley & Sons Company. The cover was printed by Lehigh Press.

Printed in the United States of America

Macmillan Publishing Company
866 Third Avenue, New York, New York 10022

Collier Macmillan Canada, Inc.
1200 Eglinton Avenue, East
Suite 200
Don Mills, Ontario M3C 3N1

Library of Congress Cataloging in Publication Data

Soldow, Gary F.
Professional selling: an interpersonal perspective / Gary F. Soldow, Gloria P. Thomas.
p. cm.
Includes bibliographical references.
ISBN 0-02-413181-4
1. Selling. 2. Customer service. I. Thomas, Gloria P.
II. Title.
HF5438.25.S65 1991
658.8′5—dc20 89-71342
CIP

Printing: 1 2 3 4 5 6 7 8 9 Year: 1 2 3 4 5 6 7 8 9 0

THE MACMILLAN SERIES IN MARKETING

Bagozzi
PRINCIPLES OF MARKETING MANAGEMENT

Beisel
CONTEMPORARY RETAILING

Berman and Evans
RETAIL MANAGEMENT, Fourth Edition

Bockus
ADVERTISING GRAPHICS, Fourth Edition

Bowersox, Closs, and Helferich
LOGISTICAL MANAGEMENT, Third Edition

Chapman and Bradley
DYNAMIC RETAILING, Second Edition

Cohen
THE PRACTICE OF MARKETING MANAGEMENT, Second Edition

Douglas
WRITING FOR PUBLIC RELATIONS

Etzel and Woodside
CASES IN RETAILING STRATEGY

Evans and Berman
MARKETING, Fourth Edition

Evans and Berman
PRINCIPLES OF MARKETING, Second Edition

Galloway, Evans, and Berman
PAINTCO III: A COMPUTERIZED MARKETING SIMULATION

Greer
CASES IN MARKETING, Fifth Edition

Hair, Anderson, and Tatham
MULTIVARIATE DATA ANALYSIS, Second Edition

Hartley
SALES MANAGEMENT

Hise and McDaniel
CASES IN MARKETING STRATEGY

Hisrich and Peters
MARKETING DECISIONS FOR NEW AND MATURE PRODUCTS, Second Edition

Johnson and Wood
CONTEMPORARY LOGISTICS, Fourth Edition

Katzenstein and Sachs
DIRECT MARKETING

Kincaid
PROMOTION: PRODUCTS, SERVICES, AND IDEAS, Second Edition

Lewison
RETAILING, Fourth Edition

Lewison
ESSENTIALS OF RETAILING

Lewison and Hawes
CASES IN RETAIL MANAGEMENT

Lill
SELLING: THE PROFESSION

Morris
INDUSTRIAL AND ORGANIZATIONAL MARKETING

Mowen
CONSUMER BEHAVIOR, Second Edition

O'Connor
PERSONAL SELLING

Onkvisit and Shaw
INTERNATIONAL MARKETING

Risch
RETAIL MERCHANDISING, Second Edition

Runyon
ADVERTISING, Second Edition

Runyon and Stewart
CONSUMER BEHAVIOR, Third Edition

Scheuing
NEW PRODUCT MANAGEMENT

Seitel
PRACTICE OF PUBLIC RELATIONS, Third Edition

Soldow and Thomas
PROFESSIONAL SELLING: AN INTERPERSONAL PERSPECTIVE

Tull and Hawkins
MARKETING RESEARCH, Fifth Edition

Tull and Kahle
MARKETING MANAGEMENT

Weeks, Perenchio, Miller, and Metcalf
MERCHANDISING MATHEMATICS

Weilbacher
ADVERTISING, Second Edition

Weilbacher
CASES IN ADVERTISING

Weilbacher
MARKETING MANAGEMENT CASES, Fourth Edition

Wood and Johnson
CONTEMPORARY TRANSPORTATION, Third Edition

To
Fred Soldow
and to
Gloria and Enoch Hughes Thomas

PREFACE

The decade that we are now beginning will undoubtedly be characterized by its own set of unique events and styles. This will, of course, affect and change the marketing environment. One likely change is that the new marketing environment will be even more sophisticated and complex. Not only will marketing professionals be more adept and aware, but, so, too, will be the people to whom they are communicating: the prospective buyers. This shift in awareness and sophistication presents an exciting challenge for the sales professional. With that challenge, however, there is a requirement for a new level of skills.

The salesperson is no longer very likely to face a prospective buyer who is easily influenced. The buyer of the 90's is well informed, intelligent, and insistent on making the right choice. It will no longer be sufficient for the salesperson to be well-informed about the product and the competitive environment. He* is going to have to be an expert in interpersonal communication. He is going to have to understand how to adapt his messages to those of his prospect. He is going to have to be sensitive to nonverbal communication, both his own and that of the prospect.

The Perspective of this Book

Because of the importance of interpersonal communication to the success of any sales encounter, we have placed a great deal of emphasis on interpersonal skills. We view the sales encounter as an interpersonal process. What happens during this process is not predetermined. It unfolds spontaneously. A skilled communicator has to know how to adapt to this unfolding process. She has to recognize that this unfolding process is more than just the words that are exchanged. Always accompanying those words is a nonverbal message.

We have preserved the traditional typology of the sales process as involving prospecting, a pre-approach, an approach, a presentation, handling objections, and a close. At the same time, because of our interpersonal perspective, we have considered each phase of the sales interaction in terms of how it forms a coherent conversation. While we show that, for example, there may be several different kinds of approaches or several different mechanisms to close a sale, we have presented these options in terms of how they can contribute to a coherent conversation. Thus, the student gains a fundamental understanding of the sales process and of which approach or close is best as a function of inherent properties of interpersonal communication.

This focuses the student's attention on the interplay of messages and allows the student to choose one type of approach, or close, or handling of an objection as a function of how his message will "fit" with the message of the prospect, and how all the messages taken together will form a coherent conversation. In order to accomplish the integration of our perspective without eliminating many of the more traditional concerns about the stages of the sales interaction, we have a number of unique features in this book that will enhance the student's experience during this course.

* Throughout the book we have alternated the gender of our pronouns to highlight the fact that selling involves both males and females.

Features of this Book that Will Foster Greater Interest and Understanding for the Student

1. We do not want the student to lose sight of the place that personal selling occupies within the broader marketing environment. In addition, we feel that true understanding is more likely if we can present our subject matter in an integrated framework. Accordingly, we have provided a model of the marketing environment and clearly located personal selling and all of the elements of personal selling in that model. That model has been the basis for the structure and organization of this book.

2. In order to present our perspective, Chapter 3 discusses the basic principles of interpersonal communication. It is here that we explain how the sales interaction is a developing process and how the salesperson can influence the development.

3. Since a major component of interpersonal communication is nonverbal, an entire chapter, Chapter 4, is devoted to nonverbal communication. While we have been careful not to oversimplify the complex area of nonverbal communication, at the same time, we have shown the student how to attend to and interpret his own nonverbal communication as well as that of a prospect.

4. Most sales interactions involve an attempt on the part of the salesperson to influence the buying decision of the prospect. Because of this, we have included Chapter 8 on persuasion. In this chapter we explore the issue of respective power of the salesperson versus that of the prospect and how that influences the persuasive ability of the salesperson. We also discuss specific things that the salesperson can do to enhance his persuasive potential.

5. Each phase of the sales interaction is discussed in terms of a dynamic interpersonal communication process. We are careful to include traditional selling techniques, but instead of merely listing and defining these techniques, we explain how they are derived from more fundamental principles of interpersonal communication. Our emphasis is on explaining why the techniques work and how they can be used.

6. Technology is something that can greatly improve a salesperson's efficiency and allow her to concentrate on her prospects' needs. We therefore have a separate chapter (Chapter 14) on technology which emphasizes specific selling applications.

7. Ethical behavior is a growing concern for business students, and this is just as true in personal selling as it is in other business areas. Chapter 15 on ethical behavior presents ethical issues in a way that we place it in the context of interpersonal communication.

Features That Occur Throughout the Book

1. Since an interpersonal communication perspective is our focus, we have made liberal use of sales dialogues to illustrate our points. We analyze these dialogues and allow the student to get involved in the analysis.

2. Each chapter begins with an outline and a list of objectives.

3. Each chapter begins with a dialogue or a vignette that roots the contents of the chapter in a context that is meaningful for the student.

4. Each chapter ends with a section called "Putting It All Together." This section provides a summary of the chapter and also places the chapter material in a larger context, thus providing additional integration of the material.

5. Each chapter includes a list of key terms, review questions, and more thought-provoking discussion questions.

6. We have an extensive list of references at the end of each chapter so that the interested student will be able to find additional information.

7. For the student's conveniences, there is a glossary at the end of the book. In addition, there is an index of subjects and an index of names.

Material That Is Provided for the Instructor

In order for this book to provide an optimal learning experience, it is essential that we provide information for the instructor. This information, together with the instructor's own area of expertise and experience should work to enhance even further the student's understanding and interest. Following are the things that will be provided to the instructor:

1. Answers to review questions and discussion questions.
2. Suggested lecture outlines and lecture notes.
3. Suggestions for class discussion topics and outside material.
4. Transparency masters to accompany lectures.
5. Dialogues of actual sales interactions on transparency masters so that the dialogues can be analyzed during class sessions.
6. Accompanying those dialogues will be notes to the instructor suggesting how specific messages illustrate points in a given chapter.
7. Suggestions for role-playing exercises.
8. A test bank including multiple-choice and true-false items.

Acknowledgments

Of the many people who have helped in the preparation of this book, we are particularly grateful to our graduate assistant, Deborah Yanofsky, without whose organizational skills we could not have completed the project. We are also grateful to our colleagues David Rachman and William Dillon for their helpful advice and support.

We would also like to give special thanks to William Oldsey, who nurtured the project in the beginning, and Michele Rhoades, who saw it through its completion.

We gratefully acknowledge the suggestions and comments of the reviewers for this text. They are:

Gordon J. Bactovick, Northern Illinois University
Richard H. Behrman, Elon College
Joseph A. Bellizzi, Arizona State University
Ken Blattner, St. Cloud State University
Marjorie Caballero, Baylor University
Ed Cerny, University of South Carolina
William Charlton, Villanova University
Theodore A. Clark, SUNY, New Paltz
Edmund A. Cotta, California State University, Long Beach
James F. Cronin, Jr., Cape Cod Community College
Ted Erickson, Normandale Community College
Ken Evans, Arizona State University
Frank Falcetta, Middlesex County College
Robert Fishco, Middlesex County College
A. Genestre, University of Houston

Jim Grant, University of South Alabama
Douglas F. Harris, University of North Dakota
Jon M. Hawes, University of Akron
Joseph C. Hecht, Montclair State College
Neil C. Herndon, Jr., Texas A & M University
Nathan Himmelstein, Essex Community College
Richard Kustin, College of Boca Raton
Arthur La Capria, Jr., El Paso Community College
William Layden, Golden West College
Frank Lospitalier, Orange County Community College
Richard A. Marsh, Greenville Technical Institute
John R. Mazey, SUNY, Old Westbury
Daniel D. Millard, Kirkwood Community College
Terry Neustrom, Westmar College
Richard D. Nordstrom, California State University, Fresno
Harold Perl, County College of Morris
Larry Peterson, County College of Morris
Robert Pollero, Anne Arundel Community College
S. Joe Puri, Florida Atlantic University
Cheryl Stansfield, North Hennepin Community College
James L. Taylor, University of Alabama
Ron Taylor, Miami University of Ohio
Lois P. Traham, Blinn College
Vernell Walker, San Antonio College
Fred Weber, Saddleback College
Wes Wedell, Columbus State Community College
Joan Weiss, Bucks County Community College
Robert Witherspoon, Triton College

Gary F. Soldow
Gloria P. Thomas

BRIEF CONTENTS

CONTENTS

PROFESSIONAL SELLING

An Interpersonal Perspective

PART ONE

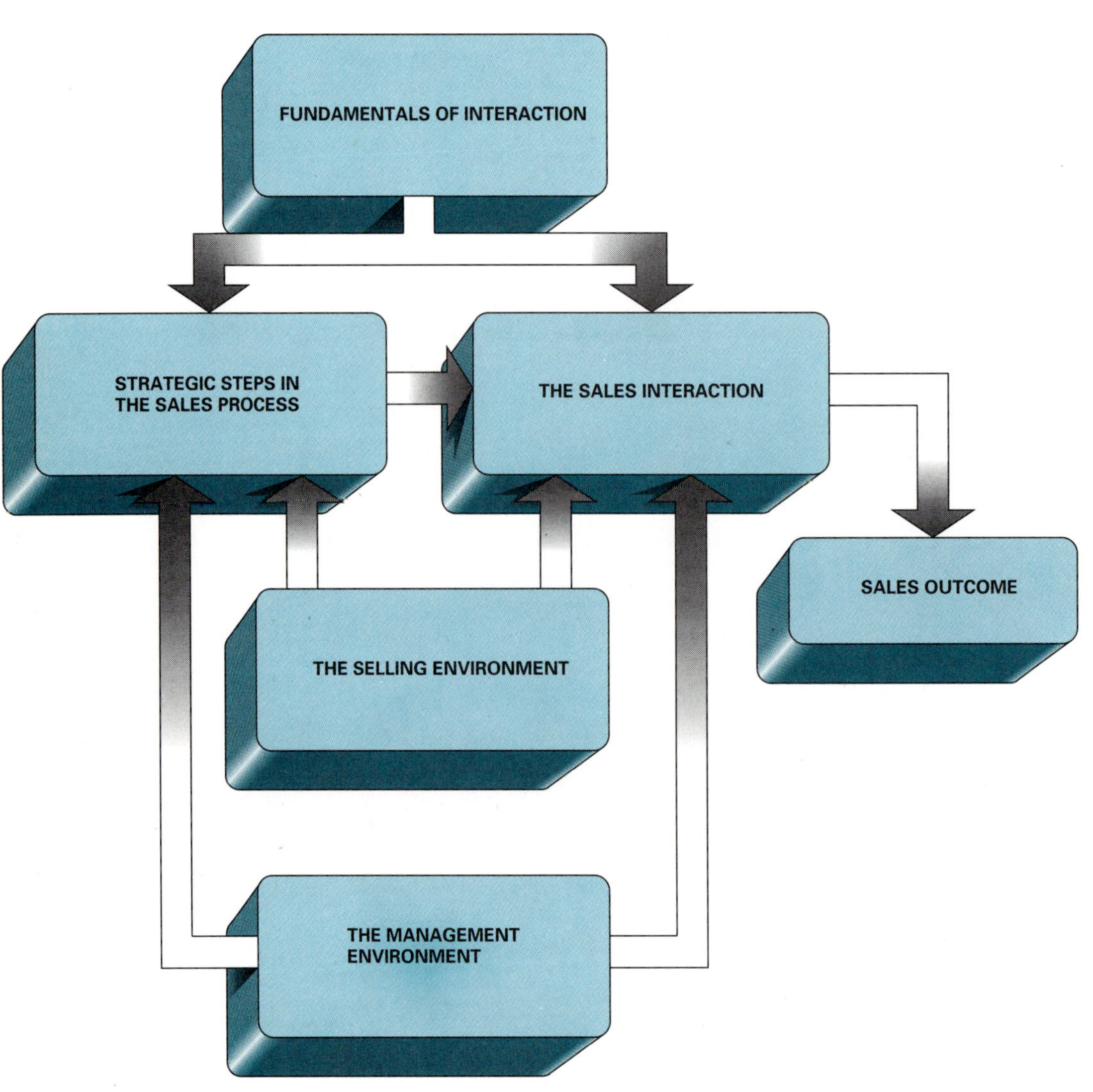

FUNDAMENTALS OF INTERACTION
STRATEGIC STEPS IN THE SALES PROCESS
THE SALES INTERACTION
SALES OUTCOME
THE SELLING ENVIRONMENT
THE MANAGEMENT ENVIRONMENT

OVERVIEW

Introduction

CHAPTER OBJECTIVES

In this chapter, you will learn:

A salesperson is a professional who must have expertise in such areas as marketing, human relations, persuasion, and at least one product category.

Selling in the 1990s involves a partnership between a salesperson and a prospect.

Today's prospects are sophisticated and demanding.

A salesperson can function as a consultant by using nonmanipulative techniques.

A successful salesperson will likely have traits such as extroversion, leadership skills, acceptance of others, stress tolerance, energy, optimism, and self-esteem.

There are many different types of sales jobs.

Sales jobs vary by task and by context.

Sales can be a rewarding career with long-term potential.

CHAPTER OUTLINE

A Sales Challenge

MS. TUKOWSKI: We're very pleased about the fuel efficiency. I still wish we could do better.

MR. SORINO: I agree, but this really is an improvement. Anyway, planes are filling up now, so costs are way down.

MS. TUKOWSKI: The thing I like about this engine is its noise level. People have been complaining more and more about airplane noise. This engine is incredibly quiet.

MR. SORINO: I'm pleased about that, too. I'll bet that we can even get some airports to lift restrictions on landings and takeoffs late at night with this engine. That would be great.

MS. TUKOWSKI: One big issue, of course, is the vibration. We certainly don't want any more problems like those we've had recently.

MR. SORINO: That's for sure. And that's another great thing about this engine; the vibration problem has also been greatly reduced.

MS. TUKOWSKI: What about the data from all the test flights? I think they look impressive, don't you?

MR. SORINO: Without question. This engine is amazing. The other thing that is great about it is the maintenance. Compared to older engines, it's a whole new ball game.

MS. TUKOWSKI: It's true. This baby can go twice as long before it has to be checked. That's going to simplify everyone's life.

MR. SORINO: All I can say is, we're really excited about this.

MS. TUKOWSKI: So are we.

An Overview

The preceding dialogue concerns a commercial airline that is considering what engines to buy for its latest airliner. At first, it appears that both Mr. Sorino and Ms. Tukowski work for the airline, and they are discussing how great the new engine is. In fact, only Mr. Sorino works for the airline. Ms. Tukowski as a sales representative for the manufacturer of the engine.

What is noteworthy about their dialogue is that they seem to be partners. There is no sense that Ms. Tukowski is persuading Mr. Sorino. In fact, Ms. Tukowski is actually working for and with Mr. Sorino. This notion of a partnership is a fundamental aspect of selling in the 1990s. Today's salespeople are problem solvers. For that reason, they are respected and valued colleagues of their clients.

The purpose of this chapter is to explain what a salesperson is and what a salesperson does. We begin by providing an overview of the salesperson and his job in order to demonstrate the professionalism that is required. Next, we quote salespeople to show how they view their jobs. With these comments, we can present a more specific description of what a salesperson is. We then discuss what kinds of people are most likely to be successful in sales. Finally, we present the range of career possibilities for professional salespeople.

The Salesperson as a Professional

What professional person has to be an expert in interpersonal relationships, an expert in the art of persuasion, thoroughly knowledgeable about marketing, extraordinarily well informed about at least one product category or service industry, sophisticated about human behavior, adept at self-management, a motivated and disciplined self-starter, and an energetic and affable individual capable of dealing with a wide variety of sophisticated and knowledgeable people?

Consider doctors or lawyers. They certainly must satisfy some of these requirements, but they can be successful without fulfilling all of them.

It is the salesperson who must satisfy every one of those requirements. Salespeople must excel at interpersonal relations and persuasion since these define a major part of their occupation. They must have some insight into human behavior because they need to have some intuitive understanding of what motivates people. They certainly must be knowledgeable about what they are selling, and they should have a broad understanding of marketing as well, since sales is part of the marketing function. Salespeople are not likely to be successful unless they are likable and affable. They need to be energetic and motivated because, unlike many professionals, they are not subject to daily supervision. For the same reason, they have to be disciplined and able to manage their time efficiently. Table 1.1 summarizes the basic requirements for a salesperson, and the relationship between the requirements and the salesperson's job.

A recent survey conducted by the editors of *Sales & Marketing Management* of 10,000 sales and marketing executives listed the following traits in describing

Table 1.1 Requirements for a Salesperson and Their Relationship to the Salesperson's Job

Basic requirements	*How the requirements fit the salesperson's job*
An expert at interpersonal relationships	The job involves one-to-one personal contact
An expert at persuasion	It is necessary to motivate prospective buyers
Knowledgeable about marketing	Sales is part of the marketing function
An expert on some service or product category	Success in sales requires extensive knowledge of the product or service
Affable and likable	Buyers prefer to deal with a salesperson they like
Disciplined and energetic	The job has little supervision, and the salesperson has to be a self-starter

EXHIBIT 1.1

Running Into the Rude Buyer

All salespeople are bound to run into a rude buyer. There is at least one in every territory. Such buyers have nothing good to say about the product or the salesperson. They seem to enjoy making snide remarks. They treat the salesperson as though he is "carrying the plague."

While the salesperson might tend to blame himself for getting such treatment, often the rude buyer is just venting his anger about some unrelated incident or from another salesperson's poor showing. It is possible to calm such a person down. All that is required is a simple question such as "Have I done something to displease you?" Such a question will cause many buyers to be reasonable and even offer an apology. In order to see if you can handle a rude buyer, answer the following questions. If you answer "yes" to at least seven, you are capable of holding your own.

1. When you meet a rude or insulting buyer, do you stay with him instead of walking out?
2. When a buyer is insulting, do you think about what you might have done on past calls to upset him?
3. Do you get right down to business with a buyer and not waste his time?
4. Do you take into consideration the fact that the buyer may be taking his resentment of other salespeople out on you?
5. Are most of your customers pleasant to you?
6. Do you think you can recognize a bad reception as a dismissal device?
7. Can you counter such a tactic?
8. Do you consider a crusty buyer as a challenge?
9. Do you perform all your obligations to the customer?
10. Is your deportment such that you are welcome in a buyer's office?

Source: G. N. Kahn (1986). Running into the rude buyer. *United States Tobacco and Candy Journal, 213* (February 20–March 12), 69, 71.

successful sales professionals: stable, self-sufficient, self-confident, goal-directed, intellectually curious, speedy, and accurate.[1]

The Impact of Sophisticated and Knowledgeable Buyers

What is particularly important here is the nature of the people the salesperson will have to deal with. We are referring to buyers. The buyers of the 1990s, whether consumers or purchasing managers for large corporations, are a sophisticated group of people. They are usually demanding and knowledgeable. They are not going to respond to the stereotypical salesperson.

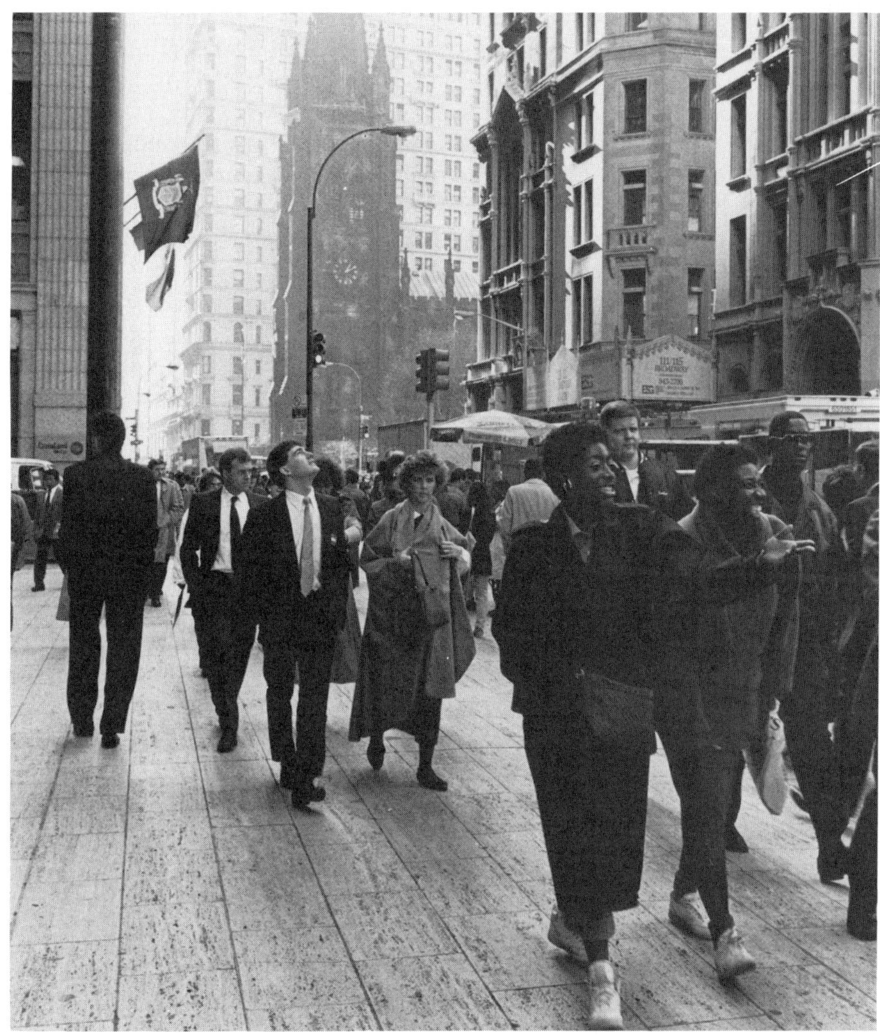

Many of the people pictured in this street are professional salespeople. They do not wear a uniform. What sets them apart is the way they function when they deal with their clients. (© Thelma Shumsky/The Image Works, Inc.)

As Dr. Herbert Greenberg, president of Personality Dynamics, a consulting firm in Princeton, New Jersey, says, "Many people think of salespeople as the gregarious, hard-driving, handshaking, backslapping, do-anything-for-the-close, buy-it-now-because-you'll-never-have-an-opportunity-like-this-again type of character. . . . And taken to an extreme, there can be a fine line, in some people's minds, between the salesperson and the con-man."[2] This stereotype is a far cry from the professional we just described. The stereotype would simply not be acceptable to the public that the salesperson now faces. In fact, there is a strong movement toward a soft-sell approach. "The principal new rule of the game: Hard-sell is out. Arm-twisting salesmen . . . no longer seem to do the trick."[3]

This can be seen at the retail level as well as in business-to-business selling. For example, the retail salespeople at Circuit City, a large electronics store, are required to dress in navy (or gray) blazers and polished shoes and are well groomed. They direct customers to equipment in their price range. "Salespeople have been schooled intensively on the distinctions between each product, and they specialize in only one category of merchandise at a time. They are assertive, and will always point out advantages of products one level more expensive than a customer has first sought out. But they are trained not to browbeat customers into making more expensive selections or denigrate less sophisticated merchandise."[4]

A sophisticated and knowledgeable buyer wants and insists upon a *partner.* Successful sales professionals of the 1990s regard their task as one involving a series of partnerships in which they help buyers solve their problems in the best possible way. To highlight this partnership view, Table 1.2 shows what purchasing agents like and dislike about salespeople.

To reflect further on this information, "In a speech to MBA students of Boston College, William E. Phillips, chairman of Ogilvy and Mather, one of New York's more creative ad agencies, once listed nine things he hoped a business school would *not* teach his daughter if she chose to attend one. One of those nine is 'that salesmanship is either ignoble or an outmoded skill. Let's face it, salesmanship is persuasion. We all do it. And the person who can find new ideas or products and then with imagination and persuasion convince others of their value—that individual performs a noble task'."[5]

Clearly, not all persuasive approaches and communication styles are equally

Table 1.2 What Purchasing Agents Like and Dislike About Salespeople

What do purchasing agents like most in a salesperson? Of the 15 characteristics they were asked to rate in the S&MM survey, the 205 respondents ranked these:

Most valued	Reliability/credibility	98.6%
	Professionalism/integrity	93.7
	Product knowledge	90.7
	Innovativeness in problem solving	80.5
	Presentation/preparation	69.7
Least valued	Supplies market data	25.8%
	Appropriate frequency of calls	27.3
	Knowledge of competitor's products	31.2
	Knowledge of buyer's business and negotiation skills (tie)	45.8

Source: Reprinted by permission of *Sales & Marketing Management,* © 1985. PAs examine the people who sell to them. *Sales & Marketing Management,* (November 11), 38–41.

well liked by all buyers. Table 1.3 shows how buyers distinguish between good, bad, and "ugly" salespeople.

What a Salesperson Is

In the broadest sense, a **salesperson** can be defined as an individual who functions as *"the intermediary . . . between the holder of goods and one who wants the goods from the holder."*[6] Beyond that, the people who are best able to explain what a salesperson is, how the salesperson is viewed, and what she does are the practitioners themselves. Following is a series of statements from practitioners.[7]

The View of Sales Practitioners

"The professional salesperson consistently earns an above-average income, has respect from his peers in other professions, has job security, and usually has a sense of high self-worth and job satisfaction." Michael D. Forrester, marketing manager, Employees Unity, Inc., Westminster, Colorado.

"My closest friend is a very successful salesperson wielding national recognition. ... This person is articulate and dedicated to helping people solve problems." Robert A. Murray, Jr., owner, Murray Marketing Services, Wausau, Wisconsin.

"The [sales] rep at a truly marketing-oriented firm is more than just a salesperson. He or she is a marketing representative who is interested in servicing the consumer's wants, needs, and problems." Paul R. Linder, International Hardware Corporation, Anaheim, California.

"Selling is a tough job. When it is done well, there is good reason to be proud because a service has been performed to the satisfaction of a very demanding and important person: the customer." Michael P. Wynne, president, International Management Consulting Associates, Naperville, Illinois.

Table 1.3 Distinguishing Characteristics of Salespeople

The Good	*The Bad*	*And the Ugly*
Honesty	No follow-up	Wise-ass attitude
Lose a sale graciously	Walking in without an appointment	Calls me "dear" or "sweetheart" (I am a female)
Admits mistakes	Begins call by talking sports	Gets personal
Problem-solving capabilities	Puts down competitors' products	Doesn't give purchasing people credit for any brains
Friendly but professional	Poor listening skills	Whiners
Dependable	Too many phone calls	Bullshitters
Adaptability	Lousy presentations	Wines and dines me
Knows my business	Fails to ask about needs	Plays one company against another
Well prepared	Lacks product knowledge	Pushy
Patience	Wastes my time	Smokes in my office

Source: Reprinted by permission of *Sales & Marketing Management*, © 1985. PAs examine the people who sell to them. *Sales & Marketing Management*, (November 11), 38–41.

"The image of a salesperson as a huckster is as antiquated as running boards on cars. Today's salesperson must be as concerned with customer needs and goals as any marketer. . . . Enthusiasm, empathy, and sensitivity to customer needs will assure a quality salesperson or marketer." E. Anthony Costa, general manager, Life Support Systems, Dedham, Massachusetts.

"Professional salespeople are problem solvers and not someone who 'does anything to make a sale." James Harris, district sales manager, Construction Products, a division of W. R. Grace & Company, North Brunswick, New Jersey.

"In a very large sense, a properly motivated salesperson is indeed the company, its values, and its culture. A salesperson is the direct link between the customer and the company. . . . Our sales management staff is part of the decision-making process in overall marketing and product matters." Al Prillaman, manager, national accounts, Aladdin Synergetics, Inc., Nashville, Tennessee.

"I have always regarded salespeople and marketers as equals in that each makes a valuable contribution to the profitability of the company. . . . Not only does the salesperson carry the necessary product knowledge, as well as information relating to the buying habits of the market in his or her territory, but he or she must also possess the necessary communication and human relations skills in order to be successful." Lynne Royse, co-founder of Professional Saleswomen of St. Louis, Missouri.

"At our company, the sales manager comes several notches above the marketing department. The sales manager and our sales force are the infantry. Everything else is support." Marshall Goldstein, dental sales representative, American Dental Supply Corporation, Alexandria, Virginia.

The Salesperson's Job

These statements are compelling in that a number of observations are consistently repeated. These observations allow us to define the job of the salesperson more specifically.

In keeping with our broad definition of the salesperson's job, the first thing to be noted is that the salesperson is viewed as a link between a customer and a company. Second, the salesperson is a problem solver. Third, the salesperson is a marketer, primarily concerned with helping customers deal with their wants, needs, and goals. Fourth, the salesperson is a skilled communicator and an expert in buyer behavior. He is articulate and understands the complex decision-making processes that the buyer goes through. Fifth, the salesperson is a major source of information regarding his product and the competing products. It is for this reason that marketers use input from salespeople to develop sales forecasts and establish sales quotas.[8] Figure 1.1 summarizes these five descriptors of the salesperson's job.

The Salesperson as Consultant

Of the five defining aspects of the salesperson's job, there is one that deserves special note: the view of the salesperson as a problem solver. This view is consis-

1. The link between the customer and the company
2. A problem solver
3. A marketer
4. A skilled communicator and an expert in buyer behavior
5. A major source of information regarding the company's product and competing products

FIGURE 1.1 The essentials of the salesperson's job.

tent with what we indicated earlier regarding a partnership between the prospect and the salesperson. In the role of problem solver, the salesperson is viewed as a **consultant.** A consultant gives *professional advice.*

What is particularly important about the salesperson as a consultant is that his own immediate goal changes. In other words, while he doesn't lose sight of the goal of making the sale,[9] the professional salesperson is equally concerned with becoming "a sustaining resource for the customer."[10] As a true consultant, this individual "must be conscious of the problems, interests, facts, feelings, prejudices, and fears that motivate the individual or the group with whom he or she is exchanging knowledge."[11]

More specifically, as a professional consultant, the salesperson has to have certain skills. The salesperson:

1. Is an aggressive listener rather than an aggressive talker.
2. Doesn't begin to present what he is selling until the prospect's needs and objectives are fully understood.
3. Never begins a sales call with a rehearsed presentation. Instead, he fosters a two-way dialogue.
4. Presents only those aspects of what he is selling to which the prospect can relate.
5. Encourages and welcomes resistance from the prospect. This resistance is handled directly and honestly.
6. Avoids closing the sale until she is certain that the product really meets the prospect's needs.[12]

To summarize, the defining skills of a consultative salesperson are as follows:

Fully understands prospect's needs and objectives.
Listens and fosters a two-way dialogue.
Deals only with what the prospect can relate to.
Encourages and deals openly with the prospect's resistance.
Closes the sale only when the product meets the prospect's needs.

PURCHASING DEPT.
LOUTHAN
"Oh . . . hold it a second . . . at this point my boss says I should ask for the order."
©Copyright, Sales & Marketing Management

FIGURE 1.2 (Reprinted by permission of *Sales & Marketing Management,* © 1985, November 11 issue, p. 40.)

Nonmanipulative Selling

The key to consultative selling is **nonmanipulative selling.** Nonmanipulative selling involves the following:[13]

1. Being other-oriented instead of self-oriented.
2. Asking questions and listening instead of telling.
3. Cultivating customers rather than sales.
4. Being people-oriented rather than product-oriented.
5. Being adaptable rather than inflexible.
6. Discovering needs rather than creating needs.
7. Establishing trust and understanding rather than fear and tension.

Much of this book will expand upon the skills and techniques that will help one to engage in truly consultative selling. A question that emerges logically is whether a good salesperson is born or made. In other words, are there certain traits that make some individuals good salespeople even without specific training? The answer is yes. While we can do a great deal to train a prospective salesperson, some people have personality traits that make them especially good candidates for the job.

Who Is Most Likely to Be a Successful Salesperson

Predicting who will be a successful salesperson is very important for most companies. In fact, some companies regard selling as so important that their star salespeople earn more than the company's president. Some salespeople earn up to $1,000,000 a year.[14] Table 1.4 shows the salaries of top salespeople in various cities.

A great deal of research has been conducted to predict salesperson success based upon personality traits. The results are not always clear-cut, but there are some traits that do seem to make a difference,[15] especially if such factors as the complexity of the specific selling task are taken into account.[16] Following is a discussion of some of those traits.[17] Note that many of the traits would benefit any professional, not only the salesperson.

1. Extroversion. Extroverted individuals enjoy dealing with people, particularly new people.
2. Leadership. Good leaders are assertive (as opposed to aggressive). This means that they are sensitive to the needs and feelings of others and behave accordingly.
3. Acceptance. These people are easy to deal with because they have wide tolerance of and respect for others, even if they have different points of view.

Table 1.4 Compensation for "Star" Salespeople

Atlanta	$150,000
	$100,000
	$70,000
Boston	$75,000
	$50,000
	$45,000
Chicago	$150,000
	$75,000
	$45,000
Denver	$50,000
	$30,000
Jacksonville	$50,000
Los Angeles/San Francisco	$52,000
	$35,000
	$30,000
New Orleans	$60,000
	$50,000
New York metropolitan area	$65,000
	$45,000
	$40,000
St. Louis	$60,000
	$50,000
	$25,000
Seattle/Portland	$60,000
	$40,000

Source: Reprinted by permission of *Industrial Distribution*, © 1986. The super salesman. (1985). *Industrial Distribution, 74* (June), 31.

4. Stress tolerance. These people enjoy stress and are able to make it work for them. They are comfortable with change and with unexpected events.
5. Energy. These people are active and enthusiastic.
6. Well-being. These people tend not to have major mood swings. They are relatively stable.
7. Competitiveness. These people are comfortable with competition but are *not* highly competitive.
8. Reserve. They are spontaneous but still tactful.
9. Self-esteem. They have a great deal of self-confidence and can handle criticism and rejection.
10. Optimism. They expect positive outcomes. When they achieve success, they attribute it to their own efforts rather than to external events.
11. Honesty. They are honest and open without being rigidly moralistic.
12. Guardedness. They are not inclined to accentuate the positive. They are comfortable showing both their strengths and their weaknesses.

Many of these personality traits hinge upon the issue of *self-confidence.* When people are self-confident, many of the other traits mentioned naturally follow. In fact, a high degree of self-confidence is extremely important for a salesperson. More than many other professionals, salespeople are subject to continual criticism and rejection. With strong self-confidence, they can cope more easily with rejection.

There are other qualities that good salespeople should have. They must be *persistent.* In order to do so, they have to like what they are doing. Obviously, viewing their job as a profession and regarding what they do as important bolster their persistence.[18]

Interestingly, another important characteristic of the successful salesperson is *creativity.*[19] This trait is useful in many ways. A creative salesperson can think ahead, anticipating a prospect's possible objections. This person can come up with new ideas for the product he is selling. Creativity can also help the salesperson adjust to new situations, new clients, and changes in the general business climate.

Finally, a salesperson should have *empathy*—the ability to sense the reactions of other people.[20] In attempting to treat each prospect as a unique person with unique needs and objectives, the ability to be empathetic will serve a salesperson well.

Obviously, a salesperson does not have to have all of the traits discussed to be successful. Some of these traits are probably more important than others. We believe that the most important one is self-confidence. However, persons who lack self-confidence shouldn't despair; a number of training programs can help them. In addition, early successes lead to self-confidence.

These facts suggest that most people could be trained to be salespeople. At the same time, the more people possess the traits just listed, the more easily they will adapt to the selling task.

The Different Types of Selling Jobs

Not all sales jobs are the same. People who are acquainted with marketing are aware of this, and even the general public distinguishes among various types of sales professionals.[21] Students are also aware of differences in sales positions. Those who are contemplating sales jobs seem to have a clear preference for positions as sales engineers or as sellers of services. They least prefer retail or trade sales positions.[22]

Actually, sales positions differ in two ways. First, they differ in terms of **task.** Second, they differ in terms of **context.** Sales tasks range from taking orders to creating orders using a complex problem-solving approach (see Figure 1.3). The primary difference between these types of tasks is the degree of persuasion involved. Order taking requires no persuasion on the part of the salesperson, whereas in other tasks, persuasion is a key activity.

When we speak of the sales context, we are distinguishing among the retail setting, the wholesale setting, the manufacturing setting, and the service setting. We now discuss in more detail the task and the context of the salesperson.

The Sales Task

Order Takers. The least-demanding sales tasks are those that require little or no persuasive activity. **Order takers** do whatever paperwork is necessary for a customer to procure merchandise. They may answer questions, but they are not usually concerned with persuading a customer. The customer who deals with an order taker usually has already made a buying decision. This does not mean that an order taker can't engage in some persuasion. Often order takers will ask customers if they need additional merchandise, particularly items that will facilitate the use of the initial purchase.

FIGURE 1.3 The sales task and the degree of persuasive activity.

Order Getters. **Order getters** are directly involved in persuasive activity. They search out prospects and persuade them to buy specific products. The major strategy that order getters use is to determine the needs of the prospect and to help the prospect see how the product will solve his or her needs.

There is some overlap between order taking and order getting. For example, order getters may have to do the same paperwork as order takers once the order getters persuade their prospects to purchase.

In addition, within each category, there is a wide range of difficulty and challenge. For example, an order getter may be a salesperson in a retail computer store who sells only to individuals for their personal use. It may be necessary to help identify the prospect's problems and tailor the offering so that it will solve the prospect's problems. But this person's job is not as complex as that of an order getter working for a computer manufacturer who is selling to a large organization.

This second order getter is concerned not only with immediate needs and problems. He must also pinpoint needs that may not occur for years. Through a complex persuasive approach, the order getter may be able to convince the organization to buy equipment that has the potential to solve future problems. On some occasions, an order getter may even influence the manufacturer to make changes in the product.

The Sales Context

The Retail Setting. The context in which we are most likely to encounter a salesperson is in a retail store. In fact, in order to get a particular item that we want, we usually have to consult a salesperson. Of course, there are many retail situations in which we can pick up an item and pay for it with no interaction whatsoever with a salesperson.

There is a tremendous variety of salespeople in retail establishments. Often the salespeople are nothing more than order takers, since many customers in retail establishments have already decided what they will purchase. For example, salespeople in department stores are likely to be order takers. However, there are also many retail establishments in which the salespeople are order getters. For example, salespeople in a furniture store are more likely to become actively involved with customers and help the customers solve their problems.

The one critical aspect of retail settings that tends to prevent salespeople from getting involved in the most complex aspect of order getting is that usually *the customer goes to the retail store.* That means that the retail salesperson does not have to generate customers directly. (Of course, retail stores do generate customers through advertising in the mass media, but that is distinct from personal selling.)

The Wholesale Setting. The salesperson working with a wholesaler can also be either an order taker or an order getter. This individual is an order taker if he responds to a retailer's request for additional units of a particular product or makes sure that the retailer has an adequate supply of the product. The salesperson is an order getter when he searches out retailers and attempts to persuade them to carry a new product.

The Manufacturer Setting. In the manufacturer setting, too, salespeople can be order takers or order getters. If they are order getters, they can function in a whole range of positions from routine selling over the telephone (telemarketing) to the more creative and complex tasks of solving long-range problems for a large organization.

In its most complex form, the job of manufacturer's representative is a respected and highly compensated sales position. At this level, salespeople often have a kind of pioneering task. They have to convince people along the channel of distribution to carry their product. The success of a product can be directly linked to the success of a pioneering salesperson. This individual has to be extraordinarily well versed both in the product she is selling and in the needs of the distributors she wants to handle the product.

The Service Setting. Salespeople who sell services are most likely to engage in order getting. They sell personal services such as insurance or investment advice or deal with nonprofit institutions such as hospitals or arts organizations. When dealing with personal services, they have to locate and persuade prospects as to the benefits their services can provide. They become personal consultants,

These jets represent a product that was created to offer a service. Many salespeople were involved in the development and manufacture of this jet. Many salespeople will be involved in selling the service this jet provides. (© Joel Gordon Photography)

helping prospects to define their needs and developing a package that will satisfy those needs. When dealing with nonprofit service institutions, they are engaged in fund-raising and other public relations efforts to persuade people to depend upon their particular institution.

Table 1.5 shows the two basic sales tasks and the form they take in each of the sales contexts we have discussed.

Specific Sales Titles and Their Functions

As in any occupation, there are many titles in sales. Often these titles are used simply to lend more prestige to a salesperson. Any of the following titles may be used:

Account Executive
Sales Coordinator
Sales Consultant
Sales Associate
Marketing Representative
Professional Representative

There are many other such titles, but essentially they all refer to a salesperson. There are, however, titles that refer to specific kinds of salespeople. These titles tend to be descriptive of the salesperson's major task. Following is a list of such titles and a brief description of the tasks associated with each one.

Service Representative. Service representatives do not sell. They become important after a sale has occurred. Their concern is with such things as delivery, repairs, warranties, or product information.

Table 1.5 Sales Tasks and Sales Contexts

	Order takers	*Order getters*
Retail	Mostly order takers	Some order getting, particularly for more expensive merchandise
Wholesale	Order takers deal mostly with keeping adequate supplies	Order getting is somewhat routinized, although it is concerned with problem solving
Manufacturer	Order taking can be routinized	Order getting can be creative and complex, with a long-term perspective
Service	Order taking is not a major concern	Order getting for personal services is consultative; for nonprofit institutions, it consists mostly of fund-raising and public relations

Account Representative. **Account representatives** deal with many already established customers. They are not concerned with developing new accounts, and they tend not to apply any pressure on their accounts.

Detailer. **Detailers** are concerned with stimulating demand for goods such as prescription medicine or college textbooks. Rather than concentrating on making actual sales, they are most concerned with developing goodwill. In other words, their main task is to engage in public relations. They deal with retailers, wholesalers, or individual customers such as physicians or college professors.

For example, when dealing with physicians, detailers represent pharmaceutical companies. Since physicians are indirect consumers of prescription medicines, the detailer's task is to communicate to them the benefits of certain drugs. It is hoped that the physicians will, in turn, order these drugs for their patients.

Sales Engineer. **Sales engineers** are salespeople who must be experts in the technical aspects of the product they are selling. At the same time, they should be experts in helping customers identify and solve problems. Sales engineers are likely to work in the chemical, machinery, and heavy equipment areas.

Service Salesperson. **Service salespeople** sell services such as life insurance or advertising space. Since they are dealing with services, they have to sell benefits that are often intangible. Such salespeople have to be expert at communicating compelling images to their prospects.

Missionary Salespeople. **Missionary salespeople** call on end users with the intent of creating sales through resellers. As an example, consider a computer sales representative who works for a manufacturer such as IBM. For her, an end user is any business in need of a computer. Her goal is to call on these end users and encourage them to place an order through the computer manufacturer's dealer. Often, detailers and missionary salespeople are considered to be the same.

Inside Versus Outside Salespeople

One additional distinction often made is between the **inside salesperson** and the **outside salesperson.** The inside salesperson generally is engaged in telemarketing. In other words, this person generally sells only over the telephone. Sometimes we use the term *inside salespeople* to refer to people who sell at the employer's place of business, whether or not the selling involves telemarketing.

The outside salesperson is what we typically think of when we think of a salesperson. This is the person who goes out into the field (and, for that reason, is often called a *field salesperson*) and has face-to-face encounters with prospects.

There was a time when inside salespeople were considered nothing more than order takers. While that may be true in many cases, inside salespeople can become critical and serve the same purpose as outside salespeople, even though they may be limited to telephone contact. Often inside salespeople service an account. For this reason, they are likely to have much more contact with the customer than the outside salesperson.[23]

A Career in Sales

At this point, it should be clear that sales should not be viewed as a job you have to take until something better comes along. While being a salesperson is often a stepping stone to other careers, it can be a career in itself. This is particularly true in the manufacturing, service, and trade contexts.

As an example, consider the situation at Marriott Hotels. Once it became clear to management that hotel properties were essentially indistinguishable from one another, the role of the salesperson became vastly more important. The salesperson was the one person who could actually make one property seem different from another. Once that became the view of management, a position in sales became a goal in itself rather than a temporary role on the way to something else. As Jon Loeb, vice president and general sales manager for Marriott, says, "Now it's chic to stay in sales and marketing."[24]

The manufacturing sales representative we referred to earlier who pioneers a new product would be particularly likely to approach selling as a career. This person is highly trained and has a critical role in the success of the manufacturing company that employs him.

In fact, in many fields, training people to be salespeople takes a great deal of time and money. People who undergo such training usually have a long-term career in mind. As an example, consider a sales engineer working for a defense contractor. Such a person has to be very knowledgeable technically. That requires extensive training.

A Salesperson or a Manager?

A decision that many people in sales may face is whether to remain in sales or go into management. This decision might be easier for salespeople to make when they consider some of the advantages they enjoy. They have a great deal of personal freedom. They can control the number of hours they work. They can structure their time and task in a way that is most suitable to them. In many cases, there is no limit on what they can earn. And, of course, salespeople enjoy the thrill of directly influencing a company's success.

A manager receives rewards as well, but they are substantially different. A good manager has to be a good leader. Satisfaction can certainly come about through successful and effective leadership, especially if it leads to company success. Managers are likely to work 10- or 12-hour days, and, of course, they are expected to be reachable during business hours. They have more structure imposed upon them than salespeople do. For many people, that is desirable. In other words, not all persons are well suited for jobs where they have to manage their own time and create their own structure. A manager can make far-reaching decisions and watch the results of these decisions lead to success (or failure). A

EXHIBIT 1.2

Check Your "Progress Pulse" to Measure Career Success

Many people are surprised to find [that] they are not doing well at their job. People often have trouble assessing their career progress because (1) they have a biased perception of themselves—they tend to remember the positive things they hear about themselves—and (2) the workplace has many confusing messages about their success.

Successful individuals maintain control over their workplace. People who react to all the different signals will end up falling behind in their progress. The following questions can help you to assess whether your ability to assess your progress, in other words, your "progress pulse," is healthy.

1. Have you had a formal or informal performance review within the last three months?
2. Have you asked your boss lately what you can do to help?
3. Do you know what your boss's goals and missions are?
4. Have you taken the initiative to do things your boss hasn't yet asked you to do?
5. Have you taken on any special projects within the past three months?
6. Have you been sought out recently for information or special advice?
7. Have you created some positive visibility for yourself?
8. Are you keeping notes on your recent accomplishments so [that] you can give them to your boss before your next performance review?
9. Are you a team player and do you help your co-workers meet their goals?
10. Do people, especially your boss, like to work with you?
11. Do people ask you to [attend] meetings and copy you on memos?
12. Have you aligned yourself with a confidential peer to get candid feedback on your performance and determine how others perceive you?
13. Have you set down where you'd like to be in two to five years?
14. Do you know how your progress compares with [that of] others in your field at your age?
15. Are you aware of training or experience you'll need to advance to the next position?
16. Are you keeping a list of contacts in your field?
17. Have you been attending professional meetings?
18. Can you name an alternative field where you could transfer your skills if necessary?
19. Have you identified a mentor—someone to keep a watchful eye to help you and serve as a good role model?

If you can answer "yes" to 14 or more of those, your "progress pulse" is fine. If you answer "yes" to less than 14, you need greater control over your work situation.

Source: Reprinted by permission of the National Research Bureau, © 1986. Check your "progress pulse" to measure career success. (1986). *The American Salesman, 31* (April), 28–30.

salesperson is usually more limited in terms of how much he alone can do to have a broad effect on the company.[25]

Clearly, there are important differences between management and selling. Both have advantages and disadvantages. It is fair to say that people who elect to become managers are more motivated by a need to achieve security and to establish a service ideal. Those who elect to become salespeople are more motivated by power, prestige, and material gain. While many salespeople go on to management positions, others choose to remain in sales. In fact, given the differences between the two jobs, not all salespeople would make good managers.

Salespeople achieve a great deal of satisfaction from making what could be called a conquest. In other words, when they actually close a sale, this is a kind of conquest. Salespeople have the opportunity to make such conquests continually during the course of their day.

People Who Switch to Sales Careers

Often people switch to sales careers later in their lives. Sometimes they do this because they are forced out of their jobs or because they are simply looking for work outside the home. Following are some anecdotal descriptions of people who have changed their careers to selling.

Norm Neeley left his job as a pilot for Braniff International to become a salesperson for Bell Chemical in Dallas. He did not leave Braniff voluntarily; the company simply stopped operating. He needed to find a profession that would allow him to rely upon his business degree earned more than 20 years earlier, as well as one that would allow him to match his $77,000 salary at Braniff. Selling was an ideal choice, since it satisfied both requirements. Neeley was very successful; within 6 weeks after taking on his new job, he had opened 21 new accounts and was highly regarded by Bell Chemical. He also enjoyed the challenge posed by sales, particularly the opportunity to be innovative and the need to be persistent.

Gary Davis, with a degree in civil engineering, had been a supervisor at International Harvester. When the company fired all its engineers, Gary had to find a new job. He decided to go into sales. He joined the Eutectic Company in Moline, Illinois, as a technical salesperson. He is pleased with his decision. He is able to give himself raises by getting more sales and no longer needs to deal with office politics.

Ken Gaskin was fired after 6.5 years as an air traffic controller for striking illegally. He found a position as an inside salesperson selling over the phone for the Scopus Corporation, which sells and maintains magnetic media packages. He enjoys dealing with people in this manner and says that it's easy to be convincing over the phone.[26]

Linda Crocker was particularly ambitious when, in her thirties, she decided to begin selling computers in New York City. She encountered a great deal of resistance from some customers simply because she was a woman. Customers just "didn't expect to hear anything technical coming out of a mouth of a woman."[27]

Now, of course, she is more comfortable as a technical salesperson, since more women are functioning in technical areas today.

What is notable about these examples is that the switch in careers often entailed a major change. In some cases, the product or service being sold was very different from what the person had been dealing with in his or her earlier career. When that happens, the person has to be trained extensively not only in selling techniques but, equally important, in the technical aspects of the product or service being sold.

How Companies View the Selling Function

Most companies regard the sales staff as extremely important. Almost all companies have to sell something to someone. If they don't sell, they can't exist. In fact, apart from some mail order companies, it is almost impossible to think of organizations that don't employ salespeople in some capacity. Companies depend heavily upon their sales force for a number of reasons: (1) to pursue profitable customer segments or products; (2) to expand into new markets; (3) to minimize problems such as short lead time or small orders, which burden their manufacturing capabilities; and finally, (4) for information on the marketplace in general, as well as on the competition.[28]

Because selling is such an important role in the organization, it is not surprising that a large portion of a company's resources is committed to its sales function. As a result, the career of a salesperson offers many exciting opportunities. It is likely to be highly regarded in any organization, since it is, in many ways, the backbone of the company.

The Cost of a Sales Call. Simply by considering the cost of a sales call, you can appreciate that it is not taken lightly by any organization. The average cost of a sales call is $229.70. Many industries, however, have average costs considerably above that figure. For example, the average cost in the computer industry is almost double: $452.60.[29] Table 1.6 shows average sales cost by industry.

Required Background for the Entering Salesperson

"One thing is certain: there will always be the need to hire and train salespeople, no matter what the method."[30] Even if people don't have recognizable sales skills, the general feeling is that these skills can be learned, according to Gary Hulgren, associate director of marketing, Moore Business Forms, Northbrook, Illinois.[31] A more important concern among people who hire prospective salespeople is their product knowledge.

An additional concern among recruiters is the salesperson's attitude toward the job. While some college students may dislike selling, there is evidence that many of them are beginning to have a very positive attitude. Robert Peters, director of industrial relations, Power Transmission Division, Dresser Industries, in Worthington, Ohio, has found this to be the case. He believes that this change has come

Table 1.6 Average Cost of a Sales Call by Industry

Computers	$452.60
Primary metals	363.90
Paper	263.70
Nonelectrical machinery	257.30
Transportation equipment	255.90
Electrical and electronic equipment	238.40
Average cost	229.70
Business services	227.20
Instruments	209.50
Fabricated metals	186.10
Stone, clay, and glass products	169.70
Chemicals	155.20
Printing and publishing	148.50
Durable goods for wholesalers	139.80
Rubber and plastics	129.30
Petroleum and coal	99.10

Source: Reprinted by permission of *Sales & Marketing Management*, © 1986. Ups and downs of cost-per-sales call. (1986). *Sales and Marketing Management, 137* (November), p. 24.

about both through sales courses and through direct attempts to eliminate the negative stereotype of the salesperson.[32]

Recruiters are not even necessarily concerned about the student's major. John Phillips, personnel manager for sales at S. C. Johnson & Son, Inc., in Racine, Wisconsin, says, "We have gone to both the business schools and the liberal arts schools, and both have produced successful salespeople. . . . A business major is not an absolute. We are primarily interested in behavioral skills, such as leadership, loyalty, and interest in a sales career."[33]

Compensation for a Career in Selling

A selling position can be very lucrative. While it is not realistic to expect to be a millionaire during one's first year, the salesperson's salary compares very favorably with those of many other professionals. Table 1.7 presents the starting salaries of sales trainees with college degrees. Table 1.8 shows the total compensation for various field sales personnel in 1990.

Future Trends in the Makeup of Salespeople

Like any other occupation, selling will experience changes in the 1990s, largely because of the aging of the baby boom generation. Nevertheless, from the perspective of the job seeker, sales is likely to remain a job seeker's market. John Lukasiewicz, an economist with the Bureau of Labor Statistics, says, "The total number of salesworkers is projected to increase a faster-than-average 20%."[34] This suggests that marketers will have to hire at a fairly rapid rate to keep their sales forces at the necessary level.

Some of these people will embark on a career in selling. (© Ulrike Welsch/Photo Researchers, Inc.)

They are expected to have a more difficult time hiring younger trainees because there will be fewer people in the 16–24 age group, where companies have traditionally found their trainees. One important implication of this situation is that companies will have to pay new recruits much more than they do currently. They will also have to retain older salespeople longer. That itself suggests that a company may have to maximize the career potential in selling so that salespeople will want to stay on longer. It may also lead to attempts to raid salespeople from

Table 1.7 Starting Salaries for Sales Trainees with College Degrees

	Averge Annual Salary, 1986
Salespersons with bachelor's degrees	
Nontechnical degree	$24,496
Technical degree	27,828
Salespersons with MBA degrees	
Nontechnical undergraduate degree	$40,008
Technical undergraduate degree	39,552

Source: Reprinted by permission of *Sales & Marketing Management*, © 1990. Survey of selling costs. Section III: Compensation and Expenses. (1990). *Sales & Marketing Management, 142* (3), 76.

Table 1.8 Compensation Range for Field Sales Personnel

Job Title	*Range*
National sales manager	$120,000–130,000
Regional sales manager	80,000–85,000
District sales manager	60,000–65,000
Senior salesperson	57,000–60,000
Regular salesperson	45,000–48,000
Sales trainee	24,000–27,000

other companies. Finally, this trend indicates that companies will have to hire more women than they have in the past.

All of these predictions suggest that tomorrow's salespeople will be even more valuable than they are today. And their employers will be the first to appreciate this. This portends well for those who seriously want to consider sales as a career. It appears that selling will have more career potential in the future than it has at any other time.

Putting It All Together

The key points presented in this chapter are summarized as follows:

- A salesperson is a professional who must be expert in a number of areas, including: interpersonal relations, in order to perform the central task of face-to-face selling; marketing, because selling is intimately linked to marketing; and a specific product or service category, because salespeople are expected to be knowledgeable about what they are selling.
- Since the salesperson's job is unstructured, with minimal supervision, the salesperson must be a self-starter who is adept at self-management, energetic, and motivated.
- The buyer whom the salesperson faces is sophisticated, demanding, and knowledgeable; therefore, the salesperson must function as a consultant who is nonmanipulative and is chiefly concerned with helping a buyer solve problems.
- Desirable qualities that will help in the success of a salesperson include extroversion, leadership ability, acceptance of others, ability to tolerate stress, energy, a sense of well-being, competitiveness, reserve, self-esteem, optimism, honesty, guardedness, persistence, creativity, and empathy.
- Many of the desirable traits for a successful salesperson hinge upon self-confidence.
- Selling jobs differ by task and by context.
- The task can involve taking an order which requires little or no persuasive activity, or getting an order which requires moderate to extensive persuasive activity.
- The context can be retail, wholesale, manufacturer, or service.

- While sales titles often vary simply to lend more prestige to a particular position, certain titles have specific meanings and functions associated with them, including service representative, account representative, detailer, sales engineer, service salesperson, and missionary salesperson.
- Salespeople can also be distinguished according to whether they work inside (i.e., deal with prospects only by telephone, or at the employer's place of business) or outside (i.e., deal with prospects out in the field).
- Selling is often pursued as a career in itself, although it can be a stepping stone to other career paths.
- Since many companies regard selling as an extremely important part of their work—a typical sales call can cost a company well over $200, a great deal of money is often spent in training salespeople.
- Companies are usually less concerned about a sales trainee's major in college than they are about such things as knowledge of the product category and attitude about the profession.
- Because of changes in our population, the future looks especially promising for salespeople as companies make it an even more lucrative career in order to attract and retain good salespeople.

Our goal in this book is to focus on the various facets of the selling process so that you will have a greater appreciation of the complexities and challenges inherent in selling. If you have a career in marketing, this information will be important to you, since, in one way or another, you will become involved in the selling process.

Key Terms

Salesperson
Consultant
Nonmanipulative selling
Sales task
Sales context
Order taker
Order getter
Service representative
Account representative
Detailer
Sales engineer
Service salesperson
Missionary salesperson
Inside salesperson
Outside salesperson

Review Questions

1. What characterizes the salesperson's job compared to those of other professionals?
2. What characterizes the prospects that salespeople have to deal with in the 1990s? Why are those characteristics important to the salesperson?
3. How is the term *partner* relevant to the salesperson?
4. What is the broad definition of a salesperson? What are the five aspects of the salesperson's job?

5. What is the definition of a consultant? What things does a salesperson do to function as a consultant?
6. What does nonmanipulative selling involve?
7. What personality traits are desirable for a salesperson? Which one is most important?
8. What are the two major aspects of the sales job? What are the components of each aspect?
9. What are some of the sales titles and their basic job descriptions?
10. What is the difference between an inside and an outside salesperson?
11. What are the advantages and disadvantages of being a salesperson compared to being a manager?
12. Why does a company depend upon its sales force?
13. What kind of background or training should a prospective salesperson have?
14. What can we predict regarding the future career potential of salespeople?

Discussion Questions

1. Provide a definition of a professional person. Based on that definition, discuss exactly how a salesperson is (or is not) a professional.
2. What groups of people are most likely to have negative views of selling? Why? How can their views be changed?
3. If you were a sales manager for a large manufacturing organization, what background, personality characteristics, and experience would you look for in screening prospective salespeople?
4. Assume that you are interested in a sales career. Explain how you might prepare for it and how you would see it unfold over the next 15 years.

CASE 1.1

Diane Newhouse was appointed president of a large professional salespeople's organization in the Northeast. The organization consists of all types of salespeople in all contexts. Its purposes are to provide (1) current research and information about selling, (2) an opportunity for salespeople to meet periodically and share ideas with one another, and (3) information to the public about what salespeople do.

The organization has been successful in dealing with the first two purposes, but not with the third. Other members of the organization have argued that the third purpose is not reasonable because the public doesn't care about salespeople and, as a result, doesn't welcome information about them. These people also believe that even if the public does care about salespeople, their views are so negative that it would be impossible to change them. They argue that the organization would be more useful if it added the following to its stated purposes: to serve as a job exchange, to provide training in selling techniques, and to encourage people to consider a career in sales. Diane's first duty as president will be to resolve this issue.

1. Do you feel that the third purpose is reasonable? Why or why not?
2. Even if people question that purpose, what things might Diane do and what kinds of information would she provide to the public?
3. Do you feel that the additional purposes recommended are reasonable? Why or why not?
4. Even if you think that they are not reasonable, how could Diane implement them?

References

1. Boone, L. E., and J. C. Milewicz. (1989). Is professional selling the route to the top of the corporate hierarchy? *Journal of Personal Selling and Sales Management, 9*, 42.

2. Kelley, B. (1985). Here's looking at you. *Industrial Distribution, 74* (September), 152.

3. Stevenson, T. H., and C. H. Paksoy. (1983). An experimental approach to improve student attitudes toward careers in selling. *Journal of the Academy of Marketing Science, 11*, 29–39.

4. Circuit city's fight for profits. *New York Times* (September 10, 1989), F-1, F-10.

5. Caballero, M. (1989). Baylor University's center for professional selling. *Journal of Personal Selling and Sales Management, 9*, 55.

6. Powers, T. L., W. S. Martin, H. Rushing, and S. Daniels. (1987). Selling before 1900: A historical perspective. *Journal of Personal Selling and Sales Management, 7*, 1.

7. The "huckster" image: The debate begins. (July 2, 1984). *Sales & Marketing Mangement, 133* (7), 183–184. The "huckster" image: The debate continues. (1984). *Sales and Marketing Management, 133* (7), 67–69.

8. Klompmaker, J. E. (1980–1981). Incorporating information from salespeople into the marketing planning process. *Journal of Personal Selling and Sales Management, 1*, 76–82.

9. Meyers, K. A. (1982). The selling professional of the 1980s. *Business, 32* (October–December), 44–46.

10. Ibid., 44.

11. Ibid., 45.

12. Ibid.

13. Alessandra, A. J., and P. S. Wexler. (1978). Non-manipulative selling: A consultative approach to business development. *Proceedings of the American Marketing Association, 42*, 59–61.

14. Moine, D. J. (1984). Going for the gold in the selling game. *Psychology Today, 18* (3), 37–44.

15. Ford, N. M., G. A. Churchill, and O. C. Walker. (1985). *Sales Force Performance.* Lexington, MA: Lexington Books.

16. Avila, R. A., and E. A. Fern. (1986). The selling situation as a moderator of the personality–sales performance relationship: An empirical investigation. *Journal of Personal Selling and Sales Management, 6*, 53–64.

17. Moine, D. J., and K. Friedenreich. (1984). What makes a sales superstar. *Industrial Distribution, 73* (November), 85.

18. Kelley, B. (1984). Having what it takes. *Industrial Distribution, 73* (November), 77.

19. Kelley, B. (1984). The creative salesman. *Industrial Distribution, 73* (July), 57.

20. Kelley, B. (1985), loc. cit., p. 152.

21. Swan, J. E., and R. T. Atkins. (1980–1981). The image of the salesperson: Prestige and other dimensions. *Journal of Personal Selling and Sales Management, 1*, 48–56.

22. Dubinsky, A. J., and P. J. O'Connor. (1983). A multidimensional analysis of preferences for sales positions. *Journal of Personal Selling and Sales Management, 3* (November), 31–41.

23. Kelley, B. (1985). The new selling team. *Industrial Distribution, 74* (February), 35–38.

24. Selling becomes chic at Marriott. (1984). *Sales & Marketing Management, 133* (December), 42.

25. Lewis, T. E. (1987). Two roads. *Managers Magazine, 62* (January), 4–8.

26. McAllister, K. (1982). Eight who switched to selling—thanks to hard times. *Sales & Marketing Management, 129* (September), 47–49.

27. Skolnik, R. (1985). A woman's place is on the sales force. *Sales & Marketing Management, 134* (April), 34.

28. Wilner, J. D. (1986). Integrating the sales force into the marketing effort. *Marketing Communications, 11* (June), 97–100.

29. Sales force highlight. (1986). *Sales & Marketing Management, 137* (June), 24.

30. Woods, B. (1982). Recruiting the best and the brightest. *Sales & Marketing Management, 129* (August), 51.

31. Ibid., 51.

32. Ibid., 54.

33. Ibid.

34. Taylor, T. C. (1986). Meet the sales force of the future. *Sales & Marketing Management, 136* (March), 59.

Marketing and Sales

CHAPTER OBJECTIVES

In this chapter, you will learn:

A broad understanding of marketing and a perspective on where selling fits into the exchange process.

The basics of a marketing plan.

How your activities as a salesperson fit into your firm's marketing efforts.

To develop a broad outline of the personal selling process.

To differentiate between basic and applied selling skills.

How the parts of this textbook fit together.

CHAPTER OUTLINE

A Sales Challenge
An Overview
Marketing and Personal Selling
- Marketing Requires a Chain of Salespeople
- Salespeople Negotiate Exchanges

The Firm's Marketing Strategy
- Target Marketing
- The Marketing Mix
- The Promotion Mix

Mass Communication Versus Personal Communication
Advertising Versus Personal Selling
- Combined Advertising and Personal Selling

Personal Selling as Part of Marketing: A Summary
The Personal Selling Process
- Searching for Potential Buyers
- Planning the Sales Call
- The Sales Call
- Postsale Activities

Background Skills
- Basic Skills
- Selling Skills

Putting It All Together
- The Textbook's Outline

Key Terms
Review Questions
Discussion Questions
Case 2.1
References

A Sales Challenge

Mike Falls was a very successful salesperson in the chemical industry. His nephew Tom had always admired him and wanted to pursue a career in sales. Mike advised Tom to take a course in personal selling when he started college, and Tom agreed. The following conversation took place between the two a week after Tom enrolled in the course.

TOM: I finished reading Chapter 1 in my textbook, and I guess I'm really convinced that I need to study selling if I'm to succeed in a career in sales. I'm learning that there's a lot more to it than I realized. But now we're supposed to read a chapter on marketing. Why do I need to learn about marketing? I thought marketing was about advertising, not sales.

MIKE: Marketing is about a lot more than advertising. Marketing is about exchange, and my whole job is really about exchange. You could say that every time I negotiate the details of a new contract, I'm doing marketing.

TOM: I didn't think of it that way.

MIKE: If you read your textbook, I bet you'll see why marketing and personal selling are closely related. Once you understand the relationship between sales and marketing, you'll be able to understand what's involved in the selling process.

TOM: Really?

MIKE: Yes. And if you understand the basic process, you'll be able to understand *why* you need the skills you do. And wouldn't you rather know why you are doing something?

TOM: That's for sure.

An Overview

The purpose of this chapter is to provide an overview of the material covered in the rest of the book. We are concerned here with two major issues: One is the way in which your selling efforts fit into the rest of your firm's marketing program. The other is the way in which the parts of your selling efforts fit each other. The chapter is divided into three major sections. First is a general explanation of marketing and a discussion of the role played by salespeople in marketing activities. From this perspective, we proceed to discuss the personal selling process and explain why each of the stages in this process is necessary. Finally, we identify the basic skills and knowledge required to engage successfully in personal selling. The outline of the book is based on these skills.

Once you understand how selling fits into marketing, you will understand the reasoning behind the second half of the chapter when we outline the actual selling process. However, after reading this chapter, you will not be expected to have mastered the entire selling process. Instead, you should have developed a basic *outline*, which you will fill in as you read the rest of the book. When you study each of the following chapters, you should refer back to this one to see how each specific topic ties into the original outline. Without such a reference point, it is easy to lose sight of the big picture as you concentrate on learning specific topics.

Marketing and Personal Selling

You can best understand the relationship between marketing and selling if we begin with a definition of marketing.

Marketing *is a social and managerial process by which individuals and groups obtain what they need and want by creating and exchanging products and value with others.*[1]

The central concept in this definition is exchange. **Exchange** is *the act of obtaining a desired object or product from someone by offering something in return.* A key idea here is that people will engage in an exchange only if *both* parties feel that it will benefit them.[2] People have been benefiting from exchange since prehistoric times.[3] Even then, when a person killed a large animal, he had too much meat to consume at once. At the same time, other people who spent their time gathering berries had too many berries and not enough meat. By exchanging meat for berries, both parties benefited. The same basic principle holds in today's complex market exchanges. Buyers will exchange their money for products when they feel that the product will benefit them more than any other use of their money.

Although there is no mention of personal selling in the definitions of exchange or marketing, most marketing exchanges could not take place without it. Even in a complex economy like ours, a great deal of marketing activity is coordinated by individual salespeople. In order to appreciate this fact, think about the last time you purchased a pair of jeans, and try to assess the role played by salespeople in your exchange. The person who will probably come to mind is the retail clerk who helped you find your size. However, this person did not represent the true role of the salesperson in your purchase. In fact, it is quite possible that you could have purchased your jeans without the assistance of this person. This does not mean that you could not have bought those jeans without the help of salespeople in general.

Marketing Requires a Chain of Salespeople

The sales clerk in the retail store is only the last salesperson in a long chain of salespeople who were needed to make your exchange happen. How do you think, for example, that your jeans got into the retail store in the first place? Most likely, a store buyer negotiated the sale with individual salespeople working for the jeans manufacturer. And before that, buyers working for the jeans manufacturer negotiated deals with salespeople working for denim and zipper manufacturers. Before that, buyers working for the denim and zipper manufacturers undoubtedly negotiated deals with salespeople representing manufacturers of machinery, computers, and raw materials. And so on.

We could trace all of this selling activity back to the natural resources used to produce the raw materials and machinery needed to make the jeans. Even the farmers who grew the cotton for the denim bought tractors and fertilizers, and each of these exchanges involved individual salespeople negotiating deals with individual buyers. Figure 2.1 illustrates such a chain of marketing activity.

You probably did not think of all of these salespeople when you bought your jeans, and you may be wondering at this point why a complex, technologically advanced economy such as ours would rely so heavily on individual buyers and salespeople to provide links in the chain. The key is that complex exchanges require negotiation.

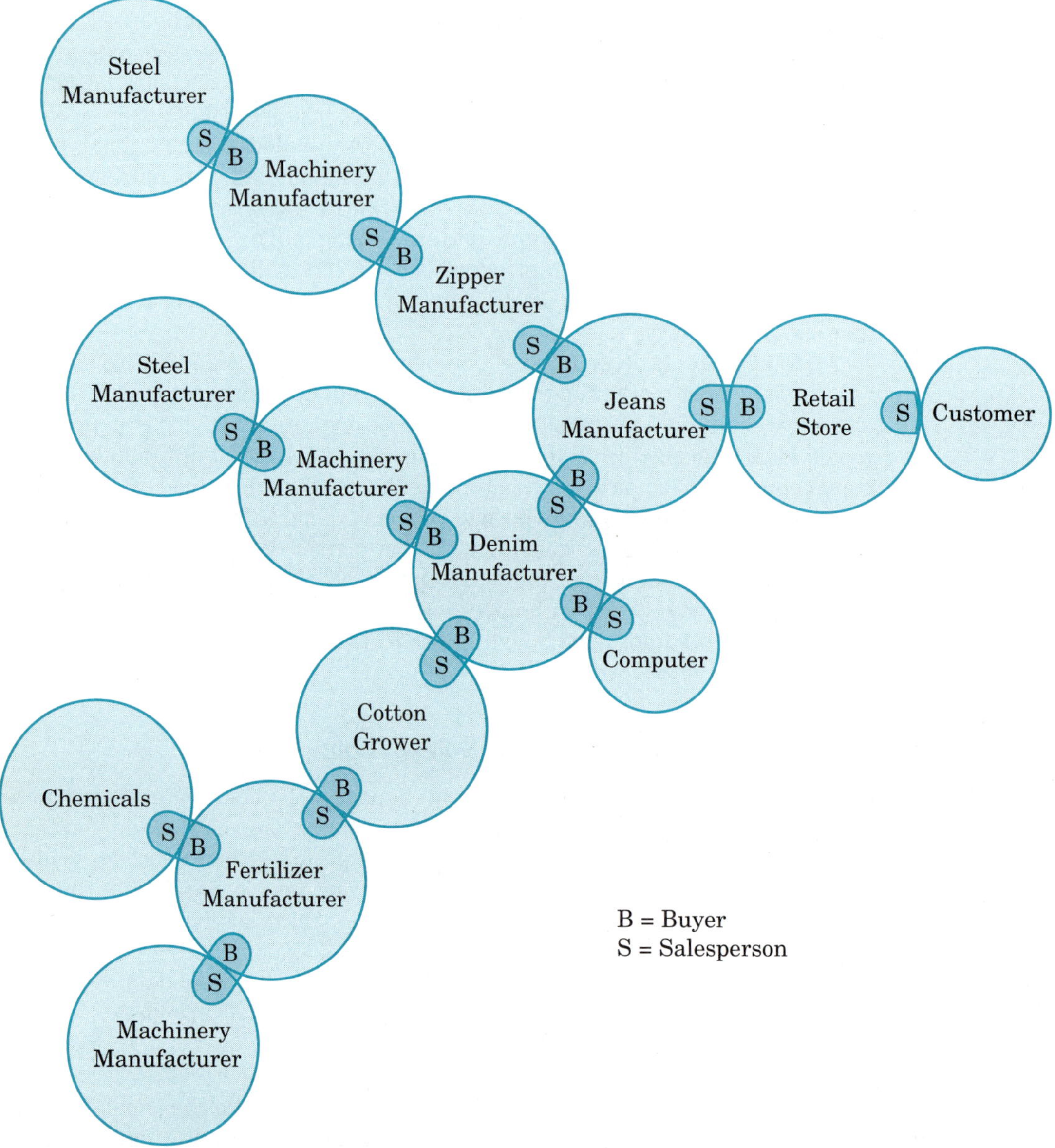

FIGURE 2.1 Marketing requires a chain of salespeople.

Salespeople Negotiate Exchanges

Because salespeople are the human element in the firm's marketing plan, they have the flexibility to *interact* with individual buyers and *adapt* as they negotiate. Remember that for an exchange to take place, the buyer and seller must agree upon suitable terms. This agreement involves *negotiation.*

You may not think of marketing in terms of *negotiated exchanges*, because you do not negotiate directly in most of your purchases. In most retail sales, the negotiation is indirect: A store sets a price for a good, and consumers "negotiate" by accepting or rejecting the offer. If enough consumers reject the price, the store will renegotiate by putting the good on sale and offering it at a lower price. Again, your part of the negotiation is a simple decision to accept or reject the product.[4]

However, in large-scale exchanges (a house or a car and most business-to-business sales), this kind of indirect negotiation is highly inefficient. With so much at stake, there is generally active negotiation where offers are made, rejected, altered, and so on as the buyer and seller interact with each other. This kind of negotiation cannot be handled efficiently through impersonal communication; it requires people to meet face to face.

It is generally true that *the more complex and important the exchange, the more central will be the role played by salespeople.* A salesperson will probably not assist you during your next purchase of toothpaste, but one certainly will play a central role the next time General Motors purchases steel for its automobiles. Without the help of individual salespeople to negotiate complex exchanges, marketing activity in our society would grind to a halt (Figure 2.2).

Type of Purchase	Large business-to-business purchase	Smaller business-to-business purchase	Large consumer purchase (house, car)	Routine consumer purchase
Salesperson's Involvement	Salesperson negotiates deal; adjusts the firm's marketing mix to suit the prospect; may adjust the product price, delivery, warranty, etc.	Salesperson negotiates deal; adjusts price, delivery	Salesperson negotiates deal; adjusts some variables like price, delivery	Transaction handled by a clerk or cashier; involves no negotiation

FIGURE 2.2 Salespeople's involvement varies with the complexity of the exchange.

But salespeople are not just neutral negotiators in the exchange process. They represent the interests of the seller. It is, therefore, important that salespeople have a thorough understanding of their firms' marketing strategies.

The Firm's Marketing Strategy

Most marketers agree that, in designing a marketing strategy, a firm should follow the **marketing concept.**[5] This means that the firm should *start* with the consumer's needs and develop marketing programs to satisfy those needs. Although this might seem obvious, there are many firms that do not have a consumer orientation. These firms start with a product idea instead of a need. They concentrate on building a "better mousetrap," even if it is a mousetrap that consumers do not like to use. Although firms occasionally succeed with this strategy, history is full of product failures that began as technological advances but did not meet the real needs of consumers. Products like picture telephones and quadraphonic stereos failed to achieve expected acceptance because consumers did not want them.[6]

As these examples illustrate, the marketing concept does *not* suggest satisfying consumers by sacrificing profits. It does *not* mean focusing on buyers' needs and forgetting about selling the product. Quite the opposite: The marketing concept says that firms and salespeople who focus on satisfying consumers will be more *profitable* than those who do not. The basic idea is that, in a competitive marketplace, you will be more successful if you satisfy consumers' needs better than your competitors do.

However, in attempting to satisfy needs, we must remember that needs differ from consumer to consumer. You cannot expect to design a single product that will meet *all* consumers' needs. Instead, consumer-oriented firms begin by dividing their markets into segments. **Market segmentation** *is the practice of dividing a market into smaller groups that share common properties.*[7] Consumer markets are frequently segmented by age, needs, or benefits sought, whereas industrial markets are segmented by such properties as the size or type of business that an organization is in.

Target Marketing

Most marketers agree that in order to design products that will effectively satisfy consumers' needs, you must aim for a specific segment (or segments) of the population. When you do this, you are said to be following a **target marketing** strategy.

A target market *is the specific segment of the population at which a firm aims (i.e., "targets") its products.* Some examples of products that are aimed at target markets are Crest Tartar Control toothpaste, My First Sony Walkman, and the Hewlett Packard Laser Jet Printer. Each of these products is targeted at a particular group: those who want to control their tartar, those who want to buy personal stereos for young children, and those who want high-speed, high-quality print for their computer output. There are many more examples of target markets. In fact, most products today follow some variation of this general strategy. The basic idea is that, because you cannot make everyone happy with a single product, you are better off aiming for a specific group and satisfying its needs well. By narrowing your focus, you can develop a marketing program that will truly satisfy your target.

In narrowing your focus, however, it is important to balance the need to have a profitably *large* target with the need to have a target that is narrow enough to be satisfied. If you aim for a target that is too large and diverse, your product may not satisfy anyone's needs. Think, for example, of how difficult it would be to develop one type of soda that would satisfy the entire population. It would be virtually impossible to attract consumers of cola and noncola, diet and nondiet, and caffeine and noncaffeine sodas with a single version of the product. Yet, at the other extreme, you could make so many variations of soda that you would not be profitable.

A key to achieving this balance is the type of product that you are marketing. If you are marketing a low-cost consumer good like soda or toothpaste, you will need to target large segments of the population in order to be profitable. However, as the value of your product increases, it becomes possible to be profitable when dealing with much smaller segments. In fact, in certain large business-to-business exchanges, where an individual transaction may involve hundreds of thousands of dollars, you may need to develop a different variation of your product for each

These products have been aimed at specific target markets. (Reproduced with permission, © PepsiCo, Inc., 1989.)

customer in order to close a deal. This happens when, for example, an appliance manufacturer produces washing machines specifically for Sears or a packaging manufacturer produces packaging specifically for Revlon. In cases like these, much of the work of targeting is carried out by salespeople. The company may develop the basic product, but salespeople are charged with locating prospective buyers and adjusting the product to fit individual needs. In marketing terms, these salespeople are putting together their firms' marketing mixes.

The Marketing Mix

The **marketing mix** includes the elements that the firm uses to create exchanges with consumers. As Table 2.1 illustrates, the marketing mix is made up of many different elements: the product, the brand, the package, warranties, coupons, the price, advertising, publicity, personal selling, and distribution, to name a few. Frequently, you will hear these elements referred to as the *4 P's.* This expression is merely a shorthand way of describing the entire mix by combining the many elements into four categories: product, price, promotion, and distribution. (In order to have a fourth *P*, the distribution element is renamed *Place.*)

As Table 2.1 indicates,

Product includes the physical product or service, the brand name, package, and warranties.

Price includes the actual price plus any discounts, payments terms, and so on.

Place includes the wholesalers and retailers, as well as the transportation and storage of the product.

Promotion includes advertising, personal selling, publicity, and sales promotion.

Marketing Mixes Are Used to Position Products. When a firm follows the marketing concept, it attempts to combine these marketing mix elements in a way that will appeal to its target market. The term **position** refers to the total image that the mix creates. Consider, for example, the positioning of Haagen Dazs Ice Cream. In order to appeal to its premium ice cream target market, Haagen Dazs adds more butter fat to the product in order to make it richer; it uses a foreign-sounding brand name in order to convey the premium image; it packages the ice cream in smaller containers than regular ice cream; and charges a higher

Table 2.1 The Marketing Mix

Product	*Price*	*Place*	*Promotion*
Features Warranties Branding Instructions Packaging	Discounts Allowances Price	Channel Kinds and location of retail stores	Salespeople Advertising Sales promotion Publicity

price. By manipulating these mix elements, Haagen Dazs succeeds in creating a total image that differentiates it clearly from regular, nonpremium ice creams.

Firms May Have Several Marketing Mixes. Many firms, in fact, develop several different marketing mixes that are positioned to appeal to different targets. Haagen Dazs follows this multiple segment strategy by differentiating between its packaged ice creams, its hand-dipped ice creams, and its novelty bars. GM also follows this strategy when it develops different mixes for the sports car, economy car, luxury car, and trucking markets. So does IBM when it develops different marketing mixes for businesses, households, and educational institutions.

Mix Elements Are Equally Important. Although we tend to think of marketing as the exchange of products, as these examples demonstrate, it is actually the entire combination of elements that is being exchanged. When buyers choose one "product" over another, they are actually choosing the marketing *mix* that best suits their needs, and their buying decisions are frequently based on something besides the product itself. This is the case, for example, where a buyer may purchase a particular brand of catsup because it comes in a squeezable bottle, or a particular stereo because it is sold in a store that provides installation and repair. In the business-to-business market, an organization may purchase equipment from a manufacturer who will train people to use it, or it may purchase raw materials from a supplier who can deliver more frequently.

Salespeople May Adjust Marketing Mixes. In each of these cases, the marketing mix creates a total package. However, as you can anticipate, based on some of these examples, the entire marketing mix is not always completely determined before the exchange. In complex, high-stakes exchanges, where target markets are defined more narrowly, salespeople *adapt* their firms' marketing mixes to suit individual customers. Although a salesperson will not adapt the catsup bottle to suit your tastes, it is salespeople who negotiate specifics like training programs or delivery schedules, which can be so important to a business-to-business sale. This is because when firms are involved in complex, high-stakes exchanges, they must compete by adapting their marketing mixes to satisfy *individual* customers. Basic products may remain the same, but other elements of the marketing mix are negotiated to meet the specifications of individual customers. There are many cases where two competitors may produce similar basic products, but the one whose sales force can best adapt the rest of the mix will win the customer.

Consider the case where two computer manufacturers are competing to sell computers to a certain airline carrier. Both manufacturers may have similar basic hardware, but the buying decision will go beyond the basic computer. Competition will involve setting up an entire information system including software, peripherals, training of the personnel who will use the system, the availability of technicians when problems occur, and so on. It will be salespeople who negotiate many of these terms. It is not surprising, then, that having professional salespeople is central to the positioning strategy of many companies.

The Promotion Mix

As Table 2.1 indicates, personal selling is included directly in the marketing mix as part of the promotion *P.* This is because promotion includes the marketing mix elements concerned with communication. When managing the communication portion of its marketing mix, the firm is said to develop a promotional mix. The **promotional mix** *is the particular combination of advertising, personal selling, sales promotion, and publicity that the firm uses to help position its products.* Some promotional mixes may stress advertising, while others may rely more heavily on personal selling or sales promotion. You will be able to understand these choices if we examine the promotional mix elements individually.

Advertising includes messages that the firm designs and pays to place in various mass media: television, radio, magazines, newspapers, billboards, and so on. Through advertising, the firm can exert control over a message that it sends to large numbers of people simultaneously.

In contrast, *publicity* represents a message carried in the mass media for which the firm does not pay directly. Firms may receive publicity for introducing innovative new products or for attempting to help good causes. Because firms do not pay for publicity, they have little control over its contents. As a result, publicity may be negative as well as positive.

Sales promotion includes a variety of short-term incentives that are often used to complement the other mix elements. Typically, sales promotion aims at getting attention for a new product or temporarily boosting sales for existing products. Common examples of sales promotions are cents-off coupons, free samples, and gifts with purchases.

Finally, *personal selling* involves the use of individual salespeople to communicate directly with prospective buyers in a one-on-one format. Personal selling is distinguished by the fact that it is based on interpersonal communication, whereas the other elements are based on mass communication.

You can appreciate the distinctions between the promotional mix elements if we examine the difference between mass and interpersonal communication.

Mass Communication Versus Interpersonal Communication

In general, **communication** is defined as *the process of transmitting information, ideas, and attitudes from one person to another.*[8] Within this basic definition, we can differentiate between interpersonal and mass communication as follows: **Interpersonal communication** is *the transmission of information from one person directly to another person's senses—sight, hearing, smell, touch, or taste.* In contrast, **mass communication** is *the process of delivering information, ideas, and attitudes to a sizable and diversified audience through the use of media developed for that purpose.*[9]

As these definitions indicate, an obvious distinction between mass and interpersonal communication stems from the fact that, in mass communication, there is an impersonal medium between the sender and the receiver of the message. As a result, the actual means of communicating are limited. Whereas in interpersonal communication there is the potential for smell, touch, and taste, as well as hearing and sight, in mass communication the sender is generally limited to communicating via sound (as in radio), sight (as in print), or sound and sight (as in television).

A more subtle but very important distinction between mass and interpersonal communication is that, in mass communication, the message's receiver has little control over the communication process. Because the message is transmitted through an impersonal medium, the receiver cannot respond directly to the source of the communication. Thus, a television viewer or radio listener can adjust the volume or turn off the communication, but cannot otherwise affect the message that is being conveyed. In interpersonal communication, however, there is active participation by both parties. In fact, we use the term *interaction* to describe interpersonal communication, because the actions of each person affect those of the other. When one party communicates a message, the other reacts, providing immediate feedback to the message sender. The feedback affects the behavior of the original communicator, who then affects the other, and so on. In mass communication, there is no direct interaction between the parties. The sender of a message has no immediate way of knowing how the receiver has reacted to it and so cannot alter the message as it is being delivered.

As you will see in the following section, these differences between mass and interpersonal communication explain many of the differences between advertising and personal selling.

Advertising Versus Personal Selling

Perhaps the single most important difference between advertising and personal selling is that personal selling involves **interaction.** As the double-sided arrow in Figure 2.3 shows, personal selling is the only truly interactive element in the firm's entire marketing mix. In personal selling, the salesperson interacts with the prospective buyer, giving him a chance to exert control over the process. While the prospective buyer benefits by being able to exercise control, the salesperson also benefits by being exposed to the buyer's feedback.

By paying close attention to feedback from the buyer, the salesperson can adjust her message continuously as the interaction proceeds. She can adjust her communication style, tone of voice, or level of aggressiveness, as well as the way she is describing the product. In cases where a salesperson senses that she may lose a sale, it is possible to stop midway through the presentation, ask questions of the prospect, and readjust the way in which she is presenting the product. For example, an office copier salesperson who begins to emphasize her machine's speed and finds the prospect unresponsive can adjust the message immediately to emphasize the clarity of the copies or some other feature.

The ability to adjust the strategy continuously is a major advantage of personal selling compared to advertising. With an advertisement, there is no way to

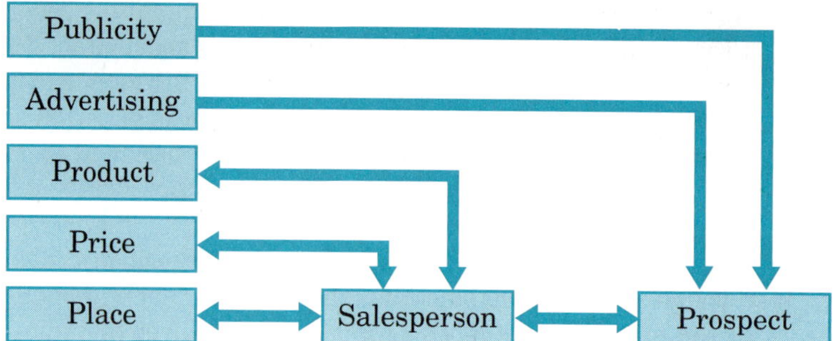

FIGURE 2.3 Personal selling is the interactive component of the promotion mix.

adjust midway through the message. If the copy machine manufacturer had opted to communicate through an advertisement instead of a salesperson, it would have been forced to decide on a positioning strategy (whether it was to stress speed, clarity, etc.), present the message to the prospective buyers, and hope for the best.

It would appear, then, that personal selling is clearly superior to advertising as a means of communicating with customers. It is certainly necessary in cases where direct negotiation is required, and if the objective of marketing is to *adapt* to consumers' needs, why would a company use any advertising at all?

The answer is quite simple. Personal selling is costly. Negotiation costs the buyer and the seller time and money. Though a single advertisement may cost up

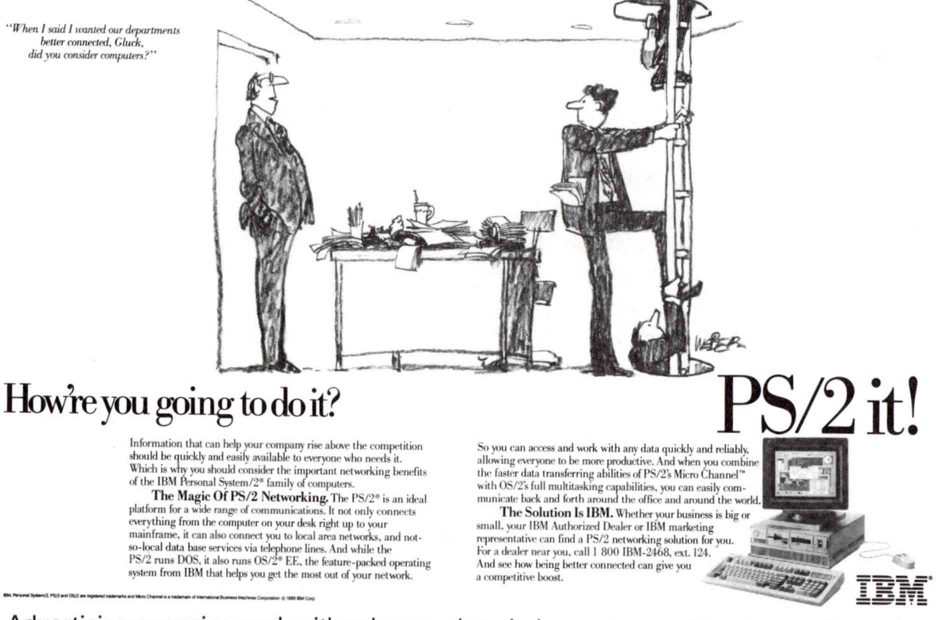

Advertising agencies work with salespeople to help create a positive image. (Courtesy of International Business Machines.)

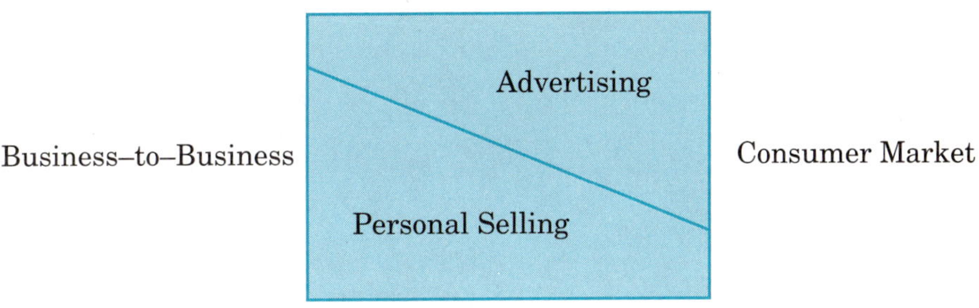

FIGURE 2.4 The advertising-personal selling mix.

to $500,000, the cost per person reached is still less than it is in personal selling. For example, a 30-second ad on prime-time television may average $100,000, but it will reach millions of people. The cost per person reached is less than $0.10. In contrast, each sales call reaches one prospective buyer and costs between $155.90 and $301.10[10] on the average. With this high cost per call and an average of four to five calls placed before a sale is closed, the average cost to land a single industrial account typically exceeds $1,000.

Combining Advertising and Personal Selling

Many firms combine advertising and personal selling in their promotional mixes. In consumer markets, they often use advertising to reach millions of final consumers and use personal selling to negotiate with individual retailers who will carry the product. In business-to-business marketing, advertising is often used effectively to enhance the efficiency of salespeople. An ad placed in a trade journal or other medium seen by purchasing agents can make prospective customers more receptive to a salesperson's call. By helping to project a quality image, the ad can help set up positive expectations before the salesperson makes the first contact. In some cases, advertising can even be used to solicit inquiries from readers so that salespeople can respond to them knowing that the person is already interested. In view of the high cost of a single sales call, it makes sense to use advertising in this way (Figure 2.4).

However, at this point, it may be hard to imagine how a single sales call could cost more than $300. The answer will become apparent when we review the relationship between sales and marketing and discuss the sales process in the second part of this chapter.

Personal Selling as Part of Marketing: A Summary

Thus far, we have discussed the role of the salesperson in the marketing process. The basic logic is quite simple: The basis of marketing is exchange, and people will exchange only when both parties feel that they stand to benefit. Exchange requires negotiation, and complex negotiation requires face-to-face interaction.

Salespeople negotiate the large, complicated exchanges in our economy. (© Jon Feingersh, 1989. All rights reserved.)

Based on this underlying logic, we can draw the following key points:

Perhaps the most basic point here is that our economy could not function without salespeople.

In general, firms compete by deciding on target markets and developing marketing mixes to satisfy these targets.

As greater value is exchanged, firms narrow their target markets and may compete by adjusting their marketing mixes to meet the specific needs of individual customers.

Therefore, complex exchanges require salespeople to carry out target marketing and adjustment of their firms' marketing mixes to suit individual customers.

If you think carefully about these points, you should be able to anticipate the following:

Personal selling must target specific people. Not everyone is a potential buyer for every product.

Personal selling involves satisfying the needs of potential buyers through negotiation and interaction.

In fact, the selling process parallels the marketing process: It begins with the identification of people (or organizations) whose needs can be satisfied and then works to satisfy those needs in an exchange. As you will see in the second half of this chapter, the selling process follows logically from the role that selling plays within marketing.

The Personal Selling Process

Personal selling begins long before a salesperson walks in the door of a prospective buyer's home or office. As the following list illustrates, personal selling is a *process* that follows a series of stages, beginning with the search for potential buyers:

- Search for prospects.
- Check whether the prospects are qualified to buy.
- Plan the sales call.
  - Plan how to secure an interview.
  - Plan whom to contact.
  - Plan a general persuasive strategy.
- Conduct the sales call.
  - Approach the prospect.
  - Present your product.
  - Demonstrate your product.
  - Handle objections.
  - Close the sale.
- Service the sale and maintain a relationship with the prospect.

It is important to see how all of these stages work together, because success at any one stage depends upon success at all of the previous stages. Successful sales calls are built on successful sales plans, and before a salesperson can interact with a potential buyer, a lot of background work needs to be done.

Searching for Potential Buyers

Unlike advertising, where the firm communicates with masses of anonymous people, as a salesperson, you must locate actual individuals in order to communicate your one-on-one message. If you are following a target marketing strategy, you cannot treat the identification of potential buyers as a hit-or-miss task. Once you have defined your target market, you must develop ways to locate people who are potential buyers of the product, so that you can avoid wasting time calling on those outside of your target.

In personal selling, we use the term **prospect** to represent the *potential buyers* of a product. This term was developed to differentiate between people who are potential buyers and people to whom the product is not targeted. A prospect for a swimming pool, for example, would be a middle- or upper-income suburban homeowner who enjoys swimming, not a couple living in a rented apartment. A prospect for a $50,000 high-speed copier would be a university or bank, but not the office of an individual dentist or country doctor.

The process of searching for prospects is called *prospecting*. Prospecting is the first stage in the selling process, and includes not only searching for potential prospects (called **leads**) but also making sure that the prospects you find are qualified to buy. If you do not begin with qualified prospects, you cannot succeed regardless of what else you do.

Planning the Sales Call

Once you qualify a prospect, you must develop a plan about how you will approach her. This planning phase is called the **preapproach** because it is done before you approach the prospect. In the preapproach phase, you map out a strategy for adjusting your marketing mix to satisfy the prospect's needs. This involves a great deal of information gathering. The more information you have when you approach a prospect, the better able you will be to anticipate her needs and plan your mix accordingly.

Further, because your role is that of a negotiator, your preapproach should also involve the development of a strategy for handling the balance of power that will exist between you and the prospect. Your approach when calling on a prospect who badly wants your company's unique product might be quite different from the one you adopt in calling on a prospect who has never heard of you or your product.

In general, the more you can plan both the marketing mix and the negotiation strategy in advance, the better off you will be when you begin to interact with the prospect, as long as you remain flexible in adapting your plan to the situation.

The Sales Call

As discussed earlier, any face-to-face conversation is an interaction. Although we are often unaware of it, most of our interactions with other people follow the same basic format. The interaction begins with a general greeting or opening (e.g., "Hi. What have you been up to lately?"). The opening is followed by a discussion of the task at hand, and the interaction concludes with a formal closing (e.g., "I've got to get going. Will you be around tomorrow? I'll see you then.").[11]

The sales interaction is no exception. It begins with a general greeting, followed by a discussion of the business at hand and a formal conclusion. In personal selling, these stages are called the *approach*, the *presentation*, and the *close*, respectively. Each stage serves an important purpose:

During the **approach,** you get the prospect's interest and "break the ice" by engaging in small talk. With a good approach, you can begin to establish yourself as a credible person who is interested in satisfying your prospect's needs.

During the **presentation,** you discuss your product with the prospect. You ask about needs and attempt to solve problems with your product. You may, at this point, use audiovisual material or conduct an actual demonstration of the product.

During the **close,** you ask for the sale. There are ways of handling this request that will increase your chances of completing the sale successfully. Most of these techniques are based on an understanding of the rules of interaction.

During any of the stages in the sales interaction, you undoubtedly will meet with frequent questions and objections. Because the sales call is an *interaction* designed for *negotiation,* much of your discussion will proceed something like this:

You make a claim.
The prospect objects.
You counter the objection.
The prospect agrees.
You make another point.
The prospect disagrees.
You counter the disagreement.
And so on.

When you engage in this back-and-forth negotiation, you are said to be *handling* **objections.** Objections occur throughout any negotiation and can provide a lot of the feedback you need to adjust your message. In fact, a major advantage of personal selling over advertising is that, with personal selling, you can hear a prospect's objections and respond immediately.

Postsale Activities

Depending upon the selling context, what you do after the sale can be as important as what you do before and during the actual negotiation. This is because success in many selling jobs depends upon developing good relationships with customers. Something simple, like a thank-you note after a sale, often can help ensure repeat business and long-term customers. Also, making sure that your customer receives prompt delivery and good service can communicate that you really are interested in satisfying needs and not just in capitalizing on a quick sale. In the end, you will see that the sales process is circular: The reputation that you create during and after the sale helps to generate new prospects and new business.

Background Skills

Having read about sales and marketing, you can appreciate that the sales process involves more than simply convincing someone to buy something. Specifically, selling involves:

Marketing knowledge and strategy development.
Target marketing.
Interaction.
Negotiation.
Follow-through.

By putting together what you have learned thus far about marketing and selling, you can undoubtedly anticipate many of the skills that you will need to succeed in a sales career.

We can begin by distinguishing between two different types of skills: basic skills and selling skills. The **basic skills** refer to those that, though needed in selling, are not specific to the sales process. Communication is an example of a basic skill: You must know how to communicate in order to sell, but knowledge of communication is not specific to the sales process. In contrast to the basic skills, **selling skills** refer to specific techniques used by salespeople to accomplish the various steps of the selling process. Prospecting, designing the preapproach plan, making the approach, presenting the product, handling objections, and closing the sale are examples of selling skills. It is a central premise of this textbook that success in selling requires mastery of basic as well as selling skills.

Basic Skills

At this point, it should be obvious that in order to succeed in selling, you need to understand something about human interaction. As the previous discussion indicates, the interactive nature of selling is what differentiates it from the rest of the marketing mix. Eventually, complex exchanges in our economy come down to individual salespeople interacting with individual prospects.

Interaction. We interact with others every day. Each time we engage in a casual conversation, we are interacting. But because we interact so often and so automatically, we take much of the process for granted. Did you realize, for example, that all of your interactions are governed by rules?[12] One of the most simple rules is that when someone says "Hello, how are you?" you respond with "Fine, thanks. How are you?" You probably follow this rule so automatically that you do not think of it as a rule. You do, however, know that something is wrong if you say "Hello" and someone fails to return your greeting.

If, as a salesperson, you understand the basic rules of interaction, you will be able to analyze why a prospect might be disagreeing. You will be able to handle the disagreement without letting it escalate into a major problem. In addition, you would know enough about interactions to realize that you should pay close attention to the prospect's **nonverbal behavior** when evaluating the situation. You would be aware of a surprising fact about interactions—that only a small percentage of our message is communicated through the spoken word. You would also know, however, that each prospect is different, and that your evaluation of the situation will require another basic skill: an understanding of human behavior.

Understanding Human Behavior. When you interact with others, you are better off if you understand what motivates them and why they might behave the way they do. This is particularly true of personal selling, where your interaction involves negotiation, uncovering needs, and persuading the prospect that your marketing mix can satisfy those needs better than other alternatives. Whether the prospect is buying for personal use, for the family, or for a large organization, he will have basic needs and problems that you should be able to understand. In order to do this, you need to have an understanding of human motivation and behavior. Uncovering needs is not as simple as asking a direct question. A prospect might not know his needs or want to admit them. How many prospects would, for example, admit to wanting a particular car because it will impress others? How many purchasing agents would admit to buying from your competitor because of free tickets to play-off games?

While no one has a perfect explanation of human behavior, we can at least discuss some basic principles that are helpful in personal selling. Based on these principles, we can answer questions such as the following: Should you ever mention negative facts about your own product or positive ones about the competition? What if a prospect says that she just doesn't like your product?

Selling Skills

As you read about the selling process, you may have wondered how you would proceed at each stage.

How, for example, would I generate a list of companies that might be interested in buying my copying machine? Once I have sold insurance to all of my friends and relatives, how would I obtain lists of other likely prospects? How would I obtain background information on prospective buyers? How would I obtain an appointment for a sales call? If I were trying to sell canning machinery to Campbell's Soup Company, who in the organization would I contact?

What would I do when I find myself face-to-face with a new prospect? Would I immediately discuss my product, or would I talk about the weather? Would I come into a presentation with a prepared speech, or would I invent one as I go? Would I bring slides or films to an average sales call? When should I demonstrate my product? What would I do if my prospect disagrees with a point I have made? If a prospect says that she needs time to think about it, should I agree or should I press her to decide on the spot? Should I wait for a prospect to say "I'll take it," or should I ask for the sale directly?

Hopefully, these questions will cause you to start thinking about some of the skills that are required in selling. Although you cannot answer them now, you can begin to analyze the skills involved. You can see that each stage of the selling process requires specific know-how. Although the basic skills will point you in the right direction, complete answers to these questions require specific selling skills—skills that you will learn as you read this book.

Putting It All Together

Although a typical salesperson does not have the time to spend thinking about her role in the marketing system, an understanding of the salesperson's role as negotiator should lead you to realize why salespeople need a combination of skills to succeed. Recall that the purpose of personal selling is to have a representative of the seller *interact* with the prospect. By its very nature, an interaction cannot be planned entirely in advance. Interactions require *flexibility.* Each person must respond to the feedback of the other. Although a salesperson cannot anticipate every need or objection that the prospect might have, he needs to respond *quickly.* As a result, successful interaction requires more than a superficial grasp of specific selling skills.

Think of what you would do if you were trained in certain sales techniques but had no understanding of the underlying basics. You would know how to prospect, how to design a presentation, and how to demonstrate a product, but with no basic skills, you would have trouble responding to anything unanticipated during the interaction. With basic skills, you understand the *underlying reasons* for what you are doing and can better adjust to each situation and each prospect.

But knowing *why* is not enough. In order to respond quickly, you need to know *what* to do and *how* to do it. The nature of interaction also requires salespeople to be able to respond quickly, and the salesperson who has developed specific knowledge will be better able to do so. It may be possible to succeed by applying common sense and basic skills, but someone who has basic skills alone will not do as well as someone who has mastered specific selling techniques.

The Textbook's Outline

The outline of this textbook is based on the premise that selling skills build on the basic skills. As a result, the book proceeds by introducing the basic skills first in Part Two, and then building on those skills to discuss specific selling skills in Parts Three and Four. However, as Figure 2.5 indicates, the personal selling process does not occur in a vacuum, and in Parts Five and Six, additional topics that affect selling success—the selling context, technology, ethics, and the sales management environment—are presented.

Part Two: The Fundamentals of Interaction—Basic Skills The first chapter in Part Two (Chapter 3) covers the fundamentals of interpersonal communication. It discusses the rules that govern all of our interactions and the ways in which you can use these rules to control your interactions with prospects. It also covers all the components of interpersonal communication and examines their roles in transmitting meaning.

Chapter 4 concentrates on one of the components of interaction: nonverbal communication. An entire chapter is dedicated to this subject because it is so important in conveying meaning in the sales interaction. In Chapter 4, you will learn how to control your own nonverbal behavior, as well as how to interpret the nonverbal behavior of prospects.

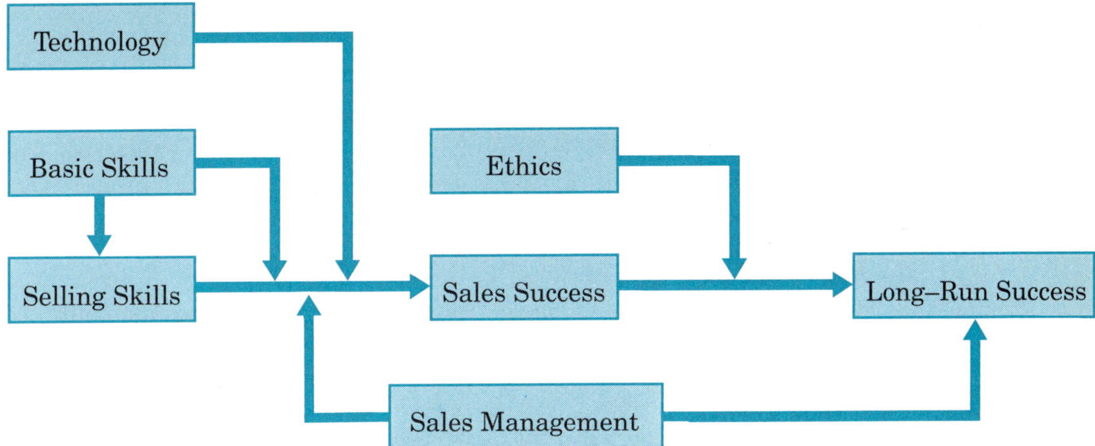

FIGURE 2.5 The relationship between skills and success is affected by the environment.

The final chapter in this part (Chapter 5) deals with the fundamentals of understanding the prospect's behavior. Here the concentration is on the prospect's motives for buying and the ways in which prospects process information and make decisions. This chapter addresses the motives and behavior of final consumers as well as industrial buyers and discusses the process through which organizations buy goods and services.

Part Three: The Strategic Stages of the Sales Process In Part Three we begin our discussion of the sales process with an analysis of the selling stages that occur before the salesperson and prospect meet face to face. Specifically covered are prospecting in Chapter 6, the preapproach plan in Chapter 7, and the development of a persuasive strategy in Chapter 8.

These initial stages of the selling process are referred to as *strategic selling activities* because of their impact on the salesperson's long-run success. If a salesperson makes an error in a strategic activity, he may not be able to compensate for it later on. For example, if the prospecting process leads to prospects who are not qualified to buy, then nothing that the salesperson does during the sales call can result in a sale.

Part Four: The Sales Interaction In Part Four, the stages of the selling process that occur as the salesperson and prospect interact with each other are discussed. Chapter 9 covers the approach and investigation of needs. Chapter 10 covers the presentation and demonstration of the product. Chapter 11 covers the handling of objections. Chapter 12 covers the close. In these chapters, you will learn how your basic skills can be used in specific selling techniques. For instance, Chapter 9 explains the impact of nonverbal behavior on first impressions. It also describes how your initial conversation can determine the pattern that will persist throughout your entire sales call. Chapter 10 shows how to apply what you learned about buyer behavior in constructing your presentations. Chapter 11 shows how to apply what you learned about interaction to handle prospects' objections. Chapter 12 shows how the rules of interaction can guide you when you close the sale.

Part Five: The Selling Environment In Part Five, we cover those aspects of the selling environment that have the greatest impact on the sales process. Our discussion in Chapter 13 begins with an analysis of the retail, business-to-business, and services selling contexts. Chapter 13 also includes a discussion of the final stage of the sales process—the follow-up activities that occur after the close. This final stage of the sales process is reserved for Chapter 13 because the nature of the follow-up activities depend upon the context in which the sale takes place.[13]

Chapter 14 covers the technological aspects of the sales environment. Although selling is and always will be a people-oriented career, the impact of modern technology is growing day by day. Chapter 14 shows how to use technology to improve your productivity and devote the time and effort saved to the human side of selling.

The final topic in Part Five is ethics. As Chapter 15 demonstrates, ethical questions pervade every step of the personal selling process. Ethical decisions are often quite difficult, and the choices made will affect your reputation and success in the long run.

Part Six: The Management Environment Part Six deals with two important management issues. Chapter 16 is about managing resources: time and territories. Specifically, it discusses how salespeople can manage their own time and territories to improve their sales performance. Time management is a particularly important issue for salespeople because selling involves so much freedom and self-motivation.

Chapter 17 deals with the concerns faced by sales managers in their management of salespeople. Although you are probably not a sales manager, this material is relevant to you for several reasons. First, most sales managers come up from the selling ranks. There is a good chance that some day you will become a sales manager. However, even if you have no interest in becoming a sales manager, this material should be of interest to you right now because it covers topics of interest to someone seeking a job in selling: selection and training of salespeople; the characteristics of successful salespeople; and compensation and reward packages for salespeople. If you understand some of these concerns of the sales manager, you will understand an important part of your environment as a salesperson.

Key Terms

Marketing
Exchange
Marketing concept
Market segmentation
Target marketing
Marketing mix

Position
Promotional Mix
Communication
Interpersonal communication
Mass communication
Interaction
Sales promotion
Prospect
Lead
Preapproach
Approach
Presentation
Close
Objections
Basic skills
Selling skills
Nonverbal behavior

Review Questions

1. What is a target market? What is a market segment? What is the difference between a target market and a market segment?
2. How and when do salespeople target market?
3. What is positioning?
4. How and when do salespeople position products?
5. How do advertising and personal selling differ? Do they have anything in common?
6. What is a promotional mix?
7. Contrast and compare interpersonal and mass communication.
8. As a salesperson, what is your most important contribution to your firm's marketing mix?
9. Why do we refer to selling as a process?
10. Describe the personal selling process?

Discussion Questions

1. Could marketing exchanges occur without salespeople? Discuss.
2. Will technology ever replace salespeople? Discuss.
3. Develop promotional mixes for the following products: toothpaste, cars, personal computers, and factory equipment.
4. What additional information would you like to have in order to respond properly to question 3? Why?

CASE 2.1

When Jeff Segal graduated from college with a degree in marketing, he began his career working for a large midwestern marketer of consumer products. His job as a sales representative involved calling on supermarket managers, persuading them to carry his company's new brands, and ensuring that his company's existing brands received good shelf space in the supermarkets. Jeff enjoyed his job and was extremely successful at cultivating relationships with customers.

After succeeding in sales, Jeff received two promotions: first to district sales manager and next to brand manager for one of the company's well-known laundry detergent lines. Jeff was pleased about the new job but concerned over the turmoil that surrounded his line of products. His predecessor had held the job for 10 years and had consistently employed a promotional mix based on heavy advertising expenditures. The emphasis on heavy advertising to consumers—a common strategy among marketers of consumers goods—is called a *pull* strategy. The idea behind this strategy is to create strong brand loyalty among consumers. If it succeeds, consumers will demand ("pull") the brand at the retail store. Store managers will then have no choice but to carry the brand, and the manufacturer will be able to call the shots. Since the balance of power favored the manufacturers, the pull strategy often led to a neglect of relationships with store managers. Salespeople were not encouraged to build relationships and were not allowed any freedom to negotiate with store managers or to offer incentives. In fact, during the era when the pull strategy predominated, powerful consumer marketers treated many large supermarket chains quite badly.

Although the strategy had worked well for Jeff's predecessor, the environment was changing as Jeff took over the job of brand manager. Despite continued advertising expenditures, consumers had begun to view all laundry detergents as basically the same. Many were basing their purchases on such factors as price or convenience, and not on specific brand advantages. As a result, the power balance shifted to retailers. Manufacturers could no longer force supermarkets to carry their brands.

In response to this change, some of Jeff's competitors had begun to rely more heavily on sales promotions—especially cents-off coupons. This strategy boosted sales temporarily but cut into profit margins. As more and more firms offered more and more coupons, they began to lose their effect.

Jeff was in a dilemma about how to proceed. He realized that it was risky to institute a totally new strategy right after starting a new job. Yet, if he did nothing new, his brand would lose sales. If he followed his competitors, he would lose profits. His instincts as a salesperson told him that a promotional mix emphasizing personal selling to store managers could solve his problems. Jeff knew that if his salespeople could develop favorable relationships with store managers, his brands would be given prominent shelf space. This can be crucial in laundry detergents, where an end of isle display can boost sales by 25 percent. Jeff also knew that there were many potential elements of the marketing mix that these salespeople could use to negotiate with store managers: They could offer promotional allowances, store displays, and slotting allowances (payments to the store for trying a new brand). They could also adjust delivery schedules, payment terms, and profit margins. However, in order to employ this strategy, Jeff would have to give much more power to the sales force than his predecessor had given them.

1. What promotional mix should Jeff use? Discuss not only the use of advertising, coupons, and personal selling, but also the extent to which the salespeople should adjust the various elements of the marketing mix.
2. Are there any risks associated with cutting out advertising altogether? Are there any problems associated with allowing individual salespeople complete freedom to adjust marketing mixes?

References

1. Kotler, P. (1988). *Marketing Management, Analysis, Planning, Implementation, and Control,* 6th ed. Englewood Cliffs, NJ: Prentice Hall, p. 11.

2. Houston, F. S. and J. Gassenheimer. (1987). Marketing and exchange. *Journal of Marketing, 51* (October), 3–18.

3. Sahlins, M. (1972). *Stone Age Economics.* Chicago: Aldine-Atherton.

4. The discussion of negotiated transactions comes from Wroe Alderson. (1957). *Marketing Behavior and Executive Action.* Homewood, IL: Richard D. Irwin.

5. Houston, F. S. (1986). "The marketing concept: What it is and what it is not. *Journal of Marketing, 50* (April), 81–87.

6. Schnaars, S. (1988). *Mega Mistakes.* New York: Free Press.

7. Kotler (1988) op. cit., p. 69.

8. Reuben, B. (1988). *Communication and Human Behavior.* New York: Macmillan.

9. Goss, B. (1988). *Communication in Interpersonal Relationships.* New York: Macmillan.

10. *Wall Street Journal* (March 21, 1988), p. 21.

11. McLaughlin, M. (1984). *Conversation: How Talk Is Organized.* Beverly Hills, CA: Sage.

12. Shimannoff, S. B. (1980). *Communication Rules: Theory and Research.* Beverly Hills, CA: Sage.

13. Hite, R. and J. E. Bellizzi. (1985). Differences in importance in selling techniques between consumer and industrial salespeople. *Journal of Personal Selling and Sales Management, 5* (November), 13–30.

PART TWO

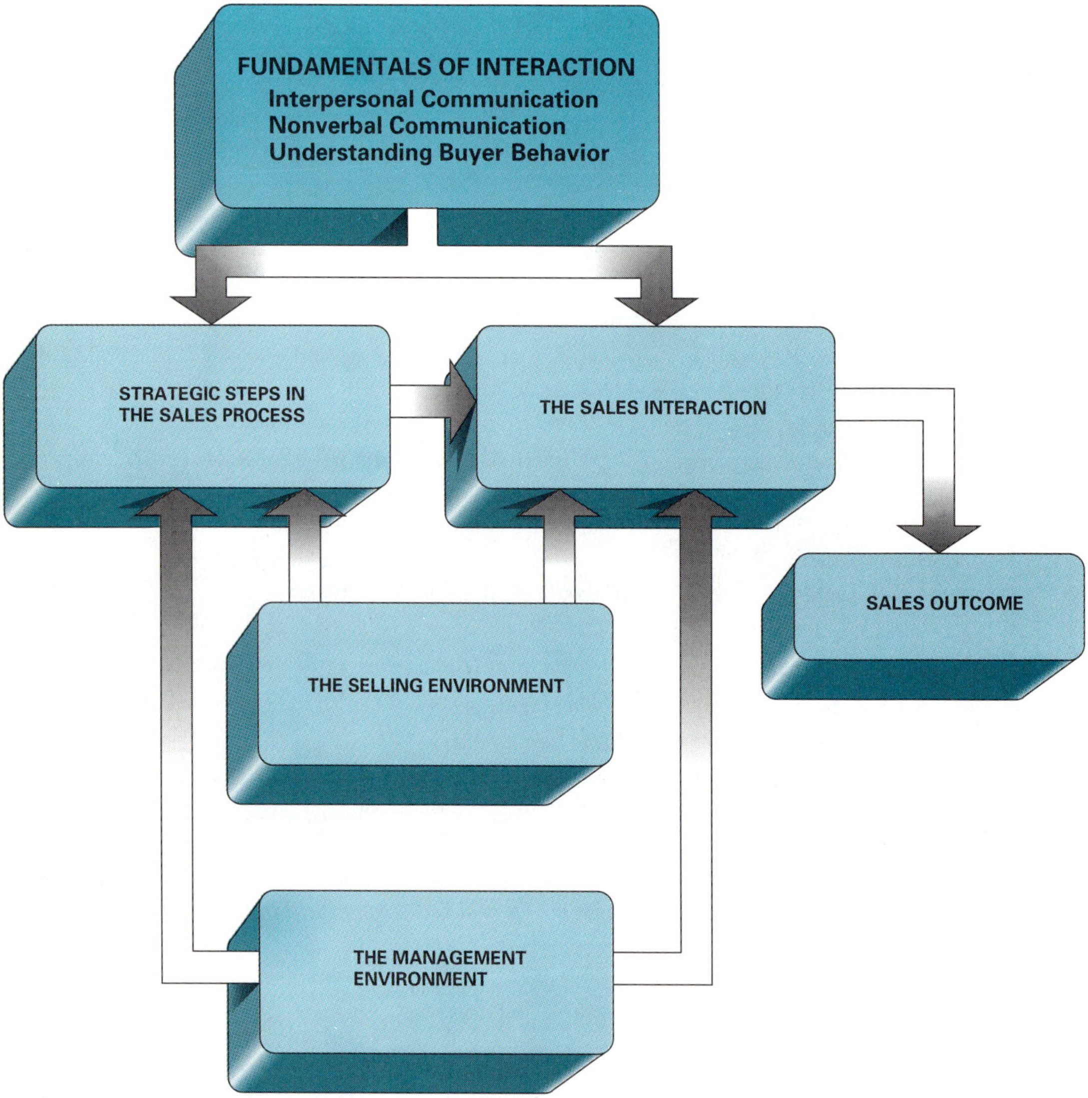

FUNDAMENTALS OF INTERACTION
Interpersonal Communication
Nonverbal Communication
Understanding Buyer Behavior

STRATEGIC STEPS IN THE SALES PROCESS

THE SALES INTERACTION

SALES OUTCOME

THE SELLING ENVIRONMENT

THE MANAGEMENT ENVIRONMENT

FUNDAMENTALS OF THE INTERACTION

3

Personal Selling as Interpersonal Communication

CHAPTER OBJECTIVES

In this chapter, you will learn:

- The basic principles of interpersonal communication.
- Whenever you are in the presence of another person, everything you do conveys a message.
- All communication has several levels of message, even though you may not be aware of them.
- How to structure your statements to control the flow of a conversation.
- People negotiate the control process without ever referring to it.
- How to avoid getting into contests for control with a prospect.

CHAPTER OUTLINE

A Sales Challenge

In Chapter 2, you read that interaction is a basic skill, and you probably wondered how something that everyone does every day can be a *skill.* The following conversation will help you understand this point. As you read it, try to predict whether Mike Wilson, a salesperson at McMann Publishing, will succeed in selling software to Mr. Brown, the sales manager at Chemcor Chemicals.

WILSON: Good morning, Mr. Brown. (Extending his hand.) Mike Wilson. We spoke on the phone earlier this week.

BROWN: That's right. You were recommended by Sara Fredricks.

WILSON: McMann has developed four new software packages that together can increase the productivity of your salesforce by 15 percent.

BROWN: Sara told me she ordered several interesting packages for the people at OCC.

WILSON: Our SMARTSELL program actually guides novice salespeople through the selling process. It advises them about how to approach each prospect and what points to emphasize.

BROWN: That sounds familiar. I think it's one that Sara ordered. She told me that . . .

WILSON: (*Interrupting.*) Our CUSTOMER will improve the way your people handle their accounts. With CUSTOMER, a salesperson can write letters, memos, and call reports, and analyze expense accounts in a single program. CUSTOMER II is adaptable to a portable computer and even reminds the salesperson when it is time to call on an account.

BROWN: I can't believe that a computer can tell a salesperson how to approach a prospect.

WILSON: It requires a machine with at least a 486 chip, and it cannot be run on a laptop computer of any kind.

BROWN: But how can it actually tell a salesperson what to do?

An Overview

Predicting the outcome of this sales call may be somewhat difficult at this point. In some ways, we would expect a positive outcome: Wilson has some excellent products that are of interest to Brown. He also has the advantage of a recommendation from a customer who knows Mr. Brown. However, something does not seem quite right. At first, Mr. Brown is very interested in the products. Yet, by the end, he has changed his tone completely.

As you read this chapter, it will become clear that the problem here is not with the products; it is with the interaction between the two people. Their conversation is not flowing smoothly. It appears almost as though Wilson is not listening to Mr. Brown. His statements do not appear to be connected to what Mr. Brown is saying.

Because we all interact every day, we tend to take conversation for granted.

We do not think of it as a *skill.* In fact, we do not appreciate its complexity until something goes wrong. But let us consider what is really involved when we speak with another person. During a conversation, each person has something he or she would like to say, and somehow a conversation evolves. A conversation is an orderly flow in which each person gets a turn to speak while the other listens. We not only give and receive specific *information,* we also form *impressions* about the other person. These impressions are based in part on the flow of the conversation.

Although friends may not think much about their ability to communicate with each other, the salesperson cannot take the interpersonal communication process for granted. If a sales conversation fails to achieve a natural flow, the resulting negative impressions may prevent the salesperson from conveying information about the product. In order to avoid this problem, salespeople should have an in-depth understanding of the basic principles of interactions.

We begin this chapter with a discussion of five basic principles of interpersonal communication:

Principle 1: Interpersonal communication is an *interaction* involving the exchange of messages between two or more people.
Principle 2: Interpersonal communication is governed by *rules.*
Principle 3: Interpersonal communication is a *sequential process.*
Principle 4: Interpersonal communication is *coherent.*
Principle 5: In interpersonal communication, one cannot *not* communicate.

Our objective is to demonstrate how a knowledge of these principles can (1) help you control the flow of your conversations with the prospect and (2) help ensure that you communicate what you want to communicate. In the second part of the chapter, we show that all interpersonal communication has three parts: a verbal message, the grammatical form of the verbal message, and a nonverbal message. Although we introduce all three types of messages in this chapter, we discuss only the verbal message in detail. Our discussion of nonverbal communication is reserved for Chapter 4, where we concentrate on that component alone.

After reading this chapter, you should appreciate the rather complicated coordination involved in conducting everyday speech. You should better understand what makes some sales call more successful than others, and you should be able to diagnose specific problems which occurred between Mr. Brown and Mr. Wilson.

A Definition of Interpersonal Communication

In Chapter 2, we defined interpersonal communication as *the transmission of information by one person directly to another person's senses.* This definition differentiated interpersonal communication from mass communication, because in mass communication, an impersonal medium (television, radio, or print) comes between the person sending the message and the person receiving it. In this chapter, we further refine the notion of interpersonal communication by discussing

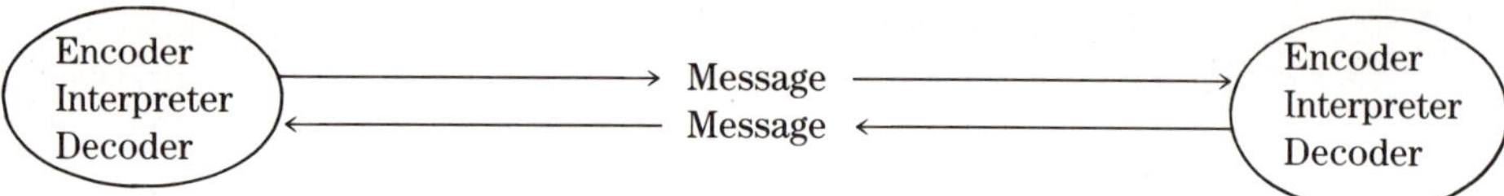

FIGURE 3.1 Schramm's Model of Communication. Source: W. Schramm and D. F. Roberts (eds.). (1971). *The Process and Effects of Mass Communication.* Urbana: University of Illinois Press.

its basic principles. Principle 1 highlights the crucial interactive nature of interpersonal communication:

PRINCIPLE 1: Interpersonal communication is an **interaction** involving the exchange of messages between two or more people.[1]

This means that, in personal selling, both the salesperson and the buyer send and receive messages. The model in Figure 3.1 provides a simple graphic illustration of this *two-way process.* Each person forms (**encodes**) a message so that it can be transmitted and receives (**decodes**) the message of the other.[2]

The key to this process is the fact that each speaker provides an immediate response to the message of the other. In fact, in interpersonal situations, this immediate response is just another term for **feedback** from the receiver of the message. And the feedback of each speaker influences the other. In fact, because interpersonal communication is interactive, it is an ongoing process of *mutual influence.* This means that when you attempt to influence another person, that person is likely to attempt to influence you. This mutual influence occurs even when a salesperson presents a memorized or "canned" message to the buyer.

PRINCIPLE 2: Interpersonal interaction is governed by rules.

A **rule** is defined as a *pattern of behavior that has come to have prescriptive force,*[3] where having *prescriptive force* means that the rule dictates (i.e., prescribes) correct or expected behavior. Because of this prescriptive force, people who violate rules are subject to criticism.

You can begin to understand the importance of rules if you think about any of the following situations: your first date, your first college class, your first job interview, or your first day on a new job. Most of us enter these new situations with a certain amount of insecurity—the insecurity of not knowing what to expect. As we become familiar with the new situation, we learn acceptable patterns of behavior. We develop expectations about how we and others should behave.

These expectations develop because these situations are governed by rules. In fact, rules govern all of our social behavior. This does not mean that there is a *written* code telling us how we should behave in every kind of social setting. Many rules are *unwritten.* In fact, we frequently follow rules without even being aware of them. It is a rule, for example, that we should not interrupt another person when she is speaking. Mike Wilson broke this rule when he interrupted Mr. Brown. Although this rule is not written, we generally become annoyed when someone interrupts us. Chances are that Mr. Brown, too, was annoyed.

A person who looked this way while you spoke to her would communicate a strong message. (© Joel Gordon Photography.)

Most often, it is these unwritten rules that allow conversations to flow smoothly. For example, there is an unwritten rule that we should take orderly speaking turns in a conversation. This rule is the basis for Principle 3:

PRINCIPLE 3: Interpersonal communication is a **sequential process.**

The two-way interaction between the prospect and the salesperson is sequential. The term *sequential* means that interpersonal communication involves a turn-taking process. One person speaks while the other listens. When the speaker is finished speaking, the two people change roles. The speaker becomes the listener and the listener becomes the speaker. This sequence continues until the two people actually leave each other.[4]

The turn-taking process seems so simple that we tend to take if for granted until it breaks down. This happens when one person interrupts the other, when both people speak at the same time, or when there are extended pauses and no one speaks. Although we do not realize it, turn taking actually requires quite a bit of complicated coordination. In fact, the sequencing of conversation actually involves specific conversational rules. How do you know, for example, when it is your turn to talk? How does the other person know when you want her to talk? When we finish our speaking turn, why do we not have to say to the other person, "I've finished speaking; it's your turn"?

Although it is unwritten, a *rule* says that we should not break into lines. A person who broke into this line would receive nasty stares and possibly verbal arguments. (© F. B. Grunzweig/Photo Researchers, Inc.)

The other person knows when her turn comes because of unwritten rules that govern turn-taking. According to these rules, certain signals mean that we have finished our speaking turn and are ready for the other person to speak. One such rule is that we drop our voices, pause, and look at the other person when we want that person to speak. When speakers follow this unwritten rule, the flow of turn taking usually occurs so naturally that no one needs to say "I have finished. Now it's your turn to speak." Instead, speakers can concentrate on the exchange of information.[5]

The exchange of information is critical in the sales interaction. For this reason, salespeople cannot take the turn-taking process for granted. If coordination breaks down, there will be awkward silences or times when both people speak at once. This problem will make the prospect feel uncomfortable and may eventually lead to the loss of a sale. A lack of turn-taking coordination was one of the problems in the conversation between Mr. Wilson and Mr. Brown, when Wilson interrupted Brown's sentence about Sara. In fact, interruptions in the *logical* flow of information violate another rule of conversation, which is Principle 4.

An unwritten rule says that we should shake hands when we greet a prospect. As a result, prospects *expect* this handshake. (© Michael Kagan/Monkmeyer Press Photo.)

PRINCIPLE 4: Interpersonal communication is coherent.

It is a basic rule of interaction that we take into account what is said by the other person in a conversation. This is another way of saying that our conversations should be coherent. **Coherence** means that something makes sense, and a conversation makes sense only when each statement is related to the statement that came before it.[6]

A sales interaction is coherent if the prospect's and salesperson's statements follow logically from each other. Each statement made by the salesperson should be related to what the prospect says; likewise, each statement made by the prospect should be related to what the salesperson says. The result is a conversation in which a topic is introduced and discussed until there is a need or a desire to change it. The new topic follows a similar sequence of introduction and discussion.

Perhaps the worst problem in the conversation between Mr. Brown and Mr. Wilson was that it lacked conversational coherence. Mr. Wilson started off with a problem when he made the statement, "McMann has developed four new software packages that together can increase the productivity of your sales force by 15 percent." There is nothing *inherently* wrong with this statement. In fact, the managers at McMann may have instructed him to use that statement to get the prospect's attention during the approach. What is wrong with the statement is that it violates the principle of conversational coherence. It does not follow logically from Mr. Brown's statement about Sara Fredricks ("That's right. You were recommended by Sara Fredricks."). In the same way, Wilson's statement,

"Our CUSTOMER will improve the way your people manage their accounts," does not follow coherently from Brown's previous statement, "I think it's one that Sara ordered. She told me that . . ."

In general, conversational coherence should not be a difficult principle to follow. You can undoubtedly think of a dozen statements that Wilson could have made that would not have violated this principle. However, problems arise when people are so intent on saying what they want to say that they are not responsive to one another. This is often the case when people rehearse scripts of what they are going to say to someone else. The reason is that the script cannot account for what the other person will say. If people insist on going through their rehearsed scripts, as Mr. Wilson did, the principle of conversational coherence is violated. What they end up communicating is that they do not care enough to listen.

PRINCIPLE 5: In interpersonal communication, one cannot not communicate.

By now, it should be clear that what we communicate may go well beyond our actual statements. Certainly we know that the words we use communicate. But there are things other than words that also communicate. In fact, in interpersonal communication, everything we do communicates.[7] Our tone of voice communicates. Whether we ask questions or make statements or disagree communicates. Our clothing communicates. So, too, does the way we comb our hair, walk, stand, and use our eyes. Even if we say nothing, we communicate.[8] This is the basis of the principle that we cannot *not* communicate.

In fact, it is impossible to be passive when engaging in interpersonal communication. When the other person finishes speaking and signals that it is your turn, you will communicate a message whether or not you actually speak. If you attempt to remain passive by saying nothing, you will communicate a lack of interest. You will also violate the rule that you should speak when the other person signals the end of a turn. The same is true of your facial expression when the other person speaks. If you attempt to remain passive and show no facial expression, your *lack* of expression will communicate something, even if you do not intend to do so.

An interruption can also convey a message—usually a negative one. When he continuously changed the subject and interrupted, Mr. Wilson communicated that he was not listening to Mr. Brown. Likewise, changing the subject can convey a negative message. When Mr. Brown began insisting on returning to his own subject ("But I don't see how . . ."), he communicated that he was getting annoyed with Mr. Wilson.

Messages in Interpersonal Communication Are More Than Words

An important conclusion to be drawn from the basic principles is that interpersonal communication involves more than spoken words. To appreciate this point, it is helpful to reconsider the communication model in Figure 3.1. Our tendency is to think of that model as showing how we exchange verbal messages. However, as the basic principles suggest, words alone convey only part of the message.

As an example, consider the following exchange between a salesperson (Sharon) and a prospect (George):

SHARON: The cost will be $500 per ton.
GEORGE: This is the best price you can come up with?

Certainly, anyone will agree that this short exchange is ordinary enough. But, even though it is ordinary, is it really all that simple?

The answer is definitely no. Based on these words alone, we cannot conclude how George feels about the price. He may be very unhappy or he may be quite pleased. It is possible that George has known Sharon for years and is just using friendly sarcasm. We cannot determine which of these interpretations is true unless we look beyond the meaning of the words.

First, it is significant that George *asks a question* about the price. He could have simply said "Okay" or "That's fine" or "I'll think about it and speak to you next week." Any of those replies would signal the end of the conversation. By asking a question, though, George indicates that he wants the conversation to continue. Because of the rule of conversational coherence, his question requires two things: (1) an answer and (2) a continuation of the topic of price.

In addition to realizing that George asked a question, if you were Sharon, you would note the way in which he asked it. Most likely, you would listen to the tone of George's voice and watch his face. Both would provide important information. For example, if George is upset about the price, we would expect him to emphasize the word *this* ("*This* is the best price you can come up with?") and to grimace as he speaks. If he is using sarcasm to negotiate in a playful way, he might emphasize the word *best* ("This is the *best* price you can come up with?"). He might also raise his voice toward the end of the question and use a wry, questioning smile.

There are two important lessons to be learned from this example:

1. In order to interpret a conversation, we must consider a mixture of verbal and nonverbal messages (as mentioned earlier, Chapter 4 focuses on nonverbal communication).
2. There is more to verbal messages than the words themselves. The grammatical form of the verbal message also conveys a message.

The Form Versus the Content of the Verbal Message

The *content* of the verbal messages refers to the actual words that are exchanged. The content in the dialogue between George and Sharon, for example, referred simply to the cost per ton of the product. The content in the dialogue between Mr. Wilson and Mr. Brown referred to Sara Fredricks, software, SMARTSELL, and so on. In general, the content of the verbal message contains the most obvious meaning.

In fact, most of us are surprised to learn that the form of our verbal communication also communicates.[9] If we examine the *form* of the conversation between Mr. Brown and Mr. Wilson, we see a series of statements that do not quite fit together. Mr. Brown spoke of Sara Fredricks. Mr. Wilson responded with a statement about software. Mr. Brown spoke again of Sara Fredricks, and Mr. Wilson responded with a statement about CUSTOMER. Mr. Brown referred to a computer's ability to advise a salesperson, and Mr. Wilson responded with a statement about the technical aspects of the hardware. In fact, it is in the analysis of the form of their interaction that we begin to detect the problem that existed between Mr. Brown and Mr. Wilson.

In general, when we consider the form of our verbal communication, we focus on issues such as the following:

Whether topics that are introduced are continued or are abruptly changed.
Whether people answer questions.
Whether one person consistently asks questions.
Whether interruptions occur.

The Form and Content Work Together

The content of a sales presentation has obvious importance. It is through the content that a salesperson conveys information about the product, its attributes, and the ways in which it can solve problems for the prospect. In fact, it would be easy for a novice salesperson to concentrate on the content to the exclusion of the form. This is what happened to Mike Wilson. He did not intend to ignore the prospect. He was simply so intent upon conveying certain facts that he caused problems in the form of the interaction.

In fact, the form and the content of a message work together. The content *conveys the information* about the product, and the form *controls the flow* of the conversation.[10] Because of the principle of conversational coherence, the content of what you say must follow logically from the content of what the prospect says. Any attempt to change a subject because you are not prepared to discuss it will interrupt the flow and communicate a problem to the prospect. To avoid this problem, you must be certain to have a great deal of knowledge about your product, your competition, and your prospect.

However, in order to discuss the content that has been prepared, a salesperson must understand the form of an interaction. This is because it is through the form that one *controls* the content of what is said. It is in the salesperson's best interests to learn ways to control the flow of the conversation. This way, the salesperson will not be forced to violate the principle of conversational coherence, particularly if she is unfamiliar with a topic brought up by the prospect. By exerting control over the flow of the conversation, the salesperson can ensure that she can communicate specific information without running into the problems that Mike Wilson encountered.

The Grammatical Form of the Verbal Message

Technically, the form of the verbal message refers to its grammatical form: Is the message in the form of a question or an assertion? The grammatical form of a statement conveys a message in addition to the one contained in the words themselves.[11] It was significant, for example, that George's response to Sharon was in the form of a question. This form led to the interpretation that George may have been using friendly sarcasm to bargain for a better price. Certainly, his question conveyed a different message than would have been conveyed by a direct assertion: "That price is way out of line."

But in order to understand the full meaning of the verbal form, we must consider the form of a statement *compared to that of the statement that preceded it.* That is, we must consider statements in pairs rather than singly. This becomes apparent when we analyze the conversation between Mr. Brown and Mr. Wilson. No single statement is wrong or bad. It is the way the statements fit together that is a problem.

Consider, for example, Mr. Brown's question, "But how can it actually tell a salesperson what to do?" On its own, this appears to be a typical question that one would expect during a sales call. It might indicate that the prospect is interested in the product. However, when we analyze this question in relation to Mike Wilson's previous statement, we see that it indicates trouble. Mike had just said, "It requires a machine with a 486 chip, and it cannot be run on a laptop computer of any kind." Obviously Mr. Brown does not want to discuss this technical information. He is intent on getting an answer to his original question about a computer's ability to advise a salesperson. This shows that it is not sufficient to look at any single statement made by Mike Wilson. We must consider each of his statements *as a response to* one of Mr. Brown's statements, just as Mr. Brown's must be considered *as responses to* Mike's.

Relational Communication as Control

The study of the verbal form of a statement compared to that of the statement that preceded it is often referred to as **relational communication** or **relational control.**[12] As the term implies, relational communication has to do with the nature of the relationship that exists between two parties who are conversing. Its primary importance is in terms of control: It indicates which party is in control or is the dominant member of the team. Thus, while **verbal content** contributes to meaning in terms of factual information, **relational form** contributes to meaning in terms of control. We can see the effect of relational communication in the contrast between the following two dialogues between Jim, a prospect, and Jack, a salesperson:

DIALOGUE I

JIM: I'm going to jog today after work.

JACK: How's the weather?

DIALOGUE II

JIM: How's the weather?

JACK: I'm going to jog today.

These dialogues show how the relational form can be considered separately from the content. Both dialogues have exactly the same words (verbal content) and even the same grammatical form. Where they differ is in the relationship of the form of the first statement to the form of the second statement. The important question here is whether that difference affects the meaning of these two dialogues.

The answer is yes. In dialogue I, the exchange is logical and natural, but in dialogue II, there seems to be something missing. What's missing is an answer to the question. Jack is not giving a direct answer to Jim's question. Although he may be implying an answer by mentioning jogging, we cannot be sure of the link between jogging and the weather. It is also possible that Jack is really saying, "I don't wish to converse with you even about something as simple as the weather, so I'm not going to answer your question. Instead, I am informing you that I am going jogging. End of discussion." Or Jack may be saying something less severe, such as, "I really don't want to discuss the weather with you. I want to discuss jogging."

In relational terms, Jim attempts to gain control of dialogue II by deciding which topic will be discussed (the weather). But Jack communicates that, instead, the discussion will be about jogging: Jack, too, wants to be in control. In dialogue I, on the other hand, Jim's initial control message is met with agreement from Jack. Jim wants to discuss jogging, and Jack responds with a related comment. Thus, Jack is allowing Jim to be in control. So, simply by changing the order of the sentences, the identical content has a completely different meaning in a relational sense.

The Variations of Relational Communication

Table 3.1 lists various relational forms that one might use in a conversation. In general, every statement that we make has a grammatical form that can be analyzed in terms of its relationship to the statement that preceded it. As the table shows, the relational communication depends upon both of these elements: the grammatical form (listed in column A) and the relationship between the statement and the one that preceded it (listed in column B). As a result, any statement in any conversation can be analyzed in terms of its relational communication.

Figure 3.2 on pp. 76–77 analyzes the conversation between Mr. Brown and Mr. Wilson according to these categories. Consider, for example, Mr. Brown's early statement, "That's right. You were recommended by Sara Fredricks."[13] This is an *assertion* (Column A) that *extended* the topic (column B) brought up by Mr. Wilson. If Mr. Brown had simply said, "That's right," it would have been an *assertion* that *supported*, but did not extend, Mr. Wilson's topic.

In fact, a person can respond to a given statement with a variety of options from Table 3.1. Consider, for example, the following dialogues:

DIALOGUE I

PROSPECT: The price of this product is quite high.

SALESPERSON: Actually, the price is quite reasonable.

DIALOGUE II

PROSPECT: The price of this product is quite high.

SALESPERSON: You're right, but the quality is really worth it.

DIALOGUE III

PROSPECT: The price of this product is quite high.

SALESPERSON: We have developed several new products in the last year.

In each case, the salesperson's response was an assertion, but in dialogue I the assertion disagreed with (offered *nonsupport*) the prospect. In dialogue II, the assertion offered *support* and *extended* the topic. In dialogue III, the assertion *changed the topic.*

Clearly, these responses have quite different implications in terms of controlling what is being said. The response in dialogue I is a *dominant* one. By disagreeing, the salesperson is refusing to accept the prospect's definition of the situation. Contrast this with dialogue II, a more *submissive* approach, in which the salesperson implicitly agrees to continue the discussion as the prospect has defined it. In dialogue III, the response choice is the most dominant of all and may very well annoy the prospect. Even though it does manage to direct the conversation to a more positive topic, it does so by breaking generally understood rules of conversation. In other words, it abruptly shifts the topic. By doing that, it violates the principle of conversational coherence.

Dominant and Submissive Relational Communication

Table 3.2 shows how specific combinations of grammatical forms and their relationship to preceding statements result in dominance (↑), submissiveness (↓), or equality (→). As you can see from Figure 3.2, we can use this information to analyze the control patterns in the conversation between Mr. Brown and Mr. Wilson.

In general, dominating the interaction means *controlling* the topic by asking

Table 3.1 Types of Relational Forms*

A *Grammatical Form*	*B* *Relationship to Preceding*
Assertion	Support
Question	Nonsupport
Talk-over	Extension
Noncompliance	Answer
Other	Instruction
	Order
	Disconfirmation
	Topic change
	Initiation/termination
	Other

* Any grammatical form from column A can combine with any relationship option from column B

Source: Reprinted by permission of International Communication Association, Austin, TX, © 1975. L. E. Rogers and R. V. Farace. (1975). Relational communication analysis: New measurement procedures. *Human Communication Research, 1*(3), 229–239.

	A	B	C
Wilson: Good morning, Mr. Brown. (Extending his hand.) Mike Wilson. We spoke on the phone earlier this week.	Assertion	Initiates conversation	↑
Brown: That's right. You were recommended by Sara Fredricks.	Assertion	Supports and extends	↔
Wilson: McMann has developed four new software packages that together can increase the productivity of your sales force by 15 percent.	Assertion	Initiates conversation	↑
Brown: Sara told me she ordered several interesting packages for the people at OCC.	Assertion	Topic change	↑
Wilson: Our SMARTSELL program actually guides novice salespeople through the selling process. It advises them about how to approach each prospect and what points to emphasize.	Assertion	Topic change	↑
Brown: That sounds familiar. I think it's one that Sara ordered. She told me that . . .	Assertion	Support and extension	→
Wilson: (interrupting) Our CUSTOMER will improve the way your people handle their accounts. With CUSTOMER, a salesperson can write letters, memos, call reports, and analyze expense accounts in a single program. CUSTOMER II is adaptable to a portable computer and even reminds the salesperson when it is time to call on an account.	Assertion	Interruption and topic change	↑
Brown: I can't believe that a computer can tell a salesperson how to approach a prospect.	Assertion	Disconfirmation	↑
Wilson: It requires a machine with at least a 486 chip, and it cannot be run on a laptop computer of any kind.	Assertion	Topic change	↑

FIGURE 3.2 An analysis of the relational communication in the conversation between Mr. Brown and Mr. Wilson. Column A labels the grammatical form; column B labels the relationship of that statement to the previous statement; column C analyzes whether the statement was dominant, submissive, or equal.

Table 3.2 Relational Control Directions According to Message Type

		Support 1	*Nonsupport 2*	*Extension 3*	*Answer 4*	*Instruction 5*	*Order 6*	*Disconfirmation 7*	*Topic Change 8*	*Initiation/Termination 9*	*Other 0*
Assertion	1	↓	↑	→	↑	↑	↑	↑	↑	↑	→
Question	2	↓	↑	↓	↑	↑	↑	↑	↑	↑	↓
Talk-over	3	↓	↑	↑	↑	↑	↑	↑	↑	↑	↓
Noncomplete	4	↓	↑	→	↑	↑	↑	↑	↑	→	→
Other	5	↓	↑	→	↑	↑	↑	↑	↑	↑	→

Source: Reprinted by permission of International Communication Association, Austin, TX, © 1975. L. E. Rogers and R. V. Farace. (1975). Relational communication analysis: New measurement procedures. *Human Communication Research*, *1*(3), 229–239.

questions, changing the subject, or disagreeing. Being submissive, on the other hand, means *refusing to control* the topic by avoiding these same behaviors.[14] There is nothing wrong with wanting to control the interaction. There is nothing wrong with wanting to be submissive, either.

However, it is very difficult for both people to be in control at the same time. Likewise, it is very difficult for neither one to be in control, since *someone* must initiate the topics to be discussed. As a result, a problem arises when both people insist on being dominant or submissive. The problem with either condition is that the two people spend too much time competing for the dominant (or submissive) role and may resort to counterproductive methods like topic changes that break interaction rules. For example, if you change the topic, and the other person's response is to change the topic, and your response is to return to your original topic, both of you are trying to be dominant. Over time, this may result in a counterproductive pattern.

Relational Communication Patterns Evolve Over Time

Whenever we meet a new person, there is a great deal of uncertainty, since we don't know anything about the person. Our immediate goal is to communicate with the person and ask questions that reduce our uncertainty. The other person has the same goal. Thus, the situation is ripe for important relational messages, since questions and, hopefully, answers abound. As the interaction proceeds, we start to get some sense of the most comfortable relational pattern. We may find that the most successful format is for us to ask the questions and, therefore, control the interaction, and that the other person prefers to submit to our control. Or we could find the reverse. Or we could find that we simply can't agree on a comfortable mode. In the last case, we may be less likely to want to see that person again.

In the first two cases, we will have an easier time dealing with the person at the next encounter. Essentially, relational patterns start to emerge, and we know intuitively what these patterns are with the different people we talk to. You probably have friends who do all the talking or who ask all the questions or who force you to ask all the questions. The point is that you have different relational patterns with each of these people, and you know what to expect before you talk to them.

The same is certainly true in the sales situation. Whether you see each of your prospects only once or many times, your first meeting involves the kind of uncertainty just discussed. In order to reduce that uncertainty, it is very likely that a pattern will evolve. This pattern will make the particular interaction and any future interactions more predictable.

Four Relational Patterns

In general, the relational *patterns* developed by people can be described in terms of dominance and submissiveness. These patterns can range from dominant-dominant, where both try to dominate, to dominant-submissive, where one dominates and the other submits. The possibilities are as follows:

1. Dominant-dominant.
2. Submissive-submissive.
3. Equal-equal.
4. Dominant-submissive.

As you might guess from the discussion thus far, certain of these patterns tend to be satisfying to both parties, whereas others are unsatisfying (Figure 3.3). The dominant-submissive pair tends to be comfortable for both parties. In this pattern, there is agreement about who will control the discussion. Similarly, a pair in which both parties communicate equality tends to be mutually satisfying. Here, control is shared. As we would expect, however, a dominant-dominant pair tends to be uncomfortable, because there is an ongoing contest for control.

We saw such a contest for control in the interaction between Mr. Brown and Mr. Wilson. By the end of the conversation, neither man was responding to what the other said. Their discussion was completely nonproductive. Chances are that Mr. Brown will never buy the software from Mr. Wilson. Mr. Wilson's problem was not simply his continued attempt to be dominant, but also the fact that he did so by changing the subject and, thus, violating the principle of conversational coherence. It is important to note that it is not always *bad* to communicate dominance, especially if the prospect's relational communication is submissive. However, if the prospect insists on dominating, the salesperson is well advised to retreat.

Fit Is Important. It is important to remember that it is the *fit* between the salesperson and prospect that counts. The salesperson cannot always avoid unsatisfying patterns by being submissive, because the submissive-submissive pair is just as uncomfortable as the dominant-dominant one. In general, both dominant-dominant and submissive-submissive pairs tend to be unstable. Because they are so uncomfortable, the people will tend to stop interacting with each other unless the behavior of one of them changes.

		Prospect		
		Dominant	Submissive	Equal
	Dominant	Unsatisfying	Satisfying	Unsatisfying
Salesperson	Submissive	Satisfying	Unsatisfying	Unsatisfying
	Equal	Unsatisfying	Unsatisfying	Satisfying

FIGURE 3.3 Some patterns of relational communication are satisfying, while others are not.

Both the dominant-dominant and submissive-submissive patterns are undesirable in a sales situation. The burden here is not on the customer but on the salesperson. Unless he adapts, the prospect will probably decide to deal with a more compatible salesperson.

However, the salesperson does not need to worry that a single mistake in relational communication will cause the prospect to go elsewhere. The existence of general relational patterns does not mean that there is never a deviation from the pattern.

Relational Communication Is Dynamic. Despite general patterns, relational communication is dynamic. Even in a dominant-submissive pattern, there can be an occasional disagreement or interruption. Thus, if we isolate any two consecutive statements, we may get a distorted picture of the relational control pattern. We always need to keep in mind that control of the interaction can change from one statement to the next. This is what happened in the conversation between Mr. Brown and Mr. Wilson. Our analysis of their conversation shows the pattern changing as the two men spoke. In the beginning, it seemed to be a stable one: Mr. Wilson dominated, and Mr. Brown allowed this domination. However, as Mr. Wilson continued to dominate by changing the topic, Mr. Brown appeared to become annoyed and changed his responses to dominant ones. The result was that the conversation turned into a contest for control.

A change in relational patterns is particularly common in sales interactions, where discussions can range from friendly small talk to hard-nosed negotiation. Although a salesperson and a prospect may have a comfortable pattern of equality during the approach, the salesperson may have a need to disagree or engage in dominant behavior as she handles objections. This could cause the relational pattern to change.

People Need Not Be Aware of Relational Form. Most people do not deliberately manipulate their relational communication. In fact, most are not even aware that relational communication exists. But this does not lessen the effect of relational communication on the control of an interaction. Think, for a moment, about Mr. Wilson's conversation. He probably did not *intend* to get involved in a contest for control. He probably did not even *mean* to be dominant. He was simply so intent on communicating certain features of the product that he failed to listen to his prospect. But as Mr. Brown's reaction indicates, relational messages affect the flow of a conversation, regardless of the intent of the speaker. An abrupt topic change has a negative effect even if it is unintended.

Similarly, the effect of a relational message does *not* depend on the awareness of the *receiver* of the message. If we had asked Mr. Brown about relational communication patterns, he probably would not have known what we were talking about. He probably did not think about whether Mike Wilson's statements were *assertions* or whether they represented *nonsupport* or *topic changes.* He simply felt uncomfortable about the interaction. We can see this by the fact that he began fighting for control by the end of the conversation.

The important message here is that a salesperson cannot avoid relational communication by ignoring it. It has an important impact on the sales call, whether or not the salesperson and prospect are aware of it.[15] As a result, salespeople who are sensitive to relational communication are at an advantage. They can make sure that they don't do such things as change the topic abruptly. They can use their knowledge to understand the control messages sent by the prospect and to facilitate their communication of information about the product.

Putting It All Together

We begin to put it all together by summarizing the key points presented in this chapter:

- Interpersonal communication is a dynamic process in which both parties are active. Someone who responds to a message is also sending a message to the original communicator.
- All messages have verbal content and verbal form.
- Whenever we say something to someone, we convey factual information through verbal content and relational control through verbal form.
- Relational communication conveys information about who is in control.
- Relational communication is meaningful only when we consider statements in pairs.
- Relational patterns evolve over the course of an interaction, particularly in a sales encounter.
- Certain patterns of relational communication are satisfying, while others are not.

Based on this summary, we can put the information in this chapter together with that presented in the rest of the book. First, after reading this chapter, it should be clear why interaction is considered a basic skill. We may interact with many people every day, but this does not mean that interacting is simple or that it requires no skill. Interaction is governed by rules, and it involves a complex combination of form and content.

These complexities may not pose a problem during casual interactions with friends. During this kind of conversation, we typically do not have a set of important information that we seek to convey. The sales situation is quite different. Here the salesperson has specific information to communicate. In many sales situations, this information may be complicated and technical. Just think of the kinds of information a salesperson has to transmit when attempting to sell an airplane, a computer, insurance, or financial products. Presenting the content alone is an accomplishment. However, the salesperson also needs to be able to control the relational part of the interaction in order to work all of this technical information into the conversation naturally.

In addition, as you will read in Chapters 9 through 12, the rules will change during different phases of the sales interaction, depending upon whether the salesperson is making the approach, presenting information, handling objections, or closing the sale. Your objective in reading this chapter was to understand the basics. In the later chapters, you will learn in detail how to apply those basics in order to make a successful sales call.

Finally, the flow of verbal communication, complicated as it may seem, is only part of the story. In later chapters, we will discuss other factors that are just as crucial to the outcome of a sales call. In Chapter 4, we analyze nonverbal communication. As you will see, nonverbal messages can even alter the meaning of verbal ones. In Chapter 8, we concentrate on power and control and explain how you can benefit by anticipating the power balance that will exist between you and the prospect. Finally, in Chapter 9, we analyze the importance of listening as we explain how a salesperson listens to the prospect's needs. As the dialogue between Mr. Brown and Mr. Wilson showed, lack of listening can lead to serious conversational problems. After reading the present chapter, you should begin to understand how all of these elements come together in the sales interaction.

Key Terms

Interaction
Encode
Decode
Feedback
Rule
Sequential process
Conversational coherence
Relational communication (control)
Verbal content
Relational form

Review Questions

1. Why is the notion of interaction so important in understanding interpersonal communication?
2. What is a rule? Give an example of a communication rule.

3. When we say that interpersonal communication is a sequential process, what are we referring to? Why is it important?
4. What is the principle of conversational coherence?
5. If you wanted to interpret the meaning of a statement, would it be sufficient to understand the words that are spoken? Why or why not?
6. What is the difference between the content and the form of a verbal message?
7. Is it possible to take any single statement from a conversation and evaluate its verbal form? Why or why not?
8. Why is the form of the verbal message referred to as relational communication?
9. Which combinations of dominance and submissiveness are likely to be most productive? Which combinations are likely to be most counterproductive?
10. How is uncertainty reduced when a salesperson and a prospect begin to talk to each other?

Discussion Questions

1. Is the salesperson better served by controlling an interaction or by allowing the prospect to control it? Explain your answer.
2. Is skill at handling relational communication a natural ability? Do you think that it can be learned?
3. When a prospect objects to something you have said, how can you counter that objection without getting into a contest for dominance?
4. Assume that you are on a sales call and a prospect says, "There is no way that your software could do all of that." Construct a dominant response and a negative response to this statement.

CASE 3.1

Mike Wilson did indeed lose the sale to Mr. Brown. He was upset about the loss, because he was not quite sure exactly what had gone wrong. He honestly felt that his products would have been of great benefit to Mr. Brown's firm, and Mr. Brown seemed to be favorable at the beginning.

Mike discussed the matter with Don Edwards, the sales manager, who had trained him. Don told Mike that he should be less intent on conveying specific information about the products and more interested in concentrating on the prospect's needs. Don advised Mike to listen carefully to what the prospect was actually saying. Mike took this advice to heart and tried to implement it when he called on Rita Danforth, a district sales manager of a firm that sold heavy machinery. Following is an excerpt from their conversation:

RITA: Come in, Mr. Wilson. I read about your new software in *Sales and Marketing Management.* It sounds interesting.

MIKE: Thanks. Which software did you read about? We have several new products that we've developed specifically for salespeople.

RITA: There was one called SMARTSELL, which really caught my attention. The ad said that it had artificial intelligence.

MIKE: That's right. We've programmed SMARTSELL with hundreds of selling rules so that it actually "knows" what to do in different situations. It will ask questions of the salespeople to help guide them through complicated selling situations. Here's our brochure. See all of these features?

RITA: I see.

MIKE: I actually brought a disc with me. If you have a computer with a 486 chip, I can show you how this works.

RITA: That would be great. Let me call in Joe Ziti. He's one of our computer people. He might be interested in seeing this.

MIKE: No problem. I'll just set this up while you're gone.

JOE: (*Extends his hand.*) Joe Ziti. I hear you have an impressive product to sell.

MIKE: (*Shakes Joe's hand.*) Mike Wilson. We certainly think so. Here, you might be interested in seeing some of these technical—(*Hands Joe a brochure.*)

JOE: (*Interrupting.*) Let me see that. I see that this requires a machine with a 486 chip. Our sales staff uses 386 machines.

MIKE: We do have a less powerful version that runs on those older machines, but you have to sacrifice some of the sophistication.

JOE: Let's just see how it works. Is this the main menu?

MIKE: Yes. As you can see, it lets the salesperson choose between paperwork activities—writing letters, handling expense accounts—and these more sophisticated functions. I'll tell it to proceed to the ADVISOR program. This is the one that—

JOE: (*Interrupting.*) How many K does this require?

RITA: Wait a minute, Joe.

MIKE: 640K for ADVISOR.

RITA: But let's not get hung up on the technical specifications. Remember, the point here is—

JOE: Well, if it won't run on our machines, it's no good to us anyway. Besides, our people use a lot of laptop computers, and I doubt if this will work on them.

MIKE: You are right. It won't help on a laptop. But the purpose of the ADVISOR is to help out in the preapproach.

JOE: What's that? I know nothing about selling.

RITA: That's when the salesperson plans the sales call before approaching the prospect. That is when a program like this would be useful.

MIKE: Just look at the material this covers. It asks about the prospect's personality and gives advice about how to deal with different types of people. It helps you make sure that you're contacting the right person in the organization. This feature—

JOE: But what do you give up in order to run this on a 386 machine?

MIKE: It doesn't analyze personalities, but it will still analyze the company's buying process and the type of purchasing problem.

JOE: I thought personalities were so important.

MIKE: Well, sophisticated computer departments have mostly moved to the 486 machines, so it's not a problem.

JOE: That's ridiculous. The 386 machines run everything we need.

RITA: I guess not. Not if they won't handle this kind of software.

Analyze this conversation according to its relational communication patterns.

1. Do you think that Mike has improved since his interaction with Mr. Brown?
2. How would you describe his communication patterns now?
3. What do the communication patterns of Rita and Joe tell you about how they feel about Mike and his software? Be sure to analyze their *form* in order to answer this question.
4. Do you think that Mike will make the sale?

References

1. Schramm, W. (1971). The nature of communication between humans. In: W. Schramm and D. F. Roberts (eds.), *The Process and Effects of Mass Communication.* Urbana: University of Illinois Press, 3–53.

2. Ibid.

3. Shimanoff, S. B. (1980). *Communication Rules: Theory and Research.* Newbury Park, CA: Sage.

4. Street, R. L., and J. N. Capella. (1985). Sequence and pattern in communicative behavior: A model and commentary. In R. L. Street and J. N. Capella (eds.), *Sequence and Pattern in Communicative Behavior.* London: Edward Arnold, 242–276.

5. Thomas, G. P., and G. F. Soldow. (1988). Information theory and communication rules in the context of interpersonal communication. In: B. Ruben (ed.), *Information and Behavior.* New Brunswick, NJ: Transaction Books, 308–328.

6. McLaughlin, M. L. (1984). *Conversation: How Talk Is Organized.* Newbury Park, CA: Sage.

7. Watzlawick, P., J. Beavin, and D. Jackson. (1967). *Pragmatics of Human Communication.* New York: Norton.

8. Weaver, R. L. (1984). *Understanding Interpersonal Communication.* Glenview, IL: Scott, Foresman.

9. Ibid.

10. Miller, F. E., and L. E. Rogers. (1987). Relational dimensions of interpersonal dynamics. In M. E. Roloff and G. R. Miller (eds.), *Interpersonal Processes: New Directions in Communication Research.* Newbury Park, CA: Sage, 117–139.

11. Soldow, G. F., and G. P. Thomas (1984). Relational communication: Form versus content in the sales interaction. *Journal of Marketing, 48,* 84–93.

12. McQuail, D. (1987). Functions of communication: A nonfunctionalist overview. In: C. R. Berger and S. H. Chaffee (eds.), *Handbook of Communication Science.* Newbury Park, CA: Sage, 327–349.

13. Rogers, L. E., and R. V. Farace. (1975). Relational communication analysis: New measurement procedures. *Human Communication Research, 1,* 222–239.

14. Ibid.

15. Fitzpatrick, M. A., and P. Best. (1979). Dyadic adjustment in relational types: Consensus, cohesion, affectional expression, and satisfaction in enduring relationships. *Communication Monographs, 46,* 167–178.

Nonverbal Aspects of Selling

CHAPTER OBJECTIVES

In this chapter, you will learn:

- What nonverbal behavior is.
- Nonverbal cues are probably more important than verbal statements in interpreting the meaning of a message.
- Nonverbal communication has a dynamic and a constantly changing sequence, just as verbal communication does.
- Nonverbal communication occurs through several channels, including the face, the eyes, the rest of the body, the voice, and the use of physical space.
- Some nonverbal channels are easier to manipulate than others.
- The face is very important in communicating emotion.
- The eyes are looked at more than any other feature.
- Our pupils dilate when we are interested in something, and this dilation cannot be controlled.
- Movement of the body can communicate such varied things as openness, aggressiveness, or liking.

We all have a sense of space that prevents us from getting too close to others in social situations.

Vocal quality is important in making inferences about personality traits and communicating an image.

Nonverbal communication is a major cue to determining deception.

Nonverbal and verbal messages can be inconsistent with one another and, when they are, the nonverbal message is considered more truthful.

CHAPTER OUTLINE

A Sales Challenge

Following is a discussion between Jim Jones, sales manager, and Christine Anderson, a sales representative for End Manufacturing. Christine has just attempted to sell cotton fabric to a large clothing manufacturer.

JIM: Well, how did it go today, Chris?

CHRISTINE: Okay, I guess. I mean, I think I made the sale, but I just can't be sure.

JIM: You can usually have some sense about it.

CHRISTINE: I guess, but George, that's the purchasing manager, was sort of tentative. He kept frowning, and every time I tried to reassure him, he'd say, that sounds fine, but he'd look down. He sort of looked unsure.

JIM: Was he friendly?

CHRISTINE: He never smiled. He kept standing up while I was sitting in front of his desk. I guess I'd have to say that he wasn't very friendly. If I had met him before, I would have a better sense about whether he is usually this way or whether it was just me.

JIM: It is a hard one to call. Maybe you'll have a better sense by his tone of voice when you call him just to thank him for talking to you.

What is significant about this dialogue is that Jim and Christine are trying to assess the probability of George's purchase based strictly on George's *nonverbal* behavior. They haven't referred once to anything George has actually said. As you will see in this chapter, Jim and Christine are quite right in considering George's nonverbal behavior as the real indicator of his buying intentions.

An Overview

It is not surprising that Judith Greene, a real estate broker, says, "I watch the face of the buyer when I show an apartment; that's the real evaluation."[1] Susan Levin, another real estate broker, says, "Nonverbal clues let you know which member of the family makes the decisions."[2]

These statements and countless others point out how much salespeople rely upon nonverbal communication in determining certain aspects of the selling process. In fact, we all rely upon nonverbal communication, even though we may not always be aware of it.

Nonverbal communication is a major component of any statement we make. As we indicated in Chapter 3, no communication can take place without it. In fact, nonverbal communication may be even more important than verbal communication. Albert Mehrabian, a scholar of nonverbal behavior, has found that when we try to interpret people's emotions, nonverbal communication contributes 93 percent to the interpretation, while verbal communication contributes only 7 percent.[3] Other people who study nonverbal communication have provided more

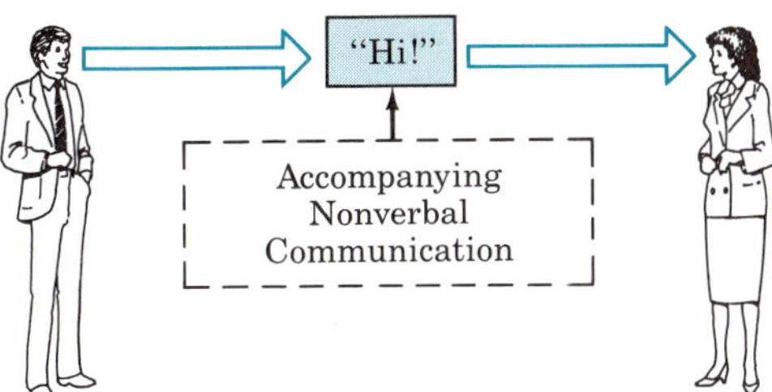

FIGURE 4.1 Even a simple "Hello" is meaningful only when we take into account nonverbal communication.

moderate estimates of the contribution of nonverbal communication ranging from 50 to 65 percent.[4] Our own experiences should confirm the importance of nonverbal communication when we interpret the messages of someone we are talking to (Figure 4.1).

The purpose of this chapter is to present the basic issues involved in nonverbal communication. We begin by discussing the meaning of nonverbal communication. Next, we describe in detail each major channel of nonverbal communication. Finally, we consider issues involved in faking nonverbal communication and deception. Throughout, we suggest specific things you can do to be more effective in your own nonverbal communication. In addition, we indicate what to look for in others to increase your skill in interpreting underlying or hidden messages.

What Is Nonverbal Communication?

A nonverbal cue can be practically anything that communicates a message but that is *not* in the form of words. More formally, we define **nonverbal communication** as follows:

> *Nonverbal communication is any behavior that has communicative potential but that is not linguistic.*

What exactly does that include? Generally, nonverbal communication includes facial expression, eye behavior, bodily movements or kinesics, spatial movement or proxemics, and voice quality or paralinguistics. It also includes such things as clothing, hair style, and makeup (Figure 4.2).

The Dynamic Nature of Nonverbal Communication

As we talk to one another, much of our nonverbal communication changes continually. Our facial expressions change, our bodies shift position, our eyes move, and we raise or lower our voices. Those nonverbal cues that are continually changing are said to be *dynamic.* Those nonverbal cues that do not change as

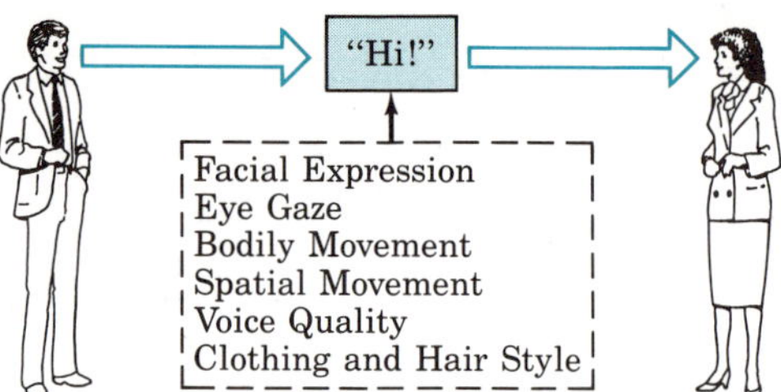

FIGURE 4.2 The elements of nonverbal communication.

we talk to one another are said to be *static.* While our clothing, hair style, or makeup may change from one day to another, they do not usually change as we converse, and they are considered to be static nonverbal cues. These cues can be extremely important in what they say about us. Our focus, however, will be on dynamic nonverbal cues, since we are concerned about the process of interpersonal communication.

Nonverbal Channels

We tend to think of nonverbal cues as operating within channels. Thus, we talk about the facial expression channel or the eye gaze channel. There are five such channels for nonverbal communication, all of which communicate simultaneously. These channels include facial expression, eye behaviors, kinesics, proxemics, and paralanguage.

Ideally, it is best to pay attention to all the channels at the same time, although that is not always possible. In what follows, we discuss each of these channels in detail. The channels vary considerably. For example, some channels are easier for us to monitor and control than others. Similarly, some channels are easier for others to observe and interpret.

Facial Expression

Facial expression *includes smiles, frowns, expressions of confusion or bewilderment or joy, and so on.* The face has a complicated muscle structure and can reveal a broad array of emotions. In fact, some people say that our facial expressions are a direct indicator of our underlying emotions.[5]

Whenever we talk to someone, the one thing we pay particular attention to is the face. If someone says that you seem to be out of sorts or, conversely, in a very good mood, chances are that your face is communicating this message. When you ask your instructor how you did on an exam, notice how you carefully scrutinize her face for an indication. Her face will probably tell you whether you performed poorly or well before you hear her verbal statement.

In the sales situation, the face is equally important for both the salesperson

EXHIBIT 4.1

The Anatomy of a Salesperson

The Hands: He uses these to hold a case which is full of literature and samples, to shake the hands of his customer-friend whom he services and has built a friendship with down through the years, to pocket commissions which are the sweet fruits of his labor.

The Eyes: He uses these to see his customer and to know him well in order to serve him better, to show his concern.

The Mouth: He uses this to speak words that will inform his customers about the merits of his product or of how it will benefit . . . their lives, to make special offers to induce his customers to buy.

The Ears: He uses these to listen to the problems of his customers, to listen for the key words from a customer during his sales presentation so as to know when to be silent, add a word and when to close.

The Nose: He uses this to smell success!

The Feet: He uses these to carry his body daily to keep appointments, visit customers and cold canvass.

The Throat: He uses this to swallow his pride when unjustly doubted by uninformed prospects, then clears it, and with sheer determination and knowledge creates a sale—and a new customer!

The Teeth: He uses these to chew his food well, but rapidly, so as not to lose precious time in diners, to display prominently when smiling at a contented customer.

The Shoulders: His customers' problems rest here, while he quickly and surely finds avenues of help with his products, building a future on their needs, strengthening a camaraderie that will last a lifetime.

The Heart: He uses this to show his customers that he is a fellow human being just like they are, that he is a warm person and shares a personal relationship with them, while helping them to achieve a better way of living.

The Brain: He uses this to ignite the motor putting all the other members of the body into motion, directing his entire being towards one primary function: To serve his customers in a professional manner, thereby filling their needs and enriching their lives!

Source: Adapted from R. Piccarelli, (1988). The anatomy of a salesperson. *The American Salesman, 33* (April), 25–26.

and the prospect. The salesperson will study the prospect's face to determine the level of interest or for signs of confusion or dislike. The prospect will study the salesperson's face looking for enthusiasm and honesty.

In all of these situations, the face has a prominent role in the interaction. It

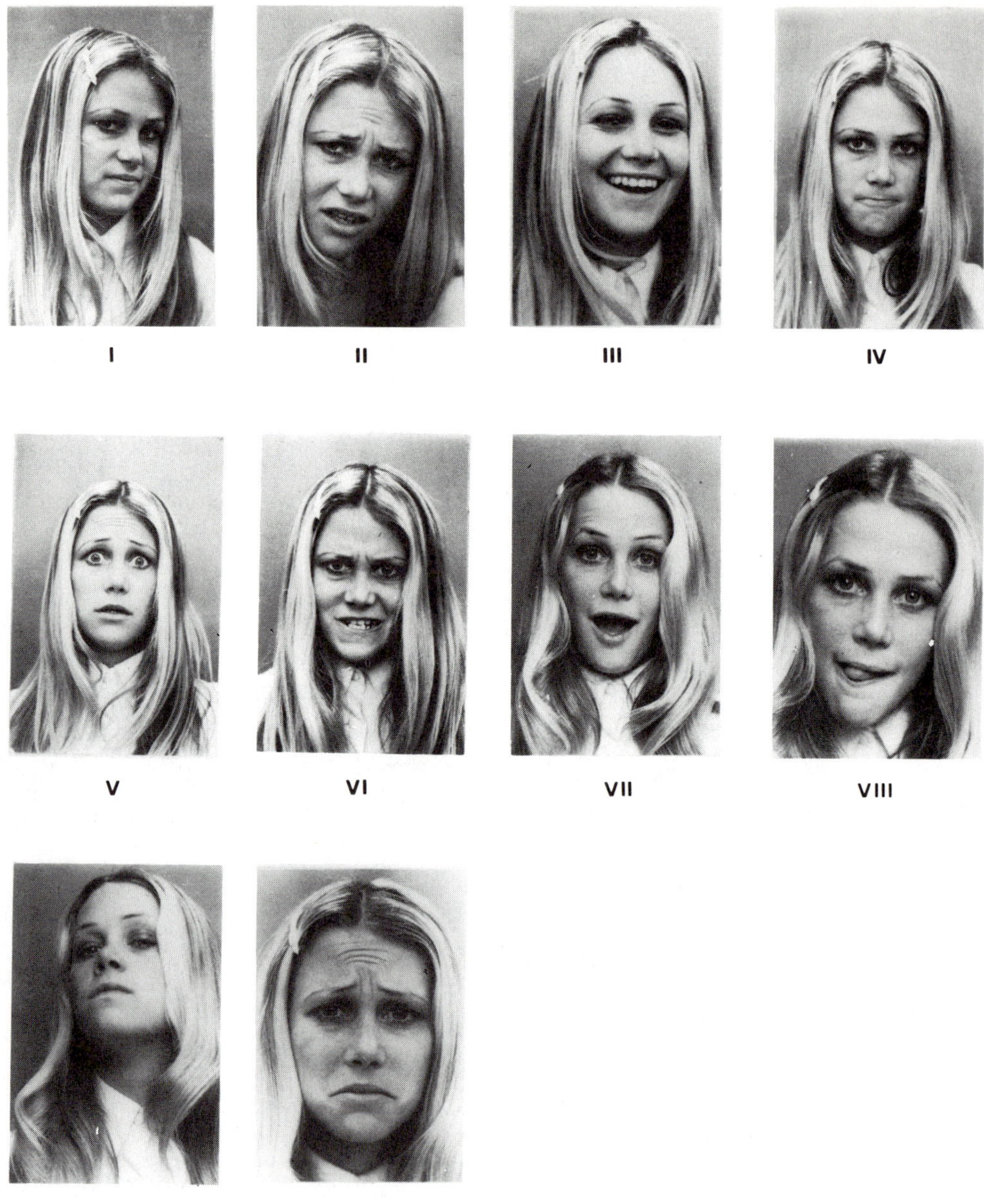

FIGURE 4.3 Facial Meaning Sensitivity Test. (Source: Reprinted by permission of Macmillan Publishing Company © 1986. D. G. Leathers. (1986) *Successful Nonverbal Communication.* New York: Macmillan, p. 24.)

is certainly revealing that we often refer to personal selling as *face-to-face* selling. This term highlights the importance of the face. It is safe to say that a successful salesperson has to be skilled at "reading" the face.

Reading the Face. As mentioned earlier, the face has a complex muscle structure that allows the face to send an elaborate set of messages. People who study the face usually break it up into three areas: eyebrows and forehead, eyes and eyelids, and the remainder of the face from the nose to the chin. It is not surprising that the various combinations of these three areas can lead to more than 1,000 different facial expressions.[6]

There are at least 10 emotions that we tend to communicate through our facial expression: happiness, sadness, surprise, anger, fear, contempt, disgust, interest, determination, and bewilderment. The 10 photographs presented in Figure 4.3 depict each of these emotions. These photographs comprise the Facial Meaning Sensitivity Test.[7]

A natural concern with regard to reading the face is accuracy. This is a difficult concern to address. First, some people's faces are more communicative than others. Second, some people are more sensitive to facial cues than others. Third, some emotions are easier to judge than others. For example, anger appears easier to judge than sadness.[8] At the same time, facial expressions appear to be universal rather than limited to certain cultures.

Fourth, the situational context can influence a response to a facial cue. For example, one study asked people to judge a smiling face. In one instance, this face was looking at a glum face. In another instance, it was looking at a frowning face. In the first case, the smiling face was perceived as vicious and taunting. In the second case, it was perceived as peaceful and friendly.[9]

In general, people are reasonably accurate in judging facial expressions. It is possible to train people to be more sensitive to facial expression and, as a result, more accurate. The best way to do this is to videotape various people expressing emotions and let the trainees see only the facial expression.

Display Rules. While facial expression is useful for communicating emotion, it is important to recognize that people tend to be very conscious of their facial expressions. This means that they can manipulate their facial expressions to communicate whatever emotions they think are necessary or appropriate. This is done by resorting to **display rules.**[10]

Display rules *dictate what is appropriate in a social situation.* Thus, we can display sadness when an acquaintance tells us about a misfortune. We can display surprise when we show up for our "surprise" birthday party, even though we have known about the party for days. A prospect can display interest in a salesperson's presentation even though the prospect has no interest whatsoever in what is being sold.

Interestingly, research[11] has shown that our ability to present false facial expressions according to display rules appears to be concentrated on the lower face. That means that we can manipulate the lower facial muscles, but we are much less successful in manipulating the eye region.

How the Salesperson Can Rely Upon Facial Expression. A salesperson should incorporate display rules when necessary. For example, if a prospect mentions that one of the salesperson's major competitors has gone out of business, the salesperson should communicate concern rather than glee. At the same time, the salesperson should try to avoid falsely presenting a certain facial expression. There is a chance that a prospect will perceive that it is false, and the salesperson runs the risk of ruining her credibility.

The salesperson should monitor the facial expressions of the prospect. These expressions can be an important indicator of the prospect's level of interest in particular points or in the product in general. These expressions can also signal lack of interest, confusion, or even dislike. The salesperson who notices such negative facial expressions can regard them as the equivalent of objections. The salesperson then has an opportunity to address the objection. Of course, the prospect can falsify facial expressions, just as the salesperson can. To check for that possibility, the salesperson has to look at the lower part of the face as well as the eye behavior.

EXHIBIT 4.2:

Even Pigeons Can Read a Face

Pigeons have been trained to distinguish among human facial expressions. In experiments at the University of Iowa, pigeons were shown photographs of different people. The people displayed happiness, anger, surprise, and disgust on their faces. The pigeons actually could distinguish between these emotions.

A noted researcher said, "Our results support Darwin's thesis that non-human animals can learn to discriminate between human emotional expressions." These results cast doubt on the theory that humans have a specialized nervous system that is capable of recognizing the subtleties of such things as facial expression.

Source: Adapted from M. W. Brown. "Is That a Grimace? Ask a Pigeon," *New York Times*, May 2, 1989, p. C7.

Eye Behavior

Eye behavior *has to do with how you look at another person—directly, indirectly, or not at all.* It also has to do with *how long you stare at another person.* Staring at a stranger communicates either intense desire or hostility. It has been said that the eyes are the window of the soul; thus, it is not surprising that eye gaze can have so much impact.[12]

We read a great deal into eyes. Some people have "hard" eyes, some people

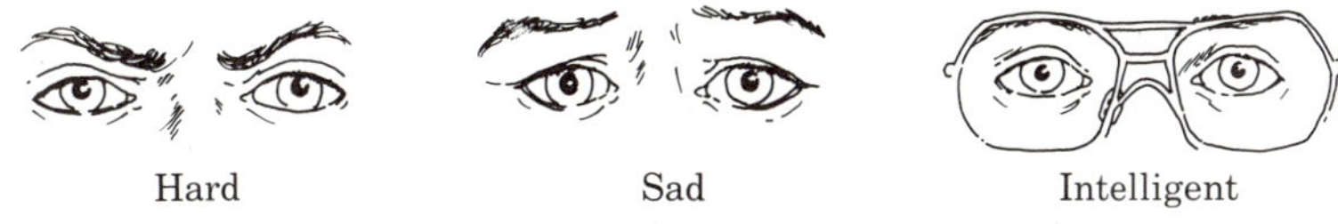

FIGURE 4.4 Eyes can communicate many things about a person.

have "mean" eyes; others look "intelligent" and still others look "sad" (Figure 4.4). You have probably asked someone to look you in the eye and make a statement. Your intent has been to discern the truth.

In fact, while the face is the aspect of a person we concentrate upon most intently, it is the eyes that we look at more than anything else.[13] Specifically, we look at the eyes over 43 percent of the time when we are talking to someone else. This suggests that the eyes serve a number of important functions.

Pupil Dilation. The first function that eyes serve is related to the face. While the face communicates emotion, the eyes communicate the intensity of the emotion. This is particularly important because emotional intensity is usually indicated by the degree of pupil dilation. When people are interested or emotionally aroused, their pupils dilate.

Pupil dilation is something we are not generally aware of and, therefore, is not subject to conscious control. This fact is particularly important for an observer. For example, pupil dilation could indicate an intense feeling about a product. A prospect might be able to maintain a passive face but would be less successful in preventing interest in the product from being reflected in his eyes. Thus, the salesperson is well advised to attend carefully to eye behavior, particularly pupil dilation.

Regulating the Conversation. A second function of eye behavior is to regulate the conversation. We use our eyes to solicit information or feedback, as well as to provide feedback. We often look at someone intently in order to communicate that we want feedback. We also look at the speaker to indicate that we are listening.

One major concern in a conversation is turn taking. Rather than saying to someone, "I'm finished talking; you now have the floor," we use our eyes as a signal. It is interesting to note that the listener looks at the speaker much more than the speaker looks at the listener. In fact, when the speaker spends too much time looking directly at the listener, the listener becomes aware of the stare and grows increasingly uncomfortable.

Defining the Relationship. The issue of eye gaze points to the third function of eye behavior: defining the nature of the relationship. In this regard, eye gaze can communicate power, particularly in situations where the two people conversing have unequal status. In such situations, the person of higher status often stares. The person of lower status either looks directly at the superior person or avoids the superior's eyes. We can also use eye gaze to determine the degree of

Affect is communicated by kinesics. One person here is very comfortable and content. The other person is tense. (© 1989 Tony Freeman/PhotoEdit.)

liking. Generally, we increase eye contact when we like someone and lessen it when we dislike someone.

How the Salesperson Can Rely Upon Eye Behavior. Eye behavior is something a salesperson should pay particular attention to, both his own and that of the prospect. The salesperson may be able to determine the degree of interest the prospect has in the salesperson's product and/or presentation. The salesperson must be careful to look directly at the prospect at least 40 percent of the time while talking in order to communicate credibility.[14] If the salesperson looks at the prospect far less often or blinks excessively, his credibility may be seriously undermined.

The salesperson should keep in mind that eye avoidance, either his own or the prospect's, can signal such things as embarrassment, anxiety, lack of interest, or dislike. The salesperson should make every effort not to avoid direct eye contact and should be attentive to any such attempts by the prospect. There is a desirable level of direct eye gaze in any situation. Since power is one potential message of eye gaze, the salesperson should be careful not to engage in prolonged staring. Generally, staring is not socially acceptable, except among people who are very intimate. Figure 4.5 conveys the frustration you might feel if you were talking to someone without the benefit of eye behavior or facial expression.

FIGURE 4.5 We rely heavily on the face and eyes when we communicate. It would be a very frustrating experience to talk to this person.

Kinesics

Kinesics *refers to body movement.* This entails such things as how you use your arms and hands or how you position your body in a chair. In this context, we note whether the person crosses the legs or points a finger, leans the head to one side, or clenches a fist.

Kinesics covers a wide range of bodily movements and is referred to in popular discussions as *body language.*[15] While we prefer not to use this term, it does demonstrate the meaning of kinesics. The face, of course, is part of the body, but because the face is so important, it is usually treated separately. When we talk about kinesics, we usually refer to the following parts of the body (in addition to the face):[16]

1. Total head.
2. Neck.
3. Trunk.
4. Shoulder-arm-wrist.
5. Hand.
6. Hip-joint-leg-ankle.
7. Foot.

Some of these bodily parts convey more nonverbal meaning than others. For example, the head and the hands can be used to communicate a great deal of meaning. The foot conveys less meaning.

Often, many body parts work together to create one general meaning. As an example, consider the act of walking. Men and women have distinctive walking styles. In general, we can tell a person's gender based upon the walk. Individuals also have their own distinctive walking styles. Walking involves all of the parts of the body listed earlier.

Probably the best way to understand bodily cues is to categorize them according to the functions they serve. There are five such functions.[17]

Emblems. **Emblems** are devices that we all use. They include such things as the peace sign, the okay signal, thumbs down, the extended arm and hand of a hitchhiker, a sign for good-bye, and, of course, strong forms of insult. Emblems *are used intentionally;* for that reason, *they don't provide as much hidden or personal information as other forms of bodily communication* (Figure 4.6).

What is unique about emblems is that they stand alone. In other words, no verbal description is required to convey their meaning. Since they can stand by themselves, they can be used even when people are physically distant from one another. We all probably know about 100 emblems.[18]

Illustrators. **Illustrators** *accompany a verbal message and, as their name states, illustrate the message.* You would be using an illustrator if you stretched out your arm horizontally with your hand extended as you describe a terrain that is flat. You would be using an illustrator if you shivered as you said, "It's cold in here."

Illustrators can be intentional or unintentional. People who use their hands a great deal when they talk are probably not aware of this tendency. Since illustrators are not necessarily intentional, they are useful in providing hidden information about a person. People often use illustrators when they are confident or want to communicate power. At the same time, illustrators can express frustration when someone is having difficulty making himself understood.[19]

This suggests that a salesperson would do well to use illustrators whenever possible. The salesperson should also watch for the use of illustrators by the prospect. The prospect may be having difficulty making himself understood when, for example, he can't find the technical term to express a product quality he is concerned about. In such cases, the salesperson should make every attempt to help the prospect. It is also possible that the prospect is using illustrators to communicate power and self-confidence. The salesperson should be aware of this and be careful not to overdo his own use of illustrators in order to prevent the interaction from turning into a contest for power.

Affect Displays. An **affect display** is *a communication of an emotion.* As suggested earlier, the face is the primary site of nonverbal display of emotion. The body, however, can also display emotion. A person in a slumped position or curled up in a chair may be communicating sadness and depression or boredom.

Affect displays are less under conscious control than emblems and illustrators. They are, therefore, better indicators of hidden information. A salesperson would do well to look for affect displays in the prospect. The salesperson should

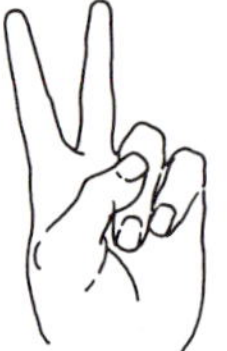

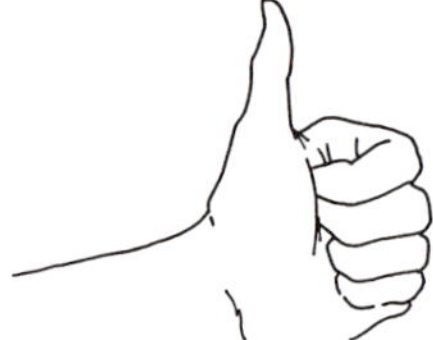

FIGURE 4.6 Some common emblems.

also be aware that the prospect may be looking at affect displays in the salesperson.

Regulators. **Regulators** *are used primarily to control the conversation.* Recall the earlier discussion of the use of eye movements for this purpose. You can raise your hand to indicate that you would like the floor. You can even go so far as to walk away to communicate lack of interest. Regulators not only control which person should speak but also provide socially acceptable ways of terminating a conversation. For example, breaking eye contact by moving the head down or sideways is considered to be a socially acceptable way of communicating that it is time to stop talking.[20]

It is important for a salesperson to be aware of bodily communication that serves as a regulator. Unawareness will likely lead to lack of sensitivity to the prospect's attempts to control the interaction. It may also cause the salesperson to use inappropriate nonverbal communication in attempting to control the conversation. For example, when greeting someone, a nod, a mutual glance, and a smile are desirable, while an open mouth and winking are undesirable.[21]

Adapters. **Adapters** *are mechanisms used to release the tension created during emotional arousal.* For example, an anxious person may try to eliminate the

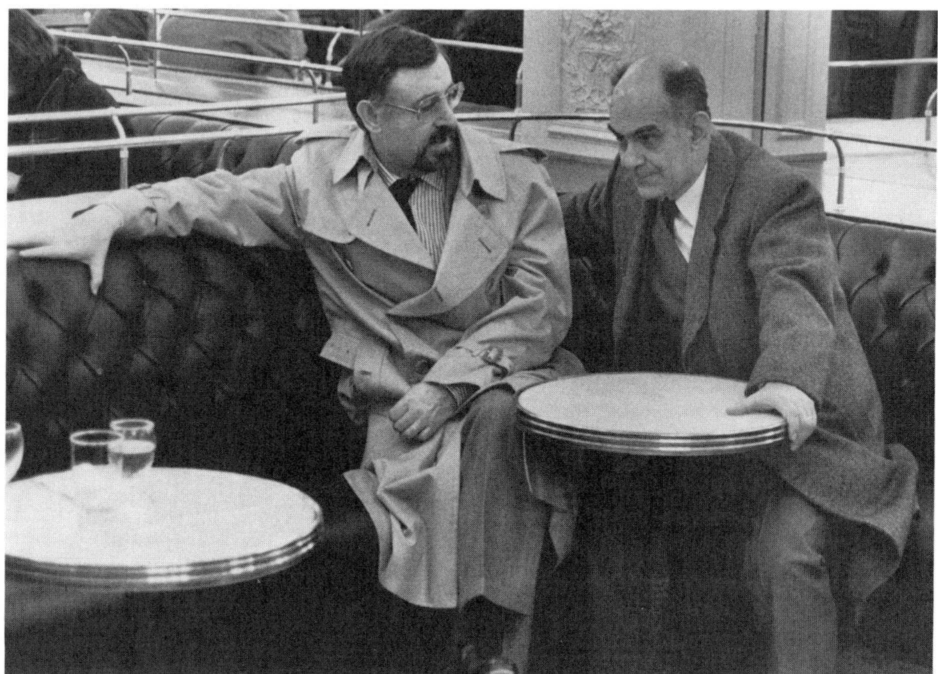

When someone's personal space is violated, the person can become very uncomfortable. (© Mark Antman/The Image Works, Inc.)

discomfort by scratching the back of his head or rubbing his arms. Adapters are usually not used consciously. For that reason, they are important sources of hidden information. Whenever a salesperson sees an adapter, she should recognize that there is some emotional arousal that the prospect is trying to ease. For example, the salesperson who notices an adapter immediately after mentioning the price may conclude that the price is of some concern to the prospect and discuss it further.

Using the Body to Communicate Openness, Assertiveness, and Liking. Generally, bodily communication that conveys openness is desirable because it also suggests that the speaker is attempting to be sincere and honest. The way to do this is through one or more of the following: unbutton your coat, uncross your legs, sit on the edge of a chair, and move as close to a desk or table between you and the speaker as possible.[22]

Similarly, assertiveness on the part of the salesperson is desirable. The best way to communicate assertiveness is to be relaxed in your gestures, lean slightly forward, maintain eye contact while avoiding staring, emphasize key words with illustrators, and avoid any indication of nervousness such as clearing the throat, a rigid posture, or avoidance of eye contact.[23]

Finally, it is useful to observe the prospect for indicators of liking. This is communicated by leaning forward, by directly facing the other person, with affirmative head nodes, eye contact, and a smile.[24, 25]

EXHIBIT 4.3

The Meaning of Gestures

When the crew of the American ship the *Pueblo* was captured by North Korea in 1968, they were forced to confess crimes against Korea. The Koreans sent a photo to prove that the crew were healthy and not forced into making their confessions. To show that this was not the case, three of the men used a common gesture: the insulting middle-finger.

When we see people nod their heads, we assume that they are indicating "yes." This is not always the case. In parts of Greece and Turkey, this same head nod can mean "no."

The thumbs-up gesture was displayed by the Roman Emperor to spare the lives of gladiators. Today, in the U.S. and most of Western Europe, it means "all right." However, in some places, such as Sardinia and Northern Greece, it is an insult meaning "up yours."

The A-okay sign means everything is fine in the U.S. In parts of Europe, though, it has a very different meaning. In France and Belgium, it means "you're worth nothing."

Source: Adapted from P. Ekman, V. Friesen, and J. Bear. (1984). The international language of gestures. *Psychology Today,* (May), 64–69.

Proxemics

Proxemics *refers to the way you position yourself when faced with another person.* In other words, it has to do with the use of space. The parties may be close together or far apart when standing opposite one another. Proxemics also refers to the way the parties position themselves at, for example, a conference table or a dinner table. Noting how close people get to one another when they speak or who chooses to sit at the head of the table are relevant proxemic concerns. As a salesperson, where you are allowed to sit when visiting a prospect's office is an important proxemic issue. Do you sit in front of the desk, next to the prospect, or at the side of the desk?[26]

Part of the reason proxemics is such an important issue has to do with **territoriality.** It seems that animals need to establish space that is their own; in other words, they establish their own territory. Humans have the same need to establish territory. Consider how upset you become when someone sits at your desk. You feel as though the person has invaded the territory that you claimed for yourself. You would be very offended if a stranger attempted to join you in a phone booth. This too would constitute an invasion of your territory.

Spatial Zones. Our sense of territory is probably what causes us to establish zones around our body as we talk to people. The **spatial zones** are shown in Figure 4.7. The **personal space zone** usually requires that we be separated from other people by 18 inches to 4 feet. This is the distance we usually use when we talk to other people with whom we are comfortable.

The person who gets closer than 18 inches has crossed over into the **intimate zone.** This zone is reserved for close friends, spouses, and lovers. In fact, even close friends should remain at the far side of this zone. The close side of this zone is usually reserved for lovemaking.

The distance between 4 and 12 feet is referred to as the **social zone.** The close side of this zone is best for a business encounter between a prospect and salesperson. If the two people are well acquainted, it would not be inappropriate for the salesperson to approach the personal zone as long as she stays on the far

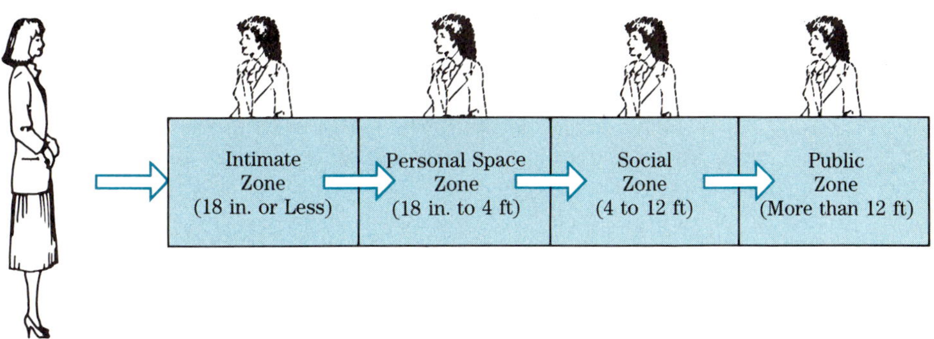

FIGURE 4.7 Spatial zones.

EXHIBIT 4.4

Some Meaningful Nonverbal Cues

The crossed-arm position can communicate defensiveness. It can also indicate disagreement or discomfort.

When the hands are joined to form a "church steeple" this can signify confidence or pride. It can also indicate smugness. This immediately communicates that the person is very sure of what he is saying.

Holding the arms behind the back and tightly clenching one wrist is an attempt at self-control. This is done in order to mask such emotions as anger or frustration.

Nose-touching or rubbing indicates doubt and can mean "no."

Rubbing the hands together indicates some expectation of receiving something.

Sources: Adapted from Nonverbal communication. (July, 1984). *Public Management, 66,* 16–18; Excerpted from G. S. Becker. (1983). Interpersonal communication. In: D. S. Arnold, C. S. Becker, and E. C. Kellar (eds.). *Effective Communication.* Washington, DC: International City Management Association.

side of that zone. Finally, the **public zone** is a distance of 12 feet or more. This is reserved for formal gatherings.[27]

There are times when we let strangers into our intimate zone, such as when we are on a crowded bus or subway. We do, however, compensate for this invasion by carefully avoiding eye contact with these persons and often by attempting to appear unaware of the invasion. We communicate this lack of awareness either by looking bored and distant or by reading a newspaper.

Violations of Personal Space. When people do violate what we consider to be appropriate distance, they may be doing so either because they come from a different culture or to show dominance and aggressiveness. Proxemics is not universal. While all cultures attend to the meaning of space and distance when conversing, the zones just described apply only to the United States. If we know that someone is from another culture, we can understand this person's violation of our norms of distance.

When people deliberately violate our space because they want to be dominant or aggressive, this can be very disruptive to the interaction. Often both people feel uncomfortable. However, there are times when we actually welcome a violation of personal space. This occurs when we find someone physically attractive or when we expect that the person can provide us with rewards.

How a Salesperson Can Rely Upon Proxemics. In a sales encounter, we would generally advise a salesperson to remain in the social zone (approximately 4 feet). An attempt to get closer to the prospect is risky, since it is likely to generate discomfort and conflict. If the prospect attempts to violate the salesperson's personal space, the salesperson can interpret this as an attempt to be aggressive, although it could also signal personal liking. The meaning of his invasion can be fully understood only by analyzing the verbal message and other nonverbal behaviors.

When the salesperson goes to a prospect's office, it is likely that both parties will be seated. The salesperson is in an inferior position if the prospect is seated behind a desk and the salesperson is forced to sit in a chair directly facing the prospect on the opposite side of the desk. If possible, the salesperson can reduce inferiority by sitting at the side of the desk rather than in front of it. In order to achieve proxemic equality, the salesperson and prospect should be seated next to one another. Figure 4.8 illustrates the various seating arrangements. It should be noted that the seating arrangement is usually determined by the prospect, although the salesperson may request that it be changed. He may do this, for example, to show the prospect a brochure.

Paralinguistics

Paralanguage is the only category of nonverbal communication that is not visual. Paralanguage *is, literally, about language. It occurs whenever you say something, since it is the vocal part of speech excluding the verbal content.*

Paralanguage has to do with *how* something is said, independently of *what* is said. People who study paralinguistics look at several things, including speech rate, volume, rhythm, and resonance.[28] They also consider such things as laughing, crying, yawning, yelling, moaning, whining, the use of words like "uh" or "un-uh," pitch, and even silences.

Personality and Vocal Quality. Vocal qualities can be very important and can enhance or detract from a message. Part of the reason for this is that we make important judgments about people, depending upon their vocal quality. We often make inferences about speakers' personalities based upon how they speak. People can sound shy or aggressive, friendly, or warm or cold. They can sound intelligent or likable. It is important to note that the assumptions made about personality on the basis of vocal quality are often wrong. However, despite the

Salesperson in Inferior Position

Salesperson in Less Inferior Position

Salesperson in Equal Position

FIGURE 4.8 Setting arrangements.

lack of accuracy, a listener will behave *as though the speaker has the particular personality characteristic.*

Judging Sex, Age, and Status by Vocal Quality. People do tend to be accurate in judging sex and age based upon vocal quality. They are also accurate in judging status based upon vocal quality. Particularly important here is a study showing that people who were judged to be of high status were considered to be more credible than people judged to be of low status. This conclusion was based upon hearing someone speak for as little as 15 seconds.[29] It certainly highlights the importance of vocal quality.

Judging Emotion by Vocal Quality. Evaluation of vocal quality is also relatively accurate in determining the emotional state. Recall that the face is particularly critical for inferring emotional state. The voice is also a major contributor, although it is less important than the face.[30]

People can identify emotions such as sadness, anger, nervousness, and happiness. They are less successful at identifying fear, love, jealousy, and pride. Interestingly, people are more successful at judging negative emotions than positive emotions from vocal quality.

Creating Images Through Vocal Quality. We can use vocal quality to create certain images. For example, we can communicate confidence through the use of rapid speech, expressiveness, and fluency. We can communicate power and status through high volume, a fast rate, and high resonance (the thickness or thinness of the vocal tone).

Paralanguage and Regulating Conversation. Paralanguage helps to signal conversational turns. Recall that eye behavior also serves that function, as do certain movements of the body. When a speaker wants to continue speaking while pausing to collect her thoughts, she uses vocalizations such as "um" or "er." This signals to the other person that the speaker has not finished her turn. A listener also communicates his willingness to continue functioning as a listener by giving reinforcing vocalizations such as "hmmm."

Paralinguistics tell the listener when the speaker has finished speaking. The speaker can do this by raising his voice at the end of a sentence as if to ask a question. Another method is to drop the intonation and follow it with an unfilled pause. Vocal cues provide the listener an opportunity to say something in the middle of a speaker's statement without actually interrupting. This can be done with similar vocalizations, such as "tsk" or "huh?" After such vocalizations, the speaker will likely ask the listener if something is wrong.

How the Salesperson Can Rely Upon Paralanguage. There are a number of important implications here for the sales interaction. First, the salesperson needs to be attentive to paralinguistics. In order for the conversation to flow smoothly, the salesperson needs to attend to vocalizations from the prospect. By doing this, the salesperson becomes aware of attempts by the prospect to interject important concerns and objections. This increased awareness also prevents the salesperson from interrupting the prospect (which is a dominant and aggressive behavior).

The salesperson also needs to be aware of the personality characteristics that the prospect can infer from the way he uses his voice. He is well advised to use his voice so that it communicates an image of confidence and high status, since these traits enhance credibility. Finally, the salesperson should look for indicators of emotional states in the prospect in order to evaluate how positively or negatively the prospect may be feeling about what he is saying.

Combining Channels and "Reading" Nonverbal Signals

Although we have discussed each channel separately, as we pointed out initially, whenever we say something, all channels communicate simultaneously. Of course, it is difficult for anyone to attend to all of those channels at the same time, and some channels may be more important than others. Whenever possible, however, it is best to attend to as many channels as you can. Consider, for example, the communication of emotion. You have learned that there are at least three channels that serve this function: facial movement, eye behavior, and paralanguage.

As a more specific example of how nonverbal elements can be combined, we can look at something called **conversational involvement**—*the degree to which people are engaged in an interaction.* Monitoring conversational involvement is important for a salesperson, because it is a good indicator of how much a prospect likes the salesperson and is interested in the product.

There are several channels that communicate conversational involvement. When partners are involved, their bodies tend to be closer, and they face one another more directly. They engage in more eye gaze, smiling, and head nodding. There are more frequent and animated hand movements, greater facial animation, fewer silences, more relaxed laughter. There are also fewer indicators of social anxiety or nervousness. This means that people are less likely to use adapters and to have deeper pitch, less random movement, and greater vocal warmth[31] (Figure 4.9).

What is striking about conversational involvement is that it is communicated by every nonverbal channel. As we suggested, however, this is no different from any other communication situation. With the exception of cases like phone conversations, where certain channels are limited, all nonverbal channels communicate simultaneously.

This doesn't mean that you can't rely upon only one or two channels in interpreting someone else's nonverbal communication. But you will be more accurate if you can observe all the channels simultaneously. One reason is that, as mentioned earlier, people have greater control over some channels than others. People have greater control over facial expression than over eye behavior. They also have greater control over bodily movements than over paralanguage. This means that people can present false nonverbal messages via those channels that are more directly under their control. This ability to falsify nonverbal communi-

FIGURE 4.9 Two people with a high degree of conversational involvement.

cation makes interpretation of nonverbal communication somewhat difficult. However, there are several potential indicators of an attempt to present a false message that an astute observer can detect. Following is a discussion of this issue.

The Presentation of False Nonverbal Cues

There are many times when we are motivated to fake our nonverbal communication. We may need to do this when we are expected to experience an emotion that we don't feel. For example, if an acquaintance has a cold, we may want to communicate concern even though we don't really feel it too strongly. We may want to appear more interested in a conversation than we really are. We may even want to present an outright lie, such as telling a salesperson that "I definitely want to buy this, but I left my checkbook at home," even though we know that is not true. In each of these cases, it is the nonverbal communication that we try to manipulate. It is also the nonverbal communication that the listener attends to, because that person is trying to find out whether what we are saying or doing reflects our true feelings.[32]

Nonverbal Communication as an Indicator of Truth

Why would nonverbal behavior be the best indicator of lying behavior? Consider the use of lie detectors. While they are not foolproof, lie detectors are sensitive machines that pick up subtle physiological changes that often accompany lying. Such changes have to do with heart rate or skin resistance or pulse rate. But these subtle physiological changes are often apparent through one or more nonverbal channels. In fact, some studies have found that human beings can outperform mechanical lie detectors just by observing a liar speak.[33]

We have all either been asked or have asked someone else to look us directly in the eye and make a statement. That request usually occurs when we think that the person may not be telling the truth. We assume that if someone is indeed lying, we will be able to see it in her eyes. If you yourself have ever been asked to do this, you know how difficult it was for you to look the other person directly in the eye and make the statement if you were, in fact, lying (Figure 4.10).

Consistency Versus Inconsistency

The essence of any attempt to fake nonverbal communication has to do with the consistency of verbal and nonverbal messages. Whenever we make a statement that is true—and most statements we make probably are true—we, of course, simultaneously communicate nonverbally. But since our statement is true, our verbal and nonverbal messages are consistent with one another. In effect, we are communicating in a way that is natural for us.

However, when we deliberately lie, or when we try to communicate a feeling that we don't really experience, an inconsistency emerges between our verbal and nonverbal messages. This inconsistency creates a certain amount of internal discomfort because we are no longer communicating in a natural manner. Instead, we are required to attend carefully to our nonverbal communication so that we won't give ourselves away. The irony of the situation is that, simply by attending consciously to our nonverbal communication, we are more likely to give ourselves away. This happens because we are more likely to reveal our underlying discomfort, since our nonverbal communication is likely to be unnatural.[34]

When our nonverbal communication becomes unnatural, the person we are talking to may notice this because of the obvious inconsistency between our verbal and nonverbal messages. Whenever that happens, there is a great deal of evidence that people attend to the nonverbal channel to determine the truth value of the statement.[35] Therefore, the listener may decide that the speaker is lying or faking some emotion.

The issue of consistency versus inconsistency can certainly extend to the salesperson and prospect. Prospects are likely to avoid telling a salesperson directly that they are uninterested in what is being sold, particularly if they expect the salesperson to attempt even more persuasion. The easiest course of action is to suggest that they need more time to think about the issue, or that they forgot their credit cards and will return later, or that they need to discuss the purchase with the purchasing manager. If these statements are made in such a way that they appear to be inconsistent with the accompanying nonverbal behavior, the

FIGURE 4.10 Eyes can signal deception.

EXHIBIT 4.5

The Language of the Prospect

Following is part of a conversation between a salesperson, Ed Philipson, a sales representative in training for business equipment, and Raymond Dreyfack, a contributor to *The American Salesman.*

ED: I guess you could say steady customers *are* communicative. . . . But prospects? Never! Or hardly ever.

RAYMOND: Prospects communicate all the time.

ED: Howzat?

RAYMOND: The explanation is simple. Bodies talk.

ED: Bodies talk?

RAYMOND: Sure. You heard of body language.

ED: Oh, that. . . . Bodies may talk, but it's not the kind of talk you can hear with your ears.

RAYMOND: That couldn't matter less. Sometimes listening with your eyes can be as effective as listening with your ears. Even more so. . . . Take Bill Schuitz. Bill sells a line of lighting fixtures and accessories. . . . He specializes in industrial customers. He called on a prospect. . . . Bill spent several hours with that purchasing manager. This P.A. *was* communicative. Very verbal. And we're not talking body language. The guy actually expressed interest, told Bill he liked his line. Bill practically had that sales commission spent in advance.

ED: What happened?

RAYMOND: The sale fizzled.

ED: So what's the point of the story?

RAYMOND: Language you can hear with your ears isn't always reliable. . . . The beauty of body language in selling is that the prospect may be giving you information without being aware that he's doing it. . . . Body language isn't planned or calculated; it's involuntary. Body language doesn't lie as a rule.

Source: Adapted from R. Dreyfack, (1988). The selling edge. *The American Salesman, 33* (August), 28–30

salesperson may recognize that they are lies. The question becomes: What specific nonverbal behaviors are indicative of this underlying discomfort?

Indicators of Underlying Discomfort

There are a number of nonverbal indicators to suggest that we are experiencing some internal discomfort about what we are saying or doing. Lack of eye contact is one indicator, but so, too, are a backward lean, excessive leg movements, rocking, speech errors, excessive hand movements, and a high-pitched voice.[36]

This issue has received a great deal of research.[37,38] Not everyone is equally observant about nonverbal communication. This means that some people are better able to detect underlying discomfort than others. At the same time, some people are better able to control their nonverbal communication than others and, as a result, are more successful in hiding their discomfort.

The Controllability of Nonverbal Behaviors

Not surprisingly, we tend to believe most in what someone is least able to control deliberately. "If one cannot control it, one cannot fake it."[39] One behavior that is relatively uncontrollable is voice pitch—the highness or lowness of the voice. It has been found that people consistently raise the pitch of their voice when they are under stress, including the stress and discomfort that lying or faking emotion generate.[40]

Recently, a detailed study of the smile provided some interesting results regarding its appearance when it is genuine and when it is false. Since the muscle structure of the face is elaborate and complex, it conveys a variety of emotions. Smiling is one of our more frequent and more important facial nonverbal behaviors. Many smiles are spontaneous and genuine. Many others, however, are deliberately presented either because people are expected to smile in certain situations or because they use the smile to cover up certain minor forms of irritation or frustration.

What is interesting is that the genuine smile actually looks different from the forced smile. The genuine smile is not accompanied by furrows between the eyebrows, and the corners of the lips tend to turn up. The forced smile results in furrows between the eyebrows, and the corners of the lips turn down as if to signal unhappiness or sadness. While the smile is just one of many nonverbal behaviors, it is instructive that the smile alone can be an indicator of lack of truth.

If someone has reason to lie, a listener is likely to be particularly vigilant about possible cues that would reveal any deception. Even the subtle differences between a genuine and a false smile can be perceived. This is especially true when a listener *expects* a speaker to lie or fake certain emotions. There are probably many instances when the salesperson becomes particularly vigilant about the prospect. Often prospects are not in a position to make an immediate purchase. Sometimes they have to discuss it with a purchasing manager or a family member. It is also possible that they simply don't want to make the purchase but say that they have to discuss it further with other people. This is when vigilance on the salesperson's part may reveal an inconsistency between the prospect's verbal and nonverbal behaviors.

In sum, perceiving lying or faking of emotion appears to be based upon how observers view (1) the demands of the situation and (2) the controllability of the behavior. That is, many situations, such as the job interview or the interaction between salesperson and prospect, involve demands that would make lying somewhat more likely than many everyday conversations such as a discussion about a test between two students or a discussion about a movie between two business people. When demands exist that make lying more likely, the observer looks to see if nonverbal behaviors that are difficult to control are in fact controlled. If they are controlled, they appear unnatural. The observer then assumes that deception has occurred.

Putting It All Together

The points we have made in this chapter are as follows:

- Nonverbal communication is at least as important as, if not more important than, verbal communication.
- Dynamic nonverbal communication occurs through five channels: face, eyes, body, voice, space.
- Some channels are easier to control than others, and those that are more difficult to control are more revealing.
- Nonverbal communication serves a number of functions, including expressing emotion and intensity of emotion, regulating a conversation, and communicating impressions.
- Faking of nonverbal communication can often be detected because it appears unnatural.

Clearly, nonverbal communication is complex. Still, most of us tend to read nonverbal cues easily and quickly. Similarly, most of us exhibit nonverbal cues that are in keeping with the expectations of other people. This usually occurs naturally.

Still, it is wise for salespeople to be vigilant regarding the nonverbal communication of prospects. They should also make every attempt to be flexible in their own nonverbal communication. Salespeople can manage the impression they create through nonverbal behaviors; these are often taught in sales training programs.[41] For example, when a buyer appears suspicious or uncomfortable, a salesperson can counter this through nonverbal communication. Specifically, he can lean forward slightly and assume a relaxed but interested posture.[42]

This brings up an important issue. Should the salesperson deliberately manipulate his own nonverbal communication? Assuming that he believes what he is saying, he shouldn't have to worry about his own nonverbal communication. It will flow naturally. Too much conscious control over nonverbal communication will make the salesperson appear unnatural and call into question his truthfulness. At the same time, the salesperson should keep in mind the importance of appearing confident, and should monitor such things as eye gaze and body position. The salesperson should attend to the nonverbal communication of the prospect. He should look for signs of interest, dislike, confusion, boredom, or discomfort. He should be particularly attentive to indicators that the prospect wishes to speak.

All of the concerns we have addressed in this chapter are embodied in a distinction between two general interpersonal styles: **assertiveness** and **aggressiveness.** Generally, people who are assertive promote their own interests, but not at the expense of someone else. Assertive people are not manipulative and don't worry a great deal about who will be dominant and who will be submissive. Instead, they communicate their needs directly, display self-confidence, and are articulate and logical, but they get their points across and do not fear being forceful.[43] They also attend carefully to what the other person says and make every effort to meet the other person's needs.

Aggressive people violate another person's rights by being domineering, by not listening, and by being insensitive. Such people view selling as an adversarial situation. They have only one goal: to achieve their own desires. They are manipulative, and use high-pressure and hard-sell techniques.

The major aspect that distinguishes assertive from aggressive behavior is nonverbal communication. The nonverbal indicators of assertiveness include a careful attempt to listen to the prospect and engage in appropriate eye contact and turn taking. The speaking volume is forceful but is not significantly louder than that of the prospect.[44] Occasional smiling is also helpful in communicating assertiveness.[45] Aggressiveness is marked either by too little eye contact or by so much of it that the prospect begins to feel uncomfortable.[46] It is also communicated by a smile that looks more like a disapproving smirk. In addition, the aggressive salesperson fails to signal turn taking and ignores such signals from the prospect. An aggressive salesperson would also be likely to communicate lack of interest nonverbally while the prospect is talking.

A salesperson should make every effort to use an assertive style. This style relies on all the nonverbal channels we have discussed. It also relies on many verbal issues that are the focus of the chapters dealing with the sales process. The salesperson should practice using the nonverbal indicators of assertiveness in order to become, in time, naturally assertive. He can then concentrate on the content of the sales presentation.

Key Terms

Nonverbal communication
Facial expression
Display rules
Eye behavior
Kinesics
Emblems
Illustrators
Affect displays
Regulators
Adapters
Proxemics
Territoriality
Spatial zones
Personal space
Intimate zone
Social zone
Public zone
Paralanguage
Conversational involvement
Assertiveness
Aggressiveness

Review Questions

1. What do we mean by nonverbal communication?
2. Why do we say that nonverbal communication is dynamic? Can nonverbal communication be static?
3. What are the five channels of nonverbal communication?
4. What are some of the emotions that the face can communicate?
5. What are display rules? Why are they relevant to facial expression?
6. Why is it particularly important to attend to pupil dilation?
7. What are the three major functions of eye behavior?
8. What are the five kinds of body movement?
9. What are spatial zones? In which zone should a salesperson be?
10. If you attend to paralanguage, what vocal qualities should you look for?
11. What are five functions of paralanguage?
12. What are the nonverbal indicators of conversational involvement?
13. Why would we look at nonverbal communication to determine if someone is telling the truth?
14. What is the difference between assertive and aggressive behavior?

Discussion Questions

1. If you were training a salesperson to sell mainframe computers to large organizations, what would you tell the salesperson to look for in the nonverbal communication of prospects?
2. How might the static nonverbal behaviors of a business-to-business salesperson be different than those of a retail salesperson?
3. When trying to sell products of multinational corporations in other countries, what difficulties might a salesperson encounter with respect to interpretation of his own nonverbal communication or with respect to the way he interprets the nonverbal communication of his prospect?
4. In general, what aspects of nonverbal communication would you include in a sales training program?

CASE 4.1

Jim Swanson was recently hired by the XY Company to develop a new sales training course. Both telemarketing and face-to-face sales are important to the company, since it sells leather to manufacturers who make shoes, handbags, belts, briefcases, wallets, and various other articles.

Up to 1982, when the company relied solely on salespeople, there was not much competition. Thus, even mediocre salespeople could be successful. By 1984, it was clear that many of the salespeople were, indeed, mediocre.

Sales had decreased dramatically at about the same time that competitors had entered the market.

As a result, the company decided to begin a sales training program in 1985. The initial program seemed to help somewhat. It consisted largely of teaching the salespeople prepared sales presentations. The program did explain how a salesperson could deviate from the presentation by making the salespeople practice various ways to present the same information. Particular attention was paid to the way the same facts could be presented in various formats.

The salespeople felt that the training was helpful, but they were still vaguely uneasy. That's when Jim Swanson was brought in. Sales had not increased sufficiently under the initial training program. Swanson was known to be an expert trainer.

Jim believed that, in any sales situation, how you say it is more important than what you say. That, of course, caused him to stress the nonverbal aspects of the sales presentation. The company's management was somewhat skeptical. They knew about nonverbal behavior, but they believed that nonverbal communication should not be emphasized to the same extent as Jim Swanson felt it should. They decided to give Jim a try anyway, wait for 6 months, and look at the bottom line: improvement in sales.

1. Do you agree with Jim Swanson that how you say it is more important than what you say? Why or why not?
2. How could you train people to deal more effectively with nonverbal behavior?
3. Should people be trained to deal with their own nonverbal communication or that of the prospect?
3. How much can salespeople control their own nonverbal communication?
4. How easy would it be to read the nonverbal behavior of a prospect? What things would a salesperson be instructed to look for?

References

1. *Manhattan Living.* (Summer 1987). 55.

2. Ibid.

3. Mehrabian, A. (1972). *Nonverbal Communication.* Chicago: Aldine-Atherton.

4. Birdwhistle, R. L. (1970). *Kinesics and Context.* New York: Ballantine Books.

5. Ekman, P., W. V. Friesen, and P. Ellsworth. (1972). *Emotion in the Human Face: Guidelines for Research and an Integration of Findings.* New York: Pergamon Press.

6. Ibid.

7. Leather, D. (1986). *Successful Nonverbal Communication.* New York: Macmillan.

8. Ekman et al., op. cit.

9. De Vito, J. A. (1986). *The Interpersonal Communication Book.* New York: Harper & Row.

10. Ekman, P. (1971). Universal and cultural differences in facial expressions of emotions. In: J. K. Cole (ed.), Nebraska Symposium on Motivation. Lincoln: University of Nebraska Press.

11. Ibid.

12. Marshall, E. (1983). *Eye Language: Understanding the Eloquent Eye.* New York: New Trend.

13. Janik, S. U., A. R. Wellens, M. L. Goldberg, and L. F. Dell'osso. (1978). Eyes as the center of focus in the visual examination of faces. *Perceptual and Motor Skills, 47,* 857–858.

14. Burgoon, J. K., and T. Saine. (1978). *The Unspoken Dialogue: An Introduction to Nonverbal Communication.* Englewood Cliffs, NJ: Prentice-Hall.

15. Montague, A. (1971). *Touching: The Human Significance of the Skin.* New York: Harper & Row.

16. Birdwhistell, R. L. (1952). *Introduction to Kinesics.* Louisville: University of Kentucky Press.

17. Ekman, P., and W. V. Friesen. (1969). The repertoire of nonverbal behavior: Categories, origins, usage, and coding. *Semiotica, 69,* 49–97.

18. Leathers, op. cit.

19. Ekman, P., and W. V. Friesen. (1972). Hand movements. *Journal of Communication, 22,* 353–374.

20. Knapp, M., R. P. Hart, and G. W. Friedrich. (1973). Verbal and nonverbal correlates of human leave-taking. *Communication Monographs, 40,* 182–198.

21. Krivonos, P. D., and M. Knapp. (1975). Initiating communication: What do you say when you say hello? *Central States Speech Journal, 26,* 115–125.

22. Nierenberg, G., and H. H. Calero. (1973). *How to Read a Person Like a Book.* New York: Pocket Books.

23. Lange, A. J., and P. Jakubowski. (1976). *Responsible Assertive Behavior.* Champaign, IL: Research Press.

24. Mehrabian, A. (1981). *Silent Messages.* Belmont, CA: Wadsworth.

25. Schlenker, B. R. (1980). *Impression Management.* Monterey, CA: Brooks/Cole.

26. Malando, L. A., and L. Barker. (1983). *Nonverbal Communication.* New York: Random House.

27. Hall, E. (1959). *The Silent Language.* New York: Doubleday.

28. Knapp, M. (1978). *Nonverbal Behavior in Human Interaction.* New York: Holt, Rinehart, & Winston.

29. De Vito, op. cit.

30. Mehrabian (1981), op. cit.

31. Coker, D. A., and J. K. Burgoon. (1987). The nature of conversational involvement and nonverbal encoding patterns. *Human Communication Research, 13,* 463–494.

32. Hocking, J. E., and D. G. Leathers. (1986). Nonverbal indicators of deception: A new theoretical perspective. *Communication Monographs, 47,* 119–131.

33. De Paulo, B., M. Zuckerman, and R. Rosenthal. (1980). Humans as lie detectors. *Journal of Communication, 30,* 129–139.

34. Harper, R. G., A. N. Wiens, and J. D. Matarazzo. (1978). *Nonverbal Communication: The State of the Art.* New York: Wiley.

35. Ibid.

36. Pryor, B., and R. W. Buchanan. (1984). The effects of a defendant's demeanor on juror perceptions of credibility and guilt. *Journal of Communication, 34,* 92–99.

37. Harper et al., loc. cit.

38. DePaulo et al., loc. cit.

39. Krauss, R. E. (1978). Verbal and nonverbal cues in the perception of lying. *Journal of Personality and Social Psychology, 36,* 380–391.

40. Streeter, L. A., R. E. Krauss, V. Geller, C. Olson, and W. Apple. (1977). Pitch change during attempted deception. *Journal of Personality and Social Psychology, 35,* 345–350.

41. King, R. H., and M. B. Booze. (1986). Sales training and impression management. *Journal of Personal Selling and Sales Management, 6,* 51–60.

42. Schwandtner, G. (1980). Nonverbal selling power. *Training and Development Journal, 34,* 62–64.

43. Jolson, M. (1984). Selling assertively. *Business Horizons, 27,* 71–77.

44. Norton-Ford, J. D., and D. R. Hogan. (1980). Role of nonverbal behaviors in social judgments of peers' assertiveness. *Psychological Reports, 46,* 1085–1086.

45. Shrout, P. E., and D. W. Fiske. (1981). Nonverbal behaviors and social evaluation. *Journal of Personality, 49,* 115–128.

46. Sitton, S. C., and S. T. Griffin. (1981). Detection of deception from clients' eye contact patterns. *Journal of Counseling Psychology, 28(3),* 269–271.

Buyer Behavior

CHAPTER OBJECTIVES

In this chapter, you will learn:

Buyers go through a series of distinct stages including attention, interest, desire, and action.

Gaining attention requires that a salesperson stand out from other salespeople.

A salesperson can get a prospect's attention by asking questions that force the prospect to get involved.

Once a salesperson encounters a prospect, it is necessary to depend upon such things as rewards, incentives, liking, and trust to be certain that the prospect hears exactly what the salesperson wants him to hear.

Getting a prospect's interest is accomplished by appealing to the basic motives of protection, satisfaction, and enhancement.

A salesperson becomes more effective by communicating interest in the prospect's well-being and by being knowledgeable.

Desire can be influenced by changing attitudes.

The best way to cause action or a purchase is to show the buyer how the purchase will solve a particular problem.

Salespeople who behave in stereotypical ways may cause a prospect not to listen to them.

CHAPTER OUTLINE

A Sales Challenge

An Overview

Attention

- Selective Exposure and Selective Attention
- Selective Exposure and Selective Attention in the Sales Situation

Interest

- Creating Interest by Appealing to Motives
- Maslow's Need Hierarchy
- The Needs of the Organization
- Emotional Versus Rational Motives
- How the Salesperson Can Utilize Motivation in the Sales Interaction

Desire

- Three Things We Can Do with Attitudes
- The Multiattribute Model
- Applying the Multiattribute Model to a Sales Situation

Action

- A Problem-Solving Perspective to Purchase
- Problem Solving in the Organization

Putting It All Together

- Automatic Reactions to Expectations That Are Confirmed
- Behaving Counter to Expectations

Key Terms

Review Questions

Discussion Questions

Case 5.1

References

A Sales Challenge

"I don't know why I bought that. I just felt I had to have it."

"I'm not prepared to make a decision just yet. I'm collecting as much information as I can, and then I'll discuss it with other people in the firm and make a decision."

"I know I didn't need another coat, but I just got tired of the same old thing."

"If I pay only the minimum on my charge card this month and next month, I can buy a new couch."

"We really do need a new computer system in this office, but we're just not very familiar with your company. I think we'd be more comfortable with a more established name."

"I just don't think they make very good products."

"We really like the design of your new aircraft, but our budget simply doesn't allow us to make a purchase at this time."

"The air-conditioning system you're proposing is impressive, but it just doesn't seem very efficient. If you can come up with a more economical proposal, we will consider it."

"Right now, what we really need is a fabric that is stain resistant. Our customers have been complaining about fabrics that are supposedly stain resistant but seem to get stained much too easily."

"I want to buy a stereo, but I really don't know very much about them."

An Overview

All of these statements made by either consumers or organizational buyers reflect various aspects of buyer behavior. Our goal in this chapter is to provide you with a better understanding of buyer behavior. Buyer behavior is actually quite complex. You need only examine your own motives, hesitations, goals, and decision processes when you make a major purchase to realize that it is not a simple matter.

To try to simplify our understanding of buyer behavior, a number of models have been suggested. These models indicate that buyers go through a series of distinct stages. They begin with awareness of a need. This is followed by gaining knowledge of the ways to fulfill that need. That process, in turn, may lead to liking and possibly a preference for a particular product that will directly fulfill that need. The final stage is purchase of the product.[1]

One model of buyer behavior is the AIDA model. This model is almost 65 years old, yet it is still regarded as a reasonable approximation of the buying process despite a number of attempts to modify it. AIDA is an acronym for attention, interest, desire, and action[2] (see Figure 5.1).

This model does not describe all buying in all situations, but it very likely applies in many cases. For example, sometimes we buy on impulse. In other words, we just buy. We may collect information after we buy. Generally, though, we collect information before we buy. The information causes interest and desire,

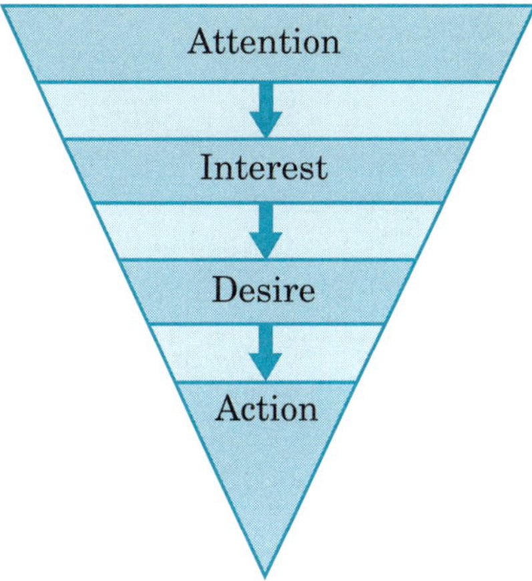

FIGURE 5.1 The AIDA model.

which lead to action. Before we collect information, we have to give our attention so that we can become aware of a product's existence.

The AIDA model is ideally suited for a buying situation that requires face-to-face interaction with a salesperson. Impulse buying situations discussed earlier usually do not require a salesperson, apart from having someone write up the order and collect money. In most sales interactions, the salesperson leads the prospect through the stages by providing information in the hope of causing interest, desire, and finally action. In this chapter, the discussion of buyer behavior is structured around the AIDA model. We begin with attention, which, in fact, is an issue of *perception.* We then discuss interest, which is an issue of *motivation.* This is followed by a consideration of desire, which is an issue of *attitudes,* and, finally by action, which is an issue of *problem solving.*

It should be understood that we are concerned with any kind of buyer in this chapter, whether a consumer in a retail store or a representative of an organization. A consumer in a retail store can be making a purchase for either personal use or as part of a family unit. A buyer in an organization may be the only decision maker or may be one of many. Organizational buyers must always be concerned with the broader needs of the organization in addition to their own needs. Consumers can be concerned with their own needs or the needs of the family unit.

Attention

The first major task facing a salesperson is getting the **attention** of the prospect. Attention is defined as *"a state of mental consciousness in which some object or idea stands out from all the rest."*[3] This definition implies that we cannot have everything in our consciousness at the same time. Thus, you can't read a magazine and watch television at the same time and give full attention to both. You can't simultaneously listen to your professor and talk to a friend and give them both your undivided attention.

EXHIBIT 5.1

Warming Up for Sales

Spring is the season for buying. "It's the birth of barter fever, retail rapture. . . . Everything is possible in May." The question becomes: How does the salesperson have the spring market to himself?

1. Arrive early.
2. Remember that people love to buy. Buying can be thrilling. It can also impress other people.
3. Remember that people hate to be sold. As soon as pressure is put on people to buy, they worry about being in a game that they can lose.
4. People buy mostly because they *want* something rather than because they need something. Don't sell people; instead, "ignite the want. Then watch them handle their own objections."

Source: Reprinted by permission of *Sales & Marketing Management*, © 1986. B. Toskich. (1986). Warming up for the sales. *Sales & Marketing Management, 136*(5), 16.

Selective Exposure and Selective Attention

The act of giving attention requires two stages. The first stage is the actual *exposure* to one thing versus something else. Since this is an act requiring *selection,* it is referred to as **selective exposure.** Selective exposure means that *you expose yourself only to certain events or information.*

Once you expose yourself to one thing, you necessarily pay attention to certain aspects and ignore others. This is the second stage of attention and is referred to as **selective attention.** Selective attention means that *you focus on certain pieces of information or certain parts of objects* (see Figure 5.2). For example, when you read, you can't take in every word on the page at the same time. Instead, you selectively attend to certain words at one time as you scan a line. Similarly, when you walk down a street, you cannot focus on every single car, person, building, and so on. You attend selectively to certain things.

Selective Exposure and Selective Attention in the Sales Situation

The concerns of selective exposure and selective attention are especially important when dealing with a prospect. The first stage, and the first major hurdle, is to get a prospect to selectively expose himself to one particular salesperson out of all of the other salespeople. Once that is accomplished, the salesperson deals with the second stage and the second major hurdle: getting the prospect to selectively attend to the points the salesperson has to make. With all the competing events in the environment, it is no wonder that the salesperson has so much difficulty gaining attention.

Consider George Griffin, a purchasing manager for a large metropolitan news-

This is the headquarters of ARCO. An organization such as this one is a fertile ground for a multitude of salespeople selling a multitude of products. Understanding the behavior of purchasing agents is critical. (Courtesy of Atlantic Richfield Co.)

paper. At a basic level, a newspaper needs newsprint and ink. It also needs various mechanical devices that allow the written word to be set in type and printed. These devices are continually being upgraded and updated as technology improves.

George Griffin receives catalogs and mailings every day from various ink and newsprint manufacturers, as well as from companies that make computer typesetting devices. On a typical day, George might receive as many as 15 or 20 of

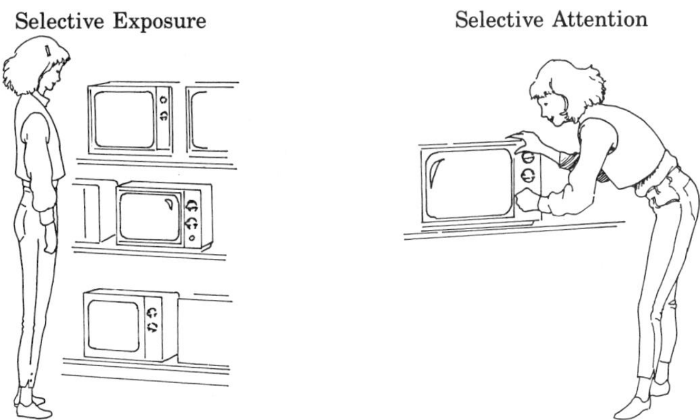

FIGURE 5.2 Selective exposure occurs prior to selective attention.

them. He is also very likely to be visited by several salespeople selling these products. These salespeople leave samples, and eventually George becomes laden with them. He reaches a point where all the samples of ink and types of newsprint look the same.

Sam Dunn is an ink salesperson who arrives at George's office at 10:30 A.M. He has no appointment, but he figures that George can always use more information about ink. When Sam Dunn is announced, George has just been informed that the newsprint currently being used is absorbing too much ink. George, therefore, is concerned with newsprint, not ink. George is also in the middle of a divorce.

How anxious do you think George is to hear from Sam Dunn, another ink salesperson? Sam has his work cut out for him. George has to be selective about who he sees and what information he deals with. Thus, the first process George will engage in is selective exposure. Usually the events we expose ourselves to are those that coincide with things we need or with information that supports our views about certain issues. The tendency for George to engage in selective exposure is the first obstacle Sam has to overcome in gaining George's attention. Sam's particular variety of ink does not coincide with the immediate crisis George is facing. This makes it very likely that George will engage in selective exposure and refuse to see Sam.

Dealing with Selective Exposure. How will Sam deal with selective exposure? In other words, how can Sam convince George to see him? If he knows Sam through previous interactions, selective exposure may be less of a problem. We will assume that George has never met Sam. We will assume further that initially Sam contacts George over the telephone.

To combat selective exposure, that is, George's refusal to see Sam, Sam should try to suggest respected sources. In other words, Sam can indicate that a major competitor uses his ink or that an important person suggested that he call George. If necessary, Sam can go so far as to have a respected newspaper person call George and tell him about Sam and his ink.

Another option to reduce the possibility of selective exposure is to offer immediately some form of reward or incentive. Sam can offer a free supply of ink for the next newspaper run if George agrees to talk to Sam after the run. Sam can also offer some incentive that is clearly superior to that offered by the competitors.

In summary, selective exposure is always a factor in attention. Two mechanisms to ensure that prospects will selectively expose themselves to a salesperson are (1) relying upon sources that the prospect knows and respects and/or (2) providing rewards and incentives (see Figure 5.3).

Dealing with Selective Attention. We will assume that Sam does, in fact, break through the barrier of selective exposure. Once Sam does have an opportunity to see George in person, he faces George's selective attention. As we suggested, George has so many things to distract him that Sam is going to have a difficult time getting George to listen to anything, not to mention Sam's main selling points.

FIGURE 5.3 Selective exposure can be overcome by using respected sources or by providing rewards and incentives.

There are four tactics that Sam can employ to control George's attention process. The first tactic should be employed during the approach, that is, at the beginning of the sales meeting. Sam should attempt to engage George in a discussion that will allow rapport to be built. In so doing, Sam will give George a basis for *liking* Sam.

The second tactic for dealing with selective attention should occur throughout the presentation. In Sam's case, he needs to communicate his *credibility* or believability. The best way to accomplish this is, first, to show that he is very knowledgeable about the product category, that is, that he has *expertise.* Second, he needs to establish that he can be *trusted.*

Trust is especially critical (1) when the prospect feels that the purchase involves risk and (2) when the prospect has incomplete information.[4] Trust can be difficult to establish, particularly if the prospect doesn't know the salesperson.[5] Establishing trust is made easier if the company the salesperson represents has a positive image and if the prospect tends, in general, to be trusting.[6] Since the salesperson has little control over these aspects, he can establish trust by engaging in the following four behaviors:[7]

1. He should indicate that he is *dependable* and *reliable.* He can communicate this through follow-up phone calls or by reference to past events in which he was dependable.
2. He should be *honest.* He can communicate this by acknowledging weaknesses in his product and highlighting its strengths. In addition, he should deal directly and honestly with a prospect's objections.
3. He should be *responsible.* He can communicate this by showing how he is committed to his profession and how he will stand by his product.
4. He should be *likable.* He can communicate this by building rapport so that the prospect perceives that he is similar to the salesperson.

A third way to focus attention is to make the item being sold seem tangible. The best way to do that is to allow the prospect to see or visualize the product in some way. This is similar to giving a speech. A speech that depends upon

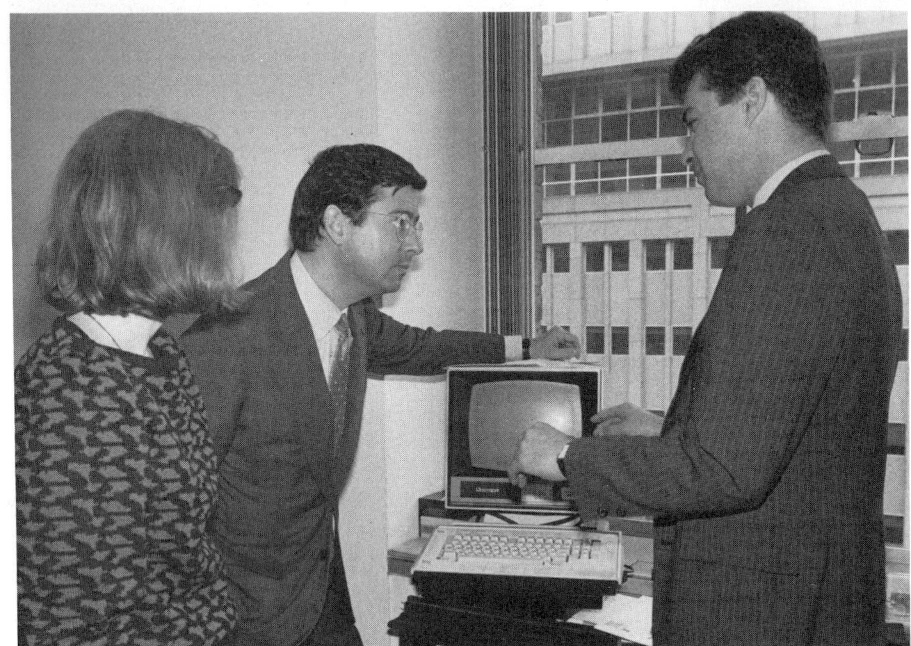

In trying to get beyond the barriers of selective attention, there is no substitute for seeing the actual product. (© Arlene Collins/Monkmeyer Press Photo.)

various visuals, such as slides, is more effective than one without such visuals because the visuals serve to focus attention. In the sales interaction, whenever there is an opportunity for a demonstration, it should be provided.

Finally, attention can be focused if the prospect can get involved in the discussion and if the prospect has a sense that the salesperson is genuinely trying to help. Both of these things can be accomplished simultaneously if the salesperson attempts to take the approach of asking a series of questions that uncover the prospect's needs. Having to think about the questions and give answers will provide some degree of involvement. In addition, the process of asking questions indicates to the prospect that the salesperson is making a real effort to uncover and solve her particular problem.

In summary, there are four tactics that the salesperson can employ to focus the prospect's attention:

1. Build rapport during the approach stage in order to get the prospect to like him.
2. Establish credibility by showing expertise about the product category and by communicating trustworthiness.
3. Provide demonstrations in order to make the product more tangible.
4. Get the prospect involved in the sales interaction by asking questions that uncover the prospect's particular problem (see Figure 5.4).

EXHIBIT 5.2

What Does It Mean to Have a Professional Approach

Following is a list of what different buyers have said:

"My idea of a good salesperson is a professional who is direct, honest, straight to the point, follows up after the sales and has a company that stands behind him/her."

"Knowledgeable!"

"Demonstrates a willingness to help potential buyers solve their problems."

"Has a sincere approach to selling."

"Researches the customer's requirements."

"Offers less-costly substitute items (if available) that can do the job as well."

"Knows enough about their products to help us meet our needs."

Source: Adapted from M. Grassell. (1986). What purchasing managers like in a salesperson. *Business Marketing, 71* (June), 76.

Interest

Once the salesperson has gotten beyond the initial barriers of selective exposure, the next major task is to get the prospect *interested.* This is not unlike the process that a newspaper editor has to go through to get our attention and then capture our interest. The newspaper headline has to gain our attention, that is, it has to "hook" us. But the story has to be written in such a way that we will be interested enough to continue reading. If the story does not maintain our interest, it is easy for us to stop reading and move on to another story.

A prospect who is face-to-face with a salesperson cannot move on so easily. Due to social expectations, the prospect will usually let the salesperson finish the presentation. The prospect has more subtle means of "moving on" while, in reality, remaining physically present. One means is selective attention. In fact, selective attention is a problem during the entire time a salesperson is with the prospect. The prospect can "tune out" what the salesperson is saying by not listening, and the salesperson may not be aware that the prospect is doing this. To combat the tendency of the prospect to engage in selective attention, the salesperson has to create interest in what is being sold.

Creating Interest by Appealing to Motives

The best way to create interest is to appeal to the basic underlying drives or **motives** of a prospect. Motivation can be defined as *"a driving force behind behavior; it is a state of tension demanding reduction. The function of an*

FIGURE 5.4 A prospect's attention can be focused.

individual's motives is to protect, satisfy, or enhance that individual."[8] People are almost continuously motivated to protect, satisfy, and enhance themselves or others to whom they are close. Anything that allows them to accomplish those goals will create interest.

If you think about the things that can protect, satisfy, or enhance, you will see that the list is very long. For example, any of the following can do one or more of those things:

> a cheeseburger, a new stereo, a sport jacket, a purse, a different hair style, sex with your spouse, a puppy, flowers, a compliment, an *A*, a vaccination, an afternoon nap, a run in the park, a movie, a day on the beach, a good novel, a paycheck, a glass of wine, nail polish, a pat on the back.

The list is probably endless. It is worth noting that these motivations to protect, satisfy, and enhance roughly correspond to Abraham Maslow's hierarchy of needs.[9]

Maslow's Need Hierarchy

Maslow developed a hierarchy of five categories of needs. He placed each category on a pyramid. The needs at the bottom of the pyramid must be satisfied before those at the next higher level take precedence, and so on.

Physiological needs have to do with getting sufficient food and water and reproducing our species. Safety needs focus on obtaining clothing and shelter so that our physical well-being is not threatened. Social needs concern our needs to belong and be loved, that is, to be part of some group. Esteem needs impel us to be respected by others as well as by ourselves. They include our need for status and recognition. Finally, self-actualization needs entail self-fulfillment, that is, to be all that we can be.

Physiological needs and security and safety needs correspond to a need for protection. Social needs and esteem needs correspond to a need for satisfaction. Self-actualization needs correspond to a need for enhancement. These relationships are shown in Figure 5.5.

In most situations, the salesperson only has to keep in mind three terms:

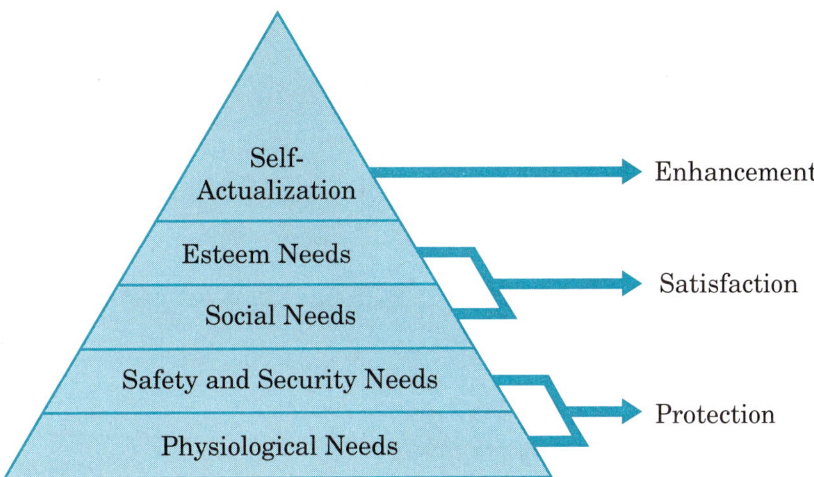

FIGURE 5.5 The relationship between Maslow's need hierarchy and the basic motives of protection, satisfaction, and enhancement.

protection, *satisfaction*, and *enhancement*. Since there is an infinite number of things that can fulfill these basic needs, the salesperson should be able to maintain interest throughout the discussion with a prospect.

The Needs of the Organization

The basic motives of protection, satisfaction, and enhancement also exist for the organization. Whenever a salesperson is dealing with a representative from an organization, she has to deal with these motives of the individual, as well as with those of the organization.

Specific organizational needs include the following:

The need for innovation.
The need for survival.
The need for profit.
The need for growth.[10]

Figure 5.6 shows how those organizational needs correspond to the basic motives of protection, satisfaction, and enhancement.

The needs of the individual representing the organization are intertwined with the needs of the organization. If the organizational buyer enhances the organization by, for example, finding an item that allows a major manufacturing improvement, which leads, in turn, to an innovative new product attribute, the buyer will likely be both satisfied and enhanced. He will be enhanced by having achieved a higher level of success. In other words, this will contribute to self-actualization. The buyer will be satisfied because he will be recognized by the organization, which will contribute to his self-esteem. This may even result in a bonus or salary increase, which will, in turn, have an impact on the buyer's need for protection by adding to his safety and security needs.

Emotional Versus Rational Motives

Whether we are dealing with a motivation for protection, satisfaction, or enhancement, and whether we are dealing with the individual or the organization, there can be an emotional component or a rational component. Emotional needs are powerful forces upon our behavior. We often are uncomfortable with our emotional needs and offer a rational explanation to justify them. Table 5.1 provides examples of buying motivations that are emotional or rational, associated with both individual and organizational needs for protection, satisfaction, and enhancement.

It is often assumed that consumers tend to be more responsive to emotional motives, while organizational buyers tend to be more responsive to rational motives. In fact, this distinction is not entirely accurate. Both consumers and organizational buyers can be responsive to either emotional or rational motives. Whether a particular person will respond more to one or the other is determined by the individual, not by whether the person is a consumer or an organizational buyer. Generally speaking, *a salesperson can introduce emotional motives, but she should justify them in terms of rational motives.*

How the Salesperson Can Utilize Motivation in the Sales Interaction

If you return to the list of the things that provide protection, satisfaction, or enhancement, you can probably begin to see ways in which a salesperson can create interest during a product discussion. This can be combined with two simple yet effective suggestions provided by Ernest Dichter regarding how someone who is recommending something to someone else should behave:

1. The person should indicate interest in the other's well-being.
2. The person's experience with and knowledge about the product should be convincing.[11]

Table 5.1 Emotional Versus Rational Buying Motives for the Individual and the Organization

		Emotional	*Rational*
INDIVIDUAL	Protection	"I want a very good computer so that I can be sure my work will be safe."	"I want a very good computer because I don't want to risk a power surge that will lose my work."
	Satisfaction	"If I buy a powerful computer, people will be impressed with me."	"If I buy a powerful computer, I will be able to work better with my colleagues at the office."
	Enhancement	"If I buy a powerful computer, I will feel proud of it."	"If I buy a powerful computer, I will be able to achieve my potential as a writer."
ORGANIZATION	Protection	"We'll go down the tubes if we don't have a powerful computer."	"The business we're in requires, as a minimum, a powerful computer."
	Satisfaction	"If we buy a powerful computer, our competition will lose and our profits will impress Wall Street."	"If we buy a powerful computer, our profits should increase by 2 percent because of our savings in personnel."
	Enhancement	"If we buy a powerful computer, we'll be able to develop so many new products that the others will never catch us."	"If we buy a powerful computer, we should be able to improve our record in new product development, which is important for long-term growth."

Armed with this background information, any salesperson should be able to generate and maintain interest during the sales interaction. Following is a summary of the major points we have suggested thus far regarding interest:

1. Interest can be created by appealing to one or more of the following motives: protection, satisfaction, enhancement.
2. All buyers respond to both emotional and rational motives. A good strategy may be to appeal to emotional motives while justifying them with rational motives.
3. A salesperson should communicate interest in the buyer's well-being.
4. A prospect is more likely to be interested if he is dealing with a convincing and knowledgeable salesperson.

Table 5.2 gives some typical salesperson statements and indicates how they create interest.

Desire

At this point, we have dealt with the barriers of selective exposure and selective attention. We have achieved interest by continually appealing to the major moti-

Table 5.2 Examples of Salesperson Statements That Create Interest

Statement	*Interpretation*
"You said your biggest concern was having a telephone system that monitors the use of personal calls. Ours can do that by having employees plug in all the numbers that they use for business purposes. Then our system keeps a record of all numbers called that are not previously designated as being for business purposes."	Deals with the need for protection; rational motive; communicates concern for the prospect's well-being; communicates the salesperson's knowledge; organization's need for profit.
"This telephone system is even more advanced than the one used by IBM."	Deals with the need for enhancement; emotional as well as rational motives; organization's need for innovativeness.
"These speakers were used at Carnegie Hall."	Deals with the need for satisfaction; emotional and rational motives; communicates the salesperson's knowledge.
"These speakers are rated as being the equivalent of speakers that cost over $3,000."	Deals with the need for protection; rational motive.
"Since you said you wanted an inexpensive wine, I recommend this one from Australia. It is inexpensive and also excellent, and it impresses people because it is imported from such an odd place."	Deals with the need for protection and satisfaction; emotional and rational motives; communicates concern for the prospect's well-being and demonstrates the salesperson's knowledge.
"This is a very conservative suit. That's what you need for any position in banking. If you don't get the job, at least you'll know that it wasn't because you had on the wrong suit."	Deals with the need for protection; emotional and rational motives; communicates concern for the prospect's well-being.
"You really look very good in that color. Much better than the other color you had on. This color even happens to be "in" this season."	Deals with the need for enhancement; emotional and rational motives; communicates concern for the prospect's well-being.

vations of the prospect. Now comes the actual task of persuasion in order to create *desire* for the product or service. Persuasion requires that the salesperson deal with attitudes and with changing those attitudes.

An **attitude** is defined as *an expression of an inner feeling that shows whether a person feels favorably or unfavorably toward some object.* An object can be anything from a person to a pair of shoes.

Three Things We Can Do with Attitudes

There are three things we can do with attitudes. We can *intensify* existing ones. When a salesperson makes a follow-up call on a prospect, the call can serve to intensify the prospect's attitude. We can *create* new attitudes. We often have to do that when we introduce a new product or when we want to teach people about some aspect of a product that they don't know anything about. Finally, we can *change* attitudes. Whenever someone does not have a favorable attitude about a product we are selling, we need to change that attitude.

These three things we can do with attitudes differ primarily in how difficult they are to accomplish. Intensifying an existing attitude is least difficult. Often prospects already have a positive attitude about a salesperson's offering. In those instances, a salesperson simply needs to reinforce this positive attitude, perhaps by giving additional information that conveys how good the offering is.

Creating a new attitude is somewhat more difficult. We are in a position to do that when a prospect has not formed an attitude about a product or service. This is still a relatively simple matter. All that is required is information showing how the offering will benefit the prospect in some important way.

Changing an attitude is the most difficult task. People don't like to be put under pressure to change an attitude, and this is what makes the process so difficult for a salesperson. People become especially resistant to information designed to change their attitudes. For example, assume that you believe that all cameras are the same. A salesperson tells you that there are vast differences among cameras. This puts pressure on you to change your attitude. Since you would prefer to avoid this pressure, you become especially resistant to the salesperson's argument. Figure 5.7 shows the relationship between what can be done with an attitude and the difficulty of each of those things.

One way to resist the salesperson is simply to believe that the salesperson is just trying to make a sale. This becomes more difficult if the salesperson is trustworthy and appears to be very knowledgeable[12]—in other words, if the salesperson has credibility. It also becomes more difficult if the salesperson does a good job of presenting the argument.

A useful approach in this situation is to consider product attributes. It has been found that our attitudes about product categories are often based upon product attributes. For certain product categories, prospects have their own list of important attributes. They will have more positive attitudes about products that they think have those attributes and more negative attitudes about products

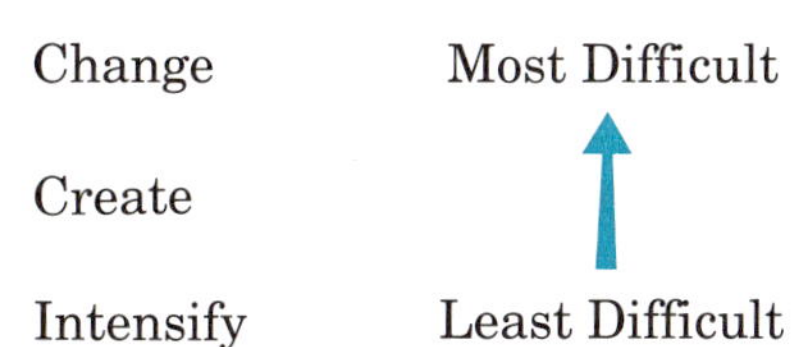

FIGURE 5.7 What can be done with attitudes and their degree of difficulty.

EXHIBIT 5.3

The Elegant Sell at Jean Laporte

Jean Laporte is a small line of original fragrances that are relatively simple in composition. It is sold throughout the world. The salespeople have a distinctive style. The best place to observe that style is to go to the first freestanding Jean Laporte shop in the U.S. It is located on Madison Avenue in New York City.

According to Edmee Mirambell, Executive Vice President of Jean Laporte, USA, it is sold in a boutique which "offers the best possible service and the best possible education. . . . When someone enters the boutique, we look at her (or his) height, style, complexion. Everything is indicative of what we should start showing. The particular floral that works for a brunette will smell too heavy for a blonde . . . if the customer has just bought a new cashmere sweater, we may suggest something with a woodsy note to wear with it. . . . What separates us from a department store is that we take an inordinate amount of time with each client to educate them about scents, to help them zero in on the ideal fragrance. . . . We have the luxury of time, and such a personalized environment . . . that people come back again and again. . . . Making a sale for the sake of selling doesn't mean anything. We want to give good advice and build total trust. . . . There is no real secret to our success; we simply treat people as we would like to be treated."

These products are not inexpensive. Eaux de toilette ranges in price from $45 to $165. Only one fragrance is available in perfume, and it sells for $160.

Source: Adapted from The elegant sale at Jean Laporte. (1987). *Product Marketing, 16*(11), 23.

that seem to lack them. For this reason, the salesperson has two courses of action in changing the prospect's attitude:

1. The salesperson can persuade the prospect that her product has the important attributes in greater degree than the competing products.
2. The salesperson can persuade the prospect that there are other attributes that are more important than those the prospect regards as important. Then the salesperson can persuade the prospect that her product has these other attributes.

There is a specific formulation that addresses the issue of attributes. This formulation is called the *multiattribute model.*[13]

The Multiattribute Model

We can understand a lot about the multiattribute model if we closely examine its name. It is called a multi*attribute* model because it defines attitudes towards products in terms of product *attributes*. Specifically, the **multiattribute model** says that *our attitudes toward products are based on beliefs about the degree to which those products possess particular attributes.*

For example, a prospect's attitude toward a Toyota Corolla would depend on her beliefs that the Corolla possessed certain attributes, such as reliability. In fact, the prospect's attitude toward the Corolla would be based upon many such beliefs. It is for this reason that the word *multiattribute* starts with *multi*. The model says that our attitudes are based on *multiple* product attributes.

A prospect's beliefs about whether or not a product has certain attributes is a major part of the multiattribute model. The other major part has to do with *how important the particular attribute is to the prospect.* For example, a prospect may believe that Toyotas are not sporty. Sportiness is an attribute. Before a salesperson tries to show that Toyotas are sporty, the salesperson should know how important sportiness is to the prospect. If the prospect regards sportiness as unimportant, there is no point in dealing with it.

For this reason, the multiattribute model rates each attribute according to its importance to the person, using a formula that combines two things:

1. Belief about whether a particular product has a particular attribute.
2. How important the attribute is.

These two things are determined for every attribute that could influence a prospect. The result is an indicator of a prospect's overall attitude toward the product. We can write the formula as follows:

$$\text{Attitude} = (\text{belief } 1 \times \text{importance } 1) + (\text{belief } 2 \times \text{importance } 2) + (\text{belief } 3 \times \text{importance } 3) + \cdots + (\text{belief } n \times \text{importance } n)$$

This formula says that attitude equals *belief about the brand on attribute 1* times *importance of attribute 1* plus *belief about the brand on attribute 2* times *importance of attribute 2*, and so on, until all of the attributes are included.

As an example, suppose that we wanted to know a person's attitude about Haagen Dazs Vanilla Ice Cream. We learn that the person thinks that Haagen Dazs is creamy, rich, and sweet. That is, the person thinks that Haagen Dazs has the attributes of creaminess, richness, and sweetness. We need to find out to what degree the person thinks that Haagen Dazs has these attributes. He may think that it is very creamy, somewhat rich, and somewhat sweet. We could assign numbers to these attributes so that creamy would get a 5, rich would get a 4, and sweet would get a 4. Next, we would find out how important these attributes are to the person in deciding which ice cream to buy. We may find that creaminess and richness are very important and that sweetness is moderately important. We would again assign numbers, so that creaminess and richness would get a 5 and sweetness would get a 3. This process is presented in Table 5.3 (page 134).

From this table, we could then get a total attitude score for the person by applying the multiattribute formula as follows:

$$\text{Attitude} = (5 \times 5) + (4 \times 5) + (4 \times 3) = 57$$

Table 5.3 The Multiattribute Model Applied to Haagen Dazs

Attribute	*Attribute Importance*	*Belief About Haagen Dazs*
Creaminess	5*	5**
Richness	4	5
Sweetness	4	3

* Measured on a scale of 1–5, where 1 is unimportant and 5 is very important.
** Measured on a scale of 1–5, where 1 is low possession and 5 is high possession of the attribute.

Of course, an attitude score is meaningful only if we can compare it to the scores on other brands of ice cream. Fortunately, a salesperson does not need to compute a mathematical attitude score for a prospect for every brand in a product category. However, by being aware of the structure of the multiattribute model, a salesperson can depend upon it to change a prospect's attitude.

Applying the Multiattribute Model to a Sales Situation

Consider the following example, in which a sales representative tried to convince the manager of a large drugstore chain to give Tic Tac mints a prominent display. To date, the manager had featured the larger sugarless mints, and Tic Tac's sales had suffered. The salesperson realized that the policy was based on the manager's attitude toward the various mints:

SALESPERSON: What qualities do you look for when you're deciding which mints to stock? [An attempt to find out what attributes the prospect regards as important.]

PROSPECT: Breath freshening. But I guess all mints do that. And calories. Many of my customers worry about their diets. [The prospect indicates that breath freshening is important but that all brands have that attribute. She then indicates that calories are also important.]

SALESPERSON: We've found that people also look at package convenience. [The salesperson attempts to introduce a different product attribute for the prospect to consider.]

At this point, the salesperson can begin to picture the multiattribute model shown in Table 5.4.

Table 5.4 Basic Elements in the Multiattribute Model Applied to Tic Tacs

Attribute	*Importance*
Breath freshening	Important
Calories	Very important
Package convenience	Possibly important

At the stage of the multiattribute model shown in Table 5.4, the salesperson doesn't have enough information to know how to change the prospect's attitude. He still needs to gather information about the prospect's *beliefs.* As the dialogue continues, you can see how he does this.

SALESPERSON: You said that all mints freshen breath. Is the calorie count at the basis of your decision, then? [The salesperson attempts to determine what attribute Tic Tac is deficient in.]

PROSPECT: Well, truthfully, it is the calories, and your Tic Tacs have sugar. I do prefer your convenient little package, but our customers are just too concerned with calories for me to feature your Tic Tacs next to the cash registers. [The prospect indicates that Tic Tacs do well with the package but poorly with calories.]

With this information, the salesperson can complete the multiattribute model as shown in Table 5.5.

Based on this structure, the salesperson knows where to begin trying to change the prospect's attitude. This is shown in the last phase of the dialogue.

SALESPERSON: Did you know that Tic Tacs have only one and a half calories per mint, while those others have nine or ten? They may be sugar free, but for dieters, they have more calories. [The salesperson tries to persuade the prospect that Tic Tacs have a better rating on calories than the other brands.]

PROSPECT: I didn't know that.

SALESPERSON: Well, you're not alone. That's the central feature in our new ad campaign.

PROSPECT: If that's the case, maybe we'll give them a try near the registers.

Certainly, not all attitudes are changed this easily. However, with the multiattribute approach, you can begin to analyze the attitude's components so that you know where to aim your efforts. Further, the multiattribute model has wide applicability, since all products or services have several attributes that consumers use to evaluate them. For example, personal computers have attributes such as the amount of internal memory, the number of disc drives, the existence of a hard disk, the quality of the monitor, the feel of the keyboard, reliability, and a host of

Table 5.5 The Completed Multiattribute Model Applied to Tic Tacs

Attribute	*Importance of Attribute*	*Belief About Tic Tacs*	*Belief About Larger Mints*
Breath freshening	Important	Good rating	Good rating
Calories	Very important	Poor rating	Good rating
Package	Important	Good rating	Average rating

others. Dog food has attributes of price, nutrition, ease of serving, appeal for the dog, and ease of storage. Stereo speakers have attributes of frequency range, power, sensitivity, and resistance. In each case, some of those attributes are regarded as more important and more positive than others, and knowledge of the attributes can be used to change attitudes.

If, for example, a salesperson is trying to sell an Apple computer system and knows what attributes a prospect likes in IBM, he needs to determine how the prospect views Apple with respect to those same attributes. With this knowledge, he will be better able to change the prospect's attitude than if he tried simply to convince the prospect that the Apple is better.

Application of the Multiattribute Model to the Organizational Buyer. The multiattribute model has particular importance for the organizational buyer. Often this buyer has a list of attributes that are dictated by the organization. This list is referred to as **specs.** The organizational buyer is expected to make a purchase that meets all of the specs listed. It is possible, however, that the salesperson is more knowledgeable about the product than the organizational buyer. The salesperson may feel that one or more of the specs is not as important as some other feature that is not specified by the organization.

When this happens, the salesperson needs to persuade the buyer that a more relevant attribute is being overlooked or that an unimportant attribute is being needlessly stressed. This puts the buyer in a more difficult position than the consumer. The buyer has to convince other members of the organization that the specs need to be changed. If successful, the buyer can proceed with the purchase.

Following is a summary of the major points we have discussed with respect to desire.

1. Three things can be done with attitudes: they can be intensified, they can be created, and they can be changed. Changing attitudes is the most difficult process.
2. People are particularly resistant to attempts to change their attitudes. This tendency can be combated by a trustworthy, knowledgeable, and convincing salesperson.
3. People's attitudes are based upon (a) their beliefs that the product or service does or does not have particular attributes and (b) their evaluations of how important those attributes are to them.
4. A salesperson can change a prospect's attitude by showing convincingly that a particular product has attributes the prospect considers important in greater degree than competing products.
5. A salesperson can change a prospect's attitude by showing convincingly that attributes the prospect considers unimportant are, in fact, important.

At this point, the salesperson has commanded attention, created interest, and generated desire. It is now necessary to accomplish the final task: **action.** By action, we mean behavior. The behavior the salesperson is interested in is a *purchase.*

Action

It seems obvious that once a prospect's attitude has been changed and the product seems desirable, the prospect will purchase it. Unfortunately, purchase does not always follow desire. Sometimes there are realities that prevent purchase. For example, you can create desire for a Rolls Royce, but it is not likely that the prospect will be able to afford to buy one. You can even allow the prospect to finance the car, but financing $120,000 for a 3-year term is still well beyond most people's financial means. Even if we can assume that there are no major barriers such as economics to purchase, we still can't guarantee that a change in attitude will automatically lead to the behavior of purchase.

People do not always act in accordance with their attitudes. One way to help make sure that they do is to get prospects to look at a product or service as a means of *solving a problem.* In other words, the salesperson approaches the sales task as one in which the prospect has a problem, and the salesperson's goal is to show how the product will directly solve that problem. If this is done, the prospect who regards himself as a rational person should be more likely to purchase the product. Rational people usually do things that solve problems.

A Problem-Solving Perspective to Purchase

In order to set up the buying situation as one involving **problem solving,** the salesperson has to question the prospect carefully so that the prospect can clearly visualize the problem. Once this is accomplished, the salesperson has only to convince the prospect that his particular product will solve the problem directly and effectively.

To begin, then, the possible problems of the prospect have to be uncovered. There are eight different problem possibilities. As you will see, some of them are more straightforward than others. Those that are most straightforward are the easiest to uncover. The specifics of taking a problem-solving approach are discussed in Chapter 10. Our concern here is simply to provide you with a brief overview of the various problem situations that a prospect can face. The eight problem situations[14] are presented in Table 5.6.

1. **Problem removal.** Here the prospect has a real problem. The prospect is motivated to make a purchase, knowing that a specific problem exists. For example, a prospect may have a phone system that requires a switchboard operator and is cumbersome and slow. The salesperson can help the prospect by showing how various alternative systems will remove the problem.
2. **Problem avoidance.** This occurs when the prospect anticipates a future problem. A prospect might have a small business in which each employee has a personal computer. The prospect may be worried that eventually a problem will occur if these computers can't communicate with one another. In this case, the salesperson can attempt to show the prospect how his product will allow the computers to be joined in a network, avoiding the anticipated problem.

Many of us might be easily convinced that we would like to own a Rolls Royce. Few of us, however, would act on that desire by purchasing the car because we could not afford to buy one. (© 1980 Pierre Berger/Photo Researchers, Inc.)

3. **Incomplete satisfaction.** Here the prospect finds that there is something incomplete in the product offering. In other words, the prospect discovers a problem that cannot be resolved—for example, that no screen on any available monitor for a personal computer is clear enough. The salesperson may try to show how his product offers the best resolution that the current technology will allow.
4. **Mixed approach-avoidance.** This actually is a combination of two or more of the first three situations just discussed. Here the prospect is in a more serious situation. Removing one problem may create a new problem. For example, the prospect might say that the only computer monitors that are clear have an amber color, but that amber gives her a headache. The salesperson can provide a device to eliminate glare. In addition, the salesperson can present evidence that green screens are more likely to cause headaches than amber screens. It may even be possible to find the prospect a green screen that is as clear as the amber screen.
5. **Normal depletion.** Here the prospect simply wants to replace an item. The salesperson wants to make sure that the prospect will either repurchase the same brand or purchase a different one, depending upon what the salesperson is selling. If the situation involves repurchase of the same brand, the salesperson needs to make sure that the prospect has no particular problem with it. If the salesperson is trying to get the prospect to switch brands, it is necessary to uncover some dissatisfaction or show how the new brand offers

Table 5.6 Problems That a Prospect Might Have and How the Salesperson Can Help Solve Them

Problem	*Salesperson Input*
Problem removal	Show alternatives for removing problem
Problem avoidance	Show how the product can avoid the problem
Incomplete satisfaction	Show how the product is the best that technology will allow
Mixed approach-avoidance	Show how the product can improve the situation or minimize its negative aspect
Normal depletion	Show how the product is the best available or an improvement over what is currently used
Sensory gratification	Show how some new attribute of the product will add gratification
Intellectual stimulation	Show some new use that provides such stimulation
Social approval	Show the broad appeal or prestige of the product

an improvement. In this case, it may be wise for the salesperson to think in terms of the multiattribute model we discussed in conjunction with desire.

6. **Sensory gratification.** In this case, the prospect has no particular problem. The purchase is merely designed to make a change in the prospect's life. Again, the salesperson should rely upon the multiattribute model and show how some new attribute will bring the prospect gratification. For example, an individual may decide to purchase a new television for no other reason than a desire to make a change. The salesperson can demonstrate the importance of stereo sound on a television. This new feature will give the prospect the sense of having made a more substantial change by buying the new product. It will also deal with sensory gratification in terms of sound.
7. **Intellectual stimulation.** Here the problem is a need to explore the product further or even to master it. This may be a function of boredom or a need to make a product more intellectually satisfying. As an example, a person may have a personal computer that is used only for spreadsheet analysis. Since a personal computer is capable of doing much more than that, the salesperson need only introduce other software for such things as word processing or games. That will allow the prospect both to explore the computer and to have a sense of mastery over it.
8. **Social approval.** Here the prospect wants to make a purchase in order to gain recognition from other people. Almost any buying situation involves some social recognition. The salesperson needs to convey to the prospect the prestige of a particular brand or the broad appeal of a particular feature such as a color. When a clothing salesperson says that something is fashionable or "in" this year, he is dealing with the need for social approval.

Problem Solving in the Organization

Both the individual consumer and the buyer for an organization go through a problem-solving process before they act and make a purchase. The buying process in the organization is somewhat more complex and elaborate than the buying process in, for example, the family. The structure of the organization is more elaborate because it contains more people than the family, as well as more levels of authority.

The decision process in the organization has six stages, as shown in Table 5.7.[15]

A salesperson can become a part of this decision at any stage. Many things can contribute to the first stage, need recognition. Something can break down, someone can run out of a supply, or someone might notice that another way of performing an operation will improve efficiency. A salesperson can also contribute to need recognition by suggesting a new piece of equipment or simply by asking a buyer to discuss her needs.

The salesperson can be of help at the second stage, determination of the characteristics and quantity of items. He can offer recommendations and help the buyer evaluate the situation. If a salesperson can get involved in the third stage, determining specifications, he can greatly influence the final selection of a supplier. The salesperson can suggest specifications that are helpful to the buyer and, at the same time, favor the product that the salesperson is selling. In other words, if he can influence the buyer so that specifications are listed that are favorable to the salesperson's firm, there is a greater probability that his firm will be among those selected at the fourth stage, the search for suppliers.

The ability to write a compelling proposal or give a commanding presentation will serve the salesperson well at the fifth stage, acquisition and evaluation of proposals. In the final stage, selection of suppliers, the salesperson usually doesn't have direct input. However, there is nothing to prevent the salesperson from supplying additional material that might influence the buyer.

Our discussion of action can be summarized as follows:

1. An effective way to cause a prospect to make a purchase is to show how the purchase will solve a problem.
2. A salesperson has to question a prospect carefully so that the prospect will see that a specific problem exists and that the salesperson's product will solve the problem.

Putting It All Together

We can begin by summarizing the key points:

- The major concerns of buyer behavior are indicated in the AIDA model: attention, interest, desire, action.
- Attention is mostly concerned with issues of perception in terms of selective exposure and selective attention.
- Interest requires that the salesperson appeal to a prospect's motivation or needs.
- The three major needs that the salesperson must be aware of are the need for protection, satisfaction, and enhancement.

Table 5.7 Organizational Buying Stages and How the Salesperson Can Influence Each Stage

Stage	*Salesperson Input*
Need recognition	Have buyer discuss the need or show how the product will satisfy the need
Determination of the characteristics and quantity of items to buy	Help the buyer evaluate the situation and make recommendations
Determination of specifications	Suggest specs that are helpful to the buyer and that favor the salesperson's product
Search for suppliers	Respond to notices seeking bidders (in addition to input at the previous stage)
Acquisition and evaluation of proposals	Write a compelling proposal or give a commanding presentation
Selection of a supplier	Provide additional supplementary information

- Creating desire often requires that the salesperson change a prospect's attitude.
- Since attitude change is difficult, the multiattribute model can be a useful basis for such attempts.
- The multiattribute model focuses upon the notion that a person's attitude about a product is based upon (1) his view that the product has or lacks certain attributes, and (2) how important these attributes are.
- Action, or purchase, is considered more likely when a salesperson uses a problem-solving approach.
- A problem-solving approach involves uncovering the specific problem of a prospect and showing how a product will directly solve that problem.

One issue that we need to highlight is the nature of the sales situation itself. By definition, the sales situation is one involving persuasion. People are generally resistant to persuasion. *We expect salespeople to persuade us.* However, when we expect someone to persuade us and they try to do so, we can never be sure if they are telling us the truth. If we get too involved in trying to decide if a salesperson is telling us the truth, we may not listen very carefully to product-related information.

Automatic Reactions to Expectations That Are Confirmed

Sometimes we just assume that salespeople selling certain products are not to be trusted. We also assume that salespeople selling certain other products are generally very trustworthy. In each of those cases, we have *expectations* about how the salesperson will behave. Because our expectations are so strong, we also have an *automatic reaction* to the salesperson, no matter what the salesperson says.

For example, if we expect a salesperson to be pushy and the salesperson is, we may say to ourselves, "This is just another pushy salesperson, so I can't really pay much attention to what he is saying." If we expect a salesperson to be helpful and dependable and the salesperson is, we may say to ourselves, "Salespeople who sell this product always seem to be especially helpful. I'm sure her recommendation is one I should seriously consider."

The product categories usually associated with negative expectations about salespeople are used cars, clothing, and household appliances. The product categories associated with positive expectations are computers and industrial products.[17]

Whether we are dealing with negative or positive expectations, if we have an automatic reaction, we fail to listen to what the salesperson is actually saying. That means that we don't listen to the product-related information the salesperson is providing. One way or another, it is important for a salesperson to get a prospect to attend to product-related information.

Behaving Counter to Expectations

The salesperson can cause the prospect to listen by behaving *counter to expectations.* How can this be accomplished? Rather than being aggressive and pushy, the salesperson who generates negative expectations can make a legitimate effort to uncover the prospect's needs, avoid saying negative things about the competition, and explain directly to the prospect how his product will satisfy the prospect's needs. This approach will likely cause the prospect to listen more carefully to the salesperson and hear the product-related information.

The salesperson who generates positive expectations should make a special point of uncovering the prospect's needs and showing how his product satisfies these needs. It is important to highlight the product's potential to provide satisfaction. Doing so will focus the prospect's attention on the product-related information.

Key Terms

Attention
Selective exposure
Selective attention
Motives
Attitudes
Multiattribute model
Specs
Problem removal
Problem avoidance
Incomplete satisfaction
Mixed approach-avoidance
Normal depletion
Sensory gratification
Intellectual stimulation
Social approval

Review Questions

1. What is AIDA? Why is it useful for the face-to-face sales interaction? What does each stage of AIDA correspond to?
2. What are selective exposure and selective attention? How can they be dealt with?

3. What are the three general motives that we all respond to?
4. How do these three motives correspond to Maslow's need hierarchy?
5. What can a salesperson do to motivate a prospect most effectively?
6. What is an attitude? What are the three things that can be done with an attitude? Which is the most difficult to accomplish?
7. What are the two issues to which the multiattribute model directs our attention?
8. If you were to depend upon the multiattribute model, how would you go about changing the attitude of someone who insists that IBM computers are superior to others?
9. What are the eight problem situations? How can a salesperson deal with each one most effectively?
10. What do we expect to happen in a sales situation?
11. What do we mean when we say that we can have automatic reactions to expectations that are confirmed? Why are we concerned about these reactions?
12. How can these automatic reactions be handled?
13. Which product categories are likely to generate negative automatic reactions to the salesperson? Which product categories are likely to generate positive automatic reactions?

Discussion Questions

1. Which of the AIDA stages do you think is most difficult? Why?
2. If you were introducing a new aspirin product that was virtually the same as every other competing product, how would you convince a manager of a large drugstore chain to stock your product, using the multiattribute model?
3. Why is a problem-solving approach most likely to result in action on the part of a prospect?
4. How is a family purchasing a house similar to an organization purchasing office space?

CASE 5.1

In the following situation, George West is trying to convince Marge Simmons to switch to an AT&T phone system. George is the sales representative for AT&T's eastern region. Marge is a director of communication services at the ABC Company, and because she has received a number of complaints about the current phone system, she is evaluating alternatives.

GEORGE: What exactly have people complained about?

MARGE: They have complained about the sound quality, for one thing.

GEORGE: Well, of course, sound quality varies according to several factors. Was there any particular time of day or season ...

MARGE: (interrupting) Sound quality is either good or bad. How would you characterize the sound quality of an AT&T system?

continued

GEORGE: We have always placed an emphasis on getting the best quality possible, and we think it is better than you'll get from anyone else.

MARGE: You're still not telling me how good it is.

GEORGE: We have never had any major complaints.

MARGE: I must say, I am uncomfortable with how vague you're being about this, but there's no point in belaboring the issue. We want everyone to have their own lines and for a call to switch to a secretary or receptionist after five rings. Can you do that?

GEORGE: We probably can, but that depends upon the number of lines you need.

At this point, it should be clear to George that Marge is not really hearing what he is saying. Why is Marge not hearing him? What should George do?

MARGE: Assuming that you can do what I just asked for, we also want to have the phone system work so that we can control and keep track of the number of local calls and long-distance calls made by each employee. We've got to keep our costs down. As you know, we do a lot of phone work, and we have to have the most efficient system we can for the least amount of money. Our current system does some of these things pretty well, but, as I said, there have been complaints about sound quality. And people are frequently being cut off in the middle of an important phone call. Can you make sure that won't happen?

At this point, George should begin to recognize that a number of attributes are being suggested. How might the multiattribute model work here to help him analyze the situation more effectively and start to respond to Marge?

GEORGE: Well, all systems have overload situations. Some have them more often than others. We have found that, during the course of a year, our system usually is able to accommodate all but the heaviest usage, and, even then, it holds up surprisingly well.

MARGE: That's not very comforting. Being cut off in the middle of a conversation has become a major concern for us. This has cost us lots of deals!

GEORGE: As I said, all phone systems have a limit to their capacity. But our system appears to perform better than any other competitor because of our advanced technology.

Clearly, George doesn't want to deliver a promise that can't be kept. He appears to be trying to persuade Marge that the AT&T system is better than the competition. Is he accomplishing this? How effective is George in creating interest? What might he do to be more effective?

Is George uncovering Marge's problems? If so, what are they? What specific solutions is he providing for each problem? What might George do that would rely more directly upon the specific problem situations listed in the chapter?

Is George generating an automatic reaction to Marge's expectations of a salesperson? How? If so, how can George overcome this reaction?

References

1. Lavidge, R. J., and G. A. Steiner. (1961). A model for predictive measurements of advertising effectiveness. *Journal of Marketing, 25,* 59–62.

2. Strong, E. K. (1925). *Psychology of Selling.* New York: McGraw-Hill.

3. Wolman, B. E. (1973). *Dictionary of the Behavioral Sciences.* New York: Van Nostrand Reinhold.

4. Hawes, J. M., K. E. Mast, and J. E. Swan. (1989). Trust earning perceptions of sellers and buyers. *Journal of Personal Selling and Sales Management, 9,* 1–8.

5. Milliman, R. E., and D. L. Fugate. (1988). Using trust-transference as a persuasion technique. *Journal of Personal Selling and Sales Management, 8,* 1–8.

6. Swan, J. E., and J. J. Nolan. (1985). Gaining customer trust: A conceptual guide for the salesperson. *Journal of Personal Selling and Sales Management, 5,* 39–48.

7. Swan, J. E., I. F. Trawick, D. R. Rink, and J. J. Roberts. (1988). Measuring dimensions of purchaser trust of industrial salespeople. *Journal of Personal Selling and Sales Management, 8,* 1–10.

8. Kassarjian, H. H. and T. S. Robertson. (1981). *Perspectives in Consumer Behavior.* Glenview, IL: Scott, Foresman, p. 136.

9. Maslow, A. H. (1943). A theory of human motivation. *Psychological Review, 50,* 370–396.

10. McCarthy, E. J. and W. D. Perrault. (1984) *Basic Marketing.* Homewood, IL: Irwin, p. 234.

11. Dichter, E. (1966). How word-of-mouth advertising works. *Harvard Business Review, 44,* 147–166.

12. Hovland, C. I., I. L. Janis, and H. Kelley. (1953). *Communication and Persuasion.* New Haven: Yale University Press.

13. Fishbein, M., and I. Ajzen. (1975) *Beliefs, Attitude, Intention, and Behavior.* Reading, MA: Addison-Wesley.

14. Fennell, G. (1978). Consumer's perceptions of the product use situation. *Journal of Marketing, 42,* 38–47.

15. Dalrymple, D. J. (1988). *Sales Management.* New York: Wiley, pp. 158–159.

PART THREE

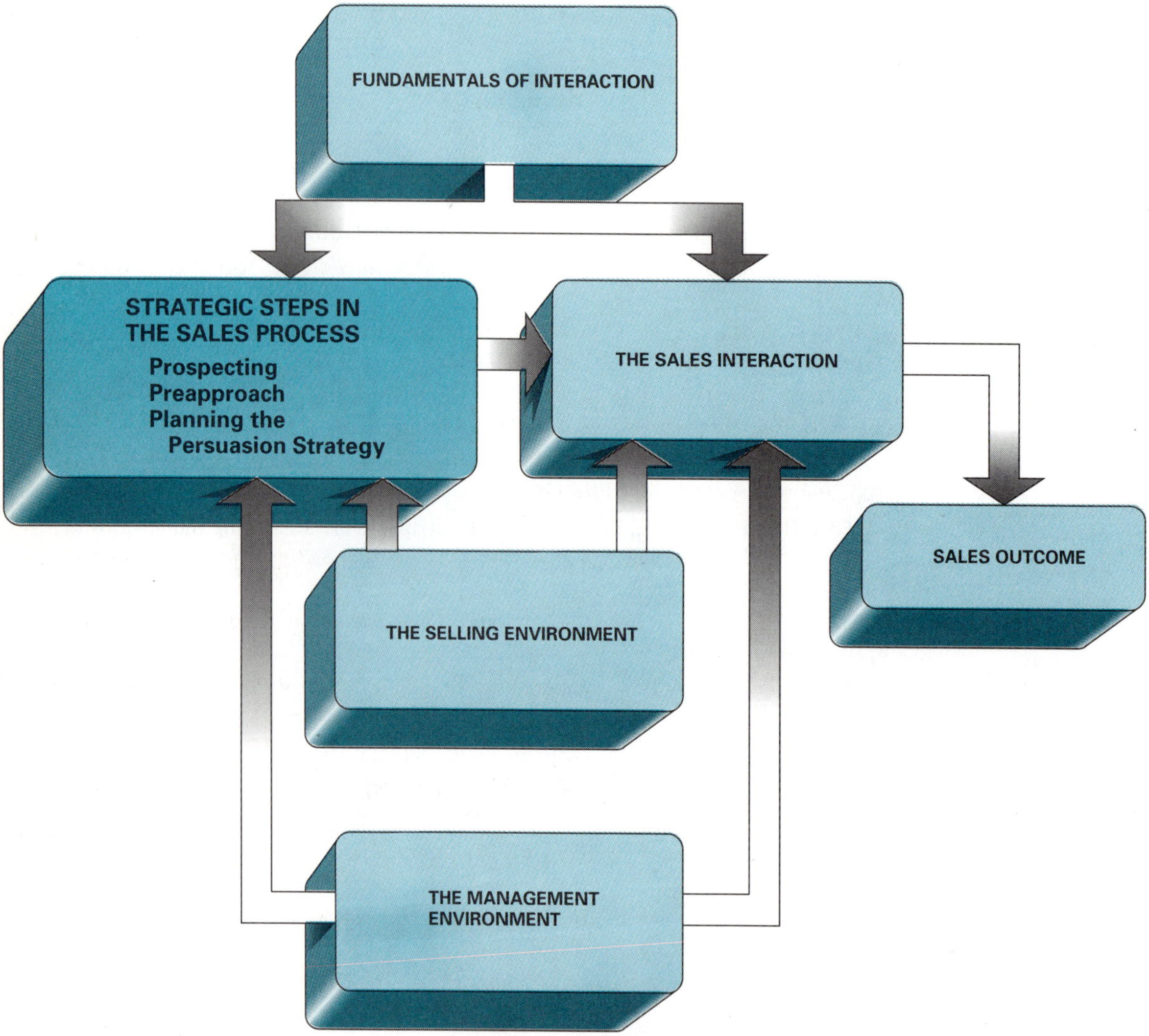

FUNDAMENTALS OF INTERACTION

STRATEGIC STEPS IN THE SALES PROCESS
Prospecting
Preapproach
Planning the Persuasion Strategy

THE SALES INTERACTION

SALES OUTCOME

THE SELLING ENVIRONMENT

THE MANAGEMENT ENVIRONMENT

STRATEGIC STAGES IN THE SALES PROCESS

Prospecting

CHAPTER OBJECTIVES

In this chapter, you will learn:

- Why your prospecting skills affect your sales productivity.
- To qualify prospects in order to ensure that they are capable of buying.
- To judge which prospecting methods are appropriate for a given sales situation.
- How to design your own prospecting strategy.
- How to design a system for managing your sales leads.
- To assess the success of your prospecting efforts.

CHAPTER OUTLINE

A Sales Challenge

An Overview

- What Is a Prospect?
- Who Engages in Prospecting?

Your Selling Strategy Begins with Prospecting

- Prospecting and Sales Productivity

Prospecting Methods

- Personal Contacts
- Secondary Sources
- Cold Canvassing
- Company-Generated Sources of Leads
- Designing Your Prospecting System

Lead Management Systems

- Lead Generation
- Response to Inquiries
- Evaluating Sources of Leads
- Lead Management by Salespeople

Putting It All Together

Key Terms

Review Questions

Discussion Questions

Case 6.1

References

A Sales Challenge

The following conversation took place as Sandy, a real estate agent, showed a condominium townhouse to Meg and Bob Dover:

Sandy: As you can see, this is a good-sized townhouse. It's 2,000 square feet all together.

Bob: How big is the living room?

Sandy: It's 18 by 30, and it looks even bigger with the picture window and this beautiful open view.

Bob: Nice view.

Sandy: Unusually nice for a townhouse priced under $150,000—and look at this brand-new kitchen.

Meg: It looks small to me.

Sandy: It's actually 12 by 15. There's plenty of room for a table and even a desk, if you want one.

Bob: But I'd rather have white appliances.

Sandy: This beige color was chosen specifically to go with these new European cabinets. Beautiful, aren't they?

Meg: I prefer oak.

Sandy: These new European cabinets are the most popular in this market, but you can replace them for about $5,000 if you like.

Meg: Well, I'm not wild about this tiled floor either.

An Overview

As you can see, Sandy tried hard to persuade the Dovers to buy this townhouse. Yet she failed to close the deal. What Sandy did not know is that *nothing* she could have said would have persuaded the Dovers. The problem occurred before she began her presentation.

Sandy assumed that the Dovers needed a townhouse, since they had answered a newspaper ad describing the one she showed them. But Meg and Bob had just bought a condominium. They were merely curious to see this one. As you will learn in this chapter, Sandy made a mistake during the prospecting stage of the selling process. Although the Dovers had responded to an ad for the townhouse, they were not qualified prospects.

What Is a Prospect?

A **prospect** is *a potential customer for your product.* In order to be a prospect, a person or organization must have a *need* that could be filled with your product. A **qualified prospect** is someone who needs your product *and* is *capable of buying it.* This means that a qualified prospect must (1) be able to afford your product and (2) have the authority to buy it. Not everyone is a prospect for every product.

The process of searching for those who are qualified to buy is called *prospecting* (see Figure 6.1). The first step in the prospecting process is to search for leads.

A **lead** (sometimes called a **suspect**) is a person or organization with the *potential* to become a prospect. As you will see later in this chapter, there are many different ways of generating leads. If, for example, you heard that a certain person or company was interested in buying your product, that person or company would be a lead, that is, someone who is suspected of having a need. Once you obtain the lead, you must decide whether the lead is a prospect. This is a step that Sandy omitted. She failed to ask the Dovers whether they needed to buy a condominium. Instead, she *assumed* that the need for her product existed. However, even if the Dovers had needed a condominium, Sandy's work would not have been complete. The second stage in the prospecting process is qualifying the prospect. This means making sure that the prospect is a qualified prospect.

Qualifying is an integral part of the prospecting process. There are several ways of accomplishing this task. First, it may be possible to qualify the prospect using background information. As you will learn in this chapter, there are many sources of background information on prospects. Some sources, like Dun and Bradstreet, can be used to check the credit ratings and financial information of many organizations. Other sources give information on the amount of sales and the number of employees. The criteria that you use to qualify your leads will depend upon your specific business.

However, there are many cases, especially in retail selling, in which you cannot rely on background information for qualifying prospects. If you cannot check the background of a lead, you may have to ask a few qualifying questions when you first come into contact with her. If Sandy had asked a few questions

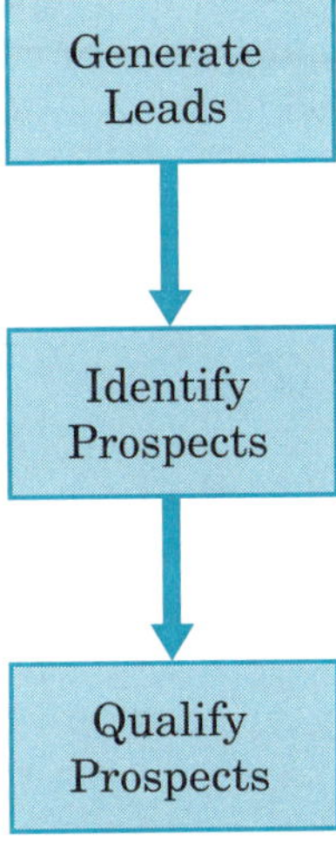

FIGURE 6.1 The prospecting process.

when the Dovers walked into her office, she might have learned that they were not actually prospects for the condominium.

Although there are many products for which this kind of qualifying questioning is not necessary, there are certain areas, like real estate, where people may want to look at products that they are not serious about buying. If you are selling this kind of product, it is important to be tactful when asking certain qualifying questions. It can be considered inappropriate for a stranger to inquire about someone's financial or personal business. In order to avoid appearing rude, some salespeople (especially in real estate) ask prospects to fill out a form that requests the information. The salesperson then reads the form and discusses any necessary information before attempting a sales presentation. With the use of a written form, the salesperson avoids having to ask about salary and the prospect does not even realize that he is being qualified.

Who Engages in Prospecting?

When you think about what is involved in a selling job, you probably envision the salesperson face to face with a prospect, talking about the product. Because most of our exposure to salespeople is through our role as customers in retail stores, we are often unaware of the prospecting process.

There are, in fact, some sales jobs where prospecting is not the responsibility of the individual salesperson. As Figure 6.2 indicates, sales jobs vary in the degree to which the salesperson does the prospecting. At one end of the continuum are situations where salespeople do not do their own prospecting. The use of advertising, telemarketing, or company-sponsored promotions ensures a steady flow of prospects for the entire sales force. Note, however, that this does not mean that there is no prospecting. It simply means that prospecting is done for the salespeople. The managers and executives take the responsibility for planning the prospecting strategies for everyone in the company.

At the opposite extreme are sales jobs in which the total responsibility for prospecting rests with the individual salesperson. These jobs range from retail stockbrokers to many business-to-business sales. In any of these positions, prospecting skills can make or break careers. The salesperson does not sell anything unless he or she is able to locate qualified prospects.

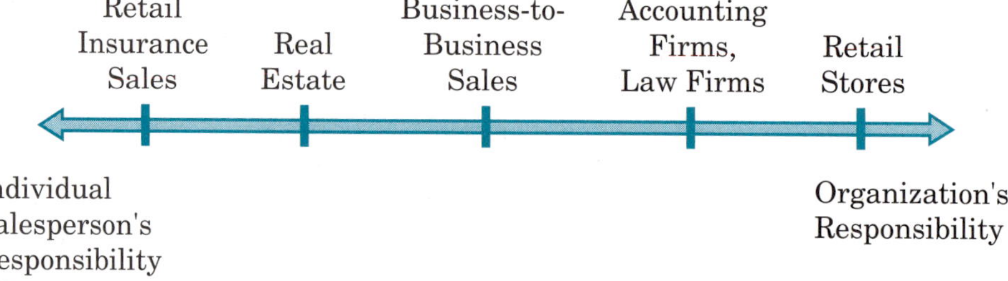

FIGURE 6.2 Responsibility for prospecting.

Between these two extremes is a host of variations. In some industrial selling situations, for example, new sales representatives may be given a list of ongoing accounts, but they are also responsible for generating their own new accounts over time. In other situations, the company generates some leads through advertising but expects the sales force to do the majority of its own prospecting. An example of this approach to prospecting would be a real estate agency. Although real estate salespeople are expected to bring in some of their own prospects, they get many prospects through office advertising or when people walk in off the street.

Although we may not think of it as prospecting, service people and organizations such as doctors, dentists, law firms, accounting firms, and advertising agencies are prospecting when they seek new business. In these operations, responsibility for prospecting typically grows with the person's position in the firm. Junior lawyers and accountants may bring in some new business, but the majority of the prospecting is done by the senior partners or account executives. In fact, the ability to prospect is frequently used as a criterion for promoting someone in this type of service firm. A doctor or dentist who works independently will have no patients without some kind of prospecting activity.

Although there is obviously a great deal of variety in the prospecting responsibilities associated with different selling positions, the need for prospecting always exists. As you will see in the next section, prospecting is a key part of your overall selling strategy.

Your Selling Strategy Begins with Prospecting

What we do not realize as customers is that the average salesperson spends only 20 hours per week making sales presentations.[1] The remaining time is spent on activities like locating and qualifying prospects and planning sales strategies. Experienced salespeople do not take these other activities for granted. They realize that the selling process begins long before they stand face-to-face with a prospect. As Table 6.1 illustrates, the selling process begins with the search for qualified prospects.

Table 6.1 The Sales Process

Search for prospects
Qualify prospects
Plan the sales call
Plan your persuasive strategy
Approach the prospect and learn about needs
Present and demonstrate your product
Handle objections
Close the sale
Follow up

As you learned in Chapter 2, selling is a *sequential process* in which success in any stage depends on success in all of the previous stages.[2] Since prospecting is the first stage, success at every other stage in the process depends upon your prospecting strategy. Because of the crucial role that prospecting plays in setting the stage for the rest of the process, it is considered a strategic activity.

In fact, we can divide the salesperson's job into two types of activities: *strategic* and *tactical.*[3] A strategic activity is one that has implications for the long run, whereas a tactical activity deals with short-run adjustments to the environment. Face-to-face selling skills are considered tactical, because making a presentation requires moment-to-moment (i.e., tactical) adjustments regarding how to deal with a particular prospect. In contrast, *prospecting and planning* are considered strategic activities because they determine *long-run* success. Although many sales have been lost through tactical errors, the best sales presentation in the world cannot result in a sale unless it is made to a person or organization that needs your product and is qualified to buy it.

Frank Carpe learned the importance of prospecting strategy in his first job as a stockbroker in a large urban area. Frank was a very bright financial planner and a persuasive salesperson. He was successful in convincing people to invest in his company's financial instruments once he spoke to them about their finances. However, his only sources of prospects were people who walked into the office or called in response to ads. Frank was not a lazy person and was anxious to do well in his first job, but he did not understand the principles of prospecting. While he sat in the office waiting for inquiries, his fellow salespeople were busy networking in the community, generating a constant flow of prospects who were interested in buying and selling real estate. Despite his tactical skills, Frank's sales were the lowest in the office.

The lesson to be learned from this case is that prospecting affects sales performance.

Prospecting and Sales Productivity

The novice may be surprised to think of prospecting activities as having an impact on total sales. However, experienced salespeople realize that smart prospecting can lead to definite improvements in selling productivity. There are several reasons why this is the case.

Frank Carpe's problem highlights the first reason: You cannot succeed in sales without an ample *quantity* of new prospects. You cannot continue to sell successfully without a steady flow of new prospects. Prospecting is not something that you stop once you have enough sales to earn a living. There is turnover among customers. Some die. Some switch to competitors. As a result, you cannot maintain sales without maintaining a steady flow of new potential customers. Quite simply, the salesperson who cannot manage to generate a supply of new prospects cannot sell as much as the salesperson who does. However, sacrificing quality for quantity is not the answer to sales productivity.

In addition, success in selling requires *high-quality* prospects. Dealing with qualified prospects increases your chances of making each sale. The greater your prospect's need for your product, the greater your chances of making the sale. Although there may be occasions when, through sheer persuasive strength, you convince someone to buy something that she does not really need, you cannot rely on your tactical skills alone to achieve sales productivity. By carefully screening prospects *before* you make a presentation, your job *during* the presentation is much easier. When dealing with someone who needs your product and is capable of buying it, you will be much more likely to succeed. There may even be cases where your product will sell itself once you present it to the right prospect.

In general, by improving your chances of success during each sales call, good prospecting will enhance your productivity by saving time and money. A very important reason why good prospecting improves sales performance is the cost of making a sales presentation to the wrong person. You may not think of a lost sale in terms of costs, but if you deal with too many unqualified prospects, the hidden costs will decrease your productivity. It is estimated that when all of the hidden costs are included, the average total cost of an industrial sales call ranges from \$155.90 for clay, glass, and stone to \$301.10 for equipment and machinery. This means that if you are the average salesperson, each call that you make to an unqualified prospect wastes \$200![4]

In fact, salespeople's time is considered so important that it has even been valued on a minute-by-minute basis.[5] Table 6.2 shows the cost of each minute of a salesperson's time, based on annual earnings and the average amount of time spent in face-to-face selling situations. As these cost figures indicate, a hit-or-miss approach to prospecting costs more than you would think. Based on these numbers, we see that by wasting an average of 1 hour per day on calls to unqualified prospects, the salesperson earning \$30,000 foregoes \$7,500 of extra income.

You can avoid wasting time and money if you have a broad understanding of the range of prospecting techniques and design your strategy accordingly. In the following sections, we present specific methods for prospecting.

Prospecting Methods

There are many different methods of prospecting, some of which are better suited for certain salespeople and selling situations than others. As you can see in Table

Table 6.2 The Cost of Each Minute of a Salesperson's Time

Annual Earnings	*Cost per Minute*	*Annual Earnings*	*Cost per Minute*
\$15,000	\$0.25	\$30,000	\$0.50
\$17,000	\$0.28	\$50,000	\$0.84
\$20,000	\$0.33	\$75,000	\$1.26
\$25,000	\$0.42	\$100,000	\$1.68

Source: Adapted from *Master Salesmanship*, (1988), *10*(7).

6.3, some prospecting methods are designed to be used by the salespeople themselves, whereas others require a centralized effort within the salesperson's company. We will begin by discussing different methods used by salespeople and then address those that the company arranges for them.

Personal Contacts

Referrals. One of the most valuable methods of prospecting, the **referral method,** is also one of the oldest and most simple. With this method, you establish what is sometimes called an *endless chain* of prospects by asking each prospect with whom you speak to give you the names of others who might be interested in your product. Although the endless chain method is straightforward, there are several points to remember.

1. Success in this method requires that you make a habit of asking for names each time you deal with a prospect. Some salespeople hesitate to ask for names, but it is important to remember that there is no cost to the prospect to give you a name, and, in fact, some people even get satisfaction out of making recommendations to others. Your request for names can be integrated quite subtly into your conversation.
2. A prospect who does not buy your product may still be a good source of names. There are many reasons why a prospect might not buy your product. Many of these reasons (e.g., lack of suitability or even finances) do not preclude giving you the names of other potential leads. In fact, a prospect who says "no" after you have taken the time to make a presentation may feel a sense of obligation: you have given time, and the prospect has not reciprocated with a purchase. By providing you with other names, this prospect may

Table 6.3 Techniques for Prospecting

Personal Contacts
Customer referrals
Leads from other prospects
Networks of friends
Cold Calls
Company-Generated Leads
Telemarketing
Direct mail
Junior salespeople
Trade shows
Secondary Sources
Newspapers
Directories
Public records
Computerized data bases

actually feel somewhat better: "I can't buy your product, but I know someone who might be interested."

3. At a minimum, ask the prospect whether you may use his name when you contact the lead. Introducing yourself to a new prospect by giving the name of a familiar person will establish instant rapport, which can be invaluable. A strange prospect who might otherwise refuse to listen to your presentation or even speak with you on the phone will generally hear you out if you begin with an opening like "I saw your friend, Sarah Smith, last week, and she suggested that I contact you." Once you establish a personal connection this way, you are no longer a total stranger, and you become harder to dismiss.
4. If possible, ask the prospect to establish contact or write a letter on your behalf. This method is even better than using the prospect's name, and it is done frequently with prospects who become customers. Someone who makes a decision to buy is often enthusiastic about the product or service and may be willing to recommend it to friends. When you ask for this kind of referral, you are taking advantage of people's tendency to want others to join them in making purchases.

The use of testimonials from satisfied customers is one of the methods that experienced salespeople tend to use. This method of lead generation has the distinct advantage of giving credibility to the salesperson in dealing with a new prospect.

The personal referral method of prospecting is extremely important for many types of salespeople. It is used heavily by insurance and real estate salespeople, stockbrokers and other service providers—lawyers, doctors, and so on—whose success depends upon their personal credibility.

Networking. One method of prospecting is to develop a **network,** or group of people who act as sources of leads. If your network consists of people who are influential in the community or industry, it is sometimes called a **center of influence.** Because networking is based upon personal contacts, it offers many of the same advantages as referrals. In fact, this method can offer additional advantages when the network is composed of influential people who themselves are highly credible. Depending upon your particular product, you may develop centers of influence with people like bankers, investment advisors, or leaders in the industry in which you sell.

You can best appreciate the way a center of influence works by tracing through an actual network of contacts (Figure 6.3). Following is part of the network developed by Tom LaTour, a top national insurance salesperson. Tom made good use of center of influence prospecting. When he sold homeowner's insurance to a stockbroker, Jane Farret, he asked that she recommend him to her clients. Since a stockbroker has credibility in financial matters, this contract resulted in many sales for Tom. Better yet, one of Jane's clients was Eric Mills, a real estate salesperson. Eric was enthusiastic about Tom's efficient service and reasonable prices. Not only did Eric buy insurance from Tom, he became another

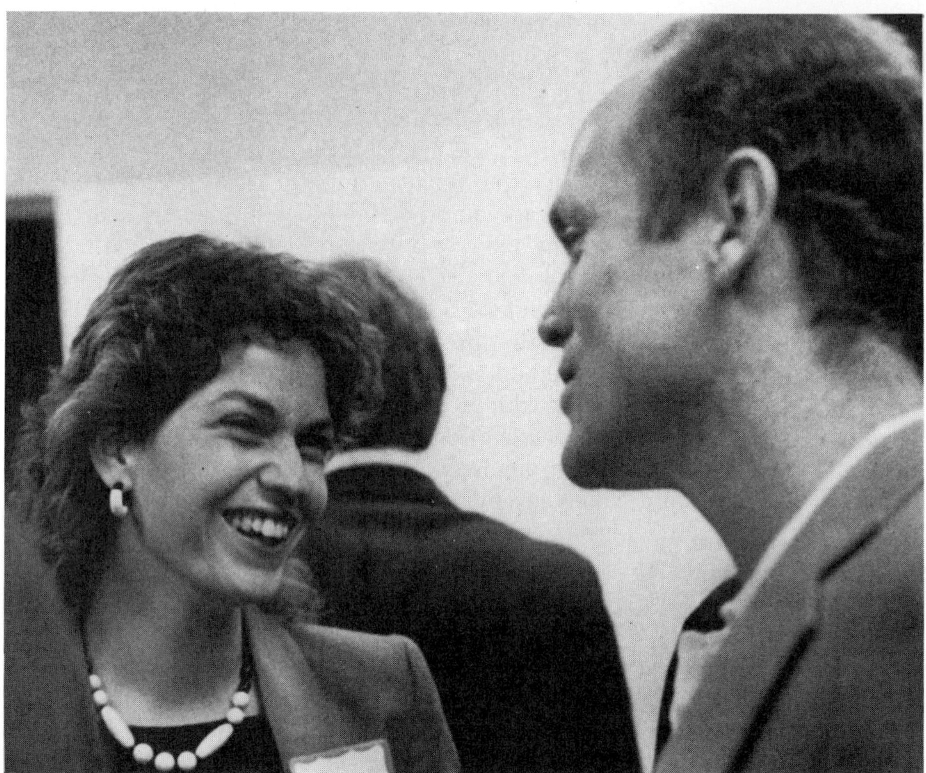

Networking can produce important prospects. (Rhoda Sidney/Monkmeyer Press Photo.)

center of influence. Whenever he sold a house or rented an apartment, he suggested Tom's name to the customer.

You may wonder why Eric bothered to generate leads for Tom. The reason explains the essence of networking. Although Eric had nothing to gain directly from Tom, he did tell his customers to use his name when they called Tom. Over time, Tom realized what an important center of influence Eric was and began sending real estate leads to him. Tom was also happy to do small favors for Eric and helped him with several insurance problems. In addition, Eric was able to provide a further service to his real estate clients by suggesting the name of a good insurance salesperson. This simplified the lives of Eric's customers, who were busy dealing with other aspects of their real estate deals.

Friends, Acquaintances, and Organizations. Personal friends and acquaintances are not to be overlooked as sources of leads. Many successful salespeople make a point of joining civic and social organizations in order to increase their personal contacts and generate new leads. However, it is important to exercise caution when prospecting with this method. If you have no interest in

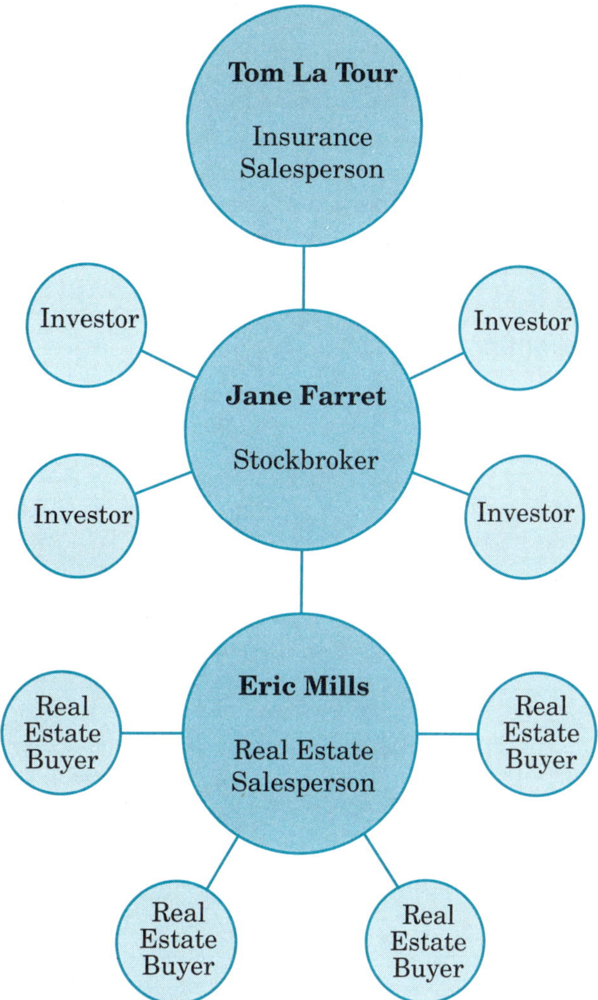

FIGURE 6.3 The center of influence.

the person or organization other than its use as a source of leads, your lack of sincerity will probably become apparent. If it does, you stand to lose the friend as well as the prospect. The issue is an ethical one, and many social and civic organizations are sensitive to it. Some even have written bylaws forbidding their members to use their membership lists for commercial purposes—including prospecting. This does not mean that the use of friends or organizations as sources of leads in itself is unethical. When contacts are used in good faith, both parties stand to benefit.

Brian Sands is a good example of a salesperson who relied heavily on personal contacts. Brian is a stockbroker with a wide circle of friends. He and his wife are active in their community. He is a member of the board of his condominium, raises funds for a local nursing home, and holds alumni parties for his college; she belongs to several civic organizations and works as a volunteer in the local art museum. Both are genuinely interested in helping people and are great assets to their community. Although the Sandses do not engage in civic activities for the sole purpose of generating leads, their network of friends and acquaintances does result in many prospects. Even the local butcher and bar owner invest their money with Brian. It is important to note here that Brian does not make unsolicited sales pitches to any of these contacts. He simply tells them what he does for a living and waits until they make inquiries regarding his services.

Secondary Sources

A **secondary source of information** is one that is *publicly available.* Publicly available information sources include newspapers, magazines, public records (births, deaths, and real estate transactions), and industrial directories. These

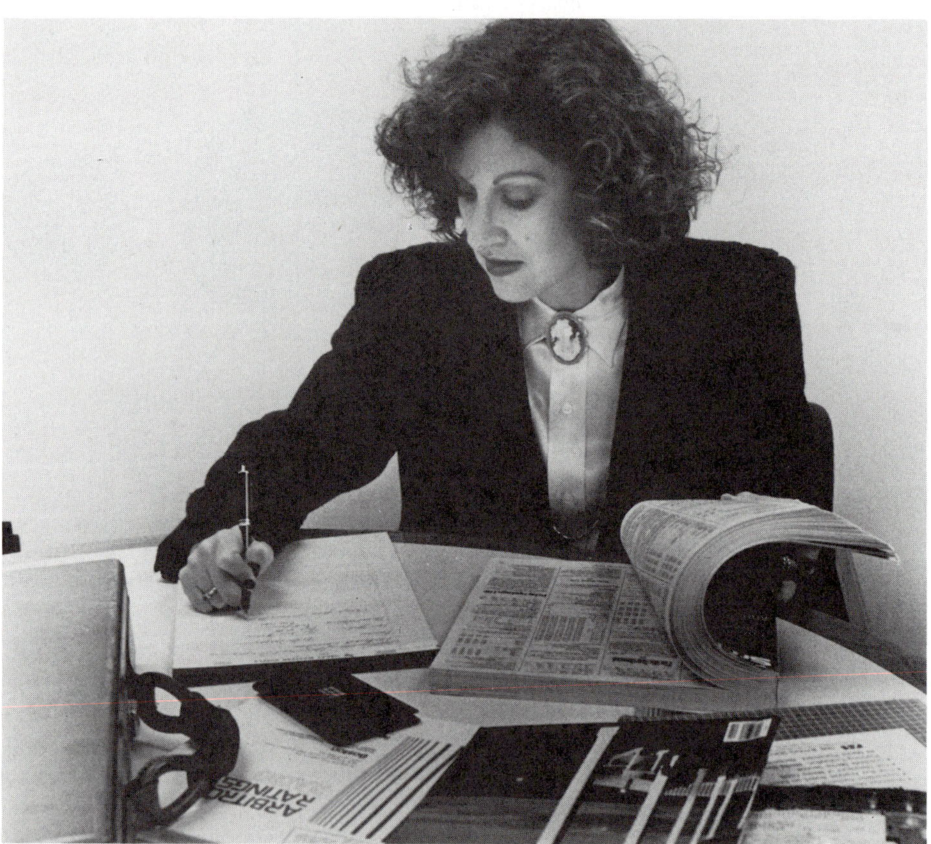

Newspapers and other secondary sources of information can provide valuable leads. (© Ulrike Welsch 1989/PhotoEdit.)

often overlooked sources of sales leads can be very valuable, especially if you use them creatively. Following are some examples of the variety of sources available. The specific secondary sources that may be of use to you in prospecting depend upon the type of product you are selling.

Newspapers, Magazines, and Journals. For some industrial salespeople, it is important to follow corporate changes in the business news. Sources like the *Wall Street Journal* are full of news items detailing the activities of individual firms. There is information about corporate takeovers and mergers, firms entering and leaving markets, and new product developments. Many successful salespeople recognize these items as important sources of leads.

Every time a firm is involved in a takeover or a change of management, there is a potential sales opportunity. When its decision makers change, an organization that had been purchasing from a competitor of yours may begin a search for new suppliers, or at least may become more receptive to outside salespeople. (Another reason to follow the business news is that if one of *your* customers is involved in a restructuring, you may be the supplier in danger of being replaced.) In addition to corporate restructuring, companies entering new businesses can become new prospects for you. If, for example, you are selling cardboard beverage containers and you read that a soda company has entered the fruit juice market, there may be a lead for you to pursue.

Joyce McFarren exemplifies the smart use of secondary sources of information. Joyce knows the value of such sources because she sells for a publisher of highly specialized financial and legal publications. Joyce makes a point of reading the *Wall Street Journal* and the *New York Times*'s business section daily in her search for new prospects. She also checks many weekly business sources of news, such as *Barron's* and *Business Week,* on a regular basis. Joyce has landed many accounts based on leads from these sources. In one case, she read that a large law firm in her district had began to develop a new legal specialty. Her firm had a publication that was targeted to that specialty, and Joyce sent a complimentary copy to one of the lawyers whose name had appeared in the paper. The lawyer found the publication extremely helpful and placed a $20,000 order with Joyce.

Many retail salespeople can also find good leads in publicly available information. For example, those who sell products and services related to weddings check newspapers for wedding announcements. Real estate salespeople often check newspaper advertisements placed by individuals seeking to sell their own properties and attempt to persuade them to use a broker's services. Even lawyers check police records to solicit business from people who have been arrested.

Directories. Suppose that you were charged with locating new prospects for a zipper manufacturer. How would you go about finding industrial leads? One very important source would be *directories.* Directories are publications that list, and often describe, specific people or companies. Perhaps the most familiar one is the telephone directory.

Directories can be used by business-to-business or retail salespeople. For retail sales, there are directories that list wealthy people or those of high social standing. Many large cities have directories called *social registers* that list socially prominent families. In addition, there are many lists of professionals (doctors, accountants, or lawyers in a given geographical area) that may be useful to salespeople selling products such as office equipment or medical supplies.

For business-to-business sales, there are many different directories that list companies and organizations. These can be particularly valuable sources for the salesperson because they often categorize the company by type of business and/or credit rating. Some of the most commonly used industrial directories are the following:

Business to Business Yellow Pages
Thomas' Industrial Directory
Dun and Bradstreet's *Million Dollar Directory*

However, there are far too many specialized directories to list here. This is something that you should check for your own industry in your own local library.

Many directories are based on the *Standard Industrial Classification*, a code developed by the U.S. government. The Standard Industrial Classification, called the **SIC Code,** uses a seven-digit number to group businesses according to their type of economic activity. The first two digits represent the major industry category (see Exhibit 6.1), and the other digits subdivide the industry into more specific categories.

If you had been charged with prospecting for a zipper manufacturer, you might begin by looking up the SIC codes for manufacturers of clothing, luggage, and upholstered furniture. Once you have the numbers, you can check one of many different directories to obtain information about specific firms in that category.

Computerized Data Bases. Many directories are now listed in computerized form. Instead of looking up the companies in a book, you search for them in a *computerized data base* (i.e., a computerized listing of firms in different categories). You gain access to the information by subscribing to the services of the organization that has computerized it. One common service that keeps information useful in solving business problems, **DIALOG,** is available in many college libraries. If your company subscribes to the organization's services, you may be able to search through the data with your own personal computer hooked up to the service with a modem. Alternatively, your company may pay others to do the searching for you.

You can best appreciate the value of these data bases if you see how they solve a specific prospecting problem. Assume, for example, that you were selling computerized equipment to firms in the printing industry, and you wanted to locate the names and telephone numbers of the top executives in printing companies in the Chicago area. Because your equipment is expensive, you are only interested in companies with net sales of over $1.5 million.[6]

How do you locate these names?

EXHIBIT 6.1

Selected Examples of SIC Codes

Construction

15	General Building Contractors
152	Residential Building Construction
1521	Single-Family Housing Construction
.	
.	
.	

Manufacturing

20	Food and Kindred Products
201	Meat Products
2011	Meat Packing Plants
2013	Sausages and Other Prepared Meats
.	
.	
.	
202	Dairy Products
2021	Creamery Butter
2022	Cheese, Natural and Processed
2023	Dry, Condensed, Evaporated Products
2024	Ice Cream and Frozen Desserts
.	
.	
.	
22	Textile Mill Products
221	Broad Woven Fabric, Cotton
225	Knitting Mills
2251	Women's Hosiery, Except Socks
25	Furniture and Fixtures
251	Household Furniture
2511	Wood Household Furniture
2512	Upholstered Household Furniture
2514	Metal Household Furniture
2515	Mattresses and Bedsprings
2517	Wood TV and Radio Cabinets
252	Office Furniture
2521	Wood Office Furniture
2522	Office Furniture, Except Wood
.	
.	
.	

Wholesale Trade

50	Wholesale Trade—Durable Goods
501	Motor Vehicles, Parts, and Supplies
5012	Automobiles and Other Motor Vehicles
502	Furniture and Home Furnishings
5021	Furniture
503	Lumber and Construction Materials

Note: The two left most digits refer to the general industry (e.g., agriculture, forestry, mining, construction, manufacturing). The additional digits refine the industry into more specific categories.

A convenient option would be to use *Dun and Bradstreet's Dun Market Identifiers.* This data base provides information on 2 million U.S. and Canadian firms with sales of over $1 million. If you accessed this information through DIALOG, the cost would be $100 per hour of connected computer time plus $2.50 for each name that you found.

Cold Canvassing

With the *cold canvassing* method of prospecting, you call on every person or organization in a certain category. This may mean calling on every house in a given neighborhood or every hospital in a given territory. When making a cold call, you have neither background information nor a personal contact before approaching the person. The idea behind this method of prospecting is that by calling on enough people (or organizations), you will find a certain percentage who turn out to be qualified prospects. The success of a cold canvassing system, therefore, rests on its use to sell products that have widespread appeal within the group being canvassed.

The obvious disadvantage of cold canvass prospecting is that because it involves little or no selectivity, each call runs a high risk of failure. A salesperson could spend an entire day calling on prospects without making a sale. On the other hand, cold canvassing can be used successfully. Judy Suttenberg, who earns $100,000 a year selling World Book Encyclopedias, takes a smart approach to cold canvassing.[7] Instead of knocking on every single door, she drives around neighborhoods looking for telltale sign of prospects: swing sets, bicycles, and station wagons. Once she sees these signs of families with children, she makes her approach.

Company-Generated Sources of Leads

Because of the central role played by salespeople in a company's overall profitability, some companies aid in the prospecting process. One common method of company-managed prospecting involves the use of impersonal communication to contact large numbers of people or organizations at a relatively low cost. The purpose of this promotional communication is to persuade interested leads to contact the company. When they do, their names are given to the sales staff.

Advertising-Generated Inquiries. An increasingly important method of prospecting is the advertising-generated inquiry. With this approach, the salesperson's company runs an advertisement that typically includes a toll-free "800" number or a tear-out inquiry slip. The purpose of the ad is to stimulate inquiries from interested parties.

The use of advertising to stimulate inquiries is not a new method of doing business. It has been used, even on a small scale, by real estate brokers, who place ads in the newspaper hoping to stimulate prospects to call. In the past, however, the large-scale use of advertising-generated inquiries on a national level had several drawbacks. With old-fashioned systems of processing leads, tear-out slips got lost in a shuffle of paperwork, and the lag time between the inquiry and a salesperson's response often dragged out to several weeks.

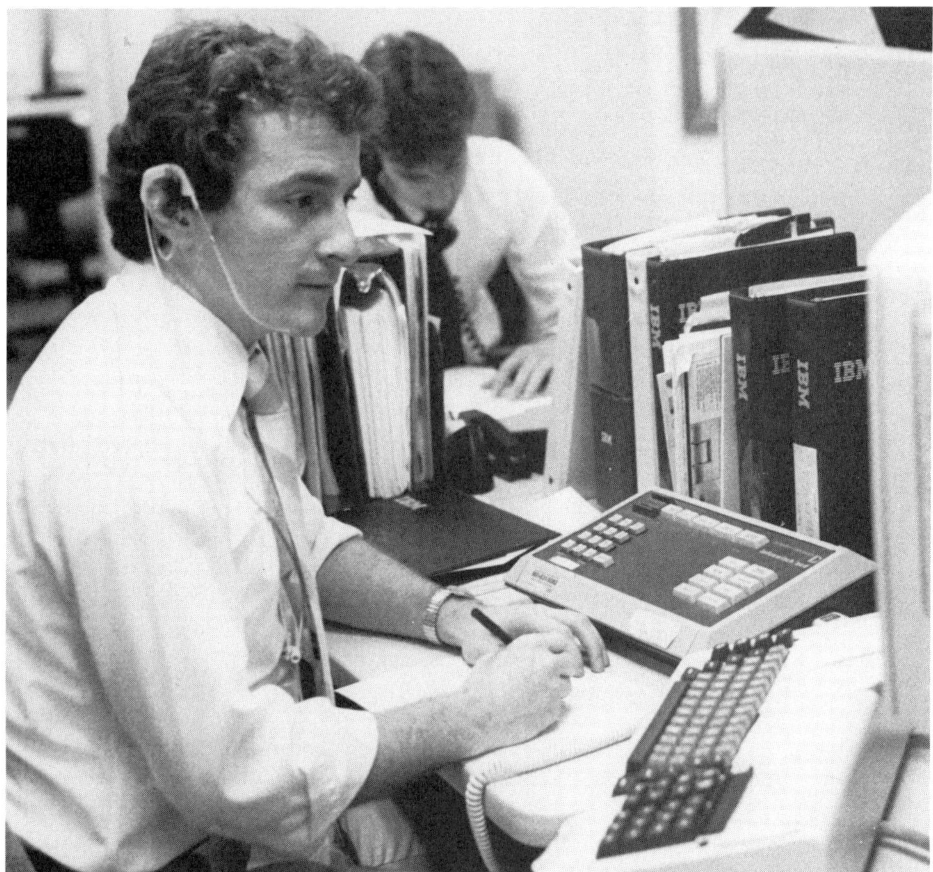

Many companies use telemarketers in their lead-generating systems. (© 1982 David M. Campione/Taurus Photos.)

However, the advent of modern technology has turned this method of prospecting into an exciting new approach. Modern systems often combine "800" numbers with computerized telecommunications to process inquiries within hours. When Honeywell, Inc., instituted such a system, its call volume increased 10-fold within 6 years. At the heart of Honeywell's system is a corporate telecommunications center that processes inquiries for Honeywell's 20 divisions.[8] When someone calls a toll-free number in response to one of Honeywell's ads, a telemarketing specialist qualifies the lead and then relays the information via computer to a salesperson in the field. The typical lag time is only 12 hours.

There are two advantages to this method of prospecting. First, by choosing the media in which the advertisement is placed, the company can target its prospecting activities to the appropriate audience. Second, the quality of the

EXHIBIT 6.2

Lawyers Use Direct Mail to Prospect

Within days of an arrest on charges of drunk driving, James H. Parker received letters from five different lawyers offering to represent him. He hired one of them for $500.

These lawyers had used public records in order to find names of leads to use in direct mail prospecting. Amidst some controversy, the practice of direct mail prospecting is growing among attorneys. Ronald J. Schweighardt, a Fort Lauderdale attorney, says he has gotten about 100 clients from more than 2,000 letters sent out over a period of six months. John Spaulding, who practices law in Washington, D.C., sends out 70 letters per week to people arrested for serious traffic offenses. He gets his prospect list directly from police records.

While critics argue that direct mail prospecting is inappropriate for professionals, many clients are happy with the results. One nurse who was charged with failing to keep accurate patient records was saved from losing her license by an attorney who solicited her business through the mail. Attorney Foster, who specializes in this kind of case, charged the nurse less than half of the quotes she had received from attorneys whom she had contacted herself.

Source: Adapted from *Wall Street Journal*, Tuesday, July 5, 1988.

prospects is increased because the method relies on inquiries, and inquiries tend to demonstrate some degree of interest on the part of the lead (see Exhibit 6.2).

Inquiries Generated by Direct Mail. Many companies use direct mail instead of or in addition to advertising to generate sales leads. The basic idea is similar: the company designs a promotion aimed at stimulating inquiries. Interested prospects phone or mail their inquiries about the product. When the company receives the inquiry, the name is given to a salesperson, who proceeds to make contact. As Table 6.4 indicates, both retail and business-to-business salespeople find these inquiries to be a very important source of prospects. A key reason is that these prospects are already interested and motivated enough to make the first move.

Direct mail prospecting can take a variety of forms, including personalized letters and brochures. A form that is gaining popularity is a direct-mail *newsletter* that the business sends out to current customers as well as potential prospects. Newsletters are well-suited to many kinds of professional offices because they offer a subtle form of promotion.

Table 6.4 Results of a Survey That Asked Retail and Industrial Salespeople How Important They Found Various Prospecting Techniques to Be

	Mean Importance	
Prospecting Technique	*Industrial*	*Consumer*
1. *Personal observation:* Look and listen for evidence of good prospects	4.36*	4.48
2. *Phone/mail inquiries:* Respond to phone or mail inquiries from potential prospects	4.16	4.14
3. *Inquiries to advertising:* Respond to customer inquiries generated from company advertising	3.93	4.11
4. *Cultivate visible accounts:* Cultivate visible and influential accounts that will influence other buyers	3.84	3.98
5. *Cold canvassing:* Make "cold calls" on potential prospects	3.40	2.79
6. *Hold/attend trade shows:* Organize or participate in a trade show directed at potential prospects	3.34	3.18
7. *Examine records:* Examine company records, directories, telephone books, membership lists, and other written documents	3.14	2.77
8. *Referral approach:* Ask each prospect for the name of another potential prospect	2.83	3.66
9. *Introduction approach:* Obtain introduction by one prospect to others via phone, letter, or in person	2.79	3.27
10. *Noncompeting salespeople:* Seek leads from noncompeting salespeople	2.75	2.92
11. *Community contact:* Ask friends and acquaintances for the names of potential prospects	2.37	3.38
12. *Contact organizations:* Seek sales leads from service clubs, chambers of commerce, etc.	2.31	2.46
13. *Bird dogs:* Have junior salespeople locate prospects that senior salespersons will contact	2.11	2.44

* 1 = not important; 5 = very important
Source: Reprinted by permission of *Journal of Personal Selling and Sales Management* © 1985. R. Hite and J. Bellizzi. (1985). Differences in the importance between consumer and industrial salespeople. *Journal of Personal Selling and Sales Management*, 5 (November), 19–30.

Chrisman, Miller, and Woodford, a 38-member design and construction firm in Lexington, Kentucky, uses its newsletter, *Perspectives*, for prospecting. "We began our newsletter as a way to keep in touch with clients and governmental agencies. . . . It also turned out to be a marketing instrument," said Jim Ball, the marketing coordinator. As Joseph Kellogg, the president, added, "Our newsletter is a low pressure way to get information to our prospects. We show prospects we have the knowledge to solve . . . problems they don't yet have, so when [the problems] occur, they call us."[9] Newsletters are also used in the retail market. Dentists, for example, send newsletters full of the latest facts on cavity prevention in order to communicate that they are current in their professional skills.

Regardless of the format used in direct mail prospecting, much of the effect depends upon the quality of the mailing list used. Although many companies use directories or other public records to obtain names for direct mail prospecting, others purchase their lists.

Selling lists of the names of people and organizations has become big business, with some companies paying thousands of dollars to obtain the names and addresses of leads. The advantage of purchased lists over names gathered from the telephone directory is that purchased lists include names that are chosen for certain characteristics. These lists may include the names of persons who subscribe to certain magazines, belong to certain clubs, or order products through the mail. The cost per name varies with the source, depending upon the characteristics of those included on the list.

When purchasing lists for prospecting, a company needs to balance the cost per name against the rate of response from qualified prospects. Some lists may be expensive but may generate a high proportion of good-quality leads. In the long run, this may be better than a list that costs less but results in fewer sales.

Trade Shows, Public Exhibitions, and Conventions. This category includes trade shows aimed at particular industries; professional conventions; and home, automobile, farm, and boat shows open to the public. Each of these outlets represents an important opportunity to locate new prospects. In fact, it is estimated that more than 91,000 firms attract more than 31 million prospects at 8,000 trade shows, at a cost of $7 billion annually.[10] When prospecting at a trade show or demonstration, salespeople typically set up a booth where there is a demonstration or exhibition of the product. As people approach the booth, they are qualified and their names are recorded for future contact. Although some sales may actually take place at the booth, there may be rules against the exchange of money during the show.

Tim McInerney, manager of trade shows for Computervision, has a well-organized system for prospecting at trade shows. When potential leads approach the Computervision booth, a demonstrator qualifies them while conducting the demonstration of the product. Qualified prospects are then taken to a conference area, where salespeople ask further questions. If a prospect is ready to buy on the spot, she is taken to a *focus center* outside of the show, because selling is forbidden on the exhibition floor. Otherwise, the prospect's name is recorded, and a salesperson follows up on the lead after the show is over.[11]

Bird Dogs and Spotters. **Bird dog** and **spotter** are names given to junior salespeople who are hired for the express purpose of locating prospects. Often part-time workers, these people allow the salespeople to devote their time to planning and conducting presentations and servicing accounts. Although they are typically hired by the company, some salespeople may hire their own spotters on a more informal basis. A real estate salesperson who maintains contact with the doorman or superintendent of an apartment building for the purpose of gaining sales leads would fall in this category.

Designing Your Prospecting System

Once you understand the basic prospecting techniques, you can begin to design your own strategy. Your prospecting system need not fall neatly into one of the existing categories. In fact, it is best if you tailor your system to your own needs and the requirements of your industry. This is evident in the results of a large survey in which a majority of salespeople found the method called *personal observation* to be the most important prospecting technique. Personal observation cuts across the techniques described earlier. It is a general method that simply means *looking and listening for evidence of good prospects.* Depending upon the industry, personal observation can involve totally different activities. If you sell to the construction industry, for example, personal observation may mean observing new construction sites or checking the papers for recorded deeds or building permits. If you sell medical supplies, personal observation may mean observing a new clinic or hospital.

The value of individualizing your prospecting method becomes even more apparent when we consider the differences in the responses of salespeople who sell *consumer* versus *business-to-business* products. As Table 6.4 indicates, salespeople who sell consumer products find personal prospecting techniques to be more valuable, while industrial salespeople favor the use of cold calls and public records.[12] This is not surprising when we consider the value of personal contacts within a community of consumers versus the availability of public records containing information on many companies.

In other cases, novel combinations of prospecting techniques can be useful to consumer or business-to-business salespeople. One successful approach uses cold telephone calls to generate inquiries.[13] With this method, salespeople, or telemarketing assistants, makes cold telephone calls in which they begin by asking whether they can send the prospect written material about the product. If the prospect shows interest, the caller proceeds to request an appointment for a face-to-face presentation. The idea behind this technique is similar to the generation of inquiries with direct mail or advertising: it results in a higher proportion of interested prospects. In addition, the novel use of the telephone allows the salesperson or telemarketer to begin with small requests ("Can I mail this to you?") while gaining a sense of how qualified the prospect is.

Finally, regardless of the specific techniques that you use, it is important to realize that your choice of prospecting strategy is *not* a one-time decision. Like any strategic decision, good prospecting strategy should be an *ongoing process.* As you try different prospecting methods, you evaluate the results and alter your strategy accordingly.

Lead Management Systems

The importance of taking a systematic approach to prospecting is highlighted by the fact that many forward-thinking companies are instituting systems for managing and evaluating their prospecting efforts. These systems are often referred to as **lead management systems** because they help manage and evaluate leads.

Although the systems vary from company to company, they tend to have several common elements: (1) a method or methods for generating leads, (2) a method for responding to inquiries, and (3) a method for evaluating sources of leads (see Figure 6.4).

Lead Generation

Lead management begins with the generation of leads. This may be done by any of the methods listed earlier. Most companies with lead management systems use some kind of company-initiated promotion (advertising, direct mail, trade show, etc.) in order to stimulate inquiries.

As mentioned earlier, the promotion generally includes some method for the lead to make an inquiry about the product (toll-free number, tear-out inquiry sheet, salesperson's business card and direct telephone number, etc.)

Response to Inquiries

Like Honeywell, many companies use a telemarketing staff to make an initial response to inquiries. In some cases, the telemarketers may make an actual sales pitch; in others, they may act as qualifiers who forward qualified prospects' names

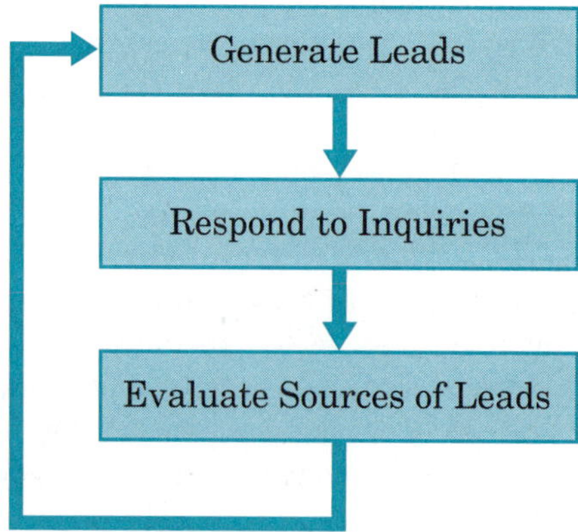

FIGURE 6.4 Lead management systems.

to the salespeople. The company may also respond by mailing printed material to the lead.

Evaluating Sources of Leads

The tracking and evaluation of sources of leads is a very important aspect of a good lead management system. In order to do this, the company must keep records of which methods it used to generate leads, how many leads were generated by each method, whether or not the leads were qualified, and the amount of any resulting sales.

The methods used to analyze this information can vary from sophisticated mathematical modeling techniques to more simple, straightforward calculations. In recent years, a great deal of computer software has been developed for managing leads. Using this software, the company can maintain and analyze a data base of all the necessary information. If, for example, a company spends $5,000 on a booth at a trade show, and the trade show generates 1,000 leads, which result in 50 sales, we can figure a cost of $5 per lead and $100 per sale. We can also compare this with the cost and business generated by, say, a toll-free number advertised in a trade journal.

When Edmond Neuberger instituted a lead management system at Westinghouse's Combustion Control Division, he obtained a 10-to-1 return on the investment. The first stage of his plan was to begin a formalized system for lead generation based on advertising, news releases, trade show exhibits, and promotional giveaways. Leads came in through toll-free numbers, return cards, and publishers' computers. A software program was used to track and evaluate these various sources of leads. Within 5 years of the system's start, leads and their conversions to sales had tripled.[14]

Lead Management by Salespeople

In addition to the use of such companywide lead management systems, many salespeople maintain their own systems for managing and evaluating leads. Today there are many simple-to-use programs developed specifically for managing leads with the use of personal computers. These programs perform tasks similar to those of the companywide systems just described. More and more salespeople are using personal computers for lead management, and some even bring a laptop model on their sales calls. However, your lead management system need not be computerized. There are also many salespeople who maintain manual files in which they record each lead, the source of the lead, and any resulting sales.

Whether you use a computer or manual files, having a system for lead management is crucial to your success. Without a formalized system for tracking and evaluating leads, you cannot improve your prospecting strategy. As you will see in the following section, maintaining a lead management system is an important part of putting it all together.

Putting It All Together

We can start to put it all together by summarizing the key points discussed thus far:

- First and foremost, prospecting is a strategic activity.
- Prospecting should be treated as an ongoing process.
- Prospecting sets the stage for the rest of the selling process.
- Prospecting affects sales performance.
- Prospecting begins with the generation of new leads.
- Qualifying is part of the total prospecting process.
- Prospecting can be done by individual salespeople or by their companies.
- Prospecting methods include personal contact, secondary information, cold canvassing, and company-generated leads.
- A systematic approach to prospecting involves (1) the use of various prospecting methods, (2) the tracking and evaluation of the various sources of leads, and (3) the constant altering of the plan to conform to the results of (2).

We can see from these key points that prospecting is a strategic process involving the *location and qualification of individual leads* as well as the *ongoing evaluation of the various sources of leads.* By understanding how these activities fit together, you can develop a coordinated prospecting plan.

A major emphasis of this chapter was that prospecting is not only the first but also a crucial stage in the sales process. Prospecting is a part of the selling process whose importance may not be understood by novices but is appreciated by experts as often making the difference between success and failure in the selling field. We can see this by putting the information on prospecting together with the material from the previous chapters. Once you understand the principles of communication and buyer behavior, you realize that there are no magic tricks or formulas for success. The most skilled communicator in the world will not be able to convince an entire buying center that it ought to spend $100,000 on equipment that it does not need. Instead, your ultimate success will depend upon your ability to present your ideas to interested, qualified prospects.

This is why prospecting is becoming increasingly prominent as modern salespeople become more highly skilled and professional. The professional salesperson does not have the time to waste on calls that have no potential to close. With wasted calls, not only do individual incomes suffer, but the profitability of the entire organization can be compromised. At costs ranging from $200 to $300 per industrial sales call, sales productivity is of obvious concern to any company. It is not surprising, therefore, that prospecting is one area of the sales process where more and more firms are stepping in to help their salespeople with high-technology, centralized, lead-generating systems.

Now that you realize the role played by prospecting, you can understand why it is done by the top people in most legal, accounting, marketing research, and consulting firms. No one who graduates from college and goes to work for an advertising agency or accounting firm will be put in charge of prospecting, but many new graduates in selling jobs will be given this opportunity to control their own productivity. Although at first prospecting may not seem to be the most glamorous part of a salesperson's job, when you think about its effect on productivity, you can realize why it is regarded as so important.

Key Terms

Prospect
Qualified prospect
Lead (suspect)
Referral method
Network
Center of influence
Secondary source of information
SIC Code
DIALOG
Bird dog (spotter)
Lead management systems

Review Questions

1. What is the difference between a lead and a prospect?
2. Why is prospecting a strategic activity?
3. Why is prospecting considered to be part of the selling process?
4. How does prospecting affect sales productivity?
5. List three different costs that might be associated with prospecting activities.
6. What are the advantages of using prospecting techniques based on personal contacts?
7. What are the advantages of company-sponsored prospecting efforts?
8. When is it appropriate to use cold canvassing?
9. What is a lead management system?
10. Why is a lead management system necessary for a good prospecting strategy?

Discussion Questions

1. Is it possible to spend too much time prospecting? Why (or why not)?
2. Prospecting is one part of the sales process in which retail and business-to-business salespeople stress very different techniques. Try to explain the reasons for the differences reported in Table 6.4.
3. Assume that you have just graduated from college and landed your first job. You will be working for a large, reputable firm, selling insurance in the consumer market. Since your compensation is highly dependent on commissions, you must start prospecting right away. Once you have spoken to your parents and all of your relatives, what do you do to establish a systematic prospecting strategy?

CASE 6.1

When Donald Thomas graduated with a degree in marketing from a university in Ohio, he landed a job selling technical publications for the Bureau of Legal and Financial Affairs (BLFA). Competition for the job had been highly competitive. Not only did the BLFA pay well, but the work was exciting and challenging.

The BLFA is a prestigious publisher of specialized information for the legal and financial professions. Their products range from subscriptions to daily information services to weekly and monthly publications describing legislative and case law developments that affect a variety of legal and financial specialties. Because of the specialized nature of the information and the high prices (some of the subscriptions can top $1,000 per year), the target markets for BLFA products tend to be large legal and financial firms with their own libraries, public and university libraries, and other major institutions.

In selling for the BLFA, Donald would be interacting with some of the brightest and most powerful people in Ohio. He had to be well versed in all of the product areas so that he could speak intelligently about the different product lines with various prospects. In addition, the BLFA has begun to add computerized information services to its product line and to expand into new geographic markets. Among those markets was Columbus, Ohio, where Donald was hired to sell. Although the BLFA had dealt directly with a few institutions in Columbus, including a university and a large public library, it had never had a local sales force west of Pennsylvania and east of California. As a result, Donald was fully in charge of his own prospecting. Unlike representatives hired on the East or West Coasts, he had no set list of clients to begin calling on.

1. How should Donald go about prospecting?
2. What methods should he use?
3. How can he generate leads in Columbus?

References

1. *Master Salesmanship.* (1988). *10*(7).

2. Szymanski, D. M. (1988). Determinants of selling effectiveness: The importance of declarative knowledge to the personal selling concept. *Journal of Marketing, 52*(1), 64–77.

3. Wagner, R., C. Rashotte, and R. Sternberg. (1988). Tacit knowledge in sales: Rules of thumb for selling to anyone. *Unpublished manuscript.*

4. Business-to-business. (1988). *Sales and Marketing Management, 140* (November 8), 27.

5. *Master Salesmanship.* (1988). *10*(7).

6. *Sales and Marketing Management.* (1988). (July), 55.

7. Kleinfield, N. R. (1988). The cheerful trudge of a world book ace. *New York Times* (March 6).

8. Kent, D. (1986). Sales lead management. *Business Marketing, 71* (March), 60–70.

9. Jenkins, T. (1988). Winning customers with a newsletter. *Sales and Marketing Management, Portfolio*, 67.

10. Kerin, R. and W. Cron (1987). Assessing trade show functions: An exploratory study. *Journal of Marketing, 51* (July), 87–94.

11. Skolnik, R. (1988). Are trade shows worth it? *Sales and Marketing Management, Portfolio*, 17–19.

12. Hite, R. and J. Bellizzi. (1985). Differences in the importance between consumer and industrial salespeople. *Journal of Personal Selling and Sales Management, 5* (November), 19–30.

13. Jolson, M. (1986). Prospecting by prenotification: An application of the foot-in-the-door technique. *Journal of Personal Selling and Sales Management, 6* (August), 39–42.

14. Kent, D. (1986), op. cit.

The Preapproach Plan

CHAPTER OBJECTIVES

In this chapter, you will learn:

The role of planning in the selling process.

To set objectives for a sales call.

What information is required to plan a sales call.

Where to obtain preapproach information.

To determine the Industrial Goods Classification of a product.

To construct a presale plan.

CHAPTER OUTLINE

A Sales Challenge

When the headquarters of the Shiply Corporation moved from New York to St. Louis, many of the employees decided to look for new jobs. After weeks of searching, Dan Mandrin and Tina Minelli, two of the top programmers in the firm, had gone on many interviews but received no good offers. They could not understand how their friend in sales, Diane Trinkaus, had found a great position almost immediately. Programmers were supposed to be in greater demand than salespeople, yet Diane was about to earn a much higher income, and they had not even received offers.

Dan: I can't understand how Diane could have found such a great job so fast. I thought that programmers were in much greater demand than salespeople.

Tina: You got me. Why don't you ask her during lunch today?
(*Lunch later that day*)

Dan: Diane, do you have any trade secrets on how to find such a great job? You'll be earning twice what Tina and I will—if we're lucky enough to get offers.

Diane: There's no secret, Dan. I just applied what I knew about preapproach planning to my job search. Before I sent out any resumes, I gathered information about each prospective employer. I figured out how my skills could fit their needs and then mapped out a specific plan for the job interview. That way, I stood out from others who were looking for the same position.

Tina: I see what we're doing wrong, Dan. We just sent our resumes to all of the companies that advertised for programmers. We never did any research on the company or tried to show how our specific skills could fit any of their needs.

Diane: Your resumes are probably on a pile with hundreds of others who did the same thing. I can show you how to develop a preapproach plan if you like.

Dan: That would be terrific.

An Overview

What Dan and Tina had not realized was that job searching requires something beyond prospecting for employment leads: it requires systematic planning. Because of her training in sales, Diane understood this principle. In fact, the key to Diane's success was the way she applied her *presale planning* skills to her job search. Table 7.1 shows where planning fits into the selling process. Based on its place in the process, we can see that planning serves as a bridge between prospecting and conducting the sales call. You develop your plan *after* you locate the prospect and *before* you approach this person. Because the plan comes before the approach, it is often referred to as the **preapproach** or **preapproach planning.**

Table 7.1 Where Planning Fits Into the Selling Process

Locate and qualify prospects
Develop a preapproach plan
Plan your persuasive strategy
Approach the prospect and learn about needs
Present your product
Handle objections
Close the sale
Follow up

Regardless of how many times you approach a prospect, each call should be preceded by a plan. The plan helps to adapt your presentation to each prospect, just as Diane fit her skills to each company.

Because of its importance, we devote two chapters to the planning process. In this chapter, we cover the basics of planning, gathering information, and adapting your presentation material to the prospect's needs. In Chapter 8, we discuss the power balance that exists between you and the prospect, and how to plan specific persuasive strategies for the content of your presentation.

Putting Planning in Perspective

We begin to put planning into perspective by recognizing that planning is a *strategic* sales activity.[1] Like prospecting, planning activities help to determine your success in the long run. With good presale planning, you work smarter, not harder,[2] by developing a general strategy to handle the sales call. How will you approach the prospect? How does your product fit the needs of the prospect? What tactics will you use?

You can better appreciate the value of planning if you compare the following two sales interactions. Both are between a professor and a textbook salesperson:

DIALOGUE I

SALESPERSON: Good morning, Professor Summers. How was your vacation?

PROFESSOR: Much too short.

SALESPERSON: It's hard to believe that the semester's half over. What courses are you teaching in the fall?

PROFESSOR: Personal selling and business ethics.

SALESPERSON: Oh, really? We have new books coming out for both of those courses.

PROFESSOR: What are they like?

SALESPERSON: They are both really comprehensive books. They come with teacher's manuals that will help you design your courses.

PROFESSOR: Well, that's not exactly what I need in personal selling. I've been teaching that course for a while now and don't need help with course design. What about cases? Does the personal selling book have cases?

SALESPERSON: I'm not sure offhand. Let me check here. (*Flips through a looseleaf notebook with textbook information*) Ah, yes, it does.

PROFESSOR: What are the cases like? I'm looking for realistically complex cases.

SALESPERSON: I'll have to get back to you on that. This promotional material doesn't actually describe the cases.

DIALOGUE II

SALESPERSON: Good morning, Professor Summers. How was your vacation?

PROFESSOR: Much too short.

SALESPERSON: It's hard to believe that the semester's half over and it's time to order books for the fall.

PROFESSOR: That's for sure.

SALESPERSON: I see that you are teaching personal selling again in the fall. You've been teaching that course for several years now, and using the Smith and Forsyth text?

PROFESSOR: That's right.

SALESPERSON: Well, we have a great new textbook that I'm sure you'll like. You use cases in personal selling, don't you?

PROFESSOR: I think cases work well in that course.

SALESPERSON: Well, look at this. (*Brings a copy of the personal selling textbook out of her briefcase and flips to the cases.*)

PROFESSOR: They look pretty comprehensive.

SALESPERSON: Students seem to learn a lot more from our cases than they do from those in the Smith and Forsyth textbook. And these seem to work particularly well for professors who have been teaching the course for a while, like yourself.

PROFESSOR: Why don't you send me a copy of the book so that I can examine it carefully?

SALESPERSON: Sure. I also brought this new business ethics textbook for you to look at. I see that you'll be one of the professors teaching this new course.

PROFESSOR: Yes, I am, and we are having trouble determining which textbook to use.

SALESPERSON: I think you'll like the approach taken in this textbook. The authors have tried to balance a philosophical approach to ethics with a mixture of very tough real-life cases on how this philosophy applies to business. I know that your ethics textbook is going to be chosen by a schoolwide committee, but I thought that you'd like to look at our new book. I think it would be well-suited to your teaching style.

After reading these two dialogues, it is not difficult to determine which salesperson did more preapproach planning. It is also not difficult to determine which salesperson will be more successful. The difference is striking, and we can learn a lot by analyzing exactly what the second salesperson did. In contrast to the first salesperson, the second one obviously had set specific objectives and had gathered detailed information before approaching the professor. Based on this information, she was able to come prepared with the relevant textbooks. She also knew how to position the books in a way that would interest Professor Summers.

A good question to ask, however, is whether the second dialogue is realistic. Could the second salesperson really have had so much information and been able to plan so much in advance? The answer is definitely "yes," and as you read this chapter, you will see how this salesperson could have prepared such a thorough plan. In fact, we will discuss the following steps involved in the preapproach:

1. Set objectives for the sales call.
2. Gather information about the prospect, her needs, and the buying process.
3. Plan the presentation format.
4. Plan the content of the presentation.
5. Plan the use of audiovisual aids, brochures, or product demonstrations.

Setting Objectives for Your Sales Call

At first, you might think that a salesperson's objectives are obvious. It is obvious that the salesperson wants to make a sale—Or is it? If the second textbook salesperson's objective had been to close a sale, we would have considered the call a failure. However, we could tell from observing the interaction that the salesperson's objectives had been to demonstrate to Professor Summers how both new textbooks could meet her needs and to persuade the professor to examine them. The salesperson knew that Professor Summers did not have the authority to choose the ethics textbook, but she succeeded in creating interest anyway.

In general, a salesperson's objectives for any given sales call should be more specific than simply making a sale, even though the sale may be the ultimate goal. The purpose of objectives is to guide actions, and an objective as general as "make the sale" offers little specific guidance.

More useful objectives might include the following:

Present your product to the person in the company who has the authority to buy.
Establish rapport with the prospect.
Persuade the prospect to look carefully at a sales brochure.
Make sure that the prospect develops certain beliefs about your product.
Convince the prospect that your product is more reliable than a competitor's.

Objectives like these give you something to aim for in planning an interaction with a prospect, and will eventually progress toward the final objective of closing a sale.

In all likelihood, you will make many sales calls where, like the book salesperson, you do not even expect to close a sale. In fact, the average industrial sale takes 4.6 sales calls before the deal is closed.[3] This means that even in cases that eventually result in a sale, an average of 3.6 of the sales calls accomplished objectives other than an actual close. If your only objective is to close the sale, you must expect to fail three-quarters of the time.

Gathering Information for Your Sales Call

As our second textbook salesperson demonstrated, good information is at the heart of preapproach planning. Without information on what courses the professor was teaching, as well as how she liked to teach those courses, the salesperson could not have developed such a thorough strategy. She would not have known which books to bring to her sales call, nor would she have known that she should stress the personal selling textbook's cases.

But how do you determine what information to gather, and how do you know where to get it? Both of these questions are addressed in the next sections.

What Information Should You Gather?

As we observed in the textbook case, important questions to address during your preapproach focus on the prospect, his buying patterns, and the needs that can be satisfied by your product (see Figure 7.1).

The Prospect. One thing that seems to distinguish successful salespeople from others is their ability to develop thorough descriptions of their prospects.[4] In general, the more traits you can use to describe your prospect, the better able you will be to tailor your strategy to fit the prospect's specific needs. Consider the example of our successful book salesperson. Instead of just regarding Professor Summers in general terms, as a professor at a specific college, the successful salesperson knew that Professor Summers taught the sales course; that she had taught that course in the past and had used a competitor's textbook; that she preferred to teach the course with cases; that she was one of several professors teaching a new ethics course; and that the choice of the ethics textbook was a committee decision. In general, when approaching a prospect, you would like to know as much as you can about the following: What is the prospect like? If the prospect is an individual consumer, what is his age, occupation, family size, and so on? What are the concerns of this person?

If the prospect is buying for an organization, what does the organization produce? How large is it? What is its corporate culture?

The Prospect's Needs. It is also easier to plan strategies if you can determine the following: Is the prospect currently using one of my competitor's products? How should I position my product? What benefits should I stress? How can I fit my product to the needs of the prospect? Prospects have different needs, and the more you know about them, the better able you will be to close a sale. As our textbook example illustrated, most products have many different features that allow them to be *positioned* in different ways. Although both textbook salespeople were selling the same book, the first salesperson stressed the design of new courses and the second stressed the cases. Because the second salesperson's

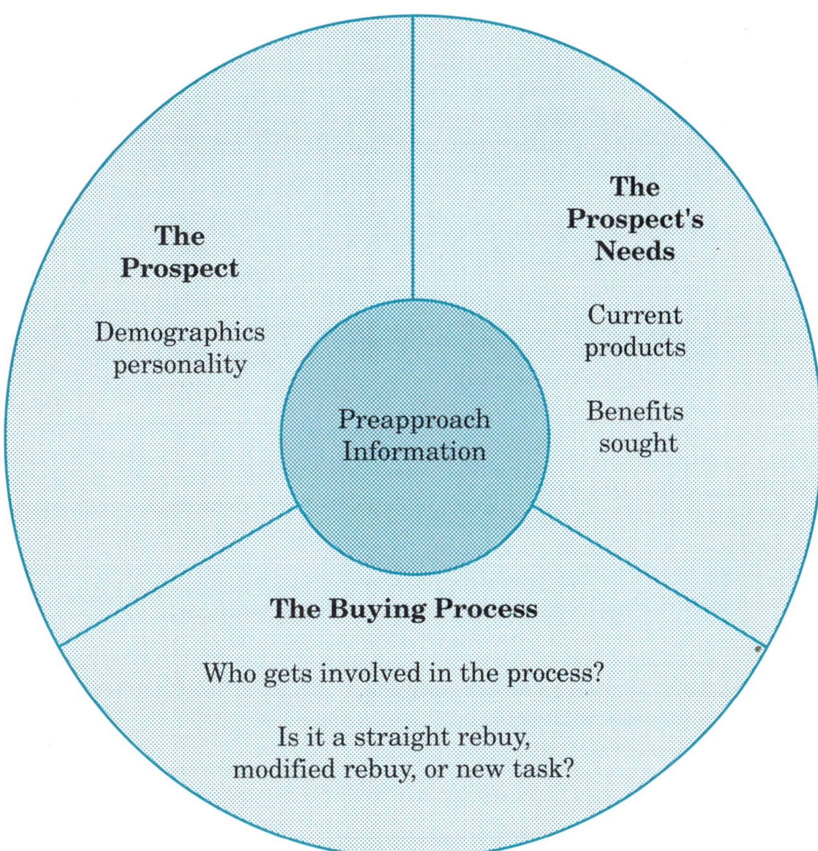

FIGURE 7.1 Information plays a crucial role in preapproach planning.

strategy was based on real information about the prospect's specific needs, it was the successful one.

The Buying Process. You can begin to answer many of your preapproach questions if you understand your prospect's buying process. This is particularly true in business-to-business sales, where the way an organization approaches buying depends largely on the type of purchasing problem it is confronting.[5] Fortunately for the salesperson about to approach an industrial prospect, a classification system called the **Industrial Goods Classification** divides industrial purchases into one of three basic categories: the straight rebuy, the modified rebuy, and the new task buy.

The **straight rebuy** is *a purchasing problem that is basically a straightforward reorder of an existing product without the consideration of competing products.* The **modified rebuy** represents *a buying situation that, though not completely new, is still important enough to warrant the investigation of different alternatives.* Finally, the **new task buy** *is a first-time purchase of an expensive or important product* and typically involves the consideration of many alternatives.[6] Table 7.2 shows the three categories and gives examples of each.

New task buying often involves committee decision making. (© Jeffrey W. Myers/ Stock, Boston.)

Using the Industrial Goods Classification in Your Plan

Knowing how your product is classified will give you information on such important questions as the following: Who makes the buying decision? How much information will the prospect gather? What benefits should I stress?

Who Makes the Buying Decision and How Much Information Will Be Gathered? When an organization makes a straight rebuy, very little new information is gathered and purchase decisions are made routinely by people in the purchasing department. The opposite is true of the new task buy. Because of the importance and novelty of the purchase, people high up in the organization get involved. Often decisions are made by committees, or **buying centers,** and it is common for an engineer or an upper-level manager to get involved. In fact, the purchasing department may have little input into the new task buy. Finally, because of its complexity, the new task buy decision may be made over an extended period of time. It is unrealistic to set an objective of closing a new task purchase on the first sales call.

Table 7.2 The Industrial Buying Classification

Category	*Example*
Straight rebuy	Secretary orders paper supplies
	Purchasing agent reorders raw materials for a manufacturing process
Modified rebuy	University committee purchases personal computers for faculty use
	Plant manager purchases new manufacturing equipment
New task buy	University hires an architectural firm to build a new science building
	Local real estate office computerizes its entire operation

Between these two extremes is the modified rebuy. In this situation, new information is considered, and the decision typically involves engineers and other technical people beyond the purchasing department. However, the group is more limited than it would be for a new task buy.

What Benefits Should I Stress? For organizations engaging in straight rebuys, the primary concern is to have a reliable supplier who will minimize problems of availability and delivery. Price may also be a concern with the straight rebuy, but in general, it is difficult to persuade an organization to adopt a new supplier as long as the existing supplier is satisfactory. As a result, the straight rebuy is a challenge to a competing salesperson.

Although the overriding concern in a modified rebuy is to ensure a reliable supply, prospects are typically open to new suppliers offering improved products or services. Therefore, with a modified rebuy, the key is to stress your special benefits without neglecting pragmatic issues such as reliability.

Knowing that your product represents a new task buy can be of great help in planning what benefits to stress during your sales calls. For one thing, organizations engaged in new task buying are less concerned with price than they are with finding solutions to their problems. As a result, buyers tend to be responsive to presentations that demonstrate how a product can work for them. Although the new task purchase is relatively rare, it is a very important category because it typically involves large sums of money and helps to establish a buying pattern that may be repeated in the future.[7]

Classifying Your Own Product

In order to make good use of the Industrial Goods Classification, you must first be able to determine which buying category your product is in. As the preceding discussion indicates, the three Industrial Goods Classifications are based on (1) the newness of the problem, (2) the information requirements, and (3) the consideration of alternatives (see Table 7.3). Unfortunately, there are no hard and fast rules for determining the buying category for your product. Many decisions fall into different categories, depending on the circumstances. Consider, for example, the classification of a textbook decision. If, for the spring semester, the bookstore reorders the textbooks chosen by professors in the fall, the buying decision is a straight rebuy. If, as was the case with the personal selling book, the professor chooses a new textbook for an existing course, the decision is probably a modified rebuy. Finally, if, as was the case with the ethics book, an entire school is adopting a textbook for a new required course, the buying decision is closer to a new task buy.

In general, you can begin to assess the classification of your product by considering the following questions:

How frequently is your product purchased? If you are selling a chemical or raw material that is purchased frequently, it may represent a straight rebuy to many firms. If your product is purchased less frequently, as is the case

Table 7.3 The Industrial Buying Classification: Dimensions Behind the Categories

Type of Buying Situation	*Newness of the Problem*	*Information Requirements*	*Consideration of New Alternatives*
New Task	High	Maximum	Important
Modified Rebuy	Medium	Moderate	Limited
Straight Rebuy	Low	Minimal	None

Source: Reprinted by permission of Allyn & Bacon © 1967. P. Robinson, C. Ferris, and Y. Wind. (1967). Industrial Buying and Creative Marketing. Boston: Allyn & Bacon, p. 25.

with major equipment or real estate, it is closer to a new task. However, you must also consider the question of importance:

How important is the purchase of your product to the prospect? If your product is an inexpensive supply item, it may never be considered a new task purchase, regardless of its purchase frequency or novelty. The purchase of novel cleaning supplies will probably never involve engineers and top-level managers, whereas the purchase of a new plant or mainframe computer will probably never be a straight rebuy.

How big is the prospect? The purchase of a copying machine may represent a straight rebuy to a large manufacturer but a new task buy to a small consulting firm.

By now, it should be clear that the answers to these questions play a crucial role in your presale plan, affecting not only which people you contact and how many people you will have to deal with, but also what kinds of information you should prepare to stress. However, knowing *what* information you need and knowing *how* to obtain that information are two different problems. In many cases, the difference between successful and unsuccessful salespeople can be the knowledge of what information sources are available and the ability to gain access to those sources.[8]

Information Sources

You may wonder how the successful textbook representative was able to know so much about Professor Summers. She seemed to have information that would not be generally available. However, if we carefully analyze her information, we see that anyone willing to make the effort could have acquired it. First, much of the information came from the professor herself. This salesperson had obviously called on Professor Summers in the past and made an effort to remember details. Information also came from *observing the environment.* Experienced book salespeople know that courses, teachers, and textbooks are listed on bulletin boards at most colleges.

In most cases, there are many different sources of preapproach information. Table 7.4 on page 188 lists some common sources and indicates their importance to retail and business-to-business salespeople. However, where you actually obtain your information will depend on whether you are making a *first call* on a new prospect, a *call back* on a new prospect, or a call on an *existing customer.*

Calling on a New Prospect. If you are making a first call on a new prospect, it may be possible to obtain information from the prospect personally, if you telephone to set up the appointment. Although this kind of call is typically brief, you may use the opportunity to gather information needed to plan your presentation. If you obtained the lead from a personal reference or other customer, that person may serve as a source of preapproach information about the prospect. It is often a good habit to ask the source questions about the prospect, such as "Who does the buying?" and "What is the prospect like?" Likewise, if you obtained the name from another salesperson or a company file, these sources may supply important preapproach information.

Call Backs. If you are making a call back on a new prospect, your first call should serve as an important source of information. This is a very valuable source that is overlooked by many salespeople. The key to using this information is that busy prospects tend to forget exactly what was said during a sales call. The typical buyer sees many salespeople. If you are careful to make a note of things that receive a positive response from the prospect during the first call, you can redesign your presentation to use these points in your call back. By tailoring your presentation to the prospect in this way, chances are that you will be able to "strike a chord" of approval and possibly close a sale that you otherwise might have lost.

This approach to information gathering can be particularly helpful in business-to-business sales where you are expected to make several calls before closing. In these cases, you might plan a sequence of sales calls, where the first is an informal interaction designed to gather information and the second is a more formal presentation incorporating that information into a proposed solution to the prospect's problem.

Calling on Existing Customers. If you are making a call on an existing customer, your own files should serve as an important source of readily available information. Although you may think of preapproach planning in terms of *new* prospects, many sales are made to *existing* customers. It is important to remember that sales calls to existing customers must also be planned. In some ways, a call on an existing customer may require more homework than a call on a new prospect, because you are expected to remember the customer, the customer's needs, and what products he has bought from you in the past. For this reason, it is important to maintain files on existing customers as well as on new prospects.

Table 7.4 Importance of Techniques for Obtaining Information About a Prospect and Gaining an Interview

Selling Technique	Mean Importance	
	Industrial	*Consumer*
1. *The prospect:* Ask the prospect direct questions to obtain some necessary information about the prospect	4.16*	4.40
2. *Phone for appointment:* Call the prospect in order to set up an appointment for a sales interview	3.93	4.12
3. *Prospect's business:* Observe the prospect's business facilities while waiting to meet the prospect	3.99	3.75
4. *Other company salespeople:* Ask fellow company salespeople for some necessary information about a particular prospect	3.08	2.68
5. *Current customers:* Ask current customers for necessary information about a particular prospect	2.86	2.79
6. *Local newspapers:* Read local newspapers to obtain some necessary information about a particular prospect	2.68	2.79
7. *Personal visit/cold call:* Call personally on the prospect unexpectedly (i.e., go through the receptionist)	2.93	2.25
8. *Personal letter to prospect:* Write the prospect a letter introducing the salesperson and requesting a sales interview	2.61	2.72
9. *Other intermediaries:* Use mutual friends, lodge brothers, etc. to arrange the sales interview with the prospect	2.10	2.42
10. *Customer letter referral:* Have a present customer write a prospect introducing the salesperson and requesting a sales interview	1.95	2.44

*1 = not important; 5 = very important.

Source: Reprinted by permission of *Journal of Personal Selling and Sales Management* © 1985. R. Hite and J. Bellizzi. (1985). Differences in the importance of selling techniques between consumer and industrial salespeople. *Journal of Personal Selling and Sales Management. 5* (November), 19–30.

Maintaining Files on Prospects and Customers. The importance of maintaining customer files cannot be overemphasized. Although both of the textbook salespeople discussed at the beginning of this chapter had met with Professor Summers earlier, only one bothered to maintain information on her. In general, good files help you maintain ongoing relationships with valuable customers. With information from your file system, you can walk into a sales call on Mr. Smith and ask about his two children or his new house. This kind of personal information is flattering and shows that you are interested in your customer. If you have no files, it is easy to forget details about each customer. You can also miss sales opportunities when, for example, you have a new product that would be of interest to a customer but no source of information to check.

Your files should contain as much information as possible about the prospect or customer, her buying patterns, past purchases, and needs. For an existing customer, you can include all of the information mentioned earlier (who has the buying authority, etc.), as well as the following additional information, which can be helpful on future calls:

What interests the prospect?
What are good times to call on the customer?
Which kinds of presentations and persuasive strategies succeeded? Which ones failed?
What products is the customer currently using?[9]

Our successful book salesperson makes notes on every professor she meets immediately following the call, when facts are fresh in her mind. In the case of new prospects, some salespeople open files as soon as they obtain a person's name.

For Gretta Larson, who sells commercial real estate, the prospect file begins on the back of a business card. At social and business functions, Gretta always asks a potential prospect for a card before offering her own. That way, she compliments the prospect and avoids appearing pushy. But the prospect's card also serves as the foundation of a file. On the back of the card, Gretta writes the event at which they met, the date, and comments about the conversation. With this information, she has something to go on when she calls on the person.

Many modern salespeople, however, use some kind of computer-based filing system. The maintenance of up-to-date file systems has been made much easier with the advent of advanced technology. With increasing availability of personal and laptop computers and software programs for salespeople, it is becoming easier to maintain large amounts of information on each customer and prospect, and to access and update your files. (Chapter 14 discusses this in detail.)

Planning the Format of Your Sales Call

Once you have obtained the appropriate information, you can plan your actual presentation. In planning for the presentation, it is helpful to distinguish between *content* and *format.*

Many salespeople maintain their own computerized customer files. (Courtesy of International Business Machines.)

The presentation's **content** refers to the *ideas that are conveyed.* This includes various facts and figures, customer needs and product benefits, and so on.

The **format** of the presentation refers to the specific *method* used to convey these ideas. Formats can range from very formal, structured ones, in which the salesperson recites a memorized speech, to very unstructured ones, in which the salesperson blends information about the product into a more casual discussion with the prospect.[10, 11]

The pros and cons of each type of presentation format are analyzed in Chapter 9. At this point, however, we must consider the presentation's format because it has an important effect on the preapproach plan. The degree to which your presentation is formally structured determines how much of it must be planned in advance. In fact, one of the first things that must be determined during the preapproach planning stage is which format you will use during the presentation.

Planning for a Formal Presentation

If you plan to follow a formal, **structured** format, the presentation contents are completely determined during the preapproach plan. Because structured formats are based on the use of a memorized speech or predetermined audiovisual aids, it is difficult, if not impossible, to adapt ideas contained in the presentation during the sales call. In many cases, the highly structured presentation will be determined by company policy. The use of certain prepared materials, including written and audiovisual materials, may be required of all salespeople. If this is the case, the extent of your own presale planning may be limited. However, it is still beneficial to know as much about the prospect's interests and needs as possible.

Planning for the Unstructured Sales Call

You might think, at first, that an informal, **unstructured** sales call requires no preapproach planning. If your presentation format involves simply talking with the prospect, asking about needs, and discussing ways in which your product can meet those needs, why would a preapproach plan be necessary? The danger in this kind of thinking was evidenced by the textbook salesperson who dropped in on Professor Summers with no advanced planning.

The unstructured presentation requires a different kind of a plan, but it *does* require a plan. A common mistake made in selling is to underestimate the amount of planning required for an unstructured presentation. Since such a presentation does not force you to use the detailed, word-for-word planning required by the memorized presentation, it is possible to think only in very general terms about how you would handle various issues. But once face to face with the prospect, you would find yourself fumbling for words.

Put Your Ideas into Words. Having a general idea in mind is definitely not the same as having a message that can be communicated. In order for your ideas to be understood by a prospect, they must be *encoded* into a form that can be transmitted. This means that the ideas must be put into words and supported with nonverbal gestures—a process that does not occur automatically in the communication of new ideas or products.

For this reason, it is important to think specifically about how you will verbalize your ideas to the prospect. This process will obviously become easier as you gain experience in selling and repeatedly practice verbalizing ideas. However, even an experienced salesperson should make a detailed plan of how she will discuss new products or ideas.

Rehearsing the Unstructured Call

One way of ensuring that you will be able to put your ideas into words is to rehearse a sales call by role playing. Even if you rehearse with yourself, you will be forced to put ideas into words before you call on the prospect.

In rehearsing for the unstructured presentation, it is important to remember to plan for different contingencies. Because the unstructured presentation consists of an *interaction* with the prospect, you will have less control over the flow of information than you would if you were presenting a more formal, structured presentation. The prospect can direct the conversation in a number of different ways, and you must be prepared to follow up on any of them. In fact, your ability to handle a range of content areas takes on added importance in the unstructured sales call (see Table 7.5).

Table 7.5 Elements of the Unstructured Presentation That Can Be Planned

- A general outline of the sales call
- An opening line
- Several topics for general discussion when you first greet the prospect
- Alternative ways of introducing your product into the discussion
- Important points that you want to mention about your product
- The use of any audiovisual aids, supporting brochures, or product demonstrations
- Specific ways of handling commonly voiced objections
- Several alternative methods for closing the sale

Planning the Content of Your Sales Call

Whether your presentation is structured or unstructured, its content should demonstrate how your product can benefit the prospect. This means that you should enter your sales call with complete knowledge about your own product and those of your competitors.

Ideally, you will be able to gather the information about the prospect ahead of time and walk into the sales call fully prepared. If this is the case, your preparation for the content of the presentation can include actual solutions to the prospect's problems that you have already worked out. This was the case when a commercial real estate broker rented office space to a large accounting firm in New York City. She used information gained during an earlier call to create a successful call back.

Salesperson: Mr. Langhorn, the last time we spoke, you were still in the market for office space priced at around \$100 a square foot. Are you still looking?

Mr. Langhorn: Yes. Have you found something?

Salesperson: I certainly have. This is a large space in the heart of the financial district. It's on the 59th floor of the Graly Building, and the rent is \$110,000—\$110 per square foot.

Mr. Langhorn: What about my computer problem?

Salesperson: I know that was a problem with the last space I showed you. Here, it's no problem. In fact, I've noted on this copy of the floor plan some ideas about how you could fit in the computer area so that there would be no rewiring problems. (Shows floor plan and points.) See, this space would fit your two receptionists, and your library could go back here—with room to grow.

Mr. Langhorn: This looks great. When can I see it?

The salesperson in this case had obviously maintained a detailed file of prospects and their needs. She knew about Mr. Langhorn's computer, reception, and library requirements and was able to offer specific solutions in presenting the new office space. With so much advance preparation on the part of the salesperson, Mr. Langhorn realized that he would not be wasting his time if he went to visit the space. This kind of situation is not uncommon in a call back or a call to an existing customer. The salesperson in this case understood that relocating an entire accounting firm is a new task buying problem, and with this understanding, she designed the content of the presentation to solve specific problems.

Planning When Information Is Lacking

Obviously, you cannot always count on having such good preapproach information upon which to base the content of your presentation. What do you do in retail selling, for example, when you have no prior knowledge about the prospect, or if you are making a first call on a new prospect with little background information?

In general, the less information you have before you begin a sales interaction, the more you must depend upon the sales call as a source of information. As Table 7.4 showed, the prospect is the most important source of information. However, relying on your interaction with the prospect to obtain crucial information does *not* mean that you cannot be prepared. It simply means that instead of planning solutions to problems, your preapproach consists of the following:

Planning specific questions that will allow you to gather the information you need.

Planning *various alternatives* to discuss, depending upon which one fits best with the information you obtain.

This definitely is not the same as "winging it." In fact, it requires a great deal of knowledge about your product and the ways that it can be used to benefit prospects. The more you have anticipated and prepared for alternative responses from the prospect, the more successful you will be.

Consider what might have happened if our successful textbook salesperson had been making a first call on Professor Summers. Although she could have learned in advance what courses Professor Summers was teaching, she would not have known in advance how to *position* the textbooks to meet Professor Summers' specific needs. The interaction might have progressed like this:

Salesperson: I understand that you are teaching personal selling in the fall.

Professor Summers: Yes, I am.

Salesperson: Tell me, how do you approach this course? Do you use anything like cases or role playing?

Professor Summers: I rely heavily on role playing. My students seem to get a lot out of it.

Salesperson: Then you might be interested in our new personal selling textbook. One of its unique features is that it is full of role-playing exercises. Along with cases at the end of each chapter, there are at least two different role-playing exercises. (Points out role-playing exercise in the textbook.)

Professor Summers: Sounds interesting. May I look at it?

In this case, it turns out that Professor Summers uses role playing and not cases. But our textbook salesperson is not at a loss. She had prepared questions in her preapproach plan that would reveal how Professor Summers likes to teach the course. She had also planned alternative strategies. She was prepared to discuss different features of her textbook, depending upon the answers given by Professor Summers. Since the textbook had cases *and* role-playing exercises, she was able to position it to fit specific needs, but without preapproach planning, she might well have fumbled. She might not have prepared specific questions or anticipated all of the product knowledge she would need to respond to Professor Summers.

Planning Audiovisual Aids

In addition to planning the ideas needed for your presentation, you must decide whether your presentation will be accompanied by audiovisual aids, sales brochures, or a demonstration of the product. This planning may be as simple as deciding which textbooks to carry when visiting a specific professor, or it may be as complex as planning and developing an entire video presentation. In fact, modern technological advances make the use of sophisticated video demonstrations quite convenient for salespeople to use during a sales call, and audiovisual aids are becoming necessary competitive tools in many industries.

If you choose to use audiovisual aids during a sales call, preapproach planning is important for two reasons.

1. It is crucial to use audiovisual aids in ways that are relevant to the prospect. Videos, slides, and printed material can have tremendous impact when they are relevant but can detract from a presentation when they are not. Relevance comes from a knowledge of the prospect's needs and concerns, which, in turn, comes from preapproach planning.
2. Planning audiovisual aids and product demonstrations also helps to ensure that they will run smoothly during the sales call. If you wish to include a video or product demonstration, your preapproach plan should include thinking through the entire sequence of the sales call: *what* you will say, *when* and *how* you plan to introduce the audiovisuals, and whether and when you plan to ask the prospect for questions.

Although you may decide to deviate from your rehearsed sequence as you interact with the prospect, the planning process will help make things run more smoothly. It will also help guard against the occurrence of technical difficulties with equipment or, worse yet, with the product when you are face to face with the prospect.

Arranging an Appointment

The final stage of preapproach planning is setting up an appointment to meet with the prospect. When you reach this stage, several important issues must be addressed:

- Do you set an appointment in advance of the sales call?
- Do you set the appointment yourself, or does someone do it for you?
- What means do you use to ask for the appointment?

We discuss each of these questions in turn.

Should You Make an Appointment?

There are many advantages to making an appointment for your sales call. The most important one is that the prospect will tend to be more receptive if she has agreed in advance to see you. The appointment-making process acts, in this sense, as a screening device: only interested prospects will grant appointments.

But there is an additional reason why a prospect will be more receptive if you make an appointment. The appointment means that the meeting time is convenient to the prospect. There are many cases when a prospect would be more receptive to a sales presentation if the time or circumstances were different. When a sales call interrupts another activity, a prospect may say "no" simply in order to return to what she had been doing before the interruption.

As you learned in Chapter 5, expectations and perceptions play a surprisingly central role in the way a prospect will respond to your sales presentation. If you have telephoned in advance, made a good impression, and left the prospect interested in hearing what you have to say, that prospect will tend to perceive the same set of facts much more favorably than the prospect who was in the midst of doing something else when you made your approach.

However, despite these obvious advantages to prearranged appointments, there are many cases when salespeople make calls without them. This is because the use of appointments is frequently determined by industry custom. In certain industries, it is customary for salespeople to make calls without prearranged appointments. The textbook industry is an example. Salespeople who sell textbooks to professors typically visit a school and call on all of the professors who are available that day. If the salesperson attempted to arrange individual appointments in advance, the result would be an extremely inefficient calling schedule requiring many visits to the same school to see different professors. Although each professor might be more receptive, the cost of arranging a schedule in this way would outweigh any benefits.

Who Should Make the Appointment?

In some companies, a secretary or other staff person makes appointments for the salesperson. The advantage of this method is that it frees the salesperson for more productive activities. The use of this division of labor within the selling task is typically determined by sales managers or other persons higher up in the company. Many different arrangements are possible. Some companies use a centralized telemarketing staff to schedule appointments. Others use a department secretary.

In some cases, an individual salesperson might choose to hire a staff person to book appointments. This is not uncommon in high-stakes selling where the salespeople operate on a commission basis. In such cases, a single commission can total thousands of dollars, and a single extra sale can pay the salary of the assistant. Having this kind of autonomy is one of the great advantages of many sales jobs, which are almost like having one's own business within a business.

How Should the Appointment Be Scheduled?

There are three basic methods for requesting an appointment: by telephone, by mail, or in person.

Telephone. In a survey of retail and business-to-business salespeople, the telephone was rated as the favored method of scheduling appointments[12] (see Table 7.4, p. 188). This is not surprising in view of the advantages of using the telephone for this purpose. The primary advantage is the fact that the telephone allows *two-way communication.* Setting up an appointment time that fits the schedule of a busy prospect and a busy salesperson will typically require two-way negotiation. The telephone is well-suited to this purpose.

In addition, the telephone is personal. When you call to set up an appointment, the person at the other end of the line will begin to form an impression of you.

The telephone is a favored method of setting up appointments with prospects. (© Arthur Glauberman/Photo Researchers, Inc.)

Based on nonverbal qualities like loudness of voice, rapidity of speech, pitch of voice, and accent, that person will make judgments about your age, social class, intelligence, and personality.[13]

In order to use the telephone to advantage, it is important to be aware of this impression formation process and to control the impression that you are creating. Some salespeople who make extensive use of the telephone practice creating a favorable impression by recording and listening to their own voices.

In addition to your voice and accent, the content of what you say has obvious importance. This kind of telephone call should be simple and businesslike. This is not the time to try to sell your product. Instead, you should simply:

- Introduce yourself and your company.
- Mention something that will interest the prospect enough to keep him on the phone. (This can be the name of a personal reference, if you have one, or a simple, direct benefit statement.)
- Ask for the appointment.

Mail. As you might expect, there are many drawbacks to the use of mail for scheduling appointments. Most obvious is the fact that a letter is a form of *one-way communication.* Although an ongoing correspondence becomes two-way communication, busy prospects and salespeople do not have the time to engage in extended correspondence in order to schedule appointments. Mail also fails to convey a sense of urgency and importance in the modern world of fax machines and instantaneous communication.

However, there are several ways in which mail can be used. Some salespeople with very large geographic territories use mail to schedule appointments far in advance. If an appointment is requested for a date in the distant future, two-way negotiation may be unnecessary. The letter can simply inform the prospect that the salesperson will be in the territory on a certain date and ask the prospect to reserve some time. An advantage of mail is that it can be used to send promotional materials along with the request. Written materials can pique the prospect's interest and increase the chances that he will grant the appointment. As a result, some successful salespeople use mail to send promotional material prior to calling for an appointment. A reference to the mail can serve as an opening statement when the call is made.

In Person. It is possible to stop at a prospect's place of business and request an appointment for a later time. Although this may be preferable to the cold call in that the prospect will be expecting your presentation, it is generally an inefficient use of your time.

Putting It All Together

We can begin to put it all together by summarizing a few key points:

- The preapproach is the point where you begin to plan how the prospect can benefit from your product.

- During the preapproach, you set sales call objectives, gather information about the prospect, and plan your presentation accordingly.
- Typical industrial sales requires four or five calls before the deal is closed, and objectives must be planned accordingly.
- Companies have different buying patterns, different information requirements, and different concerns, depending upon whether they are engaging in straight rebuys, modified rebuys, or new task buys.
- Prior sales calls serve as valuable sources of information.
- Interactions with the prospect serve as valuable sources of information, especially if you are careful to maintain files.
- The type of planning that you can do depends on whether your presentation will be structured or unstructured.
- For structured presentations, most of the content is planned in advance.
- For unstructured presentations, you can plan questions, a general outline, and audio-visual aids. You can also prepare by role playing, and plan responses to alternative points that the prospect might make.

You can see by now that the preapproach involves combining information from many different sources, developing strategies, and solving problems. In order to simplify the process, many salespeople use some kind of planning form.

A typical planning form might include the following:[14]

- Identification of the prospect.
- Identification of the prospect's wants and needs.
- A list of features and benefits that would be most useful for this prospect.
- An opening statement aimed at getting quick attention and interest.
- Materials to take along.
- Forms of proof of the product's performance like testimonials.
- Any plan for asking for the order.

Recording all of this information may sound like a lot of work, but by now, you should appreciate the value of planning as a strategic activity. You should also be ready to put it all together.

In attempting to put planning together with the information presented in the previous chapters, a logical question is, "Thus far, the book has stressed the importance of adapting—that is, that the value of personal selling is supposed to be the ability of the salesperson to adapt to the situation. If I *plan* everything in advance, how can I adapt to the prospect?" The answer to this question comes from a quote by former President Dwight D. Eisenhower: "Plans are nothing; planning is everything." The point here is that planning would be valuable even if you sat down, wrote a plan, and then threw it away. Planning forces you to *anticipate* your information needs and develop your strategies in advance of your sales call.

In fact, the knowledge and information that come from planning are what actually allow you to adapt to your prospect during the sales call. As this chapter has shown, planning does not mean adopting a rigid outline that will keep you from responding to the prospect. Quite the opposite, as we saw in our textbook sales interactions: the salesperson who had planned was able to respond to the needs of the prospect. The salesperson who winged it could not.

Key Terms

Preapproach planning
Industrial Goods Classification
Straight rebuy
Modified rebuy
New task buy
Buying center
Content
Format
Structured presentation format
Unstructured presentation format

Review Questions

1. List five different sales call objectives and the circumstances under which each one might occur.
2. What role do file systems play in the preapproach?
3. Give two examples each of a straight rebuy, a modified rebuy, and a new task buy.
4. Who would have decision-making power in the design and outfitting of an operating room in a hospital?
5. What benefits should be stressed in a new task buy?
6. What is the difference between the format and the content of a presentation?
7. Why is it necessary to consider your presentation format in developing your preapproach plan?
8. Which elements can be planned prior to an unstructured sales call?
9. What are the advantages of using scheduled appointments?
10. Why is the telephone the favored method of scheduling appointments?

Discussion Questions

1. Is it possible to plan too much? Are there any costs for planning or any circumstances in which costs might outweigh the advantages?
2. Suppose you were working for a pharmaceutical manufacturer and were responsible for persuading physicians to prescribe your company's drugs. Your company has just introduced a new prescription pain killer, and your prospects include physicians in all specialties, as well as dentists. If you were making a first call on a specific doctor, how would you proceed? What would your objectives be? What information would you seek? Would you schedule an appointment?
3. If you worked for the same manufacturer as in question 2 but were responsible for selling the drugs to hospitals, how would you proceed? (Hint: Begin by deciding how you would classify the adoption of a new pain killer by a hospital according to the Industrial Goods Classification.)

CASE 7.1

Ed McFarley was a student majoring in marketing at a large state university. His specialty was sales; he had taken a course in personal selling and one in sales management. He also had experience selling cars in his father's showroom.

The summer following his junior year, he was offered a summer internship working for a small but growing marketing research firm. Megan Foster, the president of the firm, was a skilled market researcher but had little knowledge about sales. She did know enough, however, to realize that her search for new clients was really a selling problem. She considered hiring a full-time sales and public relations person, but decided to experiment with a summer intern in order to see whether a person with selling skills could bring in enough new business to justify the additional salary.

When Ed started to work for Megan's firm, Megan was in the midst of pursuing a major new account. A large department store chain, which was considering locating in Megan's city, was interested in doing a huge market research project in order to study its image. Megan had heard about the job through a friend of a friend, and it sounded as though the total budget could run as high as $50,000. Megan's firm was particularly well-suited to do the study, since several of the employees had a background in retailing as well as marketing research.

Megan did not want to lose the account because of her lack of selling expertise and had already begun to plan how to conduct the research, but she did not know anything about planning for the sales presentations she would have to make in order to win the account. Ed's job was to work out a detailed plan of how Megan should pursue the account. Megan provided Ed with the names of the department store's president, but that was where her help ended.

1. What should Ed do?
2. Whom should he contact?
3. What objectives should he set?
4. What kinds of sales calls should he plan, and how many?
5. What sources of information can he use in planning his approach?
6. Will a formal presentation be involved?
7. Will the purchase of this kind of marketing research service be a straight rebuy, a modified rebuy, or a new task buy?

References

1. Wagner, R., C. Rashotte, and R. Sternberg. (1988). Tacit knowledge in sales: Rules of thumb for selling to anyone. *Unpublished manuscript.*

2. Sujan, H., B. Weitz, and M. Sujan. (1988). Increasing sales productivity by getting salespeople to work smarter. *Journal of Personal Selling and Sales Management, 8*(2), 9–19.

3. Business-to-business. (1988). *Sales and Marketing Management, 140* (November), 27.

4. Sujan, H., M. Sujan, and J. Bettman. (1988). Knowledge structures differences between more and less effective salespeople. *Journal of Marketing Research, 25* (February), 81–86.

5. Anderson, E., W. Chu, and B. Weitz. (1987). Industrial purchasing. *Journal of Marketing, 51* (July).

6. Robinson, P., C. Ferris, and Y. Wind. (1967). *Industrial Buying and Creative Marketing.* Boston: Allyn & Bacon.

7. Anderson et al., op. cit.

8. Weitz, B., H. Sujan, and M. Sujan. (1986). Knowledge, motivation, and adaptive behavior. *Journal of Marketing, 50*(4), 174–191.

9. *Master Salesmanship.* (1988). *10*(3).

10. Jolson, M. (1973). Should the sales presentation be fresh or canned? *Business Horizons, 16*, 81–88.

11. Jolson, M. (1986). Structured sales presentations, in Walton Beacham et al. (eds.), *Business Research: Marketing*, Washington, DC: Research Publishing, pp. 942–947.

12. Hite, R., and J. Bellizzi. (1985). Differences in the importance of selling techniques between consumer and industrial salespeople. *Journal of Personal Selling and Sales Management, 5* (November), 19–30.

13. Leathers, D. G. (1988). *Successful Nonverbal Communication.* New York: Macmillan.

14. *Master Salesman.* (1988). *10*(3).

Planning: Persuasive Strategy

CHAPTER OBJECTIVES

In this chapter, you will learn:

Persuasion is concerned with changing attitudes.

Some aspects of persuasive strategy can be planned in advance, while others cannot.

Power is one of the more important aspects of persuasion.

The prospect is usually more powerful than the salesperson because the salesperson is more dependent upon the prospect.

The salesperson can achieve certain kinds of power.

It is essential for the salesperson to have credibility in order to persuade successfully.

The best selling style is one that is assertive.

During the sales interaction there are nine ways of gaining compliance from the prospect.

CHAPTER OUTLINE

A Sales Challenge

John Anderson is a sales representative for a large maker of commercial jet engines. Once an airline decides to buy new aircraft, his task is to convince the airline to equip the aircraft with his company's engines. There was a time when the company he represented had superior-quality engines. He enjoyed a certain degree of power over airline companies because he and they both knew that his company's engines were vastly superior to those of the competitors. He called the shots.

That is no longer the case. Now there are several competitors who make engines that are just as good as those of his company. John has found his sense of power to be considerably lessened. Now he faces prospects who are in a very good bargaining position. They have power. They call the shots. Of course, John still has various tricks up his sleeve. He can negotiate on price and delivery or maintenance. He has a facility for making prospects like him. He is able to be direct and assertive, yet he projects a sense of warmth and genuineness. Most prospects consider him to be very knowledgeable and trustworthy. In a word, he is credible.

John is also very good at negotiating. He knows when to offer incentives and when to retreat. He understands instinctively when and what to do to get the prospect to comply. When he meets resistance, he remains firm, but he knows when to quit. He has always been very careful not to push a prospect too far. While his selling task is more difficult than it was when his company was the maker of the best engines, it is also much more challenging. Interestingly, John is even more successful now.

An Overview

As you begin planning how to sell to your prospect, it should be clear that part of what you are really trying to do is to decide how to persuade the prospect. In other words, you are trying to develop a persuasive strategy. In fact, persuasion is probably the major goal in a sales interaction. The purpose of this chapter is to discuss persuasion and strategies of persuasion.

While it is not always possible to plan every detail of your persuasive strategy in advance, there are certain basic strategic decisions that can be planned. Some strategic decisions apply in most sales encounters and are subject to advance planning. Others depend upon the particular interaction of the salesperson and prospect and can't be planned. Yet, even in these cases, it is helpful at least to be aware of the various options. We begin this chapter by defining persuasion. We then talk about those aspects of persuasive strategy that can be planned in advance. Finally, we discuss specific strategies that may or may not be used, depending upon the particular sales interaction. These persuasive strategies cannot be planned in advance.

A Definition of Persuasion

We all have some general idea of what persuasion means. We know that when we attempt to persuade, we want to change the thinking or the behavior of another person. We may want to change his perception that a particular brand of chocolate is creamy. Or we may want him to prefer Coca-Cola to Pepsi. We may want him to buy an American car as opposed to a foreign car. In each case, we will need to persuade the person.

Persuasion Is Changing Attitudes

We define **persuasion** as *the process of influencing attitudes or behaviors.*[1] Recall from Chapter 5 that attitudes and behavior are very closely related. If we like something, we have a positive attitude toward it. We then consider some behavior or action. The behavior that a salesperson is looking for is a purchase. Usually, before she can get a prospect to agree to a purchase, she has to persuade the prospect that the purchase is worth his while. This requires that the salesperson first determine what the prospect's attitude is and, if necessary, persuade the prospect so that his attitude will change and he will buy (see Figure 8.1).

Many different attitude statements made by a prospect are subject to persuasion on the part of a salesperson. Following are examples of such statements:

> "I don't like IBM products because they're not very innovative."
> "I like the taste of this, but it's too fattening."
> "I'm not sure that this steel will hold up under the intense force."
> "We need a softer-texture wool for our expensive line of sweaters."

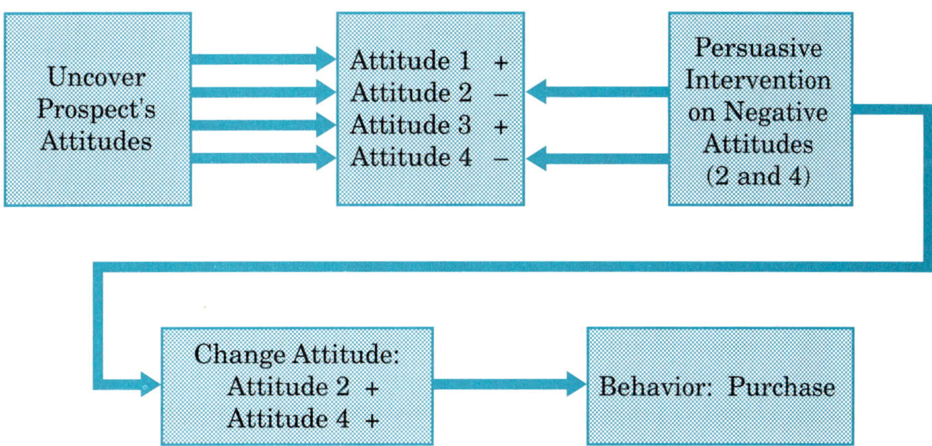

FIGURE 8.1 The relationship between attitudes and persuasion.

A salesperson has no reason to apply persuasive tactics to statements that express positive attitudes about his product. Instead, the salesperson focuses on statements that express negative attitudes about the product. Such statements are usually referred to as *objections.* The four attitude statements just listed are actually objections. As you will see in Chapter 11, objections are to be encouraged, since they give the salesperson an opportunity to zero in on specific attitudes that need to be changed before a purchase can occur.

The Role of Facts in Persuasion

Attitudes may be based, at least in part, upon facts. **Facts** are viewed as *things or events that can be observed and verified.*[2] You may have a positive attitude about IBM because you believe that IBM is a good company. This belief is likely based upon many impressions and experiences in addition to vague feelings. It may also be based upon facts, such as IBM's 1990 sales figures or an independent study on the quality of IBM products compared to those of Control Data. The impressions and feelings are not verifiable and not even clearly observable, while the facts about sales volume and product assessment are both verifiable and observable.

Persuasive communication is not concerned with changing facts. Facts can't be changed. Last year's sales figures are last year's sales figures, no matter what we say or do. However, facts can be used to make an argument more powerful. If, for example, IBM's sales figures for last year are dramatically higher than the figures for a year earlier, then the future looks promising. Thus, persuasion can change people's attitudes about the meaning of last year's sales volume.

Persuasive Strategy

A **persuasive strategy** is *a planned attempt to employ specific persuasive mechanisms.*[3] Some of these attempts can be planned in advance because they apply to most sales situations. The following mechanisms can be planned in advance:

1. Power.
2. Credibility.
3. Selling style.

Once a salesperson knows how much power she has, she knows how much persuasive clout she has. It is important to recognize that the advance planning for maximizing power depends to a great extent upon how much the salesperson knows about the prospect and his company. The more she knows, the better will be her planning of persuasive strategy.

Credibility is a necessary component of any successful attempt to persuade. There are a number of mechanisms that help a salesperson achieve credibility, and they exist regardless of the type of person the salesperson is talking to. The same is also true of selling style. Certain selling styles are generally regarded as

EXHIBIT 8.1

5 Power Points of Effective Persuasion

1. Develop a positive attitude. Believe in yourself and your company. When this happens, it will show, and you will be committed and enthusiastic.
2. Seek out prospects. Since everyone is a qualified prospect, it is up to you to qualify people and then sell to them.
3. Prepare yourself for the sale. Make sure you look good. It is important to make a good first impression. People will make judgments about character based upon appearance.
4. Perform your best. Think of yourself as being on stage, and always try to get a standing ovation.
5. Probe for customer needs. Price is not the only thing customers care about. Make an effort to get at the real needs of the customers.

Source: Adapted from D. W. Richardson. (1987). 5 power points of effective persuasion. *Sporting Goods Business*, *20* (February), 7–8.

superior. Aspects of persuasion that can be planned in advance are shown in Figure 8.2.

There are also persuasive strategies that cannot be planned in advance. These strategies involve specific mechanisms for gaining compliance and are usually referred to as *compliance-gaining strategies.* These strategies can't be planned in advance because the salesperson has no way of knowing the attitudes of a prospect until they begin to talk. However, by being aware in advance of the various compliance-gaining strategies and when to use them, the salesperson is

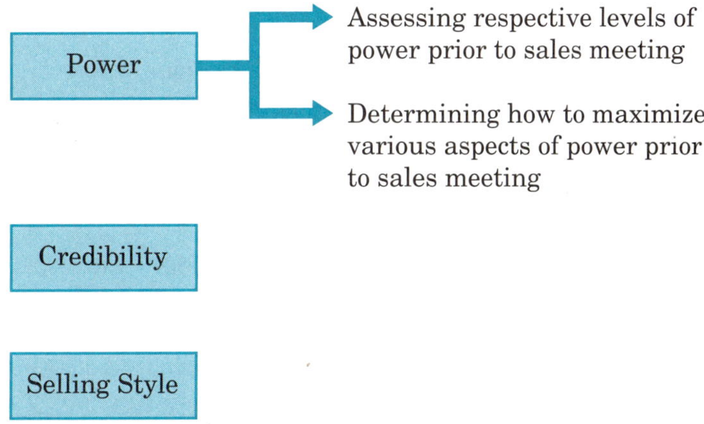

FIGURE 8.2 Persuasive strategies that can be planned in advance.

in a better position to persuade the prospect as she and the prospect converse. We begin the discussion of persuasive strategies with the first consideration that can be planned in advance: power.

Persuasive Strategies Planned in Advance: Power

Power is probably one of the major overriding concerns that affect the salesperson's ability to persuade the prospect. It is critical, therefore, for the salesperson to follow two steps before he meets a prospect:

1. He needs to evaluate carefully how much power he has at the outset of the sales interaction.
2. He needs to plan how to increase his power.

How much power he has will be important in determining how much persuasive effort he will need to exert. It will also have an effect on how successful his persuasive attempts are likely to be.

The Relationship Between Power and Persuasion

Usually the respective power of two people talking to one another is determined before they even begin their discussion. The degrees of power become obvious just by observing how much persuasive effort they have to engage in. For example, your boss doesn't have to work too hard to persuade you to do a particular task. Your instructor doesn't have to do too much to persuade you to write a term paper. Yet consider how much effort would be required for you to persuade your boss that you shouldn't perform the task or to persuade the instructor that you shouldn't have to do a term paper. The major factor that distinguishes you from your boss or your instructor is power. Both the boss and the instructor have power over you. Power, by itself, eliminates the need to exert a lot of effort with respect to persuasion. Lack of power requires a much greater persuasive effort. Figure 8.3 shows the relationship between power and persuasion.

If you evaluate the power of the salesperson versus the prospect, you will likely see a similar kind of situation. Usually, though not always, the prospect has

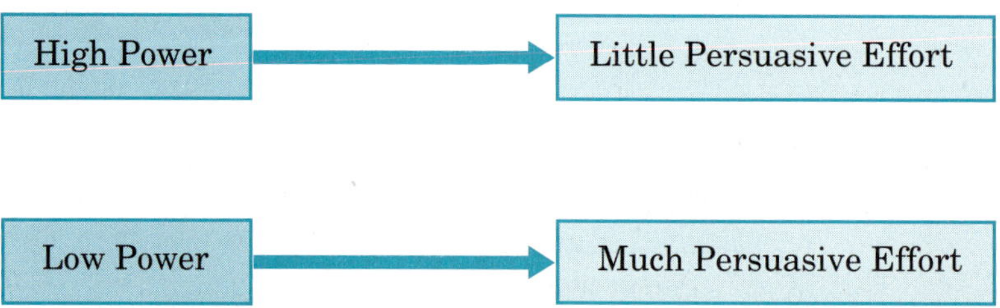

The relationship between power and persuasion.

more power than the salesperson. Since the less powerful person has the burden of influencing the more powerful person, it is most often the case that the salesperson has to make some effort in the persuasive task.

What exactly do we mean by **power?** *In an interpersonal relationship, such as that between a prospect and a salesperson, power is the capacity to influence the other person in that relationship.*[4] Influence can occur if one person can control either the rewards or the punishments of the other person.

A salesperson can control the rewards of the prospect by having the resources that would allow him to provide such things as free samples, discounts, favorable terms of sale, or even pleasant conversations and satisfying lunches involving business discussions. At the same time, of course, the prospect also has this kind of power, since she makes the decision to purchase or not to purchase, and purchase is the reward the salesperson is seeking. We need to consider more carefully, then, which person has more power, the salesperson or the prospect.

How to Determine Who Has More Power in a Two-Person Encounter

To determine who has greater power in any kind of encounter, we look to see who is more *dependent.* The more dependent person is the less powerful person. Thus, power and dependence are inversely related to one another. If the more dependent person is being persuaded, as in the case of an employee being persuaded by his boss, there is a greater likelihood of success. If the dependent person is doing the persuading, as is likely to be the case for a salesperson persuading a prospect, there is a greater likelihood of failure.[5] Figure 8.4 shows the relationship between power and dependence.

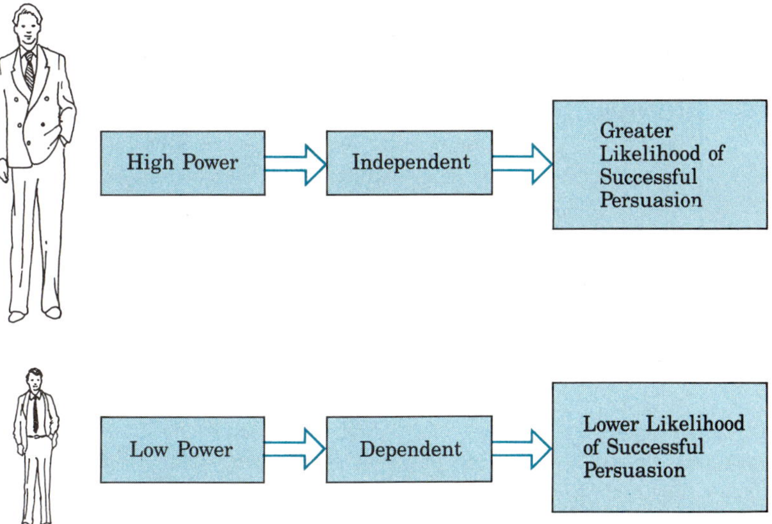

The relationship between power and dependence.

As we suggested, the prospect is not always more powerful than the salesperson. There are times when the prospect has a greater need to buy the product than the salesperson has to sell it. In such a case, the prospect is more dependent upon the salesperson. What we have to ask ourselves in evaluating the respective power of the salesperson and the prospect is: *which person has a greater need to make the sale?* In fact, this is the question that the salesperson needs to ask himself at the stage of preapproach planning. The person who has a greater need to make the sale is the more dependent person.

The Nature of the Sales Situation

To determine who has a greater need to make the sale, we need to categorize sales situations. We can identify four such categories:

1. The prospect contacts the salesperson because the prospect needs the product and the salesperson's product is the best on the market.
2. The prospect contacts the salesperson because the prospect needs the product. The product is similar to several others on the market.
3. The salesperson contacts the prospect. The prospect may or may not need the product but is not aware of this need. The salesperson's product is superior to others on the market.
4. The salesperson contacts the prospect. The prospect may or may not need the product but is not aware of this need. The salesperson's product is similar to others on the market.

It should be obvious that the power of the prospect increases directly as we move from the first category to the fourth (see Table 8.1). In the first situation, the salesperson has more power than the prospect, since the salesperson's product is superior to any competitive product (or is the only product available). In fact, this relationship does characterize certain situations in which, for example, a retailer has to convince a manufacturer to sell to her. This might be the case if a company has an exclusive product and wants to have a selective distribution pattern. A particular retailer, who does not have an appropriate image, might not be allowed to carry the product.

Table 8.1 Relationship Between the Salesperson's Power and the Nature of the Sales Situation

Sales Situation		*Power*	
Prospect's Need	*Product Quality*	*Salesperson*	*Prospect*
1. High	Best on the market	High	Low
2. High	Similar to others on the market	Medium	High
3. Low	Best on the market	Low	High
4. Low	Similar to others on the market	Low	Very high

EXHIBIT 8.2

Non-Manipulative Selling

Non-manipulative selling is based upon the philosophy that it is not desirable, or profitable, to manipulate people. There are basic distinctions between manipulative and non-manipulative selling that are easy to apply to any sales situation.

Manipulative Selling	*Non-Manipulative Selling*
me-oriented	you-oriented
tells	questions and listens
makes sales	makes customers
product-oriented	people-oriented
inflexible	adaptable
creates needs	discovers needs
creates fears and tensions	establishes trust and understanding

Source: Adapted from A. J. Alessandra and P. S. Wexler. (1978). Non-manipulative selling: A consultative approach to business development, *Proceedings of the American Marketing Association*, *42*, 59–61.

The second selling situation affords the prospect somewhat greater power than the salesperson. Here, although the prospect needs the product, alternative products are available. The salesperson has to convince the prospect that his offering is a better choice.

In the third selling situation, the prospect has even greater power over the salesperson, since the salesperson must first convince the prospect that the prospect needs the product. Once that occurs, however, the salesperson's work is done, since the salesperson's product is superior to the competition (or is the only product available).

In the fourth selling situation, the prospect has considerable power over the salesperson. In addition to convincing the prospect that he needs the product, the salesperson must convince the prospect that her product is the best available even though the prospect has viable alternatives.

Most retail situations fall into category 2. In retail settings, consumers go to the store (the salesperson); that is, they seek out the product so they are aware of their needs. The question hinges upon how many alternatives they have in terms of other stores that sell the product and/or in terms of how many other similar products exist. Industrial or trade situations may fall into any of the four categories.

The Bases of Power

We can probably conclude that, as we initially suggested, more often than not, the prospect has greater power than the salesperson. That, in turn, means that the salesperson is more dependent upon the prospect, and there is a greater likelihood that the salesperson's persuasive attempt will fail. Still, the salesperson is not without power resources. As we suggested, she can influence the prospect if she can control the rewards of the prospect. The rewards that she can control represent her resources. Methods by which these resources can be maximized should be planned in advance; this requires an understanding of the *bases of power.*

Almost 30 years ago, John French and Bertram Raven argued that power is not a simple concept but, instead, is based on several dimensions. The five dimensions they presented are still considered to be of paramount importance when the notion of power is discussed. The five are as follows: reward power, coercive power, legitimate power, referent power, and expert power[6] (see Figure 8.5). A sixth dimension was added and is called *information* or persuasion power.[7] We will discuss each basis.

Reward Power

Reward power, as its name indicates, is *the ability to provide a reward.* We know from learning theory that whenever we are rewarded for something, we are more likely to repeat our behavior. Reward is encouraging. Not surprisingly, reward is a basic factor in all of our lives and is probably the basis of much of what we know and do. Reward is what causes us to seek out something again and again.

Skinner has shown that reward is so powerful that even pigeons can be taught to peck only certain color bars because of the promise of reward in the form of food. Humans are very similar, although our rewards are considerably

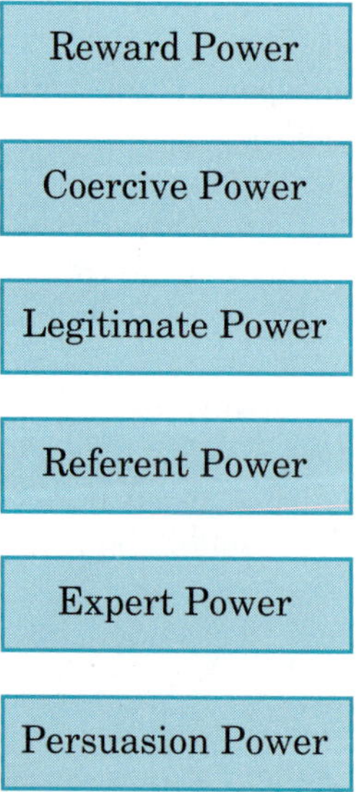

FIGURE 8.5 The bases of power.

Reward is a powerful force that causes animals and humans to behave in specific ways. (Omikron/Photo Researchers, Inc.)

more elaborate than those of pigeons. While food can serve as a reward, so, too, can such things as money, personal recognition, intellectual satisfaction, and career achievement. In terms of power, then, reward power is important. And the more reward someone can provide, the greater the power that person has.

Certainly a prospect has reward power simply because her decision to purchase is rewarding to the salesperson. And the larger her purchase, the more the salesperson is rewarded. But the salesperson can also provide reward to the prospect. He can offer various incentives to the prospect, such as quantity discounts, free samples, on-site training, or elaborate service policies. Reward tends to be a two-way street. That is, if you reward someone, chances are that he will reward you. This is referred to as the **norm of reciprocity.**[8]

The Norm of Reciprocity. We all tend to feel that *if someone does something for us, we owe it to them to do something in return. In other words, we reciprocate.* Reciprocation has actually become a rule in our society. It can take many forms. For example, the exchange of Christmas gifts is based, in part, on the norm of

The norm of reciprocity is part of the basis of exchange of gifts. (Rhoda Sidney/ Monkmeyer Press Photo.)

reciprocity. Many of us have been in the position of unexpectedly receiving a gift without giving one in return. We tend to feel very uncomfortable in this situation because we have violated the norm of reciprocity.

The norm of reciprocity also operates in business situations. It can entail buying a client a drink after the client has done the same for you. It can even exist at the level of saying hello to someone who has smiled at you.

Generally, people reciprocate by giving something roughly equal to what they received. This is particularly true in more formal relationships such as that between a salesperson and a prospect.

As an example, if you, as a salesperson, give your prospect a free sample of your product, the prospect would perceive this as a reward. Because of the norm of reciprocity, the prospect would feel a sense of obligation to give you something of similar value. This could involve increasing his order or giving you repeat business. Figure 8.6 shows various situations involving the norm of reciprocity.

Coercive Power

Coercive power is somewhat similar to reward power, but it *has to do with punishment rather than reward.* For the most part, coercive power is not part of the sales interaction, although there are some exceptions. Occasionally, the prospect may become so dissatisfied with the salesperson that she may discontinue her business. That could be viewed as punishment by the salesperson, and the prospect would therefore have coercive power.

"Hello"	Smile
Buy a Drink for Other	Buy a Drink for Other
Give Gift to Other	Give Gift to Other
Give Free Sample	Increase Size of Order
Buy Other Person Lunch	Buy Other Person Dinner
Extend Hand	Shake Extended Hand

FIGURE 8.6 The norm of reciprocity is very pervasive.

There are cases where a powerful manufacturer can force a retailer to carry a product. This is done by allowing the retailer to carry a product he regards as very desirable only if the retailer will also carry a product that he would prefer not to carry. While this practice is illegal, it does occur and is a form of coercive power. For the most part, however, coercion is not a major form of power between a salesperson and a prospect.

Referent Power

The third kind of power, **referent power,** is based on similarity. Referent power *has to do with the extent to which one person identifies with or wants to be like the other.* The more one person causes the other to identify with her, the more power she has. One major reason why someone would have referent power is because that person herself is somehow associated with a powerful person or institution or an excellent product. For example, if we were to compare J.D., a salesperson selling paper clips, to L.W., a salesperson selling Rolls Royce engines for aircraft, we would expect L.W. to have more referent power than J.D. This would be particularly true if L.W. were a close personal friend of Margaret Thatcher. In such a case, a prospect talking to L.W. would probably be inclined to identify with L.W.

Similarity. However, for identification to take place, there must first be some degree of similarity. It is not likely that a construction worker will identify with a corporate lawyer because the two people are too dissimilar. But a third-year law student might identify with that same corporate lawyer because there is some

These two people are not likely to identify with one another because they are probably too dissimilar. (© Ed Lettau/Photo Researchers, Inc.)

degree of similarity. A prospect who is the director of corporate purchasing is more likely to identify with a salesperson who is a director of marketing than with a salesperson who is a recent college graduate.

In the sales interaction, it is up to the salesperson to communicate similarity to the prospect. When this happens, the prospect is more likely to identify with the salesperson, and the salesperson will have achieved referent power. The prospect has no particular need to establish referent power except in those rare situations in which the salesperson is reluctant or unwilling to sell something to the prospect.

Rapport. The approach phase of the sales interaction (see Chapter 9) is really concerned with establishing rapport—a relationship built on mutual trust and understanding. The essence of building rapport is communicating that the two parties have much in common, that is, that they are similar. The greater the sense of rapport that a salesperson can convey, the greater is his referent power. How can the salesperson establish rapport through similarity?

To begin, the more a salesperson knows about the prospect, the more opportunity he will have to communicate similarity. Part of the goal of the preapproach phase of the sales interaction is to learn as much about the prospect as possible. Bases for similarity include the existence of family and children, hobbies and interests, and personality characteristics. For example, prospects may have pictures of their children in their offices. Such pictures provide an opportunity for the astute salesperson to initiate a discussion about the family. In that discussion, the salesperson can communicate similarity by mentioning his own children. The same thing can be done with respect to interests such as golf, tennis, or photography.

Social Class. An important concern in establishing similarity is social class. Generally, people of similar social class backgrounds feel some similarity. Social class is difficult to observe, but there are some critical indicators.

One's choice of clothing is one of the most obvious indicators. For that reason, the salesperson's choice of dress is important. While any salesperson should always be well-dressed, the exact choices of clothing should be made with some attention to the prospect's manner of dress, if that information is available. Hair style is also an indicator of social class, and it deserves the same attention as dress.

Another indicator of social class is speech patterns, especially accented speech. There are various regional accents; some of them are associated with higher social class and others with lower social class. While it is not easy to change one's accent, it may be desirable, particularly if one is going to deal with prospects who are consistently of a higher social class.

Liking. One of the major benefits of communicating similarity and achieving referent power is that these two things lead to liking. All things being equal, it is better to like than to dislike a business associate. Most people prefer to buy a product from a salesperson they like.

Following are two dialogues that illustrate how similarity and referent power can be achieved (Dialogue I) or not achieved (Dialogue II).

DIALOGUE I

SALESPERSON: Hello, Mr. Samuels. I am glad we could meet today. (*Noticing the prospect's desk.*) It always amazes me how people's desks appear so different. You seem to have yours very organized. I have been to some offices where the desks are just piled with papers in random order. My desk looks like yours. I guess I need to have things around me organized.

PROSPECT: Yeah, I know what you mean. My boss has a desk that is a mess. That would drive me crazy.

SALESPERSON: I actually get nervous if I start to have too many stray pieces of paper on my desk. I guess I can be a little compulsive.

PROSPECT: I do the same thing. But I can't help but believe that people who are sloppy about that sort of thing must be less efficient than those of us who are compulsive.

DIALOGUE II

SALESPERSON: Hello, Mr. Samuels. I am glad we could meet today. I always pride myself on remembering all my appointments, even though I never can find the piece of paper where I write them down. My desk is a mess. I just don't have time to straighten it up, and if I let my secretary do it, she'll make it so neat that it makes me uncomfortable.

PROSPECT: I couldn't stand having a desk like that. My boss is like that, and it would drive me crazy. I guess he knows where everything is, but that disorganized look is sure intimidating to me.

SALESPERSON: Well, we disorganized people usually have it all laid out in our heads.

PROSPECT: I guess you have to. But for me, it would make me pretty inefficient.

The first dialogue clearly gives the prospect some sense that the two parties are similar, and we would predict that the prospect will like the first salesperson better than the second one. Notice that the first dialogue demonstrated how a salesperson can be astute and notice certain things or listen for things that provide an opportunity to communicate similarity (see Figure 8.7).

It should be understood that not all prospects welcome such similarity. They may prefer to maintain distance and formality. If that is the case, the salesperson should suspend nontask, rapport-building talk and pursue the issue at hand. In such situations, the salesperson will simply have to accept that he will not be able to achieve referent power with this particular prospect.

Expert Power

Expert power is defined by *how much knowledge one has.* Clearly, a salesperson must have and is expected to have knowledge of her product and the competing products. In addition, a salesperson is expected to know about the prospect and the prospect's needs. This knowledge must be developed before the salesperson sees the prospect. In order for this knowledge to provide expert power, though, the salesperson must be knowledgeable *beyond what is expected.* If the salesperson merely meets expectations, she is probably not perceived as having expert power.

In order to know what the expectations are, it is necessary first to determine what the prospect knows. If the salesperson knows a great deal more than the prospect, possibly in terms of technical information, she has expert power. Note that the salesperson must be perceived as truthful in order to have expert power.

Obviously, the prospect can also have expert power. If the prospect is, in fact, more knowledgeable than the salesperson, the prospect has this kind of power. In that case, the salesperson is at a considerable disadvantage (unless, of course, the salesperson's offering is the best available and is strongly needed by the

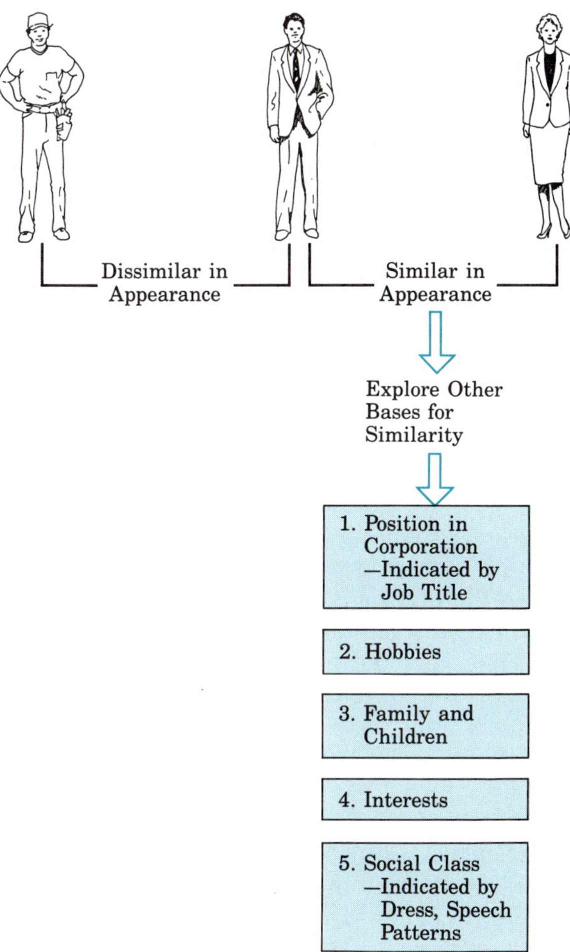

FIGURE 8.7 How to achieve similarity.

prospect). There is, however, no particular reason why a salesperson, no matter how knowledgeable a prospect, cannot have expert power.

Persuasive Power

Persuasive power, also called **information power,** is the *power to present an argument logically and persuasively.* If a salesperson is known to have the ability to persuade a prospect, then the salesperson has persuasive power. That would be the case in long-term relationships in which the salesperson has consistently persuaded the prospect through the use of convincing logic.

What is important about this kind of power is that it implies that a logical argument is more compelling than an emotional argument. Emotional arguments may work on the spot, but, in the long run, they are less desirable, particularly if the salesperson expects to develop a long-term relationship with the prospect.

Legitimate Power

Legitimate power *occurs when someone is considered to have the right to make requests.* Professors have legitimate power over students, parents have legitimate power over children, and bosses have legitimate power over subordinates. Generally speaking, a salesperson does not have legitimate power over a prospect, nor does a prospect have legitimate power over a salesperson. Thus, legitimate power is not a major factor in the sales interaction.

There may be exceptions to this situation, depending upon the respective status of the salesperson and the prospect within their own organizations. A salesperson who is executive vice president in charge of marketing has more status within his organization than a prospect who does clerical work recording orders for magazine subscriptions. Although the prospect can still make the purchase decision, the lower-status prospect may feel considerably less powerful than a prospect in a status similar to that of the salesperson. This fact can also work to the disadvantage of the salesperson if her prospect has a much higher status in his organization than does the salesperson. Nevertheless, since the salesperson and the prospect are in different organizations, even their status differences do not really constitute legitimate power.

Summary of Power

We can summarize the discussion so far by saying that of the six bases of power discussed, the salesperson has the potential to develop his own source of power, particularly through the following: expert power, reward power, referent power, and persuasion power. Coercive power and legitimate power are not major factors.

Although we have been focusing on the salesperson, it must be kept in mind that the prospect can also depend upon the same bases of power. The prospect can be more knowledgeable than the salesperson (expert power). The reward potential of the prospect's purchase may far outweigh any reward power the salesperson can offer. The prospect can also demonstrate logically and persuasively why the salesperson's product is inferior (persuasive power). Table 8.2 summarizes the power balance issue.

Planning how to maximize the four kinds of power is relatively straightforward. The salesperson should establish referent power almost immediately. As mentioned, this occurs during the approach phase of the interaction as rapport is being established. Anything the salesperson can do to establish similarity is desirable here. If the salesperson has engaged in advance planning and has learned about the prospect, he should have a number of options for establishing referent power.

As soon as the actual presentation begins, it is important for the salesperson to establish expert power. Since the goal of the salesperson is to be more knowl-

Table 8.2 Who Has and Who Needs What Kind of Power

	Who Has the Power Initially	*Who Can Achieve This Power*
Reward power	Both	Both
Coercive power	Neither	Neither
Legitimate power	Neither	Neither
Referent power	Neither	Salesperson
Expert power	Either	Both
Persuasion power	Neither	Both

edgeable than the prospect, he first needs to learn how much the prospect knows. Presale planning may reveal this. If it can't be determined during the preapproach stage, the salesperson can ask a direct question, such as "How familiar are you with __?" The salesperson can then provide factual information that the prospect is not likely to have. In so doing, the salesperson will be establishing expert power.

It is also during this phase that persuasion power can be communicated through the use of convincing logical arguments. As suggested, the salesperson should avoid presenting emotional appeals. Instead, the salesperson should use information and facts to help solve the prospect's problems. (Chapter 10 provides detailed information about problem-solving techniques.) The more facts a salesperson can bring to bear upon reasons to purchase the product, the greater will be the salesperson's persuasion power. The information necessary to achieve expert power and persuasion power must be gleaned before the salesperson sees the prospect. The salesperson will have no opportunity to learn new facts about his product or a competing product once he begins talking to the prospect.

Reward power becomes especially useful when the salesperson and prospect begin to negotiate the actual terms of the sale. For example, the salesperson can give various incentives, such as free samples, in order to induce the prospect to make even a small purchase. The salesperson can also give a quantity discount if the prospect is willing to increase the size of her order. The advance planning that the salesperson has to engage in is simply a matter of determining the acceptable discount level and the amount and kinds of incentives that he can provide. Figure 8.8 shows the power equation.

Persuasive Strategies Planned in Advance: Credibility

In any persuasion attempt, it is necessary to devise a strategy that will help the persuader achieve **credibility.** As we mentioned in Chapter 5, credibility is based upon *expertise* and *trust.*

Trust is especially important if prospects feel that a purchase has some degree of risk. It is difficult to achieve trust instantaneously, but one strategy that can be used effectively is called **trust transference.**[9] This strategy *relies on a source separate from the salesperson to enhance sales points.* An example would be a

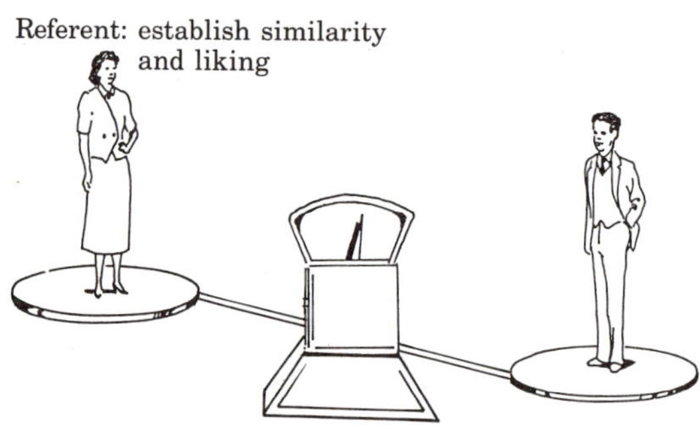

FIGURE 8.8 The power equation.

report from an independent lab or an unsolicited testimony from another purchaser or corporation.

Eventually, though, the salesperson needs to earn trust herself. Once a salesperson is considered to be credible, she will necessarily be trusted. The concern, then, is how the salesperson can establish credibility.

How to Establish Credibility

Because credibility is so important in the persuasive communication process, it has been explored through a great deal of research. One finding of this research is that credibility is not based upon expertise and trust alone but, instead, has at least five dimensions. Following is an explanation of those dimensions.[10]

1. **Competence** refers to *knowledgeability and capability.* Expertise is one aspect of competence. In general, we tend to accept the opinions of people we judge as competent. We also are less likely to try to influence a person who we think is more competent than we are in a particular area. Hence, a prospect may offer less resistance when faced with a competent salesperson.
2. **Character** is as important as, if not more important than, competence. Here we are concerned with the *person's essential goodness and decency.* These traits are strongly related to trust. In the sales situation, character emerges when a salesperson first approaches a prospect during the rapport-building stage. But character is also communicated during the presentation when the salesperson has to handle objections and refer to the competition. For ex-

EXHIBIT 8.3

Selling Your Viewpoint

When we negotiate, we are selling. Our goal is to sell our point of view. Here is how to do it:

1. Talk and listen more.
2. Don't interrupt.
3. Don't be belligerent.
4. Don't be in a hurry to bring up your points.
5. Restate the other person's position and objectives as soon as you understand them.
6. Identify the key point and stick to it.
7. Don't digress from the key point, and keep the other person from digressing.
8. Be for a point of view, not against one.

Source: Adapted from C. L. Karrass. (1987). The hardest sell of all is selling your point of view. *Purchasing, 103*(7), 43.

ample, if the salesperson belittles the competition consistently, we would begin to question his motives and, ultimately, his character.

3. **Sociability** refers to the *perception of the person as friendly, likable, and pleasant.* Even though a sales encounter is a business deal, people can also get some enjoyment out of it just because we all need to affiliate with other people. That need would not be satisfied if we encountered an unfriendly salesperson. This dimension is most likely to appear during the approach stage of the encounter.
4. **Composure** is also a desirable quality. This has to do with the *person's degree of emotional control.* What we are looking for here is a sense that the person is confident, poised, and relatively relaxed. A person who lacks composure is nervous and tense. Lack of composure might cause a prospect to question a salesperson's character. It is also possible for a salesperson to have too much composure. When people appear too confident and relaxed, they also appear to be superior. Since the prospect is usually the more powerful person, a superior salesperson might not be well received. Further, such a person might be perceived as cold and unfriendly.
5. **Extroversion** has to do with *how outgoing a person is.* Extroverted people tend to be somewhat bold and talkative, while introverted people tend to be shy. We generally find people who are extroverted to be more credible than those who are introverted. Here, too, however, there is a limit to how extroverted we want a salesperson to be. A person who is too extroverted, like the

stereotyped used-car salesperson, becomes overbearing and, as a result, less credible. Table 8.3 summarizes the dimensions of credibility and shows their relationship to power.

Planning and Credibility

While establishing credibility at the initial stages of an interaction is important, it should continue during the entire interaction. In trying to devise a strategy to communicate these various dimensions of credibility, the salesperson has to understand that different prospects will respond differently.

As with power, advance planning to achieve credibility requires a great deal of knowledge about the product, the competition, and the prospect. Achieving credibility is actually related to maximizing power, as discussed earlier. Competence is related to expert power and is communicated by the salesperson's degree of knowledge. Character is related to expert power, referent power, and persuasion power.

It should be understood that it is not always possible to know what a prospect is like as a person until the salesperson actually meets him. Advance planning is still necessary to achieve competence and character, but the salesperson may have to determine the appropriate levels of sociability, composure, and extroversion as she is talking to the prospect.

Persuasive Strategies Planned in Advance: Selling Styles

Salespeople tend to develop their own unique styles. It is possible to divide these styles into four categories. This is accomplished through a *dimensional model* of sales behavior,[11] which is presented in Figure 8.9. The two dimensions of this model are *hostile* versus *warm* and *dominant* versus *submissive.* Dominant salespeople take control in interpersonal encounters by being forceful, while submissive salespeople let others take control by not being assertive. Warm salespeople display concern for others by communicating sensitivity and caring, while

Table 8.3 What Contributes to Credibility and Its Relationship to Power

Power		*Credibility*	
Expert	→	Competence:	knowledge and expertise
Referent, Persuasive	→	Character:	essential goodness and decency
		Sociability:	friendliness, likableness, and pleasantness
		Composure:	degree of emotional control
		Extroversion:	degree of talkativeness and boldness

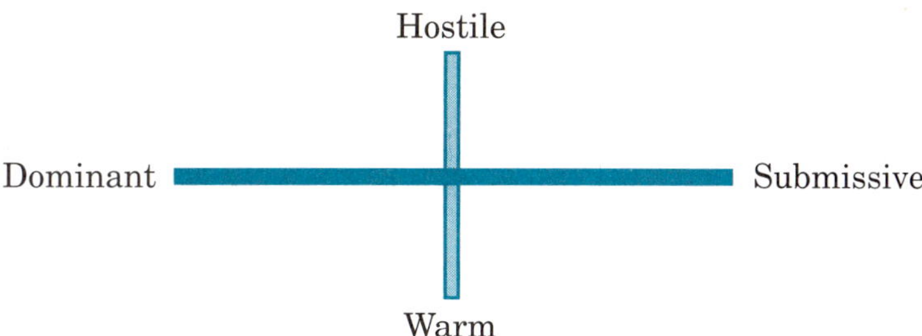

FIGURE 8.9 The dimensional model of sales behavior.

hostile salespeople don't display any concern for others and communicate that their own needs come first.

Salespeople can be categorized as dominant-hostile, dominant-warm, submissive-hostile, or submissive-warm. Recall that in Chapter 3, where we talked about relational communication, we explained that dominance and submissiveness are very important in all interpersonal encounters. Thus, it is not surprising that the dominant-submissive dimension figures prominently in categorizing a salesperson's selling style.

Jolson has argued that aggressive salespeople tend to be dominant-hostile.[12] Such people prefer never to give the prospect a chance to talk. All they wish to do is to communicate the virtues of their product or service. As a result, they have little or no opportunity to tailor their discussions to the needs of their prospects.

Submissive salespeople, while often skilled at socializing, particularly if they are also warm, are not especially enthusiastic or forceful. Whether they are warm or hostile is not as important as the fact that they are submissive. They behave submissively even when their prospects would prefer that they behave in a dominant manner and take control of the discussion. Such salespeople are not likely to generate a satisfying encounter for the prospect.

The ideal style, according to Jolson, is the dominant-warm style. People who use this style are assertive. Such people put the prospect at ease and establish rapport because of their concern and caring. They comfortably allow a true *exchange* of information and, at the same time, they avoid exaggeration. We suggest that such people are probably able to shift back and forth between dominance and submission, depending upon the demands of the interaction and the prospect's behavior. The hallmark of success is the ability to be flexible rather than insisting upon one particular style. Assertive people appear to have that flexibility and, while they are most likely dominant-warm, they can, if necessary, also be submissive-warm.

While an assertive style requires flexibility *during the course of the interaction*, a general approach to being assertive requires advance planning. Many sales training programs provide methods to cultivate assertiveness. A salesperson can practice assertiveness in encounters that do not involve actual selling. It is important for a salesperson to remember that assertive behavior is indicated both by warmth and dominance and, when necessary, by submissiveness.

Persuasive Strategies with No Advance Planning: Compliance Gaining

Compliance-gaining strategies are *tactics employed to get people to give in to requests,* including, of course, requests to make a purchase. Nine of these strategies[13] will be explained.

1. *Direct request.* This is the most straightforward strategy. It is conveyed in statements such as "Can I put you down for an order?" or "Are you interested in making the purchase?" This is a desirable strategy because it requires no manipulation of the prospect. It is best to use a direct request if a salesperson doesn't sense too much resistance on the part of the prospect. A direct request is also reasonable when the prospect is not behaving in a dominant manner.
2. *Supporting evidence.* This strategy involves using reasons why the prospect should comply. Reasons include logic, reasoning, evidence, and data. Use of this strategy is related to persuasion power, discussed earlier. Statements such as "The performance evaluation by an independent tester showed our product to be superior" would provide supporting evidence. Often a salesperson will use a direct request after providing supporting evidence. When a salesperson is dealing with a dominant or resistant prospect, supporting evidence should be used.
3. *Exchange.* This strategy involves direct negotiation and is related to reward power. It includes statements such as "If you're prepared to sign a contract now, you can take advantage of our 10 percent discount" or "If you order 500 more, we can give you a 5 percent quantity discount." This strategy is recommended in cases where the salesperson and prospect are comfortable with one another and when the salesperson expects to maintain a long-term relationship with the prospect.
4. *Face maintenance.* To use this strategy, the salesperson would refer explicitly to the prospect's good qualities or attempt to flatter the prospect. Examples include statements such as "You are clearly very knowledgeable about these products, so I guess I don't have to convince you about how good our product is" or "I'm told that you've been a major factor in helping your company. I think we have something that can help you out even more." This strategy should be used very cautiously. It can fail because the prospect may realize that he is being flattered so that the salesperson can make the sale. If no other strategy seems to work, this one can be employed.
5. *Distributive.* This strategy utilizes coercion and is related to coercive power. Statements employing this strategy include "I expect that your boss won't be pleased if you decide to switch to one of our competitors" or "We've been selling to your company for 20 years; I can't believe that you're thinking of

dealing with XYZ." Since coercive power is not a major factor in sales situations, this strategy has to be used with even more caution than face maintenance. It should be employed only as a last resort.

6. *Indirect tactics.* This involves hinting to the prospect what the salesperson wants the prospect to do. Generally speaking, it is not a necessary or a desirable strategy because the prospect knows from the beginning that the salesperson wants compliance in the form of purchase. In other words, the salesperson's goals are known at the outset. If, however, the prospect knows that the salesperson has a great deal to gain from the sale, the salesperson may opt for an indirect request. The request could be a statement such as "I'm glad you agreed to try at least one. It's surprising how many people purchased several of these."
7. *Empathic understanding.* This appeals to the prospect's liking of the salesperson. Obviously, it works only when a long-term relationship has already been established. Examples are statements such as "Have I ever sold you anything you were unhappy with?" or "Have I ever led you astray?" This strategy should be reserved for situations where there is a great deal of resistance from the prospect and when the item being sold is one that will be used for a long time.
8. *Referent influence.* As suggested by its name, this strategy is based on referent power. It involves making an explicit statement about the similarity between the salesperson and the prospect, such as "I had a setup just like yours, and I bought this model and found it was perfect" or "Like you I'm sort of compulsive, and I found this to be a perfect solution." Referent influence can be used along with other strategies. If a salesperson has been successful in achieving referent power, referent influence is simply a way of putting it to work.
9. *Other-benefit.* This strategy shows how compliance will benefit the prospect. It is similar to supporting evidence. It can and often does accompany other strategies, since part of the task of selling involves showing how the product will benefit the prospect. Statements such as "This product will really simplify your life" or "What's so great about this is its speed" are other-benefit statements. Table 8.4 provides a summary of these compliance-gaining strategies.

As we suggested, it is possible and, in fact, likely that a salesperson will use more than one and even more than two of these strategies. Which strategy or strategies are used and when depends on how the conversation progresses. Some of these strategies are employed when the sales process reaches the close stage, while others are employed during the presentation stage. Whether to employ one or more of these strategies and if so, which ones, can't be determined in advance. It depends upon what objections the prospect raises. It is helpful, however, to know in advance what each strategy is and when and how it can best be employed. Some of these strategies do depend upon knowledge, and that can only be gained before the sales encounter.

Table 8.4 Compliance-Gaining Strategies

Type	*Example*
Direct Request	"Can I put you down for an order?"
Supporting Evidence	"This air conditioning system has been shown to be 20% more effective than any other on the market by two governmental testing agencies."
Exchange	"If you order 500 or more, we can give you a 5% discount"
Face Maintenance	"You've really done your homework. I guess its safe to assume you're aware that we really have a good product."
Distributive	"Your boss happens to be a very good friend of the president of our company. I don't think he would be real pleased if you switched to a competitor."
Indirect Tactics	"Most people have wanted at least a two-year supply. Would you be interested in a two-month supply?"
Empathic Understanding	"I've never sold you anything you were unhappy with before. I certainly wouldn't do it now."
Referent Influence	"I use this model myself. Its really been a boon to my business. I'm sure it will do the same for you."
Other Benefit	"You'll be amazed at how this will free you up for other activities."

Compliance-Resisting Strategies Employed by the Prospect

It should be kept in mind that compliance-gaining strategies may likely be met with compliance-resisting strategies. In other words, the prospect will not always give in to the salesperson's attempt to get compliance. The prospect may resist by using three techniques:

1. *Justification,* in which the prospect explains why she will not comply.
2. *Negotiation,* in which the prospect wants some form of additional accommodation.
3. *Nonnegotiation,* in which the prospect simply refuses to comply.[14]

A nonnegotiation strategy is probably the most difficult to deal with, because it communicates not only an unwillingness to purchase but also an unwillingness to have further discussion. When a prospect uses a nonnegotiation strategy, the salesperson may have to discontinue the discussion rather than risk irritating the prospect.

The negotiation and justification strategies leave the prospect open to additional compliance-gaining attempts by the salesperson. The salesperson may wish to engage in *repeated attempts.* These repeated attempts will probably rely on

Table 8.5 Courses of Action for the Salesperson When the Prospect Resists Compliance

Compliance-Resisting Strategies of the Prospect	*Salesperson's Response*
Justification	Face maintenance, distribution
Negotiation	Face maintenance, distribution
Nonnegotiation	No further compliance-gaining attempt

face maintenance or distributive strategies, unless the salesperson is dealing with a long-term relationship, in which case he will more likely rely on reward strategies.[15] Table 8.5 shows what the salesperson can do, depending upon what compliance-resisting strategy the prospect uses.

Often the salesperson can be more deliberate in his approach to compliance gaining. If compliance resistance is expected, then the salesperson should initially plan on some *sequential strategy.* One is called the **foot-in-the-door strategy.**[16] This strategy *involves initially asking for a small request. When it is granted, the salesperson makes a larger request.* For example, a salesperson might ask a prospect to fit just one office with new flexible partitions. Once the prospect agrees, the salesperson might persuade the prospect to try the partitions on the entire floor.

The opposite strategy is the **door-in-the-face strategy.** Here the salesperson *asks for a very large request that is likely to be refused.* The salesperson should be careful, though, that the request not be so large that it appears absurd. *Once the request is refused, a smaller request is made.* If the prospect feels that the salesperson has given up something with the second request, she is more likely to feel obligated to grant the smaller request.[17] In this case, the salesperson might first try to persuade the prospect to utilize the new flexible partitions for each office on every floor of the company. If that request is refused, he could scale down his request to partitions on one floor or in one office.

Putting It All Together

We can begin by summarizing the key points.

- Some selling situations are more challenging than others depending upon how much a prospect wants a particular product and on how many similar products exist.
- Usually salespeople deal with situations in which a prospect has many alternatives.
- When a prospect has many alternatives, the salesperson must use persuasion in order to get the prospect to make a purchase.

- People tend to be resistant to persuasion, and the salesperson has to counter this resistance by relying upon strategies that can be planned in advance: power, credibility, and selling style.
- In terms of power, the balance generally favors the prospect, but the salesperson has potential for power through the following types of power: expert, referent, reward, and persuasion.
- Credibility is primarily concerned with truthfulness and is necessary for effective persuasion.
- An assertive selling style is generally most likely to be effective.
- Compliance gaining strategies are specific persuasive strategies that cannot be planned in advance since a salesperson cannot know ahead of time what a prospect will say.

The model provided in Figure 8.10 pictures the persuasive process.

It starts with the basic interactive communication process between the salesperson and the prospect. Each person communicates in terms of content, rela-

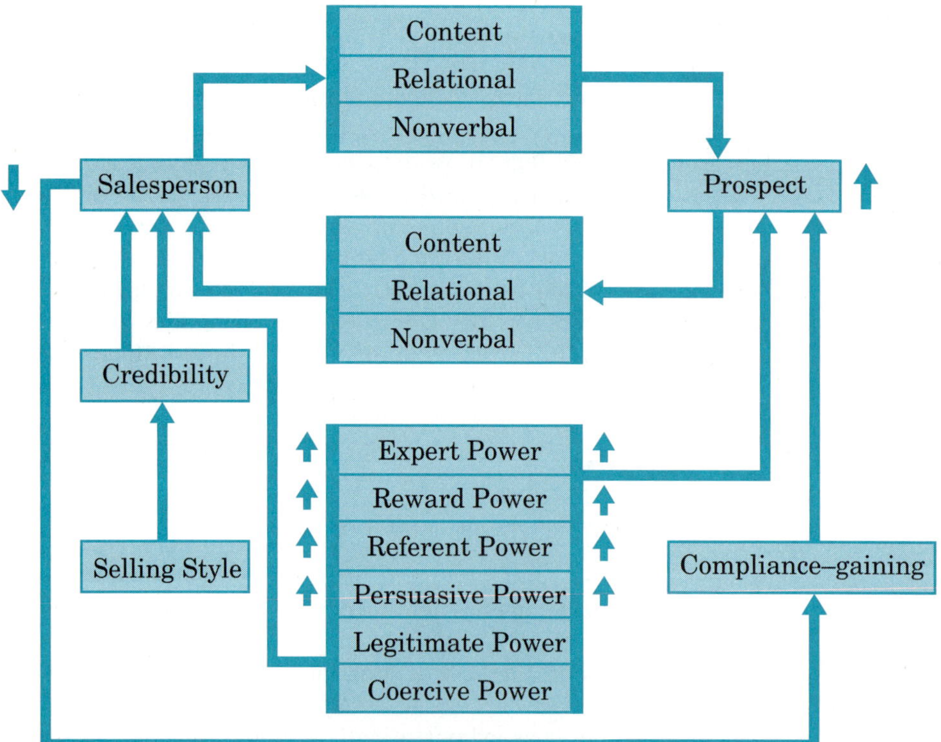

FIGURE 8.10 The persuasive process taking into account style and credibility.

tional and nonverbal messages. The six power bases are operating, and the arrows show which person has the opportunity to utilize a particular power base. The upward arrows indicate power, and the downward arrows indicate lack of power. The salesperson has a large downward arrow. Each power base that she can utilize provides her with additional power, as indicated by the small upward arrow. The salesperson has to establish credibility in order to employ compliance-gaining strategies effectively. Finally, the salesperson's behavior can be characterized in terms of a selling style.

Key Terms

Persuasion
Facts
Persuasive strategy
Power
Reward power
Norm of reciprocity
Coercive power
Referent power
Expert power
Persuasive power (information power)
Legitimate power
Credibility
Trust transference
Competence
Character
Sociability
Composure
Extroversion
Compliance-gaining strategies
Foot-in-the-door strategy
Door-in-the-face strategy

Review Questions

1. What is persuasion? Give specific examples of situations in which a salesperson would try to persuade a prospect.
2. What are facts? How can facts be used in persuasion?
3. What is a persuasive strategy? Which strategies can be planned in advance? Which strategies cannot?
4. What is the relationship between power and dependence?
5. Can a salesperson know how much power he has even before talking to a prospect? Explain.
6. What are the four possible sales situations? In which situations would the salesperson have more power than the prospect?
7. List and describe the six bases of power. Which power bases can the salesperson use to enhance personal power?
8. What does the norm of reciprocity have to do with power?
9. Why is it important for the salesperson to communicate similarity? How can the salesperson do that?
10. List and describe the five dimensions of credibility.
11. What is an assertive sales style? What does flexibility have to do with this style?

12. List and discuss the nine compliance-gaining strategies. Which strategies should the salesperson be particularly careful in using?
13. How can a prospect resist a salesperson's compliance-gaining strategy? What can a salesperson do to counteract a prospect's resistance?
14. What is the difference between the foot-in-the-door and door-in-the-face strategies?

Discussion Questions

1. Of the six power bases, which one do you think business-to-business salespeople should try to maximize, assuming that they can choose only one? Why? How would you recommend that they do this? What would you recommend for retail salespeople? Why? How would you recommend that they do this?
2. What specific kinds of statements might a salesperson make to convey each of the five dimensions of credibility?
3. Would it be possible for a salesperson to maximize power at the expense of credibility? How?
4. How can a salesperson deal with the fact that people, in general, do not like to be persuaded?

CASE 8.1

Following is a dialogue between Jim Miles, a buyer for a major department store chain, and Sally Green, a salesperson for ABC Manufacturing. Sally is in charge of men's ties and is trying to convince Jim to stock the ties in the flagship store.

SALLY: Mr. Miles? Hi. I'm Sally Green, senior V.P. in charge of sales for ABC Manufacturing. I'm sorry I didn't have a chance to meet you the last time I was in your store. It's such a great store that I often forget that I'm there for professional reasons and find myself shopping instead.

JIM: Thanks. We're certainly not going to discourage you from shopping here! What can I help you with?

SALLY: Today I'm in the men's tie business. When I was in your men's store last week, I noticed, much to my surprise, that you don't stock our Francais Ties.

JIM: That's true. But we have so many brands as it is that we can hardly move what we have.

SALLY: Yes, I understand that. I think that's the case with most department stores. But your store is the only prestigious store in the city that doesn't include our brand.

JIM: Well, we have to differentiate ourselves somehow, and besides, I don't think people look for ties by brand name.

SALLY: That's generally true. But there are some noticeable exceptions. We recently conducted a major study of men in several income brackets to see whether they shop for ties by tie brand or as a function of the store the tie is sold in. What we found is that, for the lower income brackets, people do, in fact, shop by store, just as you suggested. But the people who would fit into the bracket that would shop in your store were much more concerned with the tie's brand name.

JIM: That's interesting, but I don't seem to recall seeing much advertising for your Francais Ties.

SALLY: Actually, we have done a great deal of direct mail advertising. In addition, we have been advertising in all of the more upscale men's magazines, such as *Esquire*, *Gentleman's Quarterly*, and *M*. In fact, in a follow-up study, we found that 76 percent of men in the upper income brackets who were professionals and executives knew of our ties, and 68 percent of those owned three or more. All of the people who owned our ties said they shopped for the tie by brand. Oh, and I almost forgot—36 percent of the owners went to more than three stores until they found a Francais Tie.

JIM: Gee, that is surprising. I certainly don't look for ties by brand.

SALLY: Well, if I had the pleasure of shopping in your store, I probably wouldn't either, with, of course, the exception of Francais Ties. Actually, there is a quality difference between our ties and most of the rest. Our silk fabric is imported from China and fashioned in England. What we end up with is a very durable and resilient tie that holds its shape better than almost any other available. Part of the reason people seek out our ties is that the quality has been communicated by word-of-mouth. The result is that we have a very high-status tie.

JIM: Well, maybe we should consider this a bit further. Why don't you send me some samples?

SALLY: I'll be happy to. In fact, I have a proposal for you. Let me set you up with just one small and unobtrusive rack of our ties. If they don't sell out within 30 days, return them and we'll give you a complete refund. No obligation on your part, except a small portion of a counter top in the tie department.

1. What do you think Jim will do?
2. If Jim refuses, how should Sally proceed?
3. Who had more power at the outset? There are a number of indications that Sally tried to enhance her power by using one or more of the power bases discussed in this chapter. Point out as many indications as you

continued

can. State how successful you think each attempt was at changing the power balance.

4. There are a number of other issues that might be relevant here. For example, the issues of similarity, liking, and norm of reciprocity all come into play. Find indications of as many of them as you can. Discuss how successful Sally was in using each of them.
5. With respect to credibility, which of the five dimensions was Sally able to communicate successfully? How?
6. Were there any attempts to use specific compliance-gaining strategies? Locate them and indicate how successful they were. Locate and discuss any of Jim's attempts to resist compliance. How did Sally counter these attempts?
7. Would you describe Sally as assertive or aggressive? Explain.

References

1. Scheidel, T. M. (1972). *Speech Communication and Human Interaction.* Glenview, IL. Scott Foresman.

2. Ibid.

3. Ibid.

4. Jones, E. E., and H. B. Gerard. (1967). *Foundations of Social Psychology.* New York: Wiley.

5. Emerson, R. (1962). Power dependence relations. *American Sociological Review, 27,* 32–33.

6. French, J. R. P., and B. H. Raven. (1959). The bases of power. In D. Cartright (ed.), *Studies in Social Power.* Ann Arbor, MI: Institute for Social Research, Ch. 9.

7. Raven, B., C. Centers, and A. Rodrigues. (1975). The bases of conjugal power. In R. E. Cromwell and D. H. Olson, eds., *Power in Families.* New York: Halstead Press.

8. Cialdini, R. B. (1985). *Influence: Science and Practice.* Glenview, IL: Scott Foresman.

9. Milliman, R. E., and D. L. Fugate. (1988). Using trust-transference as a persuasion technique: An empirical investigation. *Journal of Personal Selling and Sales Management, 8,* 1–8.

10. DeVito, J. (1986). *The Interpersonal Communication Book.* New York: Harper & Row.

11. Hite, R., and J. Bellizzi. (1986). A preferred style of sales management. *Industrial Marketing Management, 15,* 215–223.

12. Jolson, M. A. (1984). Selling assertively. *Business Horizons, 27,* 71–77.

13. Goss, B., and D. O'Hair. (1988). *Communicating In Interpersonal Relations.* New York: Macmillan.

14. McLaughlin, M., M. Cody, and C. Robey. (1980). Situational influences on the selection of strategies to resist compliance-gaining attempts. *Human Communication Research, 7,* 14–36.

15. De Turck, M. (1985). A transactional analysis of compliance-gaining behavior: Effects of noncompliance, relationship contexts, and actors' gender. *Human Communication Research*, *12*, 54–78.

16. Dillard, J., H. Hunter, and M. Burgoon. (1983). Sequential request persuasive strategies: Meta-analysis of foot-in-the-door and door-in-the-face. *Human Communication Research*, *10*, 461–487.

17. Cialdini, op. cit.

FOUR

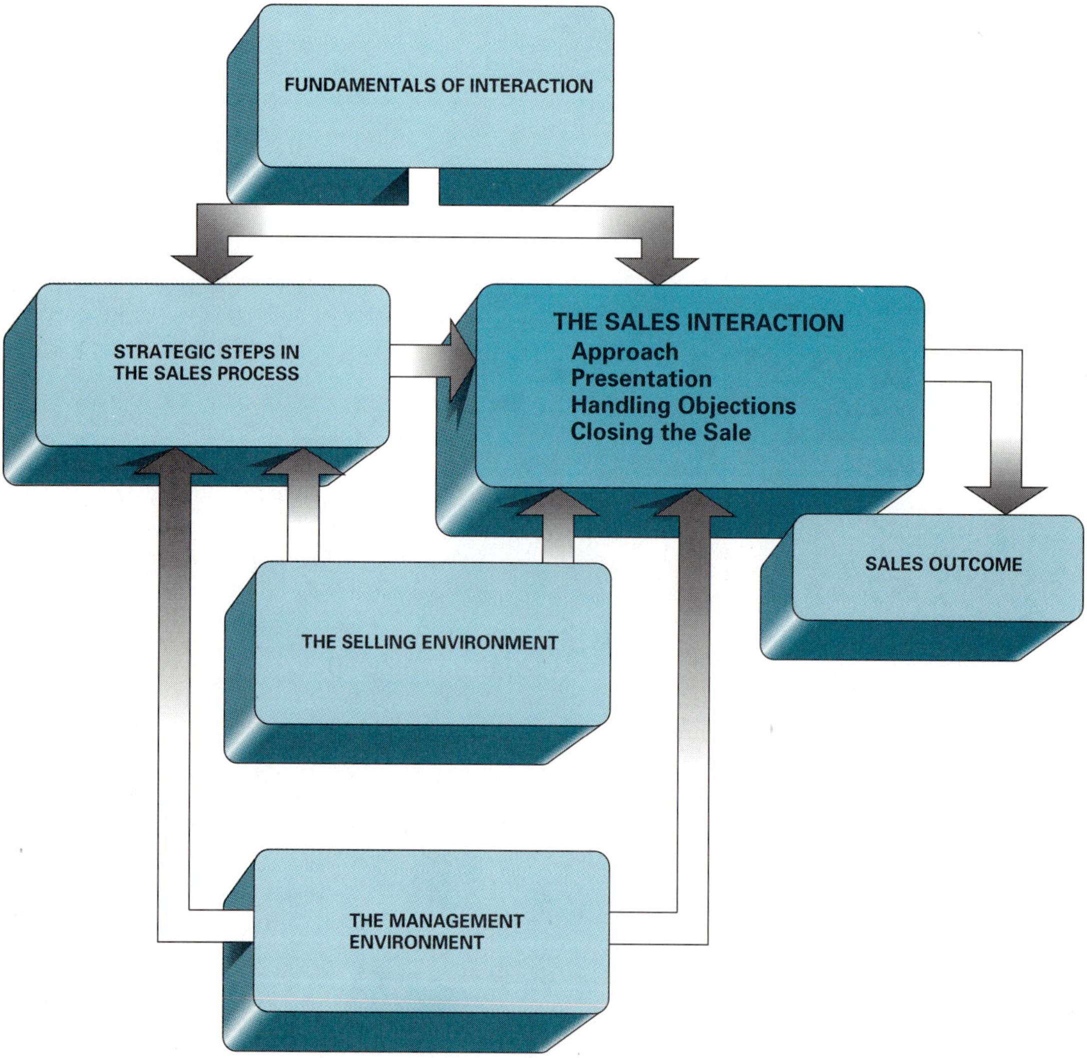

FUNDAMENTALS OF INTERACTION

STRATEGIC STEPS IN
THE SALES PROCESS

THE SALES INTERACTION
Approach
Presentation
Handling Objections
Closing the Sale

SALES OUTCOME

THE SELLING ENVIRONMENT

THE MANAGEMENT
ENVIRONMENT

THE SALES INTERACTION

9

Approaching the Prospect and Asking About Needs

CHAPTER OBJECTIVES

In this chapter, you will learn:

- To adapt your sales presentation to each situation and each prospect.
- To manage the impression you create when you approach a prospect.
- How to build rapport with a prospect.
- Several different approach techniques and when each is appropriate.
- The difference between various forms of questions.
- How to improve your listening skills.

CHAPTER OUTLINE

A Sales Challenge

An Overview

The Structure of Your Sales Call

- Adapting the Sales Call to the Prospect's Needs

The Approach

- The Purpose of the Approach
- The Basic Processes

The Content of the Approach

- Small Talk
- The Use of Specific Openers
- Advantages and Disadvantages of the Formal Opener
- Use Openers with Caution

Maintaining a Flexible Approach

- Adapting the Level of Intimacy
- Varying the Duration of the Approach

Learning About the Prospect's Needs

- Techniques for Identifying Needs: The Question's Form
- The Question's Content: Needs Versus Problems
- The Listening Process

Putting It All Together

Key Terms

Review Questions

Discussion Questions

Case 9.1

References

A Sales Challenge

Frank Dugan and Ted Parsons had been selling heavy machinery at National Machinery and Equipment for 5 years. At National, the prospecting is done through a central telemarketing office, and a standard demonstration tape is provided to all salespeople. Frank and Ted work the same number of hours and make approximately the same number of sales calls, yet Ted consistently outperforms Frank by 30 to 40 percent. The men are friends who share an office, and even they cannot figure out what accounts for the difference in sales. When they compare notes on the selling process, they appear to be using similar sales techniques, yet they must be doing something differently.

This situation is not uncommon. Two salespeople selling identical products to identical prospects with identical preapproach sales plans can differ widely in their selling effectiveness. The reason for this variation has puzzled sales executives for decades. Although no one knows exactly why such differences occur, we do know that the answer lies in what happens when the salesperson and prospect meet face to face. The beginning of this face-to-face meeting is the subject of this chapter.

An Overview

Now that you have learned the basics of communication and buyer motivation, prospecting and putting together a preapproach plan, you are ready to approach the actual sales call. Because the sales call is an *interaction*, it contains a blend of planned and unplanned elements. This is where all of your *knowledge*, *skills*, and *preparation* come together (see Figure 9.1). You enter the sales interaction with a purpose and a plan, and you must be skillful enough to alter the plan to suit the prospect and the situation. But altering your plan requires a thorough understanding of what actually happens during a sales call. This is the subject of the present chapter and the next three chapters.

Recall from Chapter 2 that the sales call proceeds from an *approach* to a *presentation* to a *close*, and that during these stages, *needs* must be uncovered and *objections* must be handled. In this chapter, we begin our analysis of the sales call with a general overview of the ways in which this basic structure can be adapted to suit different prospects. We then discuss what happens during the first stage as you *approach* the prospect. Here we concentrate on the basic processes that occur, as well as specific approaches that you can use. Next, we analyze how you learn about the prospect's needs through the processes of *questioning* and *listening*. Although these processes are important throughout the sales call, they will be discussed in detail here.

The Structure of Your Sales Call

Our division of the sales call into different chapters does *not* mean that your sales calls will be divided into neatly separated segments. Most of your calls will not

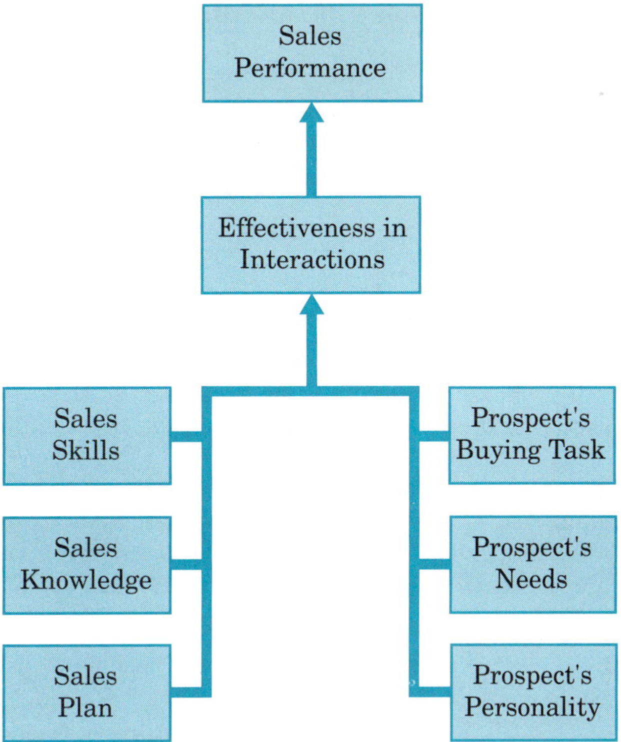

FIGURE 9.1 Skills, knowledge, and plans come together in the sales interaction.

follow a rigid scenario in which you approach, ask about needs, present your product, and then handle objections and close. You should view the stages as representing a general logical progression, but realize that there is bound to be some overlap between them. Remember, the sales call is, above all, an *interaction.* Since each prospect is unique, each sales call will be unique.

As Table 9.1 indicates, the investigation of needs, the discussion and demonstration of the product, and the handling of objections may follow a formal structure (a) or an informal structure (b).

In the formal structure, you first ask questions and then present and demonstrate the product before you handle objections. This structure is appropriate under certain circumstances. For example, if you are calling on a group of prospects concerning a major industrial sale, you might make a formal presentation, show a videotape of your product, ask for questions, and handle any objections.

However, there are many cases in which you will not use such a formal sequence. If you are showing apartments or discussing prescription drugs with a physician, for example, you would not ask *all* of your questions, present *all* of your information, and then handle *all* of the objections. Instead, you would use the more natural interaction sequence described in Table 9-1(b). In this sequence, you ask questions about certain aspects of the problem, respond to the prospect's answers, handle any objections, and then go on to ask more questions. Also, you

Table 9.1 Formal versus Informal Sales Calls

(a) The Formal Structure	(b) The Informal Structure
1. Approach the prospect	1. Approach the prospect
2. Investigate the prospect's needs	2. Ask about needs
3. Present your product	3. Present some information about your product
4. Handle objections	4. Handle objections
5. Close the sale	5. Repeat steps 2–4 until all needs are uncovered and objections handled
	6. Close the sale

will probably demonstrate the product (i.e., show the apartment or a brochure about the drugs) while you engage in the conversation.

You should note here that Table 9.1 (a and b) does not present the only kinds of sales calls. Instead, it provides *examples* of possible structures. You will undoubtedly engage in many different variations of these basic examples. In the following interaction between a drug salesperson and a physician, for example, the salesperson discovered an important need at the beginning of his approach:

SALESPERSON: It looks like you have redecorated your waiting room since I was last here. These new chairs are particularly comfortable.

DR. BLAIN: Well I've been starting to specialize in the foot problems of the elderly, and my old furniture was just too uncomfortable for many of my new patients.

SALESPERSON: I didn't realize that you were shifting your practice. I thought that you specialized in sports podiatry.

DR. BLAIN: Well, I haven't given up my sports medicine practice; I have simply expanded. There are more and more elderly people in need of medical care these days.

SALESPERSON: I'm glad that you mentioned that. I had actually come to show you something else, but now that I know you are interested in drugs that help the elderly, I can also show you this (*takes a brochure out of his bag*). We have just introduced a new anti-inflammatory drug that is ideal for the elderly. It does not have many of the common side effects and can be taken by people with heart conditions.

DR. BLAIN: That's very interesting. I read that you were in the process of developing it.

In this example, rather than following a rigid format of approach, needs discovery, and presentation, the salesperson recognized an opportunity to launch right into a presentation of product information before he had had the chance to ask formally about needs. If he had insisted on delaying his presentation until he had formally investigated needs, he would have missed the chance to discuss this new drug. Instead, he now has the option, depending upon the flow of the interaction, to return to his informal approach or to proceed to present other products. As this example illustrates, the ultimate determinant of the format of the sales call should be the prospect's needs.

Adapting the Sales Call to the Prospect's Needs

Modern salespeople recognize that satisfying the prospect's needs means more than simply finding the appropriate product. It also means adapting the selling *process* to satisfy the prospect.[1,2] You will undoubtedly be involved in many interactions in which your prospect's needs require you to deviate from the standard selling process. In cases where you have an ongoing relationship with a customer, for example, you may have developed a variation of the general sequence that is comfortable for both of you. If you are familiar with her needs and she is familiar with your products, you may make periodic calls just to maintain contact. During this kind of call, you might begin with an approach, briefly ask about any new needs or problems, and close by asking if she needs anything.

In other cases, you may intend to progress through all of the selling stages, but the prospect may not want to conform to the prescribed sequence. What do you do, for example, if a prospect mentions an objection before you have developed your presentation, or if the prospect wants to hear your presentation without discussing her problems?

In general, it is better to respond to the prospect's needs, rather than trying to force her into your predetermined outline. However, this kind of flexibility requires a thorough understanding of the underlying processes. If you understand the basic processes, you may be able to achieve the same results while deviating from the standard path.

In the following sections, we present a detailed discussion of the processes that occur as you begin your sales call.

The Approach

The Purpose of the Approach

Although we are often unaware of it, *all* of our interactions—even interactions with friends—begin with an **approach.**[3] We can appreciate the role of the approach if we consider the following conversation, in which Joan invites her friend, Sam, to a party:

JOAN: Hi, Sam. I haven't seen you in a while.
SAM: Hi, Joan. How are you doing?
JOAN: I'm fine. What have you been up to lately?
SAM: Not much. I've seen a few movies. What have you been up to?

JOAN: I've been planning a going-away party for David.
SAM: Oh, really? A big party?
JOAN: For 25 or 30 people.
SAM: In your apartment?
JOAN: Yep. Can you come on the 17th?
SAM: Sure can.
JOAN: Great. I'll call you this week with details.

Obviously, Joan is not trying to sell anything to Sam. Yet the first four lines of their conversation contain an approach. Even in a friendship relationship, beginning a conversation without an approach by jumping right into a discussion of the task at hand would appear abrupt and rude. In this case, the approach allowed Joan and Sam to make sure that they had not missed any major events in each other's lives.

When the conversation is between two strangers, the approach is even more crucial. Although the actual subject matter discussed during the approach may appear to be trivial, many important processes are occurring during this initial phase of interaction.

The Basic Processes

As discussed in Chapter 3, there is a personal element in every sales call, even though the primary focus is on the exchange of a product or service. Although the personal dimension is important throughout the sales interaction, it is the primary focus in the *approach.* With a good approach, you can begin to build *trust* and *credibility* before attempting to persuade the prospect to buy.

Although the approach serves many functions in the sales interaction, a primary objective of this phase is to lay the foundation for establishing trust and credibility. It is much easier to persuade someone to do something if that person views you as a credible, trustworthy source of information. Even though you may be quite concerned with satisfying the prospect's needs, a new prospect cannot know that you are concerned until you demonstrate this. Handled properly, the approach phase allows you to do this before beginning your persuasive argument about the product.

We can best understand the way in which trust and credibility develop if we examine the underlying processes that occur *whenever* two people meet and begin interacting. If the people are strangers, as they often are in personal selling, the following processes will occur as they begin to interact:

1. Impression formation.
2. Uncertainty reduction.
3. Rapport building.
4. Rule negotiation.

We now discuss each of these processes.

Many of our impressions of others are formed in the first few seconds of our meeting. (© The Photo Works/Photo Researchers, Inc.)

Impression Formation. We discuss **impression formation** first because it is a general process that occurs whenever two strangers meet for the first time. In fact, we even form impressions of strangers whom we may never meet, that is, of people we see on the street or in a restaurant.

First impressions are crucial because they affect the way people perceive each other, sometimes for as long as they know each other.[4–6] Thus the reality of our behavior may be less important than the way it fits with the first impression we create. Once people form impressions of us, they will actually *distort* information that does not support that impression. If they think that we are smart, they will tend to "hear" what we say as being smart. If they think that we are trustworthy, they will perceive what we say as credible.

This means that the first impression that you create when meeting a prospect can affect your ultimate success. If you create a first impression of aggressiveness or dishonesty, the prospect will tend to perceive your entire presentation that way, even if it is not. If you create a first impression that you are a "typical salesperson," the prospect will tend to pay less attention to what you have to say.[7] But if you create a first impression that you honestly believe that your product can help the prospect, the prospect will tend to take what you say seriously.

But what is the basis of this crucial first impression? Much of it is *not* based on the words we say. In fact, long before we exchange any words, changes occur in the way we perceive the other person. We begin to concentrate less on the other as a whole person and instead focus on various *nonverbal cues.* This focusing has been compared to the action of the zoom lens of a camera, which changes from a long shot of the whole person to a series of close-ups of the eye gaze, smile, general appearance, and dress.[8,9]

For this reason, it is important that you *look the prospect in the eye* and *smile* upon greeting him. As you learned in Chapter 4, these nonverbal behaviors create the impression of honesty and confidence. By contrast, eye gaze avoidance is likely to be interpreted as shifty and untrustworthy, even if you avoid eye contact because of shyness or insecurity.

It is likewise important that your dress and general appearance create an appropriate first impression. Consider the different impressions that you form when looking at the persons in Figure 9.2. Although dress may become less important as you get to know a prospect, it contributes to the prospect's initial impression of your competence, professionalism, and social class. These initial impressions are difficult to overcome. When people attribute characteristics to you based on your physical appearance, they often perceive what you say as being consistent with those characteristics.

For a salesperson, these results mean that first impressions can affect the way prospects will perceive an entire presentation. Obviously, you cannot alter physical characteristics such as height. However, you can adjust your dress and appearance to create an appropriate impression.

Uncertainty Reduction and Rapport Building. As we form our first impressions, we begin to reduce our uncertainty about the other person. Uncer-

FIGURE 9.2 Clothing and posture affect first impressions. (Randy Matusow/Monkmeyer Press Photo)

tainty is a major component of any first encounter[10]—whether a first date, a first class, or a job interview. The sales call is no exception. When you meet a prospect for the first time, the prospect will be uncertain about you, and despite your efforts at preapproach planning, you will be uncertain about the prospect. Although you may have broad impressions of each other, neither of you will really know the other's beliefs, attitudes, or values. You will be uncertain about how to reach the prospect, and the prospect will be uncertain about your motives and trustworthiness. It is important, at this point, to reduce the uncertainty in a positive way—a way that will lead to the establishment of rapport (see Figure 9.3).

Rapport is a relationship based on mutual trust and understanding. The ability to build rapport is a crucial skill in selling. Salespeople who are good at establishing rapport are more successful in general than those who do not possess this skill.[11] The salesperson who can develop rapport will have a stronger basis upon which to communicate information about her product. Even the best products will not sell if the prospect does not trust what the salesperson tells him because there is no rapport.

What mystifies some salespeople is how certain people seem to be able to build rapport almost instantly, while others have a great deal of difficulty. The key to rapport building lies in two separate abilities. Without realizing it, many of the people who appear to be naturally gifted at building rapport actually (1) read the verbal and nonverbal behavior of the other person and (2) **pace,** or synchronize, their own behavior accordingly. The result is two people acting in sync with each other. They share the same posture, tone of voice, rate of speech, and so on, and feel a sense of communality and mutual understanding—that is, rapport.[12]

One method that can be used to tell whether your efforts to establish rapport are working is to pace the prospect's behavior for a while and then gradually shift away from synchronization. You might, for example, uncross your legs while the prospect's legs remain crossed. If you have established rapport, the prospect will

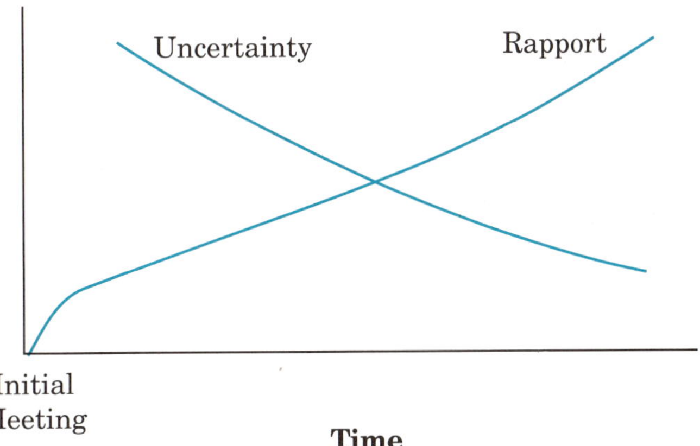

FIGURE 9.3 As rapport increases, uncertainty decreases.

begin to follow your behaviors—in this case, uncross his legs. However, caution must be used in manipulating behavior in this way.

It is very important to *avoid* obvious mimicking of the prospect. If you copy every single gesture in an obvious way, your behavior will appear forced, and you may actually reduce your rapport with the prospect. In cases where behaviors cannot be synchronized in a natural way, it is better to allow rapport to develop more gradually. There is no reason to rush this process. Although rapport building is a primary *focus* of the approach, it does not stop when you begin to discuss your product. Ideally, rapport will grow over the entire course of your relationship with the prospect.

Rule Negotiation. A frequently overlooked part of rapport building involves the negotiation of rules. As we discussed in Chapter 3, relationships are governed by rules, and prospects and salespeople determine their own sets of rules as they interact with each other. They do this by choosing to follow or violate generally accepted practices whenever they speak. If, for example, a prospect constantly interrupts what you are saying, that prospect is negotiating for a change in the standard rules against interrupting. If you allow the interruptions, you are actually agreeing to a change in the basic rule, and a pattern of interruption will result.[13]

Consider the contrast in the following two dialogues:

DIALOGUE I

SALESPERSON: We really have a well- —

PROSPECT: I have heard that your deliveries are often slow.

SALESPERSON: I'm surprised that you've heard that. Our deliveries are generally some of the fastest in the industry.

DIALOGUE II

SALESPERSON: We really have a well- —

PROSPECT: I have heard that your deliveries are —

SALESPERSON: As I was saying, we have a well-trained sales force.

If sequences like Dialogue I are repeated often enough, a *pattern* of prospect interruptions will tend to emerge. The salesperson will have agreed to a change in the basic rules against interruptions, and the prospect will be allowed to interrupt at will. Although allowing the prospect to dominate may be quite appropriate in many cases, there may be times when you will want to prevent this pattern from occurring. The salesperson in Dialogue II did just that by implicitly refusing to allow the interruption.

The important principle here is that everything you do during the approach helps to establish rules that will determine your pattern of interaction with the prospect. Your style during the approach will set the tone for the rest of your sales call. During later phases of the sales call, you will be concentrating on presenting your product, so it is important to establish a satisfying give-and-take rapport during your approach. In fact, you can think of the approach as your opportunity to establish a comfortable communication pattern before you get into the actual presentation. As the following section will illustrate, certain topics are best suited to this purpose.

The Content of the Approach

The *content* of the approach refers to the actual topics that are discussed. Although you can discuss a variety of topics during your approach, certain kinds of topics are better suited to building rapport and others are better suited to getting immediate attention. Specifically, you can use *small talk* when your primary concern is to build rapport and specific attention-getting *openers* when your primary concern is to gain immediate attention.

Small Talk

In most interactions between strangers, the content of the conversation begins with **small talk.** Though small talk may involve small or unimportant topics (like the weather), this exchange serves some very important purposes.

- Small talk allows you to concentrate on impression formation. As we discussed in the previous section, when people meet for the first time, they concentrate on forming impressions. It is because of this emphasis on general impressions that the initial content of an interaction tends to focus on small talk. Restriction

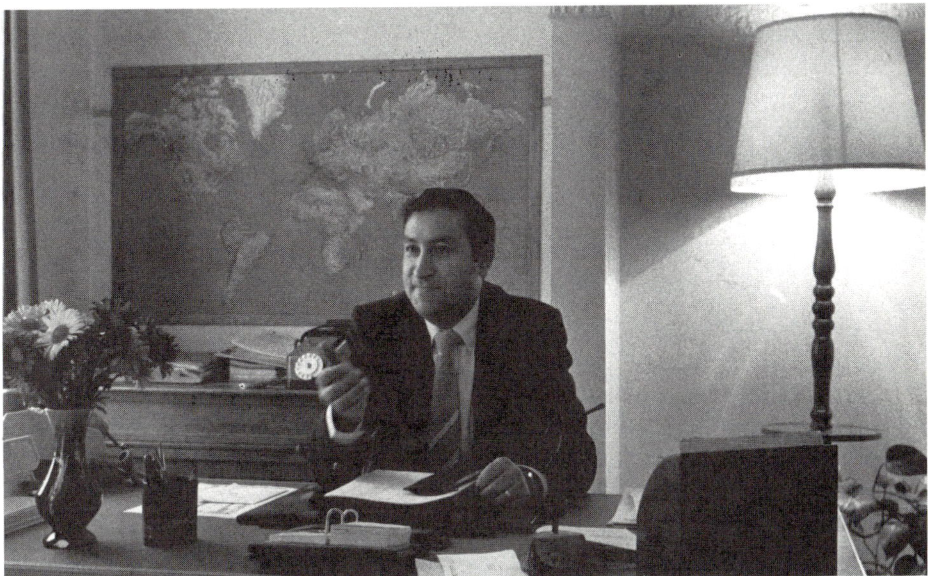

The prospect's office can be a source of small talk. (© Ulrike Welsch 1987/PhotoEdit.)

of the verbal portion of the interaction to simple, superficial topics (e.g., the weather) allows the speakers to concentrate on managing their more global impressions.

- Small talk allows you to reduce uncertainty by providing safe topics to discuss as you get to know the other person. Before you really know what the other person is like, it may be risky to discuss important subjects. Consider the risk of mentioning a recent political race or abortion decision, only to learn that your prospect actively supports the other side.
- Small talk allows you to build rapport. Engaging in small talk is particularly important in situations where your aim is to develop a long-term relationship with the prospect. While using small talk, you can search for areas of common interest and mutual agreement:

> SALESPERSON: I'm so glad that the heat wave has ended.
> PROSPECT: Me too. I was starting to get cranky and irritable.

In general, the artful use of small talk gives salespeople and prospects something to say to each other as they seek to build trust and rapport (see Table 9.2).

The Use of Specific Openers

Some salespeople plan specific openers before approaching the prospect. Openers, sometimes called *attention getters*, are designed to attract the prospect's interest immediately. In contrast to small talk, these openers make some reference to the task at hand. There are various types of openers, and different types are appropriate to different situations. One commonly used opener is the *referral.* When using the referral, you begin your approach with a statement such as "Mr. Smith, from the ABC Corporation, suggested that you might be interested in this." The referral is an ideal opener to use in situations where you have been referred by a third party. The use of a familiar name will not only get the prospect's attention but will establish an immediate link between you. Even in a cold call, it is unlikely that a person will refuse to speak with someone who mentions the name of a friend.

Some common attention-getting openers are the **benefit opener,** the **demonstration opener,** and the **question opener.** With the benefit opener, for example, you attempt to get the prospect's attention with a benefit statement such as "Good morning, Mr. Smith. How would you like to save 20 percent on your insurance costs?" In a demonstration approach, you begin by showing your product: "This vacuum cleaner will pick up dirt that your old model leaves in your carpets."

Table 9.3 on page 252 lists some commonly used openers and shows how important they are to industrial and retail salespeople.

Advantages and Disadvantages of the Formal Opener

If you use a formal opener that is related directly to the sale, the product, or the selling situation, it will be difficult to return to rapport-building small talk. Instead,

Table 9.2 Suggestions for Small Talk

Communicate similarity.
Feelings of similarity increase liking:
"Your elevator system is almost as bad as the one in my building. Ours is usually more crowded than the bus at rush hour."
"I just got the same computer that you have. How do you like yours?"

Mention a mutual friend or acquaintance.
If you have a mutual acquaintance or received the prospect's name through a personal reference, mentioning the person is a good way to begin to establish rapport. A statement such as "I spoke to Dale Roder last week, and she said to say 'hi' " may be enough to establish a common bond.

Refer to something in the immediate environment.
In cases where you call on the prospect, you might begin by discussing something about:
Your trip there: "Driving around here is really pleasant. There's almost no traffic."
The local environment: "This area has seen a lot of development since I was here last."
The prospect's office: "What a great view you have from this window."

Mention something you learned in your presale plan.
You might also make a comment based on something you learned in your presale plan:
"I understand that your company now leads the industry in growth of market share."

Personalize your small talk.
As you build a relationship with a prospect, your small talk will begin to include more personal and important issues:
"How was your trip to Toronto last week?"
"Have your kids gotten home from camp yet?"

you will typically proceed directly to your presentation. Consider how awkward it is to begin with a line about the product and then return the discussion to small talk:

> SALESPERSON: Good morning, Mr. Smith. How would you like to save 20 percent on your insurance costs?
> MR. SMITH: Well, I don't know.
> SALESPERSON: Hasn't the weather been terrific this week?

Although they rule out the use of small talk, formal openers may be appropriate in certain situations. Formal openers can be important on cold calls. In these cases, the prospect has no idea of who you are or what you are doing, and it is important that you get to the point immediately. If a prospect does not know the purpose of your call, it would be inappropriate to keep her guessing while you engage in small talk. Consider what you would do if a stranger entered your office and began to discuss the weather.

If you are in a situation that could develop into an ongoing relationship with

Table 9.3 Some Commonly Used Openers and the Importance Attached to Them by Salespeople

	Mean Importance	
Selling Technique	*Industrial Salespeople*	*Consumer Salespeople*
1. *Consumer-benefit approach:* State the benefits of the offering and see if the prospect is interested in it	4.09*	4.16
2. *Curiosity:* Offer a benefit to the prospect that has appeal to the prospect's curiosity	3.95	3.92
3. *Question approach:* Open the sales interview with a question in order to get the prospect's attention and interest	3.50	3.90
4. *The compliment:* Use a sincere expression of appreciation to get the sales interview with the prospect	3.54	3.79
5. *Referral approach:* Use a present customer's name as a reference to the prospect	3.08	3.42
6. *Survey approach:* Offer to do research for the prospect to determine if the salesperson can help the prospect	2.97	3.07
7. *Introductory approach:* Give only the saleperson's name and the company's name to the prospect	2.79	2.83
8. *The showmanship approach:* Use unusual dramatic efforts to get the prospect's attention and interest	2.21	2.05
9. *Product approach:* Place the offering in the prospect's hands with little or no explanation	2.01	1.81
10. *Premium approach:* Give the prospect a token gift for the sales interview	1.56	1.85
11. *Shock:* Put "fear" into the prospect's heart	1.25	1.31

* 1 = not important; 5 = very important.
Source: Reprinted by permission of *Journal of Personal Selling and Sales Management* © 1985. R. Hite and J. Bellizzi. (1985). Differences in the importance of selling techniques between consumer and industrial salespeople. *Journal of Personal Selling and Sales Management, 5* (November). 19–30.

the prospect, and you feel that rapport-building small talk is important, it is possible to use one of these product-related openers *after* some small talk and *before* the actual presentation.

Use Openers with Caution

While a well-designed product-related opener can get the prospect interested in listening to your presentation, it must be used with caution. In some cases, it can backfire and actually cause the prospect to *not* pay attention to what you have to say. This can occur if the opener sounds too much like a stereotypical selling line. In these cases, the prospect immediately labels you as a salesperson intent on persuasion and tunes out what you have to say. Recall from Chapter 5 that this can happen whenever salespeople behave in a way that prospects *expect* salespeople to behave. In contrast, if a salesperson acts counter to expectations, the prospect becomes more interested in listening to what he has to say.

Maintaining a Flexible Approach

Flexibility in the approach is just as important as it is throughout the entire sales call. A primary reason for *understanding* the approach process is that, with understanding, you should be better able to maintain flexibility. Memorizing many different openers is of little value if you do not understand when and where to use them. Approaches can vary tremendously from prospect to prospect and from situation to situation, so your ability to adapt is crucial.

Adapting the Level of Intimacy

Prospects differ in terms of their desire to build rapport with salespeople. Some prospects may prefer a formal relationship, whereas others may respond to a friendlier, more open approach. In some industrial selling situations, the bonds between salespeople and buyers become so strong that the buyer will continue to buy from the salesperson even if the salesperson changes jobs and begins to work for a competitor. In other cases, an industrial prospect may view rapport building as a waste of time.

There is similar variation in retail settings. In some retail situations, consumers will shop at certain stores because they have become friendly with some of the salespeople. In contrast, other consumers like to shop in large department stores because they prefer anonymity. Your attempts at small talk might be perceived as friendly or as presumptuous.

It is important to take your cues from the prospect and attempt to achieve a level of intimacy that is consistent with his preferences. You can destroy trust and credibility if you attempt to force friendship on a prospect who is not interested. However, by understanding the basic processes of impression formation and uncertainty reduction, you may learn to distinguish between a prospect who wishes to remain distant and one who is merely uncertain about what to say.

Varying the Duration of the Approach

Another facet of the approach that requires flexibility is its duration. Although the approach has been discussed at some length in previous sections, there are many cases when all of these processes can occur within a few minutes. Depending upon whether the sales interaction is a retail or an industrial sale, and whether or not you already know the prospect, there will tend to be different expectations regarding the duration of the rapport-building phase.

In addition, there are important individual differences in perceptions of time, and in the desire to engage in small talk versus getting right "down to business." If the prospect is anxious to get on with the presentation, she will probably communicate this with nonverbal signals of impatience or boredom. On the other hand, trying to cut rapport building too short could leave the impression that you are too aggressive or that you do not care about the prospect as a person.

One way to ease gradually into your discussion of the product is to talk about the prospect's needs. In fact, you can begin to blend such questions into your approach.

Learning About the Prospect's Needs

As we discussed earlier, the discovery of the prospect's needs may continue throughout your entire sales call. However, in many cases, you will have a concentrated period of needs discovery after your approach and before you begin presenting your product. Investigating prospects' needs calls for an interaction based on questions and answers. For this reason, we devote the rest of the chapter to the processes of *questioning* and *listening* (see Figure 9.4)

Although we all ask questions every day, we tend not to think about what is really involved in the question–answer process. When selling, however, you cannot afford to take this process for granted. Your success frequently depends upon your skill at delving into prospects' needs.

Joe Forester, who sells office furniture and equipment, is well aware of this

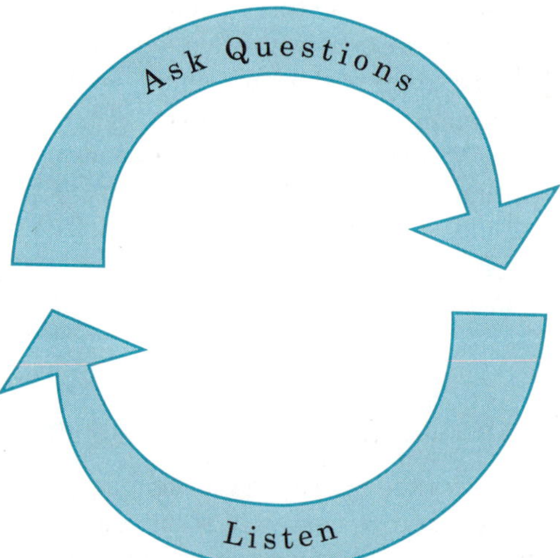

FIGURE 9.4 Questioning and listening go hand in hand.

fact. The actual furniture manufactured by Joe's company is similar to that of two other companies, both of which compete directly with Joe's firm. Yet Joe consistently outsells everyone in the industry. When asked about the secret of his success, Joe claims that it is his ability to find out what the buyer *really* wants and then plan an office arrangement to satisfy specific needs: "A lot of salespeople don't really listen to their prospects. I act as a consultant. After talking with a prospect, I often combine pieces from several different lines and adapt my equipment to solve specific problems. Other salespeople just go in there with their standard product lines and can't compete with me."

Joe's statement points out an important, but often forgotten, point about asking questions. Learning how to ask questions is only half of what is required to uncover needs. You learn about the prospect's needs by asking questions *and* listening to the answers. Listening is a crucial accompaniment to asking questions about needs. In fact, asking a prospect about needs and *not listening* to the answer is worse than not asking in the first place. In the following sections, we discuss techniques for asking questions and techniques for listening. We begin the first discussion by differentiating between the form and the content of a question.

Techniques for Identifying Needs: The Question's Form

The investigation of prospects' needs involves the extensive use of questions. It is important, at this stage, to be aware not only of the *content* of your questions, but also of their *form.* The form of the question that you ask will have an impact on the flow of your discussion. As a result, certain forms of questions cannot be used with certain presentation formats. The important distinction here is between open-ended and closed-ended questions.

Closed-Ended Questions. A **closed-ended question** is *one that specifies a choice of responses* to the prospect. In some closed-ended questions, the choices are actually listed: "Would you prefer red or black?" or "Are you interested in a station wagon or a sedan?" In other closed-ended questions, the choices are assumed but are not specified directly. For example, the question "Do you need immediate delivery?" implies a "yes" or "no" answer. You should use the close-ended question in cases where you want to restrict the response of the prospect. If you are conducting a sales call based on a prepared script, the closed-ended question allows you to gather information without leading the discussion away from the memorized speech. Because *you* are providing the prospect's response choices in the closed-ended question, you can prepare in advance what you will say following each of the possible responses.

If, for example, you are giving a *memorized presentation* about personal computers, you can stop and ask the prospect whether she will use the computer for spreadsheets or word processing. Because you know the response choices in advance of the prospect's answer (spreadsheets, word processing, or both), you can continue your memorized speech in one of three predetermined directions.

However, the closed-ended question is not limited in use to the memorized presentation. It can be used any time you want to gain information from the prospect while controlling the direction of the response.

Open-Ended Questions. An **open-ended question** is *one that does not specify responses choices for* the prospect: "What are you looking for in an investment portfolio?" or "Why do you want that grade of steel?" The open-ended question would lead to obvious problems if used during a memorized presentation. The prospect's response would lead you away from your predetermined message. For this reason, open-ended questions are excluded from most highly structured presentations.

However, the open-ended question is a very good technique to use when you are trying to uncover general needs and want to get a discussion going. The idea behind its use is that the more you can get a prospect to talk, the more information you will gather that can later help you identify problems and satisfy needs. A major advantage of the open-ended question is that the prospect can state exactly what is on her mind. By not restricting the choices open to the prospect, you might learn something that you had not considered.

However, answering open-ended questions requires more effort on the part of the prospect. Some prospects may not want to bother elaborating on their needs or explaining why they have made a particular decision. Some prospects may not even be sure why they need a particular product. In these cases, the open-ended question may generate less dialogue than a closed-ended question.

The Question's Content: Needs Versus Problems

It is extremely important to know what kind of information your questions will uncover. Questions whose content may *seem* generally similar can actually yield very different kinds of answers. Consider, for example, the following two questions asked of a sales manager-prospect who was interested in purchasing cellular phones for his salespeople's cars:

SALESPERSON: What do you need in a cellular phone?

versus

SALESPERSON: What kinds of problems do you have with your current communication systems?

Questions of the first type, which ask directly about needs, tend to yield lists of attributes from existing cellular phone promotions (e.g., "I need a phone system that will be reliable"), which may not tell you much about the prospect's actual needs. In contrast, questions about problems tend to yield more creative responses that come closer to revealing the prospect's needs.[14] A question about a prospect's problems might yield answers like "One of my salespeople had his phone stolen when he went into a prospect's office" or "When my salespeople fail to get back to me, they often say that they couldn't get through the phone lines." By working with a prospect's problems, you may gain a competitive edge by getting closer to what is actually bothering the prospect. On the other hand, if your questions yield attributes that all products claim to have (like reliability), it will be harder to build a case for the superiority of your product.

But regardless of the content of your question, it is crucial that you *listen* to the prospect's response.

The Listening Process

Without listening, we could not carry on conversations. We could not relate what we say to what the other person had said. Yet, despite its importance, listening is a process that is taken for granted. Many of us do not give a thought to the process of listening until we fail to get an appropriate response to something we say. The following conversation between Linda, a store manager, and Mildred, a salesperson, provides such an example:

LINDA: I sure hope this weather changes. If it rains for our opening, we will never draw a big crowd.
MILDRED: I'm sure tired of all of this rain.

In considering this example, try to decide whether Mildred listened to Linda. On the one hand, she must have listened, because she knew that Linda had mentioned rain. On the other hand, she could not have listened because she missed the point of Linda's concern. Can we conclude that Mildred really listened when she missed the point of what Linda was saying? The answer to this question is "yes and no."

As the example indicates, listening is a rather complicated process. It involves more than hearing. Mildred certainly *heard* what Linda had said. But listening also means *perceiving* and *comprehending* what is said. In fact, listening involves three different levels of processing.[15]

At the first level, **signal processing,** *we hear what was said and process the actual words and their structure.* In this stage of listening, we would process a string of sounds such as "andhowareyoutodaymistersmith" into understandable words: "And how are you today, Mr. Smith?"

But listening does not end when we process sounds into understandable words. In order to carry on conversations, we must make sense out of the words. As Figure 9.5 indicates, two additional levels of listening are involved in processing for comprehension. The first is called **literal processing.**

In literal processing, *we process what we hear for its literal, or simple, meaning, but we make no inference about what is said.* To understand literal processing, consider the following example.

PROSPECT: I have a meeting in ten minutes.
SALESPERSON: Oh, really? Is it an important meeting?

The salesperson in this dialogue listened for the literal meaning of the prospect's statement. At this level, the statement simply informed the salesperson that

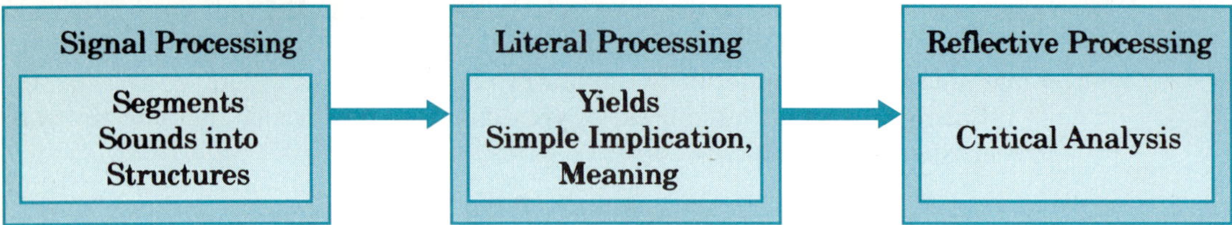

FIGURE 9.5 Listening involves more than one process.

the prospect had a meeting. By processing for literal meaning only, however, the salesperson missed the point of what the prospect said. Hopefully, no salesperson would actually respond as this one did. He missed what appears to be an obvious message: the prospect was trying to inform him that it was time to conclude the sales call.

Listening and Problem Solving. Although the real intent of the prospect's statement appears obvious, it requires a deeper level of listening than literal processing. When we listen for more than literal meaning, we are said to engage in **reflective processing.** In reflective processing, *you try to assess the point of the speaker's message.* You make inferences about the speaker's intentions and *analyze* what was said for hidden agendas or deception. In cases like the previous one, the prospect's inferences may be obvious and reflective processing may be taken for granted. In general, however, salespeople should make a point of engaging in reflective processing by analyzing all of their prospects' statements carefully.

Although some of our everyday conversations may require little reflective processing, this level of listening is at the heart of the problem-solving sales encounter. In fact, skill in combining all three levels of listening is what separates many successful and unsuccessful salespeople.

But why should listening be so difficult for salespeople? Because while the salesperson is listening to the prospect, she must also be concerned with the specific information she is trying to convey about the product. This means that during each of the prospect's speaking turns, the salesperson must accomplish four different things:

1. Hear sounds and process them into words.
2. Process the words for their literal meaning.
3. Reflect on the prospect's real intent and hidden agendas.
4. Plan how to respond to what was said.

This is where inexperienced salespeople can run into problems with their listening skills. They become so intent on planning what they want to say that they fail to listen to the prospect. This is a problem that comes from focusing on the product instead of on the prospect. It occurred in the following case, where a copy machine salesperson asked a purchasing agent about her needs:

SALESPERSON: What kind of copier do you need in this office?

PURCHASING AGENT: We do a lot of big jobs, so we need one that will copy and collate. We need a machine that will feed papers automatically, so that we don't have to put them in one by one.

But while the purchasing agent spoke, the salesperson was concentrating on the points he wanted to make next:

SALESPERSON TO HIMSELF: Don't forget to point out how easy it is to add toner to our machines. Don't forget to mention how fast it is to change the paper supply. Compare our machines to the competition . . .

While thinking about these points, the salesperson picked up on the word *paper* and missed the point that the purchasing agent was trying to make:

SALESPERSON: One thing that's particularly good about our machine is that it is easy to add paper.

PURCHASING AGENT (*annoyed*): I'm a lot less concerned about adding paper than I am about the machine's ability to feed it through automatically.

Obviously, this salesperson could benefit by improving his listening skills.

Improving Your Listening Skills. The first step in improving listening skills is to analyze your current listening habits. Do you pay close attention to what the other person is saying, or do you get so involved in planning what to say next that you forget to listen carefully? Do you prejudge what the other person is about to say and then fail to hear what he actually says? Do you stop at literal processing, or do you really analyze what the other person is saying? Do you concentrate enough to make inferences about the real point of what the other is saying?

Once you identify listening problems, you can make a conscious effort to substitute the good listening habits listed in Table 9.4.

Putting It All Together

We can begin putting it all together by summarizing the key points made in this chapter:

- The structure of the sales call should be adapted to each prospect and each situation.
- Although the interpersonal dimension is relevant throughout the sales call, it is the primary focus of the first phase of the sales call: the *approach*.
- During the approach, the prospect and the salesperson (1) form general impressions about each other, (2) reduce uncertainty and build rapport, and (3) begin to negotiate a comfortable pattern of relational communication.

Table 9.4 Improving Your Ability to Listen

1. Stop talking. Some people don't listen well because they take too many turns and take too long at each turn. You can't learn about a prospect's needs if you don't stop talking about your product long enough to listen.
2. Listen for ideas. Don't worry about the difficulties a person may be having when expressing ideas. In many cases, a prospect will be less familiar with your product category than you are. He may not have the proper terminology, and may have difficulty putting needs into words. Listen for his point.
3. Ask questions: Show the other person that you are interested. Ask questions that encourage the prospect to develop his ideas.
4. Don't respond until you know what the other person means. It is always best to listen first, then make your point. Listen patiently. You won't forget your point if it's really important to you.
5. Avoid distractions. If some irrelevant point is on your mind, dump it. If possible, write yourself a quick note, then listen to the prospect. Do whatever it takes to give the prospect your undivided attention.

Source: B. Goss and D. O'Hair. (1988). *Communicating in Interpersonal Relationships.* New York: Macmillan, p. 28. Adapted with permission.

- The content of the approach can focus on small talk or the use of attention-getting openers.
- Asking about needs can serve as a bridge to the discussion of the product.
- When you ask about needs or problems, you should consider both the form and the content of your questions.
- The form of the question will determine how the interaction proceeds.
- The content of the question will determine the type of response.
- Listening involves more than just hearing. It involves reflective processing of the meaning of what is said.

As this summary indicates, the focus of this chapter was on the interpersonal side of the sales call: getting to know the prospect and learning about his needs. It is important to remember here that these interpersonal processes do *not stop* once you begin your presentation. Although your focus may shift more directly to the product, you will continue to build trust and rapport throughout your sales call. The prospect will continue to develop his impression of you and you will continue to negotiate rules.

Likewise, the processes of questioning and listening do not stop once you begin the presentation. Although they were discussed in this chapter, these processes play a crucial role throughout the sales call. As you will see in Chapter 11, the handling of objections is done largely through a questioning and listening process. The focus will shift from *your* asking about the prospect's needs to the *prospect's* asking about points that you have made. As a result, your role will become one of encouraging the prospect to ask questions. It will be extremely important that you *listen* to the prospect's questions before responding. Frequently, an objection may hide a deeper problem or the prospect may be unsure about the precise nature of her concern, so you must learn to engage in *reflective processing* of questions.

You will also find that you can apply what you have learned here about the form of a question throughout your sales calls. When a prospect asks a question, you can pay attention to whether the question was open- or closed-ended. This kind of analysis may yield clues to the kind of response the prospect is looking for.

In fact, listening to and reflecting on what the prospect is saying should help you to adapt all phases of the sales call to the prospect's needs. We realize this by putting together the material from the beginning and end of this chapter. The chapter began with a discussion of *adapting* and ended with a discussion of *listening*. Thinking about how these topics relate to each other, we begin to formulate an important point: *adapting requires listening.*

Although we may not know precisely what makes one salesperson succeed while another fails, we do know that most successful salespeople have the ability to adapt. As this chapter indicated, you can adapt all aspects of the sales call:

The basic structure.
The approach.
Your level of intimacy and rapport building.
Your own interaction rules.
Your opening line.
Your questioning strategy.

But in order to adapt to the needs of each prospect, you must rely on cues from the prospect as guides for your actions. This means listening to what the prospect is saying. Listen for messages beyond the superficial meaning. Reflect on what is really being said, and adapt your behavior accordingly.

Key Terms

Approach
Impression formation
Rapport
Pacing
Small talk
Benefit opener
Demonstration opener
Question opener
Open-ended question
Closed-ended question
Signal processing
Literal processing
Reflective processing

Review Questions

1. Why is it important that the approach come before the presentation?
2. What functions are served by small talk during the approach?
3. What is rapport? When should you develop it with prospects?

4. How do people negotiate rules during the approach?
5. What is an opener? List five different openers. What are the pros and cons of using openers?
6. What is the difference between needs and problems?
7. Under what conditions would you use a closed-ended question?
8. Under what conditions would you use an open-ended question?
9. What does reflective processing mean?
10. Why is listening so difficult in the sales call?
11. During which stages of the sales call should you listen?

Discussion Questions

1. This chapter stressed the importance of adapting to the prospect. However, it is also important to be in control during a sales call. Does adaptation rule out control? How can you reconcile these two needs?
2. How can you engage in small talk without being uninteresting?
3. Is it possible to determine the level of listening that another person is engaging in while you are speaking?
4. Is it possible to learn many of the interpersonal skills described in this chapter? That is, can you really learn to develop rapport, control impressions, manipulate the form of your questions, and listen carefully if you do not do these things naturally?

CASE 9.1

Joan McNeal, sales manager for the AJA Company, was put in charge of finding a location for her company's annual sales meeting. Based on help from travel agents and colleagues, she had narrowed her choice to one of two locations: a luxurious new hotel/convention center in Atlantic City, New Jersey, or a graceful old hotel in Boca Raton, Florida.

The purpose of the sales meeting was twofold: (1) to conduct some sales training seminars and (2) to reward the salespeople who had exceeded their quotas for the year. Joan had polled the sales representatives in an effort to determine their preferences, but opinion seemed to be evenly split.

Since the meeting was to be held in September, the weather was not an issue; it was expected to be pleasant in either location. What did concern the sales representatives were accommodations for their families, activities for children, and access to interesting nearby sites to explore during free time.

Based on her own experience, Joan knew that she also had to consider the price, the availability of meeting rooms, refreshments to be served during the meetings, and the availability of a general hospitality room where people could gather to chat informally.

In order to conduct a thorough evaluation of her options, Joan planned overnight stays in both of the hotels. At each hotel, she met with the hotel manager in order to discuss her needs.

This case includes the initial discussions with the managers from each hotel. *Before you continue reading, stop here, and write a plan for the approach you would use with Joan.* How would you begin? What would you talk about? Would you use an opener? If so, what kind? Be sure to remember that, as the hotel manager, you do not know any of the needs stated in this case. Your knowledge about Joan is limited to a previous phone call in which she told you that she needs a site for a meeting of 350 sales representatives from Mississippi.

Sam Pinter was the hotel manager for the Palace Hotel and Convention Center in Atlantic City. His hotel featured luxurious accommodations and its own casino with nightly entertainment. When Joan entered Sam's office, the following conversation took place:

SAM: Welcome to the Palace, Joan. I trust your trip was uneventful.

JOAN: The flight was actually quite pleasant.

SAM: From our phone conversation, I gather that you are interested in holding your annual sales meeting here at our hotel.

JOAN: Yes. You come recommended by several people.

SAM: Well, I think you'll see that our recommendations are well earned. We have one of the newest, most luxurious convention centers in the country. We offer more meeting rooms than any other center on the East Coast. Our complex occupies two full acres of land and includes two swimming pools, a golf course, five tennis courts, and a health club.

JOAN: How nice.

SAM: We just spent thousands of dollars on new Nautilus equipment for the gym. So, from now on, no one will have to get out of shape while staying at the Palace. And, as if that weren't enough, we have a casino with its own nightly entertainment. Why, last week, we had Cher and Ed McMahon doing night club acts right here.

JOAN: I see. But do you have any accommodations for children?

SAM: Of course. Kids can use any of the facilities except the casino.

JOAN: And what about your banquet and meeting rooms?

SAM: I'm glad you asked. We have just finished preparing a promotional video of the convention facilities. Why don't you come into the next room and have some coffee while we watch it? I'm sure you'll be impressed.

(As the video finishes)

continued

SAM: Have you ever seen such an impressive layout? We had Blatt, Jones, and Fairchild, from New York, design the casino. We imported the game tables from England. Some of them are genuine antiques, and we offer every kind of casino game you can imagine. Why, this is a great place to stay even during the winter season!

JOAN: Well the casino and meeting rooms look nice, but the actual guest rooms look awfully small.

SAM: They're not actually small at all. Each single room is 12 by 16 feet, and each double is at least 16 by 16. We've never had a guest complain about small rooms. We have had teams of designers choose fabrics and paint to give an open, airy look to the rooms. And besides, we have brand new Posturepedic mattresses in each room. You won't have a bad back while staying here!

JOAN: What kind of rates would you give us?

SAM: Well, our usual rates are $100 for the singles and $120 to $180 for the doubles. What time of year did you say you'd need them?

JOAN: September of next year.

SAM: We could do $75 and $90 for you if you promise to take 300 rooms.

JOAN: That sounds high, given that we'd have to guarantee the 300 rooms.

SAM: High? That's a 25 percent discount. That's the best anyone will do for you.

JOAN: And what about arrangements for food during the meetings?

SAM: Why don't you speak with Vincent, our banquet and food manager for that?

Harry Treetorn was Sam's counterpart at the Palm Hotel in Boca Raton. When Joan entered Harry's office, the following conversation took place:

HARRY: Hello, Ms. McNeal. Welcome to the Palm. I hope your trip was uneventful.

JOAN: The flight was actually quite pleasant.

HARRY: I'm glad. It's always good to start a trip off with a pleasant flight. Have you been to Boca Raton before?

JOAN: No. In fact, although I've traveled quite extensively, I've never been to Florida.

HARRY: Well, if you have time when we're through talking, maybe we can show you around a little.

JOAN: I'd love it.

HARRY: Great. Then why don't we get down to business, so we'll be sure to have time? Now, I understand from our phone conversation that you are considering holding your annual sales meeting at our hotel. But I'm not sure exactly what your needs will be.

JOAN: Well, we're talking about 350 salespeople for a 4-day meeting some time in September of next year.

HARRY: That's great. We still have some space for meetings booked that far in advance. But tell me, exactly what kind of accommodations are you looking for?

JOAN: Nothing out of the ordinary. Good rates on the guest rooms, ample meeting rooms and banquet facilities.

HARRY: Well, tell me this: have you had any sales meetings in the past.

JOAN: This is our fifth. It's the third one I've been in charge of.

HARRY: Have you had any problems with your annual meetings in the past?

JOAN: Actually, we have. Last year, people complained that there wasn't enough to do with their free time.

HARRY: I see. Well we've handled a lot of sales meetings in the past, and an important issue seems to be the amount of structure planned into people's time schedules. Tell me, how much free time will your people have? Are you keeping them busy with meetings, or are you looking for sights and entertainment for them?

JOAN: Some of each. We are concerned with proximity to some interesting daytime activities. Many of the people want to bring their families.

HARRY: I see. So you'll be needing things to entertain spouses and children.

JOAN: Exactly.

HARRY: Well, from what you've said, I think we can put together an interesting package for you. Let me tell you about our meeting facilities first.

JOAN: Great.

HARRY: We have a variety of meeting rooms, ranging from accommodations for small discussion groups to large lectures. Our big rooms would easily hold your whole group. I can show them to you when we've finished talking.

JOAN: I'd like to see them. We'll need both sizes of rooms. I'd also like to know about your guest rooms.

HARRY: Of course. The room you'll be staying in tonight is typical. Although the main building of our hotel is over 70 years old, all of our guest rooms have been redecorated within the last year. Our standard rates are $100 for a single and $125 to $200 for a double, but of course, you would receive special rates: $75 and $95.

JOAN: Isn't that a little high?

HARRY: I know it sounds high, but these rates are actually discounted a

continued

full 25 percent. We could also include a suite, free of charge, that you could use as a hospitality room.

JOAN: Great.

HARRY: Oh, and don't let me forget spouses and children. We have different options for all of them. Spouses can enjoy time in our health club during the day. Or, for those who don't work out, we provide hourly shuttle buses to some interesting sites and shopping areas. We also feature baby sitters for the younger children free of charge. For teens, we have special parties at night, and during the day we run sports and game activities for all age groups. Would you like to start to tour some of our facilities while we continue our discussion?

1. Based on the preceding interactions, who will be more successful in capturing Joan's business? Why?
2. Provide an overall evaluation of both discussions.
3. What kind of impression do you think Joan formed of Sam? Of Harry?
4. Discuss the questioning and listening techniques of each manager.

References

1. Krivonos, P. D. and M. L. Knapp. (1975). Initiating communication: What do you say when you say hello? *Central States Speech Journal, 26,* 115–125.

2. McLaughlin, M. (1984). *Conversation: How Talk Is Organized.* Beverly Hills, CA: Sage, Chapter 5.

3. Szymanski, D. M. (1988). Determinants of selling effectiveness: The importance of declarative knowledge to the personal selling concept. *Journal of Marketing, 52*(1), 64–77.

4. Schul, Y. (1983). Integration and abstraction in impression formation. *Journal of Personality and Social Psychology, 44*(4), 45–54.

5. Watkins, M. and Z. Peynircioglu. (1984). Determining perceived meaning during impression formation: Another look at the meaning change hypothesis. *Journal of Personality and Social Psychology, 46*(5), 1005–1016.

6. DePaulo, B., D. A. Kenny, C. Hoover, W. Webb, and P. Oliver. (1987). Accuracy of person perception: Do people know what kinds of impressions they convey? *Journal of Personality and Social Psychology, 52*(2), 3003–3015.

7. Sujan, M., J. R. Bettman, and H. Sujan. (1986). Effects of consumer expectations on information processing in selling encounters. *Journal of Marketing Research, 23,* 346–353.

8. Mortensen, D. (1972). *Communication: The Study of Human Interaction.* New York: McGraw-Hill.

9. King, R. H., and M. Booze. (1986). Sales training and impression management. *Journal of Personal Selling and Sales Management, 6,* 51–60.

10. Berger, C. (1987). Communicating under uncertainty. In: M. Roloff and G. Miller (eds.), *Sage Annual Reviews of Communication Research (Interpersonal processes: New directions in communication research)*, Vol. 14. Newbury Park, CA: Sage, 39–62.

11. Moines, D. (1982). To trust, perchance to buy. *Psychology Today* (August), 51–54.

12. Nickels, W., R. Everett, and R. Klein (1983). Rapport building by salespeople: A neurolinguistic approach. *Journal of Personal Selling and Sales Management, 3*(November), 1–8.

13. Kent, G. G., J. D. Davis, and D. Shapiro. (1981). Effect of mutual acquaintance on the construction of conversation. *Journal of Experimental Psychology, 17,* 197–209.

14. Crawford, M. (1983). *New Products Management.* Homewood, IL: Irwin.

15. Goss, B. (1982). Listening as information processing. *Communication Quarterly, 30,* 304–307.

16. Goss, B., and D. O'Hair. (1988). *Communicating in Interpersonal Relationships.* New York: Macmillan.

10

The Sales Presentation

CHAPTER OBJECTIVES

In this chapter, you will learn:

- To help prospects frame their problems.
- To define the prospect's problem in a way that is favorable to your product.
- To solve problems in your sales presentations.
- How to choose a format for your presentation that will best accomplish your goals.
- How to develop a plan for demonstrating your product.

CHAPTER OUTLINE

A Sales Challenge

Bill Schwartz and Tina Elkins were two college seniors who had just completed summer internships with a large advertising agency. Tina had worked directly in a selling capacity, helping to put together presentations of proposed campaigns for prospective clients. Bill had worked on the other side of selling, helping media buyers decide which media should be purchased to run the ads. Both Bill and Tina had become interested in sales careers as a result of their experiences and enrolled in a personal selling course when they returned to school. On the first day of class, they found themselves debating the best techniques for making sales presentations:

TINA: I'm sold on formal presentations. When we pitched accounts, the account executive put together a really slick, professional presentation complete with slides and audiovisuals. She didn't miss a thing. An informal sales call just wouldn't have had that impact.

BILL: Well, when salespeople called on the media buyers I worked with, they didn't really make presentations. They talked informally with us, asked us about our needs, and tried to get us to buy spots in their own media. I'd much rather make that kind of sales call. It seemed really natural to me and a better way of satisfying needs.

TINA: Of course, we worked on the client's needs. But we asked about them in advance, worked behind the scenes to come up with the idea, and then presented them with the results.

An Overview

Although Tina and Bill are just beginning their personal selling course, they have hit upon an important question: How do you present your product to a prospect? Do you make a formal presentation, as Tina did, or do you persuade the prospect during an informal discussion, as Bill advocated? Do you have a list of points you want to make, or do you "play it by ear?" Do you launch immediately into an analysis of your product's features, or do you begin by showing your product?

In this chapter, we will discuss your options for making a presentation. As you will see, sales presentations can differ in terms of *content* as well as *format*. You can best understand the difference between the presentation's content and format if you think in terms of *what* versus *how*. The content of the presentation refers to *what* is communicated, and the format determines *how* the message is communicated (see Figure 10.1).

What to communicate. As you learned in Chapter 5, you can best persuade the prospect to act if your product solves some problem for him. Therefore, the *content* of your presentation should focus on problem solving,

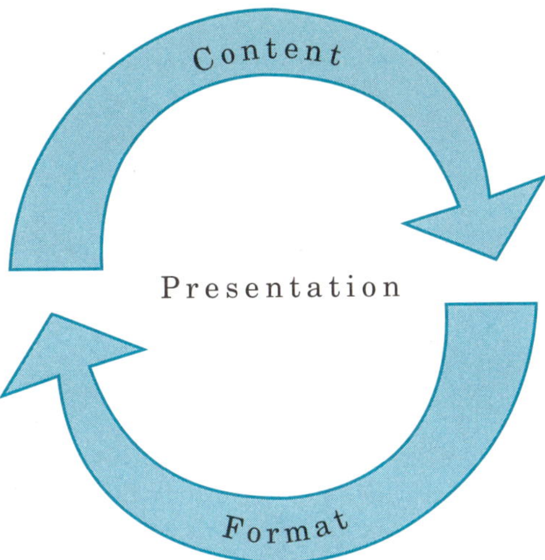

FIGURE 10.1 The content of a presentation affects the format, but the format also affects the content.

and we begin the chapter with a discussion of the problem-solving process.

How to communicate. Problem solving can be accomplished in many different presentation formats. The appropriate format depends upon the prospect, your product, and your own skills and preferences. In this chapter, we present the advantages and disadvantages of each presentation format so that you will be able to choose among them. Further, we discuss demonstration techniques for adding a visual dimension to your presentation's format. These techniques range from a demonstration of the product itself to the use of films or slides.

The Presentation's Content: Needs versus Problems

In Chapter 9, you learned that there are subtle differences between needs and problems. A prospect who is asked about his problems will be more likely to tell you about real needs.[1]

There is also a subtle difference in what happens when your presentation is designed to *solve problems* rather than to *satisfy needs.* When you attempt to solve the prospect's problems, you take on a more *active* role than when you simply match her needs with your product. The difference between satisfying needs and solving problems is illustrated in the following two dialogues, where a couple is inquiring about investments for their daughter's college education. The first salesperson uses a need-satisfying strategy, whereas the second one uses a problem-solving approach.

DIALOGUE I

SALESPERSON: (*Summarizing what the Fords have just said*) So it appears that you need a secure investment vehicle that will reinvest earnings until 2001.

MR. FORD: That's right. We would just as soon not bother with interest or dividends until Sarah is ready for college.

SALESPERSON: Our mutual fund is ideally suited to your needs. It combines stocks and bonds, and our expert money managers move funds back and forth in order to maximize the return. With this investment, you won't become rich overnight, but you should have the money when Sarah is ready for school.

Although this salesperson is not making any glaring errors, an examination of the next dialogue quickly shows which salesperson would be more successful.

DIALOGUE II

SALESPERSON: (*Summarizing what the Fords have said*) So it appears that your problem is to find a secure investment vehicle that will provide for Sarah's college tuition in 2001.

MR. FORD: That's right.

SALESPERSON: What you have here is a special investment problem. It is complicated by the fact that we don't know what tuitions will be in 2001, but we do know that they have been increasing much faster than inflation.

MRS. FORD: That's precisely our concern.

SALESPERSON: Well, there are several options. One is our debt-equity mutual fund. This fund is popular with couples saving for college education because it is aimed at long-term growth. But there's something else that might be of interest. Have you heard of the programs some colleges are developing whereby a couple pays tuition when their child is young, and is, in turn, guaranteed that there will be no additional charges when the child is ready to start her freshmen year? More and more colleges are using this plan. The school benefits by getting the use of the money for 10 to 15 years, and the couple benefits by getting a hedge against runaway tuition increases.

MR. FORD: Sounds terrific. How can we learn more about this?

SALESPERSON: We have these brochures explaining the plans and some investment packages we have developed to accompany it.

In the second case, the salesperson is acting as a consultant. She is solving the prospect's problem with *information* in addition to a product. Her willingness to take time to discuss the problem shows concern and contributes to her credibility. It is likely that prospects helped in this way will not only invest in this

EXHIBIT 10.1

A Successful Problem Solver

Barbara Cadkin, the number one Toyota saleswoman in the country, is well aware of the benefits of solving prospects' problems. One thing that Barbara will not do to sell a car is hard sell anyone: "I don't want you to leave this dealership unhappy" is a statement made commonly by Barbara. She does not believe in pressuring people, and instead, realizes the value of repeat business. Barbara wants prospects to think of her as their "car consultant"—like their lawyer or accountant, whom they can contact with car related problems for the rest of their lives. It is not surprising that Barbara ranked in the 92nd percentile (out of 12,000 salespeople) in Toyota's customer satisfaction index.

Source: N. Chesanow, (1988). Four super successful saleswomen. *New Woman*, (September), 116–122.

money fund but will also return to this salesperson for future financial planning needs.

As these examples illustrate, problem solving can differentiate you from other salespeople, who may have equally good products to sell. When you use your expertise to help the prospect solve a problem, you not only help the prospect but also create a desire for your product. It is not surprising, therefore, that comparisons between successful and less successful salespeople find that the successful ones engage in significantly more problem solving during their sales calls.[2,3]

The Problem-Solving Presentation

As Table 10.1 suggests, the general problem-solving process begins with the definition of the problem. Although problem definition may seem to be a trivial step (how can you have a problem that is not defined?), there is far more to it than you might expect. In particular, the definition of a problem means establishing a basic frame for the problem.

Table 10.1 The Problem-Solving Process

Define the problem and establish a problem frame
Search for information
Evaluate alternatives
Make the decision
Evaluate the decision outcome

The **frame** of a problem is *a reference point or perspective for considering alternative solutions.* To appreciate the importance of a problem's frame, consider a case where you offer a purchasing agent a 15 percent quantity discount, but her frame of reference is a 20 percent discount. Chances are that your offer will not be well received. However, if the same purchasing agent's frame of reference is a 10 percent discount, your offer will look pretty good. As Table 10.2 indicates, the frame of a problem refers to more than the price. It refers more generally to the way a prospect thinks about her problem. Although it may require extra work on your part, it is generally worth the effort to help the prospect frame her problem because the prospect's frame of reference will affect the way she evaluates alternative problem solutions.

The Problem Frame Affects the Prospect's Decision

The powerful effect that a frame of reference has on the outcome of a decision was illustrated in an experiment that compared different ways of framing a problem. The problem in this study involved a choice between two alternative courses of action. One group of subjects was told that the United States was preparing for an outbreak of a disease that could kill up to 600 people. If they chose Option A, they could definitely save 200 lives. If they chose Option B, there was a 1/3 chance that all 600 would be saved and a 2/3 chance that none would be saved.

In the second group, subjects were given equivalent options, but ones that were framed in terms of the number of deaths instead of the number of lives saved. These subjects were told that with Option A, 400 people would definitely die, whereas with Option B, there was a 1/3 chance that none would die and a 2/3 chance that all 600 would die.

The results of this study are quite dramatic (see Table 10.3). The options in

Table 10.2 Alternative Ways of Framing the Same Purchase Problem

Product	*Alternative Frames of Reference*
A stereo	Sound reproduction. Equipment that will be visible in her living room.
A college education	A means of acquiring specific skills to enhance one's ability to get a good job. A total social environment that will influence one's choice of friends and general outlook on life for years to come.
An office telephone system	A communication system. A means of demonstrating good decision-making skills to others in the firm.

Table 10.3 Framing the Problem in Terms of Gains Versus Losses

	Group 1	*Group 2*
Problem Frame	*Gain Benefits*	*Avoid Losses*
Option A	Save 200 lives	Avoid loss of 400 lives
Option B	1/3 chance that all would be saved 2/3 chance that none would be saved	1/3 chance that none would die 2/3 chance that all would die
Choice	72% chose A (less risk)	78% chose B (more risk)

both cases were equivalent (*no one died* is the same as *everyone lived*). However, *framing* the problem in terms of "number of lives saved" versus "number of lives lost" reversed the choices. In the first group, which was told that it could save lives, 72 percent chose the less risky option—Option A. But when the same decision was framed in terms of lives lost, 78 percent chose the riskier option—Option B. Without changing any of the facts, researchers changed the option chosen simply by framing the problem differently.[4]

The same effect has been found in a selling context. When buying decisions were framed in terms of *avoiding losses*, purchasing agents chose riskier options than when the decisions were framed in terms of *gaining benefits*.[5] What makes this finding so important is the fact that almost any buying problem can be framed in terms of gains versus losses. Consider the following alternate ways of framing the same decisions.

"Without this investment, you are sure to lose money" versus "with this investment, you are sure to make money."

"If you don't update this telecommunication network, it will start to look as though this whole office is outdated" versus "This new telecommunication system has impressed some executives to the point where the person who chose it got promoted. It really improves everybody's productivity."

"Competitors are adopting this new machinery. If you don't, you won't remain competitive" versus "This new machinery will increase efficiency on your assembly line by 10 percent as soon as it's installed."

"If you don't switch suppliers, you are going to run into problems maintaining inventories" versus "If you switch suppliers, you will have much steadier inventory levels."

In each of these cases, a salesperson who uses the first frame, based on losses, will have different results than the salesperson who uses the second frame, based on gains. Which one is *better* will depend upon the product he is presenting to the prospect: is it the riskier or the safer choice? A salesperson who is asking a prospect to change suppliers or to make some other risky choice may get better results by framing the problem in terms of *loss avoidance*.

Consider how Barbara Miller, a real estate agent, applied these principles during a conversation with prospects Frank and Mary Wilson. Frank and Mary approached Barbara when they become interested in buying their first home, a buying problem that seems risky to almost everyone:

MARY: We are looking for a three-bedroom house in the western side of town.

BARBARA: How much can you spend?

MARY: Our joint income is $55,000, but we wanted to stay in the $70,000 price range. My sister-in-law bought a beautiful house 2 years ago for $62,000, and we're looking for something like hers.

BARBARA: That may pose a problem. Three-bedroom houses in good neighborhoods are now going for around $100,000. With your income, you could easily afford those mortgage payments.

FRANK: Maybe we should stay where we are now. We'd wanted to buy because we are expecting our first baby in December, but our apartment is really quite adequate.

BARBARA: I understand your concern, but if you decide to delay your purchase, you will run the risk of being closed out of the housing market forever. Housing prices are going up much faster than inflation. Your sister's house is probably worth $120,000 by now. If you wait another year, houses will be completely out of sight. (*Thumbing through her listings*) Oh, here's a cute starter house for only $91,000.

FRANK: Maybe we should see it.

Compare this problem frame to the following one based on benefits:

BARBARA: I understand your concern, but houses are great investments. Why, your sister's house is probably worth $120,000 by now. If you buy one now, it will be worth a lot more in the future. Look, here's a cute starter house for only $91,000.

FRANK: That's really more than we wanted to pay.

In the first case, Barbara was able to interest the Wilsons in seeing the house by helping them to frame the problem in a new way. By framing the choice in terms of loss avoidance, she encouraged more risk taking. She also was able to raise the price reference by using a high frame of reference ($100,000) to make the $91,000 sound more reasonable. Finally, Barbara helped to change the frame of reference by suggesting a new set of criteria for evaluating the problem. Instead of thinking of the house simply in terms of shelter, the Wilsons were able to see the investment value of buying instead of renting.

Selecting Criteria for Solving a Problem

Before a prospect can analyze alternative solutions to a problem, she must have a set of decision criteria on which to base the evaluation of alternatives. **Decision**

criteria *are the attributes that we use to evaluate our alternatives when we make a choice* (see Table 10.4).

As an example, consider the case of Darryn and Andrew, two people who have different decision criteria for evaluating alternative health clubs. Darryn wants a club with a lot of single women that is located near his office so that he can stop by after work and socialize. Therefore, his decision criteria are (1) the number of single women members and (2) proximity to work. In contrast, Andrew is interested in a club that will facilitate his serious body building. His criteria are (1) the availability of sophisticated exercise machines and free weights and (2) expert personal trainers.

In all likelihood, Darryn and Andrew will make quite different choices of health clubs simply because their decision criteria are so different. Though we may not be fully aware of the criteria we use in evaluating problem alternatives, these criteria exert a strong influence on the outcomes of our decisions.

Gary J. Smith, director of operations for a firm that sells computerized process-control systems, recognizes that a prospect's decision criteria can be a powerful persuasive tool. Smith knows that a prospect who evaluates products based on criteria where competitors are weak will tend to go with Smith's firm. He instructs his salespeople to study competitors' products for weaknesses and then to suggest these problem areas to prospects as decision criteria.[6] If, for example, a major competitor lacks 24-hour service for the computer, Smith's salespeople will suggest the importance of this service as a decision criterion. Thus, instead of attacking competitors head on, the salespeople undermine them more subtly by influencing the prospects' decision making.

Table 10.4 Examples of Products and Some Common Decision Criteria

Product	*Decision Criteria*
Automobile	Miles per gallon Maintenance costs Sportiness Price Rear seat room
Airplane	Miles per gallon Safety record Price Maintenance costs Number of seats
Factory equipment	Payback period Compatibility with other equipment Reliability Maintenance costs

Table 10.5 Prospect Experience Affects Decision Criteria

	Type of Choice	
Prospect Experience	*Similar Products*	*Dissimilar Products*
Novice	No fixed criteria	No fixed criteria
Expert	Fixed criteria	No fixed criteria

However, you must exercise caution in attempting to influence a prospect's decision criteria. As Table 10.5 indicates, your ability to influence these criteria will depend upon the prospect's experience, as well as the type of choice being made.[7]

Decision Criteria and Prospect Expertise. If the prospect is a novice in purchasing your product, it is likely that you can exert a great deal of influence on his decision because his decision criteria will probably not be well formed. The novice prospect may, in fact, look to you for help in determining the criteria that will help solve his problem satisfactorily. This is the case when, for example, a person buys a first computer and does not know what to look for (i.e., does not have a set of decision criteria).

In contrast to novices are expert buyers. An expert buyer can be a consumer or an industrial buyer. The key difference between experts and novices is their degree of familiarity with the product category. Because the expert buyer has experience in purchasing a product category, he tends to have well-formed criteria for choosing among alternatives. However, in certain types of problems, even experts' criteria are not well formed. This occurs when the choice is between different categories of products (going out to dinner versus buying a new personal stereo; joining a health club versus buying one's own exercise equipment).

Consider, for example, a case where a secretary is making a choice between purchasing another typewriter versus a personal computer outfitted for word processing. If the choice were simply between two typewriters, the salesperson would likely have little impact on the decision criteria. To the extent that the secretary is an expert in buying typewriters, the decision criteria would undoubtedly be relatively fixed. However, in choosing between two different product categories, a typewriter and a personal computer, the secretary needs a new set of decision criteria. This will be true even if the secretary has fixed criteria for each category (e.g., when buying typewriters, base the choice on the feel of the keyboard and the ease of correction; when choosing computers, base the choice on the appearance of the screen and the size of the memory).

Working with the Prospect's Existing Criteria. In general, it is important to discover whether or not the prospect has fixed decision criteria. If the prospect is an expert buyer and has a well-formed set of decision criteria, any attempt to change these criteria may be regarded as pushy. Think of how you would regard a salesperson who attempted to do this:

PROSPECT: My primary concern is safety. I use the station wagon for transporting my kids, so I don't really care about luxury options.

SALESPERSON: Well, transporting kids doesn't mean that you have to sacrifice luxury. You haven't seen our newly designed bucket seats. They are so comfortable that you won't want to get out of the car.

PROSPECT: That's not really my concern.

SALESPERSON: Just sit on one and try it out.

When a prospect has a well-formed set of decision criteria, a salesperson will be more likely to succeed by attempting to work with the existing criteria and trying to fit her product to them. She might exert influence by pointing out new information (e.g., "Did you know that all of our luxury edition models are equipped with air bags?") but should not argue directly against the prospect's established criteria ("Transporting kids doesn't mean that you have to sacrifice luxury.")

Basing Decision Criteria on Benefits Versus Product Attributes. Although we may refer to *product benefits* and *product attributes* interchangeably in everyday speech, these terms represent very different concepts. An attribute is a feature of the actual product (e.g., protein in a shampoo); a benefit is a value that the feature provides to the prospect (e.g., silky hair). Table 10.6 provides some examples of product attributes and associated benefits. After reading this list, try to make up some of your own examples.

In general, *people seek benefits*.[8,9] This is obvious in many decision criteria:

"Buy a typewriter that makes it easy to correct mistakes."
"Join a health club where it's easy to meet people."
"Buy ball bearings that will minimize factory repair bills."

Many famous salespeople have recognized the importance of benefits in expressions like "Don't sell the drill; sell the hole that it will make" or "Don't sell the lipstick; sell the glamour it will bring." A common failing of inexperienced salespeople is that they give too much technical detail about the products and do not pay enough attention to the benefits they provide.

Table 10.6 Product Attributes Versus Benefits

Product Attributes	*Product Benefits*
Computer has 20 megahertz	Computer processes quickly
Camera is an SLR	Camera allows you to change lenses and see what the lens sees
Cream contains PABA	Cream prevents sunburn
Frozen food comes in Styrofoam box	Frozen food is microwavable
Running shoes have dual-density midsoles	Running shoes have support and cushioning

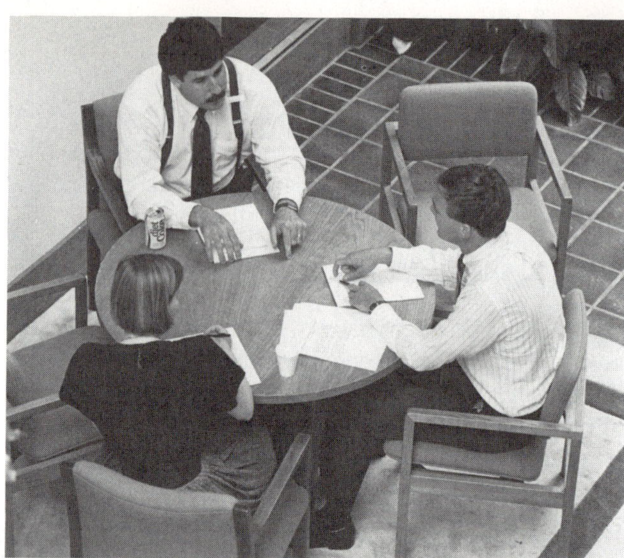

Many sales "presentations" are actually informal discussions about the product. (© Renee Lynn/Photo Researchers, Inc.)

However, it is not wise to ignore product attributes altogether. You may find that combining benefits with attributes can lead to a successful presentation. To accomplish this, you can begin by asking about the *benefits* that the prospect is seeking and then show how specific *attributes* of your product can provide them. In some cases, prospects may have learned to associate benefits with certain product attributes. Many runners, for example, have a great deal of technical knowledge about running shoes. A salesperson who sells only benefits ("This shoe will give you a lot of support") may be less convincing to the experienced prospect than the salesperson who ties the benefit to technical product attributes[10] ("This shoe will provide a lot of support because it has a dual-density midsole and sturdy heel cup.") Though these attributes may be too technical for novice runners, experienced runners may expect them to be discussed.

In deciding how much technical material about product attributes to incorporate into your discussion, you should take into consideration the background of the prospect (an engineer or a layperson), as well as his or her desire to hear about such details. A purchasing agent whose background is in engineering may be much more receptive to a more technical presentation, whereas one without such a background may prefer a much simpler style.[11]

The Presentation Format

Structured Versus Unstructured Presentations

As we mentioned earlier, the word *presentation* usually implies a certain degree of formality and one-way communication. However, sales calls differ widely in

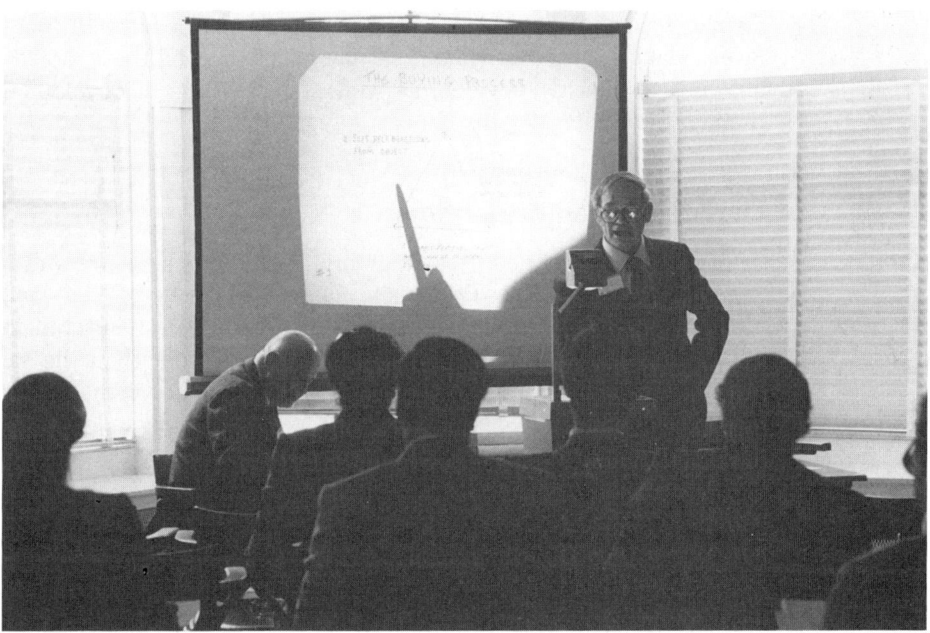

Formal presentations may be made to groups of prospects. (© Ken Robert Buck 1981/The Picture Cube.)

Use of the Automated Formats. It is possible to use the automated formats in cases where most prospects have very similar problems. The problems can be assessed prior to the sales call and the solutions worked into the automated presentation. There may also be cases where a salesperson will combine an automated presentation with other presentation formats when calling on a single account. In these cases, the salesperson typically uses an unstructured format during the initial calls but follows up with an automated presentation on a later visit. Advertising agencies use this approach to advantage by assessing needs during the initial meetings and then developing formal proposals based on their findings.

In contrast, a salesperson may attempt to attract a prospect with an automated presentation, and then, once the prospect is interested, proceed to interact with him to help solve problems. This approach is becoming popular among law firms that use videotaped presentations in their initial contacts with prospects.[13] In most cases, however, the automated formats are used when the selling company wants near-total control over the salesperson's message, especially when the salesperson is untrained and inexperienced.

Although the automated presentations are used less frequently than the alternative formats, their use appears to be on the increase. The fully automated format was used, at least occasionally, by 18 percent of major selling organizations in 1988 (compared with less than 10 percent in 1973),[14] while the semiautomated format was used by 44 percent (up from 33 percent in 1973) of major selling firms. Many experts attribute the increased use of these presentations to the growing popularity of video, as well as technological developments that make them easy to use.

The Memorized Presentation

Another type of canned presentation is the **memorized presentation.** With this presentation style, the *salesperson memorizes and recites a company-prepared speech to the prospect.* Because the salesperson is restricted to the prepared speech, she actually has little more individual input than the salesperson who delivers a semiautomated presentation. The difference is that with the memorized presentation, the prospect does not see the salesperson reading from written material. Depending upon the salesperson's delivery style, it may or may not be obvious that she is reciting a memorized speech.

Advantages and Disadvantages. An advantage of the memorized speech over the automated formats is that the prospect does not see the salesperson reading the presentation from preprinted material. As a result, the memorized presentation can give the illusion that the salesperson is giving the prospect individualized attention. However, this illusion can also be dangerous.

In the automated presentations, where it is obvious that the salesperson is there to present prepared visual or audiovisual material, the prospect does not *expect* an actual interaction to occur. However, with the memorized speech, there are no obvious cues that the salesperson is presenting a prepared speech. As a result, the prospect may form the expectation that an actual interaction will occur.

Recall from Chapter 3 that very strong rules govern interactions. Based on these rules, we expect interactions to consist of turn taking, in which each person responds to what the other has said. If the prospect expects this process to occur, while the salesperson persists in delivering the memorized speech, the salesperson may appear stubborn and unresponsive.

It is possible, however, to include *very limited* interaction in the memorized presentation. This can be accomplished with the use of *closed-ended* questions that limit the prospect to choosing between specified alternatives. For example, a memorized presentation might include questions such as "Do you have boys or girls?" Because the choices are limited to "boys," "girls," or "both," messages can be prepared in advance to follow each response. Through the use of this kind of limited questioning, a salesperson could adapt the problem frame to each prospect. However, there is always the danger that, once the prospect is allowed to speak, she will elaborate and shift the salesperson away from the memorized speech.

While you might think that memorizing a presentation should give a salesperson confidence, it can actually put her in an awkward position in cases where prospects ask questions or try to interrupt. It can be extremely difficult to answer questions and respond to a prospect in the middle of a memorized speech. Chances are that any interruption in the flow of the presentation will end in a topic that does not fit neatly into the original material. The result can make the salesperson more ill at ease than when she is allowed to interact naturally with the prospect.

Use of the Memorized Format. In a study on format utilization, many sales executives rated the memorized presentation as the worst method for achieving sales objectives, ranking it below the fully and semiautomated methods.[15] However, it can be used to aid new salespeople or to standardize telephone sales, even in the case of rather sophisticated products.

Salespeople at Prudential-Bache Securities read from a prepared script when telemarketing for new accounts. In fact, their scripts illustrate how questions can be integrated into a memorized presentation. The following excerpt from one of their actual scripts is a case in point (referring to an investment allocation program): "What it does is develop a formula showing how your investment assets should be allocated to take care of your present needs and future goals. Does that sound like it would be of value to you?"[16] (see Figures 10.3 and 10.4).

The Organized Presentation

A more popular and frequently used presentation method is the **organized presentation**. This method receives its name because *much of the content of the presentation is organized in advance, while the actual dialogue is allowed to flow naturally.* With an organized presentation, the salesperson has a set of specific objectives and points of information outlined by the company. However, once face-to-face with the prospect, the salesperson is free to follow an interactive style.

Advantages and Disadvantages. The organized presentation combines the advantages of a well-structured presale plan and an interactive presentation style.

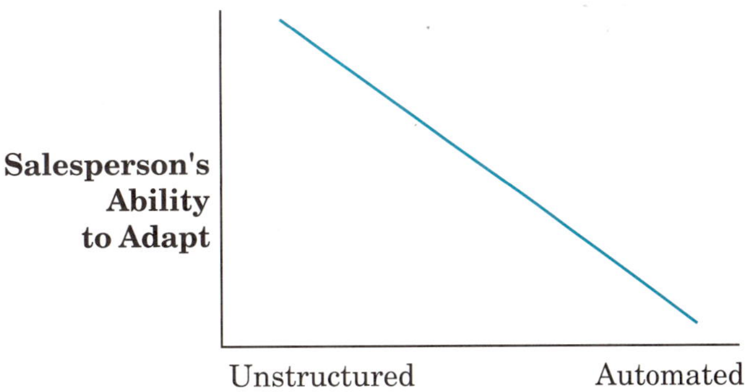

FIGURE 10.3 The ability to adapt the sales presentation to each prospect.

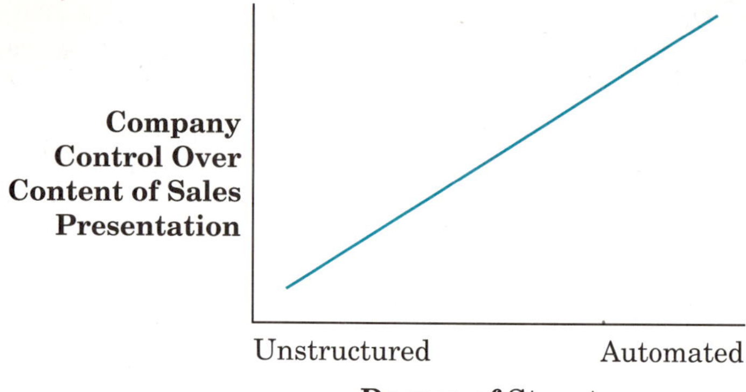

FIGURE 10.4 Company control increases as presentations become more structured.

It affords the company some control over the sales message but does not restrict the salesperson to a particular speech. This format adapts well to the problem-solving approach outlined earlier. It can be used to advantage if the salesperson proceeds by asking about the prospect's problems and solving them with the appropriate company-supplied product information. Because of the extensive advance preparation regarding the product and its benefits, the salesperson is free to concentrate on the prospect during the actual interaction.

Despite its many advantages, the organized presentation must be used with caution when a salesperson has little or no experience. In such cases, the salesperson may have problems searching for words even though he has a sense of the basic points that must be covered. A good training program that includes role playing and the observation of experienced salespeople can, however, usually overcome this disadvantage.

Use of the Organized Presentation. The organized presentation is well suited to cases where there is some commonality in prospects' problems but where prospects are different enough to require individualized attention. It is important to note that the organized presentation often includes the use of visual aids—flip charts and brochures. However, this presentation is not rigidly predetermined to focus on these devices. They are employed simply as aids in making specific points. Because the company does not control the format of the interaction, the salesperson is free to determine a suitable degree of formality based on her personal assessment of the situation.

The Unstructured Presentation

In the **unstructured presentation,** *the salesperson is free to present the product in any way that she chooses.* The company requires no checklists of specific information and does not attempt to control the content of what is said to the prospect. Although this presentation method is not the most popular among sales executives, it is viewed as the most persuasive.[17] It minimizes company control and consistency across salespeople but allows salespeople to devise entirely different arguments for each prospect.

It is important to note that the *unstructured* presentation is not *unplanned.* It simply shifts the responsibility for planning from the company to the salesperson. In this case, the salesperson should learn as much as possible about the prospect before the approach, and during the sales call should concentrate on the problem-solving process. The use of visual aids is generally the salesperson's decision.

Advantages and Disadvantages. The unstructured format can be somewhat dangerous if the salesperson is untrained and inexperienced. With no company guidelines regarding the content of the sales presentation, the novice may be at a loss about what points to make. Though trial and error will eventually teach such guidelines, many sales may be lost in the process. This is why many companies require novice salespeople to accompany experienced salespeople on sales calls before going out on their own.

However, the lack of a predetermined structure can be a big advantage for experienced salespeople. It affords the greatest freedom to tailor the form as well as the content of the presentation to the individual prospect. With this kind of freedom, today's professional salespeople can take full advantage of their expertise and skills to help prospects define and solve their problems.

Use of the Unstructured Format. The unstructured presentation is appropriate in cases where salespeople need maximum flexibility to adapt to each prospect. This occurs when prospects are so different that any companywide presale planning will be unable to solve their problems. This presentation format works best when the salespeople are highly skilled and well trained. It is particularly useful in a great deal of business-to-business selling where the salesperson acts as a consultant to the prospect or has an ongoing relationship with the prospect.

The Sales Demonstration

Thus far, we have concentrated on the verbal elements of the sales call: engaging in small talk, building rapport, framing and solving problems, and discussing benefits. Whenever possible, however, you should supplement verbal descriptions of your products with some kind of demonstration. In the **sales demonstration**, a *visual or audio dimension is added to the verbal discussion.* This does not mean that the presentation will be automated or semiautomated. There are many cases when a variety of audiovisual aids is used during organized and unstructured

Table 10.7 The Importance of Specific Presentation Techniques

Selling Technique	Mean Importance: Industrial	Mean Importance: Consumer
1. *Qualify by asking prospect question:* Ask the prospect questions during the sales presentation to establish prospect's understanding	4.26*	4.38
2. *Talk prospect's language:* Use short nontechnical words in the sales presentation	4.09	4.35
3. *Tailored sales presentation:* Make a sales presentation that is specifically tailored to each prospect	4.33	4.03
4. *Help prospect visualize offering:* Use the offering, a model, a brochure, a film, etc. to help the prospect visualize the sales offering	4.11	4.12
5. *Demonstrate:* Use a demonstration to reinforce the sales presentation	4.09	4.07
6. *Partially standardized sales presentation:* Make a sales presentation that is slightly different for each prospect	3.66	3.33
7. *Use comparisons:* Make comparisons in the sales presentation (e.g., "Our offering has twice the sales theirs does!")	3.06	2.75
8. *Use showmanship/dramatization:* Emphasize a point using unusual dramatic efforts	2.34	2.38
9. *Standardized sales presentation:* Make the same sales presentation to all prospects	1.68	2.11

* 1 = not important; 5 = very important.

Source: Reprinted by permission of *Journal of Personal Selling and Sales Management* © 1985. R. Hite and J. Bellizzi. (1985). Differences in the importance of selling techniques between consumer and industrial salespeople. *Journal of Personal Selling and Sales Management*, 5 (November). 19–30.

presentations. In fact, the value of a sales demonstration in any presentation format cannot be overstressed. As Table 10.7 shows, demonstration and visualization of the product were viewed as some of the more important elements of the presentation by actual salespeople. A well-planned demonstration can help you achieve a number of important objectives:

- Increase *credibility*. The expression "seeing is believing" applies particularly well to sales, since prospects tend to question claims made by salespeople.
- Increase the *prospect's involvement*. Adding a visual or audiovisual dimension to your presentation can help keep the prospect's interest and attention high, especially if you allow the prospect to participate in the demonstration.
- Increase *the prospect's desire* for the product. The sight, sound, touch, or use of a product has much greater immediate appeal than a verbal description, no matter how good that description is.
- Create a *lasting impression*. Adding a visual dimension to a presentation increases the prospect's ability to recall information about your product over a longer period of time.

To appreciate the appeal of a sales demonstration, consider the difference in your own responses to a simple verbal description of a product compared to an actual demonstration. No amount of technical facts about a pair of stereo speakers, for example, can equal the persuasive impact of 5 minutes in the sound room of an audio store. No verbal description of a fragrance can match the sensation of actually smelling it, and no verbal description of a sports car's engine can match the feel of actually driving the car.

Planning a Successful Demonstration

The first step in planning your sales demonstration is to determine *what* information you want to convey (Figure 10.5). In most selling situations, there are many different points that could be conveyed in a demonstration. You may choose

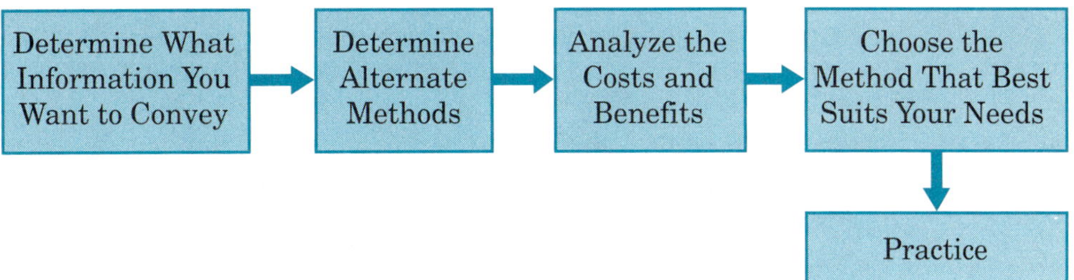

FIGURE 10.5 Planning a successful demonstration.

to highlight the way a product functions—the handling of a car, the clarity of a copying machine's copies, the speed of a chemical reaction. You may also wish to highlight the product's aesthetic qualities. In addition to function, many products are appealing simply because they are well designed; just looking at a car or seeing a piece of office equipment may be persuasive.

Once you have decided which points you want to demonstrate, you must determine *how* to demonstrate them. This means choosing a specific method of demonstration. Should you use the product itself, a model of the product, a video, or a simple brochure? In making this decision, you should begin by considering the method that will have the greatest appeal to the prospect. As researchers and salespeople are learning, prospects respond differently to information aimed at different senses. Some prospects may be more responsive to visual information, whereas others may be more responsive to hearing or feeling.

Visual versus Auditory Prospects

A new field of research in the behavioral sciences called **neurolinguistic programming** is very useful in determining which prospects will be more responsive to information described in terms of seeing versus hearing or feeling.* According to NLP, we can tell which orientation a prospect has by observing her behavior and choice of words. For example, a prospect who thinks visually will tend to use expressions such as "I *see* what you're saying" or "he *viewed* it as an insult," whereas a prospect who thinks in terms of hearing will tend to use expressions such as "I *hear* what you're saying" and "He *heard* it as an insult." A third type of "thinking" is done in terms of feelings and is represented by expressions such as "I *grasp* what you're saying" or "He *felt* insulted." Table 10.8 presents lists of words that tend to be used when people are thinking by visualizing, hearing, or feeling.

In addition to observing the prospect's word choice, you can also read cues from her eye gaze behavior. Looking up while thinking tends to indicate visualization. Looking down tends to indicate looking inward for feelings, and looking sideways tends to indicate carrying on a mental conversation—that is, hearing.

Although it may seem distracting to examine a prospect's word choice and eye behavior, many salespeople do this quite naturally. In fact, NLP researchers claim that successful salespeople—those who seem to have instant rapport with and understanding of prospects—read and use these NLP signals without realizing it.[18] Even salespeople who are not used to reading a prospect's NLP signals at every point during a sales call benefit by using them during the demonstration. By making an effort to listen for visual, hearing, or feeling words, the salesperson can determine the best points to highlight in demonstrating the product.

However, a demonstration method cannot be selected without regard for *cost*.

* Neurolinguistic programming (NLP) is based on links between brain function (i.e., *neuro*logical processes) and speech (i.e., *linguistic* behavior).

Table 10.8 Word Choice That Indicates Visual, Auditory, or Feeling Processing

Visual	*Auditory*	*Kinesthetic*
analyze	announce	active
angle	articulate	affected
appear	audible	bearable
clarity	communicate	charge
cognizant	converse	concrete
conspicuous	discuss	emotional
demonstrate	dissonant	feel
dream	divulge	firm
examine	earshot	flow
focus	enunciate	foundation
foresee	gossip	grasp
glance	hear	grip
hindsight	hush	hanging
horizon	inquire	hassle
idea	interview	heated
illusion	listen	hold
image	mention	hustle
inspect	noise	intuition
look	oral	lukewarm
notice	proclaim	motion
obscure	pronounce	muddled
observe	remark	panicky
obvious	report	pressure
perception	roar	sensitive
perspective	rumor	set
picture	say	shallow
scene	shrill	softly
see	silence	solid
sight	squeal	structured
sketchy	state	support
survey	talk	tension
vague	tell	tied
view	tone	touch
vision	utter	unbearable
watch	vocal	unsettled
witness	voice	whipped

The objective in "matching" predicates is to "match" the language in which the customer speaks, thus creating an atmosphere of rapport and understanding.

Source: Reprinted by permission of *Journal of Personal Selling and Sales Management* © 1983. W. Nickels, R. Everett, and R. Klein. (1983). Rapport building for salespeople: A neuro-linguistic approach. *Journal of Personal Selling and Sales Management. 3* (November). 1–7.

Assessing Costs Versus Benefits: Is a Demonstration of the Product Possible?

There is no denying the persuasive impact of an actual product demonstration. Whenever possible, your sales demonstrations should focus on the product itself: running the software, driving in the car, sending documents with the fax machine. The presence of an actual product can have tremendous persuasive appeal. However, there are many cases where it is impossible to show the product itself. You cannot, for example, carry a large, office-size copier from prospect to prospect or demonstrate the operation of a piece of factory machinery in the prospect's office. In these situations, you have several alternative courses of action.

- You may deem it worthwhile to bring the prospect to visit the product. Prospects have been known, for example, to visit airplane manufacturing plants to see what a new plane looks like or even to travel to a foreign country to inspect goods prior to purchasing them.
- You may rely on a scaled-down model of the product. Architects use models when they make proposals for new buildings. Though a demonstration of the actual building is obviously impossible, a three-dimensional model can be much more meaningful than a two-dimensional architect's drawings.

Sales demonstrations may involve inviting the prospect to the plant to see how the product works. (© Alan Carey/The Image Works, Inc.)

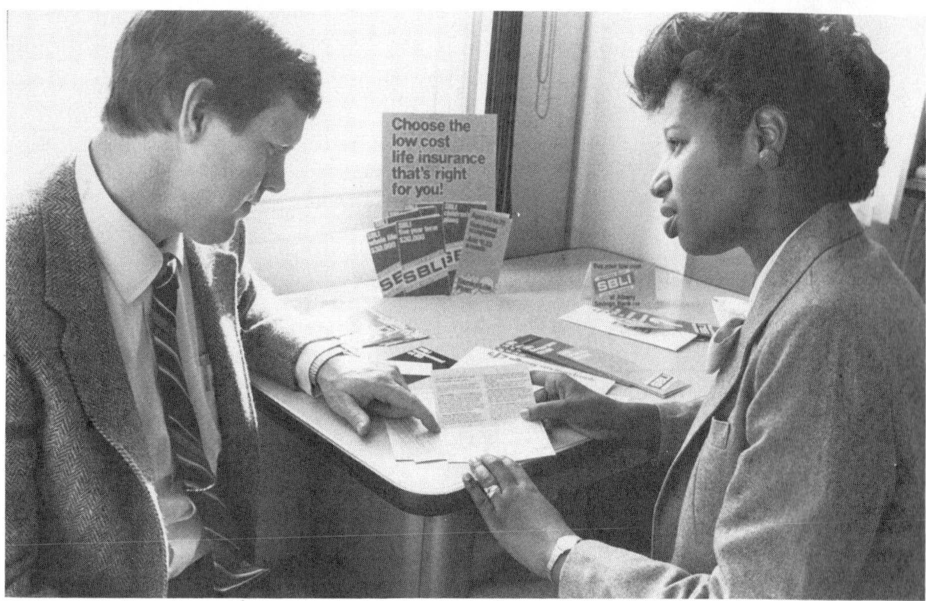

This salesperson could not bring the actual product to the prospect's office, so she is using brochures to "demonstrate" the product. (Michael Weisbrot/Stock, Boston.)

- Finally, you may rely on visual or audiovisual aids in order to demonstrate your product. These may range from something as simple as brochures containing pictures of your product to sophisticated video shows. In the case of the office copier, you might show actual copies made by the machine in order to demonstrate the machine's quality. You may also use visuals—brochures, slides, or videos—to demonstrate what the copier looks like and how it works (how to change paper, load multiple pages, etc.).

Which option you choose may depend upon your industry. In some instances, the quality of your demonstration may be fixed by industry standards. You may need to use elaborate demonstration methods in order to be competitive. If, for example, your competitors demonstrate their software by using it on prospects' own computers, whereas you use a brochure describing its capabilities, you will be at a severe competitive disadvantage.

Finally, in evaluating the cost of your options, it is important to keep in mind that a high-quality, expensive demonstration may bring intangible benefits. In one study, researchers found that people's attitudes toward a product were directly affected by their feelings about a visual aid used to promote the product. When the researchers combined identical verbal messages with pictures that people either liked or disliked, they found that the attitude toward the picture directly affected the attitude toward the product, apart from anything that was actually said about it.[19]

From this study, a salesperson can learn that it is important to consider more than the content of a demonstration. If you use a video, brochure, or slides, prospects' feelings about these visual aids can potentially affect their feelings toward the product. For example, a poorly shot, unprofessional video may demonstrate how your product functions, but it may also unintentionally convey a negative image.

Conducting the Demonstration

In addition to planning the how and what of a demonstration, you must also anticipate the practical details. In making an audiovisual presentation, you need to consider the physical environment. Something as seemingly unimportant as room size, noise level, or lighting can make the difference between a presentation that runs smoothly and one that does not. In order to ensure that things run smoothly, it is strongly advisable to *rehearse* the entire process, if possible. This is true whether your demonstration is an audiovisual representation of the product or an actual product demonstration. In the latter case, nothing can be more damaging to a sales presentation than a product that fails to work properly.

In one case, a large account was almost lost because of technical problems in a demonstration. The salesperson was attempting to use a laptop computer to demonstrate a complicated financial proposal to a group of potential investors. When the time came to compute some crucial calculations, the laptop's memory would not run the necessary software. The salesperson had been so concerned with practicing the content of his presentation that he did not worry about the "details." He had conducted his dry run using his regular desktop computer and had simply *assumed* that the laptop would function the same way. In this case, the details almost lost the account.

Putting It All Together

We begin by summarizing the key points made in this chapter:

- The presentation should help solve the prospect's problem.
- You begin problem solving by framing the problem.
- By helping the prospect to frame the problem, you can influence the decision outcome. A problem framed in terms of achieving gains encourages less risk taking than a problem framed in terms of avoiding losses.
- You can also influence the outcome of a decision by suggesting decision criteria. However, it is not advisable to attempt to change a prospect's firmly held decision criteria.
- In examining the prospect's decision criteria, try to determine whether they are phrased in terms of benefits versus attributes.

- Try to employ the presentation format that is best suited to the particular situation. Less structured formats are more appropriate when prospects' problems are unique, and more structured formats are more appropriate when salespeople are inexperienced or when the company wants to control what is presented.
- Regardless of the format you choose, a sales demonstration will help persuade the prospect.
- There are many different forms of sales demonstrations. Your choice of a method should be determined by feasibility, as well as by a cost/benefit analysis.

An analysis of these key points indicates that putting it all together for your sales presentation involves a careful consideration of what you will say, as well as how you will say it. Although the content of the presentation should always address the prospect's problems, the extent to which you can adapt your problem solving to individual prospects will depend upon the presentation format you use. Though less structured formats are more easily adapted to solve individual prospects' problems, this does not mean that problems can never be solved by an automated or memorized presentation. In some cases, a problem may be common to many prospects (e.g., the need to cut costs or improve efficiency), and you may be able to address it in a preplanned presentation. In other cases, it may be possible to combine less structured question-and-answer periods with automated segments.

It is important to realize that the sales presentation is the complex sum of many different parts. There may be times when unstructured and automated elements are blended into the same sales call. Certain parts may be memorized, while others may be organized or unstructured.[20] In either case, the use of structured versus unstructured presentation segments will have an impact on all of the steps in the selling process, from the preapproach plan to the close. With the automated and memorized presentations, for example, every word must be planned in advance. While an unstructured presentation need not be planned word for word, you must be ready to respond to a much broader range of questions. In completely structured presentations, although your canned message can attempt to frame the prospect's problems in an advantageous way, you cannot delve into individual problems. With the less structured presentation formats, you can. In the structured formats, you maintain more control, while in the less structured ones, you are free to interact.

However, it is also important to remember that even when your presentation is automated, there is *always* a personal dimension. Even when the presentation is limited to showing slides, the salesperson still makes the initial approach and answers questions. There is still nonverbal behavior. Facial expression, eye gaze, and tone of voice, for example, are important whether the presentation is read, memorized, or free-flowing. In fact, the existence of these interpersonal processes explains why salespeople differ in effectiveness even in fully automated presentations.

Key Terms

Problem frame
Decision criteria
Product benefits
Product attributes
Fully automated presentation
Semiautomated presentation
Memorized presentation
Organized presentation
Unstructured presentation
Sales demonstration
Neurolinguistic programming

Review Questions

1. Why is it important to consider form and content separately when developing a sales presentation?
2. What are the differences between a presentation based on the prospect's needs and one based on the prospect's problems?
3. What is a problem frame? Give some examples of a problem frame stated in terms of gains versus losses.
4. What are decision criteria?
5. Under what conditions will a prospect be receptive to suggestions of decision criteria?
6. How can a salesperson benefit by helping a prospect form decision criteria?
7. What are the five presentation formats? Discuss the advantages and disadvantages of each.
8. Under what conditions would you use each presentation method?
9. Describe the different types of sales demonstrations. What are the advantages of using a sales demonstration?
10. How would you determine which sales demonstration method to use?

Discussion Questions

1. Consider the following list of product attributes and benefits. Decide whether each item is an attribute or a benefit. If it is an attribute, list some appropriate benefits. If it is a benefit, list an appropriate attribute.

Product	*Attribute or Benefit*
Skin cream	Soft skin
Car	Five speed transmission
Shoes	Comfortable
Ice cream	High butterfat content

2. Recall the two students, Bill and Tina, who were engaged in a debate about presentation formats at the beginning of this chapter. Assume that you are the instructor in their personal selling class. How would you help them settle their debate? Is either one of them correct?
3. Which presentation format would adapt best to telephone selling? Explain your answer.

CASE 10.1

Casey, Inc., a tiny New York company that sells wall coverings to hotels, office buildings, prisons, and other large institutions, decided to challenge the national industry leaders for a share of the $850 million wall covering market in New York. The basis for their challenge was a strategy emphasizing safety. Casey claimed that the standard vinyl wall covering materials failed to meet New York City safety codes. The specific safety concern was with the amount of toxins given off by some vinyls when they are burned.

Though New York had always had high safety standards, it did not have a reliable method of testing the safety of a wall covering material until 1988. That year, a test was developed to determine how much of a material could burn before experimental mice were killed by the toxins. If a material was safer than paper and wood, it was legal in New York. Based on the new test, Casey developed evidence that none of the national competitors was selling safe material. Casey's wall covering proved safer than wood and paper, whereas the competitors' vinyl proved to be much more toxic. Although New York did not actively inspect and test the wall covering of every building site, builders had reason to worry about the safety of the wall covering they used. They could be legally liable if anyone died in a building fire due to inhaled toxins.

Although Casey apparently did have a product that was much safer than those of their competitors, they needed a strategy to gain the attention of the big buyers in this market, most of whom are experts—architects, designers, and purchasing agents for large hotel chains or prisons.

Assume that you are a consultant hired by Casey to determine the selling strategy for their wall covering.

1. How would you approach problem solving in the presentation?
2. How would you structure the problem in terms of a problem frame, gains versus losses, and decision criteria?
3. What presentation formats would you suggest?

CASE 10.2

Sara Meyer was a top salesperson for a large insurance company. Her sales were consistently so much higher than anyone else's that the company promoted her to sales manager. Her first task in her new job was to design a canned presentation that other salespeople could memorize and use. Sara's bosses figured that if Sara included everything that she usually discussed with prospects in her canned presentation, all of the other salespeople could achieve her performance level.

1. Is this a good idea?
2. Is a canned presentation appropriate in this case?
3. What should Sara do?
4. How should she go about developing this presentation?
5. Can she solve prospects' problems with a canned presentation?
6. What should she include?

References

1. Crawford, M. (1983). *New Product Management.* Homewood, IL: Irwin.

2. Sujan, H., M. Sujan, and J. Bettman. (1988). Knowledge structure differences between more effective and less effective salespeople. *Journal of Marketing Research, 25* (February), 41–49.

3. Sujan, H., B. Weitz, and M. Sujan. (1988). Increasing sales productivity by getting salespeople to work smarter. *Journal of Personal Selling and Sales Management, 8* (2), 9–19.

4. Kahneman, D., and A. Tversky. (1979). Prospect theory: An analysis of decision under risk. *Econometrica, 47,* 263–291.

5. Puto, C. (1987). The framing of buying decisions. *Journal of Consumer Research, 14* (3), 301–315.

6. Everett, M. (1989). This is the ultimate in selling. *Sales and Marketing Management, 141* (10), 31.

7. Bettman, J. R., and M. Sujan. (1987). Effects of framing on evaluation of comparable and noncomparable alternatives. *Journal of Consumer Research, 14,* 141–154.

8. DeVoe, M. (1956). *Effective Advertising Copy.* New York: Macmillan.

9. Stone, B. (1980). Long narrative copy: A marketer's view. *Advertising Age, 51* (August 25), 48.

10. Anderson, R., and M. Jolson. (1980). Technical wording in advertising: Implications for market segmentation. *Journal of Marketing, 44* (Winter), 57–66.

11. Bellizzi, J., and J. Mohr. (1984). Technical versus nontechnical wording of industrial print advertising. *Proceedings, Marketing Educators' Conference, 50,* 175.

12. Jolson, M. (1973). Should the sales presentation be fresh or canned? *Business Horizons, 16,* 81–88.

13. Video presentations to market legal services. (1988). *Lawyers' Digest,* July issue.

14. Jolson, M. (1989). Canned adaptiveness: A new direction for modern salesmanship. *Business Horizons, 32* (January–February), 7–12.

15. Ibid.

16. White, J. (1988). Asset allocation pitched by brokers. *Wall Street Journal*, October 6, p. C1.

17. Jolson, (1973), op. cit.

18. Nickels, W., R. Everett, and R. Klein. (1983). Rapport building for salespeople: A neuro-linguistic approach. *Journal of Personal Selling and Sales Management, 3* (November), 1–7.

19. Mitchell, A. (1986). The effect of verbal and visual components of advertisements on brand attitudes and attitude toward the advertisement. *Journal of Consumer Research, 13* (June), 12–23.

20. Jolson, (1989), op. cit.

11

Handling Objections

CHAPTER OBJECTIVES

In this chapter, you will learn:

How to view objections as a valuable part of your interaction with the prospect.

How to interpret objections as feedback.

How to analyze an objection's form and content.

Relational skills involved in handling objections.

Special communication rules involved in handling objections.

How to avoid a contest for control when handling objections.

How to solve problems when handling objections.

How to uncover hidden objections.

CHAPTER OUTLINE

A Sales Challenge

An Overview

The Role Played by Objections in the Interactive Process

- Objections Communicate Interest
- Objections Provide Feedback
- Objections Give the Salesperson a Chance to Respond

Some Common Techniques for Handling Objections

The Communication Dynamics of Objections

- Relational Communication and the Handling of Objections
- Objections Involve Special Rules
- Objections Involve Special Control Issues

Relational Communication Skills

- Begin Your Response by Approving of the Objection
- Repeat the Objection
- Respond to the Objection with a Demonstration or Case History

Handling the Content of the Objection

- Define the Problem
- Uncover Hidden Objections
- Solve the Problem
- Handling Objections by Changing Attitudes

Handling the Objection's Form Along with Its Content

Putting It All Together

Key Terms

Review Questions

Discussion Questions

Case 11.1

Case 11.2

References

A Sales Challenge

The following interaction took place when Lance Janson, a partner in a large accounting firm, met with a prospective new client—Joe Ruggero, the controller of a small manufacturing business. As you read this dialogue, try to identify the objections.

LANCE: Do you have any other questions?

JOE: Well, I'm still concerned about exactly who will work on our audit.

LANCE: Why, I would run your audit myself.

JOE: But we would be a small client to you. Right now, we're one of Forrester's biggest clients.

LANCE: We may be large, but don't forget, Joe, small business is our specialty. Our size turns out to be a plus. We can offer our small business clients a big cost advantage because of our size.

JOE: But will I be able to get you on the phone any time I have a question, or will you be out auditing someone else?

LANCE: I can always be reached, and we'll have a senior accountant assigned specifically to your audit. He can reach me any time.

JOE: A senior accountant? They're awfully young, aren't they?

LANCE: They may be young, but they are good. Because we are so big, we attract the cream of the business school crop. Our senior accountants could be partners at many lesser firms.

JOE: I'm going to have to think more about this and confer with Doris and Arthur.

An Overview

In the field of personal selling, the term objections refers to concerns voiced by the prospect. These concerns can range from direct arguments with specific points ("A senior accountant? They're awfully young, aren't they?") to disguised pleas for reassurance ("But we would be a small client to you.") to general stalling tactics ("I'm going to have to think more about this . . ."). In the preceding dialogue, every statement made by the prospect represented some kind of objection.

Despite their many different forms, objections communicate a common underlying message: "I have a problem. I am not yet ready to buy." Thus we can state the following definition:

Objections are *statements (or questions) made by the prospect that communicate directly or indirectly that there is a problem that must be solved before a buying decision can be made.*

An important point to note about this definition is that an objection represents a *problem* that the prospect has decided to share with the salesperson rather than a roadblock designed to discourage further discussion. Although objections are sometimes referred to as *resistance*, this term assumes a one-sided approach to selling: the salesperson *pushes* and the prospect *resists*. But handling objections means more than overcoming resistance. Since much of the prospect's input into the sales discussion is in the form of objections ("But what if . . . ?", "Why?", "I don't see that . . ."), handling objections has more to do with handling the *interaction* than it does with overcoming resistance. When objections are placed in the context of an ongoing interactive process, you will see why experienced salespeople welcome them. Once you understand their communication dynamics, you can use objections as valuable tools.

Because of the importance of objections in the sales presentation, this chapter is devoted to their analysis. We begin by discussing the role played by objections in the interaction and presenting the most commonly used techniques for handling objections. Next, objections are analyzed in terms of their *form* as well as their *content*. As you read this chapter, you will apply what you have learned about interpersonal communication in order to unravel the communication dynamics involved in handling objections. When you have finished studying the material, you should appreciate objections as providers of feedback. You should also have a grasp of the communication and problem-solving skills necessary to begin to handle objections successfully.

The Role Played by Objections in the Interaction Process

Instead of thinking of objections as stumbling blocks, you should learn to think of them as important sources of information about the prospect's state of mind. When properly understood, objections can give clues to the prospect's level of interest, commitment, and understanding. As we will see, the prospect who listens silently to a presentation without voicing any concerns may be harder to persuade than the one who airs problems for discussion.

Objections Communicate Interest

You can begin to appreciate the role played by objections if you think back to some of the times when you have been the prospect in a sales interaction. You can probably recall situations in which you had some objection but were not willing to mention it. Perhaps you had already decided not to buy the product and knew that if you voiced your objection, the salesperson would try to change your mind. Your decision was firm and you did not want to argue with the salesperson, so you kept quiet until the salesperson finished talking and then politely said "no." This is a common occurrence in sales situations.

An actual dialogue might sound something like this:

PROSPECT: How much is this briefcase?
SALESPERSON: The price is $149, and look at the fine quality of the leather.
PROSPECT: Very nice.
SALESPERSON: And see, the hardware is pure brass.
PROSPECT: I see.
SALESPERSON: It also comes in brown. Would you like it in brown or black?
PROSPECT: Neither one, thanks.

In other instances, you may have been a "difficult" prospect who asked many tough questions and voiced many objections:

PROSPECT: How much is this briefcase?
SALESPERSON: The price is $149.
PROSPECT: I just saw a similar one next door at Zed's for $119.99.
SALESPERSON: But look carefully at the fine quality of our leather. It's much better than Zed's.
PROSPECT: But the lining of the pockets looks like cheap vinyl.
SALESPERSON: We *have* put vinyl in the lining of the pockets, but it's definitely not cheap. We did that to make the briefcase lighter. Lift it. You can feel how light it is.
PROSPECT: I see, but won't the vinyl crack?
SALESPERSON: No, it's a very high-grade vinyl. The whole case is very well made. Even the inside hardware is made of solid brass.
PROSPECT: Is this the only color that it comes in?
SALESPERSON: No, it also comes in black. Would you prefer the black?
PROSPECT: Yes, I'll take it.

If we stopped these interactions midway through the dialogue and asked the salesperson to predict who would buy, an untrained person might say that the first prospect was more likely, but an experienced salesperson would expect greater success in the second interaction. Sales experience teaches us how important objections can be. In fact, the contrast between these two dialogues highlights several very important points about objections.

Objections Provide Feedback

As Figure 11.1 illustrates, objections provide feedback. Without specific feedback in the form of objections, it is very difficult to know what the silent prospect is thinking about your presentation. While it is true that feedback occurs continuously in face-to-face communication, much of the feedback in a sales situation

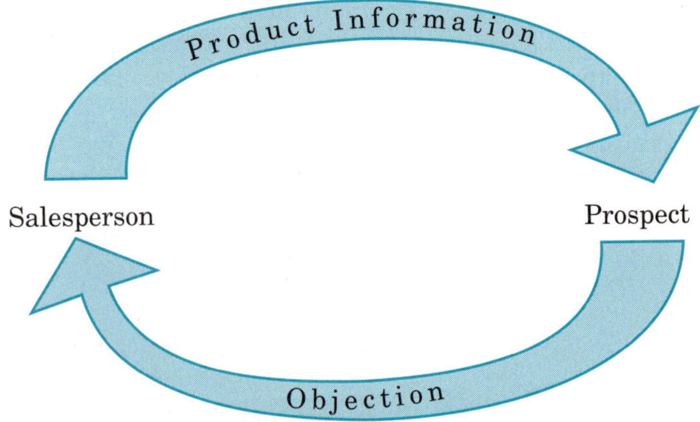

FIGURE 11.1 Objections provide feedback.

occurs in the form of simple nonverbal gestures (nods, etc.) and positive responses ("I see," "mm hmm," etc.). However, these simple responses will give little guidance as to how you should proceed with the presentation. In fact, feedback of this type does not necessarily demonstrate actual approval of what you are saying. It may indicate only that the prospect wishes to be polite, as we saw in the first dialogue.

However, as the second dialogue demonstrated, verbalized objections provide specific feedback. Based on the prospect's objections, the second salesperson learned that the briefcase's price and lining were of concern. In each case, the salesperson offered a logical argument that solved the problem, and was eventually able to close the sale. The objections provided valuable feedback and showed the salesperson where to start problem solving. If we remember that feedback is one of the important components of interpersonal communication, we can begin to appreciate the role played by objections.

Objections Give the Salesperson a Chance to Respond

You can better appreciate the role played by objections if you recall a fundamental principle from Chapter 3: The sales interaction is a *sequential* process in which each statement should relate to the one that came before it. Because of the sequential nature of conversation, every statement acts as a request for a response.[1] Thus, if you make a statement about the weather to someone ("Boy, is it hot today!"), you are requesting that the person answer with some related comment ("It certainly is hot!").

The prospect who voices an objection is probably somewhat interested in buying. (Laimute Druskis/Taurus Photos.)

When we apply this principle to objections, we realize that objections are really *requests for responses*. In general, a prospect who mentions an objection to a salesperson *expects* that the salesperson will try to address it. By stating an objection, the prospect is inviting the salesperson to respond (see Figure 11.2). This is true even if the objection does not sound like a request. Consider, for example, the objection "But I just saw one like this at Zed's for $119.99." At first, this objection might sound like a flat rejection—a signal that the prospect had no intention to buy. An untrained salesperson might indeed make such an interpretation and lose the sale. However, the trained salesperson in our example immediately recognized this as an objection and countered with a quick response. If the prospect had not wanted a response, he would not have voiced the objection in the first place. Basically, the prospect knows that the objection gives the salesperson a chance to make a persuasive argument. As a result, the objection signals at least some level of *interest* on the part of the prospect.

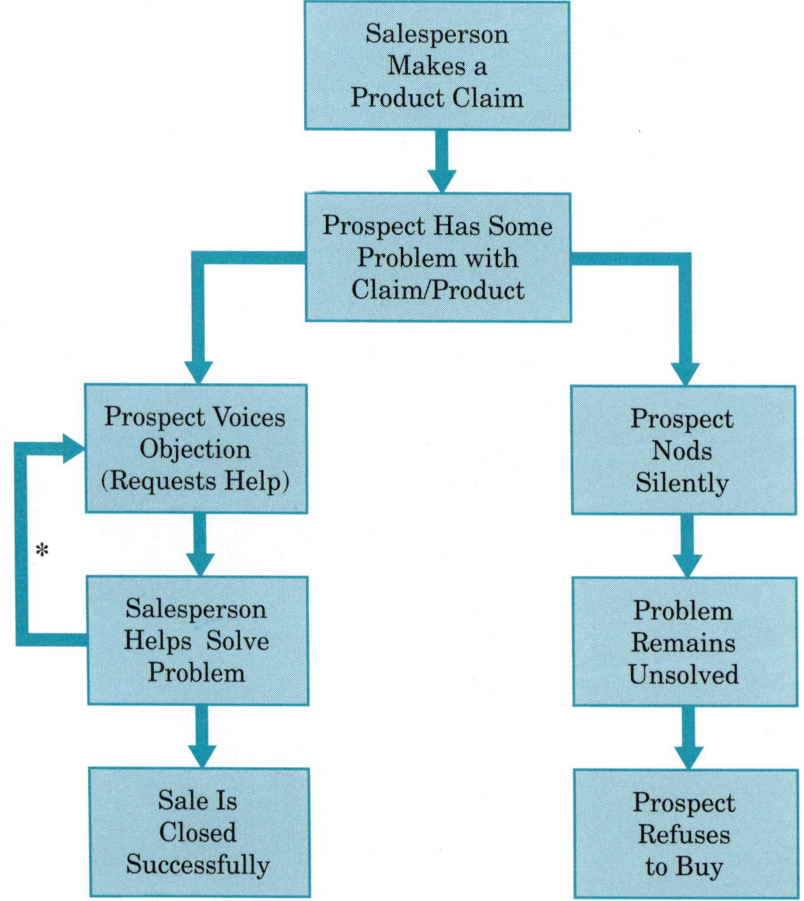

FIGURE 11.2 Objections request a response.

Some Common Techniques for Handling Objections

By now, it should be clear that, if handled properly, objections represent *opportunities* for the trained salesperson. And salespeople have developed a variety of techniques to help in this regard.[2] Table 11.1 contains a list of 17 of the most frequently used techniques for handling objections.[3] The techniques range from the simple **direct answer** (No. 1), to the use of a product **demonstration** (No. 3), to a **direct denial** (No. 15). Although these techniques can be very useful, it is important that you view this list as a starting point in your understanding of the objection-handling process. You should not rely on memorizing the techniques. Such a strategy could prove dangerous: Not all of the techniques apply to all situations. If you enter a sales call with several preplanned techniques for handling objections, you may find that they do not fit the situation. Consider, for example, the simple objection "Why is your price higher than our current supplier's?" Although a direct response works for this objection, the **yes, but** technique sounds awkward.

PROSPECT: Why is your price higher than our current supplier's?
SALESPERSON: Our basic price includes more features . . .

versus

PROSPECT: Why is your price higher than our current supplier's?
SALESPERSON: Yes, but our price includes more features . . .

In contrast, the *yes, but* technique works well with the following:

PROSPECT: Your price is much higher than our current supplier's.
SALESPERSON: Yes, it is, but that's because our basic price includes more features.

As these examples illustrate, the techniques are not interchangeable. Because of the sequential nature of conversation, the appropriate technique must follow logically from the type of objection voiced by the prospect. What would you do, for example, if you plan to use the **boomerang technique,** but the prospect never raises a *specific* objection that can be turned into a selling point? Rather than relying on memorization of certain specific techniques, you will be better equipped to handle objections if you understand their underlying communication dynamics.

The Communication Dynamics of Objections

In many ways, objections are like any other kind of statement: They have a *form* as well as a *content*, and the form and content can be considered independently. In the previous dialogues, for example, the content of the objections referred to price, while the form varied from a question to a statement. When answering objections, it is easy to get so involved in responding to the content of the prospect's statement that you forget to pay attention to the form of what you are saying. This is evident from the fact that the 17 techniques listed in Table 11.1 do

Table 11.1 Importance of Techniques for Handling Objections and Sales Resistance

	Mean Importance	
Selling Technique	*Industrial Salespeople*	*Retail Salespeople*
1. *Direct answer method*: Provide a specific response to the exact question by the prospect	4.06*	4.27
2. *Compensation method*: Admit the prospect's objections, but point out advantages that compensate for the objection	4.00	3.94
3. *Demonstration*: Demonstrate the offering to show the prospect the objection is not applicable	3.89	3.72
4. *"Yes, but" method*: Agree with prospect's objection, but then make another statement to offset it	3.68	3.79
5. *Case-history method*: Describe how another prospect purchased the offering and benefited by it	3.65	3.74
6. *Comparison with rival products*: Compare the offering to competition's to point out its advantages	3.48	3.42
7. *Answer objection with question*: Try to overcome the customer's objection by asking a question related to the objection	3.37	3.70
8. *Comparison or contrast method*: Minimize the prospect's objection by comparing it with something quite acceptable (e.g., "It costs only pennies a day")	3.34	3.53
9. *Boomerang method*: Convert the prospect's reason for not buying into a reason for buying (e.g., "That may be the very reason you should buy!")	3.41	3.40
10. *Propose trial use*: Overcome the objection by suggesting the prospect use the offering on a trial basis	3.24	2.81
11. *Indirect denial*: Give ground a little and then inoffensively dispute the prospect's objection	2.45	2.55

Selling Technique	*Mean Importance*	
	Industrial Salespeople	*Retail Salespeople*
12. *Humor*: Tell a good story to relieve the pressure	2.36	2.50
13. *Comparative-item method*: Show the prospect two or more offerings and when prospect objects to a feature in one, reject it and substitute another	2.43	2.42
14. *"It's in your hands" method*: Accept the prospect's objection and tell the prospect that the decision is up to him or her	2.10	2.44
15. *Direct denial*: Dispute what the prospect has said and then explain the "true" facts	2.25	2.24
16. *"Coming to that" method*: Tell the prospect the salesperson will answer the question later in the sales presentation	2.21	1.90
17. *Pass up method*: Smile and pass off the objection	1.81	1.98

* 1 = not imporatant; 5 = very important.

Source: Reprinted by permission of *Journal of Personal Selling and Sales Management* © 1985. R. Hite and J. Bellizzi. (1985). Differences in the importance of selling techniques between consumer and industrial salespeople. *Journal of Personal Selling and Sales Management, 5* (November), 19–30.

not make a distinction between form and content. Some refer to form (No. 1), but most address methods for handling content alone.

However, recall from Chapter 3 that the actual message you convey depends as much on the form as it does on the content. In fact, the field of **relational communication** deals specifically with how the form of your message relates to the prospect's previous message. You communicate very different messages depending upon whether your statement agrees or disagrees (disconfirms), supports or contradicts, answers or changes the topic of the previous statement.[4] As we will see in the next section, relational communication is particularly important in handling objections.

Relational Communication and the Handling of Objections

Although objections have much in common with general everyday statements, they also have some unique features. Try to discover what these features are by thinking about the relational communication in the following dialogues:

PROSPECT: Your price is too high.
SALESPERSON: You're right! It really is.

or

PROSPECT: Your price is too high.
SALESPERSON: You're right. . . and our quality is not that good either.

Both of these responses are obviously ridiculous answers to an objection. However, notice that they represent standard ways of responding to ordinary statements. The salesperson is simply *agreeing* with what the prospect has said. As you learned in Chapter 3, messages that agree or extend the topic tend to be regarded as submissive or equal, whereas messages that disagree, disconfirm, contradict, or change the subject are generally regarded as dominant.[5] Based on the *form* of her messages, the salesperson was submissive in the first example and equal in the second one. If this salesperson had given these types of responses in any context other than the handling of objections, they would have been perfectly appropriate. Consider, for example, the following exchange, which might occur during the approach phase of the sales call:

PROSPECT: The weather is too hot today.
SALESPERSON: That's for sure! And too humid too.

Contrast this response with the following one:

PROSPECT: This weather is too hot today.
SALESPERSON: Not really. I've seen a lot hotter.

In these two dialogues, the first response is more appealing. In the second case, the prospect's complaint about the weather is met with nonsupport. Essentially, the salesperson has told him that he should not be feeling too hot. In the first dialogue, however, the salesperson responds with a supportive statement, agreeing with and even extending the topic. If you were the prospect suffering from the heat, you would probably prefer to receive the supportive response.

In fact, you have probably known people who seem to disagree with everything you say. Dialogue I is an expanded version of such a conversation.

DIALOGUE I *(Relational messages printed in italics)*
PROSPECT: The weather is too hot today.
Initiates topic
SALESPERSON: Not really. I've seen a lot hotter.
Disagrees
PROSPECT: And traffic was so bad this morning.
Initiates new topic
SALESPERSON: I didn't think so.
Disagrees
PROSPECT: Well, at least my car was air conditioned.
Initiates
SALESPERSON: Mine isn't. It wastes gas.
Disagrees

After several interactions like this, you would probably start to consider the salesperson argumentative and might even try to avoid him. Yet compare this discussion of the weather with a similar dialogue involving objections:

DIALOGUE II

PROSPECT: This maintenance schedule is totally unsatisfactory.
Initiates topic

SALESPERSON: It is actually quite favorable compared to that of anyone else in the industry.
Disagrees

PROSPECT: But the price of your maintenance contract is way out of line.
Initiates new topic

SALESPERSON: It's not when you consider that we service the machines once a month, while our competitors only come eight times a year.
Disagrees

PROSPECT: But I've also heard that Sanford's has the best-trained repair people in the industry.
Initiates new topic

SALESPERSON: That's not really true. We send our repair people to a 2-month training course.
Disagrees

In the second dialogue, the salesperson responded to each of the objections with a nonsupportive statement. Although the salesperson could have handled the dialogue more smoothly, the necessity of disagreeing could not be avoided. The sale certainly would have been lost had the salesperson agreed with all of the prospect's negative points.

You can learn a lot by examining the relational communication in these two dialogues. The relational messages (printed in italics) are the same in the conversation about maintenance schedules and in the one about the heat, traffic, and air conditioning. As the contrast shows, there are special rules involved in handling objections.

Objections Involve Special Rules

As we discussed in Chapter 3, every situation is governed by specific rules.[6] Recall that a *rule* is a pattern of behavior that serves as a guideline for correct or expected behaviors. Like any other social situation, the sales interaction is governed by rules, and different rules apply to different stages in the sales interaction. In particular, there are specific rules regarding the handling of objections. One such unwritten rule is that *because the salesperson is trying to persuade the prospect to buy, she is expected to argue against the objections in defense of her product.*

It is because of this rule that the salesperson who *agreed* with the prospect's objections ("You're right, our price is too high . . . and our quality isn't good either") appeared to be ridiculous. A confirmation like this one may be expected during other types of discussions, but it violates the rules of expected behavior in the handling of objections. Stated simply, the rules governing objections dictate that the prospect is *expected* to point out concerns and the salesperson is *expected* to counter them. Based on these rules, the salesperson should not be surprised at the prospect's objections, just as the prospect will not be surprised if the salesperson tries to dismiss each objection. In each case, the behavior follows expectations. However, it is important to remember that the sales call is basically a *consultative*, not an *adversary*, situation. Objections should allow the salesperson to *help* the prospect and should not be permitted to result in a contest for control.

Objections Involve Special Control Issues

It is important that, in defending your product, you *avoid* engaging in a contest for control with the prospect. The fact that you are expected to defend your product may give you more freedom to contradict or disagree with objections than you would have in other situations, but the existence of special rules does not mean that you can or should be argumentative. If you *abruptly* contradict or disagree with everything that the prospect says, you are likely to end up in a contest for control.

Consider the control element of the following dialogue:

PROSPECT: This price is much too high for us.
SALESPERSON: This price isn't high. A lot of cars cost more than this one.

Abrupt disconfirmations like this one challenge the validity of the prospect's claim. An obvious response to this kind of challenge would be:

PROSPECT: Well, I think it's too high, and I'm not going to buy it.

In this kind of battle, the salesperson can only lose. The prospect *always* has the option of "proving" that the objection was valid by refusing to buy the product.

In handling objections, a contest for control will encourage arguments and discourage an open and honest airing of concerns. It may lead the prospect to keep quiet about a real objection or, worse yet, to make statements aimed at showing who is in control. Remember that part of the salesperson's job is to *encourage* prospects' objections. For this reason, it is important to use your relational communication skills to avoid any appearance of dominance contests when attempting to dismiss the prospect's objections. As we will see in the next section, this car salesperson could have countered the price objection without challenging the prospect.

Relational Communication Skills

At this point, you have learned enough communication theory to be able to develop skills in handling the relational aspects of objections. Before applying specifics, let us summarize what you already know (from this chapter and Chapter 3):

- Relational messages are conveyed in the *form* of a statement and are largely independent of the content. Thus, the same content can be accompanied by different relational messages, depending upon the statement's form.
- Statements that directly contradict, disagree with, interrupt, or change the topic of the previous statement are dominant, regardless of whether the speaker intends them to be.
- Salespeople are expected to argue against the content of an objection, yet simple disagreement can appear inappropriate.
- The use of dominant relational communication during the handling of objections can discourage openness on the part of the prospect and even lead to a destructive contest for control.

The logical conclusion to be drawn from these facts is that the salesperson should learn to argue against the *content* of an objection, but avoid the use of too many dominant relational *forms*. If your style of answering objections makes the prospect uncomfortable, she may stop voicing her objections and quietly refuse to buy when you try to close the sale. It is to your benefit to learn different ways to handle objections without engaging in argumentative relational communication. Following is a discussion of several techniques aimed at accomplishing this objective.

Begin Your Response by Approving of the Objection

Consider the contrast between the following two dialogues:

PROSPECT: Your price is too high.
SALESPERSON: No, it's not. Not when you consider our quality.

versus

PROSPECT: Your price is too high.
SALESPERSON: I can see why it might seem high at first, but do you realize what quality assurances we offer?

In both dialogues, the salesperson communicates the same basic message about price and quality: that the high price is justifiable because of the product's higher quality. However, in the first case, the salesperson used a relational form that appears controlling. If this salesperson continues this pattern of abrupt disagreement, he will run the risk of discouraging the prospect from voicing other concerns. In the second case the salesperson says the same thing, but also communicates that the prospect's concern has merit. The relational form here is much more equality based and will probably encourage a more open discussion of additional objections. Some alternative phrases which allow you to do this are:

"I see, that's an important issue,"
"I understand your concern."
"Your concern makes sense, but have you considered . . ."
"That issue concerns a lot of people, but did you realize that . . ."

Although the **"yes, but"** and **compensation** techniques listed in Table 11.1 do not distinguish form from content, both work well within this basic framework:

"Yes, our price is high, but . . ."
"Our price may be high, but that's because . . ."

Repeat the Objection

Another commonly used technique is to begin your response with a simple repetition of the prospect's objection. This technique is encouraged in many sales training courses because it helps to ensure that the salesperson correctly understands the prospect's concern. If a salesperson has misunderstood an objection, repeating it in her own words will give the prospect a chance to correct her before she continues.

Repetition also helps set up the response from a relational communication perspective. Repeating a statement has a neutralizing effect on the relational message. If you repeat what the prospect has said, you are no longer beginning your response with an abrupt disagreement. In relational terms, you are agreeing with the prospect and then qualifying or disagreeing with your own statement. With this technique, you communicate the same content but avoid a possible contest for dominance. The following example illustrates this concept:

PROSPECT: This looks as though it's made out of plastic. It wouldn't last for more than one season.

SALESPERSON: *I see. You're concerned with the lining material. That's certainly a legitimate concern*, but this lining is not made out of plastic. This is a new, highly durable vinyl polyester.

If we compare this to the same response minus the neutral opening statements, you can see the difference caused by the relational forms:

PROSPECT: This looks as though it's made out of plastic. It wouldn't last for more than one season.

SALESPERSON: *It certainly will last.* This lining isn't made out of plastic. This is a new, highly durable vinyl polyester.

While the second approach conveys the same information about the product, the style appears less supportive. As we have stated, there is nothing wrong with an isolated disconfirmation, but a pattern of this sort will deliver a relational message that is generally less supportive and accommodating than one in which responses begin with neutral repetition.

It is important to note here that these neutralizing techniques are not appropriate in every part of the sales interaction. In fact, the use of repetition and approval statements can appear awkward and condescending in other contexts. Consider the same type of neutral statement in a discussion about the weather:

PROSPECT: It sure is hot today.

SALESPERSON: I see, you think it's hot outside. That is a legitimate concern, but it is not really that hot.

A salesperson who made this kind of statement would be likely to offend a prospect. The prospect certainly does not need the salesperson's approval to have an opinion about the weather. Yet this kind of approval is appropriate in the case of an objection. Once again, the key difference has to do with different rules and expectations surrounding different phases of the sales interaction.

Respond to the Objection with a Demonstration or Case History

Two of the techniques listed in Table 11.1 provide a unique way of avoiding contests for control, although they do not deal directly with relational communication. With a **case history** (No. 6) or **demonstration** (No. 7), you let the facts refute the prospect's objection. In relational terms, you neither agree nor disagree directly. You simply provide outside information that supports your product without the use of a dominant relational form. The salesperson in the following example used a sales chart this way:

PROSPECT: Your formula will never get into patients' bloodstreams as fast as this one does.

SALESPERSON: (*Pointing to a graph in her sales literature*) Look at these figures. Our labs have studied that very point in several experiments, and our formula actually gets into the bloodstream 20 percent faster.

In the competitive arena of personal selling, knowledge of these fine points of style and familiarity with subtle relational rules can spell the difference between successful and unsuccessful sales calls. However, as we mentioned earlier, skill in dealing with relational communication is no substitute for preparation to deal with the content of the objections. The following discussion deals with ways to handle the content itself.

Handling the Content of the Objection

Even salespeople who have a great deal of skill in handling interactions must be ready to answer the content of any objection the prospect decides to mention. In fact, this is one instance in which a skilled salesperson should not try to manipulate the actual topics that the prospect wishes to discuss. It is crucial that you carefully address the content of each objection mentioned by the prospect and that you do not give the impression that you are trying to avoid any issues. If a prospect has a specific concern regarding your product, your attempt to change the subject might give the appearance that you have no good answer to the objection. It can also cause the prospect to feel that you have manipulated him.

To understand the importance of this point, think about times when you have been the prospect. You have probably found yourself in situations where a salesperson controlled the discussion so that you never got a chance to voice your own concerns and opinions. If the salesperson was skillful, you might not have realized what happened until you left the situation and later experienced the vague sense that you had been "had." Although this kind of manipulation may succeed in the short run, it is not an advisable approach. Remember, objections represent problems to the prospect, and your job as a salesperson is to help solve them. You begin this process by defining the problem.

Define the Problem

Although you learned in Chapter 10 to frame problems in ways that will influence the outcomes, when handling objections you should *listen* to, not influence, the problem definition. This involves detective work. You must use your insight and communication skills to help the prospect uncover any *hidden* problems that may be lying beneath the surface of the objection. In many cases, the prospect herself will not even be aware of what is really bothering her. By voicing an objection, she has halted the sales presentation and asked for your assistance. But uncovering the real problem can be complicated.

No matter what type of objection you are faced with—explicit or hidden—it is important that you not ignore the objection's stated content, even if you feel that the content masks the *real* objection. Ignoring the stated content of the objection can send one of several different messages to the prospect: "Your concern is not important to me, so I will ignore it," or, worse yet, "Our product really has a bad flaw. I have no answer to your objection, so I will ignore it."

In most cases, addressing the explicitly stated message is the easiest part of handling the objection. The trick in handling objections successfully is to determine whether the prospect's real problem is the one he has stated or whether the objection includes some hidden problem beyond the statement of fact. Deciding which type of objection you are facing requires a judgment call on your part, but there are techniques that you can use to help get to the heart of the problem.

Uncover Hidden Objections

Figure 11.3 shows the sequence involved in investigating for hidden objections. You can begin this process by deciding whether the objection is tangible and *specific* or a vague, more *general* concern. A specific objection deals with an actual attribute: "Your delivery schedule is much too slow" or "Best's has a much larger service force." In contrast, some general objections may appear to have nothing to do with your product: "I have to check this with the rest of my buying group" or "I'm just not sure. I'll get back to you next week."

If the objection is specific, you can try to respond directly:

PROSPECT: That delivery schedule is much too slow.
SALESPERSON: Well, we can be flexible if that is a real problem for you.

If the prospect appears responsive to your direct solution, then you can probably conclude that the objection did not hide some deeper problem.

PROSPECT: Well, if you can cut the lead time to 1 week, we'll be okay.

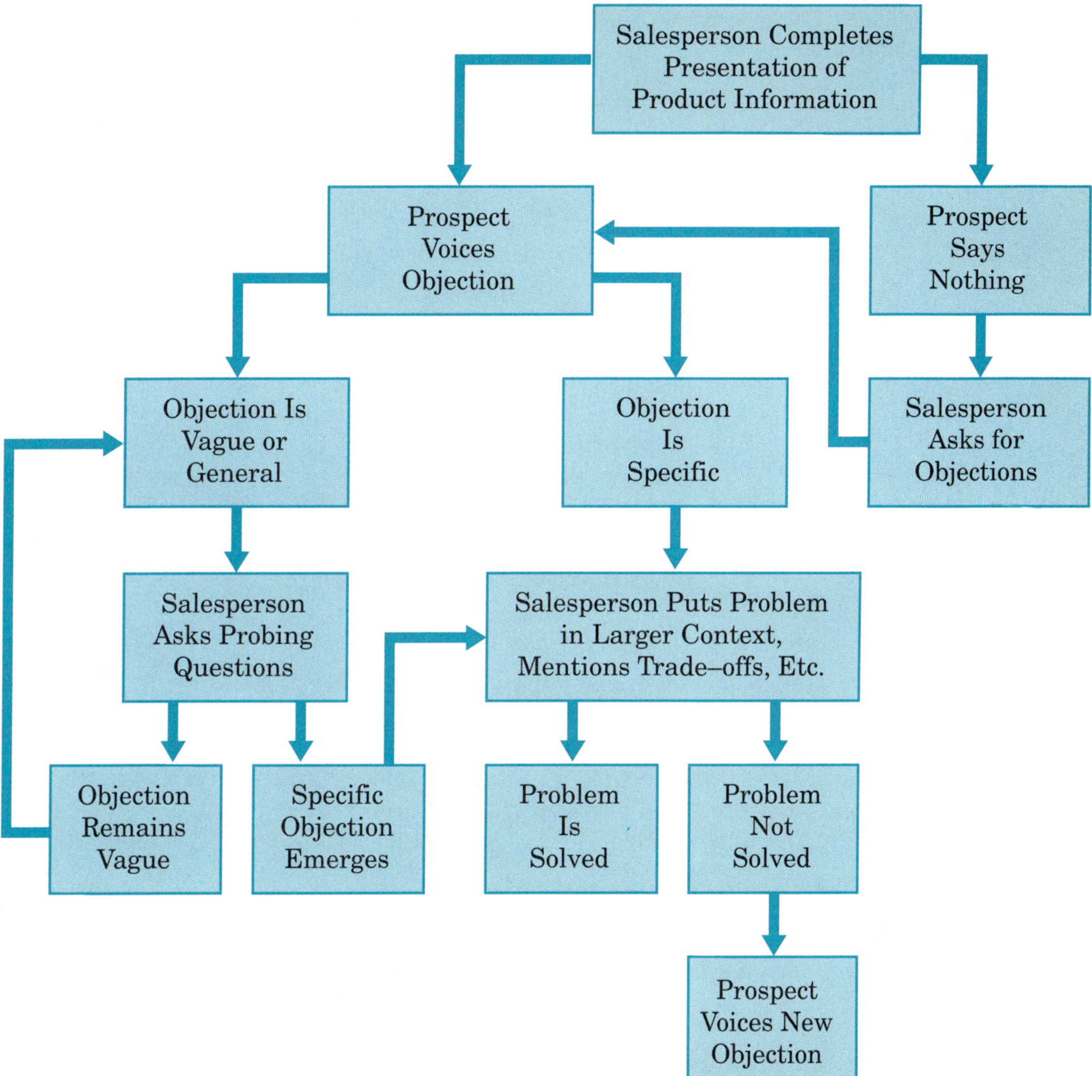

FIGURE 11.3 Probing for hidden objections.

If, on the other hand, the prospect is not satisfied and jumps immediately to some other objection, there may be some deeper problem.

Probe for Deeper Problems. If you think that there is a deeper problem or if the original objection is too vague to address properly, it is almost always a good idea to ask questions aimed at getting the prospect to expand upon the concern. By using questions, you can get a discussion going and try to probe for hidden agendas. The more information you have about an objection, the better able you are to address it properly. Here are some examples of commonly used probing questions:

> "What do you mean by that?"
> "I'm not quite sure that I understand your point. Could you explain it to me?"

The following dialogue illustrates the use of this type of question:

PROSPECT: I'd be interested in your machines, but your service contract just isn't satisfactory.
SALESPERSON: In what ways do you find it unsatisfactory?
PROSPECT: Well it just doesn't meet our needs.
SALESPERSON: What is your company looking for in a service contract?
PROSPECT: Well, we want to have a repair person here within an hour after we call for help.
SALESPERSON: I see, so the timing of our response is a concern. Well, you're right. The contract does not specify a specific time limit, but in the past, we have always been one of the fastest in the industry to respond to repair calls.
PROSPECT: I see.
SALESPERSON: What other concerns did you have about the contract?

In this example, the salesperson used open-ended questions to get to the bottom of a vaguely stated objection. Once he uncovered some specific issues, he was better able to address the real problem.

But what if the objection is of the very general **stalling** type (e.g., "I'm just not sure. I have to think about it.")? Once again, you can try to get more information to go on by asking probing questions:

> "What is it that you're not sure about?"
> "Is there some other information that would help you make a decision?"

Once you have uncovered the problem, you can help the prospect solve it.

Solve the Problem

The proper approach to solving a problem depends on the problem itself. Perhaps the easiest type of objection to overcome is one based on a misconception. If the prospect has some misconception about a specific issue and you have facts to the contrary, simply presenting your facts may be sufficient. This was the case in the following interaction:

PROSPECT: But I know for a fact that two of your competitors have longer warranty periods than you do.
SALESPERSON: That was true in the past, but we have recently extended ours to 5 years. We now have by far the best warranty.
PROSPECT: I didn't realize that. That makes a big difference.

Unfortunately, your job will not always be this easy. What would you do, for example, if your warranty actually is shorter? Certainly, you cannot misrepresent the facts. That strategy will only hurt you in the end. Instead, you can help to solve the problem with creative combination and application of the facts that you have learned. The following dialogue illustrates several approaches to creative problem solving when the problem involves a *specific product attribute*:

PROSPECT: I know for a fact that two of your competitors have a longer warranty period than you do.

SALESPERSON: That's true. Two of our competitors do offer a longer warranty period. But you can't consider warranties in isolation from other factors. Warranties don't tell the whole story. Have you seen these data on the frequency with which our products require service? (*Shows a report published by an independent source*)

PROSPECT: No, I haven't.

SALESPERSON: This is a report published by an independent testing agency. You are right. Those other firms have longer warranty periods, but their machines break down, on average, 17 and 13 percent more often than ours. That means that, even with the longer warranty, their total maintenance costs are 15

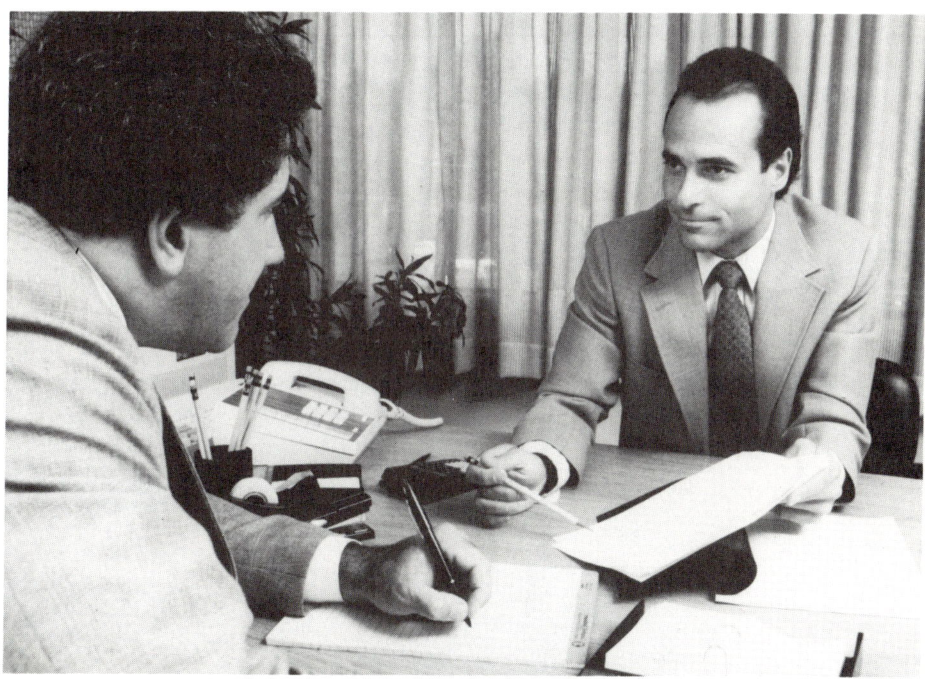

Objections may be overcome with reference to factual information. (Frank Siteman/ Taurus Photos.)

percent higher than ours at the end of the third year. By the end of the fifth year . . .

The salesperson in this example used each of the following problem-solving techniques in responding to the content of the objection (see Figure 11.4).

Place the Problem in a Larger Context. It is often helpful to see a problem as part of a bigger picture. The salesperson in the preceding dialogue helped the prospect to do this by placing the problem in a larger context. In this case, the larger context was the overall cost. It is often true that an objection to a specific cost issue can be explained when it is viewed as part of an overall cost. The prospect's concern about the warranty was really a concern about the cost of repairs after the warranty period was over.

Once he placed the objection about the warranty in a larger context (e.g., overall cost), the salesperson was able to explain what looked like a major shortcoming of his product. He was also able to balance the problem with a more positive feature (product reliability) and point out that one compensated for the other.

Analyze the Problem in Terms of Trade-Offs. You can appreciate the usefulness of the **trade-off** approach if you think of your own purchase decisions. Many times your concern is with overall value, and in seeking it, you balance one

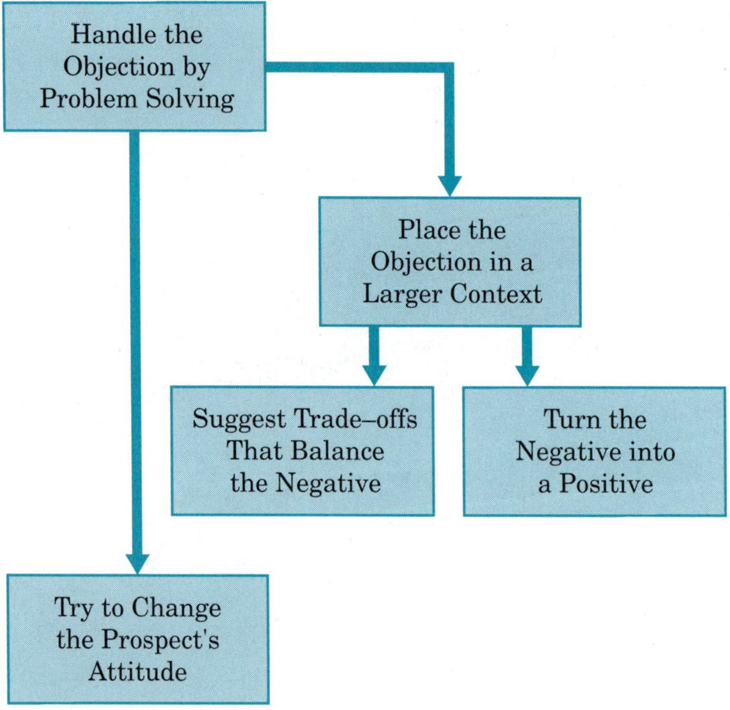

FIGURE 11.4 Problem solving.

attribute against another. It is hard to think of a case where this kind of trade-off is not made. We constantly trade off price for quality, energy efficiency for price, and so on. Yet we are not always aware that we are making such trade-offs. We might complain to a salesperson that a price is too high and have to be reminded that it is because the cost of maintenance is so low.

A salesperson who is prepared to help the prospect think in these terms will be better prepared to answer the content of objections. If the salesperson in the previous example had responded to the objection about warranties with information about warranty periods, he might have lost the sale. The fact is that his company does *not* compare well when you look at the warranty alone. Yet, in the broader perspective of the overall cost of maintenance, the salesperson's company comes out on top. Although the cost of repair was the basic concern behind the warranty objection, the prospect did not make the connection. It was up to the salesperson to make this link, solve the objection creatively, and satisfy the prospect.

This general notion of trading off is the idea behind the content of the *compensation* and *yes but* techniques for handling objections. In each case, the salesperson offers a feature that compensates or trades off for the problem feature.

Turn the Disadvantage into an Advantage. Turning a disadvantage into an advantage is the basis of the *boomerang* technique listed in Table 11.1. This technique differs from the trade-off approach in that it involves looking at a single attribute from a different perspective. The first salesperson in this chapter turned a disadvantage into an advantage when the prospect complained about a vinyl lining in the pockets of a briefcase. The salesperson was quick to point out that there was a good point to the use of vinyl: It made the briefcase lighter. The technique of turning a disadvantage into an advantage can be used in a variety of situations, given that many things have a good as well as a bad side. Here is a different application of the same idea:

PROSPECT: But your account rep is new and inexperienced.

SALESPERSON: Sure, she is new. Yours would be her first account. I remember my first account well. I put more effort into that account than all of the more experienced reps put together. That client ended up making the highest profits too. From what I've been able to see of June, the same would be true for you.

As this example illustrates, the techniques listed in Table 11.1 can be combined once you understand the underlying reasoning. In this case, the salesperson turned a disadvantage into an advantage by giving a **case history.** In general, we can see from these examples that responding to the content of a specific objection involves more than employing a series of memorized facts. It involves *listening* to what the prospect is really saying, *diagnosing* the problem, putting it into a larger context, and *solving* it creatively.

However, there may be cases that cannot be addressed by problem solving alone. In these instances, the problem may be the prospect's basic attitude, and handling the content of an objection may involve attitude change.

Handling Objections by Changing Attitudes

There may be cases where you cannot seem to handle an objection with the use of the previous techniques alone. If you are faced with an objection that states a general preference (e.g., "Well, I really prefer Kraft's cheese spread to yours."), you cannot use a technique that is designed to attack a specific complaint. Instead, you may judge that it is time to try to change the prospect's attitude. This might be true in the following case, where a salesperson is arguing for more shelf space in a retail store:

> PROSPECT: We seem to do quite well selling Kraft's products. We really don't have room for two brands of cheese spread.

By applying what you learned in Chapter 5, several things should come to mind in handling this kind of objection.

- The problem in this case is the store manager's basic attitude: He prefers Kraft.
- Based on the *multiattribute attitude model*,[7] we realize that this general preference is based on certain beliefs and that changing some of these beliefs should change the attitude. We begin by trying to uncover the underlying beliefs. As this example shows, the basic beliefs are not always obvious at first, so the salesperson needs to probe.

> SALESPERSON: What is it about Kraft's spread that makes you prefer it?
> PROSPECT: They advertise so heavily that people demand it. Other brands just wouldn't move off the shelf as fast.

Here the salesperson has uncovered a basic belief—that competitors' brands will not sell as rapidly. The logical next step is to attempt to change this belief. However, caution must be exercised here. It is dangerous to try to change beliefs without having some sense of the prospect's involvement with the product. If the prospect is highly involved with the product, attempting a drastic change of belief can backfire.[8,9] Instead of changing the belief in the direction you had hoped, you can cause the prospect to think worse of you and your product.

In this case, if the prospect believes strongly that other brands will not sell quickly, and the salesperson makes a claim such as "If you put our brand next to Kraft's in your refrigerator case, Kraft won't even sell," the attempt to change the belief could have the opposite effect. The result may very well be that the prospect will think that Kraft is even better than he did before the salesperson attempted to change his attitude. If a prospect is highly involved with a product and has very strong beliefs, it is better to attempt to change his belief a little bit at a time. "Actually, ours will sell better than you think. Here, look at the sales figures we've achieved in other markets."

Handling the Objection's Form Along with Its Content

At this point, you may be wondering how you would handle an actual objection. Although we have discussed each aspect separately, every real-life objection has a form and a content that must be handled together. In this section, we present and analyze an extended example that combines what you have learned about form and content. The salesperson in this example is trying to convince the buyer in a drugstore chain to carry her company's new shampoo.

1 PROSPECT: Well, it sounds good, but I'll have to ask my district manager about it.

2 SALESPERSON: I can make an appointment to see her if it's convenient. Would that help?

3 PROSPECT: Actually, she's too busy for that.

4 SALESPERSON: Well, do you have any concerns that I can address?

5 PROSPECT: No, not really.

6 SALESPERSON: Do you think that the district manager will be favorable?

7 PROSPECT: Actually, I'm not optimistic.

8 SALESPERSON: Why not?

9 PROSPECT: Well, to tell you the truth, our shelf space is very limited, and we just agreed to add Clairol's new shampoo to our line.

10 SALESPERSON: What made you decide to carry theirs?

11 PROSPECT: They are backing it up with the biggest ad budget in the history of the industry. I've already seen the TV ads, and they're really good.

12 SALESPERSON: What did you like about them?

13 PROSPECT: I think they'll create quite a stir—people will talk about them. In fact, I've already heard comments about them.

14 SALESPERSON: So have I. That is an important issue. We actually considered a similar campaign for our new shampoo, but our research people found that those sexy ads don't stimulate as many sales as you would think. Also, in the shampoo market, even the sexiest ad won't get many people to shell out $4.99 to try another new brand. We decided to stick with a price of $2.29. Our research people say that will lead to 30 percent higher initial trial rates.

15 PROSPECT: I don't care what they say about the price. Once people smell this, they'll try it.

16 SALESPERSON: I know what you mean. Scent is one of the big enticers in the initial trial phase, and Clairol's does smell good. But we are concerned with repeat business. We actually compared theirs to ours in an extended in-home trial and found that people preferred our body-building qualities to theirs by 2 to 1. We spent a long time developing that new conditioning agent I was telling you about, and in repeat purchase, we've found that body counts more than smell.

17 PROSPECT: You mean you actually compared theirs to yours? Maybe we should try a few cases.

In this case, the salesperson combines many techniques for handling objections. We see that a primary concern at the beginning of the interaction is defining the problem. The salesperson is apparently suspicious of a stall and probes for the hidden objection with the use of a series of questions (lines 2, 4, 6, and 8). Although the salesperson does not appear controlling, the persistent use of questions makes it difficult for the prospect to continue to stall. Finally, a specific objection emerges (line 9).

With a specific objection to go on, the salesperson starts problem solving. In this phase, the salesperson balances the handling of relational and content aspects of the objections. He has been careful to begin potentially argumentative responses with neutral approval statements (lines 14 and 16). Yet each neutral statement is followed by an astute argument about the content of the objection. Specifically, the salesperson begins by probing the comment about the competitor's shampoo (line 10) to learn that an underlying reason for the decision is the advertising campaign. Searching for underlying beliefs (line 12), the salesperson attempts to change the prospect's attitude about the ad (14). Here the salesperson is careful only to suggest that the ad won't sell "as much as you would think" instead of claiming that it will be a complete failure. Next, the salesperson links the ad to another attribute in which his own company is superior: price (linc 14). When the prospect discusses another attribute in which the competition excels, scent, the salesperson ties it to a larger context, repeat purchase, and argues that his own company will win here too (line 16). By linking scent to repeat purchasing, the salesperson is able to tie in the major attribute of his own product: manageability. Here the salesperson presents enough facts to persuade the prospect.

We can see from the way this interaction flows that the form and content of objections can be handled together quite smoothly. The salesperson moves from problem definition to attitude change and problem solving so naturally that one does not even notice that the argument is carefully constructed to follow specific principles. With familiarity and a little practice in applying these principles, you can learn to make the handling of objections seem almost effortless.

Putting It All Together

At this point, we can summarize the chapter's material:

- Objections are necessary and should not be avoided.
- Objections provide feedback and request a response.
- Objections have form as well as content.
- Objections involve special rules.
- In handling objections, you are often expected to disagree with the content while avoiding a contest for control.
- An objection's content cannot be ignored.
- Handling the content involves problem solving and attitude change.

We can also summarize specific conclusions that should help you handle the form and content of objections successfully:

- In handling the form of the objection (the relational communication), begin your response with some neutral statement (approval and/or repetition) or make your point with some neutral information source (demonstrate your product, mention a case history).
- In handling the content of a specific objection, mention an attribute in which you excel, put the problem in a larger context, mention trade-offs, or turn the disadvantage into an advantage.
- In handling objections by changing attitudes, ask questions to uncover basic beliefs, but do not attempt too drastic a change in a strongly held belief.
- Because every objection has form as well as content, make sure that you do not concentrate on one to the exclusion of the other. As we saw in the final dialogue, form and content must be handled together.

However, putting it all together requires more than combining the form and content of each objection. It means putting what you have learned in this chapter together with the rest of the sales process. In earlier chapters, you learned how to approach the prospect, what *you* should say as you approach, how *you* should ask questions and listen to responses, what *you* should say in the presentation, and how *you* should say it. Each of these topics stressed one direction of the communication process: the information *you present to the prospect.*

By now, however, you are well aware that the sales call is an *interaction.* To complete the picture, you need to include the material presented in this chapter, which covers the *prospect's* role in the presentation. As we discussed earlier, any question, concern, or stall voiced by the prospect is considered an objection. Therefore, handling objections really involves knowing how to respond to anything the prospect says during and after your presentation. This may require responding to questions, explaining specific issues, justifying weaknesses in your product, or getting to the bottom of general stalls. And, with the exception of formal presentations, the objection handling process will occur throughout your entire presentation (see Table 11.2).

In fact, once we put objections in their proper perspective, we realize that

Table 11.2 Placement of Objections in the Sales Presentation

Formal Sequence	*Informal Sequence*
Investigate needs	Investigate some needs
Present product information	Present some product information
Handle objections	Handle objections
	Investigate more needs
	Present more product information
	Handle more objections*

* This sequence can be repeated until all needs are uncovered, product information is discussed, and objections are handled.

this chapter might better have been called "Handling the Interactive Aspect of the Sales Presentation." It is easy to see why the salesperson who cannot handle objections will not be able to succeed. Not handling objections means not being able to interact with the prospect.

Key Terms

Objection
"Yes, but" technique
Direct answer technique
Direct denial technique
Boomerang technique
Relational communication
Compensation technique
Case history technique
Demonstration technique
Stall
Trade-offs

Review Questions

1. What functions do objections serve in the sales interaction?
2. Why are objections a benefit to the salesperson?
3. What is special about the communication dynamics of objections?
4. Why are objections likely to lead to a contest for control in the interaction?
5. How can you avoid a contest for control in handling objections?
6. How can a demonstration avoid a contest for control?
7. What is the first stage in problem solving when handling an objection?
8. How can you tell whether there is a hidden objection?
9. What are the three different ways of solving a problem contained in an objection?
10. Why must you exercise caution when attempting to change a belief?

Discussion Questions

1. Following are four different objections. How would you respond to each one? Think about how you would handle the form as well as the content of each.
   a. Prospect at a university copy center: "I'm not convinced that this copy machine will stand up to the amount of stress we will give it."
   b. Prospect at a car dealership: "When you add in that destination charge, this car costs more than the bigger Japanese model."
   c. Prospect in a clothing store: "I don't know about this suit. I think I should ask my girlfriend about it."
   d. Prospect ordering personal computers for an accounting firm: "I simply prefer the IBM."
2. Respond to each of the objections in question 1 with two different techniques from the list in Table 11.1.

CASE 11.1

Now that you understand the dynamics of objections, turn back to Case 9.1 and consider both sales presentations in terms of their objections. Did Joan have any objections in these dialogues? If so, how were they handled by Sam and Harry? Be sure to analyze the handling of the form as well as the content of any objections.

CASE 11.2

As you have just seen, Case 9.1 ended when Sam referred Joan to Vince, food and banquet manager at the Palace. In this case, we listen to the conversation that took place between Joan and Vince. We begin with some background information on Vince.

Everyone at the Palace agrees that Vince is a talented food and banquet manager. His sense of what pleases guests is undeniable. In the 2 years since Vince has managed this area, the Palace has gained a reputation for world-class food. Groups from all over the Northeast travel to the Palace for their banquets. The banquet rooms are booked several years in advance.

In addition, Vince is quite good at handling problems with the food staff. The chefs, in particular, are known to be temperamental, and Vince manages to keep them all happy and productive.

There is only one potential problem with Vince's performance. Sam, Vince's boss, is concerned about Vince's ability to sell his services. Sam believes that a good salesperson needs to be outgoing and aggressive. Whenever Sam and Vince have a conversation, Vince is quite shy and never seems to say very much. Although Sam appreciates the good work that Vince has done, he is considering hiring a person whose job would be to deal directly with the public instead of Vince. Sam could train such a person in his own selling style and would leave Vince to handle the personnel and food problems.

In order to evaluate Vince's selling skills, Sam has decided to observe him in action. He begins by listening to the conversation that takes place after he refers Joan to Vince:

VINCE: Nice to meet you, Ms. McNeal. Do you plan a stay at the Palace?

JOAN: I'm just here overnight. I'm trying to decide about having my annual sales meeting here. I've spoken with Sam, and he tells me that you are the person who handles food and banquet arrangements.

VINCE: That's right. So what can I do for your meeting?

JOAN: Well, we're planning a 4-day meeting. We'd need food for a welcoming party on the first night, refreshments during the seminars and lectures, and a large banquet for the final night. Otherwise, the reps are on their own.

VINCE: I see. Well, we are pretty flexible in our offerings. What kind of food are you interested in?

JOAN: Well, we'd like pretty elaborate hors d'oeuvres for the first night—though I'm not sure what.

VINCE: We have several options that are popular with large groups. You can have hot hors d'oeuvres, cold hors d'oeuvres, or a combination. Here are the actual menus. The prices are listed.

JOAN: Normally, we'd want the combination, but you have nothing here for dieters or health-conscious people.

VINCE: (*looking at the menu*) You mean you're concerned about the calorie counters? I guess we don't have a lot of diet foods on this menu. Well, we could—

At this point, Sam, who has been listening with frustration to Vince's laid-back style, is worried that Vince will agree to do something special that will cost too much. He interrupts Vince)

SAM: (*pointing to the menu*) A lot of our choices are healthy. Look at these, Ms. McNeal. Snow peas stuffed with lobster salad are very healthy. We even make our own mayonnaise for the lobster.

JOAN: Well, that's part of the problem. Mayonnaise is very fattening, and for that matter, lobster has cholesterol.

SAM: Not so. All the health experts tell you to eat fish oils now, and lobster is a fish.

JOAN: Yes, but dieters worry about calories.

VINCE: I understand your point, Ms. McNeal. Well we could leave the snow peas plain and arrange them next to a yogurt dipping sauce. To keep things interesting, we could add some caviar.

JOAN: Great. But what about the cost?

VINCE: It would depend on the type of caviar that you chose. Here's our price list.

JOAN: That's way out of line with what we can afford.

SAM: These caviar prices are from a wholesale list. We don't make any money on caviar.

JOAN: I'm not questioning your pricing margins. I just think this is too much for us.

VINCE: That's a reasonable point. Well what about this? We could arrange a vegetable platter with the yogurt dipping sauce and no caviar, but include some unusual miniature vegetables for interest. (*Vince points to a picture and price in a brochure*) It would cost less, and have you ever had these? They're delicious!

JOAN: That sounds like a reasonable solution. Now what about refreshments for the meetings?

After observing Vince in action, Sam was even more convinced that someone else should be hired to deal with the public. Sam felt that Vince was not forceful enough and that Joan was just covering up a hidden objection about price. He was certain that if Vince had held his ground, Joan could have been convinced to stick with the snow peas and lobster salad.

1. What is your opinion of this interaction? Be sure to analyze the conversation in terms of relational communication as well as content.
2. Which of Joan's statements (or questions) could be considered objections?
3. How was each objection handled?
4. Do you think that Joan was covering up a hidden objection about the price? (If so, what should have been done about it?)
5. Should Vince have stood firm with Joan?

References

1. McLaughlin, M. (1984). *Conversation: How Talk Is Organized.* Beverly Hills, CA: Sage.

2. Hite, R. and J. Bellizzi. (1985). Differences in importance of selling techniques between consumer and industrial salespeople. *Journal of Personal Selling and Sales Management,* (November), 13–30.

3. Peterson, R. T. (1987). Sales representative utilization of various widely-used means of answering objections. *Proceedings, American Marketing Association Educators' Conference, 53,* 119–124.

4. Millar, F. E. and E. Rogers. (1987). Relational dimensions of interpersonal dynamics. In: M. Roloff and G. Miller, eds., *Sage Annual Reviews of Communication Research. Interpersonal processes: New Directions in Communication Research,* Vol. 14. Newbury Park, CA: Sage, 117–139.

5. Thomas, G. and G. Soldow. (1988). Information theory and communication rules in the context of interpersonal communication. In: *Information and Behavior,* Vol. 2. New Brunswick, NJ: Transaction Books, 309–321.

6. Shimanoff, S. (1980). *Communication Rules: Theory and Research.* Beverly Hills, CA: Sage.

7. Fishbein, M. and I. Ajzen. (1975). *Belief, Attitude, Intention and Behavior.* Reading, MA: Addison-Wesley.

8. Hovland, C., O. J. Harvey, and M. Sherif. (1957). Assimilation and contrast effects in reactions to communication and attitude change. *Journal of Abnormal Psychology, 55* (July), 244–252.

9. Anderson, R. E. (1973). Consumer dissatisfaction: The effect of disconfirmed expectancy on perceived product performance. *Journal of Marketing Research, 10* (February), 38–44.

12

Closing the Sale

CHAPTER OBJECTIVES

In this chapter, you will learn:

- All interactions, not just sales interactions, end with a close.
- The close is the natural conclusion to the sales call.
- It is the salesperson's responsibility to close the sale.
- Closing is part of the interaction.
- Closing attempts can be tried as often as desired, as long as they are integrated into the discussion.
- Closing attempts should follow a signal given by the prospect.
- The salesperson who is in doubt about the prospect's signals can attempt a trial close to learn more information.

CHAPTER OUTLINE

A Sales Challenge

We can learn an important lesson about the closing of a sale from the following conversation, which took place between two graduate students at a university in New York City:

PATRICK: So, did you buy your computer yesterday?

PENNY: Yes, but I'll never go back to that store again.

PATRICK: Why not?

PENNY: The salespeople were terrible.

PATRICK: Gee, I've always liked that store. The salespeople have never pushed me to buy.

PENNY: They didn't push me either. Why, they wouldn't even help me. When I'm spending $2,000 of my hard-earned money, I expect some decent information. Those salespeople could not have cared less. Not only did I have to do all of the talking, I finally even had to *ask* them if they would sell it to me! Something is definitely wrong when you have to ask whether you can spend $2,000.

An Overview

Penny's complaint brings up an important point. With the exception of certain retail situations, in which the salesperson functions as an order taker, it is generally considered part of the salesperson's role to *ask for the sale.* When you ask the prospect to buy your product, you are said to *close the sale.*

You will see the term *close* used in a variety of ways:

"Joe *closed* that sale in a hurry!"
"Salespeople must know how *to close* successfully."
"That sale wasn't *closed.* They just couldn't agree on a price."
"Sandy used an assumptive *close.*"

Most often, the **close** is defined as *that point in the sales call when the salesperson secures the prospect's agreement to purchase.* However, we can see from the way the term is used that the close frequently is considered to be something that the salesperson *does.* As a result, we can speak of *closing techniques,* which are *strategies that a salesperson can use to secure a purchase agreement from the prospect.*

The purpose of this chapter is to help you understand the close from an interactive point of view. Our discussion is based upon the underlying communication dynamics of closing a sale. Like any interaction, the close is governed by rules. We begin with a discussion of these rules. Next, we discuss signals that prospects may send when they are ready to buy. Finally, we present commonly used closing techniques, and analyze the underlying dynamics of each.

When you finish this chapter, you will understand the following points about the close of a sale:

- *The close is not magic.* A glance at any book on selling will tell you that there are many different techniques for closing a sale. Some claim that there is one "sure-fire" way to close successfully. These sources attach almost magical properties to specific closing techniques. Unfortunately, there are no sure-fire closing techniques. In fact, there is not even one *best* technique for closing a sale.
- *The close is the natural conclusion to the sales call.* It is no more mysterious than any other part of your interaction with the prospect. If you have not convinced the prospect to buy during your presentation, the use of a "magical" close will probably not win her over. This does not mean, however, that you can treat closing lightly, because you certainly can lose a sale at this point. Further, the close has significance beyond the immediate sale. Because it is the final part of the interaction, the close affects the impression that you leave on the prospect.
- *The close is an interaction.* Despite the fact that people refer to the close

Not every sales call is expected to result directly in a sale. This call concluded when the salesperson succeeded in setting up an appointment to make a formal presentation to this purchasing agent's buying committee. (© Tim Barnwell/Stock, Boston.)

as something the salesperson does, it is important to remember here that the close is part of your interaction with the prospect. In fact, the key to success in the close is to realize this simple fact and to begin to treat the close as an *interaction.* It is not something that you do *to* the prospect, but rather the culmination of your communication process *with* the prospect.

Once you understand the communication dynamics of the close, you will not have to rely on magic to achieve success. In fact, with an understanding of the underlying processes and rules, you will be able to judge which techniques are appropriate for different selling situations. You will even be able to invent some of your own techniques.

The Close Is Governed by Rules

Recall from Chapter 3 that all interactions are governed by rules. Rules guide our interactions by prescribing what is *correct or expected behavior* in each situation. Rules of this sort are often unwritten. In fact, we frequently follow rules without even being aware of them.[1]

Although a rule may not be written, people who violate it will be open to criticism. In fact, a rule violation was responsible for the criticism that Penny made at the beginning of this chapter. The computer salesperson violated a basic rule: that salespeople are expected to ask for the sale.

Following are three important rules that apply to the closing of a sale (see Table 12.1).

Rule I: Salespeople Are Expected to Close the Sales Call

In certain basic ways, the sales call is like any everyday interaction. Although we do not think in terms of these formalities, *all* of our interactions must be closed, and in general, the person who initiates a conversation is responsible for closing it.[2] In the sales interaction, it is generally the salesperson who initiates the conversation, and it is the salesperson's responsibility to close by asking for the sale. In fact, the salesperson who does not ask for the sale (directly or indirectly) is assuming that the prospect will do part of the selling job. Although the untrained salesperson may be timid about asking for the sale, with training

Table 12.1 Rules Govern the Close

Rule I	Closing the sale is the salesperson's responsibility
Rule II	The close should follow the principle of conversational coherence (The close should flow logically from something that the prospect says)
Rule III	The timing of the close should follow from the prospect's signals (Signals may be verbal or nonverbal)

you realize that making a presentation and *not* asking for the sale may appear unprofessional.

Remember that in the sales interaction the prospect is fully aware of the purpose of the meeting. When a salesperson calls on the prospect and presents a product, there is an unspoken understanding that the salesperson wants the prospect to buy something. Because of this understanding, the request for the sale is an *expected* conclusion to the presentation. Without some close, the prospect can be left wondering why the salesperson went through the whole presentation and did not ask him to make a purchase. A prospect should not be put in this position.

Rule II: Closes Should Follow Conversational Coherence

Recall from Chapter 3 that one of the most basic principles of interaction is the **principle of conversation coherence.** This means that conversations should *make sense,* that is, be *coherent.* Because of this principle, each statement in a conversation should follow logically (coherently) from the other speaker's previous statement. Interactions are supposed to be *two-way* processes, and it is the principle of conversational coherence that keeps conversations flowing smoothly back and forth between speakers. If people were not expected to link their statements coherently, we could not have conversations at all.

Conversational Coherence and the Close. Conversational coherence plays two roles in closing a sale.[3] First, coherence acts as a constraint on what you are able to say. It is because of this constraint that we hear people say, "I had planned to ask her to buy it, but I just couldn't find the right moment." Because each of your statements must flow logically from statements made by the prospect, you cannot make an arbitrary closing attempt whenever you feel like it. As with any conversation in which you *plan* to say something, you must wait until you can work your close into the conversation logically.

If you attempt a close without linking it to something the prospect has said, it will appear as though you are not paying attention to him. Consider, for example, the contrast between the following two closing attempts, and try to decide which one violates the rule of conversational coherence.

CLOSING ATTEMPT I

PROSPECT: I'm really not certain how much we will need this month.

SALESPERSON: I can write up the order right now if you like.

CLOSING ATTEMPT II

PROSPECT: I'm really not certain how much we will need this month.

SALESPERSON: Well, why don't I write up a small order now, and then I'll call you around the 15th to see if you need more.

But conversational coherence is not just a constraint on what you can say. It can also provide important *opportunities* to ask for the purchase. By linking your close to something the prospect has just said, you can make it appear perfectly natural. Consider the following opportunity created by a prospect's comment regarding the color of a car:

PROSPECT: Would I have to wait if I wanted to get this in red?
SALESPERSON: I'm sure we have one red one left on the lot. *Would you like it?*

In this case, the salesperson linked the close (indicated in italics) to the prospect's statement by following the principle of conversational coherence. The question "Would I have to wait . . .?" was a signal that the prospect was ready to decide, and the salesperson responded appropriately with a relevant close.

In general, though it is the salesperson's responsibility to ask for the sale, it is crucial that this request follow coherently from some signal given by the prospect (Rule III).

Rule III: The Timing of the Close Should Follow the Prospect's Signals

The timing of the close should occur when the prospect communicates readiness to decide, not simply when you feel that you have finished your presentation. If you ask for the sale before the prospect indicates readiness, your attempt to close may be considered pushy and receive a negative response. Consider the contrast in these two conversations between a prospect and a television salesperson:

DIALOGUE I
PROSPECT: Who makes this TV? (*pointing to a floor model*)
SALESPERSON: Panasonic. It's an excellent choice.
PROSPECT: Do you have this model in stock?
SALESPERSON: We certainly do. Would you like to take it with you today?
PROSPECT: Yes, my car is parked outside.

DIALOGUE II
PROSPECT: Who makes this TV?
SALESPERSON: Panasonic. It's an excellent choice. Would you like to buy this one?
PROSPECT: No, thank you. I'm just looking.

In the first case, the prospect has indicated a readiness to buy. Questions about the *availability* of a product are signals of interest. In the second case, however, no such signal has been given. The close violates the principle of conversational coherence because it is not linked to anything the prospect has said. It communicates that the salesperson is more interested in making a sale than in satisfying the prospect.

However, this attempt does not mean that you should always delay closing attempts. It is just as bad to keep on talking once the prospect has made a decision. By waiting too long, you communicate that you are more interested in hearing yourself talk than you are in satisfying the prospect's needs. You may even lose a sale this way.

This is what happened to the salesperson in the following example:

SALESPERSON: This camera has all of the features you're looking for. It is fully automatic. You don't even need to focus or advance the film. It also costs $40 less than the other model. I—

PROSPECT: *(interrupting) Could you ship it to New Jersey without damaging it?*

SALESPERSON: Of course. This camera is so sturdy that it could be shipped anywhere. I bought one for my 12-year-old, and you should see the abuse that it can take. It comes with a well-padded carrying case too. Even the shoulder strap is padded for comfort . . .

Although the closing signal (indicated in italics) in this example may seem obvious, there are many cases where a salesperson misses closing signals because he is so intent on delivering all of his arguments. This salesperson should have followed up on the prospect's signal:

PROSPECT: Could you ship it to New Jersey?

SALESPERSON: We certainly can. I'll make sure that the order goes out today.

As both of these examples indicate, the key to correct "timing" of the close is not really a function of time. It is a function of your ability to relate the close to the prospect's closing signals.

Recognizing the Prospect's Closing Signals

Signals in Everyday Interactions

You probably have more ability to recognize signals than you realize. Most of our everyday interactions are based on sending and receiving a variety of subtle signals.[4,5] In many cases, we are not even aware that we are sending or receiving these signals. For example, every time you take your speaking turn in a conversation, you respond to signals given by the other person. Without realizing it, that person looks at you, drops her voice, and pauses when it is your turn to speak. You respond to these signals automatically by starting to talk and, just as automatically, give the same signals when you are finished with your speaking turn.

There are many cases in which people follow fairly complicated signaling patterns without even thinking about them. Frequently, it takes researchers who study interaction to identify these patterns. Researchers have, for example, found standard patterns of signals that we all use when we close our telephone conversations. Although the specific behaviors vary according to whether the conversation is between friends or strangers, there is a definite pattern to the signals at the conclusion of the call.

The "closing" sequence begins as we near the end of our discussion of the "business" of our conversation. At this point, our responses tend to become shorter. Instead of elaborating on what the other person says, we respond with simple phrases such as "Mm hm." Next, someone summarizes the discussion, often beginning with "So" or "well": "So, it sounds like you had a really rough day." Following these summary statements are statements justifying the end of the call: "Well, I won't keep you on the phone if you have that exam tomorrow" and, finally, statements referring to future contact: "Thanks. Will I see you at school tomorrow?"[6,7]

Although this sequence may sound long and involved, we follow it without having to think about it. Likewise, you can learn to respond automatically to closing signals in the sales call.

Stay Attuned to Changes in Nonverbal Behavior

As you learned in Chapter 4, there is no simple dictionary for assigning meaning to nonverbal signals. Specific nonverbal signals vary with individual people and with situations. The close is no different. There is no definitive list of closing signals that apply to all prospects and all sales calls. However, this lack of uniformity is not a critical problem. Although each prospect is different, most prospects *do* send subtle signals as they become ready to buy. The important point to remember is that you should be *attuned to looking for the prospect's signals.* In many cases, salespeople miss these signals simply because they fail to look for them.

The key is to look for *changes* in the prospect. Changes in the prospect's appearance and behavior often reflect internal changes in thinking. If he has appeared tense while processing new information and thinking through his decision, the prospect may appear to relax as he reaches a decision. His posture and facial expressions may become friendlier and more open. This is not surprising: Once he decides to buy from you, your role changes from that of someone who is trying to persuade him to that of someone who is going to provide him with something he wants.

Look for Verbal Cues

There is also an important set of verbal cues that stem from the fact that, as a prospect nears the purchase decision, her thinking shifts from "Is this what I want?" to "Now that I want this, can I get it?" This shift is reflected in questions about product *availability, payment methods,* and *delivery dates.* If a prospect says anything like the following, it is probably a good time to attempt a close:

"Do you have this in stock?"
"Do you accept Visa?"

"Do you charge for delivery?"
"When could I get it?"

Consider the following dialogue, in which a salesperson and a prospect are discussing an alarm system for a small business. Try to determine whether the prospect is ready to buy:

SALESPERSON: This alarm system serves two purposes. It guards against fire and break-ins.

PROSPECT: Does it just ring here, or does it alert the fire and police departments?

SALESPERSON: We have models that do either one. Our low-end models set off a screeching sound on the premises when they sense smoke or when an intruder breaks in a door or window. Then we have high-end models that set off alarms on the premises here but also buzz the police and fire departments.

PROSPECT: How often do they set off false alarms?

SALESPERSON: Well, truthfully, no alarm system can guard against them completely. But ours have the best record in the industry. You see, ours have this special protection device (*shows the model*). If you happen to break your own doors or windows, you can punch in a special code and prevent a false alarm.

PROSPECT: How much does the expensive one cost?

SALESPERSON: $1,600.

PROSPECT: Does that include installation?

SALESPERSON: It sure does. We install it ourselves.

PROSPECT: How long would the installation take?

In this case, we have some good clues that the prospect is ready to buy. She stops asking about product features and starts asking about price and availability. She also changes to the conditional form of question: "How long *would* the installation take?" The conditional form implies the question "How long would this take *if I were to purchase it*?" The fact that the prospect used this question form instead of asking "How long *does* the installation take?" indicates that she is already thinking of owning it.

Some prospects may not give such a clear indication that they are ready to buy. This is where an understanding of the communication dynamics of closing techniques can come in handy. Some closing techniques are designed specifically to help determine interest on the prospect's part while allowing the discussion to continue.

The Communication Dynamics of Closing Techniques

You can best understand the purpose of the various closing techniques if you examine the role played by the close in the sales call. When you reach the point in your sales call where you think that you may need to close, you have already sensed some change in the prospect that has led you to believe that he may be ready to buy.

Your *objectives* at this point are as follows:

1. You want a clearer indiction of what the prospect is thinking.
2. You want to ask for the sale *but*
3. You want to avoid creating a potential dead end in the conversation in case the prospect is not ready to buy.

Meeting these objectives is not as difficult as it may seem at first. The key is to remember the principle of conversational coherence and integrate the closing attempt into the conversation. If the close is indirect and follows coherently from something the prospect says, the prospect may not even recognize that a closing attempt was made. Consider the following sequence between a carpet salesperson and a prospect:

PROSPECT: Do you deliver to Delaware?

SALESPERSON: We sure do. In fact, orders placed today can go out on Friday's delivery schedule. Do you want me to write up the order?

PROSPECT: Well, I'm still worried about how it will look in my living room.

SALESPERSON: Let's look at that fabric swatch again.

The salesperson handled this case well. She followed a common closing signal with a question that *could have* resulted in the sale but did *not* end the discussion. The close followed the principle of conversational coherence so smoothly that the prospect was probably unaware that she had rejected a closing attempt. In fact, this kind of subtle closing technique can be used as often as desired. It has no particular drawbacks and can even provide you with useful information. In this case, the closing attempt uncovered an *objection* that will give the salesperson something new to go on.

This represents an important guideline for constructing closes: Try to avoid placing the prospect in the position of having to defend a negative response to a close. You can reduce the sales call to an argument in this way:

SALESPERSON: *(Bringing a pair of shoes to the prospect)* Here, try these. *(Prospect tries on the shoes.)*

SALESPERSON: These shoes fit you perfectly. Do you want to take them?

PROSPECT: No, thanks. I really don't like this heel height.

SALESPERSON: But this height is much better for your circulation.

PROSPECT: I know. But it looks dowdy to me.

SALESPERSON: I think it looks good on your leg.

Chances are that this salesperson will never make this sale. By asking a premature and unrelated direct closing question, he has forced the prospect to defend a negative position. Further, by arguing in this way, the salesperson is making matters worse. He is putting the prospect in the position of having to defend her right to make her own buying decision. If we analyze their conversation, the *underlying messages* would read as follows (underlying messages are in italics):

SALESPERSON: These shoes fit you perfectly. Do you want to take them? *(I think you should buy these shoes).*

PROSPECT: No, thanks. I don't really like this heel height. *(Thanks, but I don't want to buy them.)*

SALESPERSON: But this heel height is much better for your circulation. *(But I know better than you, and I think you should buy them.)*

PROSPECT: I know. But it looks dowdy to me. *(It's my decision, and I will not buy them.)*

How could this salesperson have handled the case differently? A better technique would have been to use indirect questions to determine the prospect's readiness to buy:

SALESPERSON: Why don't you try these on? . . . They seem to fit you perfectly. How do they feel to you?

PROSPECT: They're okay.

SALESPERSON: Would you like them better in black?

PROSPECT: The problem isn't the color. It's the heel. I don't like this heel height.

SALESPERSON: You mean it's too high or too low?

PROSPECT: Too low. It looks dowdy.

SALESPERSON: Well, maybe you'd rather try these.

In this case, the salesperson avoids risking an unsuccessful direct close by asking a question aimed at determining the prospect's willingness to buy. She learns that she should not close at this point and also gains some further information about the prospect's preferences. Questions of this sort are frequently used before the actual closing attempt. They are called *trial closes.*

The Trial Close

The **trial close** is *a question that aims at indirectly determining the prospect's readiness to buy.* Although it is called a *close,* the objective of the trial close is not to secure an immediate purchase. Rather, the trial close is used *before* a final close. In the previous dialogue, the question "Would you like them better in black?"

was a good example of a trial close. It represented an indirect way of asking whether the prospect liked the shoes.

The trial close frequently uses a conditional question format:

"*Would* you put this in your living room?"
"*Would* you change over to this new system right away?"
"What *would* you wear that with?"

In each of these questions, the phrase "If you were to buy this" is implied. Typically, when a prospect gives a direct answer to such a question, he is agreeing implicitly to having an interest in the product. Table 12.2 shows three such positive responses to trial closes.

However, there are cases in which a trial close will receive a negative response. In fact, the trial close is designed specifically to handle these situations. Since the trial close is not a direct request for a purchase, the prospect who is not yet ready to buy is *not* forced to give a definite "no" response. Table 12.2 also

Table 12.2 Positive and Negative Responses to Three Trial Closes

	Positive Responses
Trial Close I	
Salesperson:	*Would you put this in your living room?*
Prospect:	No. I think I'd rather put it in my dining room.
Trial Close II	
Salesperson:	*Would you change over to this new system right away?*
Prospect:	Well, we would have to retrain about 50 employees first.
Trial Close III	
Salesperson:	*What would you wear this with?*
Prospect:	I'd wear it with the suit I just bought for work.
	Negative Responses and Salesperson "Retrievals"
Trial Close I	
Salesperson:	*Would you put this in your living room?*
Prospect:	Well, I'm not sure. I'm afraid it's too formal.
Salesperson:	A lot of buyers use this with the country look. Although you might rather consider this (*pointing to a different sofa*).
Trial Close II	
Salesperson:	*Would you change over to this new system right away?*
Prospect:	Well, I'm still concerned about the extra training our personnel would require.
Salesperson:	We do have several staff members who specialize in training employees to use our new systems. If you're interested, I can see about having them run some seminars for you.
Trial Close III	
Salesperson:	*What would you wear this with?*
Prospect:	Well, that's the problem. I'm afraid this doesn't go with anything in my wardrobe.
Salesperson:	A lot of women wear this with their basic navy suits. It's very nice.

shows three possible negative responses to trial closes and highlights the ease with which the salesperson can continue the discussion. In each case, the trial close uncovered an *objection* and conveyed valuable feedback to the salesperson.

Because they carry almost no risk of ending the conversation, and because they often lead to valuable feedback, trial closes can be used frequently during a sales call. In fact, a common trial close sequence might proceed like the one in Table 12.3.

Once you receive an indication of interest with a trial close, you can go on to a final closing technique. In the following section, we will discuss some commonly used closing techniques. As you will see, some of them are indirect and not very different from the trial close.

Techniques for Closing the Sale

Figure 12.1 shows the most commonly used techniques for closing a sale. If we examine the role played by each of these techniques in the interactive process, we see that not all of them are equivalent. In fact, we can identify three different categories of techniques:

Table 12.3 An Example of a Trial Close Objection Sequence

Salesperson:	Would you put a computer in everybody's office, or would you locate them centrally? *(Trial close)*
Prospect:	Your machines are far too expensive for us to put one in everyone's office. *(Objection)*
Salesperson:	If you wanted to buy fewer machines, we could easily upgrade their memory to handle your needs. *(Handles Objection)*
Prospect:	*That's an interesting idea. (Signals Interest)*
Salesperson:	Would five machines do it if they were located in this central room? *(Trial Close)*
Prospect:	But there's another problem. If the machines are centrally located everyone will have access to all of our data files. *(Objection)*
Salesperson:	That's actually less of a problem than you think. Some of our models can be locked so that no one without a key can turn them on, let alone search through files. How many keys would you need for each computer? *(Handles Objection—Trial Close)*
Prospect:	Four per computer would do it. But do the lockable models cost more than we had discussed? *(Signals Readiness to Buy)*
Salesperson:	If you order five, I can get them for you at the same price. Shall I order them for delivery this week? *(Close)*

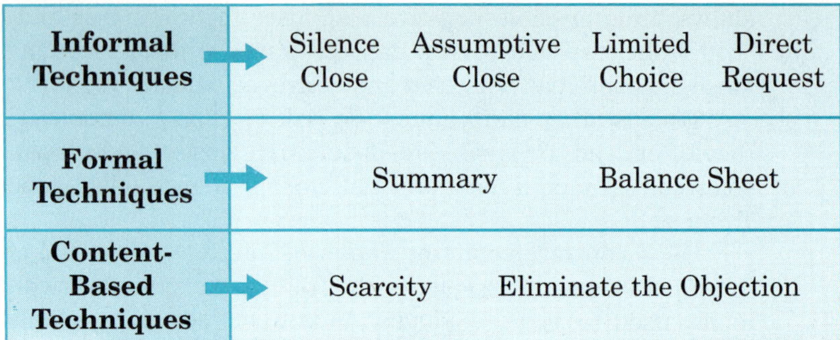

Informal Techniques
Silence Close
Assumptive Close
Limited Choice
Direct Request
Formal Techniques
Summary
Balance Sheet
Content-Based Techniques
Scarcity
Eliminate the Objection

FIGURE 12.1 Categories of closing techniques.

Informal Requests for the Purchase

The first category of techniques includes (1) the *silence close*, (2) the *assumptive close*, (3) the *limited choice close* and (4) the *direct request*. All four represent methods of actually requesting the sale. These techniques are called *informal* because they consist of simple questions that can be inserted into the natural flow of the conversation. As Figure 12.2 illustrates, the informal closing techniques vary in terms of how directly they make the request for the purchase. At one extreme is the silence close, which is so indirect that you do not actually ask for the sale verbally. Instead, you rely on nonverbal signals to request the purchase. At the other extreme is the direct request: "Do you want to order this one?"

Formal Summary Techniques

The second category of closing techniques includes (1) the *summary close* and (2) the *balance sheet close*. As we will discuss, both of these techniques summarize major points of the presentation. Because they are actual summaries, they are categorized as formal techniques. They cannot be inserted indirectly into the flow of the interaction but, instead, signal formalized conclusions to the sales presentation.

Content-Based Techniques

The techniques in this category are not necessarily formal or informal. They are distinguished by the *content* of their arguments rather than by the *form* of their

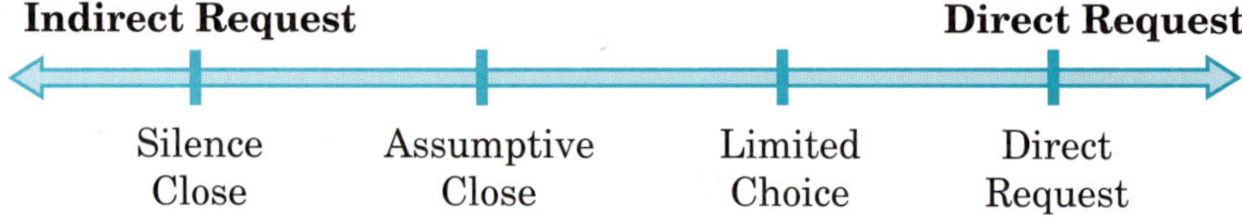

FIGURE 12.2 Direct versus indirect requests.

requests. The content-based techniques contain specific persuasive arguments that you might make when you ask for the sale. Included in this category are (1) the *scarcity close* (sometimes called the *standing room only close)* and (2) the *eliminate the objection close.*

In the following sections, each of these techniques is discussed in detail.

Informal Techniques

The Silence Close

The **silence close** is the most indirect of the informal closing techniques. With this close, you make some statement that would naturally be followed by a request for an order, but instead of asking, you merely pause and look at the prospect.

It may seem simple, but the silence close is actually one of the most difficult techniques to master. Although this close does not ask for the sale directly, it is one of the most dominant ways to request a purchase. With this closing technique, you take advantage of rules of nonverbal communication and combine a *pause* with a *stare* to "demand" that the prospect respond.

A pause is not, by itself, a dominant signal. As we have mentioned elsewhere, pausing is a natural part of speech. A pause is, in fact, one of the indicators that a speaker uses to signal the end of her speaking turn. However, natural pauses last for only 3 seconds or less. A silence of more than 3 seconds tends to be very uncomfortable for both parties.[8] Therefore, if you intentionally delay speaking for more than 3 seconds, the prospect will probably feel pressured to say something. This is particularly true when the extended pause is coupled with a controlling stare. The combination serves to demand a response from the prospect.

In addition to pressuring the prospect to respond, you exert control over the *contents* of the response by the type of statement you make before your pause. Based on the principle of conversational coherence, the prospect will respond to your stare with a statement that flows from the last thing you said. A typical example is:

SALESPERSON: In view of what you've told me, this seems to be your best choice (*pause*).

PROSPECT: You're right. I think I'll take it.

There is little question regarding the effectiveness of silence in forcing a response. The problem with the silence close is that it forces a response with such controlling means. Making the prospect feel uncomfortable runs counter to everything that the interactive salesperson stands for. However, as with all communication strategies, there is a great deal of variation from person to person. Recall from Chapter 3 that some people prefer to be submissive in conversation.

Therefore, depending upon the prospect and your own natural communication style, you may be able to use the silence close appropriately.

The Assumptive Close

The **assumptive close** does exactly what its name implies: It *assumes* that the prospect has made a decision to buy. With the assumptive closing strategy, you never actually ask the prospect to buy the product. You simply follow his readiness to buy signals with statements or actions that assume that the decision has been made. If the prospect responds to these statements, he agrees implicitly that he wants to make the purchase.

Although *assuming* that a decision has been made when in fact it has not may seem awkward, this technique can be quite natural. The key to using it smoothly is the principle of conversational coherence: Make sure that your assumptive statement follows *naturally* and *logically* from the prospect's previous statement. Consider, for example, the following three dialogues, and try to decide whether any of the closes will be successful:

DIALOGUE I

PROSPECT: This model seems to be what we need.

SALESPERSON: Shall I charge it to your account?

DIALOGUE II

PROSPECT: This model seems to be what we need, but I would really have to check which one my wife wants before making my final decision.

SALESPERSON: Shall I charge it to your account?

DIALOGUE III

PROSPECT: This model seems to be what we need, but I would really have to check which one my wife wants before making my final decision.

SALESPERSON: No problem. I'll just write a note on this order that you'll phone to confirm the exact model number (*writing up the order*).

We can see from these three dialogues that the key to a successful assumptive close is not so much the specific closing statement as the fit between that statement and the prospect's preceding statement. In fact, the same closing statement is used successfully in Dialogue I and unsuccessfully in Dialogue II. The prospect in Dialogue II added a qualifier that made the assumptive statement "Shall I charge it to your account?" sound out of order. Yet we can see in Dialogue III that this qualifier does not rule out the use of an assumptive close. It simply requires that a different one be used. The statement "I'll just write on this order that you'll phone in the model number . . ." follows logically from what the prospect has said. It could be followed by another statement, such as "Do you want this charged to your account?", but this is not necessary.

The Limited Choice Close

The **limited choice close** is sometimes referred to as the *alternatives close.* It uses questions of the form "Which one do you want?" as opposed to "Do you want this?" Because the "Which one" question assumes that the prospect wants one or the other, the limited choice close is actually assumptive. However, this close is used so extensively that it merits its own analysis. As Figure 12.2 indicates, the limited choice close is an indirect close. It never asks the prospect directly whether she wants to buy the product. Instead, it offers a *choice* that *assumes* that the purchase decision has been made.

Some typical limited choice closes are:

> "Will this be cash or charge?"
> "Do you want the red one or the blue one?"
> "Do you want me to include the service contract in your order, or do you want to wait on that?"

At first glance, the limited choice close resembles some of the trial closes discussed earlier. A direct comparison, however, shows that there is a difference. Consider the following two questions, and try to decide which one is the limited choice close:

> "Do you want one or two dozen of these?"
> "Would you need one or two dozen?"

The first one is the limited choice close. Because it *assumes* that the prospect has decided to buy, it is a *final* closing technique. Upon examination, we see that the second question is the trial close. It uses the conditional *would* and does not assume that a decision has been made. The difference between these two questions is highlighted if we compare possible responses to them. A positive answer to the trial close would indicate interest, but it would not represent a definite decision to buy. "I'd need two dozen" is still a conditional statement and implies that "I *would* need two dozen *if* I were to place an order." In contrast, it is difficult for the prospect to give a conditional response to the limited choice close. The question "Do you want *A* or *B*? is a forced choice question to which the natural response is "*A*" or "*B*."

The limited choice close is a very easy technique to use. Because it is an indirect request, it minimizes the risk of direct rejection. In addition, it requires less dominance than the other indirect techniques. Not everyone can stare at a prospect until he agrees to buy, and some people may even feel uncomfortable with some of the assumptive techniques. But anyone can ask a question such as "Do you want the red one or the blue one?"

There are, however, several things to remember when using a limited choice close. First is the principle of conversational coherence. The limited choice close is like any other close in that it must follow logically from what has been said. The second point is indicated in the name of the limited choice close by the word *limited.* Although this close is extremely easy to use, you must be certain to offer a *limited* choice, that is, a choice with limited options. In order to appreciate this point, consider the implications of using an open-ended question such as "What color do you want?" This question could lead unnecessarily to a problem by allowing the prospect to specify a color that is not available. Instead of closing the sale, it initiates a new objection.

The Direct Request Close

The **direct request close** is, quite simply, a direct request for the sale. Any question, such as "Would you like me to write up the order?" represents a direct request close. This technique is obviously the most straightforward of all the techniques for requesting a sale. Because of the simplicity of the direct request's structure, mastering the actual technique requires little practice. What does require expertise is knowing when to use the direct request.

Because of the directness of this technique, there is the risk of receiving a flat "no" from the prospect. Therefore, before using it, you should be fairly certain that one of the following two conditions exists: (1) the prospect has given such a strong readiness to buy signal that she will almost certainly say "yes" or (2) you feel that you have enough control over the situation to be able to retrieve the conversation should a "no" occur. Such a "no" was given in the following instance, but the salesperson was able to overcome it:

SALESPERSON: So, Bill, can I put you down for an order?

PROSPECT: Not today. You have to give me more time to think about it.

SALESPERSON: That's what you say every time I bring a new product in here. Remember how happy you were with the Model 730 after I coaxed you into signing on the dotted line?

PROSPECT: You're right. I do procrastinate about everything, and you've never steered me wrong in the past.

Obviously, this salesperson and prospect are on quite friendly terms. In such a case, the direct request may be quite appropriate. More will be said about the conditions under which you should choose various techniques after the remaining closing techniques have been discussed.

Formal Summary Techniques

The Summary Close

Although the **summary close** generally is considered a closing technique, it does not contain an actual request (direct or indirect) that the prospect make the purchase. Rather, the summary close represents a conclusion to the sales call in which the salesperson summarizes the key points. Because the summary close does not make an actual request for the purchase, it is typically combined with one of the previously discussed methods of asking for the sale.

The following example illustrates the use of a summary:

> SALESPERSON: So, Ms. Freeman, let me summarize some of these options. We can provide the motherboard with 640k, the Seagate hardcard with 40 megabytes, and the 1070 color monitor for $1,995. As I mentioned, we would throw in the new DOS and the printer cable. Shall I write up the order?

There are several important reasons for including a summary before you make a request for the sale. One obvious advantage is that the summary allows you to highlight your strong points before making the actual request. People often weigh the *last* information they hear rather heavily.[9] This is particularly important in cases where there is a great deal of complicated information, as in the previous example.

In addition, the combination of a summary and a request for the purchase provides a more *formal* closing than the use of a simple indirect question. There are times when the use of one of the more simple methods is not appropriate to

It is best to accompany your close with a written order that the prospect signs. (Susan Kuklin/Photo Researchers, Inc.)

the selling situation. As we will see in the following sections, formal presentations often deserve more formal closing techniques. Finally, the summary close can be a very good way of ending a sales call in which you have no intention of closing a deal. Remember that many sales require multiple calls. If you are on a sales call where your objective is to establish contact, present initial information, and request permission to draw up a proposal, a summary of your discussion will provide an excellent conclusion.

If you decide that a summary is appropriate, there are several variations from which to choose. The most obvious one is a straight summary. However, you may also use the **balance sheet close.** With the balance sheet, your summary explicitly mentions the advantages and disadvantages of your proposal. Although you try to highlight the advantages, your inclusion of disadvantages can lend credibility to your close. The balance sheet may literally be written on a sheet of paper, with one column labeled "Advantages" and another labeled "Disadvantages."

Content-Based Techniques

The content-based techniques do not control the *form* of your request, that is, whether it is a direct question, an either-or question, or a summary statement. Rather, these techniques define the *content* of what you say as you ask for the sale. Based on theories of persuasion from social psychology, these techniques, when used judiciously, can help convince the prospect to buy.

The Scarcity Technique

The **scarcity close** is based on the principle of scarcity: that things appear to be more valuable as they become harder to get. In order to apply this principle at the close of a sale, you must have a *legitimate* argument that if the prospect does not buy now, he may not be able to get the same deal in the future. Two examples of scarcity would be that (1) prices are about to increase or (2) stock is limited.

This closing technique has somewhat limited application because it must be reserved for situations in which the scarcity actually exists. The use of this technique when no scarcity exists is not only unethical but will hurt your business and personal reputation in the long run.

Eliminate the Objection/Final Concession Close

Additional persuasive arguments are based on the principle that people feel obliged to return favors. With these techniques, you make a **final concession,** often in order to eliminate an objection, at the last moment of the close. This approach is often effective because prospects tend to feel a need to match the gesture by agreeing to buy. However, when you use this technique, you should be careful to phrase it in a way that will ensure that you are making the *final* concession. The salesperson in the following example did just that:

PROSPECT: Your price is too high.
SALESPERSON: If I can get it down 10 percent, will you give me the order?

If this salesperson had simply said "I can lower the price by 10 percent," the prospect would have had room to bargain for additional concessions and the 10 percent price reduction would have been wasted.

Finally, a word of caution must be added in regard to some of these content-based closing techniques. The use of behavioral rules to manipulate prospects is dangerous. In the long run, no one benefits if the prospect is manipulated to buy something that she does not really want. In general, the key to choosing these or any other techniques lies in knowing when the situation is appropriate.

Adapt Your Close to the Situation

In order to appreciate the importance of adapting the close to the specific selling situation, consider the following scene:

The discussion takes place about 10 minutes into an *initial* call by a computer salesperson on a prospect in charge of buying computers at a large bank:

PROSPECT: What would be the advantage of buying this upgraded mainframe?
SALESPERSON: This new one will take care of your needs into the next decade. It will allow you to connect with banks worldwide, as well as with all of the computers throughout your own branches.
PROSPECT: Would this model run all of our existing software?
SALESPERSON: It certainly would. Shall I write up the order?

In this case, the salesperson interpreted the prospect's question about software to be a closing cue. She proceeded to ask for the sale before she should have. Although it is true that this kind of question might have been a closing cue under different circumstances, it should *not* have prompted a closing attempt in this case.

We can begin to understand the reason if we contrast this discussion with a similar one taking place between a sporting goods salesperson and a prospect:

PROSPECT: But what would be the advantage of buying this new gym bag?
SALESPERSON: This new model is designed specifically for swimmers. It's waterproof and has special compartments to hold your goggles and ear plugs.

PROSPECT: Yes, but will it fit my running shoes too?

SALESPERSON: They'd fit in perfectly right here, but if you're worried, you could get this triathlete bag. It's designed to hold swimming, running, and biking equipment. Would you prefer to take this one?

The dialogue is similar in both cases. Both prospects asked a question that indicated that they were seriously considering how the product would adapt to their needs. Yet in one case a close was appropriate, whereas in the other, it was not.

The important difference in these two cases is that they represent very different *selling situations.* The computer is a major industrial purchase, while the gym bag is a $20 consumer item. The computer salesperson should not even expect to close this sale 10 minutes into the first call. As indicated in Chapter 7, this prospect probably does not even have the authority to make this purchase on the spot. Attempting a close here shows lack of understanding of the situation. In contrast, the swimmer is likely to make a purchase decision after a preliminary examination of several gym bags. If this salesperson does not attempt a close, he may lose the sale.

Figure 12.3 summarizes the characteristics of the situation that should be considered when you are determining a closing strategy. Many of these distinctions stem from principles that you learned earlier.

Industrial Versus Retail Settings

We would expect a major industrial purchase to require a different closing technique than a simple consumer purchase. As you read in Chapter 5, many industrial situations involve multiple buyers. You may contact the purchasing agent, but she may have to deal with many others in the organization. The selling process is likely to extend over a number of visits and may even continue for a year before contracts are actually signed. You should not expect a $200,000 deal to be negotiated in 10 minutes!

In addition, it is likely that the industrial sales call will be conducted in a relatively *formal* way. When selling a $100,000 computer, you would undoubtedly use visual or audiovisual aids. You would probably prepare an entire presentation with facts and figures linking your computer to the specific needs of the prospect's organization. Further, at some point in the process, you may make a formal presentation to a group of decision makers from the organization. After such a formalized procedure, you would not expect to end with an indirect, informal close such as "And that, ladies and gentlemen, concludes our presentation. Oh and by the way, how would you like to pay for this mainframe?"

Yet, in contrast, such a simple, indirect question slipped into the conversation may serve the retail salesperson quite well. In fact, as mentioned earlier, many retail sales are closed with the question "Will this be cash or charge?"

The Prospect	
Is she dominant or submissive?	If dominant, do not use the Silent Close
Is she pressed for time or does she want attention?	If busy, do not use extended Summary Close

Your Relationship with the Prospect	
Are you friends?	Direct closes are less risky with friends than with strangers
Are you strangers?	Trial closes should be used subtly
Is your relationship formal or informal?	Informal relationships carry less risk of dead ending with a close

The Selling Situation	
Is it industrial or retail?	Do not attempt immediate informal closes in large industrial sales

Your Presentation	
Was it formal or informal?	Formal presentations call for formal closes. Either may be used in an informal presentation

FIGURE 12.3 Conditions affecting the choice of closing technique.

The Prospect's Needs

As with other aspects of the selling process, it is important to adapt your closing strategy to the needs of your prospect. This means taking into consideration the prospect's time needs, as well as his personality and preference for a dominant or submissive role in the interaction. Do not, for example, attempt a lengthy summary if you face a prospect with limited time. On the other hand, if you face a prospect who wants a great deal of your attention, a lengthy summary may be appropriate.

By the time you reach the close, you should have a sense of your prospect's need for dominance. You should not try a silence close if you are facing a dominant prospect. Such an aggressive strategy could result in a contest for dominance. On the other hand, you may face a prospect who exhibits a tendency to communicate directly in an equality-based, businesslike manner. With this kind of prospect, you may close with a direct request.

Your strategy for handling prospect differences will also change depending upon the nature of your relationship with the prospect.

The Nature of the Salesperson–Prospect Relationship

As Figure 12.3 indicates, an additional characteristic affecting the closing strategy is the nature of the relationship between the salesperson and the prospect. If you have an ongoing, friendly relationship with a prospect, you may use a more direct closing technique than you would with a stranger. The reason for this difference is simple: In cases where there is an ongoing relationship, there is much less risk that a direct closing question will end the discussion, even if the prospect is not ready to buy. Once you have established a relationship based on trust and credibility, you do not have to be as concerned with "dead-ending" a sales call with the wrong type of close.

In this respect, the prospect–salesperson relationship is like any interpersonal relationship. As a relationship develops over time, any one statement made by either person will have less effect on the impressions that the two people have of each other. Thus, any one statement exchanged between friends will have relatively little impact on the relationship. A premature closing attempt made in the context of an ongoing salesperson–prospect relationship will probably not mean the end of the discussion. In contrast, in the dialogue between two strangers who know nothing about each other, every statement plays a major role in contributing to the overall impression. In that case, a premature closing attempt runs the risk of creating a negative impression and possibly losing the sale.

Your Own Communication Style

Although it is obviously important to adapt your close to the situation, the prospect, and your relationship with the prospect, this does *not* mean that you must be prepared to use closing techniques which are inconsistent with your own communication style. Not all salespeople excel at every technique. One reason for studying many different techniques is to find several that you can learn to use comfortably.

An important part of a natural-sounding close is a technique that fits the style of your whole presentation. If your style is direct and dominant, you may do better to use a direct, dominant close. In contrast, a less dominant presentation style may make a dominant close sound forced.

Putting It All Together

Although the close of a sale is considered mysterious by some, you should realize by now that it is only one more aspect of your interaction with the prospect. At this point, we can summarize what you have learned about closing a sale:

Table 12.4 Different Closing Techniques and Their Importance to Salespeople

Selling Technique	Mean Importance: *Industrial Salespeople*	Mean Importance: *Consumer Salespeople*
1. *Direct Close:* Ask for the order in a straight-foward manner	4.32*	4.33
2. *Summary close:* Summarize the benefits already covered in the sales presentation, thus inducing the buying decision	4.06	4.09
3. *Single obstacle close:* The prospect is favorably disposed toward the offering except for one factor, so the salesperson attempts to eliminate that obstacle	4.00	4.00
4. *Assumption close:* Assume the prospect is ready to buy and focus on transaction details such as the delivery date	3.80	4.14
5. *Choice close:* Ask the prospect which of two or more versions of the offering he or she prefers	3.62	3.68
6. *Report close:* Tell the prospect about another prospect with a similar problem who made the purchase and benefited by it	3.40	3.40
7. *Demonstration close:* Demonstrate the offering to close the sale	3.16	3.29
8. *Minor-decision close:* Seek approval on the smallest possible decision encompassing the full order—substitute a minor decision for a major one	2.93	2.94
9. *Use silence:* Let the prospect make the decision	2.87	2.96
10. *Concession close:* Make the presentation and then offer some incentive/concession to the prospect (e.g., a price reduction for buying now)	2.70	2.72
11. *Comparison cost:* Compare the salesperson's offering's features with those of a well-known competitor	2.52	2.57
12. *"Buy now" close:* Instill an urgency in the prospect by explaining that unless the purchase is made now, the desired offering may be unavailable	2.24	2.46
13. *Emotional close:* Appeal to the prospect's emotions—fear, love, status, competitiveness, recognition	2.10	2.35

* 1 = not important; 5 = very important.

Source: Reprinted by permission of *Journal of Personal Selling and Sales Management* © 1985. R. Hite and J. Bellizzi. (1985) Differences in the importance of selling techniques between consumer and industrial salespeople. *Journal of Personal Selling and Sales Management, 5* (November), 19–30.

- First and foremost, the close is an interaction.
- Like all interactions, the close is governed by rules.
- Closing the sale is the salesperson's responsibility.
- Regardless of the technique used, the close should follow from something that the prospect has said (principle of conversational coherence).
- The timing of the close should be adapted to the prospect's needs.
- If in doubt, use a trial close as often as needed.
- Tailor the close to the prospect, the selling situation, and your own style.
- Closing techniques can be combined creatively.

At this point, you should have enough of an understanding of the dynamics of the close to practice the techniques mentioned and to determine which ones will suit your own style. However, the techniques described in this chapter should not be regarded as a definitive list. You should view them as illustrating various types of closes that you can employ in different situations. There are, in fact, many different variations on these techniques (see Table 12.4).

In putting it all together, you should realize that memorizing a standard list of techniques will not make you a successful closer. Rather, the salesperson who has a strong background in the basic skills described earlier, and who can apply them to closing, will be more successful in closing sales than the salesperson who simply memorizes some techniques. This is because successful closes must be worked *coherently* into the sales interaction. This requires basic interaction skills. Further, since the timing of the close follows the prospect's signals, successful closing requires an ability to recognize nonverbal behavior. In general, the close is like all the other parts of the selling process: It requires a blend of basic skills and specific selling techniques.

Key Terms

Principle of conversational coherence	Direct request close
Trial close	Summary close
Silence close	Balance sheet close
Assumptive close	Scarcity close
Limited choice close	Final concession close

Review Questions

1. What are the rules that govern closing?
2. Why is the close considered the salesperson's responsibility?
3. What is conversational coherence?
4. Write an example of a dialogue in which a limited choice close (a) follows the principle of conversational coherence and (b) violates the principle of conversational coherence.
5. When is it appropriate to attempt a close?
6. What is the most significant nonverbal signal to look for in determining whether the prospect is ready to close?

7. What are the characteristics of verbal closing signals? Give three examples.
8. What is a trial close? When should it be used? How often should it be used?
9. Under what circumstances should you *avoid* the summary close?
10. What are the advantages of informal closing techniques? What are the disadvantages?

Discussion Questions

1. Write plans for a series of closes that combine the various techniques. Specifically, combine the scarcity and summary closes with (a) an assumptive close, (b) a limited choice close, and (c) a direct request close.
2. Give some examples of trial closes that a salesperson might use when selling a refrigerator to newlyweds.
3. Would you attempt a close after these comments by the prospects in question 2?
   a. Is that the only color this model comes in?
   b. Would we be able to get it in almond?
   c. Do you charge for delivery?
   Be specific in determining exactly what you would say.
4. Would it be possible to adapt the close to the prospect's signals if you were giving a memorized or automated presentation?

CASE 12.1

The following conversation between Margaret Spokes and Dave Cushing was overheard in the employees' dining room at Babbit Packaging. Margaret had been with Babbit for 4 years, and Dave had just been hired. The conversation was actually a heated debate about the merits of various closing techniques. Margaret and Dave had reason to get excited about the topic of closing a sale: Both were sales representatives at Babbit. They sold labels and boxes for perfumes and creams in the cosmetics industry.

The precise nature of the manufacture of these products meant that the stakes were quite high. The commission on a single deal typically ranged in the thousands of dollars. Six-figure salaries for salespeople were the industry norm. But those salaries were earned. The job was a high-pressure one. It was not uncommon for an entire order to be abandoned if the exact shade of coloring was not achieved, and satisfying the buyer was the salesperson's responsibility. The salespeople at Babbit had to act as liaison between the manufacturer and the buyer. In addition to knowing about packaging techniques in general, they had to be experts in color theory and production.

But the job required interaction skills even more than technical expertise. Much of the business involved establishing ongoing relationships with people in the cosmetics houses. Getting a new order often required a year of "courting" the prospect. However, once a solid relationship was formed, it tended to be stable. In fact, there were several instances in which cosmetics companies changed package suppliers in order to stay with an individual sales representative who had changed jobs.

Dave had initiated the debate about closing techniques. He had overheard Margaret telling her colleagues that she had just landed a million-dollar account that she had pursued for over a year.

MARGARET: And so, yesterday afternoon, after lunch at the Water Club, I finally asked him if we could have his business.

DAVE: You mean you used a simple direct close in a million-dollar deal? Do you think you're selling toothpaste?

MARGARET: Of course not, but I almost always use a direct close. You just don't understand this business. By the time I get to the close, I've become quite friendly with the people involved. By then, I don't want to pull anything fancy. I just ask.

DAVE: Sounds risky to me. So what do you do if they say "no"? You're up a creek without a paddle.

MARGARET: Your problem is that you can't read the signals. I know nonverbal communication. When I ask for the sale, I'm *sure* that I'll get it.

DAVE: I still think you're asking for trouble. With sales of this size, I always use a summary technique. There are too many complicated facts to just breeze into an informal close. Besides, formal situations deserve formal closes.

MARGARET: Talk about risk. Once you've gone through a formal buildup to the close, it's even harder to save a negative situation.

DAVE: Well, I cover myself there. I always use two or three trial closes before my summary and a limited choice close when I've hit all the major points.

MARGARET: Talk about selling toothpaste. I never use the limited choice close for a deal bigger than $10.

The debate between Margaret and Dave continued for 20 minutes until half of the sales staff at Babbit had gathered around the lunch table. One of their mutual friends, Bill Fitzwater, tried to settle the debate by arguing that the close didn't really matter anyway: By the time you get to that point, you've either got the account or you haven't. Bill did succeed in stopping the debate. Both Margaret and Dave teamed up to argue with him about the value of a good closing technique.

1. Summarize the major issues highlighted in the discussion. Include a list of all of the points made by each sales representative and an analysis of the pros and cons of each.
2. What would you have said to Margaret, David, and Bill?
3. On what issues would you have agreed with any of them?

References

1. Shimanoff, S. (1980). *Communication Rules: Theory and Research.* Beverly Hills, CA: Sage.

2. McLaughlin, M. (1984). *Conversation: How Talk Is Organized.* Beverly Hills, CA: Sage, Chapter 5.

3. Hobbs, J. R., and M. H. Agar. (1981). Planning and local coherence in the formal analysis of ethnographic interviews. Menlo Park, CA: SRI International. Unpublished manuscript.

4. Leathers, D. (1986). *Successful Nonverbal Communication.* New York: Macmillan.

5. Duncan, S., and D. Fiske. (1977). *Face-to-Face Interaction: Research, Methods and Theory.* Hillside, NJ: Lawrence Erlbaum.

6. Clark, H. H., and J. W. French. (1981). Telephone goodbyes. *Language in Society, 10,* 1–19.

7. Schegloff, E. A., and H. Sacks. (1973). Opening up closings. *Semiotica, 8,* 289–327.

8. McLaughlin, M., and M. J. Cody. (1982). Awkward silences: Behavioral antecedents and consequences of the conversational lapse. *Human Communication Research, 8,* 299–316.

9. Webster, F. (1971). *Marketing Communication.* New York: Ronald Press.

PART FIVE

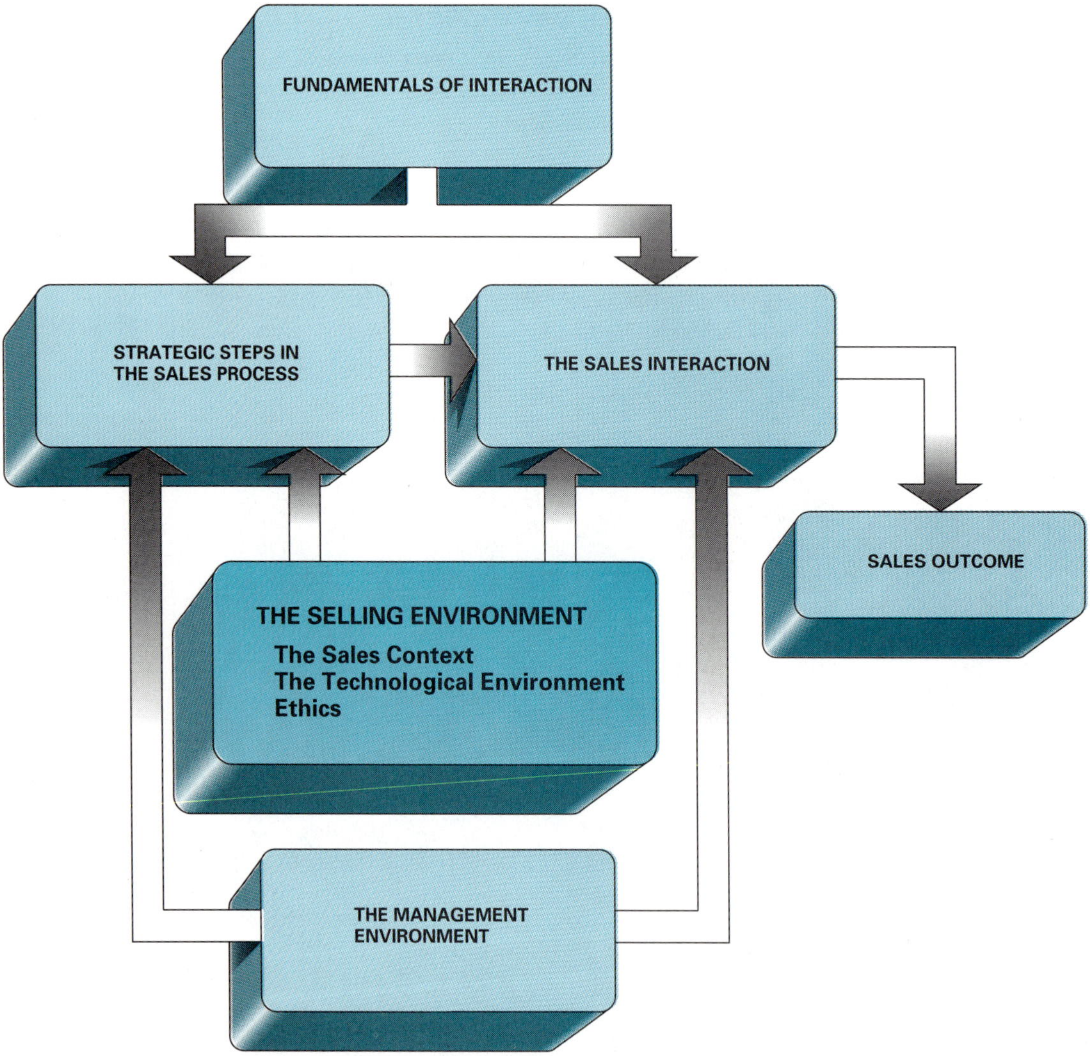

FUNDAMENTALS OF INTERACTION
STRATEGIC STEPS IN THE SALES PROCESS
THE SALES INTERACTION
SALES OUTCOME
THE SELLING ENVIRONMENT
The Sales Context
The Technological Environment
Ethics
THE MANAGEMENT ENVIRONMENT

THE SELLING ENVIRONMENT

13

The Context of the Sales Interaction

CHAPTER OBJECTIVES

In this chapter, you will learn:

No matter what selling context exists, personal selling is an interactive process, and the salesperson can make a difference between whether a product is sold or not.

The selling context can influence whether or not the prospect and salesperson have a long-term relationship.

The input of a salesperson is determined by how routine the purchase decision is.

The business-to-business salesperson has special considerations that require awareness of the needs of the buyer, external influences on the buyer, and the type of buyer.

Prospects expect the retail salesperson to be courteous, charming, and ingratiating, as well as knowledgeable and credible.

In selling services, the sales interaction becomes part of the service.

CHAPTER OUTLINE

A Sales Challenge

Janet Means usually has a busy day. She tries to make all her face-to-face sales calls in the morning and her phone calls right after lunch, and do her paperwork until late in the evening. She is a manufacturer's sales representative for a major producer of expensive glassware. She enjoys calling on department stores and small but expensive shops. Her biggest complaint is that the paperwork can sometimes be overwhelming. Although she is based in New York, she travels throughout the country and to Europe. Because Janet is very conscientious about follow-up and servicing her accounts, she has developed long-term relationships with her customers. Those relationships have turned out to be one of the things she most enjoys about her job.

George Sanders puts in a long day at a large personal computer store in Chicago's Loop. His customers range from students who want an inexpensive personal computer to small and medium-size businesses that want a network of personal computers. George prefers to work with businesses, not only because he can make considerably more money, but also because finding a solution for a specific business is more challenging. He has found that if he provides installation and on-site training, his business customers tend to make repeat purchases and, as a result, have often become customers of long standing.

Sharon Healey sells watches at I. Magnin in San Francisco. She finds dealing with a wide range of both men and women to be very interesting. She views each customer as a closed book and regards her task as trying to tease out some of the pages in the book. She is continually amazed both at how similar everyone is and how different they are. She makes a strong effort to ensure that the watch she sells a customer suits the customer's personality.

Jim Jackson is a sales representative for a major airline in Miami. He travels throughout the South, promoting the airline and various travel packages the airline offers to travel agents. He is amazed at how difficult it can be to persuade many of these agents. Agents tend to have very strong views about various airlines based either on their own experiences or on reports of their customers. He finds it quite a challenge to convince some of these agents about the benefits of his airline when they have had a negative experience with it. It seems that only one bad experience is enough to cause the airline to be strongly disliked.

Notice that all four of these people can be categorized as salespeople, and certain aspects of their jobs are common to all. Yet it should be clear that each of their positions is distinctly different. Janet Means is an industrial salesperson. George Sanders and Sharon Healey are both retail salespeople. Jim Jackson is a service salesperson.

An Overview

What distinguishes one type of selling job from another is the context. The **context** is *the circumstances in which an event occurs.* Generally, in selling we can identify three contexts: *business-to-business, retail, and service.* People who sell services can function in either a retail or a business-to-business setting. However, since selling services has its own special concerns, we treat it as a separate context regardless of whether it is concerned with the consumer or with business-to-business selling. Each context has important characteristics that make it unique. Our purpose in this chapter is to discuss, first, those aspects of selling that occur in all contexts and, second, the unique aspects of each context.

In discussing the special concerns of each selling context, we will highlight the role of follow-up and servicing an account. As you will recall, follow-up is the last part of the sales process and occurs *after a purchase has been made.* Follow-up is strongly influenced by the sales context. For that reason, we have deferred the discussion to this chapter, where we elaborate upon the differences in context to discuss follow-up.

Aspects of Selling That Occur in All Contexts

Much of our discussion in this book has been devoted to the selling process. As you will recall, the process begins with prospecting, followed by a preapproach, an approach, a presentation, a close, and, finally, follow-up. One way or another, all the parts of the selling process occur in any sales interaction, no matter what the context. Beyond that, there are two other major aspects that occur in all sales contexts.

1. All sales encounters are interactive. As we indicated at the beginning of this book, any sales encounter, no matter what the context, involves an interaction between a salesperson and one or more prospects. Since selling is an interaction, all of the concerns about interpersonal communication are relevant for the salesperson. No matter how perfunctory the encounter, it still involves a dynamic exchange of messages. This means that anyone who has developed interpersonal communication skills should be able to apply those skills in any sales context.
2. In almost any sales encounter and any sales context, the salesperson can make the difference between whether a product is sold or not. A salesperson can have an important impact on the sales of any organization, whether it be a department store or a major manufacturer of heavy machinery. Figure 13.1 summarizes the common features of all sales interactions.

Aspects of Selling That Differ by Context

While the three contexts have many of the same characteristics, they also have important differences. There are only two major differences, but these differences have broad implications for the job of the salesperson. The first difference has to do with *the expected duration of the relationship between the salesperson and the prospect.*

Generally speaking, the relationship between the business-to-business sales-

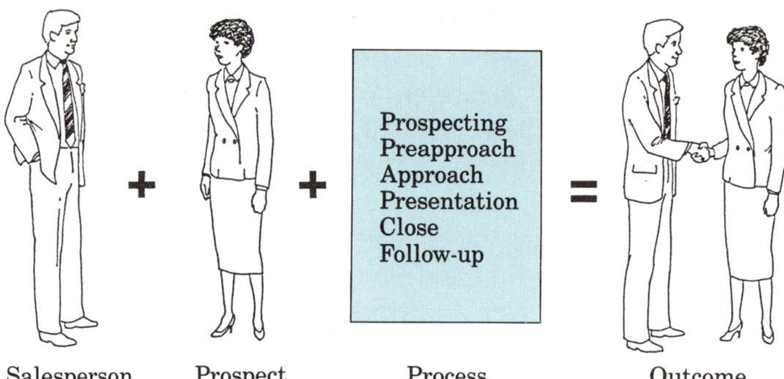

FIGURE 13.1 Aspects of the sales encounter that are common to all contexts.

person and the buyer can be, or at least has the potential to be, long term. In contrast, the relationship between the retail salesperson and a prospect is likely to be short term and is often a one-time interaction. As you will see, the duration of the relationship has an effect on the follow-up stage of the sales process.

The second difference has to do with *the degree of formality of the decision.* The formality of decision is based upon two properties:

1. How many people are involved in the purchase decision.
2. How much information they are likely to have.

Some decisions are made by one individual who has little information. This situation describes many retail purchases. Other decisions are made by one in-

This is a large wholesaler. Salespeople will try to sell products to this company. The wholesaler's salespeople will, in turn, try to sell the product to a retailer. Finally, the retailer will try to sell the product to the final consumer. (Michael Kagan/Monkmeyer Press Photo.)

dividual who has a great deal of information. This situation describes some retail purchases, particularly those involving large expenditures, as well as purchases by proprietors of small businesses.

Decisions that involve several people with a great deal of information describe many business-to-business purchases. The *people making the purchase decision are referred to as* **buying center.** This situation can also describe a retail purchase in which a major purchase is being made and the entire family is involved in the decision-making process. Generally speaking, there are few purchase situations that involve many people with minimal information. Figure 13.2 summarizes the context of the purchase as a function of the formality of the decision-making process. We now turn to a discussion of the buying contexts in order to show the unique aspects of each.

The Business-to-Business Context

Any selling situation that does not involve a consumer is considered to be **business-to-business selling.** Generally, we distinguish between two broad categories: industrial sales and trade sales. **Industrial sales** *involve merchandise that is bought to make items that are then resold to the final user.*[1] **Trade sales** *involve selling merchandise to wholesalers and retailers who, in turn, resell the products to the consumer.* Since in both cases the transaction involves goods that are resold, the term *industrial sales* is often used to refer to all business-to-business transactions. We will use that convention here.

We should first consider what industrial customers are likely to buy. The industrial customer can buy anything from paper towels to buildings to wheat. Industrial goods cover a wide range of products. These products are listed and classified in Table 13.1.

The Importance of the Industrial Salesperson

In addition to being important for our economy, the industrial context is vital to many companies. The industrial salesperson can become the chief link to the buyer of the product. While companies rely on other forms of promotion, such as advertising, direct mail, and catalogs, most sales of industrial goods occur through a salesperson.

		Amount of Information	
		Little	Much
Number of People	One	retail	retail; small business
	Many		business to business

FIGURE 13.2 Formality of the purchase decision and context of the decision.

Steel produced in this steel mill will be used to make a wide variety of other products. The steel mill employs salespeople who try to sell the steel to other manufacturers. (Gerald Fritz/Monkmeyer Press Photo.)

Because of the importance of his position, the industrial salesperson has a challenging and difficult job, as suggested by the following quotation:

> The job of the salesperson in the industrial market may be one of the most exacting and complicated in all of marketing. The industrial salesperson must call on people in various positions within customer firms and sell them on the merits of his or her products and/or services. This means, of course, that the salesperson must fully understand how the customer firm will use those products and services. . . . With little doubt, technical competence is a requirement for effective selling in many parts of the industrial market. . . . At the same time, industrial selling requires more than just technical competence. . . . Understanding the motives of these people, commonly called "buying influences," is critical if effective selling is to take place.[2]

It is not surprising that selling an industrial product through a salesperson is very expensive. The average cost of a sales call to a buyer is $229. However, to complete a single sale requires, on the average, 5.5 sales calls. This brings the actual cost of getting an order through a salesperson to an average of $1,250.[3]

This situation has a number of implications. The first is that the relationship between the industrial salesperson and the buyer is important. As indicated earlier, this relationship tends to be long term. A long-term relationship is almost a given, since it takes many calls to complete a sale.

Long-Term Relationships. When a relationship is expected to be long term, the success of a salesperson is tied directly to that relationship. This means that the salesperson has to nurture the relationship and be certain that she is doing

Table 13.1 Goods Classification in the Industrial Market

I. Goods entering the product completely—materials and parts
- A. Raw materials
  1. Farm products (examples: wheat, cotton, livestock, fruits and vegetables)
  2. Natural products (examples: fish, lumber, crude petroleum, iron ore)
- B. Manufactured materials and parts
  1. Component materials (examples: steel, cement, wire, textiles)
  2. Component parts (examples: small motors, tires, castings)

II. Goods entering the product partly—capital items
- A. Installations
  1. Buildings and land rights (examples: factories, offices)
  2. Fixed equipment (examples: generators, drill presses, computers, elevators)
- B. Accessory equipment
  1. Portable or light factory equipment and tools (examples: hand tools, lift trucks)
  2. Office equipment (examples: typewriters, desks)

III. Goods not entering the product—supplies and services
- A. Supplies
  1. Operating supplies (examples: lubricants, coal, typing paper, pencils)
  2. Maintenance and repair items (examples: paint, nails, brooms)
- B. Business services
  1. Maintenance and repair services (examples: window cleaning, typewriter repair)
  2. Business advisory services (examples: legal, management consulting, advertising)

Source: P. Kotler, *Marketing Management: Analysis, Planning, and Control*, 4 ed., © 1980, p. 172. Reprinted by permission of Prentice Hall, Inc., Englewood Cliffs, NJ.

what is best for her customer. Since the time horizon is long term, the salesperson is well advised to avoid using high-pressure tactics. Instead, the salesperson should take an approach that is *cooperative and consultative.*

The Salesperson as a Consultant. We discussed consultative selling in Chapter 1. A salesperson who functions as a consultant is trying to solve the customer's problem with the best available product. The salesperson functions as though he works for the same company as his customer. As a result, the salesperson and the customer are not adversaries but cooperative partners.

In terms of the selling process itself, the industrial salesperson has a number of concerns that do not affect the retail salesperson. These concerns make the industrial salesperson's job unique. In what follows, we will discuss these unique concerns of the industrial salesperson.

Unique Concerns of the Industrial Salesperson

The unique aspects of the industrial salesperson's job begin at the prospecting stage. We devoted an entire chapter (Chapter 6) to prospecting because it is a major step in the sales process. There we explained that, for the most part, retail salespeople don't engage in prospecting, whereas industrial salespeople do.

Because of the importance of prospecting for the industrial salesperson, several attempts have been made to develop mathematical models that can be used to determine who is a viable prospect. While we are not concerned with the mathematical aspects of those models, we present the factors here so that you can gain an appreciation of the complexities of prospecting for the industrial salesperson. The factors are as follows:[4]

1. Expected revenue from a particular sale minus the cost of converting a prospect to a buyer.
2. The cost of maintaining a prospect's account. This includes such things as distribution costs, service costs, inventory costs, and production costs.
3. The prospect's future value. A new account is always expected to grow, since a prospect should purchase more when he becomes more familiar with a supplier.
4. A prospect's strategic value. This is an assessment of a prospect's worth beyond a monetary concern. As an example, a prospect's reputation in the community can have an impact on a salesperson's future sales to other prospects. This factor has to be coupled with the probability of obtaining the prospect's account. The higher the probability and the better the reputation of the prospect, the greater is his strategic value.
5. Conversion costs. This is the cost of expenses incurred prior to the initial sale. It includes such things as transportation costs, hotel expenses, and entertainment expenses. Table 13.2 summarizes the factors involved in evaluating a prospect.

Once prospecting has been accomplished, the industrial salesperson has several other unique concerns. The industrial salesperson is selling to a company, but she is always dealing with one or more individuals who represent that company. "Companies themselves do not buy—it is people within those companies that affect the decisions to buy various goods and services."[5] This means that the industrial salesperson must know as much about the people who make the buying decision, and their positions and influence within the organization, as possible.

There are three broad areas of concern for the industrial salesperson: (1) the *needs* of the buyer, (2) the *external influences* on the buyer, and (3) the *type of buyer.* We will now discuss each of these concerns.

The Needs of the Buyer

The salesperson is concerned with three categories of needs for each individual who influences the buying decision:[6]

Table 13.2 Factors in Evaluating a Prospect by the Industrial Salesperson

Expected revenue
Cost of maintaining a prospect's account
Prospect's future value
Prospect's strategic value
Conversion costs

1. Personal needs.
2. Job-related needs.
3. Organizational needs.

Personal Needs. Personal needs include concerns about the individual's own job security and physical comfort. The industrial buyer is also concerned about how he appears to his co-workers as well as his supervisors. He wants to be perceived as a competent and wise decision maker. Ultimately, he wants more than basic job security. He also wants to advance in the organization. Making a prudent purchase decision or directly influencing someone else to make such a decision can have a major impact on his success.

Job-Related Needs. The individual wants to work with and use products that are safe. She wants products that are cost effective and of high quality. She wants to be certain that delivery and inventory will be effectively handled by the seller. Since resale is usually involved, she wants to be sure that her company's customers are satisfied and that the products that are purchased will enhance the company's reputation so that it can compete and grow effectively.

Organizational Needs. The industrial buyer wants his organization to provide workers with safe, pleasant working conditions. He wants it to be valued in the community. He wants it to be perceived as an industry leader. He wants it to be the direct influence on competitive moves rather than having to respond to competitors. He wants it to be a place where people will want to work and invest. He wants it to be innovative so that it can grow physically and financially.

Given these three levels of needs, the salesperson clearly has a great deal of work to do at the preapproach stage. He not only has to be prepared in advance to deal with information that is relevant to those needs, he also has to understand that these needs will vary, depending upon what individual he is talking to.

External Influences on the Industrial Buyer

A number of external factors will influence the industrial buyer. They can be categorized into four areas:[7]

1. *Influences of the environment.* These are general business conditions such as inflation and growth, as well as political or legal trends such as governmental regulation or outbreaks of war. Environmental concerns can have a major effect on a buyer's willingness or ability to buy and to what extent she can negotiate with a salesperson. For example, a buyer for a major builder will not want to discuss the purchase of steel if there is a major downturn in construction due to an economic slowdown.
2. *Influences of the buyer's organization.* The organization can have a centralized or a decentralized buying process. In a centralized buying process, the buyer with whom the salesperson is dealing may not have a major input into the decision-making process. If the organization has a decentralized process, the buyer may have a much greater influence on the decision.

   Another aspect is the organization's reliance on the computer for evaluating

EXHIBIT 13.1

How Organizational, Job-Related, and Personal Needs of the Industrial Buyer Can Be Satisfied

	Organization Needs	*Job-Related Needs*	*Personal Needs*
Physical safety	To provide safe working conditions for employees; to provide a clean environment for the surrounding community	To purchase products that are safe to operate; to purchase products that are not ecologically harmful; to buy from multiple sources to protect the company, and so forth	To avoid products and/or suppliers whose products could have detrimental effects on the buyer's own environment; to avoid decisions that could prove harmful to the buyer in keeping his or her job or position
Material security	To purchase products that work properly—that do not require excessive service, returns, defects, and so on; to earn enough income to stay in business	To purchase from reliable suppliers; to purchase products that are most cost effective; to purchase quality products at the lowest possible price; to purchase products that add to the salability of the buying company's products	To maintain his or her source of income and thus material security; to avoid instances that could affect job security
Material comfort	To provide clean, comfortable working conditions; to have adequate inventories on hand for production; to provide attractive facilities and offices for employees	To purchase products at optimum inventory levels; to purchase from suppliers who will guarantee delivery; to avoid stock-outs and back orders; to purchase facilities and equipment to provide	To obtain material objects that add to the buyer's material comfort both on and off the job; to work in attractive facilities such as a well-lit, well-decorated office with adequate budget and staff

	Organization Needs	*Job-Related Needs*	*Personal Needs*
		comfortable working conditions for officers and employees	
Acceptance by others	To be accepted as a good corporate citizen; to be accepted by customers as a reputable and fair supplier; to be accepted as a good place to work	To purchase locally when possible to foster good community relations; to purchase components that add good value to customers; to purchase in a fair and equitable manner from suppliers; to purchase in such a manner that other departments will accept what is bought	To be accepted by others in the company as knowledgeable and competent; to be recognized by suppliers as competent and fair; to be accepted by top management as a competent employee; to be accepted in the buyer's community and neighborhood
Recognition from others	To be recognized as an asset in its immediate community; to be recognized as a leader in its industry; to be recognized by competitors as fair and honest; to be recognized as a place where people would want to work and where people would want to invest	To purchase in such a manner that purchased products add to the recognition of the company's products; to purchase from reputable and well-known suppliers for supplier recognition; to purchase in such a manner as to lower cost and develop a reputation as a shrewd buying company	To be recognized by others in the company as a good buyer; to be recognized by top management as a member of the company team; to be recognized as a shrewd and wise buyer by suppliers; to be recognized by peers in professional groups; to be recognized in the community
Influence over others	To exert influence over competitors' actions rather than vice	To purchase products that would provide the company with a	To influence other buying influences (department heads)

(continued)

	Organization Needs	*Job-Related Needs*	*Personal Needs*
	versa; to influence governmental agencies toward more positive policies; to exert influence over channel members, suppliers, and customers	competitive edge; to purchase in such a manner (volume, and so on) as to place the firm in a position where it could influence suppliers on price, service, and so forth; to purchase products that would add to channel components' ability to sell, and so on	when the buyer believes that one product or supplier is better than what is specified; to influence others outside the company (salespeople, middlemen, suppliers) to add to the company's purchasing prowess
Professional growth	To grow in sales and profits; to grow in reputation; to grow in its industry and not fall behind competition; to be innovative and aggressive	To purchase from innovative and aggressive suppliers to help the company grow; to purchase products that will add to increased return on investment; to purchase products that will add to the company's marketing program	To advance in the company or outside it; to grow with the purchasing position; to become more knowledgeable in many facets of the business to foster advancement; to grow intellectually

Source: Reprinted by permission from *Business* magazine. "Using the Buyer's Needs to Improve Industrial Sales" by Michael A. Belch and Robert W. Haas, September–October 1979.

and selecting suppliers. The more the organization relies on a computer, the more structured the buying decision is likely to be.

3. *Influences of the buying center.* The buying center itself will have an effect on the purchase decision as a function of which particular organization members are part of the buying center.

The buying center has its own methods of reaching a purchase decision and its own criteria for selection. In addition, the dynamics of the interaction within the buying center will have an effect on the decision. Some buying center members will have greater influence on the purchase decision than others.

4. *Influences of the nature of the purchase itself.* In Chapter 7 we discussed the three major classes of purchase: new task buys, modified rebuys, and straight rebuys. Obviously, the new task buying situation will require much more deliberation on the part of the buying center than the straight rebuy. Which kind of purchase is involved can be easily determined.

The Type of Buyer

A great deal has been written about the things purchasing agents like or dislike about a salesperson. For example, it was found that purchasing agents regard a good salesperson as someone who is "friendly but professional."[8] In addition, purchasing agents don't like salespeople who are "pushy, egotistical, know-it-all, long-winded, and glad-hander."[9] Greg Vollendorf, a purchasing supervisor for Detector Electronics in Minneapolis, says, "I can't stand the salesman who comes in here with a full line of the latest jokes."[10]

While it is useful to keep these things in mind, the salesperson must also remember that not all buyers are the same. In keeping with the theme that we have established in this book, the salesperson has to be flexible and deal appropriately with different types of people.

For example, the buying center may consist of a purchasing agent who may be price conscious, an engineer who is concerned with product quality, a marketing person who is concerned about what impact the purchase will have on the eventual sale of the final product, a financial analyst who is concerned about the financing of purchases, and, depending upon the nature of the purchase, the actual user of the product, who is concerned with the product's performance.

Thus the industrial salesperson is required to understand and accommodate a wide variety of people, each with unique concerns. It is useful, therefore, to consider the general types of buyers the salesperson is likely to encounter. Six such types have been identified, and each has its own approach to the buying task (see Table 13.3). Following is a discussion of these types of buyers and suggestions on how a salesperson can deal with each type.

1. The **hard bargainer.** This buyer is difficult and resists consummation of the sale. He may require salesperson clearance. He will likely want several price quotes and will use several sources of supply for the same item. The salesperson should make every effort to negotiate with this person. Maximizing

Table 13.3 A Classification of Industrial Buyers

The hard bargainer
The sales job facilitator
The straight shooter
The socializer
The persuader
The considerate

Source: Reprinted by permission of *Journal of Personal Selling and Sales Management,* © 1982. A. J. Dubinsky and T. N. Ingram. (1981–1982). A classification of industrial buyers: Implications for sales training. *Journal of Personal Selling and Sales Management, 2,* 46–51.

her power, as we discussed in Chapter 8, will be especially important for the salesperson. She should also be adept at handling objections and emphasizing competitive product knowledge.

2. The **sales job facilitator.** This person will try to make the interaction go smoothly. She is receptive to the salesperson. She rarely asks for free samples. The salesperson dealing with such a person should convey the importance of having a satisfied customer base and should make every effort to achieve a *quid pro quo* (something for something).
3. The **straight shooter.** This person behaves with integrity. He doesn't procrastinate or use his buying power to gain any concessions. He also tends not to use price to pit one supplier against another. The salesperson dealing with a straight shooter should focus on the substantial aspects of the product she is selling and be straightforward in handling objections.
4. The **socializer.** This person enjoys the personal aspect of the buyer–seller interaction. He likes to socialize with salespeople and enjoys free gifts and entertainment. He is more likely to purchase from a salesperson he likes. A salesperson dealing with such a person should be careful not to violate company policy regarding free gifts and socializing with customers. He should also be careful to maintain a balance between socializing and conducting business.
5. The **persuader.** This person tends to sell her company to the salesperson. She wants the salesperson to have a favorable view of her firm. The salesperson dealing with such a buyer should be certain that he is dealing with a realistic prospect in terms of one that can or should buy the product he is selling.
6. The **considerate.** This buyer is concerned with the salesperson and has compassion. She will accept substitute products and will allow a salesperson to requote. In return, the salesperson should be considerate to such a buyer.

No matter what type of buyer the salesperson is dealing with, he should always ensure that the sales presentation deals with tangible product qualities.[11,12] In addition, since an average industrial sale requires many visits from the salesperson, he should be careful not to press for closing the sale prematurely.

Follow-Up Concerns for the Industrial Salesperson

As we mentioned, the industrial salesperson is likely to have a long-term relationship with her customers. The part of the sales process that contributes to the length of this relationship is follow-up and servicing of the account. The salesperson communicates that she is concerned about her customer through follow-up. The salesperson benefits herself by having an opportunity not only to get repeat sales from the same customer but also to cross-sell. **Cross-selling** involves the *sale of related products.*

During follow-up, the salesperson becomes a true consultant. As a consultant, he behaves as though his company has bought the product rather than sold it. As such, the industrial salesperson becomes an overseer of his account. Not surprisingly, he often devotes more time to follow-up than to getting the sale.

As an overseer, he makes sure that his products are delivered on time and in good condition. In order to do this, he remains in contact both with his own company and with his customer. He may be instrumental in helping the customer make decisions about how or where a product will be used. He may also be helpful in instituting a formal training program.

Frequently, a sale in this context will involve a formal contract that states specific service requirements. While it is not the salesperson's job to regularly perform services such as maintenance or installation, it is desirable for her to be on hand occasionally so that her presence will communicate concern and foster the consultative approach.

Since a major goal of follow-up is to generate repeat sales of the product, the salesperson needs to be aware of the buyer's purchase cycle. She can do this by monitoring the past purchase patterns of the buyer or of other similar buyers. Once it appears that a repurchase may be in order, the salesperson will want to call on the customer. Such a call will communicate the salesperson's availability, as well as present the customer with the option of a repurchase.

In the long run, effective follow-up will enhance the salesperson's reputation both within her own organization and, more importantly, on the outside. Buyers have their own informal communication network. One likely topic of conversation among buyers is salespeople. A salesperson who provides excellent follow-up is likely to be mentioned and recommended. This is probably one of the most desirable forms of recommendation.

The Retail Context

Retail selling involves a wide variety of situations. This form of selling takes place in large department stores, small boutiques, discount electronics stores, and corner grocery stores. Not surprisingly, consumer purchases in these different environments will vary in terms of *uncertainty* and *importance.* When consumers are considering a new or expensive product such as a car or a home, they face an *extended decision* with a great degree of uncertainty. They are likely to engage in much deliberation before reaching a buying decision.

Consumers often face buying decisions that are less important and involve less uncertainty, such as an upgraded television or stereo system. Such decisions involve *limited problem solving.* Finally, a great deal of consumer purchasing is routine and involves a *habitual decision.* It has little uncertainty and is not deemed very important. A good example is a typical grocery store excursion (see Figure 13.3).

The Role of the Salesperson

As you might expect, the greater the uncertainty and the more important the buying decision, the more work the salesperson has. In fact, in retail situations involving a routine purchase, there is frequently no salesperson with whom to deal.

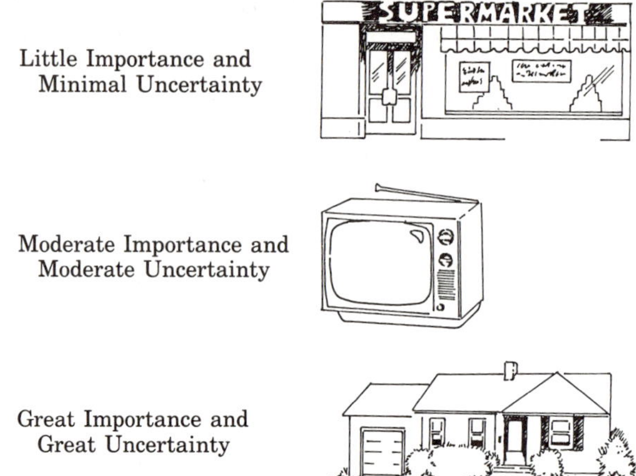

FIGURE 13.3 Importance and uncertainty in the retail context.

Short-Term Relationships. As we indicated earlier, salesperson–customer relationships in the retail context tend to be one time. That is not always the case, of course. There are some retail salespeople who do maintain long-term relationships with their customers. This depends upon the kind of store and the product being purchased. Expensive products such as furniture or designer clothing may be purchased repeatedly from the same salesperson, particularly in a store devoted solely to that particular product. This suggests that the salesperson in such a store needs to be mindful of the impact of follow-up.

When the expectation is that a salesperson–customer interaction will be one time or very short term, both the salesperson and the customer are more concerned about maximizing their own gain. While the salesperson should always be mindful of the potential for repeat business, he is usually more concerned with making a sale. Since he may have only one opportunity to make the sale, he may be more likely to engage in high-pressure tactics. While we would argue that such tactics are generally not desirable, salespeople often feel that they cannot be avoided because of the limited time available to make a sale.

In a short-term relationship, the salesperson may be more likely to appeal to emotional motives for buying. Prospects do not always make purchases based on logic and information, and the salesperson needs to be prepared to deal with these situations. This is particularly true of products that have high social visibility, such as clothing, furniture, or make-up.

Unique Concerns of the Retail Salesperson

Recall that the retail salesperson usually does not engage in prospecting in the same way as the industrial salesperson. Prospecting is done for the retail salesperson through advertising and other forms of promotion that generate store traffic. People who enter the retail store have some interest in what is being sold there.

This is a retail salesperson trying to sell a dress. Because the dress is expensive, the consumer will likely engage in limited problem solving. As a result, the salesperson's input is important in determining whether the sale is eventually made. (Comstock)

Inside the store, the behavior of the salesperson can determine whether the prospect will purchase. "In a large variety of retail transactions consumer buying decisions ultimately depend upon the customer–salesman interaction."[13] This is particularly true with respect to consumer durables.[14]

It is noteworthy that retail customers look for *courtesy, charm, and ingratiation.*[15] While all of these qualities can be communicated during the course of the sales interaction, they are particularly likely to emerge during the approach phase, since the impression of the salesperson is made during the first few minutes of interaction with the prospect.

During the presentation, retail prospects look for *credibility and patient buying assistance* from the salesperson.[16] Taking the time to determine the prospect's needs communicates both of these characteristics. *Product knowledge* is ranked highly by retail prospects, just as it is by business-to-business prospects, in their evaluation of a salesperson.[17] A product demonstration is desirable during the presentation. Often retail prospects are uneducated about the features of a particular product. During the demonstration, the salesperson can teach the prospect about the product. Again, credibility can be communicated whenever a question arises in regard to a competing product not available at the salesperson's store. If the salesperson does not attempt to undermine this competing product or the store that sells it, she enhances her credibility. Table 13.4 summarizes what prospects look for in retail salespeople.

The following dialogue illustrates how many of these qualities can be communicated. Jim Colby is a salesperson in an expensive stereo equipment store. Jack West is his customer.

> JIM: I see you have a Walkman. You were smart to buy that one, because it's probably the best on the market. *(Building rapport by discussing a nontask issue; this serves to ingratiate the salesperson with the customer.)*
>
> JACK: Yeah, I'm really pleased with it. But it was expensive.
>
> JIM: Well, sometimes it is the case that you get what you pay for. Are you looking for anything in particular today?
>
> JACK: I want to upgrade my speakers. But I get confused when I hear a bunch of speakers in a sound room.
>
> JIM: What kind of speakers do you have now?
>
> JACK: Boston Acoustics.
>
> JIM: Well you can't get too confused—those are some of the best around (*ingratiation, charm, and credibility*). I'll tell you what, why don't you pick out any record that you're familiar with from our selection. I'll play it and let you have as long as you want to make comparisons among speakers (*courtesy*).

This approach is very different from one that begins "What can I help you with today?" followed by an immediate attempt to present the equipment. In fact, it is probably best to avoid such a question. A more desirable approach might be to say something like "If there's anything I can help you with, just let me know."

Generally speaking, retail salespeople try to close by actually making the sale. Many retail purchases can be made on the spot, so making the sale is a

Table 13.4 What Prospects Look for in a Retail Salesperson

1. Product knowledge: "This is an excellent air conditioner. It has 9,500 BTU's, which will cool a room of about 250 square feet unless the room has a great deal of sun exposure."
2. Courtesy: "Feel free to look around. I'll be standing in the back. Come over whenever you have a question."
3. Charm: "You look as though you can use an air conditioner. I know I looked as though I could use one when I walked in this morning."
4. Ingratiation: "You seem to be very knowledgeable about computers. It is a pleasure to deal with someone who is up on the field."
5. Credibility: "I was almost going to buy one of these myself, but when I studied what the experts were saying, I decided that the less expensive version was a much smarter buy."
6. Patient buying assistance: "Have you used one of these before? . . . What do you think you'll be using it for? . . . Do you think your needs will remain pretty much the same over the next 1 to 2 years?"

EXHIBIT 13.2

The Retail Salesperson

Some retail clerks I've talked to make a point when they say that not only do they receive little training, but much of the rudeness and lack of product knowledge they exhibit can be traced to dealing with unruly customers. If I ever had any doubts about that, they vanished after my friend Bob told me about the time he encountered an irate little old lady while looking around a department store for a present to give his wife.

"Where are the dresses?" the woman asked him.

"I don't work here," he told her.

"But where are the dresses?" she persisted.

"Lady," Bob replied patiently, "I don't know, because I don't work here."

"It's a good thing you don't!" she snapped. "You're not very helpful."

Besides reminding us that there are plenty of rude shoppers out there, the story conjures up memories of times when all the salespeople in a store seem to have vanished and *no one* was around to tell where the dresses were. In fact, a good retail salesperson stands out so clearly in a world of mediocrity these days that he deserves special recognition.

For example, there is Mike Disimone of our local Lincoln-Mercury dealer. He actually let me sell myself a new car.

The car carries an unlimited warranty of three years or 30,000 miles, and Mike could tell right away that I didn't enjoy the prospect of driving it in for servicing. Thus he closed the sale by offering to pick up the car, leave a loaner in its place, and deliver the serviced car to me at my house.

"That sounds like a clincher, Mike," I told him, "but what assurance do I have that you'll be here at the dealership for three years or 30,000 miles?"

"Mr. Lavenson," he said, "I was just appointed sales manager, so you can see that I'll be around for a while." He handed me a business card with "Sales Manager" clearly imprinted under his name. I shook his hand and went into the manager's office to buy a car.

Later, as I waited for the keys, I wandered around the showroom thinking that perhaps the good guys are winning and that salesmanship isn't dead. Then, glancing down at the other salespeople's desks, I detected a disturbing trend: *everybody's* card had the title "Sales Manager."

Source: Reprinted by permission of *Sales & Marketing Management* © 1986. J. Lavenson, (1986). The right (sales) stuff. *Sales & Marketing Management*, (April), p. 12.

reasonable goal. There are exceptions, however, and these generally have to do with the expense of the product. For example, when selling personal computers, homes, or even cars, it is not realistic to expect a prospect to make an on-the-spot decision. Since such purchases require a sizable portion of the prospect's income, the prospect will usually want to have an opportunity to pursue other alternatives or to think about the purchase in a nonpressure situation. When it is not feasible to expect the prospect to make an immediate decision, the salesperson should do the same thing as her business-to-business counterpart. She should define intermediate sales goals such as obtaining the prospect's phone number so that he can be contacted or arrange for a future meeting.

The Family as a Buying Center

As we suggested earlier, the consumer in a retail store is sometimes making a purchase for the family. In this case, the consumer is acting the same way as an industrial buyer. They are both part of a buying center. The consumer in the store may be the equivalent of the head of the buying center, in which case she has the final authority to make the purchase. She may or may not want to consult further with her family, and the astute salesperson should be able to determine this. If the prospect does not have final authority, then the salesperson is wasting time trying to force a closing of the sale. Generally, the more expensive the item being considered, the more the salesperson should think in terms of the family as a buying center and act accordingly.

Follow-Up for the Retail Salesperson

Follow-up service in the retail context differs from that in the business-to-business context. Maintenance is usually performed by the buyer. Repair is usually handled through a warranty arrangement between the buyer and the manufacturer, so the retailer is not directly involved.

This does not eliminate the need for the retail salesperson to attempt some follow-up as a matter of courtesy. This is particularly true for a sale involving a large expenditure. A simple phone call from a car salesperson to the customer to make sure that the car is operating properly and the customer is pleased can result in a repeat sale 2 or 3 years later. It is simply a matter of the salesperson's taking a longer-term perspective.

Even when retail salespeople sell relatively inexpensive items, they can engage in a form of follow-up that at least communicates to their customers that they value their business. Such follow-up often takes the form of sending a catalog or a calendar. Even sending a special announcement of a sale communicates a continuation of the retail salesperson–customer relationship.

The Service Context

Services are not the same thing as goods. Services have to do with "activities and processes (health care, entertainment, travel) rather than objects (soap powders, cars). . . . [Goods can be defined] as objects and services as deeds or efforts."[18] When goods are being sold, the salesperson can rely to some extent on the good itself to help him make the sale. This is not the case when selling services. The decision to buy a service may depend solely on the encounter between the prospect and the salesperson. In fact, *the encounter itself becomes part of the service.*[19]

An airline offers a service that is intangible. For a salesperson to sell such a service requires a different kind of effort than is required for selling a product. (Mimi Forsyth/ Monkmeyer Press Photo.)

As we mentioned, because of the special nature of services, it is not necessary to make a distinction between those sold directly to consumers (retail) and those sold to businesses (business to business). In all cases, *the success of a salesperson depends upon the ability to build a positive image.*

The Role of the Service Salesperson

Since the impression that the salesperson makes is of critical importance to the service encounter, the approach becomes especially important. The approach is probably more important in the service context than in the retail or business-to-business context when goods are being sold.

The personal relationship between the salesperson and the prospect is the essence of the service.[20] It is for this reason that the impression made by the salesperson becomes so important. The salesperson can't depend upon demonstrating an actual product to convince the prospect. She can only depend upon how well the prospect likes and respects her, that is, upon how successful she is in creating a favorable impression.

People form impressions of one another very quickly, often during the first few minutes of an interaction. This means that the service salesperson can fail or succeed during the approach phase. If she creates a negative impression, she will very likely fail to sell her service. If she creates a positive impression, she is more likely to succeed. Above all, the salesperson needs to create an impression of *competence, honesty, and sincerity.*

Unique Concerns of the Service Salesperson

Prospects regard buying services as more risky than buying goods. This is not surprising, since services are not tangible. They can't be touched and seen. Prospects are also less likely to be objective when they purchase a service. They spend less time comparison shopping for a service than for a good.

Determining the Needs of the Prospect

These facts imply that the salesperson has to take special care to probe a prospect to find out exactly what his needs are. This requires that the salesperson be very knowledgeable, as well as genuinely interested in other people. Such an interest causes a natural inclination to ask questions, and asking questions is necessary to determine the prospect's needs.

To be successful, the salesperson has to have "more personal involvement, more personal contact, and more customer input" to sell services than to sell goods.[21] In order to get customer input, the salesperson must be adept at getting the customer to indicate what she wants. Often customers are very vague about their needs.

As an example, consider a prospect who goes to a travel agent and wants a 2-week vacation in a warm place. While there are some automatic choices (e.g., Florida, Mexico, the French Riviera), a travel agent would be unwise to suggest any of these immediately. Determining the customer's needs requires that the agent learn how much the customer wants to spend, whether the customer wants a beach or a city that happens to be warm, whether the customer wants a U.S. destination or a foreign one, whether the customer is comfortable with long distances, what kind of hotel and airline accommodations are desired, how much pre-trip planning the customer wants to engage in, what degree of comfort the customer is used to, and so on.

Clearly, there are many aspects to the selling of any service, and it is up to the salesperson to find out the customer's needs in each of these areas. It is likely that the salesperson will have to spend more time with a customer when selling a service than when selling a good. Not only must he find out the customer's needs, he must continually reassure the customer that he has exactly what the customer says she wants.

As in all sales contexts, it is desirable for the salesperson to get the prospect to voice objections. What makes the service context different from the retail and business-to-business contexts involving goods is that the prospect for services may be less able to state his objections. Since prospects are often vague about what they want to begin with, it is unlikely that they will have specific objections, although objections may crop up as the salesperson tries to determine their needs.

Probably the best way for the salesperson to handle objections is to treat them as potential objections. In other words, the salesperson should anticipate objections and present what she is offering in such a way that these objections will never even emerge. This will further help reassure the customer and make the customer feel that he is not engaged in such a risky venture.

Since the customer tends to do less comparison shopping for services than for goods, it is reasonable for a salesperson to try to bring the sale to a close with a formal signing of a contract during the first encounter. This, of course, depends upon what service he is selling and to whom. For example, if a health care service is being sold to a large corporation, it is likely that many people are involved in the decision, and an attempt by the salesperson to force a close would not be well received. On the other hand, if a travel package is being sold to an individual, a close is sensible. Table 13.5 summarizes the aspects of the service encounter that make it unique.

Follow-Up for the Service Salesperson

Some form of follow-up is especially important when dealing with a service. Since a service is performed by people who are usually in the seller's organization, the service salesperson should make a point of contacting the customer at regular intervals to ensure that everything is operating as expected and that the customer is satisfied. Whether the purchaser is a consumer or a businessperson, there is a reasonable probability of a long-term relationship between the customer and the salesperson. The best way to allow that relationship to flourish is to provide follow-up. Sending mailings of interest to the customer and even making occasional phone calls at times when it is likely that the service can be repurchased are important forms of follow-up.

It is also wise for a salesperson to make and keep notes regarding a customer's preferences and dislikes. When the customer returns to the salesperson, she then has an opportunity to communicate that she remembers her customer's

Table 13.5 Aspects of the Service Encounter That Make It Unique

Services, unlike products, are intangible.
Prospects regard purchasing services as more risky than purchasing goods.
The interaction between the salesperson and the prospect becomes part of the service being sold.
The salesperson must have more personal involvement with a prospect who is purchasing a service than with one who is purchasing a good.
The salesperson must spend more time with a prospect who is purchasing a service than with one who is purchasing a good.
The salesperson must work harder to uncover a prospect's needs when selling services than when selling goods.
Prospects have a harder time stating objections when purchasing a service than when purchasing a good.
A salesperson dealing with services can often expect to close the sale during the first encounter with the prospect.

specific needs. This demonstrates to the buyer that he is viewed as a valued customer.

Putting It All Together

The key points presented in this chapter can be summarized as follows:

- While all selling jobs offer their own set of challenges, they have a number of things in common.
- Any selling job requires a concern with the interpersonal nature of the selling process since any sales encounter is interactive.
- All sales encounters involve prospecting, a preapproach, an approach, a presentation, a close, and follow-up.
- A salesperson can make a difference between selling and not selling.
- The business-to-business salesperson sells products that will be resold to a final customer; he can sell to industry or to the trade.
- Industrial salespeople perform an important job in an organization and usually have long-term relationships with their customers.
- Unique aspects of the industrial salesperson's job emerge almost immediately in the prospecting phase where elaborate and complex models may be employed.
- The industrial salesperson has to consider that the buyer has personal needs, job-related needs, and the needs of the organization.
- There are a number of external influences on the industrial buyer including the general economy, the internal structure of the organization, influences of the buying center, and influences of the purchase itself in terms of whether it is a completely new purchase, a straight rebuy, or something in-between.
- The industrial salesperson must also take into account the personality of the buyer.
- Unlike a retail salesperson, an industrial salesperson cannot reasonably expect to close a sale during the first encounter.
- While retail salespeople usually have short-term relationships with buyers, they are still expected to be knowledgeable, courteous, charming, ingratiating, credible, and willing to provide patient buying assistance.
- The service context provides a unique set of challenges because services are intangible.
- The relationship between the service salesperson and the prospect becomes part of the service that is being sold.
- The service salesperson usually has to spend more time and become more involved with a prospect than a salesperson selling a good.
- Since prospects purchasing a service often have a hard time voicing objections, the service salesperson has to anticipate these objections ahead of time in order to help the prospect.
- Like the retail salesperson, the service salesperson can usually try to close the sale during the first encounter.
- Follow-up is very important in any sales context because, in addition to being

a natural and logical extension of the actual sale, it will very likely lead to repeat sales opportunities.

- Follow-up can range from nothing more than a telephone call to ensure that the buyer is satisfied with the purchase to becoming involved with installation and possibly maintenance and service.
- Follow-up communicates that the relationship between the buyer and seller continues beyond the actual exchange of goods and services for money.
- Follow-up serves to assure the buyer that the salesperson is genuinely behind the good or service that is being sold.

It is important to keep in mind that we have talked about context differences in a broad sense. In other words, our discussion simply distinguished between the business-to-business, retail, and service contexts. You should be aware, however, that the context of a sales encounter can be defined much more narrowly. It may, for example, be defined in terms of the office or store in which the encounter takes place. Since every office and every store is unique, there are additional aspects that we have not discussed.

Fortunately, our emphasis on flexibility on the part of the salesperson accommodates these more narrowly defined differences in context. A flexible salesperson who is aware of the basic nature of the contexts discussed in this chapter will be able to handle any situation comfortably, whether it involves selling for Boeing Aircraft or Joe's Plumbing Supply Company.

Key Terms

Context
Buying center
Business-to-business selling
Industrial sales
Trade sales
Hard bargainer
Sales job facilitator
Straight shooter
Socializer
Persuader
Considerate
Cross-selling

Review Questions

1. What are the two aspects of the selling situation that occur regardless of the context?
2. What are the two aspects of the selling situation that differ according to the context?
3. What are the factors that should be considered in prospecting for the industrial salesperson?
4. What are the three levels of needs that are of concern for the industrial buyer? What is involved in each level?
5. What are the four external influences on the industrial buyer? What is involved in each?
6. What are the six types of buyers that the industrial salesperson is likely to encounter? Describe each type.
7. Is it reasonable for the industrial salesperson to close a sale during the first encounter? Why or why not?

8. Describe the nature of the follow-up phase for the industrial salesperson.
9. What two dimensions allow us to classify retail contexts?
10. Does the retail salesperson engage in prospecting? Explain.
11. What do retail customers look for in a salesperson?
12. How are services different from products?
13. How is the job of the service salesperson different from that of the retail or industrial salesperson?

Discussion Questions

1. Would you agree with the claim that selling in the industrial context is more challenging than selling in other contexts? Explain.
2. In addition to the factors mentioned in this chapter as being common to all sales interactions, what factors could you add to the list? Explain.
3. If someone were trained to be a retail salesperson, do you think she could easily make the transition to being an industrial salesperson? What about the reverse transition from being an industrial salesperson to being a retail salesperson?
4. Why is it that something as basic as the intangibility of services as compared to goods results in a selling process that is so different?

CASE 13.1

Jack Hansen is just about to graduate from college with a degree in marketing. He has specialized in marketing management, and he has taken a course in personal selling. He is finding that, as with many new graduates, the most likely place to begin his career is in sales.

Jack has had numerous interviews and he has received three job offers. One offer is with Neiman-Marcus in Dallas. The job entails selling expensive men's clothing to people who make appointments to see the clothing. The possibility of the job leading to a sales management position is very good.

The second offer is with Texas Instruments, also in Dallas. Another sales job, the task is to sell various computer parts to computer manufacturers. This is a very competitive industry, and the position offers many challenges. As with the first position, there is a good chance of advancement to a sales management position.

The final offer is with Continental Airlines, again in Dallas. The job is to sell Continental's air travel services to in-house travel agencies of corporations or to travel agencies that focus on business travel. The goal of the airline is to be a major factor in business travel. In this case, too, there is an excellent chance for advancement to a sales management position.

1. Which job would you recommend that Jack take? Why? Consider the important differences and similarities in context that were discussed in this chapter in making this evaluation. (Assume that the money, location, hours, and so on are roughly equivalent for each position.)

References

1. Dalrymple, D. J. (1988). *Sales Management: Concepts and Cases.* New York: John Wiley & Sons.

2. Belch, M. A., and R. W. Haas. (1979). Using the buyer's needs to improve industrial sales. *Business* (September–October), 8.

3. Cardozo, R. N., S. H. Shipp, and K. J. Roering. (1987). Implementing new business-to-business selling methods. *Journal of Personal Selling and Sales Management, 7,* 17.

4. Brady, D. L. (1987). Determining the value of an industrial prospect: A prospect preference index model. *Journal of Personal Selling and Sales Management, 7,* 27–32.

5. Belch and Haas, op. cit.

6. Ibid.

7. Hutt, M. D., and T. W. Speh. (1989). *Business Marketing Research.* Chicago: Dryden, p. 512.

8. PA's examine the people who sell to them. (1985). *Sales and Marketing Management* (November 11), 38–41.

9. Ibid., p. 39.

10. Ibid.

11. Dubinsky, A. J., and W. Rudelius. (1980). Selling techniques for industrial products and services: Are they different? *Journal of Personal Selling and Sales Management, 1,* 69–75.

12. Hite, R. E., and J. A. Bellizzi. (1985). Differences in the importance of selling techniques between consumer and industrial salespeople. *Journal of Personal Selling and Sales Management, 5,* 19–30.

13. Etgar, M., A. K. Jain, and M. K. Agarwal. (1978). Salesmen–customer interaction: An experimental approach. *Journal of the Academy of Marketing Science* (Winter), 1.

14. Hawes, J. M., C. P. Rao, and K. E. Mast. (1987). Consumer perceptions of the importance of salesperson attributes. *Proceedings of the American Marketing Association Educator's Conference, 53,* 113–118.

15. Ibid.

16. Ibid.

17. Ibid.

18. Solomon, M. R., C. Surprenant, J. A. Czepiel, and E. G. Gutman. (1985). A role theory perspective on dyadic interactions: The service encounter. *Journal of Marketing, 49,* 99.

19. Ibid., p. 100.

20. George, W. R., and J. P. Kelly. (1983). The promotion and selling of services. *Business* (July–September), 14–20.

21. Ibid., p. 18.

14

The Changing Technology of Selling

CHAPTER OBJECTIVES

In this chapter, you will learn:

- The ways in which computers can improve your efficiency as a salesperson.
- To evaluate software programs designed to manage customer and prospect files.
- How portable computers can help solve prospects' problems, communicate with the home office, and decrease paperwork.
- The advantages and disadvantages of alternative channels for distance communication (FAX and voice mail).
- Why technology has professionalized telemarketing.

CHAPTER OUTLINE

A Sales Challenge

An Overview

Information Management Technologies

- Managing Your Databases
- Relational Versus Nonrelational Databases
- Analyzing the Information in Your Database
- Integrated Software

Using Technology to Analyze Prospects' Problems

- Two-Stage Problem Solving
- Analyzing Problems During the Sales Call
- Laptop Computers
- Hand-Held Computers

Advanced Communication Technologies

- Facsimile Machines
- Voice Mail

Advances in Telemarketing

- Cost Savings
- Better Service
- Technological Advances

Putting It All Together

Key Terms

Review Questions

Discussion Questions

Case 14.1

References

A Sales Challenge

When Susan Gitten was put in charge of training and development for Zanko Corporation's staff of 400 salespeople, she was unsure about how to approach the area of computers and information technology. On the one hand, Susan was well aware of the many experts who believed in the importance of technology in sales. Computers were revolutionizing the salesperson's job, and Susan felt compelled to introduce them into her training courses. Yet some people at Zanko argued that computer technology should not be taught in a sales training course. They thought that salespeople should concentrate on *people* and not on machines.

Susan faced a dilemma. As modern technology revolutionizes the selling profession, it is becoming increasingly important for salespeople, especially those beginning their careers, to have a fundamental understanding of this revolution. As an expert from the *New York Times* pointed out, "For years [selling] was mostly a matter of amiability, portability and motivation. But these days, . . . as information technology advances, as products get more complex and as competition intensifies, a new kind of sales force is emerging: men and women with more education—and with computers . . . in their briefcases."[1]

But were the others at Zanko completely wrong? Isn't it true that salespeople should concentrate on their prospects rather than on their computers?

An Overview

The answer to Susan's dilemma lies in the approach taken to the study of computers in sales. Computers and information technologies are becoming far too important for a salesperson to ignore. But technology should not become the focus of a sales training effort. The same argument applies to the material presented here. Your objective in reading this chapter should be to learn how you can use advanced technologies to enhance your efficiency and professionalism as a salesperson. It is important for you to think of these technologies as *tools* that can help you concentrate on solving the prospect's problems. You should *not* expect to become a technical expert.

Specific technologies will evolve continuously over the course of your career. There will be constant improvements in computers, their capacity and portability. More and more software programs will be designed to help salespeople manage their customer and prospect information. Improvements in audiovisual technologies will make presentations more exciting, and integrated telemarketing systems will mean that more business will be conducted over telephone lines.

In order to remain competitive, you will need to keep abreast of these changes. However, given the rapid pace of change, technical knowledge becomes outdated quickly. Rather than concentrating on technical details, you should focus on learning how you can apply technology to improve your performance as a salesperson. Consider, for example, the revolution in computers and software. If you focus on learning the technical details of any one machine or software program, you will need to devote constant effort to relearning systems. If, however, you emphasize understanding the ways in which computer technologies can improve your filing and communication systems, you will be able to adapt that knowledge to each new generation of computer.

With this objective in mind, our focus in this chapter will be on the *applications* of technology to sales. Therefore, we have organized the material according to specific tasks to which technology has been applied: the management of customer and prospect information, the analysis of prospects' problems, communication with the home office as well as with the prospect, and telemarketing. Within these application areas, we discuss the use of computerized databases, spreadsheets, graphics, and artificial intelligence; laptop computers, facsimile machines, and voice mail; and computerized telemarketing systems (see Figure 14.1).

Information Management Technologies

As you have read throughout this book, the management of information is an extremely important part of the salesperson's job. Salespeople need to organize information on their sales leads, their customers, and their own time allocation in order to prospect, plan sales calls, and make presentations. As a result, one of the most important applications of modern technology to selling involves the use of computers to manage databases.

You read about *computerized databases* in Chapter 6. There the discussion was confined to information services that provide on-line access to public information. However, the term *database* is not limited to these on-line systems. You can also maintain your own private information in a database. In fact, any collection of information can be considered a database.

There is nothing mysterious about the subject of database management. *Data* is simply another term for *information*, and a **database** is any *collection (or base) of information.* Your list of sales leads is a database. So are your lists of customers, sales, and call records. Each is a collection of information about something.

Although the term *database* is used in conjunction with computers, technically we are managing a base of data when we maintain written files on any of

- Managing information on prospects and customers
- Simplifying and facilitating paperwork
- Analyzing prospects' problems
- Providing more exciting presentations
- Improving communication efficiency
- Lead generation and selling through telemarketing

FIGURE 14.1 Selling functions that can be enhanced with technology.

these subjects. In fact, the term *file* is used in computerized systems to refer to a collection of a *specific type of information.* A salesperson may keep a file of new leads and another file of sales and expenses. Each file would be a separate collection of data stored in the computer.

Managing Your Databases

Many different programs are available for managing databases. Some are general database programs designed to manage any kind of information. These programs can be used to store everything from tax records to addresses and phone numbers to cooking tips and recipes. More useful, however, are the database systems designed specifically for salespeople.

Software for Maintaining Files on Customers and Leads. Because of the widespread need for database management among salespeople, many programs are designed specifically for managing sales databases. Exhibit 14.1 on pp. 396–397 presents a list of some of the programs available to salespeople. These specialized programs make it easier to maintain customer and lead files for the person who is not expert at designing a customized database system. Typical programs will prompt the user with specific questions or commands. For example, when the program appears on the computer's screen, it might list a series of options such as these:

1. To review prospect list, press the "L" key;
2. To alter the prospect list, press the "A" key;

By pressing the appropriate key, you command the program to follow your instructions. In this case, an "L" will show the list of prospects on the screen and an "A" will allow you to type in changes to the list.

The programs vary widely in terms of how much information they hold, as well as the ease with which you can retrieve information from them. Some basic programs list records based on the customer's name but cannot select cases based on other characteristics. More sophisticated programs allow you to select cases based on a variety of characteristics, such as prospect size, location, income, or sales.

The ability to select specific cases in a file can play an extremely important role in prospecting. If, for example, you were making sales calls in a certain area, you might want a list of every customer within a certain zip code who purchased one of your products within the last 6 months. Or you might want to list all leads who are currently using one of your competitor's products. A drug salesperson whose company had just introduced a new heart medication could list all physicians with specialties in cardiac, vascular, or internal medicine. There is almost no end to the possibilities for classifying information in computerized data files. The key to using these systems is determining what information you will need and organizing your files accordingly. The computer cannot list prospects according to characteristics that you have not entered into your files!

Relational versus Nonrelational Databases

A **relational database** allows you to *combine information that you have stored in different files.* For example, you might save records of all of your sales calls in one file. This call record file might give the prospect's name and number of employees, the number of calls you made on the account, and what purchases have been made to date. In another file, you might keep records of your expenses (see Table 14.1).

These two files would certainly be useful in their own right. But what if you wanted to assess whether your expenses were paying off? A relational database would allow you to examine the relationship between the number of calls you had made, the amount of your expenses, and the size of any resulting sales by accessing information from both files at once. With a *nonrelational database,* you would have to list expenses and customer accounts separately and do the comparison manually.

In general, a program with more options will be more useful. However, these systems also tend to be more complicated, so it is important to decide how much flexibility you really need. You do not want a system that is so sophisticated that it becomes your focus instead of a tool (see Figure 14.2).

Analyzing the Information in Your Database

Although the software previously discussed allows you to store and retrieve information, those database programs do not allow you to analyze the information in a sophisticated way. There will be many instances when some analysis can help

Table 14.1 Excerpts from a Prospect File and an Expense File

Prospect	*No. of Employees*	*No. of Calls Made*	*Purchase*	*Model*
Comcor	14,000	4	$12,000	arj4401
ABC	60,000	1	—	—
Barns	25,000	6	13,500	arj4501
			11,500	ark5500

Expense	*Account*	*Amount*
Air fare	Comcor	$ 845
	ABC	520
	Barns	1,090
Hotel	Comcor	$ 300
	ABC	—
	Barns	610
Meals	Comcor	$ 450
	ABC	230
	Barns	600

EXHIBIT 14.1

Some Software Programs Developed Especially for Salespeople

Vendor	Software	Applications	Memory	Price	Hardware	Demo/ Cost	Systems
Account Management							
Computer Masters	Client Master	Preprogrammed database. Keynotes, form letters, envelopes, labels, rolodex, auto-dialer. Menu driven.	320K	$149	IBM PC-XT, -AT; PS/2 & compatibles; MS-DOS	Yes/$10	50
EMIS	EMIS II (Executive Management Information System)	Management system for large client databases or, with auto-dial, can run massive telemarketing compaigns.	512K	$1295 & up	IBM PC-XT, AT, PS/2 & compatibles	Yes/$37.25	140
Pinetree Software	The Maximizer Plus	Menu-driven program organizes information on lead generation, account development, and management. Including: letters, payment analysis, personal management.	512K (hard disk recommended)	$295	IBN PCs & compatibles; MS-DOS, PC-DOS 3.0 or greater	Yes/free	1,100
Valor Software	Info-XL	No setup. Handles freeform, data, contacts, histories, notes, letters.	384K	$265	IBM PCs & compatibles	No	New
Direct Marketing							
Group 1 Software	ArcList	Mailing list manager: finds duplicates, merges lists, presorts, imports/exports, produces list analysis and reports.	640K (hard disk required)	$595	IBM PC-XT, -AT & compatibles	No	950 +
Lead Tracking							
Arlington Software & Systems	PCAT: Professional Contact & Tracking System	Fully integrated lead-tracking system. Reports, auto-dialer, word processing, scripts, script analysis. Fifty user-definable fields.	384K (hard disk required)	$1,295-$6,400	IBM PCs & compatibles; PS/2	Yes/$10	1,850
ASH	Leads & Sales Plus	For nontechnical salespeople. Lead-tracking, coding, tickler, prewritten reports, merge-file, labels, lead cards, sorting, coding.	512K (hard disk required)	$229	IBM PCs & compatibles	Yes/$5	New

CCX Network	MarketManager	Targeted lead generation and tracking using analysis, sorting, import/export, labels, report outputs.	256K (2 disks required)	$295	IBM PC-XT, -AT; PS/2 and compatibles	No	500
Commercial Micro	Sales Busters	Client and prospect tracking system. Database search, tickler, calendar, letter, rolodex, import/export.	512K (hard disk recommended)	$295	IBM PCs & compatibles	Yes/$15	250 +
GoldData Computer Services	Sales Prospect Tracking System	Tracks leads, offers: mail-merge, letters, labels, on-line telemarketing, back-end reporting.	192K	$124.95	IBM PCs & compatibles	Yes/$10	400
IDSC Rental	marketrieve PLUS	Sales-lead tracking (esp. for multiple contacts at same co.) and market analysis. Batch and form letters, on-line notes, forecasting, sales management reports.	256K (hard disk recommended)	$1,500	IBM PCs & compatibles; MS-DOS, PC-DOS	Yes/$25	New
Information Research	ActionTracker	Best for tracking multistep selling cycles. Reports built in, pop-up windows. Designed for local area network.	384K-512K	$198-$1,498	IBM PCs & compatibles	No/30-day guarantee	500 +
Nelson Business Systems	Client Tracking System	Organizes and tracks clients and prospects, features individual notepads for each record and letter file, labels, mount-field, interal dial.	512K	$495–1,095	IBM PCs & compatibles, MS-DOS, PC-DOS	Yes/$10	New
PowerHouse Systems	Lead Management System	Lead tracking, mailings, word processor, spreadsheets, expenses, sales costs, daily to-do, labels.	640K	$99.95–$395	IBM PCs & compatibles	Yes/$5	New
Practical Marketing Software	Sales Leader	Tracks and qualifies leads generated from advertisements, news releases, trade shows, direct mail. Direct modern transfer.	640K	$895	IBM PCs & compatibles; OS2 Series	Yes/30-day trial	150 +
Pyramid Software	Lead Manager	Tracks contacts, products, rates, histories, products. Word-processing, labels, envelopes.	256K	$79.95	IBM PCs & compatibles	Yes/$15	2,500 +
Supersell Software	Sales Generator Plus	User-friendly lead tracker for nontechnical salespeople. Includes sorting by any code of client profile, labels, letters, auto-dial.	256K	$99.95	IBM PCs & compatibles	No/brochure	2,500 +

Source: Reprinted by permission of *Sales & Marketing Management* © 1988. T. Taylor and B. Voss. (1988). Spring update: Software with Sales and Marketing Applications. *Sales & Marketing Management*, (May), 55–56.

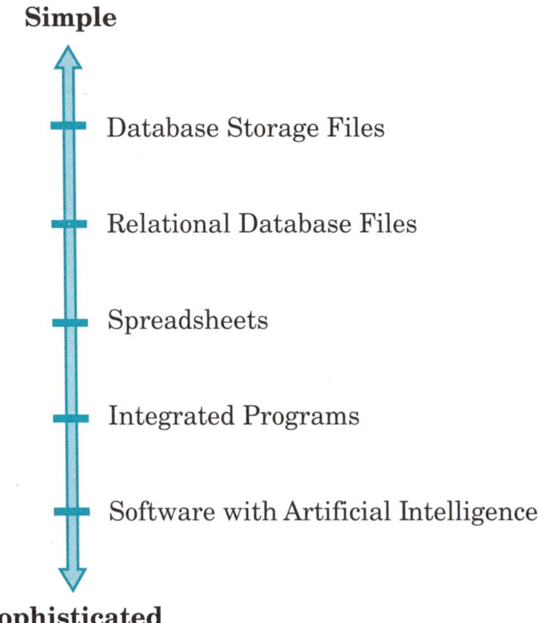

FIGURE 14.2 Software comes in a range of sophistication.

you direct your prospecting efforts or improve your presale planning. If you wanted to answer a question such as "Will medium-sized firms buy my machinery if inflation goes up to 6 percent?", you would need to do some numerical analysis on your files. Numerical analysis such as this is the focus of a **spreadsheet** program.

Spreadsheets. Figure 14.3 shows a typical spreadsheet. A *spreadsheet* program is one in which *columns and rows of numbers can be spread out before you for*

First Quarter Sales/Expenses: Models Arj, ARK

A Account	B Sales	C No. of Calls	D = C x $200 Cost of Calls	E Travel Expenses	F = D + E Total Cost	G = B − F Account Profit
Comeon	12,000	4	800	2,455	3,255	8,745
ABC	60,000	1	200	910	1,110	58,890
Barns	25,000	6	1200	1,280	2,480	22,520
RTE	—	3	600	800	1,400	1,400
Total	97,000	14	3800	5,445	9,245	87,755

FIGURE 14.3 A portion of a spreadsheet comparing sales and expenses for certain models.

analysis. Lotus 1-2-3 is a popular example of software that allows you to analyze spreadsheets. Many people think of spreadsheets as tools of accountants. However, there are many reasons why a salesperson might want to use a spreadsheet to analyze some of the numbers in her data files.

Spreadsheet analysis can improve efficiency. Time is one of the salesperson's most valuable resources. Yet poor time management is a common problem. Many salespeople do not realize, for example, that their efforts follow the *80-20 rule*, which states that 20 percent of their effort is generating 80 percent of their sales. If your sales follow the 80-20 rule, 80 percent of your effort is being spent inefficiently (to generate only 20 percent of your sales), while a small portion of your time is resulting in most of your sales. Although the 80-20 rule is extremely common, most people are unaware of it because they do not analyze their time expenditures carefully enough to know which activities or prospects are paying off more than others.

With spreadsheet analysis of your sales activities, you can analyze the problem by answering questions such as these:

"Is there a relationship between the amount of time I spend in dealing with a prospect and the eventual size of the sale?"
"Is the time I'm spending at trade shows paying off in sales?"
"Are larger companies spending more on my products than smaller companies?"

In order to analyze questions such as these, you compare the figures from your time allocation file with figures from a sales file and analyze them together with your spreadsheet program.

Integrated Software

As software becomes more sophisticated, some programs **integrate** many of the functions that are important to salespeople into a single package. For example, programs like Symphony, Framework, and WordPerfect Executive combine information management, word processing, and spreadsheets. Typical integrated programs include a calendar for listing appointments, a "to do" list, expense account worksheets, directories for filing prospect data, word processing, and memo and letter forms. With programs such as WordPerfect Executive, which are designed for use with portable computers, you can use all of these functions on an airplane while returning from an out-of-town call.[2]

You might, for example, use the word processor to write a report on your sales call and then switch to the expense account function to enter your expenses for the trip. By pressing a series of keys, you could call up the calendar function to record any future appointments that you made with the prospect and add notes to yourself under the "to do" function (e.g., "call Jim to check on shipment"). Finally, the letter and memo functions will call up standard letter and memo forms so that you can write a letter to the prospect thanking him for his time and send a memo to the shipping department about the details of the order.

Of course, salespeople have been accomplishing all of these tasks without computers for years, but this much paperwork would have taken at least an entire morning the day after a trip. With a program like WordPerfect Executive, the paperwork is handled quite simply during the flight, and the salesperson is ready to call on other prospects as soon as she returns from her trip.

Software with Artificial Intelligence. In addition to helping you manage account information and paperwork, some software with artificial intelligence can actually advise you about how to proceed with an account. **Artificial intelligence** means that the *software has been programmed with complex series of rules so that it can "reason" through a problem.* Such programs integrate certain "smart" functions with the more routine database management and spreadsheet analysis. An example of this type of program, called SELLSTAR, includes six different functions, which are listed in Table 14.2. The CONSULT function is the unique feature that uses artificial intelligence.[3] This part of the software has been programmed with rules relating to the Industrial Goods Classification (discussed in Chapter 7), the stage in the buying process (from Chapter 5), the personality of the prospect, and her level in her organization. The software "knows," for example, that in order to succeed with a *new task purchase*, you must contact the actual decision maker. By combining all of its internal rules, CONSULT will ask questions and give advice aimed at ensuring that you take this action.

CONSULT will also ask questions to determine whether the purchasing problem is a new task or a modified rebuy, whether the prospect is in the information-gathering or specifications stage of the process, whether the prospect needs the product badly or is unaware of it, whether a given person in the organization is a decision maker or an advisor, and whether the prospect is positive or negative about the purchase. Based on these determinations, CONSULT will advise you about how to proceed. If, for example, a prospect is still in the first stage of the buying process—that is, unaware of a need for the product—after two sales calls, it may be time to move to another prospect. If the prospect has already established product specifications and you do not know who the competitors are, SELLSTAR will advise you to make another sales call to gather this information. SELLSTAR will also alert you when it is time to call on an account whose purchase cycle is about to begin again.

Table 14.2 The Functions of SELLSTAR

1. ACCOUNT	used for entering, editing, or deleting information about an account.
2. TO DO	generates lists from the activity data in each account.
3. REPORTS	generates common sales reports, account history, call reports, monthly reports, and so on.
4. CONSULT	artificial intelligence advises the salesperson about how to proceed with an account.
5. FORECAST	generates forecasts for specific time periods.
6. UTILITIES	allows transfer of data, renaming of accounts, generation of address lists.

Source: Reprinted by permission of *Journal of Personal Selling and Sales Management* © 1988. H. Hennessey. (1988). Microcomputer applications: Accelerating the salesperson learning curve. *Journal of Personal Selling and Sales Management 8* (3), 77–82.

Exhibit 14.2 lists questions that are typical of those asked by CONSULT. They offer a major advantage to the novice salesperson who is confronted at once with learning about his firm, his product, his competition, and his market, as well as the buying process and the basic rules of selling. With programs like SELLSTAR to help make the sales *process* more productive, salespeople are free to concentrate on solving their *prospects'* problems.

Using Technology to Analyze Prospects' Problems

There are many cases in which answering a "what-if" question for a prospect can help you make a sale. These applications range from calculating the benefits of life insurance policies to doing a sophisticated cost/savings analysis to present to an industrial prospect. By combining figures supplied by your own company with data about your prospect's needs, you might, for example, calculate that one of your new machines installed in the prospect's plant would pay for itself within 2 years. With facts like this, your sales presentation is bound to be more persuasive than one that simply makes a vague claim that the equipment will save money.

In general, you will be more helpful to the prospect if you can analyze problems using your prospect's own facts and figures. You will arrive at better solutions and appear more professional than the salesperson who does not tailor her problem solving to the prospect's specific data. But incorporating the prospect's information into the proposed solution requires more sophisticated analysis than simply stating a "canned" solution to a problem. An example of a canned solution might be as follows: For a 40-year-old man of average health, this insurance policy will be worth $200,000 in 25 years. But a personalized solution requires analysis: Since you are a healthy, nonsmoking woman, aged 39, if you invest the amount we've been discussing, this policy will be worth $400,000 when you reach the age of 65. The personalized solution may require more complicated analysis, but it is much more helpful to the prospect.

There are many modern technological advances that can help you address prospects' problems directly. The appropriate tools will depend upon your preferred approach to problem solving. If you prefer a two-stage approach, in which you meet with the prospect first to discuss needs and later return to present your solution, you can use modern technology to work through the problem and enhance the quality of your presentation. If the situation requires you to solve the problem while you interact with the prospect during a single sales call, you can rely on portable computer technology to work through problems while you are in the prospect's office.

Of course, many selling situations require a combination strategy. You might call on a prospect to inquire about needs, work through the more complicated parts of the problem in your own office, and return to the prospect with a formal presentation, but alter the solution when necessary as you interact with the prospect. In the following sections, we discuss the ways in which technological advances can help you accomplish all of these tasks.

EXHIBIT 14.2

Some Examples of the Questions Asked by CONSULT

CONSULT Profiles Each Contact Person

Contact Data File-Profile for: Robert Scott

Enter a 1 if the statement on the left is more accurate or a 3 if statement on the right better applies. Enter a 2 if you can't decide between them.

1.	Accepts more than disputes	=1 2 3=	Disputes more than accepts
2.	More questions than statements	=1 2 3=	More statements than questions
3.	Vague, confusing communication	=1 2 3=	Crisp, clear communication
4.	More slow deliberate speech	=1 2 3=	More quick, fast-paced speech
5.	More calm, patient	=1 2 3=	More active, impatient
6.	Usually leans back/faces away	=1 2 3=	Usually leans forward/faces you
7.	Seldom emphasizes with voice	=1 2 3=	Emphasizes with voice
8.	Indifferent handshake	=1 2 3=	Firm handshake
9.	Guarded and aloof	=1 2 3=	Outgoing and approachable
10.	Prefers facts/details	=1 2 3=	Prefers concepts/opportunities
11.	Mostly logical	=1 2 3=	Mostly intuitive
12.	Infrequent eye contact	=1 2 3=	Frequent eye contact
13.	Little body/hand movement	=1 2 3=	Many gestures
14.	Seems controlled/businesslike	=1 2 3=	Seems responsive/attentive
15.	Reserved facial expression	=1 2 3=	Animated facial expressions
16.	Cool and formal	=1 2 3=	Warm and friendly

CONSULT Identifies Types of Buyer Needs

Level of Need?	*Need Explanation*
Very High	Needs solution to bail him out
High	Needs solution for better results
Low	Everything going OK—why change?
Very Low	Everything going great—no need
?	Not sure of player's level of need

CONSULT Identifies Roles

Player's Role	*Player's Role Explanation*
Decision Maker	The final authority for this purchase
User/Recommender	Recommends which product/service to buy
Influencer	Can lock you out from competing
Inside Helper	Can steer/advise you for this purchase
?	Not sure of this player's role

CONSULT Identifies the Company Buying Stage

Pick the Best Description of the Buying Stage
Account not aware of any problem, need, or opportunity
Account has general idea of a problem, need, or opportunity
Problem/need/opportunity isolated. Funding (budget)/justification uncertain
Problem/need/opportunity isolated. Funding (budget)/justification certain
Specifications being developed. Vendor selection criteria unknown
Specifications established. Vendor selection criteria known
Short list established. Formal quote/proposal/references requested
Best and final requested

Source: Reprinted by permission of *Journal of Personal Selling and Sales Management* © 1988. H. D. Hennessey. (1988). Microcomputer applications: Accelerating the salesperson learning curve. *Journal of Personal Selling and Sales Management, 8* (3), 77–82.

Two-Stage Problem Solving

There are many reasons why you might want to solve the prospect's problem in a two-stage process. An important consideration is the nature of the problem. Some problems are so complicated that they cannot be solved during a single face-to-face meeting with a prospect. In these cases, the solution to the problem may involve a lot of sophisticated, creative thinking that cannot be done while you are interacting with another person. Salespeople who develop computer systems, who adapt plant equipment to specific manufacturing problems, or who sell financial services to institutions engage in this kind of problem solving on a regular basis. The problems they work on may take weeks to solve and are generally too complicated to handle during a single sales call.

Consider, as an example, the case of Don Edwards, a banker who makes formal group presentations whenever he pursues a new account. Don's prospects are city and state governments that need his help in financing large building projects. In Don's types of sales, a single presentation can mean millions of dollars worth of business. The problem solving involves complex financial analysis that is more sophisticated than the prospects themselves can understand. Don says that the key to his success is his ability to gather information from the prospect and use it to come up with a financing arrangement that will solve the prospect's problem. He may work through 10 different solutions over a period of weeks before he determines the financing plan that best suits the prospect's interests.

After initial meetings and fact gathering, Don uses sophisticated spreadsheet programs to analyze questions such as "What if you need to raise more than $20,000,000?" and "What if interest rates increase by 2 percent?" However, Don's reliance on technology does not end with the solution to his problem. Once the solution is determined, Don must prepare the formal presentation, and much of his success comes from realizing that complicated facts and figures are difficult for a prospect to understand. As a result, Don spends almost as much time determining how he will depict the information in visual aids, graphs, or charts as he did working through to the solution. In trying to present his solution in a way that will be understandable to the prospects, Don works with spreadsheets that include graphics options.

Using Graphics Software to Prepare a Presentation. A *graphics* feature added to your spreadsheet program can help you develop visual aids for your presentations. Programs like Lotus 1-2-3 offer graphics features that allow you to display your numerical analysis graphically. Figure 14.4 shows some examples of the ways in which numerical analyses can be displayed in an integrated spreadsheet-graphics program.

The use of graphs and other visuals in sales presentations is not new. In fact, it has been estimated that schools, businesses, and other institutions make between 15 and 30 million presentations per day and that an estimated 1.5 billion overhead transparencies and slides are produced in a single year in the United States.[4] Although salespeople have used visual aids for years, technology is changing the way in which this is done. With modern equipment, you can use your own personal computer system to produce professional-quality slides or overhead transparencies directly from your own spreadsheet graphs. Although this technology will not guarantee *artistically* pleasing results, it will save the time and money required to have visuals produced by outside professionals. The saving can be substantial when a single slide can cost $100 and take days to produce.[5]

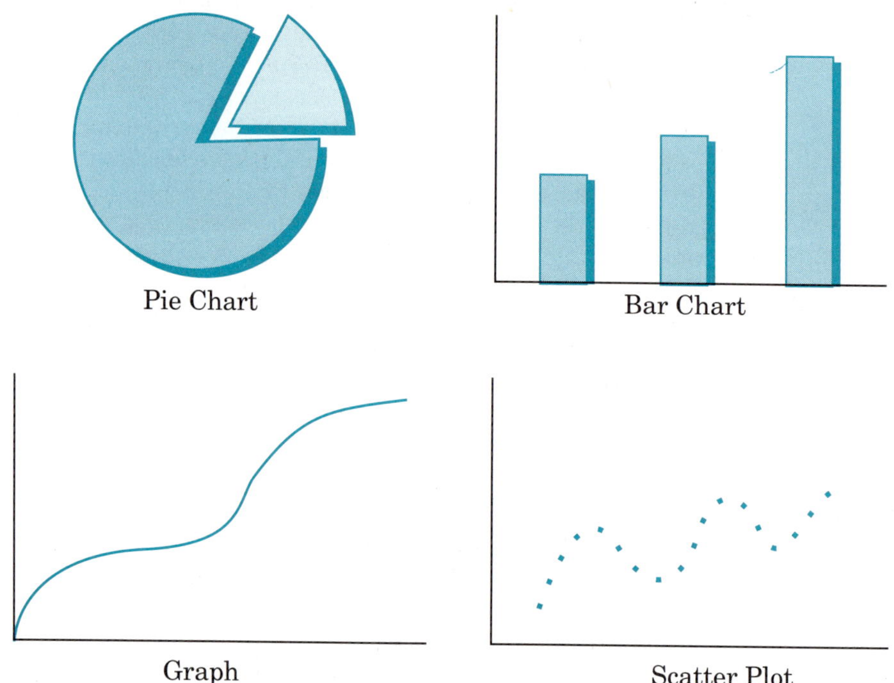

FIGURE 14.4 Computers can generate many different kinds of graphic displays.

Another interesting option for presenting graphic information during a formal group presentation is to connect a personal computer directly to a projection television. With this setup, you project the screen of your computer monitor onto the screen of the television. Instead of relying on prepared graphics, you can analyze questions posed during your presentation and project graphic solutions to your audience. This technology can be particularly helpful if you are working through problems as you interact with your prospect, and therefore can be used when you solve problems in a single sales call.

Analyzing Problems During the Sales Call

There are times when it is inconvenient or impossible to analyze a prospect's problems in your office and return with a presentation of the solution. In fact, if the prospect's problem is not as complicated as those described in the previous section, a two-stage approach to problem solving may hinder your ability to arrive at a good solution. If your concern is to tailor an insurance policy or an investment program to a consumer, or to calculate how much inventory a company might need to order, you may be better off analyzing the problem while interacting with the prospect. In fact, you can solve a variety of fairly complicated problems this way:

- Analyze an investment portfolio.
- Analyze insurance needs.
- Determine an inventory/delivery schedule.
- Calculate the best way to stock a retailer's shelf space.
- Determine how many computers a school will need to purchase, depending upon various conditions.

The ability to analyze complicated technical problems without having to return to your home office has been made possible by the growing technology of portable computers. With a laptop computer programmed to do appropriate calculations, you can work through any of these problems while you speak with the prospect.

Laptop Computers

A **laptop computer** is simply a personal computer that is the size of a briefcase. Although size limitations mean that many laptops do not equal the standard-size personal computer in screen size or storage capacity, their portability makes them an important tool for salespeople. With advancing technology, laptops are becoming very powerful.

More and more companies are outfitting their salespeople with laptop computers. There are several important advantages to this technology in cases where you do not need to prepare a formal presentation. First is the fact that, for the kinds of problems previously listed, you can respond to the prospect's needs more efficiently if you can work with the prospect to solve problems. Without portable

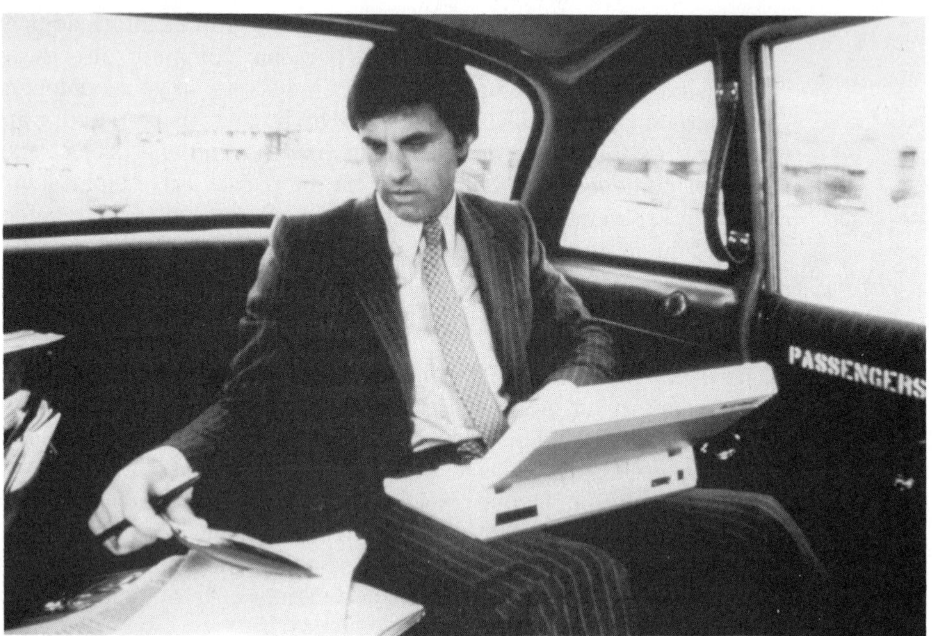

Many laptop computers weigh as little as 4 pounds. (Courtesy of Hewlett Packard.)

computer capability, you have to gather information from the prospect, return to your office to work out technical details, and then go back to the prospect with a proposed solution. Chances are that it will be impossible to anticipate all possible questions, so you will have to return to your office every time the prospect asks a question that requires a computer-assisted answer.

For reasons like this, Thomas Schlein of the Schlein Insurance Agency in Cuero, Texas, says that "There's no way that anybody who's going to be successful with universal life is going to do it without a computer." In one instance, Schlein spent 2.5 hours crunching numbers for a prospect on his laptop computer. After Schlein answered a variety of tough "what-if" questions, the prospect concluded that his current type of life insurance was a bad investment and ordered $500,000 worth of universal life coverage.[6]

Chances are that this sale would not have been closed if Schlein had had to delay his response to each question by running back and forth between his office and the prospect's or responding by telephone. The ability to interact with the computer saved the day.

In another case, a large oil company handed 150 laptop computers to its salespeople to take on their sales calls to gas stations. With this new technology, the salespeople could calculate which lubricants and additives were most profitable without having to return to their offices.

However, the applications of the laptop computer are not limited to solving

Laptop computers are becoming important tools in presentations. (© Joel Gordon Photography.)

complex prospect problems. In fact, sales experts like the one quoted at the beginning of this chapter believe that in the foreseeable future almost every salesperson will have a laptop computer precisely because of their ability to save time in planning, ordering, paperwork, and communication.

Time Saving with Laptop Computers. The House of Seagram's recognized these applications when it gave 100 laptops to its sales force in an effort to fight a declining market for hard liquor products. Now the retail account managers enter information on their laptops to build account databases, track sales activities, plan sales calls, and communicate with headquarters. Says Julie Hardesty, a regional account manager, "I've cut the time it takes to make out call and call planning reports from ten and fifteen minutes to one or two because it's easier to work on a keyboard than to fill out forms by hand."

Pat Sanders, another manager, likes the ability to transmit information from her laptop to her company's central computer. "Rather than depend on regular mail, which can take days, I send out information at 4 P.M., knowing that managers will read it that night."[7]

James Chambers, a sales director at Nabisco, says that laptops are invaluable for salespeople such as his. He describes a typical situation in which a supermarket manager might say to a salesperson, "Okay, you want me to buy the coffee that's on special, but what about that order of batteries we're expecting?" With a laptop computer, the salesperson can check the status of the battery order on the spot.[8]

Handheld Computers

Even smaller than laptops, **handheld computers** can save hours of paperwork for many salespeople. Tyrone Howze, a salesperson for Nabisco, uses his handheld computer to keep track of his inventory when calling on supermarkets. With the handheld computer, Mr. Howze can record information while standing in the store isle, and later transmit the information directly to headquarters by plugging the computer into a phone. Though simple and unsophisticated, the handheld computer allows Mr. Howze to spend more time calling on customers and less time on technical details.[9]

Advanced Communication Technologies

Facsimile Machines

A striking example of the application of modern technology to the problem of communicating over distances is the **facsimile (FAX) machine.** A FAX machine allows its user to transmit a copy (facsimile) of a printed document over telephone lines to another FAX machine. With a FAX machine, you can send written material to another person without waiting even for overnight mail.

Some experts predict that in the near future, every salesperson will have a FAX machine in her home.[10] Others predict that portable FAX machines will be connected to cellular telephones in the cars of many salespeople. Although these predictions may be somewhat extreme, FAX technology does offer several important advantages to the salesperson.

Salespeople have many occasions for transmitting written materials. There is a constant need to send orders, product specifications, and similar materials that cannot be easily described without printed words. In many of these cases, the spoken word cannot be substituted for the actual printed document. If, for example, the information must be written on specific forms or a signature is required, a telephone call will not do. The communication must be transmitted in printed form. For these occasions, the obvious advantage of the FAX technology is saving time. FAX transmits documents instantaneously, so there is no need to wait for mail. In addition, FAX machines are less expensive to use and are certainly more convenient than the postal service.

However, some experts warn about the overuse of FAX machines in sales. As with any technology, there is always the danger that the FAX machine will become the focus of attention rather than a tool for accomplishing some goal. This is the case when salespeople enjoy FAX technology so much that they begin to substitute FAXing for personal contact with customers.[11]

It is important to remember that the FAX machine is an efficient substitute for mail when it is necessary to transmit written material, but it is not a substitute for a telephone call when maintaining contact with a customer. As you have learned, *human communication includes much more than spoken words,* and the FAX machine can capture only the written word.

Therefore, in cases where a written document is not required, some companies are adopting communication systems based on voice mail.

Voice Mail

Voice mail systems are based on personal security-coded "mailboxes" that are stored in a central computer. The basic principle of voice mail is similar to that of a centralized telephone answering machine. A caller communicates with another person by calling that person's voice mailbox and leaving a recorded message. The other person listens to the message at a later time, whenever he contacts his mailbox for messages. Companies can adopt a voice mail system either by developing their own mailbox systems or by subscribing to a voice mail service that provides mailboxes for many different subscribers.

At first, the concept of voice mail may appear needlessly complicated. An obvious question is "Why not just call the other person? A simple phone call is easier and more direct than this complicated system of recorded messages." Although this observation may appear to be true to the layman, more and more companies are adopting these systems.

The advantages of voice mail are immediately obvious to many experienced salespeople. The typical salesperson spends a lot of time in the field calling orders into the main office, calling sales managers to report activities, and calling people to check inventory levels. Every time one of these lines is busy, the salesperson must keep calling or interrupt her schedule later to call again. There are also many times when a salesperson needs to receive a message from someone but does not want to stay in the office to wait for a call. With a voice mailbox, the salesperson can go out into the field and check for the message at her convenience.

The Chicago Iron and Tube Corporation represents a typical case of a company that has adopted voice mail for its salespeople. This manufacturer has a staff of 30 outside and 40 inside salespeople who must coordinate their efforts in order to fill customers' orders. Says Don McNeeley, executive vice president, "Our salespeople work harder, making more calls, which leaves them less time to call in during business hours. This makes it critical that they and their internal support staff stay in touch. With fifty-four mailboxes on our system, it's much easier for an inside person to let the outside person know about the latest activity such as an inquiry or a phone-in order before he or she calls on a customer so that they can demonstrate they're on top of things. . . . With voice mail, you eliminate time wasting chitchat. . . . [It] has increased my own productivity fifteen to twenty percent."[12]

In addition to improving productivity, voice mail can make life easier for some salespeople. Since the Thomas J. Lipton Company adopted voice mail, its 850 salespeople can leave messages for their managers at their own convenience. "Before we had voice mail, salespeople were on the phone every night bringing their managers up-to-date. . . . Now their evenings are free."[13] It is important to note, however, that the growing popularity of voice mail is not making the telephone obsolete. With voice mail, there is no direct interaction between the communicators; for this reason, it has not replaced the telephone for interacting with prospects.

In general, there are tradeoffs in using any new technology. Table 14.3 summarizes the advantages and disadvantages of the communication technologies discussed in this section.

Advances in Telemarketing

Telephones were first used in selling in the early 1900s.[14] Until recently, however, selling via telephone was reserved for small-scale, mostly retail selling. People associated telephone sales with the salesperson who called prospects at home, often interrupting their dinners in order to ask them to buy something.[15]

Advances in modern technology have changed this image. Telemarketing is no longer limited to small-ticket retail sales. Instead, it is a quickly growing method of conducting business-to-business sales. According to Richard J. Huether, manager of telemarketing development at General Electric, the company's telemarketing efforts have resulted in extremely large sales. In one case, a system designed to produce steam and electricity at a price in excess of $100 million was sold through telemarketing. In another case, the product was a $400,000 control system.[16]

Certainly, these cases do not represent the average telemarketing sale. However, sales of products that cost thousands of dollars are closed frequently through telemarketing efforts. A typical example is Monarch Marking Systems (a subsidiary of Pitney Bowes), which routinely sells products costing between $2,000 and

Table 14.3 Advantages and Disadvantages of Communication Technologies

Technology	*Advantages*	*Disadvantages*
Telephone	Immediate, personal, interactive	No visuals, may be inefficient
Voice mail	Personal, efficient	Not immediate, no visuals, no direct interaction
FAX	Immediate, visual, cost efficient	Less personal
Express mail	Visual	Less personal, more costly than FAX, less immediate than FAX

Telemarketing will be gaining in importance in the 1990s. (© 1981 Sarah Putnam/ The Picture Cube.)

$10,000 over the telephone. In addition, Statistical Package for the Social Sciences (SPSS) relies exclusively on telemarketing efforts to sell software products ranging from several hundred dollars to around $10,000.[17]

An obvious question to ask at this point is "Why now? What has caused the increase in the use of telemarketing in these big-ticket business-to-business sales?" There are several factors behind this trend:

- Cost savings.
- Better service.
- Technological advances.

Cost Savings

A reduction in the cost of doing business is one of the factors that makes telemarketing an attractive complement to face-to-face sales. With major reductions in travel expenses and salesperson time, the savings can be very impressive. Marketing officials at the Air Compressor Group, a large industrial company, estimate that it costs them $8 per call to maintain contact through telemarketing compared to $250–$300 for each face-to-face call made by a competitor. Similarly,

Linda Sullivan at SPSS estimates a cost of $40 per telemarketing sale compared with a "hi-tech industry average of $300 per personal sales call."[18]

However, in a competitive marketplace, reductions in costs cannot be the sole motivating factor in the choice of sales approaches. A cost saving of $200 or $300 is not a saving if it loses a sale worth several thousand dollars. The reason companies are able to achieve efficiencies with telemarketing is that the prospects are often receptive to the idea.

Better Service

An important but often overlooked point is that telemarketing can make more efficient use of the prospect's time as well as the salesperson's. This point is particularly important for today's professional buyers, who are concerned with efficiency at the buying end of the exchange process. Although no one would argue for an end to the personal sales call, there are many cases where face-to-face selling may not be necessary.

With software such as that sold by SPSS, the product's benefits can be described over the telephone quite adequately. Similarly, a steam and electricity generator need not be seen by the prospect. At best, a personal sales call could include a video of the generator in action. In this case, however, the buying decision is based on the product's technical specifications and cost, which can be described over the telephone.

The key in both of these cases is that the professional buyer knows basically what the product consists of and can make an informed judgment based on a verbal description.

Another important application of telemarketing in business-to-business sales is the telephone call aimed at generating new sales from an existing customer. A salesperson who must call on a customer in person will, of necessity, maintain less frequent contact than a salesperson who relies on the telephone. With telemarketing efforts, salespeople can "call" on their customers with great regularity, check their inventory levels, point out new products, and maintain relationships. If telemarketing is handled properly, customers can be given very attentive, conscientious treatment based largely on telephone contact.

According to officials at General Electric, "Many buyers are looking to lower their inventory costs by placing orders more frequently and in smaller quantities, and they need a rapid response system to do that."[19] Modern telemarketing can provide this rapid-response system because of recent technological advances.

Technological Advances

It is certainly possible to conduct a telemarketing campaign without advanced technology. Technically, a company needs only a salesperson and a telephone to run a telemarketing department. Such a simple system would, however, be very limited in scope. The salesperson would have to devote a large portion of her time to paperwork: finding prospects' names and telephone numbers, writing reports on the calls, filling out order forms, and sending written materials to prospects who had requested them. Even an efficient telemarketer would have limited time to spend on the phone doing actual selling.

With modern technology, the picture is quite different. Sophisticated modern technology is a major force behind the growing importance and professionalism of telemarketing. There are two major reasons for this development:

Automation of much of the paperwork has made telemarketing an efficient part of the selling effort.

Technology has linked the telemarketer to other computerized systems aimed at follow-up and lead processing.

Each advantage will be discussed in turn.

Automation and Efficiency. With an automated telemarketing system, each salesperson works at a workstation or terminal that is linked to a central computer. Often this central computer houses a relational database similar to the ones described earlier in this chapter. With a single keystroke on her computer, the telemarketing salesperson can list an entire profile of a prospect on the screen of her terminal (Figure 14.5). Records might contain descriptive facts as well as a history of the account. Because the computer can actually dial the prospect's number, the salesperson can use this time to plan what she will say to the prospect once the call goes through. Though having a computer dial a phone number might

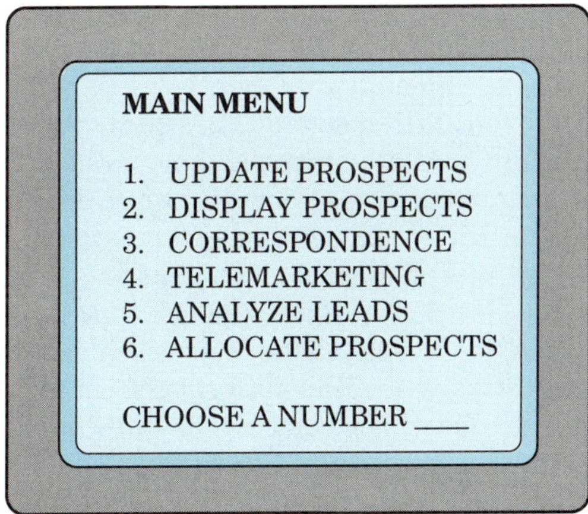

FIGURE 14.5 A typical menu from an integrated telemarketing program. The number that is selected determines which function will appear on the screen next.

not seem to be a major saving, it is quite important because of all of the busy signals and no answers that confront a telemarketer in a single day. With a computer dialing numbers, recording busy signals and no answers, and either automatically redialing or prompting the salesperson to call the next day, a great deal of time is saved.

There are also major efficiencies to be achieved through the maintenance of prospect files. Instead of filling out detailed written records of each call, the salesperson can enter the relevant facts directly into the computer.[20] Often the computer will automatically enter the time spent on the call directly into the file and provide the telemarketer with a choice of preprogrammed options to describe the outcome of the call. Thus by punching single keys, the telemarketer can enter information about whether a sale has been closed, whether a call back is needed, or whether the prospect is using a competitor's product. Additional information can be entered into the main file simply by using the terminal as a word processor. These facts can serve as valuable information for follow-up calls.

Automated Follow-Up. In addition to simplifying paperwork and record keeping, automated telemarketing systems improve follow-up with something called a **tickler system.** With a tickler system, the computer has a *daily automatic display listing the calls that the salesperson should make that day.* The tickler list includes call backs scheduled for that day, previously missed follow-ups, and newly assigned calls. Some systems even allow the salesperson to assign priorities to important calls to ensure efficient follow-up.

Consider, for example, a case where a software telemarketer had an automated system that combined many of these different advantages. During an initial call, the telemarketer learned that the prospect, a major university, was planning to install a new computer system. Although they were not yet at the stage of determining specific software needs, they were able to tell the telemarketer some of the specifications of the computer hardware that they were purchasing. They also told him that they would need to assess programs to manage student and staff records within another month.

The telemarketer entered these notes into his prospect file. A month later, his computer prompted him with a note reminding him to call the prospect. Upon seeing the reminder, the telemarketer retrieved the record from the main databank in order to review the details of his original conversation. Based on this call history, he was able to include relevant information in his presentation, and eventually closed a software sale in excess of $10,000.

In addition to helping the telemarketer conduct follow-up calls, computerized telemarketing systems can perform certain follow-up activities automatically. If a telemarketer determines that a prospect would be interested in literature, she can choose from a selection of literature printed on the computer's screen. With the touch of a key, she can have the computer print a cover letter, forward the literature request to the proper person, and record the mailing in the prospect's computer file.[21]

Putting It All Together

The purpose of this chapter has been to provide you with a broad understanding of the advantages that modern technology can offer you as a salesperson. At this point, we can begin to put it all together by summarizing the key points:

- The ultimate focus of selling is the prospect, and regardless of how sophisticated technology becomes, salespeople should maintain a person-oriented focus.
- Technology can actually enhance this orientation by freeing up time that would otherwise be spent on paperwork.
- Computerized databases improve the maintenance of files on prospects and customers.
- Modern integrated software allows you to combine database management, spreadsheet analysis, and paperwork.
- Presentation graphics and visuals can be produced with a personal computer.
- Laptop computers allow you to solve complicated problems while interacting with the prospect.
- Facsimile machines and voice mail can improve your efficiency by simplifying communication.
- Telemarketing can save time and money for you and the prospect.
- With modern integrated technology, telemarketing can be used to sell almost anything.

When we put these technologies together with the information presented in previous chapters, we see that technology can help you in many different stages of the sales process. To begin with, it can improve your *prospecting* efforts. Computerized telemarketing can be used to generate leads. In addition, computerized management of your prospect and customer files can help you select those leads that you think will be qualified prospects. By maintaining databases of sales leads, you can have the computer select cases according to characteristics that you think will result in sales. In many cases, you might have discovered these characteristics through your own spreadsheet analysis of your sales: You might have discovered, for example, that large manufacturers of a certain type of plastic are particularly likely to want your product. At this point, it may even be possible to pursue the prospects through telemarketing and avoid the expense of personal calls.

If you decide to call on the prospect, technological advances can help you *plan sales calls.* Smart software such as SELLSTAR can assist you in planning which people to approach, how frequently to call, and what kinds of approaches to take. You can also use sophisticated software to plan a *formal presentation,* including the visuals and graphics. If you have a sales call that requires you to solve complex problems *during* your presentation, a laptop computer will allow you to analyze the prospect's answers to your questions without interrupting your interaction.

Once you *close* a sale, advanced communication systems allow you to complete the actual order and relay it to your home office with a minimum of paperwork and inconvenience. And with modern telemarketing systems, you may be able to get additional sales with fewer actual visits to the prospect.

As these examples illustrate, modern technology can enhance the job of selling in many different ways. Indeed, the applications seem to be so far-reaching that we are led to believe predictions that all salespeople will soon be armed with laptop computers and FAX machines. At first, this prediction might meet with resistance. Computerization can seem unsettling to some who are about to enter a sales career, because, traditionally, sales attracts people-oriented individuals rather than technicians.

However, those who are drawn to sales because they are people-oriented should not be discouraged by the growing role played by computers. Far from making sales more complicated or difficult, these modern technologies can automate many tasks like record keeping, order filing, and call reports, which many salespeople find burdensome. By saving the time required to perform these nonproductive activities, technology allows salespeople to concentrate on what they should be doing—*planning*, *problem solving*, and *communicating*.

Key Terms

Database	Laptop computer
Relational database	Handheld computer
Spreadsheet	Facsimile (FAX) machine
Integrated software	Voice mail
Artificial intelligence	Tickler system

Review Questions

1. What is a database? List five ways in which databases can be used in sales.
2. What is a relational database? What kinds of sales problems do *not* require a relational database program?
3. What is a spreadsheet? List five problems that can be analyzed with a spreadsheet program. (Two examples should also require the use of integrated graphics.)
4. List five ways in which a salesperson can use a laptop computer.
5. What are the advantages of FAX technology?
6. Are there any disadvantages to using FAX machines in sales?
7. What is voice mail? Under what circumstances would a company benefit from a voice mail system?
8. What are the primary reasons for the increased use of telemarketing in business-to-business sales?

9. What functions can be automated in a telemarketing system?
10. In what ways can a telemarketing system fit into a personal selling program?

Discussion Questions

1. Could a prospect be put off by a computer and a great deal of sophisticated technology? Discuss. If the answer is "yes," is there anything that could be done to prevent this reaction?
2. Will it be possible to succeed in sales in the 1990s and beyond if a person has no understanding of technology? Discuss.
3. Will an emphasis on technology change the people-oriented nature of selling? Can it affect the type of person who is attracted to the selling profession?
4. Can software such as SELLSTAR really capture the knowledge of an experienced salesperson? If you were responsible for assisting a programmer in developing software like CONSULT, which selling rules would you include in it? What questions would you suggest that it ask of a user?

CASE 14.1

When Joyce Fairbanks was promoted to sales manager at Royco, Inc., her first assignment was to develop a complete plan to "bring Royco into the twenty-first century." Royco was a medium-sized insurance company, located in the Southeast, with a sales force of 130. Their primary target market was individuals, but they also sold insurance to condominiums, cooperative apartments, and some small retailers. The sales territories were spread out geographically, so the average representative spent a great deal of time traveling.

Joyce was given the assignment of modernizing the sales force because she had sold personal computers before coming to Royco. Top management thought that she would be good at designing integrated computer systems. The assignment was not an easy one: Royco's sales force had remained almost untouched by computers, and most of its personnel feared anything that seemed to be technologically sophisticated. The manager who had preceded Joyce in the job had spent thousands of dollars on a computer system that was never used. He had purchased expensive personal computers for everyone on the sales staff. However, because he did not understand computers, he left the purchase of software to each salesperson. A few purchased general database management programs but could not customize them for sales applications. No one really knew what to do with the machines.

How should Joyce proceed with her assignment? Be specific in your comments about the following:

1. The purchase of additional computer hardware.
2. The purchase of software.
3. The purchase of any other advanced communication technology.
4. The use of any telemarketing systems.
5. The institution of a training program to teach the sales force to use the new technology.

References

1. "Moving Beyond Patter and Persistence," *New York Times*, January 1, 1989, p. F6.

2. Collins, R. (1988). Microcomputer applications: The perfect travelling companion. *Journal of Personal Selling and Sales Management, 8* (May), 67–70.

3. Hennessey, H. D. (1988). Microcomputer applications: Accelerating the salesperson learning curve. *Journal of Personal Selling and Sales Management, 8* (November), 77–82.

4. Thompson, K. (1988). Another hot market. *Macintosh Business Review*, (September), 31–33.

5. Collins, R. (1989). Unleash the power of desk top presentations. *Journal of Personal Selling and Sales Management 9*, 70–75.

6. *InfoWorld Special Report No. 2*, September 24, 1984.

7. Seagrams looks to laptops for help. (1989). *Sales & Marketing Management, 141* (January), 67.

8. *New York Times*, January 1, 1989, p. F6.

9. Ibid.

10. Walsh, J. (1988). Fax to the max: How marketers are finding ways to use facsimile. *Marketing News*, November 7, p. 1.

11. Graham, J. R. (1988). Avoid being snared by the FAX trap. *Marketing News*, November 7, p. 9.

12. Taylor, T. (1988). Voice mail delivers. *Sales & Marketing Management, 140* (July), 62.

13. Ibid.

14. Johnson, E. M., and W. Meiners. (1987). Telemarketing: Trends, issues and opportunities. *Journal of Personal Selling and Sales Management, 7* (November), 65–68.

15. Don't call me; I'll call you. (1988). *Nation's Business*, (February).

16. Taylor, T. (1988). Telemarketing goes for the big ticket. *Sales & Marketing Management, 140* (October), 100–107.

17. Ibid.

18. Ibid.

19. Ibid.

20. Collins, R. (1985). Microcomputer systems to handle sales leads: A key to increased salesforce productivity. *Journal of Personal Selling and Sales Management, 5* (May), 77–83.

21. Gallucci, S. (1988). "Automated telemarketing has benefits manual systems lack. *Marketing News,* (August 15), p. 9.

15

Ethical Issues in Selling

CHAPTER OBJECTIVES

In this chapter, you will learn:

Ethics is the study of customs involving what is considered to be morally right and wrong.

Objective morality concerns society's view and subjective morality concerns the view of the individual.

One good way to figure out whether or not something is morally right is to take the view of the other.

Lying and manipulation are major ethical issues throughout the sales process.

A half-truth is unethical if it causes harm to a prospect.

Unethical behaviors not directly related to the actual selling process include devious methods of learning about a competitor's product, tampering with a competitor's product displays, moonlighting, cheating to win sales contests, and abusing travel and entertainment benefits.

Behaving ethically will contribute to both a positive self-concept and a good reputation.

CHAPTER OUTLINE

A Sales Challenge

James T. has just completed the sales training program for the AAA Company. AAA manufactures glass bottles, and James' task is to sell these bottles to a wide variety of users. He will concentrate on perfume makers and wine makers. He was hired 9 months ago right out of college as a sales representative. He had no sales experience. He is about to begin his first week as a salesperson. Like any other salesperson, he has to find prospects, set up appointments, and sell his bottles.

It so happens that a colleague of his who was hired 2 years earlier left a prospect list on his desk. While answering his colleague's phone, James notices this list. He sees that many of the prospects giving firm orders have peculiar notations after their names. Looking further, he notices that these notations correspond to cash amounts. As James puzzles over this information, he sees a note from one of these accounts thanking his colleague for a "gift." It finally dawns on James that his colleague is giving kickbacks to prospects who place large orders.

James is in a dilemma. He knows that his colleague was engaged in unethical (and probably illegal) behavior. He also knows that he himself is behaving unethically by invading the privacy of his colleague. He has a number of options. He could say nothing. That would be unethical because he would be allowing this practice to exist. He could confront his colleague. That would be uncomfortable because he would have to admit that he looked through his colleague's personal papers. He could report it to his sales manager. That would also entail admitting that he invaded the privacy of his colleague. He would also run the risk of reporting a practice that is condoned by the sales manager. That would put James' job in jeopardy.

James did not enter the profession of selling with any expectation of engaging in such practices, let alone having to confront them. Unfortunately, there is no easy solution to James' dilemma.

An Overview

We are all faced with moral dilemmas every day. This is as true of the salesperson as it is of any other kind of professional. We can usually select a course of action when we are faced with such dilemmas because we know "right" from "wrong." Or do we? In fact, the issue of right and wrong is the fundamental basis of moral behavior. But it is not always clear-cut. In fact, it usually is not.

This chapter considers the essentials of ethics. We then look at ethics with respect to the salesperson. We first consider the dilemmas that a salesperson faces as she goes through the stages of the selling process. We then discuss ethical issues facing a salesperson that are not directly involved in the selling process. Finally, we look at the impact of unethical behavior on the salesperson's self-concept.

In recent years, Wall Street has achieved a new kind of publicity because of the exposure of a number of professionals who were engaging in unethical (and illegal) activities. (James R. Holland/ Stock Boston.)

It is important to understand that since the whole issue of ethical behavior is often ambiguous, we cannot always state that something is or is not unethical. When we feel that the morality of a situation is reasonably clear, we say as much. Unfortunately, we are not always able to do this, and you, as a reader, will have to make your own decisions. There is reason to believe that even conscientious salespeople do not always know when something is or is not unethical. There is evidence that salespeople want guidelines from their sales managers to help them deal with ethical problems.[1]

It is also important to understand that most salespeople choose the ethical course of action once they know what it is. Nevertheless, as with anything else, a few salespeople will choose to act unethically. The unethical behaviors we discuss are not widespread. In fact, if anything, they are decreasing in frequency. Nevertheless, they do exist. For that reason, we feel that it is important for any prospective salesperson to be aware of them. To be forewarned is to be forearmed.

Ethics and Morality

Although we are not aware of it, we have been learning about ethical behavior since we were children. Our parents, our schools, our government, and our employers have all attempted to teach us how to live the "good" life. In other words, we have been socialized into a society where we have a sense of a "right" way and a "wrong" way of living. Basically, a sense of ethics has been instilled in each of us.

Ethics can be defined very simply as *"the study of human customs."*[2] When we consider ethics, we need to distinguish customs that are mere conventions, such as table manners and forms of etiquette, from customs that are more fundamental, such as being honest, respecting other people's property, caring for our children, and obeying our parents. *Customs that are conventions are more properly called* **manners.** Customs that are more fundamental and can be considered to be right or wrong are called *morals.* When we study ethics, we are not concerned with manners. Instead, we are concerned with morals. **Morality** *is the aspect of human activity that allows us to call it right or wrong.* Since ethics is really a concern with a moral philosophy, we can use the terms *ethics* and *morality* interchangeably.

Subjective Morality Versus Objective Morality

There are two kinds of morality: *subjective* and *objective.* **Subjective morality** *is based upon an individual and his own knowledge, consent, background, training, and personality.* **Objective morality** *is based upon whether any normal person would be allowed to engage in a particular act.* When we consider subjective morality, we ask such questions as "Did this person intend to do that?" or "Did this person realize what he was doing?" When we consider objective morality, we ask such questions as "Is it wrong to steal?" or "Is it wrong to lie?" Figure 15.1 summarizes the distinction between subjective and objective morality.

A salesperson is constantly faced with these two aspects of morality. For example, he knows that it is wrong to lie to a prospect. If he says, for example, that a fabric will not fade and he knows that the fabric fades, the salesperson is *objectively* immoral because he is lying.

However, when we evaluate his behavior, we also need to question his *subjective* morality. If the salesperson deliberately lied, we can easily say that he was subjectively immoral. If he was unaware of the fabric's tendency to fade, we can only say that he is uninformed. In that case, we cannot say that the salesperson behaved unethically. We would have to direct our criticism to his lack of product knowledge.

Right Versus Wrong

One of the great difficulties with the study of ethics is determining what is *right* and what is *wrong.* This means that we have to define those words. Since this is not a simple task, we must first agree on a few basic assumptions.

First, we all have desires, and we know how to satisfy many of them.[3] Second, we are all entitled to attempt to satisfy our desires. Third, we can't achieve our desires whenever and however we choose because doing so will interfere with other people's attempts to satisfy their desires.

Because of those three assumptions, we have to consider ethics and morality.

Objective Morality
"Is it wrong to lie?"
"Is it wrong to steal?"
Subjective Morality
"Did he do that deliberately?"
"Did he realize what he was doing?"

FIGURE 15.1 Objective versus subjective morality.

In other words, when two or more people wish to satisfy a desire, even though they are entitled to do so, they may do it in such a way that they will interfere with one another. As a result, one of them will not be able to satisfy her desire. As an example, consider a salesperson who risks being short of her quota. She certainly desires to meet her quota, and she is entitled to try to do so. But what happens when a salesperson from a competing firm also has the same desire, and they have both independently found the same prospect? Both salespeople will not be able to satisfy their desire using the same prospect.

Is it right or wrong for one of them to try to sell to this prospect, knowing that the other person will not be able to do so as a result? The answer is, *it depends*. In fact, it depends upon how the successful salesperson influences the prospect's decision. If she engages in bribery, we would say that she is ethically wrong. If she uses the customary means of influence, such as offering better terms for quantity discounts or providing a free trial, we would say that she is right.

Why is one action right and the other wrong? One action is in keeping with an agreed-upon custom, and the other violates that custom. The custom is that competitive actions are right as long as their success is achieved through honest practices. The person who engages in bribery is engaging in a dishonest practice. While she is being competitive, she is violating the custom of negotiation. The person who offers quantity discounts or free trials is also being competitive, but

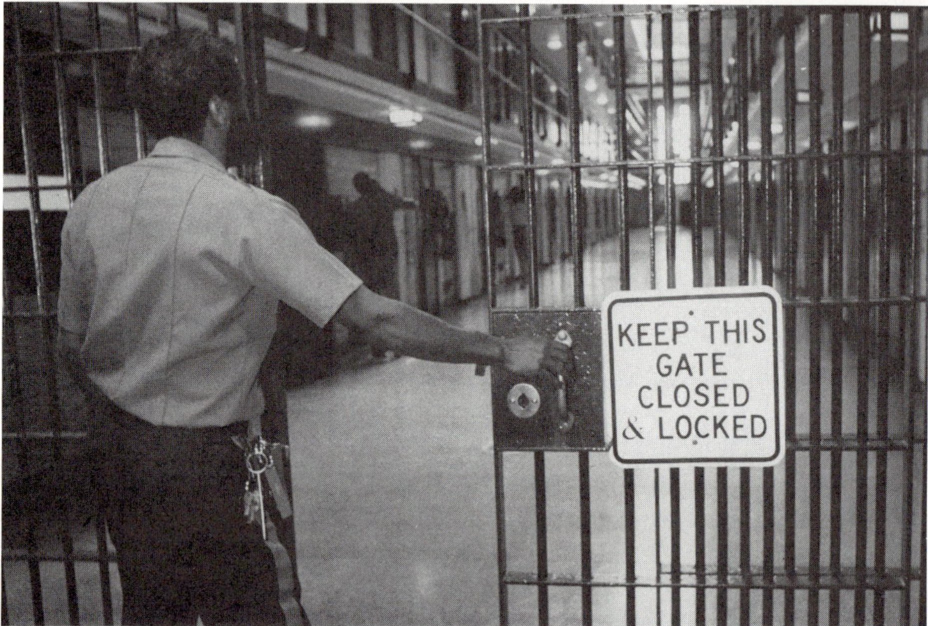

Certain unethical behaviors are also considered illegal. Murder is one such behavior. People who commit such acts will be severely punished and will usually end up at an institution such as the one pictured here. (© Laima Druskis/Photo Researchers, Inc.)

she is adhering to the custom of negotiation. The first person, then, is morally wrong. The second person is morally right.

The Definition of Right

Now we are in a position to define right. **Right** *is any act that is consistent with the norm of morality.* The **norm of morality** *has to do with that which is equitable or fair.* For example, we all have a desire to thrive economically. This means that we engage in productive work that allows us to succeed. Since economic rewards are scarce, we have to compete for them. As long as we compete within the norm of morality, we are right. When we violate that norm, we are wrong. If we were to engage in stealing, cheating, or lying, we would be in violation of the norm of morality. We would be wrong.

We all have a desire to stay alive. We are entitled to do what is necessary to achieve that desire. But we are not entitled to do it in such a way that it interferes with another person's ability to achieve that desire. For that reason, we consider as a moral norm that murder is wrong. We have a number of moral norms:

Murder is wrong.
Arson is wrong.

Stealing is wrong.
Lying is wrong.
Cheating is wrong.
Destroying someone else's property is wrong.

Often moral norms have laws associated with them. If we violate a norm of morality, we are also likely to violate a law. In that case, we will be punished.

Knowing Right from Wrong

Many situations arise in a sales context that require us to distinguish right from wrong behavior. That can be difficult, but there is reason to assume that most of us do, in fact, know right from wrong. We know that it is wrong to lie; therefore, telling a prospect that our product will do things that it can't do is unethical. We know that it is wrong to cheat; therefore, cheating to win a sales contest is wrong. We know it is wrong to steal; therefore, taking customers away from our colleagues is wrong. We know it is wrong not to respect privacy; therefore, spying on a competitor is wrong.

Shades of Gray in Ethics

Unfortunately, the question of ethics is not always as simple as knowing right from wrong. In many situations there are shades of gray, and that is where application of ethical standards becomes especially critical. Figure 15.2 depicts the concern about gray areas in ethics.

As an example, consider the issue of reporting the number of hours worked to an employer. Any report that states more hours than were actually worked is a lie and, hence, unethical. Unfortunately, many people distort their reports of hours worked. Some of them convince themselves that if the distortion is only slight, it is not unethical. This is where we run into difficulty with ethics. At what point is distortion acceptable, and at what point does it become unethical? We will see that this question emerges in other contexts regarding ethics. There is no easy answer to it, and in fact, different people have different answers. And that is precisely the problem.

If we all accepted the basic notion of simply being honest, we would not have to grapple with this issue. Even then, different people have different views of honesty. Much of this subjectivity is a function of the customs of a particular profession or even a particular organization. It is also a function of how an individual views honesty.

FIGURE 15.2 Shades of gray in ethics.

Ultimately, we have to live with ourselves, and we each determine our own code of ethics. In terms of reporting hours worked, some people say that it is not unethical to round up to the nearest hour, others say that it is not unethical to round up to the nearest day, and still others say that it is not unethical to round up to the nearest week. In all cases, of course, they are rounding up rather than down. If you were the employer instead of the employee, which of these positions would you consider to be ethical?

Taking the Role of the Other

Very likely, you indicated that most of these distortions would be unethical. And that may be the key to dealing with shades of gray in ethics. *Whenever a behavior occurs that has the potential to be unethical, assuming that it has an impact on someone else—whether it be an employer, a colleague, a competitor, or a prospect—it is important to look at it from the other's perspective.* In other words, put yourself in the role of the other person. When you do that, you will quickly decide what is ethical and what is unethical.

Taking the role of the other person is how we frequently deal with difficult issues. For example, when we inadvertently hurt someone's feelings, we are often surprised to learn that we did so. But when we consider how we would feel if someone did that same thing to us, we understand why the person was hurt. If we give a noisy party in an apartment, we are surprised when neighbors complain. Yet we would probably complain if they were to give a noisy party. We can avoid the complaining to begin with if we take the role of our neighbors and recognize that it is not pleasant to be forced to live with excessive noise. We therefore make every effort to keep our party quiet.

In both of these examples, we are taking the role of the other. We all have experiences that are varied enough to make this possible. If a salesperson wants to take customers away from a co-worker, he can easily know how he would feel if his co-worker did that to him. He will immediately know that it is unethical. We have all been prospects. We know how upset we become if a salesperson lies or misrepresents the product. By recalling such experiences, we can take the role of the prospect and easily recognize that misrepresenting the product is unethical.

The Role of Ethics for the Salesperson

The job of a salesperson includes a number of situations in which it is possible to be unethical. For example, a salesperson often has the use of a company car and is reimbursed for business trips and business meals. She should be careful not to use these perquisites for her personal pleasure. The salesperson can also enter company-sponsored contests that may entail winning merchandise or trips. She should compete fairly and avoid doing anything to increase her sales volume artificially to win these contests.

EXHIBIT 15.1

How the Sales Manager Can Prevent Valuable Information from Leaving a Company with the Departing Salesperson

When salespeople move to a rival company, they often take with them trade secrets, lists of customers, and even confidential information having to do with prices and manufacturing processes. If this information gets out, it can interfere with a company's ability to maintain a competitive edge. How can management prevent this from happening? Following is a list of several things a manager can do.

1. It is first important to know what constitutes a trade secret. A trade secret is usually involved when

   The company guards the secrecy of the information.

   The company has spent large sums of money in developing the information.

   It is difficult to acquire the information from outside the company.

   Employees are explicitly told that the information represents a trade secret.

There are explicit laws governing trade secrets. For example, while a salesperson can use a customer list from a previous employer, it is illegal for him to use it in such a way that his knowledge of a given customer's buying habits will give him a competitive edge. It is recommended that management remind salespeople about the legal issues involved in using trade secrets when they move to a new employer.

2. Create a climate of confidentiality. Employees should from the very beginning be told about the importance of confidentiality of trade secrets. Posters can reinforce this, and the issue can be mentioned in company newsletters.
3. Employees need to be advised of the seriousness of the problem. Many states now have laws making it a criminal offense to steal trade secrets. Informing salespeople about this appears to have a big impact on reducing the problem.
4. Include restrictive covenants in all employment contracts. If newly hired employees have to sign these contracts, the company will have an easier time in court should going to court be necessary. The covenant should provide a reasonable time limit such as six months.
5. Establish effective exit procedures. All company material should be returned before an employee leaves. Employees should be reminded of their obligation to maintain the confidentiality of trade secrets.
6. If any problem should develop, the company should act quickly. Sometimes a company can act before a problem develops by sending a competitor a letter to remind the competitor of the ex-employee's continuing obligation to adhere to any restrictive covenant.

Source: Adapted from S. M. Sack. (1985). You *can* keep a secret. *Sales & Marketing Management*, (February 4), 39–41.

The salesperson is usually competing with salespeople from other firms who sell the same product. A good salesperson should allow this healthy competition to exist. He deals with prospective and actual buyers of his products. He should behave in such a way that he is consistently honest. That means, for example, that he should avoid offering excessive incentives to the prospective buyer, since such incentives can be interpreted as bribes.

These are not easy issues to deal with. We all tend to take advantage of certain situations. Some of us do and some of us don't. It takes a reasonably strong person to resist the temptations that surround unethical behavior. Often our legal system prevents certain unethical behaviors from occurring. Corporations can also help prevent unethical behaviors by imparting the ethical values of the organization.[4] Sales managers can also work to prevent unethical behavior.[5] Usually, though, it is the individual salesperson who must work to avoid engaging in unethical behavior.

Are Some Things More Unethical Than Others?

As we suggested earlier, people often think that some things are more unethical than others. We all have a sense of that difference in our own lives. For example, many people are less likely to inform a salesperson in a large department store about being mistakenly undercharged than in a small neighborhood store. The

It is very easy for us to be undercharged at a retail store. When this happens, we have to ask ourselves whether it is unethical not to report this to the salesperson or clerk. (© Alan Carey/The Image Works, Inc.)

perception is that the large store, being impersonal and uncaring, isn't as deserving as the small store. The underlying argument is that it is more unethical to fail to inform the small store about this mistake than the large store.

Is that, in fact, the case? While an argument could be made justifying the distinction between a large store and a small one, allowing a mistake to occur that is in the customer's favor would seem equally unethical in both cases. Such a mistake by a small store takes money away from the people whose livelihood depends upon the success of that store. This also happens in a large store, although more indirectly. Ultimately, in the large store, this mistake comes back to the customer because the large store will be forced to raise prices to compensate for the loss of revenue. Thus, the size of the store is irrelevant. The question is whether it is ethical to allow the mistake.

We can ask a variation of this question. Is it more ethical to allow oneself to be undercharged than to actually steal an item? While there are explicit laws about theft, in both cases something is being stolen, but in the situation involving a mistake, it is not outright theft.

Clearly, the issue of degree of ethicality is very difficult. For the salesperson, the same issue occurs. Is it more unethical for a salesperson to lie to a potential customer about a product or to lie to an employer about the number of hours worked? In both cases a lie is being told, but it can be argued that if the employer is large enough, the lie is less harmful than it is to an individual customer.

Is it more unethical to lie about the quality of a product to a buyer representing a large company or to an individual representing a small household? Some people would argue that the large company is impersonal and can withstand the lie, while the small household is directly affected by it. In both cases, however, a lie is being told. And that should be viewed as unethical.

We would argue, therefore, that one should try to be ethical in any situation where ethics exist. While some unethical behaviors can be more harmful than others, the end result of unethical behavior is that, in the long run, everyone will be harmed. Further, when one says that it is acceptable to be ethical in one situation but not in another, what is to keep that person from progressively extending the number of situations in which it is acceptable to be unethical? Following is a discussion of ethical dilemmas that can occur during the sales process.

Ethical Concerns That Can Emerge During the Sales Process

Since personal selling is essentially an interactive process, our first concern is with ethical issues that can arise as the salesperson seeks out and interacts with prospects. There is usually some pressure for the salesperson to make a sale. As a result, the salesperson is faced with a number of ethical dilemmas. Two dilemmas that can occur in almost any phase of the sales interaction are lying and manipulation. We discuss those issues first. Then we consider dilemmas that are specific to each phase of the sales interaction.

Lying

Lying can occur during the approach, during the presentation, in handling objections, and during the close. It can also occur in situations not directly related to the sales process, such as lying to the employer about the number of hours worked. As we have already indicated, lying is wrong from the perspective of objective morality. If a salesperson unknowingly presents inaccurate or incorrect information, he is not wrong from the perspective of subjective morality. Nevertheless, he risks losing a customer if the customer learns of his mistake. If a salesperson deliberately presents false information, he is wrong in terms of subjective morality.

The difficulty here is that presenting inaccurate information is not always an **outright lie.** In other words, there is a gray area with respect to ethics. An outright lie is not only unethical but is also considered to be fraud.[6] The situation in regard to other forms of misrepresentation is not so clear-cut. We can make some distinctions:

1. An outright lie.
2. A half-truth.
3. Exaggeration.

The Outright Lie. As suggested, the outright lie is illegal. A salesperson who engages in such fraudulent behavior is not only jeopardizing her own job, she is placing her entire company at risk. The customer can sue the selling company. For an outright lie to be clearly illegal, it must have to do with a statement of fact. A **fact** is *something known to have happened or to be true.* Since a misstatement of a fact is an outright lie, it is both objectively and subjectively unethical.

The Half-Truth. Where we run into complications is when a factual statement is made, but an additional relevant factual statement is not made. For example, while it may be true that the condensers in an air conditioner may not freeze, it may only be true if the filter is thoroughly cleaned before the air conditioner is run for several days at a time. If the salesperson neglects to give this information, he is telling a half-truth. This is also referred to as a *sin of omission.*

A **half-truth** is a *statement that may be wholly true, but it may not be the whole truth.* For example, assume that a professor asks whether you studied for your exam. The whole truth is that you studied for 30 minutes. If you answer "yes," your statement is wholly true. If you neglect to provide the information about how long you studied, you have not told the whole truth.

Deciding to omit relevant information is unethical, particularly if this information can harm a prospect. A salesperson may be inclined to make true statements about a product's advantages and positive qualities. He may, however, fail to make any statement that informs the prospect about its disadvantages or negative qualities. This practice is unfortunate because he loses an opportunity to enhance his credibility by revealing the negative aspects of the product. We suggest that engaging in half-truths is objectively unethical when the omitted information is of critical importance. Whether it is objectively unethical when the omitted information is not critical is less clear and can't easily be determined. It is subjectively unethical for the salesperson to omit important information deliberately. If he is unaware of the information, he is not being subjectively unethical.

Exaggeration. Of course, salespeople make statements that reflect their own opinions. Often these statements contain some exaggeration. They are not unlike advertisements in which a product is claimed to be the best in the world. This kind of exaggeration is considered to be **puffery,** *the embellishment through adjectives or metaphor.*[7] While puffery in advertising is an area that is increasingly being scrutinized by the Federal Trade Commission, it is assumed that the public understands that puffery is just that. In other words, it is assumed that the public doesn't literally believe claims that are based upon puffery.

Similarly, in a sales context, opinions that use obvious exaggeration are sometimes expected. Such statements are not illegal. Whether or not they are ethical depends on how clearly they are presented as exaggerated opinion statements. If an exaggerated claim is treated as a statement of fact (e.g., "Independent tests showed our product to be vastly superior to the competition in durability"), it is unethical and potentially fraudulent. That same statement expressed as an exaggerated opinion (e.g., "This product puts the others to shame when it comes to durability") is not fraudulent, and it probably is not unethical either objectively or subjectively. In the same way that people don't literally believe puffery in advertising, it can be assumed that they don't literally believe exaggeration from the salesperson.

There is a risk, however, in giving exaggerated opinion statements. If the prospect does buy the product and doesn't agree with the salesperson's opinion, the prospect is not likely to trust the salesperson again. This suggests that a salesperson should use such statements very cautiously because he is risking his credibility.

Manipulation

A major aspect of any sales interaction is persuasion. You will recall from Chapter 8 that persuasion is a process of influencing someone else. Many people consider persuasion to be **manipulation.** When we manipulate someone, we *influence them in a clever or crafty way; we alter information to suit our purposes.* Table 15.1 presents a number of statements that could be considered manipulative.

Almost all salespeople engage in persuasion. Often that also entails manipulation. For example, an attempt to achieve rapport by communicating similarity is an attempt to manipulate the prospect into liking the salesperson. In trying not to make negative statements about the competition, even if they are justified, the salesperson is manipulating the prospect into thinking that she is above such behavior.

Another form of manipulation involves gifts and special treatment. Often this

Table 15.1 Examples of Manipulative Statements

Statement	*Interpretation*
"You sure know your computers. You must be pretty smart."	Flatters the prospect.
"I think our competitor makes a good product. I would be worried about service. Don't quote me, but I heard that they may be taken over. It's just a rumor, but you never know."	Presents information that, while not an outright lie, cannot be checked because it is deliberately vague.
"Very simply, we make the best office furniture you can buy."	Exaggerates.
"I usually don't do this, but I will give you a break."	Gives a special favor that is not really special.
"I've been in this business a long time. I wouldn't sell this product if I thought it was inferior."	Communicates regard for the product that may or may not be genuine.

problem is caused by customers who expect special treatment. This situation varies by industry, but when a customer does expect special treatment, the only way a salesperson can have a reasonable chance of making a sale is to accommodate the customer.

Special treatment includes anything from inexpensive gifts, nice lunches, and tickets to sporting events to lavish gifts and weekend trips. Expensive gifts and weekend trips can be so lavish as to constitute bribes or kickbacks, which are clearly illegal. A few salespeople provide special treatment of their own volition. By doing this, they are inadvertently creating customer expectations for special treatment in future sales.

It is difficult to determine whether manipulation is ethical or not. It is not objectively unethical to persuade someone else. Nor is it subjectively unethical. But when the persuasion entails such manipulative tactics as special treatment, it is more difficult to argue that it is ethical. For example, it is perfectly acceptable for a salesperson to take a customer out to lunch or dinner if they discuss business. It is less ethical, but still acceptable, if the salesperson takes a customer to lunch or dinner when business is not discussed. It is not considered ethical for a salesperson to send a customer on an all-expense-paid weekend to Las Vegas. Thus, a determination of ethics here is a function of the *degree* of special treatment rather than simply whether or not special treatment exists.

When special treatment is in the form of a gift, the salesperson is approaching the practice of bribery. A token gift of something worth $10 would not be considered a bribe. In fact, any gift worth $25 or less is considered legal.[8] This suggests that such gifts can reasonably be considered ethical as well. Thus, whether a gift is ethical depends on how much it is worth.

When gifts become too lavish, they can be considered bribes. This means that in addition to being illegal, they are also unethical. That is not to say that

EXHIBIT 15.2

Keeping It Clean, and Legal

Consider the following attempts by salespeople to make inroads:

A new salesperson in town circulates a letter among his competitor's customers that points out the failures in the competition's products and services. As a result, a number of the competitor's customers refuse to renew their contracts.

A group of distributor salespeople leave their company and form a competing company. Many of their old customers follow. Salespeople from the original company try to win these customers back by telling them things such as [that] the new company's equipment is faulty, it cheats its customers, and it bills irregularly.

Whether these practices are done out of innocence or maliciousness, a salesperson is responsible for what he says in a sales presentation. "Many times, when libelous or slanderous statements are made, the verdicts that are coming down are substantially large, very large," says Steven Mitchell Sack, a New York City attorney and author of *The Salesperson's Legal Guide.* In a case similar to the first scenario above, the company was forced to pay $100,000 in damages for circulating the letter. In a case similar to the second scenario above, the original company paid $25,000 for a defamation settlement and about $25,000 more in legal fees.

As a result, a salesperson should know what constitutes libel and slander. *Business slander* is an oral form of defaming the competition, either the reputation of the company or the reputation of an individual in that company. *Business libel* is the written form of defaming the competition. *Product disparagement* involves false and unfair comparisons or deceptive claims. *Unfair competition* involves misstatements regarding the salesperson's own product or services. Sales puffery is allowed by the courts. But once this puffery is passed off as factual, it becomes business defamation or unfair competition.

In a libel or slander suit, "you don't have to prove damages by the remark. The law allows a recovery, sometimes a substantial recovery, because the damages are presumed . . . from their utterance," says Sack.

Sack recommends never repeating unconfirmed trade gossip. He suggests avoiding remarks that can be interpreted as impairing the reputation of another business. The best policy is to make accurate comparisons that have documentation.

Source: Adapted from P. Frichtl. (1985). Keeping it clean, and legal. *Industrial Distribution.* (December), p. 45.

Business lunches are common. It is legitimate for a salesperson to be reimbursed for a business lunch if it really involves a discussion of business. Unfortunately, such things as business lunches are abused when employees ask for reimbursement for meals that are not business related. (Comstock)

gifts worth more than $25 are not given. In fact, it is estimated that about $7 billion is spent on bribes and kickbacks.[9]

It should be noted that many customers bridle at attempts to give them special treatment. In those cases, the salesperson only diminishes her own credibility, as well as that of her organization. Companies themselves often have policies that prevent an employee from accepting a gift from a salesperson. Certainly a company has a vested interest in preventing its buyers from being bribed. Bribery can easily cause a buyer to make a purchase decision that is not based upon the merit of the product but rather on the amount of the bribe. We can conclude that special treatment and gifts can be either ethical or unethical objectively, depending on the nature of the special treatment and the amount of the gift. In terms of the subjective aspect, we have to consider whether the salesperson is aware of acceptable industry practice.

The issue of manipulation is a moral dilemma that we cannot easily resolve. The only way to deal with it is to consider that there are degrees of manipulation. Manipulation that is more likely to cause harm to a prospect is more likely to be considered morally wrong than manipulation that causes no harm. Fortunately, most persuasive attempts fall into the second category. The reason is that the prospect recognizes that the sales encounter is one involving persuasion. As a result, she is aware of how manipulation can be used.

While we can conclude that manipulation is probably not harmful to the prospect, it is important to keep in mind that many people today insist upon nonmanipulative selling. As we discussed in Chapter 1, **nonmanipulative selling** *involves selling as a mechanism of problem solving with the total absence of manipulative techniques.* This suggests that while manipulative selling may not be unethical, it is probably not considered desirable. We now turn to specific ethical issues that can arise during the various phases of the sales process.

Ethical Dilemmas with Respect to Prospecting

We have discussed the importance of prospecting. In fact, there is a great deal of pressure on a salesperson to search for and qualify prospects so that he can make productive use of his time. The prospecting methods we discussed in Chapter 6 can be regarded as *customary* techniques.

There are, however, prospecting techniques that are not customary and, possibly, of questionable morality. Consider a technique mentioned at the beginning of the chapter: using a list of prospects from a colleague. Since many companies assign salespeople to specific territories, this situation does not always occur. There are, however, a number of instances in which territories are not assigned, such as in retail selling and selling of investment services.

When territories are not assigned, is it unethical to use a colleague's list of prospects? If the list is utilized without the knowledge of the colleague, we believe that it is unethical. It is wrong because it is stealing, and stealing is regarded as wrong.

If we return to our assumptions, we can see how this is unethical. Both salesperson *A* and salesperson *B* want to satisfy their desire to make money. They know how to satisfy that desire. The first step is successful prospecting. The number of prospects is not unlimited. It is likely that these salespeople will compete; that is customary. If salesperson *A* meets with a prospect before salesperson *B*, the custom is that *B* retreats and lets *A* try his luck. It is assumed that *A* used one of the acceptable and customary techniques for prospecting. On the other hand, if *A* contacts the prospect because he has stolen the name from *B*'s list, this is a violation of the custom and can be regarded as unethical.

Further, if we consider whether the behavior is objectively versus subjectively immoral, we will see that it must be both. It is certainly objectively immoral because it involves theft, and stealing is wrong. It is likely to be subjectively immoral as well. Certainly the salesperson knows that he is taking private information surreptitiously. Therefore, it is hard to argue that it is not done intentionally. It is also hard to argue that the salesperson is unaware that he is violating a custom.

In fact, there are other customs he is violating beyond that of not stealing. He is seeking out confidential information and perusing personal property. Therefore, he is violating the norm of respecting personal privacy. Again, we have to distinguish between objective morality and subjective morality. Objectively, violating the personal property of another is wrong. Subjectively, we have to know whether the actor is doing it deliberately. Once again, however, it would be difficult to argue that a salesperson would be doing it accidentally. In addition, if he encountered the personal property of a colleague accidentally, he wouldn't have to use the information.

Moving to Another Company. Often salespeople are hired by a competitor. The prospects they had at their original company become prospects for them at their new company. Is it wrong for them to continue to sell to the same prospects? The ethics of this issue are difficult to determine. In fact, the new employer may have hired the salesperson precisely because of the potential of the salesperson's existing prospects. Is the salesperson stealing prospects from her original company? Objectively, we can't answer this question. Subjectively, the salesperson knows that she is, in fact, using the same prospects. But in this case, given customs of the particular business, this may be considered an acceptable practice. Therefore, the salesperson is not being unethical in a subjective sense. Table 15.2 summarizes the ethical issues involved in prospecting.

Ethical Dilemmas with Respect to the Preapproach

The essence of the preapproach is gathering information about the prospect. A good salesperson will collect as much information as she possibly can. However, she may collect information that puts her in the position of knowing more than she should know. In this situation, she can be faced with an ethical dilemma.

Use of Personal Information About a Prospect. A salesperson can uncover information about a prospect that could be used to force the prospect to make a purchase. For example, the prospect might be in a vulnerable position in his company. The salesperson might attempt to use this information in such a way that the prospect feels so vulnerable that he makes a purchase. It is objectively

Table 15.2 Ethical Issues Involved in Prospecting

	Ethical	*Objectively Unethical*	*Subjectively Unethical*
Competing through normal selling activities	Yes	No	No
Getting customers from another salesperson's prospect list	No	Yes	Yes
Moving to another company and taking prospects along	Uncertain	Uncertain	Uncertain

unethical to threaten someone's livelihood for personal gain. Since this must be a deliberate act, it must be subjectively unethical as well.

The salesperson may also learn personal information about the prospect that the prospect would not want repeated to anyone else. A salesperson might threaten the prospect with revealing this information if he chooses not to make a purchase. It is objectively wrong to blackmail someone. It is subjectively wrong to the extent that the person who reveals the information to someone else does so deliberately with the intention of causing harm. Table 15.3 summarizes the ethical issues involved in the preapproach.

Ethical Dilemmas with Respect to the Approach and Presentation

It is during the approach phase of the sales interaction that the salesperson has an opportunity to build rapport with a prospect. Recall from Chapter 5 that one aspect of building rapport is establishing similarity. How far should a salesperson go in communicating similarity? If his prospect has two children and he has none, is it unethical for him to say that he also has children? If his prospect enjoys golf and he enjoys tennis, is it unethical for him to say that he also plays golf?

In both of these cases, the salesperson is lying. It is objectively wrong to lie. But is this behavior unethical subjectively? While we can't provide a definitive answer, we can suggest that such a lie will not cause any harm to the prospect. Nevertheless, the salesperson is deliberately lying. In that sense, we suggest that his lie is subjectively unethical.

Failure to Divulge Information. Once the approach phase has ended, the presentation phase begins. During this phase, the content of the information, particularly its accuracy, is important.

A salesperson may learn that a particular version or model of a product she is selling is about to be replaced. If she fails to tell the prospect, she is omitting information. Omitting information is a half-truth. A half-truth can be considered unethical if it causes harm to a prospect. It is difficult to say whether it is unethical if the omission does not harm the prospect.

Often a replacement model involves nothing more than a cosmetic change or a minimal technological improvement that will have little or no impact on a

Table 15.3 Ethical Issues Involved in the Preapproach

	Ethical	*Objectively Unethical*	*Subjectively Unethical*
Use of information about the status of the prospect in the firm to harm the prospect	No	Yes	Yes
Use of personal information about the prospect as a threat	No	Yes	Yes

prospect. We suggest that omitting this information, while not desirable, is probably not objectively unethical. On the other hand, a replacement model may involve significant improvements. Failure to inform the prospect about this would more likely be objectively unethical. Deciding whether the omission is subjectively unethical is a function of whether the salesperson has the information. If the salesperson does have the information, failure to disclose it is subjectively unethical.

In an extreme case, a replacement model may be introduced because the older model is defective. In this case, selling the defective product involves not only lying but potential harm to the prospect, either directly or indirectly. It is wrong to knowingly allow harm to occur to another person. This case is a more clear-cut situation involving both objective and subjective ethics. We suggest that this action is unethical.

Using Information Manipulatively. A salesperson can certainly be privy to insider information such as a takeover or merger. This information is regarded as confidential. Objectively, it is ethically wrong to betray a confidence or to divulge confidential information. If a salesperson chooses to use this information in order to make a product or service more attractive to a prospect, is he being unethical subjectively? If the salesperson is not aware that this is confidential insider information, it could be argued that he is not behaving unethically. On the other hand, if he is aware of the nature of this information and still chooses to divulge it, he is being unethical. It should be noted that, in addition to being unethical, this behavior is illegal. Table 15.4 summarizes the ethical issues involved in the approach and presentation.

Ethical Dilemmas with Respect to Handling Objections and Closing the Sale

Handling objections involves responding directly to any expression of concern from the prospect. The most obvious forms of response range from an acknowl-

Table 15.4 Ethical Issues Involved in the Approach and Presentation

	Ethical	*Objectively Unethical*	*Subjectively Unethical*
Communicating a greater degree of similarity than actually exists	No	Yes	Uncertain
Use of an outright lie	No	Yes	Yes
Use of a half-truth	No	Uncertain	Yes
Failure to divulge information that is not critical	Uncertain	Uncertain	Yes
Failure to divulge information that is critical	No	Yes	Yes

edgement that the objection is legitimate to a statement that the objection is not legitimate. Acknowledging a legitimate objection, even when the salesperson counters the objection, is ethical.

Falsely saying that a legitimate objection is not legitimate is objectively unethical, since this involves lying. It could only be considered subjectively ethical if the salesperson genuinely thought that the objection was not legitimate. Basically, then, the ethical concern hinges upon whether the response to the objection is true or not.

Suggesting Scarcity. Bringing a sale to a close is a major concern to the salesperson. Often the salesperson is inclined to force the issue in ethically questionable ways. For example, a salesperson can introduce the notion of *scarcity.* We discussed this in Chapter 12. When a salesperson utilizes scarcity, she communicates that the prospect must hurry to make his purchase decision because there is a limited supply or because a discount will soon be discontinued. Using scarcity is not ethically wrong if it is legitimate. It is ethically wrong if it is not legitimate because it constitutes a lie.

Pressuring the prospect to make a decision through any tactic is a form of manipulation. Again, it is difficult to state conclusively that this tactic is morally right or wrong. Any prospect foresees that he might be pressured to make a decision. For this reason, the prospect is not likely to be harmed by this kind of manipulation. It can reasonably be concluded that, since both parties have a general knowledge of the sales process, manipulative behavior designed to lead to a close that does not bring harm to either party is not unethical. Table 15.5 summarizes the ethical concerns in handling objections and the close.

Ethical Issues That Are Not a Direct Part of the Sales Process

It is not only the sales process that is ripe for ethical dilemmas. Unethical behaviors can also occur in dealing with competitors and employers. While some of

Table 15.5 Ethical Issues in Handling Objections and the Close

	Ethical	*Objectively Unethical*	*Subjectively Unethical*
Acknowledging that an objection is legitimate and countering it	Yes	No	No
Stating that a legitimate objection does not exist	No	Yes	Uncertain
Suggesting that scarcity exists when it does not	No	Yes	Uncertain
Manipulatively pressuring the prospect to close	Uncertain	Uncertain	Uncertain

these behaviors can be indirectly related to the sales process itself, any potential damage falls more on the competitors and the employer than on the prospect.

Ethical Issues with Respect to Competitors

If a salesperson were lucky enough to be selling a one-of-a-kind product, the issue of competition would not exist. Of course, the salesperson's job would not be particularly challenging either. Usually the salesperson is selling a product for which there are many alternatives. Some of these alternatives are better than others.

It would simplify the salesperson's life if most of these alternatives did not exist. For that reason, there might be a tendency for an occasional salesperson to at least prevent these alternatives from existing in the prospect's mind. The easiest way to do this is to lie about a competitor's product. We have already talked about ethical concerns with respect to lying to the prospect.

Devious Methods of Learning About a Competitor's Product. Unfortunately, lying about a competitor's product is relatively minor compared to certain other ethical violations. These practices include learning the contents of secret bids by bribing secretaries or spying on the competitors. These behaviors are morally wrong objectively as well as subjectively. It is objectively wrong to bribe people, and it is wrong to spy. It seems clear that a salesperson engaging in these behaviors would be doing so deliberately. Therefore, these actions would be morally wrong subjectively as well.

Tampering with a Competitor's Product Displays. Another practice is tampering with competitors' product displays. Often companies have point-of-purchase displays in retail outlets. A few unethical salespeople have been known to damage these displays. Similar attempts have involved displays at trade shows. Destroying the property of someone else is morally wrong objectively. Since the act of destruction must be deliberate, it is also morally wrong subjectively. Rather than directly tampering with the product, some salespeople have gone so far as to pose as prospects and complain about competitive offerings to a competitor's distributor. This, too, undermines the product, although less directly than tampering with a display. Table 15.6 summarizes the ethical concerns of dealing with competitors.

Table 15.6 Ethical Issues with Respect to Competitors

	Ethical	*Objectively Unethical*	*Subjectively Unethical*
Obtaining information by bribing secretaries	No	Yes	Yes
Posing as a prospect	No	Yes	Yes
Tampering with product displays	No	Yes	Yes

Ethical Dilemmas with Respect to Employers

Dealing with an employer is a situation ripe for exceeding the bounds of ethical behavior. People often view an employer as impersonal and unresponsive to the individual. For this reason, they justify engaging in behaviors that are unethical.

Moonlighting. Consider, first, the issue of hours and accountability. Remember that the salesperson has a unique job in that she is not accountable on a daily basis to an employer the way many other professional people are. Employers vary in their policies of salesperson accountability, but there are many situations in which the salesperson can, if she chooses, moonlight. *Moonlighting* is the practice of having two jobs. Because of the lack of supervision in many selling jobs, it is possible for a salesperson to work on her second job during the time she is supposed to be working as a salesperson. That means that she is being paid by one employer to collect money from another employer.

The question becomes, is this ethical? This is not an easy question to answer. From the employer's perspective, it is unethical. It may also violate company policy, in which case it is not only unethical but becomes grounds for dismissal. From the salesperson's perspective, it may not appear so unethical. If the salesperson can do a good job in both positions but feels that she needs extra money to support her family and home, she can certainly justify moonlighting. The probability is, however, that the salesperson will not be able to perform two jobs as well as she can perform one.

If the salesperson works on her second job *on her own time*, moonlighting could be viewed as objectively ethical. On the other hand, if the salesperson works on her second job *on the company's time*, it should be viewed as objectively unethical. Whether or not moonlighting is unethical subjectively is more difficult to determine, particularly if the salesperson genuinely feels that she can perform well in both jobs.

Contests. Another area of potential abuse is the *company-sponsored contest.* Employers often try to motivate their salespeople by sponsoring contests. Salespeople who sell the greatest volume win. That seems straightforward enough.

However, some salespeople have discovered ways to ensure that they win the contest. Unfortunately, these methods go beyond simply trying to sell the product in the normal fashion. For example, if the contest deals with August sales, it is possible for a salesperson not to submit his July orders until August so that it appears that both his July and August orders occurred in August. Obviously, that gives him a tremendous edge over people who don't choose to do this. Another ploy is for a salesperson to convince a good customer to order more than she needs. Once the contest is over, the customer is allowed to return the excess merchandise at no penalty.

These two practices are clearly unethical objectively because they involve cheating as well as lying. Because they involve deliberate planning, they must also be regarded as subjectively unethical. If enough people in an organization engage in these practices, those who choose to remain ethical have no chance of winning the contest. They, too, may decide that the only way they can compete is to engage in the same unethical behavior. Thus, unethical behavior can spiral into a very serious situation.

Travel and Entertainment Benefits. Many companies provide a company car for use by a salesperson *when the salesperson is engaged in selling activities.* Similarly, many companies provide expense accounts so that the salesperson can take clients out to lunch or dinner or even to an entertainment event *when the primary purpose of the meeting is business.* Salespeople often have to travel a great deal, and company expense accounts pay for their lodging and meals. These benefits are subject to abuse in a number of ways.

The company car can be misused as a form of personal transportation or a second car for another family member, rather than existing simply for business purposes. Similarly, the expense account can be misused to pay for lavish lunches that have nothing to do with business. Such practices are a form of theft and, as such, are objectively unethical. Since it is likely that company policy will clearly indicate how travel and entertainment benefits are to be used, if they are misused, it can be assumed that the salesperson is aware of the situation. Therefore, we consider these practices to be subjectively unethical. Table 15.7 summarizes the ethical issues with respect to employers.

Ethical Behavior and the Self-Concept

In Chapter 16, we introduce the notion of **self-concept.** Your self-concept is *your attitude about yourself.* This attitude is a function of a variety of experiences that you have. For example, if you consistently get *A*'s in your college courses, you may feel competent and smart. If others consider you a competent person, this attitude will heighten your feeling of competence. Eventually, your self-concept will include the belief that you are a competent person.

Table 15.7 Ethical Issues with Respect to Employers

	Ethical	*Objectively Unethical*	*Subjectively Unethical*
Moonlighting on person's own time	Uncertain	Uncertain	Uncertain
Moonlighting during time paid by employer	No	Yes	Uncertain
Misreporting of monthly sales or getting a customer to order more than is necessary to win a contest	No	Yes	Yes
Use of a company car for personal use	No	Yes	Yes
Use of an expense account for personal use	No	Yes	Yes

This is generally true of many other situations. Our self-concept may include such descriptions as *attractive, ugly, easy to get along with, difficult, fun, intelligent, boring, fascinating, honest, straightforward, happy, moody, deceptive, trusting, fair, standoffish,* or *hard-working.* Most people prefer to have a positive attitude about themselves rather than a negative attitude. In other words, most people prefer to have a positive self-concept rather than a negative self-concept. Thus, we are more comfortable describing ourselves as happy than as moody. We are also more comfortable describing ourselves as honest than as deceptive. And, of course, we are more comfortable describing ourselves as ethical than as unethical.

We all have to live with ourselves. This is much easier and more pleasant if our self-concepts are positive. While ethical behavior is only one part of a self-concept, it does touch on other parts, such as honesty, trustworthiness, truthfulness, and fairness. We suggest, then, that if for no other reason, ethical behavior is worthwhile because it contributes to a positive self-concept.

Putting It All Together

The key points made in this chapter are summarized as follows:

- The study of ethics is essentially a study of customs.
- When we consider ethics, we are really concerned with making moral decisions regarding what is right and wrong.
- Defining what is right or wrong hinges upon the assumption that we are all free to pursue what we desire as long as we do not interfere with other people who are doing the same thing.
- Lying, stealing, cheating, murder, and destruction of another's property can interfere with someone else's ability to pursue his own desires, and for that reason, they are considered wrong, hence, immoral and unethical.
- There are two kinds of morality: objective and subjective.
- Objective morality refers to what is acceptable from the perspective of the society.
- Subjective morality refers to an individual's awareness of a particular act; a person who deliberately engages in something he knows to be wrong is subjectively immoral.
- There are many opportunities for the salesperson to make decisions regarding what is right or wrong, often during the selling process.
- Lying and manipulation are two major forms of unethical behavior that can occur during any phase of the selling process.
- Outright lies that distort facts are clearly unethical as well as illegal.
- Half-truths that omit certain information can also be unethical if the omitted information results in harm to the prospect.
- Exaggeration is probably not unethical, since it represents a salesperson's opinions, and prospects understand that a salesperson may be inclined to exaggerate.

- The persuasive process itself, even though it can involve manipulation, is probably not unethical since both the prospect and salesperson understand and expect manipulation to occur.
- Prospecting can be unethical if it involves knowingly taking prospects from a colleague, but it is probably not unethical for a salesperson to take prospects with her if she goes to another company.
- Using personal information about a prospect to force the prospect into making a sale is unethical.
- Presenting false or inaccurate information, while subjectively unethical, is objectively unethical only if it causes harm to a prospect.
- Unethical behavior can also occur outside of the actual selling process and includes such things as spying on a competitor, tampering with a competitor's product displays, moonlighting while working on another employer's time, or abusing travel and entertainment benefits.

The concern about ethics has taken on much greater importance in recent years due to the proliferation of unethical and illegal business activities on Wall Street and elsewhere. The salesperson has an especially strong responsibility to try to maintain the highest ethical standards.

Most salespeople are ethical. But, as in any other area, a few unethical salespeople receive a great deal of public attention. Even those few salespeople who engage in unethical behavior would do well to consider the impact of their behavior on their reputations.

While behaving unethically can lead to immediate sales, this is true only in the short term. Over time, people who consistently behave unethically see their reputations suffer. On the other hand, people who consistently behave in accordance with the highest ethical standards see their reputations enhanced. A favorable reputation will do more to create sales and overall success on a long-term basis than any amount of unethical behavior.

Key Terms

Ethics
Manners
Morality
Subjective morality
Objective morality
Right
Norm of morality
Outright lie
Fact
Half-truth
Puffery
Manipulation
Nonmanipulative selling
Self-concept

Review Questions

1. What is meant by ethics?
2. What is the difference between subjective morality and objective morality?

3. What are the three assumptions that form the basis of knowing right from wrong?
4. What is the definition of right?
5. What is a good way to know whether or not something is unethical?
6. What are the three kinds of misrepresentation? Are they all unethical?
7. What is manipulation? Is it unethical?
8. What are the ethical dilemmas with respect to prospecting?
9. What are the ethical dilemmas with respect to the preapproach?
10. What are the ethical dilemmas with respect to the approach and presentation?
11. What are the ethical dilemmas with respect to handling objections and closing the sale?
12. What are the ethical dilemmas with respect to competitors?
13. What are the ethical dilemmas with respect to one's employer?
14. How is ethics related to the self-concept?

Discussion Questions

1. Why is it important to make a distinction between objective morality and subjective morality?
2. Do the norms of morality of the United States apply in all countries? How might a salesperson run into difficulty in a country that had different norms of morality?
3. It is difficult to determine whether or not exaggeration and mild forms of manipulation are ethical, yet salespeople often resort to these tactics. Can you propose a way of making a clear-cut distinction so that it would be possible to decide when exaggeration and manipulation are or are not ethical?
4. What traits could a prospective employer look for in a salesperson in order to predict whether the salesperson will be ethical? Why do you think that someone who has every reason to behave in an ethical manner would choose to behave unethically?

CASE 15.1

Jim James has been working as a salesperson for 2 years. He sells professional video equipment to organizations that use video for training, as well as to organizations whose business is totally dependent upon video equipment.

Jim failed to fill his quota during his first year with the company. One reason for his failure is that he didn't work too hard. He used his free time to relax and enjoy the nice weather. He is far from meeting his quota as his second year comes to an end, and he knows that if he fails again, he will probably lose his job.

He can make a sale of over $230,000 if he makes a deal with the XYZ Company. XYZ is negotiating with Jim. The company, however, expects something in return.

The purchasing manager has made it clear that Jim should do something

continued

for him and his family as a goodwill gesture. Jim admits to himself that he can be lazy. But he also prides himself on being honest. He doesn't think that it's right to give the equivalent of a kickback.

He discusses the issue with Carol Ames, his sales manager. Carol explains that this happens all the time and that as far as she is concerned, as long as he keeps it quiet, it's acceptable to her. After all, a trip to Hawaii doesn't hurt anyone. All it does is to make the purchasing manager happy and a likely prospect for a repeat purchase.

This situation is making Jim uncomfortable. To make matters worse, he has just learned from a fellow salesperson that a lot of salespeople in this industry compete by forcing shorts in a company's current equipment so that the company will be more likely to switch to a different brand. He also discusses this with Carol. Carol finds it very disturbing and argues that it is unethical. She asks Jim to report to her anyone whom he knows engages in this action.

Jim is somewhat confused. He certainly has a motivation to give a kickback; his job is at stake. But he wonders how he can continue to function if he has to confront even more blatantly unethical behavior such as forcing shorts in a prospect's current equipment. Jim wonders where this unethical behavior stops.

1. Could it be argued that if everyone gives kickbacks, this is customary and, hence, ethical? If it is ethical, should Jim go along with the purchasing manager's expectation of special treatment? Should he do so if it is unethical?
2. Can we distinguish between kickbacks and tampering with equipment, so that we can argue that one is more unethical than the other? Explain.
3. If you were a career counselor, what would you advise Jim to do about the situation he is confronting? What would you advise him to do regarding his job in general?
4. Do you think Carol is behaving ethically? Why?

References

1. Chonko, L. B., and J. J. Burnett. (1983). Measuring the importance of ethical situations as a source of role conflict: A survey of salespeople, sales managers, and sales support personnel. *Journal of Personal Selling and Sales Management, 3*, 41–47.

2. Fagothey, A. (1972). *Right and Reason.* St. Louis: Mosby, p. 1.

3. Cooney, T. J. (1985). *Telling Right from Wrong.* Buffalo: Prometheus Books.

4. Hunt, S. D., V. R. Wood, and L. B. Chonko. (1989). Corporate ethical values and organizational commitment in marketing. *Journal of Marketing, 53*, 79–90.

5. Bellizzi, J. A., and R. E. Hite. (1989). Supervising unethical salesforce behavior. *Journal of Marketing, 53*, 36–47.

6. Futrell, C. (1987). *Sales Management.* Chicago: Dryden.

7. Weilbacher, W. M. (1984). *Advertising.* New York: Macmillan.

8. Anderson, R. E., J. E. Hair, and A. J. Bush. (1988). *Professional Sales Management.* New York: McGraw-Hill.

9. Friedman, J. A. (1986). A traveler's guide to gifts and bribes. *Harvard Business Review,* (July–August), 122–136.

PART SIX

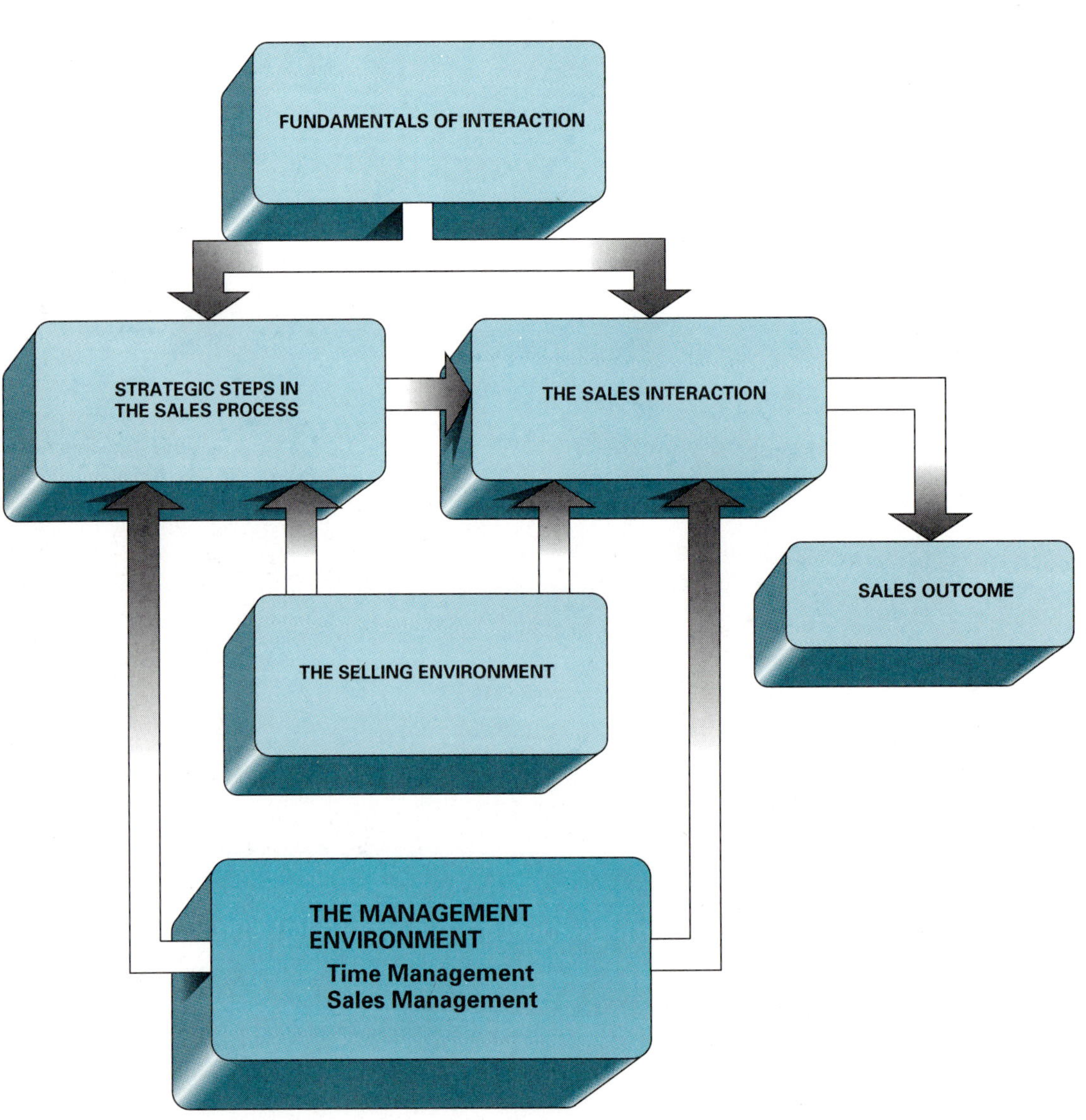
FUNDAMENTALS OF INTERACTION
STRATEGIC STEPS IN THE SALES PROCESS
THE SALES INTERACTION
SALES OUTCOME
THE SELLING ENVIRONMENT
THE MANAGEMENT ENVIRONMENT
Time Management
Sales Management

THE MANAGEMENT ENVIRONMENT

16

Self, Time, and Territory Management

CHAPTER OBJECTIVES

In this chapter, you will learn:

The way you feel about yourself will affect your work, and vice versa.

The more positively you feel about yourself, the more productively you will use your time.

Stress, procrastination, fear of failure, and impatience can cause you to feel negatively about yourself.

To manage time effectively, you have to turn sales goals into specific tasks that will allow you to achieve those goals.

The typical salesperson spends only one-third of his time actually selling.

Most of a salesperson's time is spent on various administrative tasks and on such things as planning and travel.

Planning one's time often begins with a detailed analysis of activities which prioritizes the more important and urgent tasks.

Most salespeople have specific territories they must cover.

Twenty percent of a salesperson's accounts usually generate eighty percent of a salesperson's business.

Routing for a salesperson is based upon the same logic we provide for ourselves when we have a number of errands to run.

CHAPTER OUTLINE

A Sales Challenge

Imagine that you have just been hired as a salesperson by the XYZ Company. You've completed a 1-month training program, and you are now ready to go out into the field. This means calling on medium-sized and large corporations to sell business forms. That seems relatively straightforward.

It's the Sunday before your first day on the job, and suddenly it occurs to you that you don't know what to do with your time on Monday. Should you call and make appointments? Should you show up at companies? Should you plan your presentation in case you have appointments? But how much time should you allow for each appointment? How much time should you allow for travel between appointments? When will you organize your paperwork? When will you contact the head office in case you need to have orders filled?

An Overview

A major concern we all share is how to organize our time. You already have an inkling of how difficult that is if you are a full-time student. How do you decide when to study and when to write? What about that movie you want to see? How will you manage to get to your 8 A.M. class on time? Once again, the central problem is how to organize your time.

If you organize your time incorrectly, whether at school or on the job, the results can be disastrous. For example, if you don't have enough time to study, you will fail your exam. If you insist on watching late-night television, you will probably miss your early-morning class.

If, as a salesperson, you don't leave enough time between appointments, you will be late for some of them. And being late is likely to cost you a sale, if not completely eliminate the prospect as a potential one for you. On the other hand, if you have too much time between appointments, you will end up wasting time unless you can fit in other tasks, such as processing orders or setting up other appointments.

The salesperson has a unique situation in terms of time management. Most professionals have an office to go to, and their time is fairly rigidly structured. By contrast, salespeople usually function independently and do not have such structure. They have to provide it for themselves. In this chapter, we discuss time management. As you will see, this issue is also directly related to territory management.

Both time and territory management rest on something even more fundamental: your attitude toward your work and toward yourself. Success in any endeavor depends to a great extent upon knowledge and competence. But no matter how competent you are, your underlying attitudes about yourself and how you feel about your work may be the most important determinant of success. For that reason, we begin with a discussion of work- and self-related attitudes. Then

A clock is a major fact of life for any salesperson. The concern is how to use it in the most efficient way. (© Frank Siteman/Taurus Photos.)

we discuss how to manage your time and your territory. All of the questions we posed at the beginning of this chapter will fall into place and will be answered as we proceed.

Attitudes About Your Work and About Yourself

You can't expect to manage either your time or your territory unless you can first feel good about yourself. The reason is that you have to have a positive feeling about yourself before you can be motivated to manage your time and territory effectively. The best indicator of how you feel about yourself is your self-concept.

Self-Concept

Your **self-concept** is *your attitude about yourself.* It is composed of various traits that you consider yourself to have. For example, if you think of yourself as assertive, likable, honest, and straightforward, you should have a positive self-concept. On the other hand, if you think of yourself as shy, friendless, untrustworthy, and lazy, you should have a negative self-concept. Table 16.1 is a short test that allows you to evaluate your self-concept.

To evaluate yourself on the test in Table 16.1, give yourself one point each for agreeing with items 1, 2, 4, 6, and 7 and 1 point each for disagreeing with items 3, 5, 8, 9, and 10. The closer your score is to 10, the highest possible score, the higher your self-esteem and the better your self-concept.

The Relationship Between Self-Concept and Work

Basically, the more positive your self-concept, the more successful you will be as a salesperson. In fact, a positive self-concept is especially important for a salesperson because of the nature of his job.

A salesperson often works independently. He doesn't usually have a supervisor looking over his shoulder. As a result, he has to be self-motivated and ambitious. A salesperson also has to be prepared to be rejected through no fault of his own. For example, he can't control product design, advertising programs, or economic fluctuations. As a result, he has to be able to withstand rejection and to be assertive. All of these requirements demand a positive self-concept.

Your self-concept is intertwined with your occupation. For example, one aspect of your self-concept has to do with how competent you think you are. Competence is determined by how effective you think you are at your work. If you are successful, you will feel competent. That competence will be a positive contributor to your self-concept, and you will be motivated to display even greater competence, which will make you more successful. This is a pattern in which self-concept and work performance reinforce each other.

Table 16.1 A Test to Evaluate Your Self-Concept*

1. I feel that I'm a person of worth, at least on an equal basis with others.
2. I feel that I have a number of good qualities.
3. All in all, I am inclined to feel that I am a failure.
4. I am able to do things as well as most other people.
5. I feel I do not have much to be proud of.
6. I take a positive attitude toward myself.
7. On the whole, I am satisfied with myself.
8. I wish I could have more respect for myself.
9. I certainly feel useless at times.
10. At times I think I am no good at all.

* See text for explanation of test scoring method.

Source: Reprinted by permission of Princeton University Press © 1965. M. Rosenberg. (1965). *Society and the Adolescent Self-Image.* NJ: Princeton University Press.

EXHIBIT 16.1

How to Gain Back Confidence Once It Has Been Lost

Almost anyone, including salespeople, can lose confidence. This can happen, for example, when sales from steady customers are lost, or when the company is in a slump, or when there just isn't enough money around the house.

When self-confidence does begin to get shaky, the last thing you should do is question your ability. Robert E. Eastman, the author of *The Winning Edge in Selling*, argues that "it is essential to build your confidence—bounce back . . . after a string of losses." Eastman offers a plan to gain back your confidence. The plan has six points as follows:

1. Assume that you are doing something wrong.
2. Reexamine and carefully study all facets of your sales methods.
3. Discuss your lost sales with a respected associate, your sales manager and possibly your spouse.
4. Avoid justifying the losses by blaming customers, blaming the competition or putting the flaw to your product.
5. Find some sparkling-new elements to work into your selling.
6. And—it's simple, but infallible—augment your work schedule. Give it more hours, more thought, more calls. Reduce your pleasure time until you are firmly back on the track.

Source: Adapted from B. Kelley. (1984). The confidence game. *Industrial Distribution, 73,* 43.

They can also reinforce each other in a negative way. If you have a negative self-concept, you may feel incompetent. If you feel incompetent, you may not be very effective in your work. That, in turn, will heighten your feeling of incompetence, which will further lower your self-concept. Once again, a pattern emerges.

The Relationship Between Self-Concept and Time

The issue of self-concept is directly related to how you structure your time. As a salesperson, it is up to you to construct your day and make it work for you. If you don't feel good about what you have to do that day, you will not be strongly motivated to structure your day so that it is productive. That, in turn, will further lower your self-concept, which, in turn, will cause you to be unmotivated to structure the next day, and so on. As Table 16.2 shows, your feelings about yourself and about your work are so tied together that a vicious cycle can start if either of these factors turns negative.

Compare Table 16.2 to Table 16.3, in which the same cycle begins on a positive note.

It is not surprising that our self-concept is so closely intertwined with our competence at work that it is difficult to separate them. In our culture, our worth

Table 16.2 The Negative Interplay of Self- and Work-Related Attitudes

You have a lowered self-concept (e.g., depressed because of loss of a sale the previous day).
You can't manage to accomplish much on Monday.
You feel more negative about yourself because nothing was accomplished on Monday.
You feel even worse, so you can't accomplish much on Tuesday.
You feel even worse about yourself because nothing was accomplished on Tuesday.

.
.
.

By Friday, you are so depressed that you feel terrible about yourself because you are failing at your job.
You live in dread of facing Monday.

is determined in large part by our work and by how successful we are at our chosen profession. While it is difficult to determine which comes first, your attitude about your work or your attitude about yourself, for the sake of argument, let's assume that it is your attitude about your work. To ensure that you maintain a positive attitude about your work, it is useful to list some potential pitfalls that are especially likely to affect a salesperson because of the special nature of the salesperson's job.

Obstacles to Success: Things That Can Cause a Salesperson to Have a Negative Self-Concept

Edward Barkas[1] suggests a number of obstacles to success and how they can be overcome. Ross Webber[2] also offers a number of obstacles. They include (1) stress, (2) procrastination, (3) fear of failure, and (4) impatience. We discuss each of these briefly.

Table 16.3 The Positive Interplay between Self- and Work-Related Attitudes

You have a very productive Monday (even though you lost a sale on Friday).
You feel pretty good about yourself (i.e., you have an improved self-concept).
You are particularly motivated to have an even more productive Tuesday, and you accomplish that goal.
You feel even better about yourself.

.
.
.

By Friday, you are on a roll and have a great day.
You feel that you are a success, and it shows. You really look forward to Monday so that you can continue your success.

Stress. Stress is a major concern in today's fast-paced world. As a beginning, then, the most important thing you can do is *relax.* People who are relaxed are more likely to feel better about themselves and have a greater sense of control over their lives. In fact, it is well documented that stress, the opposite of being relaxed, takes a major toll on people both in terms of their efficiency and in terms of their psychological and physical well-being.

Having a great deal of time on your hands or, at the other extreme, having too little time to accomplish what you need to do, can cause a great deal of stress. Depression or worry can cause stress. Even being in love can cause stress, as can family problems. While it is not realistic to create a life with no stress, there are ways to deal with stress when it does occur. One important method is to make a deliberate attempt to relax your body. Barkas suggests such things as eating well, exercising, planning, or doing an optional activity that is of interest.[3] The important thing is to reduce stress as much as possible.

In fact, managing stress is a major concern for many people who work under pressure. Certainly salespeople work under pressure, and they need to deal with the resulting stress. Many companies understand the need to manage stress, and they have instituted exercise programs as one method of reducing it. Meditation and formal relaxation techniques are also very effective. Stress management must

A good way to manage stress is to have a formal exercise program. (© J. Berndt/ Stock Boston.)

be employed regularly and consistently. In other words, it must be built into the salesperson's daily routine.

Procrastination. Procrastination is something we all probably know too well. It occurs whenever we do something, especially something pleasurable, when we should be doing something else. As a salesperson, you might find it easier and more pleasant to talk on the phone with a friend than to call strangers and try to arrange appointments so that you can try to make a sale.

There are a number of ways to cure procrastination. One is to reward yourself when you have done what you should do. An even better way is to do obligatory activities first during the day. You can also set aside time to procrastinate. Thus, if you like to read magazines, allow yourself 1 hour in the afternoon to read them after you have accomplished your work-related tasks.

Fear of Failure. We all harbor some fear of failure. This fear is probably even more significant for a salesperson than it is for many other professionals because salespeople continually face possible rejection in the form of a lost sale. Unfortunately, one way to deal with a fear of failure is not to put oneself in a position where one can fail (i.e., not to try).

A much better way to overcome this fear is to become accomplished and competent. Your own sense of accomplishment will itself diminish this fear. However, it is inevitable that you will fail occasionally. The best way to handle this situation is to change your response to failure. Be realistic and say to yourself, "I can't expect to succeed all the time, and an occasional rejection allows me the opportunity to learn and do things differently the next time." You can also remind yourself about what we said earlier: Failure to make a sale can often occur through no fault of your own.

Impatience. We all tend to want immediate results. When that is all we want, we become impatient. Our impatience causes us to hurry others and pay little attention to what they say. That itself can be a problem if we are dealing with a prospect and fail to listen to her.

There is no easy way to force oneself to become patient. The best approach is simply to consider what you are doing as a process rather than an outcome. That process should be viewed as important and enjoyable in itself, no matter what the outcome. This attitude is not necessarily easy to achieve, but a good time to start is the next time you find yourself becoming impatient. For example, if being put on hold as you are waiting to speak to a prospect makes you impatient, use the time to plan what you will say. You can also glance at your calendar or handle paperwork. If you consistently do such things, you will find your general level of impatience start to decrease. Figure 16.1 summarizes the obstacles to success and the suggestions for their resolution.

There are a number of other obstacles that you need to be on the lookout for, since they, too, can interfere with your success. For example, overreacting to events and continually complaining can waste a lot of time and make you angry and anxious. Similarly, overreacting to criticism can make you feel threatened and

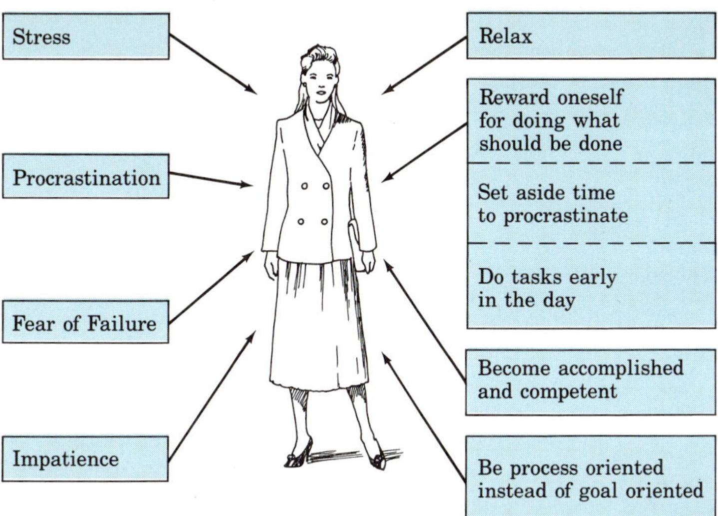

FIGURE 16.1 The salesperson's obstacles to success and their resolution.

interfere with your ability to work. In both cases, the best way to handle the situation is to try to evaluate things carefully and take them in stride—*relax.*

Now that we have discussed obstacles to success and how to overcome them, we assume that you are in the right frame of mind to pursue your career goals. Those career goals, of course, have to be broken down into more tangible goals that can be accomplished on a particular day. The process of identifying daily goals is the beginning of how to manage your time effectively.

Time Management

To begin managing your time, you have to turn big goals into little ones. This is what a company does when it turns its broad goals into specific goals for an individual salesperson. This is also what a salesperson must do when she turns her broad goal of generating sales on an annual basis to the specific daily goals or tasks that will cause that to happen.

Determining Goals

Almost all companies have broad goals based upon expected sales revenues. However, it would be virtually impossible for a salesperson to manage his time based upon broad company sales goals, since those goals are far removed from the goals of the individual salesperson. From those company goals, however, it is possible to develop goals for each salesperson through a number of intermediate steps. Think of a pyramid that reaches a point, and that point represents the goals of the individual salesperson. This is depicted in Figure 16.2.

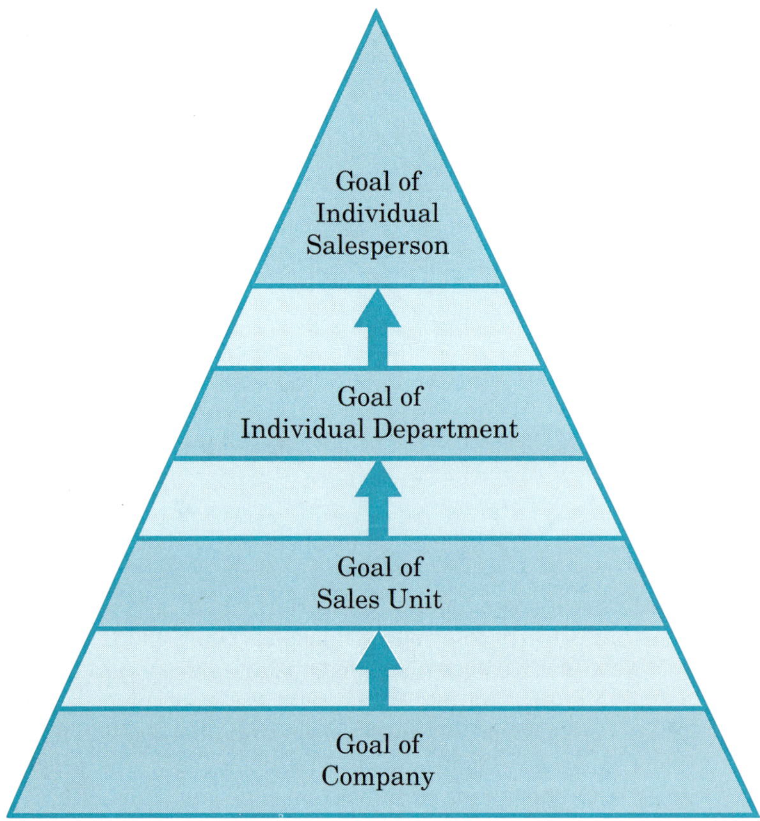

FIGURE 16.2 From company goals to salesperson's goals.

Goals as Sales Quotas. As a salesperson, it is very likely that you will have to fulfill a quota. That quota is determined on a basis similar to that of the pyramid in Figure 16.2. As suggested, a company will have a sales forecast. That forecast will be based upon a number of things, including the following:

1. An understanding of general economic conditions.
2. The industry's total market potential for a particular product category.
3. A forecast of the sales of the actual product.[4]

This forecast will be based upon expert judgment and various forecasting methods. While it is understood that forecasting is not an exact science, the company's forecast will have implications regarding what the salesperson is expected to accomplish.

From the company's forecast, responsibilities will be parceled out to individual departments (depending upon how the company is organized). The sales managers will become involved and will determine what sales are expected of their individual units. Finally, quotas will be established for individual salespeople based upon what is expected of each unit.

Once those quotas are established, the salesperson has an actual sales goal to accomplish. This goal is the benchmark upon which the salesperson's success or failure will be based. But it is really a broad, long-term goal. Through a funneling procedure similar to what the company does, the sales goal can be reduced to specific goals that can be accomplished in the short term. It is up to the salesperson to break down the sales goal into these specific goals and allocate the appropriate time and effort to them.

Allocation of Time to Specific Goals That Comprise Selling

The specific goals that lead to the sales goal refer to the daily routine tasks involved in selling. The first thing we need to do, then, is to determine what these tasks are.

The most obvious task for the salesperson is face-to-face selling. That activity is the one that is most challenging and very likely the most rewarding. Surprisingly, however, it is not necessarily the task that has the greatest amount of time allocated to it. Generally, less than one-half of a salesperson's time, and often less than one-third, is spent in actual face-to-face selling. Today, in fact, actual selling hours are becoming fewer and fewer.

Basically, we can distinguish two major categories of a salesperson's time: **selling activities** and **nonselling activities.** More time is now being spent on nonselling activities. According to Howard A. Berrian,[5] we can further divide nonselling activities into **organizational activities** and **investment activities.** That leaves us with three essential categories in which to allocate time. Table 16.4 shows these activities and the percentage of time generally allotted to each one.

The Role of Planning

Needless to say, the role of planning is critical in managing time. The 20 percent of time spent on selling activity will not happen if appointments are not arranged to begin with. This means that it is crucial to use nonselling time efficiently. You may, for example, accomplish some organizational activity during investment time. Thus, if you are waiting for an appointment, you can work on correspondence.

Table 16.4 The Major Tasks of the Salesperson

Selling Activities

Selling time (20%) (also referred to as *payoff time*): the time spent with a potential or current prospect.

Nonselling Activities

Organizational time (25%): the time devoted to preparing reports, handling correspondence, and various other administrative tasks such as filing.

Investment time (55%): time spent traveling, waiting for appointments, setting up appointments, and servicing accounts.

EXHIBIT 16.2

Salespeople Spend Almost Half of Their Time on Routine Activities

"Even good salespeople sometimes get locked into a routine that costs them commissions and robs their companies of new business. They travel their sales territories as a habit each week and miss opportunities for new customers. . . . In an average day, a salesperson may spend only half an hour prospecting for new business. The rest of the time is spent in nonsales activities or in servicing existing accounts."

Interestingly, while salespeople say they spend only about 9% of their time trying to get new acounts, their sales managers think they spend 27% of their time doing this. Salespeople say that they spend 43% of their time on "routine." Routine includes such things as "paperwork, reports, meetings, etc."

Source: Adapted from H. L. Mathews. (1985). Sales reps spend 43% of time on "routine" activities: Survey. *Marketing News, 19*(6), 4.

Or, if you are traveling by train or plane, you can engage in a host of organizational activities.

Thinking in Terms of the Future. The key to planning is to think in terms of the *future.*[6] There is often a tendency to think only in terms of the present. Yet a simple adjustment in thinking toward the future will lead to a natural path of planning.

As you might expect, you have to define what you mean by the future. The best way to think about this is to go back and consider the funnel of goals discussed earlier. Recall that the goals become progressively more specific as you near the narrow point of that funnel. When you think about the future, you need to keep in mind the broad, long-term goals as well as the more specific weekly ones. The former are referred to as **high-payoff activities** and the latter are referred to as **low-payoff activities.**[7]

A long-term goal may be defined in terms of a year or more and would probably have to do with your total sales quota. To achieve that quota, however, you must make specific daily plans that often will not result in an immediate payoff such as a sale. But eventually, some of the daily encounters will lead to a sale, and the sum total of those sales will allow you to achieve your long-term goal. The point is that low-payoff activities should not be viewed as ends in themselves. We continually need to link them to high-payoff activities that are more future oriented.

This is the same thing you must do as a student. A low-payoff activity, such as reading a chapter early on in the term, contributes to a higher-payoff activity such as a final examination. Successfully completing a course, a low-payoff activity, contributes to your receiving a degree, a high-payoff activity. One of the problems we all have, whether we are in school or selling in the field, is that we tend to find low-payoff activities less enjoyable and may even neglect them. If, however, we keep in mind the high-payoff activity to which the low-payoff activities are related, our view of them becomes very different and they take on added importance and meaning. Table 16.5 shows the relationship between low- and high-payoff activities.

Specific Techniques for Planning Time

Since planning your time is such an important activity, it is often necessary to do it in a formal way rather than just making a casual mental list of how you will spend a given day. This means compiling lists and creating logs.

Activity Analysis. A particularly good way to plan your activities is to follow Joseph Trickett's activity analysis.[8] This analysis is a bit more complicated than some, but it has been found to be very effective and it has important applications for a salesperson. This analysis requires not one list, but five, as follows:

1. A list of all activities that are part of your job. As a salesperson, then, you would include most if not all of the following:

   Talking to a new prospect to try to make a sale.
   Checking secondary sources of information for new leads.
   Checking that orders have been filled as promised.
   Talking to a customer to be certain that the person is satisfied.
   Arranging appointments.
   Determining how best to travel from one appointment to the next (i.e., routing yourself in the most efficient manner).
   Handling paperwork (including correspondence, filing, and preparation for advertising).
   Maintaining contact with the home office and your supervisor.

Table 16.5 The Relationship Between Low-Payoff and High-Payoff Activities

Low-Payoff Activities	*High-Payoff Activities*
Having a date	Getting married
Eating a healthy lunch	Lowering your cholesterol level
Arranging an appointment	Adding to your list of prospects
Getting a new prospect	Making a sale
Making a sale	Exceeding the sales quota
Checking up on a customer who has made a purchase	Building customer loyalty
Making sure that the home office processes a new order	Earning the trust of customers
Reading new product information	Becoming an expert in the field

Preparing for sales demonstrations.
Reading product literature.
Traveling.

Notice that this list is not concerned with the order of importance of these activities. All you need be concerned with is trying to come up with a list of all your activities associated with selling.

2. Activity analysis for intrinsic importance. This list has four columns:

   Activities that are very important and must be done.
   Activities that are important and should be done.
   Activities that are not so important, but are useful even though they are not necessary.
   Activities that are unimportant and can be eliminated.

   In order to complete this list, take all the activities from list 1 and put them into one of the four columns in list 2. It is important that each activity appear under only one heading. It is also important that you have some activities under each heading.

3. Activity analysis for urgency. This list also contains four columns:

   Very urgent, must be done now.
   Urgent, should be done soon.
   Not urgent, long-range.
   Time not a factor.

   Again, take each activity on list 1, and place it in one of these categories. Each category should have some activities.

4. Activity analysis for delegation. Here the purpose is to decide what you should do yourself versus what you can delegate. Before doing this, you need to compare the second and third lists you have just completed. The activities that end up in both the "very important, must be done" column and the "very urgent, must be done now" column should be completed by you.

   In this list, you begin with a column headed "must be done by me." The activities just referred to that end up in the left-hand column from the previous two lists would be placed in the "must be done by me" column. Other activities that don't need your personal attention can be delegated to others. Thus, you have several other columns headed "delegated to ——." Of course, it is up to you to decide who the person is in each case. The home office will have a number of support staff members who can do various tasks. For example, a secretary can complete correspondence or even check to make sure that orders are processed and received. You may have an assistant assigned to you who can do various activities related to servicing accounts. The purpose of this fourth list, then, is to decide what you must do and what can be delegated.

In fact, delegating tasks is an important issue that any salesperson must confront. Failure to delegate is as much a problem as delegating too many tasks. The purpose of the fourth list is to determine what can legitimately be delegated. You certainly don't want to delegate an important and urgent task, because you run the risk of losing control over its completion and outcome. At the same time, you lose precious time by trying to do everything yourself. Hence, you should be able to delegate less important and less urgent tasks. Most likely you will find that very few tasks are both very important and very urgent. Peter Drucker has suggested two important guidelines[9] for determining what to do yourself and what to delegate to someone else.

Keep what is unique for yourself and delegate routine tasks. You will undoubtedly find that unique tasks are also important and sometimes urgent.

Keep those tasks in which your performance is superior and delegate those you handle less effectively. If you are not a good letter writer or record keeper, you are better off delegating those activities to support personnel rather than handling them poorly yourself.

5. Activity analysis for communication. This list contains four columns:

   People I must talk to every day.
   People to talk to frequently.
   People to talk to regularly.
   People to talk to infrequently.

   The way to deal with this analysis is to return to your original list, which contains all the activities associated with your job. Next to each of those activities, write down the names and telephone numbers of people you communicate with in performing the activity. Then place each of these names in one of the four columns just described.

   Separating people you talk to from activities performed allows you to determine who you will talk to separately from the important activities. In other words, there are likely to be people you must talk to every day, even though they have nothing to do with one of your more urgent and important tasks. By maintaining contact with those people, you develop a wider range of prospect contacts. In addition, you stay in touch with supervisory personnel at the home office, which also contributes to your success. In effect, you now have an additional activity to add to your original list: communicating with people either in person or by telephone.

A Time Allocation List. R. Alec Mackenzie[10] provides a way of monitoring and scheduling time. His time inventory is pictured in Figure 16.3.

This is a weekly form, but it can be used continually. Its use requires three simple steps:

1. Determination of ideal time allocation. This is entered in the lower left part of the form. Start by listing under "Category" the major tasks associated with your job. It is important that these tasks be stated in broad terms, such as maintaining customer contact or keeping up with new product information.

Daily Goals	MON 1. 2. 3. 4. 5.	CATEGORY #	TUE 1. 2. 3. 4. 5.	CATEGORY #	WED 1. 2. 3. 4. 5.	CATEGORY #	THU 1. 2. 3. 4. 5.	CATEGORY #	FRI 1. 2. 3. 4. 5.	CATEGORY #	SAT 1. 2. 3. 4. 5.	CATEGORY #	
9:00													
9:30													
10:00													
4:00													
4:30													
5:00													

ALLOCATION Category	%	Time Spent	% of Day	Time Spent	% of Day	Time Spent	% of Day	Time Spent	% of Day	Time Spent	% of Day	Time Spent	% of Day	SUMMARY Total Time Spent	% of Goals
1.															
2.															
3.															
4.															
5.															
6.															
7.															
8.															
Estimate of Effectiveness															

FIGURE 16.3 R. Alec Mackenzie's executive time inventory. (Source: Reprinted by permission of publisher from, *The Time Trap,* by R. Alec Mackenzie, p. 23, © 1972 AMACOM, a division of American Management Association, New York. All rights reserved.

Then determine your ideal time allocation for each task. This decision should be based on your own view of what you think would be best for you.

2. Actual time expenditure. For each day, also in the lower portion of the form in Figure 16.3, keep a record of daily activities and the amount of time you actually spend on them. Ignore any discrepancies between actual and ideal time expenditures. Finally, at the end of the week, summarize the time spent under the "Summary" category.
3. Setting time goals. Now you are ready to use the top part of the form. After dealing with just the bottom part of the form for a few weeks, you will be able to decide if and how you want to change your time expenditure so that your actual time is closer to your ideal time. Begin by listing your daily goals at the top and indicating to which category they correspond (from the bottom left). The daily goals will be more specific than the categories listed at the bottom. For example, calling to check on whether orders have been received would be part of maintaining customer contact. So, too, would telephoning old customers just to communicate that you are still thinking about them. But each of those activities would be listed as a daily goal. Then decide during which hours you want to deal with these goals.

While this seems a bit complicated, after a few weeks it will likely increase your efficiency, since you will learn how each daily goal contributes to your broader categories of job tasks and how the daily goals together add up and approach your ideal time expenditure. It becomes relatively easy to modify your daily goals or the hours spent on those goals so that you get closer to your ideal time allocation.

It should be clear that the Trickett approach together with the MacKenzie approach will provide important information and strategies for managing your time effectively. There are several other issues that will also have an effect. The most critical of those issues is the nature of your territory and how you manage it.

Territory Management

Territory management actually entails two related issues. The first concern is to establish the territory itself. After you have been selling for a few years, you may have many accounts within a given territory, but only some will be of importance. Therefore, the second concern is to identify those few accounts that generate the most sales. When both of these issues have been addressed, specific actions that will affect scheduling (e.g., routing) can be implemented. We will discuss in turn each of these issues.

Establishing the Sales Territory

Usually a sales territory is determined for the salesperson by management. There are a number of reasons for establishing sales territories. First, having a defined territory allows you to cover a region more efficiently than attempting to sell in an unbounded area. Second, having a territory helps keep costs down. If you were able to sell anywhere and ended up with accounts scattered all over the country, you would undoubtedly spend a great deal of time (and money) traveling. By having a territory that is more concentrated, some of these costs can be eliminated. Third, since a sales territory provides a more limited number of total prospects, it allows you more time to deal with each individual customer and, thus, to develop and maintain close relationships.

There are other benefits that are more important to the sales manager, such as allowing the company to hire and train salespeople specifically with the requirements of a certain territory in mind. Assigning salespeople to territories also makes it easier to evaluate a particular salesperson's performance.

How Territories Are Determined

How exactly is a territory created? Not surprisingly, the usual method is in terms of geographical boundaries. The goal is to make a territory manageable for a salesperson. Territories typically are created based upon already existing boundaries. That means that a territory can be a state, a county, a metropolitan area, a city, or even a zip code. Another mechanism for determining a territory is the trading area. A trading area is based upon the natural flow of goods and services. Usually it consists of a city and the surrounding area.

There are advantages and disadvantages to each of these methods. For ex-

New York County (Manhattan) could be unwieldy as a geographical unit. (Charles Marden Fitch/Taurus Photos.)

ample, a state may be too large a geographical unit. Some counties may be too unwieldy when, for example, they comprise part of a large city such as New York County or Los Angeles County. How a territory is finally defined will be a function of the nature of the company's business and the distribution and location of actual and potential customers. Eventually, though, as a salesperson, you will likely have a territory that is your responsibility.

Occasionally companies elect not to establish territories. This would be the case for a very small company. It would also occur when potential sales are so great that every salesperson will have more than enough sales. Still, more often than not, particularly with larger companies, a sales territory will be established. Once you have been assigned a particular territory, it is up to you to organize it and cover it in the most efficient manner, keeping in mind what has been discussed thus far with respect to time management. As a beginning, then, you will immediately recognize that some accounts generate more sales than others. Those accounts will also be more demanding in terms of what services and follow-up they expect from you.

The 80/20 Rule

In fact, the importance of some accounts compared to your total number of accounts has been formally recognized through the **80/20 rule,** which can be stated as follows:

> Eighty percent of a territory's sales are likely to come from only 20 percent of its prospects.

The most important thing this rule tells us is that not all accounts are equal. For that reason, we usually divide accounts into three categories: *a*-, *b*- and *c*-accounts. This division is based on (1) how likely a particular account is to help meet a salesperson's sales quota and (2) what proportion of the quota a particular account will provide. The greater the likelihood and the greater the proportion, the more important the account.

Segmentation of Accounts

In effect, a salesperson is engaging in an analysis of each account so that they can be segmented. By segmenting accounts into most important to least important categories, the salesperson can utilize his time more efficiently. Accounts that are most important will require more of the salesperson's time than those that are least important. For example, recall the last part of the Trickett time inventory, which deals with communication. The most important accounts may require some form of communication from the salesperson several times a week, while the less important ones may not require anything more than once a month.

The most important accounts are ***a*-accounts** and are typically referred to as **key accounts.** These accounts *are very profitable and very good customers.* Loss of these accounts would have a major impact on a salesperson's quota. The

EXHIBIT 16.3

Salespeople May Be Gaining More Sales Time

A survey by McGraw-Hill on how salespeople spend their time shows that they are increasing their use of telephone selling. The average industrial salesperson spends 25% of his time selling face-to-face and 17% of his time selling by phone. This compares to a survey in 1977 that showed [that] a salesperson spent 39% of his time selling face-to-face.

There is reason to believe that salespeople are gaining more selling time because the proportion of time spent travelling decreased from 32% in 1977 to 25% currently.

Source: Adapted from Are salespeople gaining more selling time? (1986). *Sales & Marketing Management, 137*(1), p. 29.

next level of account is a ***b*-account** and can be referred to as a **regular account.** These accounts *have potential sales, but their loss, while having some effect on a salesperson's quota, would not be dramatic.*

Finally are the accounts that are much more limited, the ***c*-accounts.** These accounts *make occasional purchases but are not usually very profitable.* This is not to say that they can't be made profitable. They do require time and service, and they can be responsive to direct mail. How much effort can be allocated is a function of the salesperson's time. It might be advisable for a salesperson to anticipate this and allocate a specific portion of her time to devote to *c*-accounts. Table 16.6 summarizes the segmentation of accounts and provides a suggested time allocation.

Clearly, the majority of time and effort should be devoted to the key accounts. This is where the 80/20 rule directly applies. Key accounts represent approximately 20 percent of the salesperson's accounts, but they generate 80 percent of the sales. Regular accounts cannot be neglected, but they must receive a lower priority than key accounts. As we suggested, *c*-accounts can be turned into regular accounts, but this does require additional time. That extra time should accrue only after all other accounts have been adequately serviced and maintained.

Table 16.6 Segmentation of Accounts

Kind of Account	*Importance*	*Time Allocation (%)*
a-accounts (key accounts)	Very important	50–60
b-accounts (regular accounts)	Important	30–40
c-accounts	Less important	10

Routing

Another aspect of territory management is routing. No matter how a territory is defined, there will necessarily be some travel from one account to another. Which accounts will be visited in person will, of course, be a function of how they are classified. *C*-accounts can probably be handled by telephone. Regular accounts can be handled either by telephone or in person, or both. Key accounts should probably receive as much in-person attention as possible.

Once it is determined which accounts are to be visited on a given day and appointments are scheduled, a route must be selected. This route must allow adequate time between appointments so that various conditions, such as travel or unexpected waits to see people, can be accommodated. A great deal of attention has been given to routing.

The Logic of Routing. We all engage in routing several times a week. Whenever a series of errands has accumulated over several days, we finally reach a point where they have to be handled. You may have to take laundry, buy coffee, buy envelopes, buy stamps, take a radio to be repaired, and buy a birthday present. It is very likely that you will have to go to different establishments to complete each of these errands. Further, you probably need to complete these errands quickly, possibly on a Saturday morning. While you may not engage in a formal routing procedure, you are likely to make an informal plan.

You may start by going to the farthest point and work your way back home, stopping at the next farthest stop, and so on. This may not work out so well, however, if, for example, one of your errands requires buying groceries. If the grocery store is the farthest point, rather than carrying the groceries as you complete all the other errands, you may instead elect to go to the establishment closest to home first and work your way to the grocery store. If the grocery store is at an intermediate point, it may be necessary for you to retrace some of your steps in order to avoid carrying the groceries.

A similar problem exists when you need to call on several accounts on a given day. You may be able to do the routing plan yourself simply by getting a detailed map showing the location of your accounts. You can then schedule visits by developing a plan based upon such factors as where your most important prospects are located, their distance from one another, and accessibility in terms of traffic patterns.

Specific Routing Plans. You will immediately notice that some plans are logical, whereas others are, for all practical purposes, not really plans at all. Thus, you may be able to travel in a circle. Or you may have to establish a hub, as do the airlines, and travel to accounts located near the hub, then establish another hub and travel to the accounts near it, and so on. You can use a cloverleaf plan with a central base and cover a loop each day. Figure 16.4 depicts these three routing patterns. Of course, there are many other possibilities. Keep in mind that the routing plan is based in part on the way you have segmented various accounts.

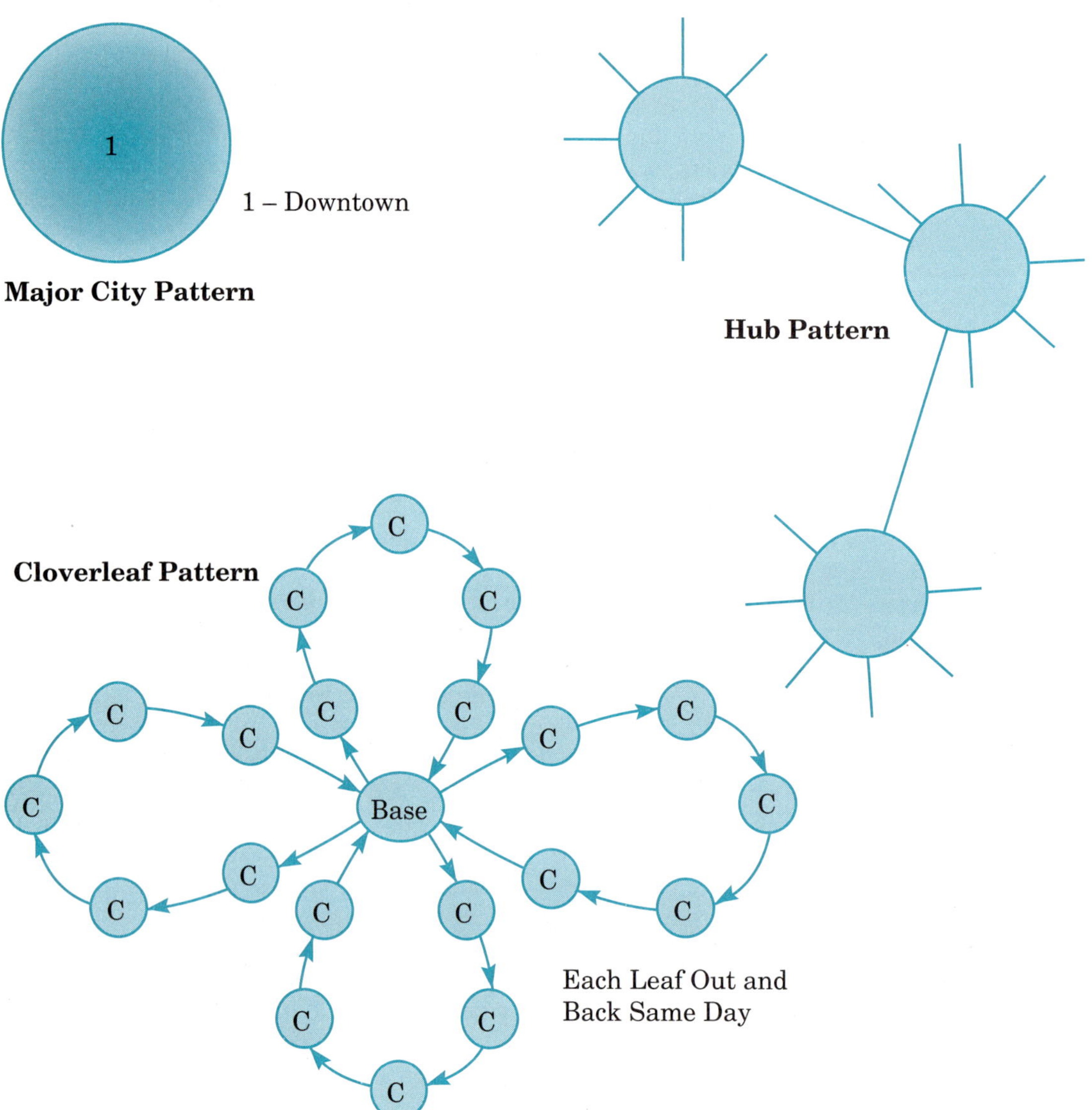

FIGURE 16.4 Typical routing patterns.

Computer Routing Plans. Routing plans can become so complicated that a computer analysis is often necessary. That is the province of the field of operations research. One computer-based model that has been directly applied to routing for salespeople is **CALLPLAN.**[11]

To utilize CALLPLAN, a salesperson has to estimate how customers will respond to various sales call frequencies. In other words, for a given account, what impact will one call have versus two versus three, or more? With this information, sales territories can be divided into account groupings based upon frequency of sales calls, travel times, length of the call, and sales potential. Obviously, this model requires input from the salesperson. The better the input, the better the output. CALLPLAN is one of several computer-based models.

Putting It All Together

The key points in this chapter are summarized as follows:

- Self, time, and territory management are all interrelated since managing the self hinges upon having a positive self-concept, and by having a positive self-concept we are motivated to succeed, which, in turn, enhances our self-concept, leading to greater success, and so on.
- A salesperson has to combat problems such as stress, procrastination, fear of failure, and impatience, all of which can lower the self-concept.
- A positive self-concept helps the salesperson deal with unique aspects of his job such as the degree of independence that requires the salesperson to provide his own structure on his time.
- How the salesperson structures his time can have a major impact on his success.
- To structure her time, the salesperson must first set her goals and then allocate blocks of time to be used in achieving these goals.
- In allocating blocks of time, the salesperson needs to plan and separate high-payoff from low-payoff activities.
- Specific planning techniques include activity analysis and making a time allocation list.
- Territory management has a major effect on time management.
- To manage a territory, the salesperson first has to establish its exact boundaries and second determine how best to cover the territory or the most effective route to use.
- Not all of a salesperson's accounts are equally important.
- The 80/20 rule states that 80 percent of a territory's sales are likely to come from only 20 percent of its prospects.
- The 80/20 rule will influence how the salesperson's territory is managed, since he will have to pay particular attention to the key accounts that comprise a small portion of his prospects.

Perhaps the best way to appreciate the process of time and territory management is to consider a more extended example. We reiterate that through careful planning of time and territory, your self-concept will be enhanced because you will have a sense of satisfaction at having successfully completed rewarding tasks.

John is a new salesperson for IBM. His task is to sell minicomputers to medium-sized companies in New York City. His territory is defined as midtown Manhattan. Figure 16.5 shows a map of John's territory. John decides to use the Trickett activity analysis. He begins by listing some of the specific activities on his job.

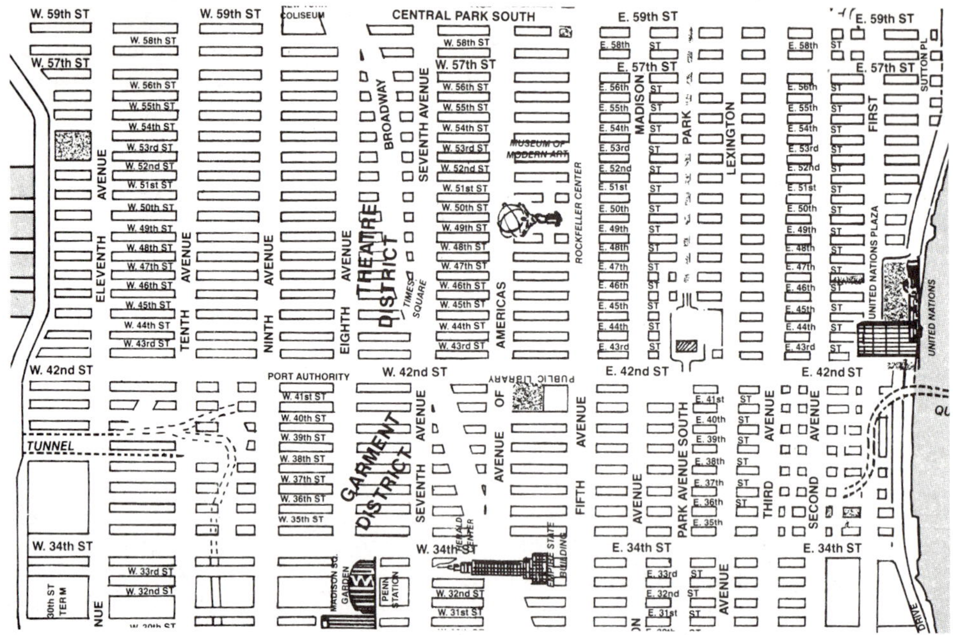

FIGURE 16.5 Midtown Manhattan. (Courtesy of *City in the Pocket* © 1986.)

1. He has to call —— to make sure that the system that was just installed at ABC is working properly.
2. He has to go to DEF to help them start their system.
3. He wants to call on GHI to see if he can persuade them to expand their system.
4. He needs to phone eight new prospects to see if he can arrange appointments.
5. He has already made appointments for Monday, Tuesday, and Thursday afternoons, and he must first be certain that he is still expected.
6. He has to arrange with the home office in White Plains to get more literature and to have them send literature to people he visited last week.
7. He has paperwork left over from last week, since he had too many appointments to complete it. This includes writing several follow-up letters and recording the outcomes of his sales attempts.

This completes step 1 of the Trickett analysis. Step 2 requires that he order these activities in terms of their importance. Items 1 and 2 are very important; they must be done now. Item 5 is also very important and must be done now, because no salesperson can afford to break an appointment. Item 4 is important and should be done, while items 3 and 6 are not so important. Item 7 can be eliminated from the list of tasks he must complete himself.

For step 3, urgency needs to be determined. Very urgent is item 1. Urgent are items 2 and 5. Not urgent are items 3 and 4. Time is not a factor for items 6 and 7.

Now he can delegate these tasks. Items that are both very important and very urgent must be done by John. That means he must do item 1. Item 2 is less urgent but still very important and must also be done by John. Item 5 must also be done by John, since these represent potential prospects. Item 3 can be done by his assistant, as can item 4. John's secretary can deal with items 6 and 7.

Finally, in terms of communication, John must list the people he must see or speak to every day. These include his supervisor, his secretary, and his assistant. He can call each of them early in the morning. People he must contact frequently include his district sales manager. People to contact regularly are those who are responsible for purchasing and maintaining equipment he has sold to his best accounts. Finally, people to deal with only infrequently are those who have expressed only mild interest in the product or those who are very small purchasers. Calls to *a*- and *b*-accounts are handled in his listing of daily activities.

This analysis reveals that John's agenda now has a structure that it didn't have earlier. John can now make an actual schedule for his week, using the MacKenzie inventory. Part of that inventory will already have been filled out based upon previous weeks on the job. Thus, John will need to deal only with his daily goals, which are determined in part by the Trickett analysis, already completed. His actual schedule will entail a routing program based upon John's knowledge of midtown Manhattan. He wants to visit his best accounts. It so happens that these accounts are located at the far corners of the territory, but several are concentrated at these corners. Thus, he needs to arrange to see people in one corner on the same day. This becomes the equivalent of a cloverleaf pattern.

If John consistently takes this approach every day of the year, he will certainly meet his broad sales quota. He may even exceed it. Clearly, his schedule is complicated enough that he cannot be successful if he attempts to work out all of the details in his head.

Key Terms

Self-concept
Selling activities
Nonselling activities
Organizational activities
Investment activities
High-payoff activities
Low-payoff activities
80/20 rule
Key accounts (*a*-accounts)
Regular accounts (*b*-accounts)
C-accounts
CALLPLAN

Review Questions

1. What is a self-concept? What is the relationship between a self-concept and success at work? What is the relationship between self-concept and time?
2. List and discuss four things that can cause a salesperson to have a negative self-concept.
3. What are the three major categories of a salesperson's time?
4. How much time is spent in actual selling activities?
5. What is meant when we say that the key to planning is thinking in terms of the future?

6. What are the five lists you would make if you were using Trickett's activity analysis to plan your time?
7. What are some of the ways that sales territories are determined?
8. What is the 80/20 rule?
9. What are the three categories into which sales accounts are usually divided? Why are they segmented this way?
10. What is the purpose of routing? Is it based on logic? Explain.

Discussion Questions

1. Would you advise someone with a low self-concept to avoid the selling profession? Why?
2. How would you counsel a salesperson who has been on the job for about 3 years and is thinking of leaving the profession because she has found that her sales are beginning to decline?
3. Assume that you are a salesperson for General Motors. Your job is to sell cars to car rental agencies in Minnesota, North Dakota, South Dakota, and Iowa. Using the Trickett activity analysis, structure your time for 1 week.
4. Assume that your key accounts are in metropolitan areas with a population of 250,000 or more. At the same time, there are many car dealers in rural parts of the states listed in question 3. In order to maintain contact with key accounts, as well as with regular accounts and even *c*-accounts, how would you route yourself during 1 week based upon this information?

CASE 16.1

Janet has just been hired by Pillsbury for a summer sales position. Her job is to sell Pillsbury packaged goods to retailers in Minnesota, Iowa, North Dakota, and South Dakota. She is surprised that she has been given very little direction by the company. The only thing they have told her is that she has a sales quota, and if she exceeds the quota, she'll be given a bonus.

Janet has gone through a 2-day orientation program to learn about Pillsbury and its products, but not too much was said about her actual job. All she knows is that the company expects her to check in with her sales manager twice a week. Janet received her degree in marketing just 2 weeks ago, but her concentration was in advertising. She knows very little about sales, but like many new college graduates, if she wants a career, she has to start out by selling.

Assume the role of an experienced salesperson and advise Janet about how to proceed in terms of the following:

1. Organizing and planning her time.
2. Segmenting her accounts.
3. Covering her four-state territory in the most efficient manner possible.

References

1. Barkas, E. (1984). *Creative Time Management.* New York: Prentice-Hall.

2. Webber, R. (1980). *Time Is Money.* New York: Free Press.

3. Barkas, op. cit., p. 13.

4. Andersonn, R. E., J. F. Hair, and A. J. Bush. (1988). *Professional Sales Management.* New York: McGraw-Hill, p. 120.

5. Berrian, H. A. (1988). *Sales & Marketing Management: Portfolio 1988,* p. 24.

6. Webber, op. cit.

7. Rutherford, R. D. (1988). *Just in Time.* New York: John Wiley & Sons.

8. Trickett, J. (1962). A more effective use of time. *California Management Review, 4,* 4–15.

9. Drucker, P. (1967). *The Effective Executive.* New York: Harper & Row.

10. Mackenzie, R. A. (1972). *The Time Trap.* New York: Amacon.

11. Lodish, L. M. (1971). CALLPLAN: An interactive salesman's call planning system. *Management Science,* (December), 25–40.

17

Sales Management

CHAPTER OBJECTIVES

In this chapter, you will learn:

The sales manager is concerned with hiring, training, motivating, and evaluating salespeople.

The job of the salesperson is very different from the typical corporate position, since it involves little supervision and little structure.

The sales manager should seek out as prospective salespeople those who are self-starters and can take rejection in stride.

Salesperson training entails imparting knowledge about the company's policies and techniques for selling.

Motivating the salesperson involves more than monetary compensation: salespeople are especially responsive to recognition for doing a good job.

It is not sufficient to look at sales volume alone in evaluating the performance of a salesperson.

CHAPTER OUTLINE

A Sales Challenge

An Overview

Criteria for Selecting Salespeople

- Unique Aspects of the Sales Job
- Desirable Personality Characteristics
- Selection Concerns of Various Companies

The Role and Extent of Company Sales Training Programs

- The Degree of Salesperson Experience
- Knowledge and Information
- Style and Technique

Motivation of the Sales Force

- External Motivation
- Internal Motivation

Evaluating Salespeople

- The Varied Tasks of the Salesperson
- Systems to Evaluate Salesperson Performance

Putting It All Together

Key Terms

Review Questions

Discussion Questions

Case 17.1

References

A Sales Challenge

Jack L. has moved up through the ranks. He started working for LM Manufacturing 8 years ago, right out of college. LM manufactures an expensive line of office furniture, and it was Jack's job to sell this furniture to medium-sized and large corporations in the northeastern United States. He was fortunate for three reasons. First, the Northeast is the home of many large corporations. Second, many corporations were moving out of some of the larger central cities into new suburban offices, and this made them ideal prospects for new office furniture. Third, Jack was a very good salesperson. After 4 years in the field, he was promoted. He became a district sales manager. He now supervised field salespeople who were doing exactly what he had been doing. Once again, Jack proved himself very capable. Through his supervision, the field sales force was able to increase sales by more than 15 percent for 3 years. Finally, Jack was promoted to regional sales manager. Now his task was to oversee the work of the district sales managers. At this point, Jack's next possible promotion was to national sales manager and then, possibly, to vice president of marketing. He had a reasonable chance to reach this position since, once again, sales were increasing in his region during his first year in his new job.

An Overview

It is often the case that people who start their careers as salespeople end up in sales management after as little as 1 or 2 years. However, this process can take anywhere from 6 months to 5 or 6 years depending upon company policies, the product being sold, and the ability and goals of the salesperson.

Not every salesperson aspires to become a sales manager. Many people prefer to remain as salespeople in the field; for them, sales management is not a desirable position. Others, however, want to get involved in the planning and control of the sales program. These people would manage the sales program rather than sell directly in the field.

To envision the task of the sales manager, imagine that you are the head of a medium-sized manufacturing company, and you have just completed the manufacture of a new product. Your major task now is to sell that product to companies throughout the United States and Europe. What do you do? Of course, you hire salespeople. That seems simple enough. But where are you going to find these people? How will you train them after you hire them? How will their jobs be defined? How will they be compensated? How will you evaluate their performance?

These questions are critical because the selling function is often the foundation of any successful organization. Ronald W. Tidmore, senior vice president of sales for Pepsi, argues that "quality management" is the most important factor in sales force success.[1] Obviously, a company has to sell in order to survive and flourish. Fortunately, we have people called *sales managers*. It is their function to address directly the questions raised in the preceding paragraph.

Thus far, we have talked about the process of selling itself. An equally important area, and one that constitutes a field in itself, is how to select, train, organize, and manage the sales force. These are the broader concerns of sales management and the focus of this chapter.

We will deal with only some of the more basic issues of sales management. In fact, the job of sales manager entails many other concerns. To show you how varied this task can be, some of the possible concerns of the sales manager are listed in Table 17.1.

If we were to deal with all of these issues, we would have an entire course in the area. Actually, we have talked about the last four concerns elsewhere in this book. As for the rest of them, we will cover some of the major issues that are most relevant to a salesperson. Specifically, the following topics will be addressed:

1. What criteria should be used in selecting salespeople?
2. Should there be a formal company sales training program, and if so, how extensive should it be?
3. Once the salespeople are hired and trained, how can the company ensure that they will be motivated to perform well?
4. How can the performance of a salesperson be evaluated?

Criteria for Selecting Salespeople

"The proper selection of salespeople is the key activity in the management of a sales force. . . . A well selected sales force should be more productive than a poorly chosen one."[2]

In trying to decide how to select salespeople, many people have asked

Table 17.1 Tasks and Concerns of a Sales Manager

1. How many salesforces should the company have?
2. How large should each salesforce be?
3. How should each salesforce be organized into sales districts and/or sales territories?
4. How should the effort of each salesperson be allocated to trading areas, customers, prospects, and/or products?
5. What type of salespeople should be employed?
6. What type of training should the salespeople receive?
7. What type of supervision should the salespeople receive?
8. How should the salespeople be motivated?
9. How should the performance of the salespeople be evaluated?
10. How should salespeople adapt to customers?
11. What influence bases should salespeople use?
12. What influence techniques should salespeople use?
13. How should salespeople control the interaction?

Source: Reprinted by permission of American Marketing Association © 1983. R. W. LaForge, S. J. Grove, and G. M. Pickett. (1983). Sales management research: A call for integration. *Proceedings of the American Marketing Association, 49*, p. 212.

whether there are factors that predict salesperson success. In other words, are there certain personality traits or characteristics that are especially desirable for a salesperson? A great deal of research has focused on this issue and, not surprisingly, has found that some people are more suited to selling than others. You might try yourself to list what you think are important personality characteristics before reading any further. You will probably find that this task is relatively easy.

Some of the characteristics that have been identified include a high energy level, high self-confidence, a strong desire for money, a habit of working hard with minimal supervision, perseverance, and competitiveness.[3] Other characteristics include empathy (the ability to identify with another person) and ego drive (the desire to compete, persuade, and win).[4]

You will probably have found some similarity between your list of important characteristics and those just listed. Certain personality characteristics of the salesperson are obvious, due to the nature of the sales job itself. In other words, there are certain things about functioning as a salesperson that make this job very different from that of a marketing manager or an account executive or even a sales manager.

Unique Aspects of the Sales Job

In the jobs listed, there is usually a great deal of structure. People are expected to work in an assigned office during specific hours. Their success is not directly tied to a continual stream of encounters with people they must persuade. The job of the salesperson is just the opposite. The salesperson does not have a specific time assigned or a specific place to work (apart from appointments she herself makes with prospects). In addition, the salesperson must persuade each of her prospects—some more easily than others, but nevertheless, she must persuade them. Table 17.2 provides a comparison between a typical manager and a salesperson.

Table 17.2 Things That Make a Salesperson's Job Special

Typical Manager	*Salesperson*
Works 9 to 5, Monday through Friday	Can work anytime, any day
Hours set by the company	Hours set by salesperson
Has a boss who is seen every day, several times each day	Has a boss who may not be seen for several days at a time
Has an assigned office that is used every day, all day	May have an assigned office that may not be used very often
Has various tasks, which may include supervision, administration, and some persuasion	Has one central task: selling through persuasion
Success often measured by how well liked and competent the person is	Success measured by sales volume

Desirable Personality Characteristics

From the preceding discussion and Table 17.2 we can derive a number of personality characteristics, some of which were referred to earlier. Consider first the issue of not having a fixed time or an office to go to. The salesperson is almost like a student who, while he has papers to write, can write them whenever and wherever he chooses, as long as the paper is completed on time. No one is watching over the student's shoulder.

That basically describes the job of the salesperson. The salesperson has to sell a certain amount, but she can do it whenever and wherever she chooses, given certain constraints. She doesn't have a boss who is constantly supervising her. Under these circumstances, it is very easy to procrastinate. Just as a student can procrastinate in doing papers, a salesperson can procrastinate in regard to selling in the field. What kinds of traits would make such a person less likely to do that?

A salesperson has to be able to work well with little supervision. Not everyone can do this. People who want to work hard and who are *self-starters* are more likely to work well with minimal supervision. A salesperson must also be *self-disciplined.* Imagine how easy it would be to decide to take off on a beautiful summer day instead of forging ahead and making sales calls.

But minimal supervision is only part of the picture. The task of continually making sales calls has a number of pitfalls. The major one is the possibility of being rejected by the prospect. Rejection can take many forms, such as the prospect's canceling an appointment or shortening a half-hour appointment to only 5 minutes. Rejection can also be experienced when the salesperson fails to make the sale.

A person who wishes to be a salesperson must be able to handle rejection. Some people are better at this than others. What characteristics relate to such an ability? First, it is necessary for the salesperson to have a high degree of *self-confidence* and *self-esteem.* Those two qualities allow the salesperson to avoid taking rejection personally. A need to be *competitive* is also helpful, since the competitive salesperson will push on in spite of actual or potential rejection. In addition, the salesperson has to be *assertive* in order to approach people who might reject her or who have rejected her in the past.

There are several other personality traits that serve a salesperson well. These traits probably characterize what we expect of any professional person but are especially important for a salesperson, since he is selling by persuasion. These traits include *intelligence, the ability to communicate ideas effectively, the ability to deal with a wide range of people, competence, enthusiasm, and loyalty to the profession.*

To summarize, an effective salesperson is comfortable working with little supervision, a self-starter, self-disciplined, and hard-working. In addition, the person must be able to handle rejection, have high self-confidence and self-esteem, and be competitive and assertive. Finally, the effective salesperson is intelligent, competent, enthusiastic, has an ability to handle a wide range of people to whom ideas must be effectively communicated, and is loyal to the profession. Table 17.3

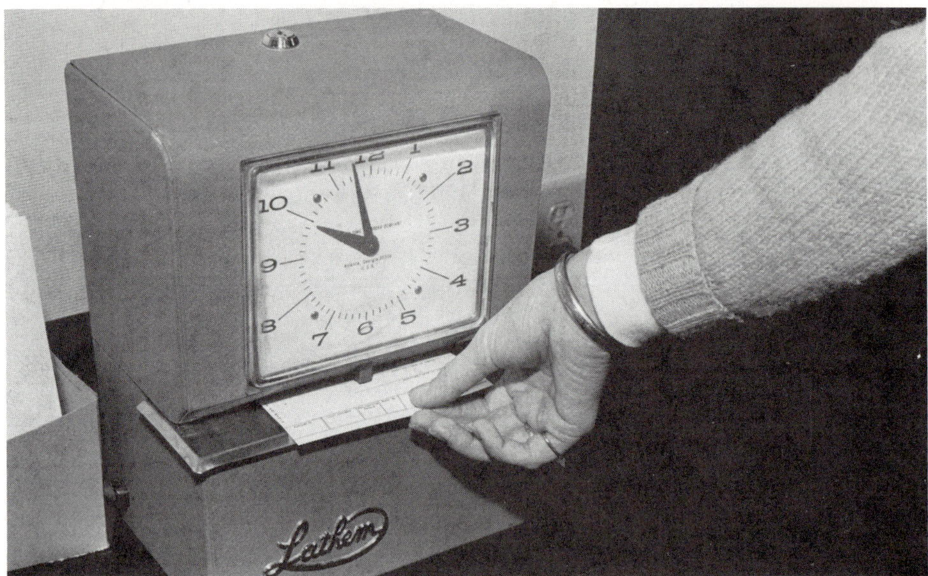

A time clock is one thing salespeople do not have to face. Salespeople set their own time schedules. (© Margaret Thompson/The Picture Cube.)

lists some relevant aspects of the salesperson's job and the personality characteristics that are required.

It is useful to be aware of one additional issue regarding the hiring of salespeople. Generally speaking, salespeople appear to be more motivated by a desire for "prestige, power, and material gain than they are by a service ideal or the need for security."[5] This is very important to keep in mind in predicting who will be a successful salesperson. It indicates that a person who has a high need for security would not be a good candidate for a sales position. A better candidate would be a person who has a strong need for high status.

Table 17.3 Relationship Between Personality Characteristics and the Special Nature of a Salesperson's Job

Features of the Job	*Personality Characteristics*
No fixed time or office	Self-starter Well disciplined
Likelihood of rejection	High self-confidence and self-esteem Competitive Assertive
Selling through persuasion	Intelligence Ability to communicate ideas effectively Competence Enthusiasm Loyalty to the profession

EXHIBIT 17.1

How Customers Recognize the Pros

A study was conducted to determine what sales practices are indicative of salespeople who are considered to be true professionals. Following is a list of those practices.

How Customers Recognize the Pros

Sales Practice	*Significance Level**
Makes effort to understand concerns	.01
Presents logical arguments	.01
Gives evidence of product effectiveness	.05
Prepares effective responses to objections	.05
Asks questions about customer's needs	.05
Asks about needs of customer's company	.05
Explains product drawbacks	.05
Answers questions about product	.05
Is concise and to the point	.05
Maintains eye contact	.05
Shows enthusiasm	.05
Is aware of customer's needs	.10
Understands economic conditions	.10
Is entrusted with confidential information	.10
Is sensitive to customer's personal situation	.10
Is able to restate accurately	.10

* A statistical analysis assigned "significance" scores based on how customers rated 43 sales practices that they considered important. The highest significance level of .01 means there is 1 chance in 100 that a cited practice was due to coincidence; .10, 1 chance in 10. That customers expect salespeople to do their planning before they make a sales call is underscored by the high significance level of "makes effort to understand concerns" and "presents logical arguments."

Source: Reprinted by permission of *Sales & Marketing Management* © 1986. T. C. Taylor. (1986). Anatomy of a star salesperson. *Sales & Marketing Management, 136*, (May), p. 50.

Selection Concerns of Various Companies

What do specific companies look for when hiring salespeople? Executives at Mark I, a company in Chicago that manufactures and sells stickers, feel strongly that only people with excellent selling skills should be recruited.[6] This is probably not difficult because it appears that there are many qualified salespeople looking for work.[7]

At other companies strong product knowledge is emphasized over sales skills. This is true of Moore Business Forms in Northbrook, Illinois, where it is believed that sales skills can be trained in-house and that, therefore, knowledge is more important.

Managers at Dresser Industries of Worthington, Ohio, argue that a particularly important criterion is "an extremely healthy attitude toward selling. . . . [Salespeople are] professionals. . . . They're not only selling a product. They are, in effect, an adviser to the customer."[8]

Educational Background. What should prospective salespeople study in school? Here, too, there are many different emphases. John Phillips, personnel manager for S. C. Johnson in Racine, Wisconsin, considers people with business degrees as well as those with liberal arts degrees: "A business major is not an absolute. We are primarily interested in behavioral skills such as leadership, loyalty, and interest in a sales career. . . . So we rely heavily on experience on campus."

Lederle Laboratories in Wayne, New Jersey, prefers most of its recruits to have science backgrounds, since the sales task is to promote prescription drugs to doctors and hospitals. But even here, a science background is not essential. John Rose, a manager at Lederle, says, "If I had my druthers, I'd like to get people who have the behavioral characteristics that go with a successful salesperson and then have us give him the technical wherewithal. . . . [Salespeople have to be] self-motivated and interested in the kind of job they're doing because in the main they will be managing themselves."[9]

The Dr. Pepper Company seeks people with "character, intelligence, and personality." In addition, Dan Craft, vice president of sales, explains that not only must Dr. Pepper want the recruit, but the recruit must want Dr. Pepper.

The Successful Salesperson. A recent issue of *Sales & Marketing Management* presented the results of a survey of 400 salespeople in six industries conducted by a Boston sales and training management company called the Forum Corporation. In comparing very successful and moderately successful salespeople, they found several qualities that a sales manager might look for in making hiring decisions:[10]

1. Successful salespeople exchange information rather than present products. They ask questions in such a way that prospects are forced to evaluate and analyze their situations.
2. Very successful salespeople know *when* to close the sale. Usually the closing attempt occurs only after it is clear that the product satisfies a specific need.
3. Successful salespeople deal with people as individuals and try to meet customers' needs.
4. Successful salespeople are thought by their customers to be genuinely interested in the customer's needs.
5. Successful salespeople are considered a valuable source of expertise by their customers.
6. Successful salespeople spend as much time making sure that their staff and managers trust and share information with the salespeople as they do actually selling.
7. Very successful salespeople maintain more eye contact, show greater enthu-

siasm, restate more accurately, ask more questions about customers' needs, and are better prepared to handle objections than moderately successful salespeople. Figure 17.1 summarizes these qualities.

The Salesperson of the Future. One important area of speculation has to do with the nature of the salesperson of the future. One likely trend is that the number of salespeople will be greater in 1995 than today. Compared to 1984, there should be about 20 percent more workers in sales in 1995. Perhaps more important than that is the age of the salesperson. It is predicted that salespeople will be older than they are today. This age difference is a major advantage, since it suggests that salespeople of the future will be more experienced than they are now.

At the same time, there will be a shrinking pool of younger new sales trainees. This means that organizations will likely have to pay salespeople more to compensate them for their increased experience. One other major change is that the number of women in sales is expected to increase.[11]

Assessment Centers. It should be clear by now that salesperson selection is an important issue. In fact, because of the importance of the initial hiring decision, assessment centers have been instituted. "**Assessment centers** *are sophisticated selection devices used most frequently for hiring. . . . [They] are intense testing environments that place candidates in realistic problem settings, where they must prioritize activities, make decisions, and act upon them.*"[12] Many large corporations, such as Merrill Lynch, use assessment centers, and they can be very effective. Other corporations depend upon more standardized testing. This method, too, appears to be a very good way of screening applicants for sales positions.[13]

It is important to be aware that predicting the success of a new hiree is difficult. All things being equal, a sales manager is better off selecting a salesperson who has the characteristics we have discussed thus far. Unfortunately, even if a newly hired salesperson does possess those characteristics, there is no guarantee

They exchange information rather than products

They know when to close a sale

They treat people as individuals

They are genuinely interested in their customer's needs

They are a source of expertise

They devote time to gaining the trust of their staff and managers

They have more eye contact, enthusiasm, ask more questions and provide more accurate restatements, and better handle objections than moderately successful salespeople.

FIGURE 17.1 Qualities of very successful salespeople.

of success. For this reason, salesperson training becomes valuable. Effective training can be crucial because the company has an opportunity to impart information and selling techniques that it feels will contribute to success. In fact, training programs are often used as recruiting devices. The more extensive a company's training program is, the more desirable the company is to an inexperienced salesperson.

The Role and Extent of Company Sales Training Programs

There is a widespread belief that good salespeople are born, not made. Few sales managers today would wholeheartedly accept this belief. Based on our discussion of the selection process, it should be clear that not everyone can be or would want to be a salesperson. In addition, even people who would make good salespeople need to be trained.

We can modify this belief and say that good salespeople are both born and made. They are born to the extent that they have the right personality characteristics to undertake the particular challenges that sales offers. But they are also made to the extent that training can sharpen their abilities to persuade and communicate effectively.

The issue of training is not taken lightly by organizations. In fact, one-third of all firms require that employees have at least 1 year of training and other company experience before they actually sell. And close to one-half of all companies have training programs ranging from 3 to 6 months.[14] Because of its duration, training is a major expense. Dartnell has estimated that the average cost of training a sales representative is $12,500.[15]

The Degree of Salesperson Experience

There are two essential areas for training. The first area focuses on *knowledge and information*. The second area concerns *technique and style*. In both areas, a newly hired salesperson may have either no background or an extensive background. More likely, this person will fall between these two extremes. The range of possibilities is depicted in Figure 17.2.

A salesperson who has recently graduated from college will be in the no-

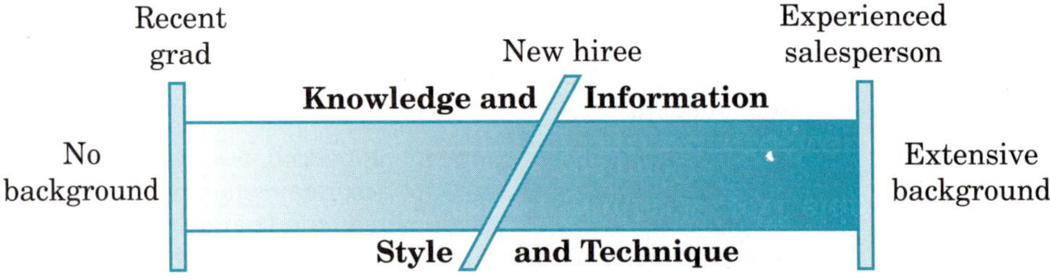

FIGURE 17.2 The salesperson's background.

background category for both areas. This person will need the maximum amount of sales training that the company can provide. A salesperson with several years of experience will need some training, depending upon what he has been selling. For example, if a salesperson who has several years' selling experience with over-the-counter drugs is hired to sell prescription drugs to doctors and hospitals, he will need more training than someone who has worked for another prescription drug company. The person with over-the-counter experience will have to learn how to talk with doctors as opposed to owners of drugstores. In addition, that person will have to learn about the company's products as well as competing products.

No matter how extensive the background, the salesperson will need some training in both areas. Every company has its own way of doing things, as well as a particular image it wants its representatives to project. A newly hired salesperson will have to be taught a company's policies.

Table 17.4 lists training topics that have to do with a particular company's policies. The list of topics is based upon a survey given to 200 sales managers who are members of the Sales and Marketing Education Association of Chicago.[16] These topics were considered to be important in sales training programs. Note that they cover material that is relevant to both knowledge and information (e.g., customer benefits), as well as style and technique (e.g., questioning techniques).

Knowledge and Information

As we discussed in Chapter 7, it is essential that a salesperson be very knowledgeable about the product she is selling. In addition, she must be knowledgeable about the company, competing companies, and competing products. In part, obtaining this knowledge is the responsibility of the salesperson. But the company she works for wants to be certain that its own views are imparted to the salesperson. For that reason, one major aspect of any sales training program is to provide what the company feels is important information.

Table 17.4 Training Topics That Have To Do with a Particular Company's Policies

1. Time utilization
2. Customer benefits
3. Closing techniques
4. Objections
5. Professional standards
6. Salesperson self-attitude
7. Questioning techniques
8. Listening techniques
9. Buyer behavior and motivation
10. Change of attitude about salespersons

Source: Reprinted by permission of The Dartnell Institute of Financial Research, © 1980, Dartnell Corporation, Chicago, IL.

EXHIBIT 17.2

Different Perspectives of Desirable Traits of Star Salespeople

Not all people the salesperson deals with have the same concerns as to what are the most desirable qualities the salesperson should have. Below is a table indicating how important the various traits are to three major groups salespeople have to deal with. You will notice that about the only quality that all three groups seem to agree upon is *interpersonal.*

Three Perspectives of Star Salespeople*

	Importance to three groups surveyed		
Characteristics of Top Salespeople	*Customers*	*Internal Support Staff*	*Salespeople*
Aggressive	14.8%	8.0%	3.4%
Creative	16.6	4.5	10.0
Disciplined	9.4	15.2	16.9
Interpersonal	14.8	16.1	16.9
Knowledgeable	17.3	25.9	15.7
Professional	12.9	23.2	29.2
Verbal	7.4	7.1	4.5
Well-groomed	6.8	0.0	3.4

* Each of the three groups surveyed by Forum has its own ideas on the high performer's single most important trait. Salespeople, by far, singled out "professionalism" indicating a strong sense of pride in their craft. Both customers and internal support personnel, placing "knowledgeable" at the head of their lists, expect the high performer to know his products and services and the situation he is selling into. Significantly, internal support people also gave "professionalism" a high score. Note, too, how the three groups debunked some popular myths about selling, giving very low scores to "aggressive" and "verbal."

Source: Reprinted by permission of *Sales and Marketing Management* © 1988. T. C. Taylor, (1988), Anatomy of a star salesperson. *Sales and Marketing Management:* Portfolio 1988, 39.

Specific Information Provided by a Training Program. What general areas of information are considered to be important? Some of them are as follows:

1. Knowledge about the company. Every company has its own way of doing things and its own policies. Companies have policies with regard to such things as expense accounts, credit, use of a company car, and access to upper-level management. Taken together, these policies lead to what is sometimes referred to as the *corporate culture.* The unique policies that comprise a corporate culture help to give the employees the sense of belonging to a special organization.

   As an example, the Marriott Hotel Corporation has recently undergone a major change in its corporate view. It now regards the job of selling as a goal in itself rather than as a stepping stone to other positions. Jon Loeb, vice president and general sales manager, says, "Now it's chic to stay in sales and marketing."[17]

2. Knowledge about the product. Many people feel that this is the most important part of the training program. Information in this area includes almost everything that can be utilized in evaluating a product. This means that a salesperson should understand the advantages and benefits that a prospect can immediately appreciate, as well as things that are less immediately apparent, such as technical information.
3. Knowledge about the marketing program for the product. The salesperson needs to be well informed about the four *P*'s of marketing. Pricing information would be necessary, as well as information about advertising approaches and sales promotion. Finally, the salesperson needs to be well informed regarding distribution issues.
4. Knowledge about the competition. The salesperson needs to know the policies of competing companies. It is also important to know as much about the four *P*'s of every competing product as possible.
5. Knowledge about potential and actual customers. The more the salesperson knows about the customer, the more likely he will be to adapt to that person and make the sale.
6. The company's view of the role of selling. Different companies have different ideas about the approach to selling. Some companies prefer a problem-solving approach, while others emphasize servicing. Frequently, a company's view of the role of selling is based upon ethical standards. The training program will provide information on this issue.

   As an example, Blue Bell, the maker of Wrangler jeans and Jantzen sportswear in Greensboro, North Carolina, puts great emphasis on "consultative selling, wherein the sales rep takes an active part in everything from local advertising and promotion to actually stocking the shelves in retail outlets."[18] Kodak's philosophy is that "the customer is king." This places a strong emphasis on keeping old customers and being certain to provide follow-up servicing.[19]

Style and Technique

Being armed with a great deal of information is a major part of the preparation for a successful salesperson. How to provide that information most effectively is the next major concern of a sales training program. This has to do with style and technique. How extensive training must be depends upon the company's view, as well as upon the experience of the salesperson.

Training in the Actual Sales Process. The information on the sales process presented in this book in Chapters 6 to 12 is, in effect, the heart of the style and technique of selling. Most selling requires a process involving prospecting, preapproach, approach, presentation, demonstration, closing, and, at whatever point is necessary, handling objections. Any or all of these components of the sales process can be part of a training program.

Obviously, the experienced salesperson has an immediate understanding of these things, while a beginner requires direct training. In all cases, however, certain company philosophies serve to guide the process. The Kodak philosophy, that the customer is always king, would result in a somewhat different approach to the sales process than a philosophy that the buyer is simply a means to making a sale.

It is interesting to note that the Campbell Soup Company recently changed its perspective in this regard. Initially it regarded its chief buyer, the retail grocer, as a trade merchant. It now considers the grocer as a sophisticated marketer. This shift in philosophy has changed the relationship between the buyer and seller from an adversarial one to one of greater respect and equality.[20]

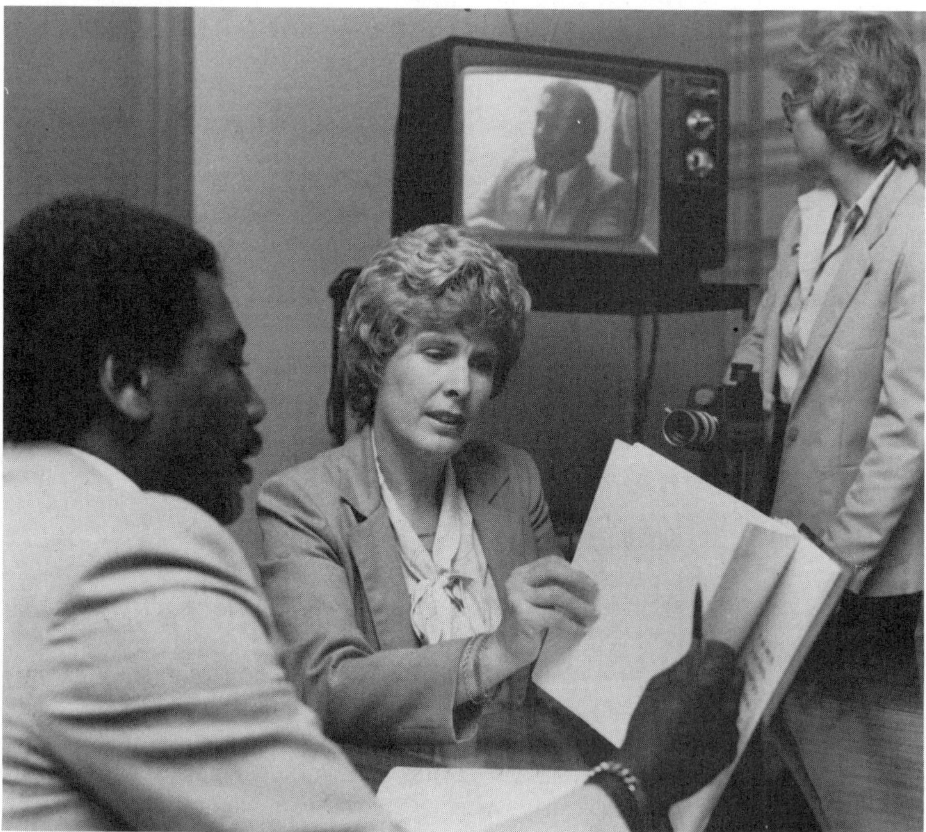

Role playing is a common exercise used to train salespeople in their style and technique. Videotaping gives the salespeople an opportunity to observe themselves and make any necessary improvements. (© Roy W. Hankey/Photo Researchers, Inc.)

EXHIBIT 17.3

Training for the Trade Show

Even something such as handling a trade show might require some additional training. Trade shows are actually very demanding and, in many cases, very different than the typical situation an industrial or trade salesperson would find himself in. For example, in a trade show, the salesperson has to get the job done in a few minutes as opposed to getting the job done in a more conventional 30-minute meeting in the prospect's office. What kinds of training information would be appropriate for a sales training show? Honeywell tells its salespeople not to have soft drinks at their booths and not to congregate with co-workers. They also suggest that salespeople arm themselves with a pad of paper and write down information about the prospect. Other companies deal with such issues as where the salesperson should stand so as not to block the entrance to a particular exhibit and how to gauge reactions. Gould, Inc., of Rolling Meadows, Illinois, sells electronic products and is a multi-billion-dollar corporation. The salespeople it brings to trade shows are particularly knowledgeable about their products. The company trains the trade show salespeople and gives pointers about such things as dress, posture, and grooming. Thus it has pointers such as the following:

Avoid attention-getting clothes
If you smoke, don't let your habit annoy others
Don't congregate with colleagues in the booth
Don't sit or lean, just stand
Wear a badge so that it can be easily seen
Don't ask "May I help you?"; instead use openers such as "Have you seen our new model?"
Don't use the booth phone to conduct personal business
Don't prejudge a potential customer based upon looks

Koch Supplies in Kansas City sells equipment to the meat industry. In preparing for its trade show for the American Meat Institute, it provides sales representatives with a full day of training before the show. This focuses on the sales sequence (approach, qualify, handle objections, close). Role playing is used extensively.

Source: Reprinted by permission of *Sales & Marketing Management* © 1988. R. Skolnik. (1988). Pre-show sales training makes the difference. *Sales & Marketing Management: Portfolio, 1988,* 47–48.

A number of other issues are important in considering technique and style training. Not surprisingly, many sales training programs use role playing as an effective means of improving skills. Trainers have to decide how much to concentrate on nonverbal skills. They must consider what content (or factual information) should be conveyed to a prospect. A decision has to be made about how much freedom a salesperson has during the course of a sales encounter. The result of this decision determines whether the company will use structured or unstructured presentations (see Chapter 10).

Impression Management. One approach to sales training involves impression management. **Impression management** refers to *"the ways people manipulate their communications (voice, facial expressions, and appearance) to create a certain type of impression."*[21] Clearly, impression management places a heavy emphasis on nonverbal communication. It can also depend upon content issues. These content issues can be individualized for a specific company or product. Table 17.5 shows an example of content issues that can contribute to impression management.

Many companies elect to have an outside organization provide sales training for style and technique. This decision is a function of the size of the sales force and the complexity of the sales task, as well as the ability of the company to provide an elaborate training program. One thing should be clear, however: training is a necessary and important part of any salesperson's career. It is also necessary for the broader success of the company's overall sales efforts. For this reason, it becomes an important concern in managing salespeople.

As an example of how effective training is, consider the case of Molex. Molex sells terminals, switches, and connectors to high-technology customers. Tim Moore, the first training director they hired, found that the company's salespeople were expert technically but knew little about selling. That is, they had knowledge and information but knew little about style and techniques. They rarely agreed on what they were selling, and almost half of the salespeople had never gone through a formal training program.

Clearly, a major training program was necessary. Moore found an outside company that tailored its program for Molex by using Molex's own vocabulary and products. Within 3 months, every salesperson had completed the course. When sales before and after the training program were compared, the annual return on investment was found to be 37:1; 3 months after that, it rose to 40:1. In addition, everyone who had been through the program used the newly learned skills, and more than half of the salespeople expressed interest in taking an advanced course.[22]

Motivation of the Sales Force

It is fair to say that salespeople, almost by definition, are motivated. In fact, part of the selection process consists of finding those salespeople who are most highly

Table 17.5 Content Issues That Can Be Managed by a Salesperson and Individualized for a Specific Company or Product

Remember the actual presentation is entirely up to you. This is a general format which merely provides suggestions for the content.

I. Possible openers
  1. Show something and talk about it
  2. Render free service
  3. Point out current conditions that you can help improve
  4. Appeal to single buying motive if one appears predominant in prospect
  5. Refer to some personal interest of the prospect
  6. Sincerely compliment or congratulate the prospect
  7. Ask the prospect a question
  8. Make a statement or claim
  9. Use a curiosity-arousing opening
  10. Relate a case history

II. Principles of approach
  1. Make maximum use of advance information
  2. Ask questions if necessary
  3. Give out what prospects should absorb
  4. Secure control at the beginning
  5. Promise buyer benefit early
  6. Make prospect feel important
  7. Observe the law of self-interest
  8. Like and be liked

III. Suggested presentation techniques
  1. Convince and persuade
  2. Use logical reasoning
  3. Demonstrate
  4. Use testimonials or case histories

IV. Suggested techniques for overcoming objections
  1. Fail to hear
  2. Compare products
  3. Give a case history
  4. Demonstrate
  5. Guarantee
  6. Admit and counterbalance
  7. Direct answer

V. Suggested closing techniques
  1. Close on a choice
  2. Assume a close
  3. Dispose of single objective
  4. Summarize benefits
  5. Direct appeal
  6. Special concession

Source: Reprinted by permission of *Journal of Personal Selling and Sales Management* © 1986. R. H. King and M. B. Booze. (1986). Sales training and impression management. *Journal of Personal Selling and Sales Management, 6* (August), 59.

motivated or who can be motivated. The company itself, however, has a great deal of influence on how motivated a salesperson can be. One major aspect of motivation is, of course, compensation. Everyone prefers to make more money. That does not mean that salespeople require $750,000 a year in order to be motivated. They expect to earn amounts that are consistent with what other salespeople earn, although they would like to be at the high end of that range. Money, however, is not the only thing people look for. They are also motivated by things that have to do with a sense of competence and achievement.

Basically, we have just suggested two kinds of motivation: external and internal. **External motivation** *is related to things such as monetary compensation, vacation time, and bonuses.* It can also include various ways the sales manager can give the sales representative a "pat on the back." **Internal motivation** *has to do with a sense of accomplishment and achievement of such things as status and prestige.* The differences in these kinds of motivation are shown in Table 17.6. We will discuss each of them separately, although they are related to one another. For example, compensation, if it is great enough, allows one to purchase material possessions that will contribute to status.

External Motivation

A great deal has been written about how to motivate people by providing external rewards. The reward most often discussed is money. This is a controversial topic, especially in sales.

Compensation. There are three general approaches to salesperson compensation:

1. Salary.
2. Commission.
3. Combination plan: salary plus commission.

Each of these plans has advantages and disadvantages. In addition to each plan, various incentives can be provided, such as bonuses or prizes from sales contests.

Since we have all been customers at one time or another, we can readily appreciate the importance of this issue. Salespeople who are more dependent

Table 17.6 Kinds of Motivation for a Salesperson

Kinds of Motivation
External motivation
Monetary compensation
Vacation time
Bonuses
Pats on the back
Internal motivation
Personal sense of accomplishment
Achievement of prestige
Achievement of status

upon commissions appear to be more motivated to make a sale than salespeople who are paid the same salary no matter how much they sell. This fact is an important consideration for sales managers in deciding upon various compensation options. Following is a discussion of the three basic compensation plans available to salespeople.

Salary Plan. The **salary plan** *ensures a steady income* and is easy to administer. John Steinbrink argues that this plan is best when a salesperson spends a great deal of time doing missionary work.[23] This makes sense, since spending time this way would prevent even a good salesperson from making many sales. Since the other two compensation plans are tied to the amount of sales, such a salesperson would end up being poorly paid.

Still, there are major disadvantages with this plan. Since the salesperson's income is guaranteed, she is not likely to make that extra effort. Still, this plan, while not the most popular, is used in companies which have cyclical sales, such as durable goods companies. It allows a salesperson to maintain a steady and consistent income despite seasonal fluctuations in demand.[24]

Jay Schuster and Patricia Zingheim argue that most successful corporations use a compensation plan that requires the salesperson to depend, at least in part, on his own effort for his monetary reward.[25] That would suggest more serious consideration of the other two compensation options.

Commission Plan. In a **commission plan,** a salesperson's *income is based solely on how much she sells.* Therefore, if she sells nothing, she is paid nothing. This is an easy plan to administer, and it is directly related to the salesperson's performance. At the same time, it has a number of disadvantages.

It encourages salespeople to neglect nonselling duties and can cause wide fluctuations in their earnings depending upon the product being sold and economic conditions. It is recommended that, when using this plan, a guarantee of a base salary or fringe benefits be given in order to provide a salesperson with some kind of security. This recommendation makes the commission plan similar to the combination plan.

Combination Plan. The **combination plan** is the most popular compensation approach. There are many variations, but they all include *a base salary and various commission options.* These plans are more complex to administer than the other two options, and there remains the difficulty of determining what proportion of the combination plan should be salary versus what proportion should be commission. An 80/20 split is very common, but many companies also use a 70/30 or a 60/40 split. Under this plan, a decent base salary is $25,000 to $36,000.[26]

This plan provides more security than a commission plan but also greater earning possibilities than a salary plan, thereby motivating the salesperson to place greater emphasis on selling. Its major disadvantage is its complexity.

Generally speaking, although the salary plan and the commission plan deserve serious consideration, based upon what the most successful companies do, the combination plan is the most desirable approach to external motivation. The compensation plans are summarized in Table 17.7.

Table 17.7 Compensation Plans for Salespeople

Kind of Plan	*Description*	*When to Use*
Salary plan	Fixed pay regardless of amount of sales	When salespeople do a great deal of missionary work For durable goods companies with seasonal sales
Commission plan	Pay based solely on what is sold	When it is necessary to find a plan that is easy to administer and is tied directly to performance
Combination plan	Pay based on salary plus commission	When some degree of security and great earning potential are considered desirable

There are other aspects of external motivation in addition to compensation. For example, job promotion provides greater compensation and greater responsibility. Clearly, we have to compensate people so that, economically, they can have a satisfying life. But, no matter how much someone is paid, if she is unhappy with her job, she will not work hard. Happiness comes, in part, from the pat on the back provided by the sales manager.

Pats on the Back. The sales manager can do a number of things to motivate the salesperson that have nothing to do with money, either directly or indirectly. Following is a list of some of those things.

1. Recognition. This is probably the most important external motivator, assuming, of course, that the salesperson's basic monetary needs are being met through a compensation plan. As DiBari points out, the salesperson is "a 'crusader' by nature and *needs* everyone to know when he has conquered his quest. This acknowledgment shouldn't be implemented via a 'private' meeting with his manager. He *must* be recognized in front of his entire peer group."[27]
2. Awards. This is a symbolic way of highlighting an accomplishment. It is a tangible indicator of recognition, particularly when an award is presented in front of one's peers.
3. Trust. Trust is important in any relationship, including the relationship between a salesperson and a sales manager. When someone knows he is trusted, this itself becomes a motivator.
4. Involvement. The more a salesperson is involved in the company, including such things as formulating and carrying out the company's goals and strategies, the more she will be motivated to perform well for the company.

The other major component of happiness on the job is internal motivation. While the term *internal motivation* suggests that it comes from within, there are many things that a sales manager can do to foster this.

Internal Motivation

Finding ways to motivate the salesperson internally is difficult for the sales manager. Often, the sales manager at the home office is far away from the salesperson whom he supervises. There are, however, a number of things that can be done to enhance internal motivation.

The Pygmalion Effect. As in other areas, people get what they expect. In fact, several years ago, Ron Markin and Charles Lillis argued that sales managers who have high expectations of their salespeople usually get better results than sales managers who have low expectations. A basic principle is operating here: *"people oftentimes become what we expect from them."*[28] This is referred to as the **pygmalion effect.** Of course, it is not sufficient for a sales manager simply to have high expectations for the sales force. Much of internal motivation comes from a need for self-esteem and satisfaction.

Key Job Dimensions. Not surprisingly, there are specific aspects of the sales job itself that can affect the salesperson's self-esteem and internal satisfaction. Following is a list of **key job dimensions** that influence the salesperson's level of motivation.[29]

1. Skill and variety. This has to do with how much a salesperson is able to use his skills, as well as how varied his job is. The greater the use of skills and the greater the variety of the job, the more motivated is the salesperson.
2. Autonomy. Many people, particularly self-starters, like to function as though they are their own bosses. The ability to do this is referred to as *autonomy*. The greater the autonomy, the more motivated is the salesperson.
3. Importance. The more a salesperson feels that her job is important and makes a contribution to the organization, the more motivated she will be.
4. Task identity. This has to do with whether a salesperson can do a job from beginning to end and see the results of his efforts. The more a salesperson can be involved in the whole process, the more motivated he will be.
5. Feedback. This is a necessary component of any job. It occurs when the manager gives the salesperson information about her performance and effectiveness. Of course, the more positive the feedback, the greater will be the motivation.

A good sales manager can maximize these key job dimensions in order to give a salesperson a strong sense of satisfaction and achievement. These things enhance self-esteem, which, in turn, further motivates the salesperson. In fact, recent research has demonstrated that motivators such as personal growth, accomplishment, liking, and respect are more important than pay or job security.[30]

Evaluating Salespeople

After having hired, trained, and motivated a salesperson, the logical question is, "Was it worth it?" In other words, the sales manager needs to know how well the salesperson actually performed on the job. Of course, performance is a major concern for any job in any organization. Often, however, employees do so many things that there is no neat way to measure performance.

The Varied Tasks of the Salesperson

Consider, for example, the job of a product manager. It includes preparing annual marketing plans, sales forecasts, and budgets; developing long-range competitive strategies; teaching the sales staff about the product; working with advertising agencies; continuously gathering marketing research; and finding ways to improve existing products and create new ones.[31] Measuring the performance of a product manager, while it can be done, is not an easy task. It is not sufficient to measure her contribution to the sales of the product or products she is in charge of, since she is dealing with so many other tasks.

By comparison, consider the salesperson. He has one essential task: to sell a product. The logical way to evaluate his performance, therefore, is to look at sales volume. And, in fact, many sales managers do just that. More often than not, though, this is not the most effective way to evaluate a salesperson. Salespeople whose main task is to prospect with the goal of finding leads cannot reasonably be evaluated in terms of sales volume. But even when salespeople are placed in the field and told that their major task is to sell, their jobs are more complicated than simply selling.

Salespeople have to service accounts; they have to present an image to a prospective buyer that the company finds desirable; they have to gather relevant information about the market and provide it to the company; they have to keep accurate records; they have to distinguish major accounts from less important ones; and they have to manage their own support staffs at the home office.

It is fair to say, then, that salespeople have to engage in marketing research, reporting research, public relations, administrative tasks, managerial tasks, and, finally, selling. Thus, it does not seem reasonable to evaluate their performance strictly as a function of sales volume. As a result of the complexity of the sales job, a number of systems have been developed to evaluate salesperson performance.

Establishing Goals and Objectives. Whichever system is applied, it is important that sales goals and objectives be established by management. **Goals** *are usually long-term concerns*, such as having the sales force be recognized as the most efficient one in the industry. These goals are usually vague and, thus, difficult to measure. For that reason, objectives are also established. **Objectives** *are short-term and are usually directly tied to sales.* For example, a sales objective might be to increase sales by 8 percent or to keep sales expenses within the assigned budget.[32] Specific techniques that follow the establishment of goals and objectives can be used to evaluate a salesperson's performance.

Systems to Evaluate Salesperson Performance

One technique that has been used for many years in evaluating managerial personnel has recently been applied to sales personnel. It is called **management by objectives.** This program requires both a salesperson and a manager to set up specific objectives that are to be achieved within a certain time period. The salesperson is then evaluated annually or semiannually to determine if the objectives have been met. Table 17.8 depicts the management by objectives process.

This approach has been criticized because it is very time-consuming. It is also difficult to apply consistently to every salesperson because it requires that a manager and a salesperson negotiate to determine what are reasonable and realistic objectives. Objectives for one salesperson may be different from those for another salesperson with a similar territory.

Behavioral Anchored Rating Scale. As an answer to some of the shortcomings of management by objectives, another technique has been developed. It is based upon the use of **behavioral anchored rating scales.** *These scales tie the notion of specific desirable activities or behaviors to specific desirable outcomes.* These scales require the identification of what are called **critical incidents,** or *certain actions that are critical to success.* These might include such things as the number of sales calls per day.[33] By agreeing upon certain critical incidents, it is relatively easy for a manager to evaluate a salesperson because the required actions are easily measured. An example of a behavioral anchored rating scale for a sales manager is shown in Table 17.9.

IBM, whose sales force is considered to be second to none in the computer industry, uses a combination of management by objectives and a behavioral anchored rating scale. They do this by establishing a personal performance plan for each sales representative.[34]

As an example of management by objectives, the performance plan provides specific objectives based on the revenues the salesperson is expected to bring in. As an example of a behavioral rating scale, the plan describes specific behaviors, such as getting all administrative reports in on time. Thus, getting reports in on time becomes a critical incident that should lead to a successful outcome such as providing market information to the company. In addition, the salesperson is evaluated so as to take into account other tasks associated with being effective. This includes determining how satisfied his customers are and measuring the effectiveness of his leadership skills among his peers.

Table 17.8 The Management by Objectives Process

1. Based on the mission of the organization and its business plan, organizational goals are established.
2. From the organizational goals, each employee, together with a supervisor, sets individual goals to be achieved during a specified period of time. They also mutually decide upon the performance criteria that will determine if these goals have been achieved.
3. The employee develops a specific plan of action to accomplish the goals set in step 2.
4. The employee and supervisor hold review sessions at least once every three months.
5. At the end of the specified period of time determined in step 2, the employee and supervisor meet so that the employee's performance can be evaluated.
6. The first five steps are repeated beginning with the establishment of a new set of individual goals for the employee.

Table 17.9 A Behavioral Anchored Rating Scale for a Sales Manager

Instituting a new procedure:

a. Describes the details of the procedure to salespeople.

Almost Never	1	2	3	4	5	Almost Always	NA

b. Explains why the procedure is necessary.

Almost Never	1	2	3	4	5	Almost Always	NA

c. Discusses how the procedure will affect the salesperson.

Almost Never	1	2	3	4	5	Almost Always	NA

d. Listens to the concerns of salespeople.

Almost Never	1	2	3	4	5	Almost Always	NA

e. Asks salespeople for help in making the new procedure work.

Almost Never	1	2	3	4	5	Almost Always	NA

Total = ________

Scores set by management:

5—the employee's specified behavior is 95–100% of the time appropriate.
4—the employee's specified behavior is 85–94% of the time appropriate.
3—the employee's specified behavior is 75–84% of the time appropriate.
2—the employee's specified behavior is 65–74% of the time appropriate.
1—the employee's specified behavior is 0–64% of the time appropriate.
NA—not applicable; The rater circles NA when there was no opportunity to observe the behavior.

Below Adequate	Adequate	Good	Excellent	Superior
6–10	11–15	16–20	21–25	26–30

The Importance of Evaluation. There are many other means for evaluating salespeople. The important point here is that sales volume, by itself, is not adequate. The whole range of activities that comprise the salesperson's job needs to be taken into account. Evaluation does become an important issue for a number of reasons. It determines whether a salesperson is or is not promoted or given extra compensation. This evaluation allows salespeople who are not performing as well as they should to correct their deficiencies. In that sense, an evaluation can serve to motivate a salesperson.

Evaluation is necessary to help improve a poor performance and to reward a performance that meets or exceeds expectations. The evaluation process also establishes the specific expectations that are to be met. There is, however, another important benefit of evaluation. It protects management if and when it becomes necessary to dismiss a salesperson.

There was a time when salespeople could be dismissed easily. The laws have changed now, and salespeople are now more protected from firing as well as from on-the-job discrimination, sexual harassment, and the requirement to take lie detector tests. Still, a manager will find it necessary to discharge a salesperson who is not performing well. Since there is a risk that the salesperson can sue the company for unfair discharge, the manager must protect herself. This is where the importance of evaluation emerges.

First of all, the salesperson can have access to his personnel file. If a file has only good evaluations of a salesperson and he is discharged, he can file a lawsuit. This suggests that evaluations *should be accurate and not be inflated.*[35] It also suggests that the company's work rules and other policy manuals should be worded so as not to make any promises or stipulate any provisions that an attempt to dismiss would violate.

Ultimately, it should be clear that evaluation benefits both the employer and the employee. It involves both motivational and legal issues, but if it is done carefully and regularly, it can only benefit all concerned. Good salespeople want good evaluations from good sales managers. In fact, a survey of what were considered to be high performers showed that they do, in fact, want feedback from their managers. They also want this feedback to emphasize recognition rather than criticism. Finally, they want evaluations that allow the salesperson enough leeway to correct her own errors.[36]

Putting It All Together

The key points in this chapter are summarized as follows:

- The sales manager's job as coordinator of the selling activity of the organization is especially important because the success of an organization is often directly based upon the success of its salespeople.
- There are four major areas of sales management: selection, training, motivation, and evaluation.
- There are many criteria that can be established for selecting salespeople; often these have to do with personality traits that are related to the unique aspects of the salesperson's job.
- Sales managers need to select salespeople who can work with minimal supervision, who are self-disciplined, and who can handle rejection.
- Because of the importance of initial selection of salespeople, assessment centers that provide intense testing and interviews are often used.
- While some people are better suited to be salespeople than others, any person who pursues a sales career has to be trained.
- Training focuses on knowledge and information and on style and technique.
- All salespersons have some basic motivation to succeed (internal motivation), however, external motivation is also necessary.
- External motivation involves a consideration of compensation and pats on the back.
- Compensation plans include straight salary, commission only, or a combination of the two.
- Pats on the back include recognition, awards, trust, and involvement.

- Internal motivation can be enhanced through key job dimensions that include skill and variety, autonomy, importance, task identity, and feedback.
- Since the selling job involves more than just making a sale, evaluation is a complex issue.
- Systems to evaluate salespeople include management by objectives and behavioral anchored rating scales.

When we consider training in particular, much of what has been discussed in this book becomes relevant. Training includes acquiring knowledge and information, such as information about the company, the competition, the customers, and the general environment. Gathering this information was discussed in Chapter 7. Training also includes developing style and techniques for selling. The chapters dealing with the approach (Chapter 9), the presentation (Chapter 10), handling objections (Chapter 11), and the close (Chapter 12), are directly concerned with style and technique.

Key Terms

Assessment center
Impression management
External motivation
Internal motivation
Salary plan
Commission plan
Combination plan
Pygmalion effect
Key job dimensions
Goals
Objectives
Management by objectives
Behavioral anchored rating scale
Critical incidents

Review Questions

1. List the major tasks and concerns of a typical sales manager.
2. Compare the job of a typical manager with the job of a salesperson.
3. What are some of the desirable personality characteristics of a successful salesperson?
4. What are some behaviors that distinguish successful from moderately successful salespeople?
5. Is it true that a salesperson is born rather than made? Discuss.
6. What are the two major areas included in sales training? Discuss each area.
7. Distinguish between external and internal motivation. What concerns are included in each?
8. What are the three basic compensation plans? Is one necessarily best? Explain.
9. What does a pat on the back provide for the salesperson?
10. List some of the key job dimensions that provide internal motivation for the salesperson.
11. Is it true that the best way to evaluate a salesperson is to see how much he has sold? Discuss.
12. Describe a behavioral anchored rating scale. Give an example of how it would apply to evaluation of a salesperson's job performance.

Discussion Questions

1. What qualities would you look for in hiring a sales manager?
2. Do you think that the best sales managers come from the ranks of the sales force? Why?
3. Would it be possible to train someone to be an effective salesperson if that person had poor self-discipline and low self-esteem?
4. Apart from the two evaluation procedures discussed in this chapter, what additional methods would you recommend? Would you recommend different procedures for retail versus business-to-business salespeople? Would you recommend different procedures depending upon the size of the organization?

CASE 17.1

John Simmons has just been hired as the new sales manager of the CDE Company, located in a large metropolitan area. The company manufactures a wide variety of computer parts, including microchips, disk drives, and monitors. It is a very large company, employing 250 salespeople.

John was hired because the company found a great deal of dissatisfaction among the salespeople. This dissatisfaction was translated into poor sales for the last 3 years.

John first found it necessary to learn how the salespeople were selected and compensated. He found that most of them had a great deal of previous experience, but in almost all cases, the experience was in areas that had little to do with computer sales. At CDE their main task was to sell to computer companies such as IBM, as well as to retailers that sold computers. They were paid on a straight salary basis and were given a 2-day training program in which they were exposed to all of the company's products. Their performance was evaluated on the basis of sales volume.

John clearly had to engage in a major shakeup. He was willing to keep all the salespeople, but he felt strongly that substantial changes were needed. He also felt that future hiring practices had to be revised.

As a beginning, John decided that the compensation program needed to be changed. This met with a great deal of resistance from management, but John insisted. He also felt that the salespeople should be given an extensive 2-month training program. John also wanted to institute a more elaborate and rigorous evaluation system. In addition, he made a formal policy change with respect to future hiring. He felt that new salespeople had to have previous experience in the computer field, even if that experience did not involve actual selling. He was even willing to hire new college graduates as long as they had a strong background in computers and computer programming.

1. In terms of compensation, should John change the program? What compensation plan should he use?

continued

2. Is it necessary for John to suddenly force the salespeople to engage in an extensive training program?
3. What things might he do with respect to evaluating the salespeople?
4. Do you agree with John's new hiring policy? Why?

References

1. How Pepsi keeps its sales sparkle. (1984). *Sales & Marketing Management*, (December 3), 46.

2. Stanton, W. T., and R. H. Buskirk. (1978). *Management of the Sales Force.* Homewood, IL: Irwin.

3. McMurry, R. N., and J. S. Arnold. (1968). *How to Build a Dynamic Sales Organization.* New York: McGraw-Hill, p. 3.

4. Mayer, D., and H. M. Greenberg. (1964). What makes a good salesman? *Harvard Business Review, 42* (July, August), 119–125.

5. McMahon, L. (1981). Salespeople: How to find them, how to keep them. *Business Horizons, 24* (March–April), 46.

6. A stickler for product knowledge. (1984). *Sales & Marketing Management*, (July 2), 31.

7. Woods, B. (1982). Recruiting the best and the brightest. *Sales & Marketing Management, 129* (August 16), 51–52.

8. Ibid.

9. Ibid.

10. Qualities to look for when you're hiring. (1984). *Sales & Marketing Management*, (August 13), 84, 86.

11. Taylor, T. C. (1988). Meet the sales force of the future. *Sales & Marketing Management: Portfolio 1988*, 3–4.

12. Fleenor, C. P. (1987). Assessment center selection of sales representatives. *Journal of Personal Selling and Sales Management, 7*, 57.

13. Nelson, R. (1987). Maybe it's time to take another look at tests as a sales selection tool? *Journal of Personal Selling and Sales Management, 7*, 33–38.

14. Riso, O. (1980). *The Sales Manager's Handbook*. Chicago, IL: Dartnell.

15. Ibid.

16. Ibid.

17. Selling becomes chic at Marriott. (1984). *Sales & Marketing Management*, (December 3), 42.

18. Blue Bell's Mann with a mission. (1984). *Sales & Marketing Management*, (December 3), 28.

19. Kodak's reputation makes a pretty picture. (1984). *Sales & Marketing Management*, (December 3), 14.

20. Skolnik, R. (1986). Campbell stirs up its sales force. *Sales & Marketing Management*, (April), 56.

21. King, R. H., and M. B. Booze. (1986). Sales training and impression management. *Journal of Personal Selling and Sales Management*, *6*, 51–60.

22. Brass, A. (1988). When the problem is skills, start from scratch. *Sales & Marketing Management: Portfolio 1988*, 46.

23. Steinbrink, J. (1988). How to pay your sales force. *Harvard Business Review*, (July–August), 111–122.

24. Ibid.

25. Schuster, J. R., and P. K. Zingheim. (1986). Sales compensation strategies at the most successful companies. *Personnel Journal*, *65* (6), 112–116.

26. Dibari, N. (1988). Compensation vs. motivation. *Sales & Marketing Management: Portfolio 1988*, 13.

27. Ibid.

28. Markin, R. J., and C. M. Lillis. (1975). Sales managers get what they expect. *Business Horizons*, *18* (June), 52.

29. Tyagi, P. K. (1985). Relative importance of key job dimensions and leadership behaviors in motivating salesperson work performance. *Journal of Marketing*, *49* (Summer), 76–86.

30. Bellenger, D. N., J. B. Wilcox, and T. N. Ingram. (1984). An examination of reward preferences for sales managers. *Journal of Personal Selling and Sales Management*, *4*, 1–6.

31. Kotler, P. (1984). *Marketing Management*. Englewood Cliffs, NJ: Prentice Hall, p. 721.

32. Anderson, R. E., J. F. Hair, and A. J. Bush. (1988). *Professional Sales Management*. New York: McGraw-Hill.

33. Cummings, W. T., and M. R. Edwards. (1984). How to evaluate your sales force. *Business* (April–June), 30–36.

34. Georgia–Pacific blazes trails/The IBM salesperson is king. (1984). *Sales & Marketing Management*, *133*, (8).

35. Taylor, T. C. (1988). Anatomy of a star salesperson. *Sales & Marketing Management: Portfolio 1988*, 41.

36. Ibid.

GLOSSARY

Account Representative A salesperson who deals with established customers rather than developing new accounts.

Adapters Bodily cues that are used to release tension created during emotional arousal.

Affect Displays Bodily cues that communicate emotion.

Aggressiveness An interpersonal style characterized by violating another person's rights through dominance, failure to listen, and insensitivity. Aggressive people are concerned only with achieving their own desires; they are manipulative and use high-pressure techniques.

Approach The first stage of the sales interaction.

Artificial Intelligence Software is said to have artificial intelligence when it has been programmed with a complex series of rules so that it can "reason" through a problem.

Assertiveness An interpersonal style characterized by promoting one's own interests, but not at the expense of someone else. Assertive people are not manipulative and communicate their needs directly, display self-confidence, are articulate and logical, do not fear being forceful, and pay attention carefully to what the other person says so that they can meet the other person's needs.

Assessment Center Sophisticated selection devices used most frequently for hiring. They place candidates in realistic environments and conduct tests concerned with prioritizing activities and making decisions.

Assumptive Close A statement or question (such as "Shall I have this shipped to New Jersey?") that assumes that the purchase decision has been made.

Attention A state of mental consciousness in which some object or idea stands out from all the rest.

Attitude An expression of an inner feeling that shows whether a person feels favorably or unfavorably toward some object.

Balance Sheet Close A formal summary close in which the salesperson summarizes the advantages and disadvantages of the product or service before asking for the sale.

Basic Skills Abilities, such as the ability to communicate, which are necessary for effective selling but which do not require knowledge of specific selling techniques.

Behavioral Anchored Rating Scale Scales based on the notion of specific desirable activities or behaviors as leading to specific desirable outcomes.

Benefit Opener Beginning an approach with a statement about something that the product can do for the prospect.

Bird Dog Junior salesperson hired for the express purpose of locating prospects. A spotter.

Boomerang Technique (for handling objections) A technique for handling objections in which the salesperson converts the prospect's reason for not buying into a reason for buying.

Business-to-Business Selling Any selling situation that does not involve a consumer.

Buying Center The people in an organization who make the purchase decision.

***C*-accounts** Limited accounts that are not usually very profitable.

CALLPLAN A computer-based routing plan for estimating how customers will respond to various sales call frequencies.

Case History Technique (for handling objections) A technique for handling objections in which the salesperson describes how another prospect purchased the offering and benefited by it.

Center of Influence A method of prospecting based on a network of people who are influential in the community.

Character A person's essential goodness and decency.

Close The final stage of the sales interaction in which the salesperson asks for the sale.

Closed-Ended Question A question that specifies the choice of responses.

Coercive Power The ability to punish someone.

Combination Plan A form of compensation in which a salesperson is paid with a combination of salary and commission.

Commission Plan A form of compensation in which a salesperson is paid on commission.

Communication The process of transmitting information, ideas, and attitudes from one person to another.

Compensation Method A technique for overcoming objections in which the salesperson contrasts the problem area with a more favorable aspect of the product.

Competence Knowledgeability and capability.

Compliance-Gaining Strategies Tactics employed to get people to give in to requests.

Composure The degree of emotional control that a person has.

Considerate A buyer who is concerned with the salesperson and has compassion.

Consultant Someone who is a problem solver and gives professional advice.

Content (of a verbal communication) The meaning of the words which are spoken.

Content (of a presentation) The specific ideas which are conveyed in the presentation.

Context The circumstances in which an event occurs.

Conversational Coherence A principle of conversation that holds that each statement should follow logically from the statement preceding it.

Conversational Involvement The degree to which people are engaged in an interaction.

Credibility A quality that is based upon expertise and trust.

Critical Incidents Actions that are critical to success.

Cross-Selling The selling of related products.

Decision Criteria Attributes that are used to evaluate alternatives when a choice is made.

Decode The process in which a receiver attaches meaning to a message.

Demonstration Opener A technique in which the salesperson begins the sales call with a demonstration of the product.

Demonstration Technique (for handling objections) A technique for handling an objection in which the salesperson demonstrates the offering to show the prospect that the objection is not applicable.

Detailer A salesperson concerned with stimulating demand and developing goodwill rather than actually making a sale.

DIALOG A service offering a computerized business database.

Direct Answer Technique A technique for handling an objection in which the salesperson responds to the prospect's concern in a simple, straightforward manner.

Direct Denial A technique for overcoming objections in which the salesperson states that the objection is not true.

Direct Request A closing technique that employs a simple, direct request for the sale.

Display Rules Rules that dictate what is appropriate in a social situation.

Door-in-the-Face Strategy A strategy in which a very large request is made that is likely to be refused. This is followed by a smaller request that is more likely to be granted, since the person receiving the request may have some sense of obligation.

80/20 Rule A rule that states that 80 percent of a given territory's sales are likely to come from only 20 percent of the territory's prospects.

Emblems Bodily cues that are used intentionally and have a specific meaning. Included are such things as the peace sign, the okay signal, and thumbs down.

Encode To translate one's thought into a message that can be transmitted to another person.

Ethics The study of human customs.

Exchange The act of obtaining a desired object or product from someone by offering something in return.

Expert Power The amount of knowledge one has.

External Motivation A device to motivate people, usually in the form of such things as monetary compensation, vacation time, and bonuses.

Extroversion How outgoing a person is.

Eye Behavior How someone looks at another person: directly, indirectly, or not at all. It is also concerned with how long someone stares at another person.

Facial Expression Movements of facial muscles that lead to such things as smiles and frowns and communicate such emotions as confusion, bewilderment, or joy.

Facsimile Machine Device that transmits images printed on paper over telephone lines so that they can be reproduced by a second machine at the remote site.

Fact Something known to have happened or to be true; things or events that can be observed and verified.

Feedback Information conveyed from the receiver of a message back to the sender of the message.

Final Concession Close Also called the *eliminate the objection* close, this closing technique involves the salesperson's giving in to some request in order to close the sale.

Foot-in-the-Door Strategy A strategy in which an initial request is small. When this is granted, a larger request is made.

Fully Automated Presentation Sales presentation in which the audio and visual dimensions of the message are completely predetermined and delivered via film or slides and a recording.

Goals Long-term concerns that are often vague and difficult to measure.

Half-Truth A statement that may be wholly true but that may not be the whole truth.

Handheld Computer A computer that can be held in one hand, typically used for entering data while a salesperson is in the field.

Hard Bargainer A difficult buyer who is resistant to the consummation of the sale.

High-Payoff Activities Activities that are concerned with long-term goals.

Illustrators Bodily cues that accompany and illustrate a verbal message.

Impression Formation A process that occurs when people meet for the first time and begin to get to know each other.

Impression Management The ways people manipulate their communications to create a certain type of impression.

Incomplete Satisfaction A situation in which the prospect faces a problem that cannot be resolved. The salesperson shows how his product will offer the best resolution that current technology will allow.

Industrial Goods Classification A system for categorizing business-to-business purchases based on the newness and importance of the purchase.

Industrial Sales The selling of merchandise that is bought to make items that are then resold to the final user.

Inside Salesperson A salesperson who sells over the telephone or at the employer's place of business.

Integrated Software Software that combines different functions, such as word processing and spreadsheets, into a single program.

Intellectual Stimulation A situation in which the prospect's problem is to explore a product further or even to master the product.

Interaction A two-way communication process characterized by mutual exchange.

Internal Motivation A form of motivation concerned with a person's sense of accomplishment and achievement of such things as status and prestige.

Interpersonal Communication The transmission of information by one person directly to another person's senses.

Intimate Zone A spatial zone of less than 18 inches that is reserved for close friends, spouses, and lovers.

Investment Activities Time used for traveling, waiting for appointments, setting up appointments, and servicing accounts.

Key Accounts (*a*-accounts) The salesperson's most important accounts; they are very profitable and are very good customers.

Key Job Dimensions Aspects of a salesperson's job that influence his level of motivation. They include skill and variety, autonomy, importance, task identity, and feedback.

Kinesics Movements of the body, including such things as how the arms and hands are used or how the body is positioned in a chair.

Laptop Computer A personal computer that is the size of a briefcase or smaller.

Lead A potential prospect.

Lead Management System A system for generating and evaluating leads.

Legitimate Power Power that comes about when someone has the *right* to make requests.

Limited Choice Close An assumptive close in which the salesperson asks an "either-or" question (such as "Will that be cash or charge?").

Literal Processing A level of listening in which one processes what one hears for its simple meaning but makes no inferences about what is really being said.

Low-Payoff Activities Activities that allow one to realize specific short-term goals.

Management by Objectives A method used for evaluating managerial personnel. It requires that both a salesperson and a manager set up specific objectives against which a salesperson can be evaluated periodically.

Manipulation A process of influence in which the person is clever or crafty; information is altered to suit the person's purposes.

Manners Customs that are conventions.

Market Segmentation *See* Segmentation.

Marketing A social and managerial process in which individuals and groups obtain what they need and want by creating and exchanging products and value with others.

Marketing Concept A marketing philosophy that states that firms should focus their marketing programs on the needs of consumers.

Marketing Mix The elements which the firm has at its disposal in order to create exchanges with consumers.

Mass Communication The process of delivering information, ideas, and attitudes to a sizable and diversified audience through the use of media developed for that purpose.

Memorized Presentation A presentation format in which the entire content of what the salesperson says has been memorized.

Missionary Salesperson A salesperson who calls on end users with the intent of creating sales through resellers.

Mixed Approach-Avoidance A situation in which the prospect finds that removing one problem creates a new problem.

Modified Rebuy An industrial buying situation that, though not completely new, is still important enough to warrant the investigation of different alternatives.

Morality The aspect of human activity that allows us to call it right or wrong.

Motives Driving forces behind behavior; states of tension demanding reduction. They serve to protect, satisfy, or enhance the individual.

Multiattribute Model A model that says that our attitudes toward a product are based on beliefs about the degree to which the product possesses a particular attribute or attributes.

Network A group of people who can act as a source of leads.

Neurolinguistic Programming A field of research in the behavioral sciences that links brain function to speech in order to determine whether the person is processing information visually, auditorially, or through touch.

New Task An industrial buying decision involving a first-time purchase of an expensive or important product.

Nonmanipulative Selling A nonmanipulative approach to selling that involves being other-oriented, asking questions, cultivating customers, being people-oriented, being adaptable, discovering needs, and establishing trust and understanding.

Nonselling Activities Activities devoted to organizational and investment concerns.

Nonverbal Communication Any behavior that has communicative potential but is not linguistic.

Norm of Morality That which is equitable or fair.

Norm of Reciprocity A norm that states that when you reward someone else, that person will reward you in return.

Normal Depletion A situation in which the prospect simply wants to replace an item.

Objection A statement (or question) made by the prospect that communicates, directly or indirectly, that there is a problem that must be solved before a buying decision can be made.

Objective Morality A form of morality based upon whether any normal person would be allowed to engage in a particular act.

Objectives Short-term concerns that are usually tied directly to sales.

Open-Ended Question A question that does not specify response choices. Open-ended questions often begin with words such as *why* or *how.*

Order Getter A salesperson who is directly involved in persuasive activity. Such a person searches out prospects and persuades them to buy specific products.

Order Taker A salesperson who engages in little or no persuasive activity. Such a person does whatever is necessary for a customer to procure merchandise.

Organizational Activities Time devoted to preparing reports, doing correspondence, and performing various other administrative tasks such as filing.

Organized Presentation Presentation method in which the content is organized in advance according to company guidelines but the dialogue of the sales interaction is allowed to flow naturally.

Outright Lie A deliberate presentation of false information.

Outside Salesperson A salesperson who goes out into the field and has face-to-face encounters with prospects.

Pacing Synchronizing one's behavior, especially one's nonverbal behavior, to coincide with the behavior of another person.

Paralanguage Nonverbal communication that is about language and is not visual; it is the vocal part of speech excluding the verbal content.

Personal Space A spatial zone that separates the person from other people by a distance of 18 inches to 4 feet.

Persuader A buyer who tends to sell his company to the salesperson.

Persuasion The process of influencing attitudes or behavior.

Persuasive Power The ability to present an argument logically and persuasively.

Persuasive Strategy A planned attempt to employ specific persuasive mechanisms.

Position An image of a product or service created in the consumer's mind.

Power The capacity to influence the other person in an interpersonal relationship.

Preapproach The stage of the selling process in which the salesperson establishes plans for the sales call. It occurs immediately prior to the approach.

Presentation The stage in the sales call in which the salesperson conveys information about the product.

Problem Avoidance A process in which a salesperson shows a prospect how his product will allow the prospect to avoid anticipated problems.

Problem Frame A reference point or perspective for considering alternative solutions to a problem.

Problem Removal A process in which a salesperson shows a prospect how various alternatives can eliminate a particular problem that the prospect is having.

Product Attribute Feature of a product.

Product Benefit Value provided to a consumer by a product attribute.

Promotional Mix The particular combination of advertising, personal selling, sales promotion, and publicity that the firm uses to help position its product.

Prospect A potential buyer.

Proxemics The way people position themselves in space when they communicate with another person.

Public Zone A spatial zone of 12 feet or more that is reserved for formal gatherings.

Puffery Embellishment through adjectives or metaphors.

Pygmalion Effect Getting people to perform better by expecting them to perform better.

Qualified Prospect A potential buyer who has a need for a product as well as the ability to purchase it.

Question Opener An attention-getting opening line in which the salesperson greets a prospect with a question related to the product.

Rapport A relationship based on mutual trust and understanding.

Referent Power The extent to which one person identifies with or wants to be like the other person.

Referral Method A prospecting method in which the names of new prospects are solicited from existing customers.

Reflective Processing Listening for more than the literal meaning of what is said; listening for the point of what is said.

Regular Accounts (*b*-accounts) Accounts that, while important, are less important than key accounts. Their loss would not have a dramatic effect upon a salesperson's quota.

Regulators Bodily cues whose purpose is to control the conversation.

Relational Communication Control The form of interpersonal communication, generally the grammatical form of an utterance considered in light of the utterance that preceded it.

Relational Database A database that allows the user to combine information stored in different files.

Relational Form The grammatical form of one person's statement relative to the grammatical form of the immediately preceding statement of the other person.

Reward Power The ability to provide a reward.

Right Any act that is consistent with the norm of morality.

Rule A pattern of behavior that has come to have prescriptive force.

Salary Plan A form of compensation in which a salesperson is paid a straight salary with no commission.

Sales Context The setting in which the salesperson works. It can be retail, wholesale, manufacturing, or service.

Sales Demonstration Audio or visual dimension added to a sales presentation. The sales demonstration may include the demonstration of the actual product or the use of films, brochures, or other visual aids.

Sales Engineer A salesperson who is an expert in the technical aspects of the product being sold.

Sales Job Facilitator A buyer who tries to make the sales interaction go smoothly.

Salesperson A person who serves as a link between a customer and a company. This person acts as a problem solver, a marketer, a skilled communicator, an expert on buyer behavior, and a major source of information regarding his product and the competing products.

Sales Promotion Part of the promotional mix that includes a variety of short-term incentives such as cents-off coupons or free samples.

Sales Task The nature of the salesperson's job that determines the degree of persuasive activity in which the salesperson engages.

Scarcity Close A closing technique in which the prospect is informed that he will not be able to obtain the product at the offered price unless he acts immediately.

Secondary Source of Information Publicly available information sources such as newspapers, public records, or the census.

Segmentation The practice of dividing a market into smaller groups that share common properties.

Selective Attention Focusing on certain pieces of information or certain parts of objects.

Selective Exposure Exposing oneself to certain events or information.

Self-Concept One's attitude about oneself.

Selling Activities Activities in which time is spent with a potential or current prospect.

Semiautomated Presentation A sales presentation consisting of visual aids accompanied by written material that is read by the salesperson.

Sensory Gratification A situation in which the prospect has no specific problem but simply wants to make a change in his life.

Sequential Process A process that occurs in stages. The term refers to the turn-taking process of conversation.

Service Salesperson A salesperson who sells services such as insurance, investment advice, hospital services, or the services of an arts organization. Such a salesperson is most likely to be an order getter.

Service Representative A salesperson who doesn't actually sell, but who becomes important after the sale has occurred by dealing with such things as delivery, repairs, warranties, or product information.

SIC Code Abbreviation for the Standard Industrial Classification, a system that assigns numbers to a variety of industries.

Silence Close The technique of "asking" for the sale by pausing and staring at the prospect until the prospect feels compelled to respond.

Small Talk Conversation about seemingly unimportant topics such as the weather. It allows people to form impressions of each other.

Sociability How friendly, likable, and pleasant a person is.

Social Approval A situation in which the prospect wants to make a purchase in order to gain recognition from other people.

Socializer A buyer who enjoys the personal contact of the buyer–seller interaction.

Social Zone A spatial zone of between 4 and 12 feet. This is the zone in which a business encounter would take place.

Spatial Zones Zones established around the body characterized by varying degrees of space that separate the person from other people in conversation.

Specs A list of product attributes that are dictated by the organization of the buyer.

Spreadsheet Software that displays data in matrix format so that computations can be performed across rows or columns.

Stall A tactic used by a prospect in order to delay making a buying decision.

Straight Shooter A buyer who behaves with integrity. He doesn't procrastinate or use buying power to gain any concessions.

Straight Rebuy An industrial buying situation in which no new alternatives are considered; the current product is simply reordered.

Structured Presentation A format in which the content of the presentation is determined in advance of the sales call.

Subjective Morality A form of morality based upon the individual and his own knowledge, consent, background, training, and personality.

Summary Close A formal closing technique in which the salesperson summarizes the major points that have been made and then asks for the sale.

Target Market The specific segment of the population toward which a firm aims its product.

Target Marketing A marketing management perspective in which the firm aims its marketing mix at a specific segment of the population.

Territoriality A need to establish space, or territory, that is one's own.

Tickler System Feature of some filing systems in which files requiring calls or other activity are flagged by the computer.

Trade-Off Balancing the advantages and disadvantages of a product.

Trade Sales The selling of merchandise to wholesalers and retailers who, in turn, resell the product to the consumer.

Trial Close A question designed to determine indirectly the prospect's readiness to buy.

Trust Transference A strategy in which a source separate from the salesperson is relied upon in order to enhance sales points.

Unstructured Presentation A presentation format in which neither the content nor the dialogue of the sales interaction is controlled by management. The planning is left to the discretion of the individual salesperson.

Verbal Content The words that are exchanged in interpersonal communication.

Voice Mail A communication system in which callers leave recorded messages in personal security-coded "mailboxes" stored in a central computer.

Yes, But Technique (for handling objections) A technique for handling objections in which the salesperson agrees with the prospect's objection but then makes another statement to offset it.

INDEX OF NAMES

INDEX OF SUBJECTS

D

N

O